W9-AQI-337

Index of American Periodical Verse: 1981

by
Rafael Catalá

in association with
James Romano
and
James D. Anderson

The Scarecrow Press, Inc.
Metuchen, N.J., & London
1983

Library of Congress Catalog Card No. 73-3060
ISBN 0-8108-1602-4
Copyright © 1983 by Rafael Catalá
Manufactured in the United States of America

CONTENTS

PREFACE

This is the eleventh annual volume of the Index of American Periodical Verse. The first ten years of the Index were guided by Sander W. Zulauf and his associate editors. Sander conceived of this index, recognizing the need for access to the work of poets scattered in hundreds of literary and general periodicals published in the United States and Canada, and nurtured it through the first ten years of its life to the point where it has become a standard reference source. He has now passed on the "parenting" responsibility to new editors. I only hope that we, his successors, can maintain the high quality of the work which he began.

A major addition to this year's index is the inclusion of important United States and Puerto Rican literary journals published in Spanish. Spanish, after all, is also an important medium for more and more poets in these countries. With the addition of many more poets with compound surnames and surnames containing various prefixes, we have recognized the need for systematic cross references from alternative forms of the surname to that chosen for entry in the index. In choosing the form of entry, we have followed the standard of the Anglo-American Cataloguing Rules, which is also followed by every major library in the United States and Canada. We have included cross references from alternative forms of surname when the form used for entry did not fall under the last element.

The basic format and style of the index remain unchanged. Poets are arranged alphabetically by surname. In creating this alphabetical sequence, we have adopted some of the principles included in new filing rules issued in 1980 by the American Library Association and the Library of Congress. Names beginning with "Mac" and "Mc" are no longer interfiled, but are filed as spelled, just as in most telephone books. Accents are no longer considered in filing, so that, for example, "ö" and "o" are filed in the same way. We follow an older tradition, however, in not considering spaces within surnames, so that "Van der SEE" and "VANDERSEE" would file next to each other.

Under each poet's name, her/his poems are filed alphabetically by title or, if there is no title, by first line. Poem titles and first lines are placed within quotation marks. All significant words of titles are capitalized, but in first lines, only the first word and proper nouns are capitalized. Excerpts from larger works are preceded by the word "from," followed by the title of the larger work, but the "from" is ignored in the arrangement of titles. The title or first line of the excerpt, within quotation marks, follows the title of the larger work. Numbered excerpts are placed within parentheses. For example:

> from Lumb's Remains: "A primrose petal's edge."
> from The Impossible: (85, 87, 93, 182).

When more than eight poems by the same poet are published contiguously in the same journal, these poems are not indexed separately, but are described as "Eight poems," "Nine poems," etc. Notes about dedications, joint authors and translators, if any, follow each title, enclosed in parentheses. A poem with more than one author is entered under each author. Likewise, a translated poem is entered under each translator, as well as its author(s). Each entry includes the names of all authors and all translators. Multiple authors or translators are indicated by the abbreviation "w/" standing for "with." Translators are indicated by the abbreviation "tr. by," standing for "translated by," and original authors are indicated by the abbreviation "tr. of," standing for "translation of." For example:

> CENDRARS, Blaise
> "Hotel Notre-Dame" (tr. by Perry Oldham and Arlen Gill). WebR (5:1) Wint 80, p. 32.
>
> GILL, Arlen
> "Hotel Notre-Dame" (tr. of Blaise Cendrars w/ Perry Oldham). WebR (5:1) Wint 80, p. 32.
>
> OLDHAM, Perry
> "Hotel Notre-Dame" (tr. of Blaise Cendrars w/ Arlen Gill). WebR (5:1) Wint 80, p. 32.

The journal citation includes an abbreviation standing for the journal title, volume and issue numbers, date, and pages. The journal abbreviation is underlined. An alphabetical list of these journal abbreviations is included at the front of the volume, along with the full journal title, name of editor, address, the numbers of the issues indexed in this volume of the Index, and subscription information. A separate list of indexed periodicals is arranged by full journal title, with a reference to the abbreviated title. Volume and issue numbers are included within parentheses, e.g., (16:5) stands for volume 16, number 5; (21) refers to issue 21 for a journal which does not use volume numbers. Years are abbreviated throughout, as 81 for 1981; (27) 80 means issue 27, 1980. Dates are given using abbreviations for months and seasons. Please see the separate list of abbreviations.

Compiling this year's index has been an adventure into the wealth and variety of poetry published in United States, Puerto Rican and Canadian periodicals as well as the intricacies of bringing this wealth together and organizing it into a consistent index. We are also beginning to explore the possibilities of using computer technology to facilitate and improve the quality of our work. A large part of this index was compiled using an Osborne 1 microcomputer, which proved to be a great time-saver. We are now studying procedures for increasing the number of operations which computers can do for us more efficiently than humans, such as sorting and formatting.

I want to express my sincere appreciation to my associate editors James Romano and James D. Anderson, and to the indexers who assisted us in this new (for us) venture: Paul Romano, Pat Marino, Janet Friedman, May Matosian, Leonard Stein, Alex Greenberg, Sato Moughalian, and Anca Mendelovich. I know that we have made mistakes. Most of us are primarily poets, and the intricacies of information organization and indexing are new to us. We were most fortunate in having the constant advice of James D. Anderson, Associate Professor of Library and Information Studies and Chairperson of the Library & Information Studies Department of Rutgers, the State University of New Jersey. We solicit your corrections and suggestions, which you may send to me at the address listed below.

Rafael Catalá, Editor
RD 1, Box 356
Hampton, NJ   08827

ABBREVIATIONS

ad.	adaptation
arr.	arrangement
back:	back issue copy price
ed. (s.)	editor(s)
exec.	executive
(ind.)	price for individuals
(inst.)	price for institutions
(lib.)	price for libraries
p.	page
pp.	pages
Po. ed.	Poetry editor
pub.	publisher
sing:	single copy price
SI	Special Issue
(stud.)	price for students
tr. of	translation of
tr. by	translated by
U.	University
w/	with
$10/yr	ten dollars per year
$10/4	ten dollars for four issues
(1:9)	volume one, number 9
(80)	issue eighty

Months

Ja	January	Jl	July
F	February	Ag	August
Mr	March	S	September
Ap	April	O	October
My	May	N	November
Je	June	D	December

Seasons

Aut	Autumn, Fall	Spr	Spring
Wint	Winter	Sum	Summer

PERIODICALS ADDED

Areíto
Caliban
Caribe
Claridad
Inti
Letras Femeninas
Lugar Sin Límite
Mairena
Maize

Meadows
Mester
Metamorfosis
Noticias de Arte
Puerto Norte y Sur
Revista/Review Inter-
    americana
Sin Nombre
Sulfur

PERIODICALS DELETED

The Andover Review
Bits
— Boston University
    Journal
Carleton Miscellany

The Falcon
Glassworks
Mouth of the Dragon
Small Farm
Water Table

CORRECTIONS

The following corrections to the 1980 Index have been incor-
porated in this volume:

Ritchie, Elisavietta "Fait Divers." Vis (4) 80.

Strahan, Barak "Last Door." Vis (3) 80.

The title was incorrectly spelled in the first entry, and the
second title was accidentally attributed to B. R. Strahan.

PERIODICAL ABBREVIATIONS

Arranged by acronym with names of editors, addresses, issues indexed, and subscription information.

AAR: ANN ARBOR REVIEW, Fred Wolven, ed., Washtenaw Community College, Ann Arbor, MI 48106
Issues Indexed: None received in 1981; Subscriptions: $6/3 issues; Single issues: $2

Academe: ACADEME: BULLETIN OF THE AAUP, D. S. Green, J. Kurland, J. Horton, eds., Suite 500, One Dupont Circle, Washington D.C. 20036
Issues Indexed: (67:1-6); Subscriptions: $24/yr.

Agni: THE AGNI REVIEW, Sharon Dunn, ed., Box 349, Cambridge, MA 02138
Issues Indexed: (14-15); Subscriptions: $11/2 yrs., $6/yr.; Single issues: $3

AmerPoR: THE AMERICAN POETRY REVIEW, David Bonnano, Kathleen Sheeder, Stephen Berg, et al., eds., Dept. S, Temple U Center City, 1616 Walnut St., Room 405, Philadelphia, PA 19103
Issues Indexed: (10:1-6); Subscriptions: $19/3 yrs.; $13/2 yrs., $7.50/yr.; Single issues: $1.50

AmerS: THE AMERICAN SCHOLAR, Joseph Epstein, ed., 1811 Q St. NW, Washington D.C. 20009
Issues Indexed: (50:1-4); Subscriptions: $30/3 yrs., $12/yr.; Single issues: $4

Annex: ANNEX 21, Richard & Lorraine Duggin, eds., U of Nebraska at Omaha, Omaha, NE 68182
Issues Indexed: None received in 1981; Single issues: $3.95

Antaeus: ANTAEUS, Daniel Halpern, ed., The Ecco Press, 18 W 30th St., New York, NY 10001
Issues Indexed: (40-43); Subscriptions: $14/yr.; Single issues: $4

AntR: THE ANTIOCH REVIEW, Robert S. Fogarty, ed., Sandra McPherson, Po. ed., Box 148, Antioch College, Yellow Springs, OH 45387
Issues Indexed: (39:1-4); Subscriptions: $15/yr. (inst.), $12/yr. (ind.); Single issues: $3.50

Areíto: *AREITO, Max Azicri, Emilio Bejel, et al., eds., GPO Box 1913, New York, NY 10116

---

*New titles added to the Index in 1981.

Issues Indexed: (7:25-28); Subscriptions: $18/yr. (inst.), $8/yr. (ind.); Single issues: $2

ArizQ: ARIZONA QUARTERLY, Albert Frank Gegenheimer, ed., U. of Arizona, Tucson, AZ 85721
Issues Indexed: (37:1-4); Subscriptions: $5/3 yrs., $2/yr.; Single issues: $0.50

Ark: THE ARK, Geoffrey Gardner, ed., Box 322, Times Square Station, New York, NY 10036
Issues Indexed: None received in 1981; Single issues: $10

ArkRiv: THE ARK RIVER REVIEW, Jonathan Katz, Anthony Sobin, et al., eds., Box 14, Wichita State U., Wichita, KS 67208
Issues indexed: (5:1); Subscriptions: $6/2 issues

Ascent: ASCENT, The Editors, English Dept., U. of Illinois, 608 South Wright St., Urbana, IL 61801
Issues Indexed: (6:2-3) (7:1); Subscriptions: $3/yr.; Single issues: $1 (bookstore), $1.50 (mail)

Aspect: ASPECT, Ed Hogan, ed., 13 Robinson St., Somerville, MA 02145
Issues Indexed: (77/79); Single issues: $4.95 (a 10 year retrospective)

Aspen: ASPEN ANTHOLOGY, J. D. Muller, ed., Box 3185, Aspen, CO 81612
Issues Indexed: None received in 1981; Subscriptions: $6.50/yr.; Single issues: $3

Atl: The ATLANTIC, William Whitworth, ed., Peter Davison, Po. ed., 8 Arlington St., Boston, MA 02116
Issues Indexed: (247:1-6) (248:1-6); Subscriptions: $45/3 yrs., $33/2 yrs., $18/yr.; Single issues: $1.75

Bachy: BACHY, F. X. Feeney, Prose Ed., Leland Hickman, Po. Ed., Papa Bach Paperbacks, 11317 Santa Monica Blvd., West Los Angeles, CA 90025
Issues Indexed: None received in 1981; Subscriptions: $10/yr.; Single issues: $3.50

BallSUF: BALL STATE UNIVERSITY FORUM, Dick Renner, Frances M. Rippy, eds., Ball State U., Muncie, IN 47306
Issues Indexed: (21:4) (22:1-4); Subscriptions: $5/yr; Single issues: $1.50

BaratR: THE BARAT REVIEW, Lauri S. Lee, ed., Barat College, Lake Forest, IL 60045
Issues Indexed: None received in 1981; Subscriptions: $15/2 yrs., $8/yr.; Single issues: $4.50

BelPoJ: THE BELOIT POETRY JOURNAL, Robert H. Glauber, et al., eds., Box 2, Beloit, WI 53511
Issues Indexed: (31:3-4) (32:1-2); Subscriptions: $17/3 yrs., $6/yr.; Single issues: $1.50

BerksR: BERKSHIRE REVIEW, Stephen Fix, et al., eds., Williams College Box 633, Williamstown, MA 01267
Issues Indexed: (16); Subscriptions: No information given.

BlackALF: BLACK AMERICAN LITERATURE FORUM, Joe Weixlmann, ed.,
PH 237, Indiana State U., Terre Haute, IN 47809
Issues Indexed: (15:1-4); Subscriptions: $8/yr., Statesman Towers
West 1005, Indiana State U., Terre Haute, IN 47809

BlackF: BLACK FORUM, Julia Coaxum, ed., Box 1090, Bronx, NY 10451
Issues Indexed: No issues received in 1981; Subscriptions: $3/yr.;
Single issues: $2

Bound: BOUNDARY 2, William V. Spanos, ed., Robert Kroetsch, Po. ed.,
Dept. of English, SUNY-Binghamton, Binghamton, NY 13901
Issues Indexed: (9:1-3) (10:1); Subscriptions: $20/yr.(inst.), $13/yr.
(ind.), $10/yr. (stud.); Single issues: $8 (double), $5 (single)

Calib: *CALIBAN, Roberto Márquez, ed., Box 797, Amherst, MA 01004
Issues Indexed: (3:2); Subscriptions: $10/yr. (inst.), $5/yr. (ind.);
Single issues: $2.50

CalQ: CALIFORNIA QUARTERLY, Elliot L. Gilbert, ed., Sandra M. Gil-
bert, Robert Swanson, Po. eds., 100 Sproul Hall, U. of California,
Davis, CA 95616
Issues Indexed: (18-20); Subscriptions: $5/yr.; Single issues: $1.50

CapeR: THE CAPE ROCK, Ted Hirschfield, John Bierk, et al., eds.,
Southeast Missouri State U., Cape Girardeau, MO 63701
Issues Indexed: (15:3) (16:2) (17:1); Subscriptions: $1.50/yr.; Single
issues: $1

Caribe: *CARIBE, Miguel Santiago Santana, ed., Box 995, Estación Viejo
San Juan, San Juan, PR 00902
Issues Indexed: (2:2/3); Subscriptions: $4/yr. (ind.), $5/yr. (inst.)

CarolQ: CAROLINA QUARTERLY, Davis A. March, ed., Marc K. Manganaro,
Po. ed., Greenlaw Hall 066-A, U. of North Carolina, Chapel Hill, NC
27514
Issues Indexed: (33:1) (34:1-2); Subscriptions: $12/yr. (inst.), $9/yr.
(ind.); Single issues: $4; Back issues: $4

CEACritic: CEA CRITIC, Elizabeth Cowan, ed., Dept. of English, Texas
A&M U., College Station, TX 77843
Issues Indexed: (43:2-4) (44:1); Subscriptions: $18/yr. (lib.), $14/yr.
(ind.)

CEAFor: THE CEA FORUM, Elizabeth Cowan, ed., Dept. of English, Texas
A&M U., College Station, TX 77843
Issues Indexed: (11:3-4) (12:1-2); Subscriptions: $18/yr (lib.), $12/yr.
(ind.)

CentR: CENTENNIAL REVIEW, David Mead, ed., Linda Wagner, Po. ed.,
110 Morill Hall, Michigan State U., East Lansing, MI 48824
Issues Indexed: (25:1-4); Subscriptions: $5/2 yrs., $3/yr.; Single
issues: $1

CharR: CHARITON REVIEW, Jim Barnes, ed., Division of Language and
Literature, Northeast Missouri State U., Kirksville, MO 63501
Issues Indexed: (7:1-2); Subscriptions: $7/4 issues; Single issues: $2

Chelsea: CHELSEA, Sonia Raiziss, ed., Box 5880, Grand Central Station,
New York, NY 10163

Issues Indexed: (39-40); Subscriptions: $7/2 issues; Single issues: $4

ChiR: CHICAGO REVIEW, Molly McQuade, John L. Sutton, eds., Thomas Bonnell, Keith W. Tuma, Po. eds., U of Chicago, 5700 S. Ingleside, Box C, Chicago, IL 60637
Issues Indexed: (32: 2-4) (33: 1); Subscriptions: $27/3 yrs., $18.50/2 yrs., $10/yr., $6/yr (ind.); Single issues: $3

Chowder: CHOWDER REVIEW, Ron Slate, ed., Floyd Skloot, Associate ed., Box 33, Wollaston, MA 02170
Issues Indexed: None received in 1981; Subscriptions: $8/3 yrs. (inst.), $7/3 yrs. (ind.); Single issues: $2.50

ChrC: THE CHRISTIAN CENTURY, James M. Wall, ed., 407 S. Dearborn St., Chicago, IL 60605
Issues Indexed: (98: 1-43); Subscriptions: $45/3 yrs., $30/2 yrs., $18/yr.; Single issues: $0.60

CimR: CIMARRON REVIEW, Neil J. Hackett, ed., Terry Hummer, Po. ed., 208 Life Sciences East, Oklahoma State U., Stillwater, OK 74078
Issues Indexed: (54-57); Subscriptions: $10/yr.; Single issues: $2.50

Claridad: *CLARIDAD, Juan Mari Bras, ed., Ave. Ponce de Leon 1866, Pda. 26 1/2, Santurce, PR 00911
En Rojo: EN ROJO, Literary Supplement, Luis Fernando Coss, ed. Issues Indexed: (22: 1458-1484, 1486-1495, 1498-1507); Subscriptions: $24/yr., $13/6 mo., Box 318, Cooper Station, New York, NY 10276

ColEng: COLLEGE ENGLISH, Donald Gray, ed., Brian O'Neil, Po. cons., Dept. of English, Indiana U., Bloomington, IN 47405
Issues Indexed: (43: 1-8); Subscriptions: NCTE, 1111 Kenyon Rd., Urbana, IL 61801; $30/yr. (inst.), $25/yr. (ind.); Single issues: $3

Columbia: COLUMBIA, Eva Burch, Harvey Lillywhite, eds., Kate Daniels, Po. ed., 404 Dodge Hall, Columbia U., New York, NY 10027
Issues Indexed: No issues received in 1981; Single issues: $3

Comm: COMMONWEAL, James O'Gara, ed., Rosemary Deen, Mary Ponsot, Po. eds., 232 Madison Ave., New York, NY 10016
Issues Indexed: (108: 1-23); Subscriptions: $39/2 yrs., $22/yr.; Single issues: $1

ConcPo: CONCERNING POETRY, Ellwood Johnson, ed., Robert Huff, Po. ed., Dept. of English, Western Washington U., Bellingham, WA 98225
Issues Indexed: (14: 1-2); Subscriptions: $4/yr.; Single issues: $2

Cond: CONDITIONS, Elly Bulkin, et al., eds., Box 56, Van Brunt Station, Brooklyn, NY 11215
Issues Indexed: (7); Subscriptions: $22/yr (inst.), $11/yr (ind.) (free to women in prisons and mental institutions); Single issues: $4.50

Confr: CONFRONTATION, Martin Tucker, ed., English Dept., Brooklyn Center of Long Island U., Brooklyn, NY 11201
Issues Indexed: (21-22); Subscriptions: Business Manager, Eleanor Feleppa, Office of the Director of Public Relations, Southhampton College, Southhampton, NY 11968; $15/3 yrs., $10/2 yrs., $5/yr.; Single issues: $3; Back issues: $2

CreamCR: CREAM CITY REVIEW, Tony Kubiak, ed., Ken Pobo, Po. ed.,
English Dept., U. of Wisconsin-Milwaukee, Milwaukee, WI 53201
Issues Indexed: (6: 1-2) (7: 1); Subscriptions: $5/yr.; Single issues:
$2.50

CropD: CROP DUST, Edward C. Lynskey, ed., Route 2 Box 392, Bealeton,
VA 22712
Issues Indexed: No issues received in 1981; Subscriptions: $8/yr.;
Single issues: $3

CutB: CUTBANK, Sandra Alcosser, Jack Heflin, eds., Dept. of English,
U. of Montana, Missoula, MT 59812
Issues Indexed: (16-17); Subscriptions: $9.50/2 yrs., $5/yr.; Single
issues: $3

DacTerr: DACOTAH TERRITORY, Mark Vinz, Grayce Ray, eds., Moor-
head State U., Box 775, Moorhead, MN 56560
Issues Indexed: No issues received in 1981; Single issues: $2

DenQ: DENVER QUARTERLY, Leland H. Chambers, ed., U. of Denver,
Denver, CO 80208
Issues Indexed: (15: 4) (16: 1-3); Subscriptions: $14/2 yrs., $8/yr.;
Single issues: $2

Durak: DURAK, Robert Lloyd, D. S. Hoffman, eds., 166 S. Sycamore St.,
Los Angeles, CA 90036, or RD 1, Box 352, Joe Green Rd., Erin, NY
14838
Issues Indexed: No issues received in 1981; Subscriptions: $7/2 yrs.,
$3.50/yr.; Single issues: $1.95; Back issues: $2.50; Set: $10

EngJ: ENGLISH JOURNAL, Ken Donelson, Alleen Pace Nilsen, eds., Col-
lege of Education, Arizona State U., Tempe, AZ 85207
Issues Indexed: (70: 1-8); Subscriptions: NCTE, 1111 Kenyon Rd.,
Urbana, IL 61801, $30/yr. (inst.), $25/yr. (ind.); Single issues: $3

EnPas: EN PASSANT, James A. Costello, ed., 4612 Sylvanus Dr., Wilm-
ington, DE 19803
Issues Indexed: (12); Subscriptions: $11/6 issues, $6/3 issues; Single
issues: $2.25; Back issues: $1.75

Epoch: EPOCH, James McConkey, Walter Slatoff, eds., 245 Goldwin Smith
Hall, Cornell U., Ithaca, NY 14853
Issues Indexed: (30: 1-3); Subscriptions: $5/yr.; Single issues: $2

Field: FIELD, Stuart Friebert, David Young, eds., Rice Hall, Oberlin
College, Oberlin, OH 44074
Issues Indexed: (24-25); Subscriptions: $10/2 yrs., $6/yr.; Single
issues: $3; Back issues: $10

Focus: FOCUS/MIDWEST, Charles L. Klotzer, ed./pub., Dan Jaffe, Po.
ed., 8606 Olive Blvd., St. Louis, MO 63132
Issues Indexed: (14: 89-90) (15: 91); Subscriptions: $100/life, $29/30
issues, $19.50/18, $14/12, $8/6; Single issues: $1.25

FourQt: FOUR QUARTERS, John Christopher Kleis, et al., eds., Richard
Lautz, Joseph Meredith, Po. eds., La Salle College, 20th & Olney
Aves., Philadelphia, PA 19141
Issues Indexed: (30: 2-4) (31: 1); Subscriptions: $7/2 yrs., $4/yr.;
Single issues: $1

GeoR: GEORGIA REVIEW, Stanley W. Lindberg, ed., U. of Georgia, Athens, GA 30602
Issues Indexed: (35: 1-4); Subscriptions: $10/2 yrs., $6/yr.; Single issues: $3

GreenfieldR: THE GREENFIELD REVIEW, Joseph Bruchac III, ed., Carol Worthen Bruchac, Managing ed., Greenfield Center, New York 12833
Issues Indexed: No issues received in 1981; Subscriptions: $5/2 issues; Single issues: $3

GRR: GREEN RIVER REVIEW, Raymond Tyner, ed., Saginaw Valley State College, Box 56, University Center, MI 48710
Issues Indexed: No issues received in 1981; Subscriptions: $6/yr.; Single issues: $2

HangL: HANGING LOOSE, Robert Hershon, et al., eds., 231 Wyckoff St., Brooklyn, NY 11217
Issues Indexed: (39-40); Subscriptions: $15/9 issues, $10/6, $5.50/3; Single issues: $2

Harp: HARPER'S MAGAZINE, Lewis H. Lapham, ed., Hayden Carruth, Po. ed., Two Park Ave., New York, NY 10016
Issues Indexed: (262: 1568-73) (263: 1574-79); Subscriptions: $18/yr.; Single issues: $2

Hills: HILLS, Bob Perelman, ed., 30 Clyde St., San Francisco, CA 94107
Issues Indexed: No issues received in 1981; Single issues: $2

HiramPoR: HIRAM POETRY REVIEW, David Fratus, Carol Donley, eds., Box 162, Hiram, OH 44234
Issues Indexed: (29-30); Subscriptions: $2/yr.; Single issues: $1

HolCrit: THE HOLLINS CRITIC, John Rees Moore, ed., Hollins College, VA 24020
Issues Indexed: (18: 1-5); Subscriptions: $5/yr. (Note: The Hollins Critic was mistakenly deleted from the 1980 Index)

Hudson: THE HUDSON REVIEW, Paula Dietz, Frederick Morgan, eds., 65 E. 55th St., New York, NY 10022
Issues Indexed: (34: 1-4); Subscriptions: $12/yr.; Single issues: $3.50

Humanist: HUMANIST, Lloyd L. Morain, ed., 7 Harwood Dr., Amherst, NY 14226
Issues Indexed: (41: 1-6); Subscriptions: $12/yr., $20/2 yrs., $27/3 yrs.; Single issues: $2

Im: IMAGES, Gary Pacernick, ed., Dept. of English, Wright State U., Dayton, OH 45435
Issues Indexed: (7: 2-3); Subscriptions: $3/yr.; Single issues: $1

Inti: *INTI, Revista de Literatura Hispánica, Roger B. Carmosino, ed., Dept. of Modern Languages, Providence College, Providence, RI 02918
Issues Indexed: (9-11); Subscriptions: $14/yr. (inst.), $8/yr. (ind.)

Iowa: IOWA REVIEW, David Hamilton, Fredrick Woodward, eds., 308 EPW, The U. of Iowa, Iowa City, IA 52242

Issues Indexed: (11: 2-4) (12: 1); Subscriptions: $15/yr. (inst.), $12/yr. (ind.); Single issues: $4

JnlONJP: JOURNAL OF NEW JERSEY POETS, V. B. Halpert, Managing
ed., M. Keyishian, et al., eds., English Dept., Fairleigh Dickinson
U., 285 Madison Ave., Madison, NJ 07940
Issues Indexed: No issues received in 1981; Subscriptions: $3/2 issues; Single issues: $1.50

JnlOPC: JOURNAL OF POPULAR CULTURE, Ray B. Browne, ed., Popular
Culture Center, Bowling Green U., Bowling Green, OH 43403
Issues Indexed: No issues received in 1981; Subscriptions: $25/2 yrs.,
$15/yr.; Single issues: $5

KanQ: KANSAS QUARTERLY, Harold Schneider, et al., eds., Dept. of
English, Kansas State U., Manhattan, KS 66506
Issues Indexed: (13: 1-4); Subscriptions: $10/yr., $18/2 yrs.; Single
issues: $3

Kayak: KAYAK, George Hitchcock, ed., Marjorie Simon, Assoc. ed., 325
Ocean View Ave., Santa Cruz, CA 95062
Issues Indexed: (56-57); Subscriptions: $5/4 issues; Single issues: $1

LetFem: *LETRAS FEMENINAS, Victoria E. Urbano, ed., Asociación de
Literatura Femenina Hispánica, Box 10023, Lamar U., Beaumont, TX
77710
Issues Indexed: (7: 1-2); Subscriptions: $15/yr.

LitR: THE LITERARY REVIEW, Martin Green, Harry Keyishian, eds.,
Fairleigh Dickinson U., 285 Madison Ave., Madison, NJ 07940
Issues Indexed: (24: 3-4) (25: 1); Subscriptions: $9/yr.; Single
issues: $3.50

LittleBR: THE LITTLE BALKANS REVIEW, Gene DeGruson, Po. ed.,
The Little Balkans Press, Inc., 601 Grandview Heights Terr., Pittsburg, KS 66762
Issues Indexed: No issues received in 1981; Single issues: $3.50

LittleM: THE LITTLE MAGAZINE, David G. Hartwell, Carolyn Kirkpatrick, eds., Box 207, Cathedral Station, New York, NY 10025
Issues Indexed: (13: 1/2); Subscriptions: $11/yr. (inst.), $8/yr.
(ind.); Single issues: $1.50

LittleR: THE LITTLE REVIEW, John McKernan, ed., Little Review Press,
Box 205, Marshall U., Huntington, WV 25701
Issues Indexed: (15); Subscriptions: $2.50/yr.; Single issues: $1.25

Lugar: *LUGAR SIN LIMITE, Ivan Silén, Myrna Nieves Colón, et al., eds.,
Boricua College, 2875 Broadway, New York, NY 10025
Issues Indexed: (1: 1); Single issues: $1.50

Mairena: *MAIRENA, Manuel de la Puebla, ed., Himalaya 257, Urbanización Monterrey, Río Piedras, PR 00926
Issues Indexed: (2: 5-6) (3: 7-8); Subscriptions: $10/yr. (inst.),
$6/yr. (ind.); Single issues: $3

Maize: *MAIZE, Alurista, Xelina, eds., Centro Cultural de la Raza, Box
8251, San Diego, CA 92102

Issues Indexed: (4: 1-4); Subscriptions: $9/yr. (inst.), $8/yr. (ind.); Single issues: $5

MalR: THE MALAHAT REVIEW, Robin Skelton, ed., Box 1700, Victoria, BC Canada V8W2Y2
Issues Indexed: (57-60); Subscriptions: $40/3 yrs., $15/yr.; Single issues: $6

MassR: THE MASSACHUSETTS REVIEW, John Hicks, Robert Tucker, eds., Memorial Hall, U. of Massachusetts, Amherst, MA 01003
Issues Indexed: (22: 1-4); Subscriptions: $12/yr.; Single issues: $4

Meadows: *THE MEADOWS, Mary Burrows, et al., eds., Art Dept., Truckee Meadows Community College, 7000 El Rancho Dr., Sparks, Nevada 89431
Issues Indexed: (2: 1); Subscription: no information given.

Mester: *MESTER, John Akers, et al., eds., Dept. of Spanish and Portuguese, U. of California, Los Angeles, CA 90024
Issues Indexed: (9: 1-2) (10: 1-2); Subscriptions: $12/yr. (inst.), $8/yr. (ind.), $5/yr. (stud.); Single issues: $4

Metam: *METAMORFOSIS, Erasmo Gamboa, ed., Centro de Estudios Chicanos, GN-09, U. of Washington, Seattle, WA 98195
Issues Indexed: (3: 2) (4: 1); Single issues: $5

MichQR: MICHIGAN QUARTERLY REVIEW, Laurence Goldstein, ed., 3032 Rackham Bldg., The U. of Michigan, Ann Arbor, MI 48109
Issues Indexed: (20: 2-4); Subscriptions: $15/yr. (inst.), $13/yr. (ind.); Single issues: $3.50; Back issues: $2

MidwQ: THE MIDWEST QUARTERLY, V. J. Emmett, Jr., ed., Michael Heffernan, Po. ed., Pittsburg State U., Pittsburg, KS 66762
Issues Indexed: (22: 2-4) (23: 1); Subscriptions: $4/yr.; Single issues: $1.50

MinnR: THE MINNESOTA REVIEW, Roger Mitchell, ed., Dept. of English, Oregon State U., Corvallis, OR 97331
Issues Indexed: (NS16 - NS17); Subscriptions: $15/2 yrs. (inst.), $11/2 yrs. (ind.), $9/yr. (inst.), $6/yr (ind.); Single issues: $3

MissouriR: MISSOURI REVIEW, Speer Morgan, ed., Dept. of English, 231 Arts and Science, U. of Missouri, Columbia, MO 65211
Issues Indexed: (4: 3) (5: 1); Subscriptions: $12/2 yrs., $7/yr. (Note: 5: 1 is a special fiction issue.)

MissR: MISSISSIPPI REVIEW, Frederick Barthelme, ed., The Center for Writers, Southern Station, Box 5144, Hattiesburg, MS 39401
Issues Indexed: (28/29); Subscriptions: $14/2 yrs., $8/yr.; Single issues: $3

ModernPS: MODERN POETRY STUDIES, Jerry McGuire, Robert Miklitsch, eds., 207 Delaware Ave., Buffalo, NY 14202
Issues Indexed: (10: 2/3); Subscriptions: $9/yr. (inst.), $7.50/yr. (ind.)

Montra: MONTEMORA, Eliot Weinberger, ed., Box 336, Cooper Station, New York, NY 10276
Issues Indexed: (8); Single issues: $5.95

Mund: MUNDUS ARTIUM, Rainer Schulte, ed., U. of Texas at Dallas, Box
—— 688, Richardson, TX 75080
        Issues Indexed: (11: 2) (12/13); Subscriptions: $10/2 issues (inst.),
        $8/2 issues (ind.); Single issues: $4.50

Nat: THE NATION, Victor Navasky, ed., Grace Schulman, Po. ed., 72
—— Fifth Ave., New York, NY 10011
        Issues Indexed: (232: 1-25) (233: 1-22); Subscriptions: $50/2 yrs.,
        $30/yr., $15/half yr.; Single issues: $1.25

NegroHB: NEGRO HISTORY BULLETIN, J. Rupert Picott, ed., 1401 14th
—— St., N.W., Washington, DC 20005
        Issues Indexed: No issues received in 1981; Subscriptions: $16/yr.;
        Single issues: $4.50

NewEngR: NEW ENGLAND REVIEW, Sydney Lea, ed., Box 170, Hanover,
—— NH 03755
        Issues Indexed: (3: 3-4) (4: 1-2); Subscriptions: $12/yr.; Single
        issues: $4

NewL: NEW LETTERS, David Ray, ed., U. of Missouri-Kansas City,
—— 5346 Charlotte, Kansas City, MO 64110
        Issues Indexed: (47: 2/3-4) (48: 1); Subscriptions: $10/yr. (ind.),
        $12/yr. (lib.); $18/2 yrs. (ind.), $21/2 yrs. (lib.); Single issues: $3

NewOR: NEW ORLEANS REVIEW, John Giguenet, ed., Box 195, Loyola
—— U., New Orleans, LA 70118
        Issues Indexed: (8: 1-3); Subscriptions: $19/3 yrs., $13/2 yrs.,
        $7/yr.; Single issues: $2.95

NewRena: THE NEW RENAISSANCE, Louise T. Reynolds, ed., Stanwood
—— Bolton, Po. ed., 9 Heath Road, Arlington, MA 02174
        Issues Indexed: (14); Subscriptions: $8/3 issues; Single issues: $4

NewRep: THE NEW REPUBLIC, Martin Peretz, ed., Robert Pinsky, Po.
—— ed., 1220 19th St., N.W., Washington, DC 20036
        Issues Indexed: (184: 1/2-13); Subscriptions: $28/yr., $17/yr.
        (stud.); Single issues: $1.25

NewWR: NEW WORLD REVIEW, Marilyn Bechtel, ed., 162 Madison Ave.,
—— 3rd Flr., New York, NY 10016
        Issues Indexed: (49: 1-6); Subscriptions: $5/yr.; Single issues: $1

NewYorker: THE NEW YORKER, Howard Moss, Po. ed., 25 W. 43rd St.,
—— New York, NY 10036
        Issues Indexed: (56: 46-52) (57: 1-45); Subscriptions: $46/2 yrs.,
        $28/yr.; Single issues: $1.25

NewYRB: THE NEW YORK REVIEW OF BOOKS, Robert B. Silvers, Barbara
—— Epstein, eds., 250 W. 57th St., New York, NY 10107
        Issues Indexed: (28: 1-20); Subscriptions: $20/yr.; Single issues:
        $1.25

Nimrod: NIMROD, Francine Ringold, ed., Jean Flint, Mike Lowery, et al.,
—— Po. eds., Arts and Humanities Council of Tulsa, 2210 So. Main, Tulsa,
        OK 74114
        Issues Indexed: (24: 2) (25: 1); Subscriptions: $5.50/yr.; Single is-
        sues: $3

NoAmR: NORTH AMERICAN REVIEW, Robley Wilson, Jr., ed., Peter
Cooley, Po. ed., U. of Northern Iowa, 1222 West 27th St., Cedar
Falls, IA 50614
Issues Indexed: (266: 1-4); Subscriptions: $9/yr.; Single issues:
$2.50

Northeast: NORTHEAST, John Judson, ed., Juniper Press, 1310 Shorewood
Dr., LaCrosse, WI 54601
Issues Indexed: (3: 10-11); Subscriptions: $15/yr.; Single issues:
$2.50

NorthSR: NORTH STONE REVIEW, James Naiden, ed., U. Station, Box
14098, Minneapolis, MN 55414
Issues Indexed: No issues received in 1981; Subscriptions: $7.50/3
issues (inst.), $6.50/3 issues (ind.); Single issues: $3

Notarte: *NOTICIAS DE ARTE, Frank C. García, ed./pub., Florencio
García Cisneros, Director, 172 E. 89th St. #5-A, New York, NY 10028
Issues Indexed: (6: 1-5) (6: 11-12) (special eds.: Je/Jl and N);
Subscriptions: No information.

NowestR: NORTHWEST REVIEW, John Witte, ed., John Addiego, Po. ed.,
369 PLC, U. of Oregon, Eugene, OR 97403
Issues Indexed: (19: 1/2-3); Subscriptions: $14/2 yrs., $8/yr.,
$13/2 yrs. (stud.), $7/yr. (stud.); Single issues: $3

Obs: OBSIDIAN, Alvin Aubert, ed./pub., Wayne State U., Detroit, MI
48202
Issues Indexed: (6: 1/2-3); Subscriptions: $8.50/yr.; Single issues:
$3

OhioR: OHIO REVIEW, Wayne Dodd, ed., Ellis Hall, Ohio U., Athens, OH
45701
Issues Indexed: (26); Subscriptions: $25/3 yrs., $10/yr.; Single issues:
$3.50

OntR: ONTARIO REVIEW, Raymond J. Smith, ed., 9 Honey Brook Dr.,
Princeton, NJ 08540
Issues Indexed: (14-15); Subscriptions: $18/3 yrs., $13/2 yrs., $7/yr.;
Single issues: $3.95

OP: OPEN PLACES, Eleanor M. Bender, ed., Box 2085, Stephens College,
Columbia, MO 65215
Issues Indexed: (31/32: a retrospective of issues 1-30); Subscriptions:
$11/2 yrs., $6/yr.

Os: OSIRIS, Andrea Moorhead, ed., Box 297, Deerfield, MA 01342
Issues Indexed: (12-13); Subscriptions: $5/2 issues; Single issues:
$2.50

Outbr: OUTERBRIDGE, Charlotte Alexander, ed., Margery Cornwell-
Robinson, Asst. ed., English Dept., College of Staten Island, 715
Ocean Terrace, Staten Island, NY 10301
Issues Indexed: (6/7); Subscriptions: $4/yr.; Single issues: $2

Paint: PAINTBRUSH, Dr. Ben Bennani, Dept. of English, U. of Riyadh,
Box 2456, Riyadh, Saudi Arabia
Issues Indexed: No issues received in 1981; Subscriptions: Jelm Moun-

tain Pubs., Suite 205, Laramie, WY 82070, $12/2 yrs., $7/yr.;
Single issues: $4

Pan: PANACHE, David Lenson, pub., Candice Ward, ed., Box 77, Sunder-
land, MA 01375
Issues Indexed: No issues received in 1981; Single issues: $3

ParisR: THE PARIS REVIEW, George A. Plimpton, et al., eds., Jonathan
Galassi, Po. ed., 45-39 171 Place, Flushing, NY 11358
Issues Indexed: (79-82); Subscriptions: $20/8 issues, $11/4, $100/life;
Single issues: $3.50

PartR: PARTISAN REVIEW, William Phillips, ed., Boston U., 128 Bay
State Rd., Boston, MA 02215
Issues Indexed: (48: 1-4); Subscriptions: $12.50/yr. (ind.), $23/2
yrs., $18/yr. (inst.); Single issues: $3.50

Paunch: PAUNCH, Arthur Efron, ed., 123 Woodward Ave., Buffalo, NY
14214
Issues Indexed: No issues received in 1981; Subscriptions: No infor-
mation.

Peb: PEBBLE, Greg Kuzma, ed., The Best Cellar Press, 118 S. Boswell
Ave., Crete, NE 68333
Issues Indexed: (21 special issue: Forty Nebraska Poets); Subscrip-
tions: $15/4 issues (lib.), $12/4 issues (ind.)

Pequod: PEQUOD, David Paradis, ed., 536 Hill St., San Francisco, CA
94114
Poetry Mss.: Mark Rudman, Po. ed., 817 West End Ave., New York, NY
10025, Issues Indexed: (12-13); Subscriptions: $12/3 yrs., $9/2 yrs.
$5/yr.; Single issues: $4

Pig: PIGIRON, Jim Villani, Managing ed., Rose Sayre, Associate ed.,
Box 237, Youngstown, OH 44501
Issues Indexed: No issues received in 1981; Subscriptions: $7/yr.;
Single issues: $4

PikeF: THE PIKESTAFF FORUM See PikeR

PikeR: THE PIKESTAFF REVIEW, James R. Scrimgeour, Robert D. Suth-
erland, eds., Box 127, Normal, IL 61761
Issues Indexed: (2); Subscriptions: $6/3 issues; Single issues: $2;
Back issues: $2

Playb: PLAYBOY, Hugh M. Hefner, ed., 919 N. Michigan Ave., Chicago,
IL 60611
Issues Indexed: (28: 1-12); Subscriptions: $18/yr.; Single issues:
Varies.

Ploughs: PLOUGHSHARES, DeWitt Henry, Peter O'Malley, Dirs., Box 529,
Cambridge, MA 02139
Issues Indexed: (6: 4) (7: 1-4); Subscriptions: $12/yr.; Single issues:
$4.95

Poem: POEM, Robert L. Welker, ed., U.A.H., English Dept., Huntsville,
AL 35899
Issues Indexed: (41-43); Subscriptions: $5/yr.

PoetC: POET AND CRITIC, David Cummins, ed., 203 Ross Hall, Iowa
State U., Ames, IA 50011
Issues Indexed: No issues received in 1981; Subscriptions: $7/2 yrs.,
$4/yr.; Single issues: $2

Poetry: POETRY, John Frederick Nims, ed., 601 S. Morgan St., Box
4348, Chicago, IL 60680
Issues Indexed: (137: 4-6) (138: 1-6) (139: 1-3); Subscriptions:
$20/yr.; Single issues: $2 plus 0.25 postage; Back issues: $2.25
plus 0.25 postage

PoetryE: POETRY EAST, Kate Daniels, Richard Jones, eds., Star Route
1, Box 50, Earlysville, VA 22936
Issues Indexed: (4-6); Subscriptions: $10/yr.; Single issues: $3.50
No. 6, $5 No. 4/5

PoetryNW: POETRY NORTHWEST, David Wagoner, ed., 4045 Brooklyn
Ave. NE, U. of Washington, Seattle, WA 98105
Issues Indexed: (22: 1-4); Subscriptions: $8/yr.; Single issues: $2

PoNow: POETRY NOW, E. V. Griffith, ed./pub., 3118 K Street, Eureka,
CA 95501
Issues Indexed: (30-33); Subscriptions: $13/12 issues, $9/8, $7.50/4;
Single issues: $2

PortR: PORTLAND REVIEW, Gene Van Troyer, ed., Portland State U.,
Box 751, Portland, OR 97207
Issues Indexed: (27: 1-2); Single issues: No. 1 $1.50, No. 2 $5

PottPort: THE POTTERSFIELD PORTFOLIO, Lesley Choyce, ed., Potters-
field Press, RR # 2, Porters Lake, Nova Scotia B0J 2S0 Canada
Issues Indexed: (3); Subscriptions: $10/3 yrs.

PraS: PRAIRIE SCHOONER, Hugh Luke, ed., 201 Andrews Hall, U. of
Nebraska, Lincoln, NE 68588
Issues Indexed: (55: 1-4); Subscriptions: $20/2 yrs. (ind.), $11/yr.
(ind.), $15/yr. (lib.); Single issues: $3.25

Prima: PRIMAVERA, Julie Auburg, et al., eds., 1212 E. 59th St., U. of
Chicago, Chicago, IL 60637
Issues Indexed: (6/7); Single issues: $5 (6/7); Back issues: Varies

Puerto: *PUERTO NORTE Y SUR, José M. Oxholm, ed., 19454 Woodbine,
Detroit, MI 48219
Issues Indexed: Wint 81; Subscriptions: No information given.

QRL: QUARTERLY REVIEW OF LITERATURE, T. & R. Weiss, 26 Haslet
Avenue, Princeton, NJ 08540
Issues Indexed: No issues received in 1981; Subscriptions: $20/2 is-
sues (cloth), $10/2 issues (paper); Single issues: $13 (cloth), $5.95
(paper)

QW: QUARTERLY WEST, David Baker, Lex Runciman, eds., 317 Olpin
Union, U. of Utah, Salt Lake City, UT 84112
Issues Indexed: (12-13); Subscriptions: $10/2 yrs., $5.50/yr.; Single
issues: $3

RevIn: *REVISTA/REVIEW INTERAMERICANA, John Zebrowski, ed., GPO
Box 3255, San Juan, PR 00936

Issues Indexed: (9: 4) (10: 1-3); Subscriptions: $35/2 yrs. (inst.),
$20/2 yrs. (ind.), $20/yr. (inst.), $14/yr. (ind.), $9/yr. (stud.);
Single issues: $5

RusLT: RUSSIAN LITERATURE TRIQUARTERLY, Carl R. Proffer, Ellen-
dea Proffer, eds., Ardis Publishers, 2901 Heatherway, Ann Arbor, MI
48104
Issues Indexed: No issues received in 1981; Subscriptions: $25/3 is-
sues (inst.), $16.95/3 issues (ind.), $13.95/3 issues (stud.); Back is-
sues: Prices on request; Cloth: Add $10 to each rate

Salm: SALMAGUNDI, Robert Boyers, ed., Peggy Boyers, Exec. ed., Skid-
more College, Saratoga Springs, NY 12866
Issues Indexed: (52/53); Subscriptions: $25/2 yrs. (inst.), $16/yr.
(inst.), $15/2 yrs. (ind.), $9/yr. (ind.); Single issues: $4

Sam: SAMISDAT, Merrit Clifton, Robin Michelle Clifton, eds., Box 129,
Richford, VT 05476, or Box 10, Brigham, Quebec J0E 1J0 Canada
Issues Indexed: (104-109; 111-117; 119-121); Subscriptions: $15/500
pages, $25/1000 pages, $150/all future issues; Single issues: Varies

SeC: SECOND COMING, A. D. Winans, ed., Box 31249, San Francisco,
CA 94131
Issues Indexed: No issues received in 1981; Subscriptions: $6.50/yr.
(lib.), $4/yr. (ind.)

SenR: SENECA REVIEW, James Crenner, Bob Herz, eds., Hobart & Wil-
liam Smith Colleges, Geneva, NY 14456
Issues Indexed: (10:2/11:1) (11:2) (12:1/2); Single issues: $3.50;
Double issues: $7

SewanR: SEWANEE REVIEW, George Core, ed., U. of the South, Sewanee,
TN 37375
Issues Indexed: (89: 1-4); Subscriptions: $15/yr. (inst.), $12/yr.
(ind.); Single issues: $4. (Note: The Sewanee Review was accidentally
deleted from the 1980 Index.)

Shen: SHENANDOAH, James Boatwright, ed., Richard Howard, Po. ed.,
Washington and Lee U., Box 722, Lexington, VA 24450
Issues Indexed: (31: 3-4) (32: 1-2, and 4); Subscriptions: $18/3
yrs., $13/2 yrs., $8/yr.; Single issues: $2.50; Back issues: $4

SinN: *SIN NOMBRE, Nilita Vientós Gastón, Dir., Box 4391, San Juan,
PR 00905-4391
Issues Indexed: (12: 2); Subscriptions: $20/yr. (inst.), $15/yr.
(ind.); Single issues: $4.25

Sky: SKYWRITING, Martin Grossman, ed., 511 Campbell Ave., Kalamazoo,
MI 49007
Issues Indexed: No issues received in 1981; Subscriptions: $5/2 issues;
Single issues: $2.50

SlowLR: SLOW LORIS READER, Patricia Petrosky, ed., 923 Highview St.,
Pittsburgh, PA 15206
Issues Indexed: No issues received in 1981; Subscriptions: $10/4 is-
sues, $5.50/2 issues; Single issues: $3

SmPd: SMALL POND, Napoleon St. Cyr, ed./pub., Box 664, Stratford, CT 06497
Issues Indexed: (51-53); Subscriptions: $4.75/yr.; Single issues: $2

SoCaR: SOUTH CAROLINA REVIEW, Richard J. Calhoun, Robert W. Hill, eds., Dept. of English, Clemson U., Clemson, SC 29631
Issues Indexed: (13: 2) (14: 1); Subscriptions: $5/2 yrs., $3/yr.; Back issues: $2

SoDakR: SOUTH DAKOTA REVIEW, John R. Milton, ed., Box 111, U. Exchange, Vermillion, SD 57069
Issues Indexed: (19: 1-3); Subscriptions: $17/2 yrs., $10/yr.; Single issues: $3

Some: SOME, Alan Ziegler, et al., eds., 309 W. 104th St., Apt. 9D, New York, NY 10025
Issues Indexed: No issues received in 1981; Subscriptions: $9/yr. (inst.), $5/yr. (ind.); Single issues: $2.50

SouthernHR: SOUTHERN HUMANITIES REVIEW, Barbara A. Mowat, David K. Jeffrey, eds., 9088 Haley Center, Auburn U., Auburn, AL 36849
Issues Indexed: (15: 1-4); Subscriptions: $8/yr.; Single issues: $2.50

SouthernPR: SOUTHERN POETRY REVIEW, Robert Grey, ed., English Dept., U. of North Carolina, Charlotte, NC 28223
Issues Indexed: (21: 1-2); Subscriptions: $4/yr.; Single issues: $2

SouthernR: SOUTHERN REVIEW, Donald E. Stanford, Lewis P. Simpson, eds., Drawer D, U. Station, Baton Rouge, LA 70893
Issues Indexed: (17: 1-4); Subscriptions: $12/2 yrs., $7/yr.; Single issues: $2

SouthwR: SOUTHWEST REVIEW, Margaret L. Hartley, ed., Southern Methodist U., Dallas, TX 75275
Issues Indexed: (66: 1-4); Subscriptions: $10/2 yrs., $6/yr.; Single issues: $1.50

Sparrow: SPARROW, Felix & Selma Stefanile, eds., Sparrow Press, 103 Waldron St., West Lafayette, IN 47906
Issues Indexed: (41); Subscriptions: $6/3 issues; Single issues: $2

Spirit: THE SPIRIT THAT MOVES US, Morty Sklar, ed., Box 1585, Iowa City, IA 52244
Issues Indexed: (6: 1); Subscriptions: $5/3 issues, $9/6 issues, $6.50/ volume (lib.), $12/2 volumes (lib.), $17/3 volumes (lib.); Single issues: $2

Stand: STAND, Jon Silkin, et al., eds., Jim Kates, American ed., 45 Old Peterborough Rd., Jaffrey, NH 03452
Issues Indexed: (22: 1-4); Subscriptions: $19.50/2 yrs., $10/yr.; Single issues: $2.50

StoneC: STONE COUNTRY, Judith Neeld, ed., 20 Lorraine Rd., Madison, NJ 07940
Issues Indexed: (8: 3) (9: 1/2); Subscriptions: $7/5 issues (ind.), $8/5 issues (lib.); Single issues: $2 & $4

Sulfur: *SULFUR, Clayton Eshleman, ed. , Box 228-77, California Institute
of Technology, Pasadena, CA 91125
Issues Indexed: (1: 1-3); Subscriptions: $18/yr. (inst.), $12/yr.
(ind.); Single issues: $5

SunM: SUN & MOON, Douglass Messerli, Literary ed. , 4330 Hartwick Rd.
#418, College Park, MD 20740
Issues Indexed: (11); Subscriptions: $15/3 issues (inst.), $10/3 issues
(ind.); Single issues: $4. 50

Tele: TELEPHONE, Maureen Owen, ed. , 109 Dunk Rock Rd. , Guilford,
CT 06437
Issues Indexed: (17); Subscriptions: $7/2 issues

Tendril: TENDRIL, George E. Murphy, Jr. , ed. , Box 512, Green Harbor,
MA 02041
Issues Indexed: (10-11); Subscriptions: $10/3 issues (inst.), $8/3
issues (ind.); Single issues: $3

13thM: 13th MOON, Ellen Marie Bissert, ed. , Drawer F, Inwood Station,
Inwood, NY 10034
Issues Indexed: (5: 1/2); Subscriptions: $17. 85/3 issues, $11. 90/2
issues; Single issues: $5. 95

ThRiPo: THREE RIVERS POETRY JOURNAL, Gerald Costanzo, ed. , Three
Rivers Press, Box 21, Carnegie-Mellon U. , Pittsburgh, PA 15213
Issues Indexed: (17/18); Subscriptions: $5/4 issues; Single issues:
$1. 50

Thrpny: THE THREEPENNY REVIEW, Wendy Lesser, ed. /pub. , Box 335,
Berkeley, CA 94701
Issues Indexed: (4-7); Subscriptions: $10/2 yrs. (ind.), $6/yr. (ind.),
$8/yr. (inst.); Single issues: $2

TriQ: TRIQUARTERLY, Elliot Anderson, Jonathan Brent, eds. , 1735 Ben-
son Ave. , Northwestern U. , Evanston, IL 60201
Issues Indexed: (50-52); Subscriptions: $35/3 yrs. , $25/2 yrs. , $14/
yr. ; Single issues: $5. 95

UnmOx: UNMUZZLED OX, Michael Andre, Erika Rothenberg, eds. , 105
Hudson St. , New York, NY 10013
Issues Indexed: (22); Subscriptions: $9/4 issues, $15/8 issues, Single
issues: $4. 95

Ur: URTHKIN, Larry Ziman, ed. /pub. , Box 67485, Los Angeles, CA
90067
Issues Indexed: No issues received in 1981; Single issues: $3. 95

US1: U. S. 1 WORKSHEETS, Deborah Boe, Dina Coe, Jack Wiler, eds. ,
US 1 Poets Cooperative, 21 Lake Dr. , Roosevelt, NJ 08555
Issues Indexed: (14/15); Subscriptions: $5/7 issues; Single issues:
$1. 50; Back issues: Prices on request

UTR: UT REVIEW, Duane Locke, ed. , U. of Tampa, Tampa, FL 33606
Issues Indexed: No issues received in 1981; Subscriptions: $9/4 is-
sues; Single issues: $2. 50 & $5

VirQR: VIRGINIA QUARTERLY REVIEW, Staige D. Blackford, ed. , Greg-
ory Orr, Po. cons. , One West Range, Charlottsville, VA 22903
Issues Indexed: (57: 1-4); Subscriptions: $24/3 yrs. , $18/2 yrs. ,
$10/yr. ; Single issues: $3

Vis: VISIONS, Bradley R. Strahan, ed. /pub. , Black Buzzard Press, 5620
South 7th Place, Arlington, VA 22204
Issues Indexed: (5-7); Subscriptions: $7/3 issues; Single issues: $2. 50

WebR: WEBSTER REVIEW, Nancy Shapiro, ed. , Webster College, Webster
Groves, MO 63119
Issues Indexed: (6: 1-2); Subscriptions: $4/yr. ; Single issues: $2

WestHR: WESTERN HUMANITIES REVIEW, Jack Garlington, ed. , U. of
Utah, Salt Lake City, UT 84112
Issues Indexed: (35: 1-4); Subscriptions: $20/yr. (inst.), $15/yr
(ind.); Single issues: $4

Wind: WIND, Quentin R. Howard, ed. , RFD Route 1, Box 809K, Pikeville,
KY 41501
Issues Indexed: (10: 39) (11: 40-43); Subscriptions: $6/4 issues
(inst.), $5/4 issues (ind.); Single issues: $1. 50

WindO: THE WINDLESS ORCHARD, Robert Novak, ed. , English Dept. ,
Indiana-Purdue U. , Fort Wayne, IN 46805
Issues Indexed: (38-39); Subscriptions: $20/3 yrs. , $7/yr. , $4/yr.
(stud.); Single issues: $2

WorldO: WORLD ORDER, Firuz Kazemzadeh, ed. , 415 Linden Ave. ,
Wilmette, IL 60091
Issues Indexed: (15: 1-4) (16: 1); Subscriptions: $11/2 yrs. , $6/yr. ;
Single issues: $1. 60

WormR: WORMWOOD REVIEW, Marvin Malone, ed. , Ernest Stranger, Art
ed. , Box 8840, Stockton, CA 95208-0840
Issues Indexed: (81-84); Subscriptions: $15/4 issues (patrons), $6/4
issues (inst.), $5/4 issues (ind.); Single issues: $2

YaleR: THE YALE REVIEW, Kai Erikson, ed. , J. D. McClatchy, Po.
ed. , 1902A Yale Sta. , New Haven, CT 06520
Issues Indexed: (70: 3) (71: 1); Subscriptions: $18/yr. (inst.),
$12/yr. (ind.); Single issues: $4; Back issues: Prices on request

Zahir: ZAHIR, Diane Krunchkow, ed. , Weeks Mills, New Sharon, ME
04955
Issues Indexed: (11); Subscriptions: $4/2 issues (ind.), $6/2 issues
(inst.); Single issues: $2. 50; Back issues: $2

ALPHABETICAL LIST OF JOURNALS INDEXED, WITH ACRONYMS

ACADEME: BULLETIN OF THE AAUP--Academe
THE AGNI REVIEW--Agni
THE AMERICAN POETRY REVIEW--AmerPoR
THE AMERICAN SCHOLAR--AmerS
ANN ARBOR REVIEW--AAR
ANNEX 21--Annex
ANTAEUS--Antaeus
THE ANTIOCH REVIEW--AntR
AREÍTO--Areíto
ARIZONA QUARTERLY--ArizQ
THE ARK--Ark
THE ARK RIVER REVIEW--ArkRiv
ASCENT--Ascent
ASPECT--Aspect
ASPEN ANTHOLOGY--Aspen
THE ATLANTIC--Atl

BACHY--Bachy
BALL STATE UNIVERSITY FORUM--BallSUF
THE BARAT REVIEW--BaratR
THE BELOIT POETRY JOURNAL--BelPoJ
BERKSHIRE REVIEW--BerksR
BLACK AMERICAN LITERATURE FORUM--BlackALF
BLACK FORUM--BlackF
BOUNDARY 2--Bound

CALIBAN--Calib
CALIFORNIA QUARTERLY--CalQ
THE CAPE ROCK--CapeR
CARIBE--Caribe
CAROLINA QUARTERLY--CarolQ
CEA CRITIC--CEACritic
THE CEA FORUM--CEAFor
CENTENNIAL REVIEW--CentR
CHARITON REVIEW--CharR
CHELSEA--Chelsea
CHICAGO REVIEW--ChiR
CHOWDER REVIEW--Chowder
THE CHRISTIAN CENTURY--ChrC
CIMARRON REVIEW--CimR
CLARIDAD--Claridad
COLLEGE ENGLISH--ColEng
COLUMBIA--Columbia
COMMONWEAL--Comm
CONCERNING POETRY--ConcPo

17

CONDITIONS--Cond
CONFRONTATION--Confr
CREAM CITY REVIEW--CreamCR
CROP DUST--CropD
CUTBANK--CutB

DACOTAH TERRITORY--DacTerr
DENVER QUARTERLY--DenQ
DURAK--Durak

EN PASSANT--EnPas
ENGLISH JOURNAL--EngJ
EPOCH--Epoch

FIELD--Field
FOCUS/MIDWEST--Focus
FOUR QUARTERS--FourQt

GEORGIA REVIEW--GeoR
GREEN RIVER REVIEW--GRR
THE GREENFIELD REVIEW--GreenfieldR

HANGING LOOSE--HangL
HARPER'S MAGAZINE--Harp
HILLS--Hills
HIRAM POETRY REVIEW--HiramPoR
THE HOLLINS CRITIC--HolCrit
THE HUDSON REVIEW--Hudson
HUMANIST--Humanist

IMAGES--Images
INTI--Inti
IOWA REVIEW--Iowa

JOURNAL OF NEW JERSEY POETS--JnlONJP
JOURNAL OF POPULAR CULTURE--JnlOPC

KANSAS QUARTERLY--KanQ
KAYAK--Kayak

LETRAS FEMENINAS--LetFem
THE LITERARY REVIEW--LitR
THE LITTLE BALKANS REVIEW--LittleBR
THE LITTLE MAGAZINE--LittleM
THE LITTLE REVIEW--LittleR
LUGAR SIN LIMITE--Lugar

MAIRENA--Mairena

MAIZE--Maize
THE MALAHAT REVIEW--MalR
THE MASSACHUSETTS REVIEW--MassR
THE MEADOWS--Meadows
MESTER--Mester
METAMORFOSIS--Metam
MICHIGAN QUARTERLY REVIEW--MichQR
THE MIDWEST QUARTERLY--MidwQ
THE MINNESOTA REVIEW--MinnR
MISSISSIPPI REVIEW--MissR
MISSOURI REVIEW--MissouriR
MODERN POETRY STUDIES--ModernPS
MONTEMORA--Montra
MUNDUS ARTIUM--Mund

THE NATION--Nat
NEGRO HISTORY BULLETIN--NegroHB
NEW ENGLAND REVIEW--NewEngR
NEW LETTERS--NewL
NEW WORLD REVIEW--NewWr
THE NEW RENAISSANCE--NewRena
THE NEW REPUBLIC--NewRep
NEW WORLD REVIEW--NewWR
THE NEW YORK REVIEW OF BOOKS--NewYRB
THE NEW YORKER--NewYorker
NIMROD--Nimrod
NORTH AMERICAN REVIEW--NoAmR
NORTH STONE REVIEW--NorthSR
NORTHEAST--Northeast
NORTHWEST REVIEW--NowestR
NOTICIAS DE ARTE--Notarte

OBSIDIAN--Obs
OHIO REVIEW--OhioR
ONTARIO REVIEW--OntR
OPEN PLACES--OP
OSIRIS--Os
OUTERBRIDGE--Outbr

PAINTBRUSH--Paint
PANACHE--Pan
THE PARIS REVIEW--ParisR
PARTISAN REVIEW--PartR
PAUNCH--Paunch
PEBBLE--Peb
PEQUOD--Pequod
PIGIRON--Pig
THE PIKESTAFF FORUM--PikeF
THE PIKESTAFF REVIEW--PikeR
PLAYBOY--Playb
PLOUGHSHARES--Ploughs
POEM--Poem
POET AND CRITIC--PoetC
POETRY--Poetry
POETRY EAST--PoetryE

POETRY NORTHWEST--PoetryNW
POETRY NOW--PoNow
PORTLAND REVIEW--PortR
THE POTTERSFIELD PORTFOLIO--PottPort
PRAIRIE SCHOONER--PraS
PRIMAVERA--Prima
PUERTO NORTE Y SUR--Puerto

QUARTERLY REVIEW OF LITERATURE--QRL
QUARTERLY WEST--QW

REVISTA/REVIEW INTERAMERICANA--RevIn
RUSSIAN LITERATURE TRIQUARTERLY--RusLT

SALMAGUNDI--Salm
SAMISDAT--Sam
SECOND COMING--SeC
SENECA REVIEW--SenR
SEWANEE REVIEW--SewanR
SHENANDOAH--Shen
SIN NOMBRE--SinN
SKYWRITING--Sky
SLOW LORIS READER--SlowLR
SMALL POND--SmPd
SOME--Some
SOUTH CAROLINA REVIEW--SoCaR
SOUTH DAKOTA REVIEW--SoDakR
SOUTHERN HUMANITIES REVIEW--SouthernHR
SOUTHERN POETRY REVIEW--SouthernPR
SOUTHERN REVIEW--SouthernR
SOUTHWEST REVIEW--SouthwR
SPARROW--Sparrow
THE SPIRIT THAT MOVES US--Spirit
STAND--Stand
STONE COUNTRY--StoneC
SULFUR--Sulfur
SUN & MOON--SunM

TELEPHONE--Tele
TENDRIL--Tendril
13th MOON--13thM
THREE RIVERS POETRY JOURNAL--ThRiPo
THE THREEPENNY REVIEW--Thrpny
TRIQUARTERLY--TriQ

UNMUZZLED OX--UnmOx
URTHKIN--Ur
US 1 WORKSHEETS--US1
UT REVIEW--UTR

VIRGINIA QUARTERLY REVIEW--VirQR
VISIONS--Vis

WATER TABLE--WatT
WEBSTER REVIEW--WebR
WESTERN HUMANITIES REVIEW--WestHR
WIND--Wind
THE WINDLESS ORCHARD--WindO
WORLD ORDER--WorldO
WORMWOOD REVIEW--WormR

THE YALE REVIEW--YaleR

ZAHIR--Zahir

AAL, Katharyn Machan
  "The Beets Poem." Hangl (40) Aut 81, p. 3.
  "Confessions." PoNow (6:1, issue 31) 81, p. 21.

AARNES, William
  "Three Memories." CarolQ (34:1) Sum 81, p. 39.
  "What Shall I Do?" SoCaR (13:2) Spr 81, p. 74.
  "Yard Work." SoCaR (13:2) Spr 81, pp. 72-73.

AARON, Jonathan
  "Auras." YaleR (70:3) Spr 81, pp. 408-409.
  "Betty & John." Iowa (11:2/3) Spr-Sum 80, p. 201.

ABBOTT, Anthony S.
  "After." NewEngR (3:3) Spr 81, pp. 430-1.
  "Daisies." SouthernPR (21:2) Aut 81, p. 33.

ABBOTT, Steve
  "How Lovely Wound Up" (for Rob & Pat Flores). Tele (17) 81, pp. 36-
    37.
  "Knockout Punch." Tele (17) 81, p. 37.
  "Pastoral Poem." Tele (17) 81, p. 35.
  "Trying To Fight Sexism With Snapshots As If Ockham's Razor Weren't
    Still A Guillotine." Tele (17) 81, p. 34.

ABBOTT, Ward
  "Here It is October." PoNow (6:1 issue 31) 81, p. 34.

'ABD al-SABŪR, Salāh see al-SABŪR, Salāh 'Abd

ABDEL HAI, Muhammad
  "The Poet." Stand (22:1) 80, p. 8.

ABERG, W. M.
  "The Artist in Charcoal." Chelsea (40) 81, p. 126.
  "The Listening Chamber" (for Renê Magritte). Chelsea (40) 81, pp.
    127-128.
  "The Party." Chelsea (40) 81, p. 128.
  "The Sleepers" (for Tom Duke). Chelsea (40) 81, p. 127.

ABERG, William
  "The Iron Knee of Dinner." Kayak (57) 81, p. 33.

ABINADER, Elmaz
  "Making It New" (for Greg). Nimrod (25:1) Aut-Wint 81, p. 98.
  "We Move by Water." Nimrod (25:1) Aut-Wint 81, p. 98.

ABLEY, Mark
    "The Dead Are Watching Over." MalR (58) Ap 81, p. 114.
    "On Holy Island." MalR (58) Ap 81, p. 115.
    "Shepherd's Bush Aubade." MalR (58) Ap 81, pp. 112-113.

ABLON, Steven
    "New Year's Eve Concert at Lincoln Center." Ploughs (7:2) 81, pp. 142-
    143.

ABRAMS, Doug
    "Bringing Out the Light." Wind (11:41) 81, pp. 3-4.
    "Reply Without Grace." CapeR (16:2) Sum 81, p. 9.
    "Turning Out the Mountains." Wind (11:41) 81, p. 3.

ABRAMS, Mary
    from Lessons To A Fourth Grade Class ("Lesson II," "Lesson III,"
    "Lesson VIII," "Lesson X"). Tele (17) 81, pp. 42-44.
    "Post-Partum Blues." Tele (17) 81, pp. 45-48.

ABRAMSON, Glenda
    "A Meeting with My Father" (tr. with Tudor Parfitt of Yehuda Amichai).
    Poetry (138:3) Je 81, p. 138.
    "Rain in a Foreign Land" (tr. with Tudor Parfitt of Yehuda Amichai).
    Poetry (138:3) Je 81, p. 139.
    "Things That Have Been Lost" (tr. with Tudor Parfitt of Yehuda Ami-
    chai). Poetry (138:3) Je 81, p. 137.

ABRAMSON, Leslie H.
    "Mango Notes." LitR (24:3) Spr 81, pp. 383-385.

ABSHER, Tom
    "Abandoned Farm." PoNow (6:3 issue 33) 81, p. 21.
    "Hunting with My Father." PoNow (6:3 issue 33) 81, p. 21.
    "Resting Place." PoNow (6:3 issue 33) 81, p. 21.

ACCONCI, Vito
    "(he asked) (what happened) (when it went) (on)." Chelsea (39) 81, p.
    204.
    "(here) (   ) (   )." Chelsea (39) 81, p. 200.
    "Page 1." Chelsea (39) 81, pp. 204-205.
    "A poster...." Chelsea (39) 81, p. 201.
    "A store is a supply of that (Over there, that's it)...." Chelsea (39) 81,
    pp. 202-203.

ACKERSON, Duane
    "Moonlight In Any City...." (tr. of Carlos Drummond de Andrade, w/
    Ricardo da Silveira Lobo Sternberg). Mund (12/13) 80-81, p. 271.

ADAM, Bruce Ormsby
    "The Inventory." WormR (84) 81, pp. 117-118.
    "The Spell." WormR (84) 81, p. 117.
    "Spring." WormR (84) 81, pp. 116-117.

ADAMS, Anna
    "Two Minutes Silence." Stand (22:3) 81, p. 28.

ADAMS, Barbara
    "Mother's Analysis, 1944." ModernPS (10:2/3), pp. 116-117.

ADAMS, David J.
    "Something Else." Wind (11:43) 81, p. 3.
    "The Bluebird." CentR (25:4) Aut 81, pp. 382-383.
    "North into Love." CentR (25:4) Aut 81, pp. 383-38[

ADAMS, Jeanne Nall
    "Absolutes." ChrC (98:26) 26 Ag-2 S, 81, p. 830.
    "Funeral Feast." ChrC (98:8) 8 Mr 81, p. 255.

ADKINS, Allen
    "Air tight." Obs (7:1) Spr 81, p. 27.
    "The death of uncle funk." Obs (7:1) Spr 81, p. 28.
    "Poem: I met a holy woman...." Obs (7:1) Spr 81, p. 26.
    "Uptown republic." Obs (7:1) Spr 81, p. 26.
    "Visions of the woman they almost lynched." Obs (7:1) Spr 81, pp. 26-
        27.

ADKINS, Geoffrey
    "Island Irrigation System." AntR (39:2) Spr 81, p. 203.

ADLER, Carol
    "it is the pure shape." Mund (12/13) 80-81, p. 114.

ADLER, Hans
    "Senior Citizen." ChrC (98:19) 27 My 81, p. 611.

ADONIS
    "A Dream for Any Man." Mund (12/13) 80-81, p. 31.
    "Elegy in Exile." Mund (12/13) 80-81, pp. 28-30.
    "The Fire Tree." Stand (22:1) 80, p. 7.
    "Invasion." Stand (22:1) 80, p. 7.
    "The Minaret." Nimrod (24:2) Spr/Sum 81, p. 47.
    "The Past" (tr. by Samuel Hazo). Mund (12/13) 80-81, p. 27.
    "The Sleep of Hands." Mund (12/13) 80-81, p. 27.
    "You Have No Choice." Nimrod (24:2) Spr/Sum 81, p. 47.

ADŪNĪS see ADONIS

AGUERO, Kathleen
    "Istanbul." PoNow (6:3 issue 33) 81, p. 1.

AGUILA, Pancho
    "Marilyn." Maize (4:3/4) Spr-Sum 81, pp. 44-5.

AGUILAR, Ricardo
    "Genesis of Teponaxtle." DenQ (16:3) Aut 81, p. 23.

AGUSTINI, Delmira
    Ten poems (four tr. by Beth Tornes; one tr. by Beth Tornes with Linda
        Wine). SenR (12:1/2) 81, pp. 96-109.

AHERN, Tom
    "Fascination." Chelsea (39) 81, p. 40.
    "One Hundred and One Signs of Failing Water Pressure." Chelsea (39)
        81, p. 41.
    "P.S. (etc.)." Chelsea (39) 81, p. 39.
    "A Postcard to a Friend." Chelsea (39) 81, p. 42.

AI
"Blue Suede Shoes." Iowa (11:4) Aut 80, pp. 87-91.
"Salome." Antaeus (40/41) Wint-Spr 81, pp. 252-253.

AI, Qing
"Coal's Reply" (tr. by Marilyn Chin). Iowa (12:1) Wint 81, p. 92.
"The North" (tr. by Marilyn Chin). Iowa (12:1) Wint 81, pp. 89-91.
"Snow Falls on China" (tr. by Marilyn Chin). SenR (12:1/2) 81, pp.
    114-16.
"Sun" (tr. by Marilyn Chin). Iowa (12:1) Wint 81, p. 93.

AICHINGER, Ilse
"Glimpse from the Past" (tr. by Allen H. Chappel). NewOR (8:2) Sum
    81, p. 189.
"Old View" (tr. by Stuart Friebert). Field (25) Aut 81, p. 65.
"Subtracted" (tr. by Stuart Friebert). Field (25) Aut 81, p. 64.
"Timely Advice" (tr. by Stuart Friebert). Field (25) Aut 81, p. 63.

AIKEN, William
"Urban Renewal: Boston." Sam (116) 81, p. 34.

AJAY, Stephen
"Tolstoy's Estate." Confr (21) Wint 81, p. 92.

AKERLUND, Erik
"I: The thewed horses slept" (tr. by John Currie and Leif Sjoberg).
    SenR (12:1/2) 81, p. 182.
"I: De tunga hästarna sov." SenR (12:1/2) 81, p. 180.
"II: De tar inte mycket med sig." SenR (12:1/2) 81, p. 181.
"II: They don't carry away much" (tr. by John Currie and Leif Sjo-
    berg). SenR (12:1/2) 81, p. 183.

AKERS, Ellery
"Camping at Night in the Desert." NowestR (19:3), p. 17.

AKHMATOVA, Anna
"Ah! You've Come Back" (tr. by Judith Hemschemeyer and Anne Wilk-
    inson). Hudson (34:4) Wint 81, pp. 553-554.
"Confession" (tr. by Judith Hemschemeyer and Anne Wilkinson). PoNow
    (5:6 issue 30) 81, p. 1.
"For Us to Lose Freshness" (tr. by Judith Hemschemeyer and Anne
    Wilkinson). Hudson (34:4) Wint 81, p. 553.
"I came as the poet's guest" (to Alexander Blok) (tr. by Judith Hemsche-
    meyer and Anne Wilkinson). Stand (22: 2) 81, p. 4.
"In a secret region for the intimate." (tr. by Mary Maddock). ChiR
    (33:1) Sum 81, p. 80.
"Kiev" (tr. by Judith Hemschemeyer and Anne Wilkinson). Hudson (34:
    4) Wint 81, pp. 552-553.
"Muse" (tr. by Paul Thorfinn Hopper). Vis (5) 81, n. p.
"My imagination obeys me" (tr. by Judith Hemschemeyer and Anne
    Wilkinson). Stand (22: 2) 81, p. 4.
"My pillow is hot on both sides" (tr. by Mary Maddock). ChiR (33:1)
    Sum 81, p. 81.
"One heart isn't chained to another" (tr. by Judith Hemschemeyer and
    Anne Wilkinson). PoNow (5:6 issue 30) 81, p. 1.
"Song of Our Last Meeting" (tr. by Judith Hemschemeyer and Anne
    Wilkinson). PoNow (6:1 issue 31) 81, p. 43.
"They didn't bring me a letter today" (tr. by Judith Hemschemeyer and

Anne Wilkinson). PoNow (5:6 issue 30) 81, p. 1.
"The Twenty-First" (tr. by Judith Hemschemeyer and Anne Wilkinson).
Hudson (34:4) Wint 81, p. 554.
"Under the Icon" (tr. by Judith Hemschemeyer and Anne Wilkinson).
Hudson (34:4) Wint 81, p. 552.
"Verses about Petersburg" (tr. by Judith Hemschemeyer and Anne
Wilkinson). Stand (22: 2) 81, p. 3.
"We are drinkers and fornicators here, one and all" (tr. by Judith
Hemschemeyer and Anne Wilkinson). PoNow (5:6 issue 30) 81, p. 1.
"When you're drunk you're so much fun!" (tr. by Judith Hemschemeyer
and Anne Wilkinson). PoNow (5:6 issue 30) 81, p. 1.

AKIN, Gulten
"Laughing Stock" (tr. by Talat Halman and Brian Swann). PoNow (5:6
issue 30) 81, p. 2.

AKTAN, Feriha
"Come, when you can" (tr. by Murat Nemet-Nejat). Mund (12/13) 80-
81, p. 115.

ALBAN, Laureano
"Here Everything" (tr. by Reginald Gibbons). Mund (12/13) 80-81, p.
293.

ALBERT, Frank J.
"African Violet." BlackALF (15:2) Sum 81, p. 72.

ALBERTI, Rafael
"Comet" (tr. by Brian Swann). PoNow (5:6 issue 30) 81, p. 2.
"Danger" (tr. by Brian Swann). PoNow (5:6 issue 30) 81, p. 2.
"Do Not Dump Rubbish Here" (tr. by Brian Swann). PoNow (5:6 issue
30) 81, p. 2.
"Lizard" (tr. by Brian Swann). PoNow (5:6 issue 30) 81, p. 2.
"A Pair of Threes" (tr. by Brian Swann). PoNow (5:6 issue 30) 81, p.
2.

ALBERT ROBATTO, Matilde
"Ahora." Mairena (2:5) Aut 80, p. 64.
"Así." RevI (10:1) Spr 80, p. 120.
"Habrás de Saber." Mairena (2:5) Aut 80, p. 64.
"Hoy." RevI (10:1) Spr 80, p. 122.
"No hay tiempo para versos." RevI (10:1) Spr 80, p. 121.
"Otra vez." Mairena (2:6) 81, pp. 66-7.
"Poco a poco." Mairena (2:5) Aut 80, p. 64.

ALBERTUS, Alexander
"Bit of an Elegy." Poetry (139:3) D 81, p. 157.
"A Novel of Jane Austen's." Ploughs (7:1) 81, p. 137.
"Now and Again." Poetry (139:3) D 81, p. 157.
"The Way A Man Chooses to be Photographed is Always Significant
(--Gore Vidal)." Ploughs (7:1) 81, p. 138.

ALBORNOZ STEIN, Suzana
"Despertar María" (with Graciela Paternó Ibarra). LetFem (7:1) Spr
81, pp. 90-91.

ALCOSSER, Sandra
"Each Bone a Prayer." Poetry (138:2) My 81, p. 102.

"The Entomologist's Landscape." Poetry (138:2) My 81, pp. 103-104.
"Ruddy Glow Against a Black Background." Poetry (138:2) My 81, pp. 105-106.
"The Trap." PoNow (6:3 issue 33) 81, p. 2.

ALCUIN
"An Elegy" (tr. by Fred Beake). Stand (22: 4) 81, p. 47.

ALDERDICE, Eve
"Endangered Species." Wind (10:39) 80, pp. 3-4.
"The Owl Drugstore." Wind (10:39) 80, p. 3.

ALDRICH, Marcia
"Something Shocking." PoetryNW (22:1) Spr 81, pp. 32-33.

ALEIXANDRE, Vicente
"Adolescence" (tr. by Donald A. Yates). Mund (12/13) 80-81, p. 405.
"Come, Come Always" (tr. by Alan Brilliant). Mund (12/13) 80-81, pp. 402-403.
"Con Todo Respeto." Lugar (1:1) 79, p. 23.
"El Más Bello Amor." Lugar (1:1) 79, p. 23.
"Fire" (tr. by Muriel Rukeyser). Mund (12/13) 80-81, p. 405.
"For Whom I Write" (tr. by Ben Belitt). Mund (12/13) 80-81, pp. 395-396.
"Idea" (tr. by Louis M. Bourne). Mund (12/13) 80-81, p. 404.
"It's Not Possible Now" (tr. by Lewis Hyde and David Unger). PoNow (5:6 issue 30) 81, p. 3.
"Love's Cutting Edge" (tr. by Lewis Hyde and David Unger). PoNow (5:6 issue 30) 81, p. 3.
"My Voice" (tr. by Willis Barnstone). Mund (12/13) 80-81, p. 403.
"No Man's Land" (tr. by Lewis Hyde and David Unger). PoNow (5:6 issue 30) 81, p. 3.
"Poet" (tr. by Ben Belitt). Mund (12/13) 80-81, pp. 400-401.
"They Who Dance Are Consumed" (tr. by Ben Belitt). Mund (12/13) 80-81, pp. 398-399.

ALESHIRE, Joan
"The Concord String Quartet Plays Rutland High." PoNow (6:3 issue 33), 81, p. 1.
"Family Man." PoNow (6:3 issue 33) 81, p. 1.
"Immune to Spring." PoNow (6:3 issue 33) 81, p. 1.

ALEXANDER, Michael
"Mr. Bradbury's Ohio Lawns." PortR (27: 2) 81, p. 50.

ALEXANDHROV, Aris
"Flavius Marcus to Himself" (tr. by Kimon Friar). Poetry (139:2) N 81, p. 89.
"The Knife" (tr. by Kimon Friar). Poetry (139:2) N 81, p. 89.
"No Man's Land" (tr. by Kimon Friar). Poetry (139:2) N 81, p. 88.
"Perturbation" (tr. by Kimon Friar). Poetry (139:2) N 81, p. 87.

ALFANI, Gianni
"Guido, Quel Gianni Ch'a Te Fu L'Altr' Ieri" (tr. by Ezra Pound). Iowa (12:1) Wint 81, p. 46.

ALFRED, William
"To a Friend in Fall." NewYRB (28:2) 19 F 81, p. 33.

al-HAJ, Unsi
"Is This You or the Tale?" (tr. by Sargon Boulus).   Mund (12/13) 80-
    81, pp. 166-167.

ALI, Agha Shahid
"Flight from Houston in January."   Poem (43) Nov 81, p. 32.
"The Previous Occupant."   Poem (43) Nov 81, p. 31.

ALIESAN, Jody
"Letter."   NowestR (19:1/2), p. 78.

ALKANA, Joseph
"Ephemera."   PortR (27: 2) 81, p. 82.

al-KHAL, Yusuf
from "The Long Poem."   Stand (22: 1) 80, p. 6.

ALLEN, Dick
"A Winter Morning."   Poetry (138:1) Ap 81, pp. 20-21.

ALLEN, Gilbert
"The Mother, Ironing."   SouthernPR (21: 1) Spr 81, p. 38.
"Testament" (to Barbara).   KanQ (13:3/4) Sum-Aut 81, p. 18.

ALLEN, Heather
"Walking with My Father."   NewEngR (3:3) Spr 81, p. 428.

ALLEN, James
"Birthday for the Father."   SewanR (89:2) Ap-Je 81, pp. 176-177.
"Farmer."   SewanR (89:2) Ap-Je 81, pp. 177-178.

ALLEN, Judith
"Lucy: In Memoriam."   Tendril (10) Wint 81, p. 10.

ALLEN, June
"Fallen Tree."   Wind (11:42) 81, p. 8.

ALLEN, Paula Gunn
"Beloved Women."   Cond (7) Spr 81, pp. 65-66.

ALLEN, Robert
"City Burning."   BallSUF (22:4) Aut 81, pp. 18-19.

ALLEN, Winifred
"Alphabet."   PoNow (6:3 issue 33) 81, p. 2.

ALLMAN, John
"Eugene O'Neill at Tao House."   PoetryNW (22:4) Wint 81-82, pp. 45-
    46.
"Marie Curie at the Grand Canyon."   PoetryNW (22:4) Wint 81-82, pp.
    43-45.

ALLWOOD, Martin S.
"The Wind-Bent" (tr. of Carl Frederik Prytz).   OntR (14) Spr-Sum 81,
    pp. 57-58.

al-MAGHUT, Muhammad
"Tourist."   Stand (22: 1) 80, p. 7.

ALMON, Bert
"Under Orders." MinnR (17) Aut 81, p. 27.
"Which Way the Wind Blew (for Robert Solomon)." MinnR (17) Aut 81, p. 26.

al-NAWWAB, Muzaffar
"Jerusalem" (Michael Beard and Andy Tenner). Nimrod (24: 2) Spr/
Sum 81, pp. 135-138.

ALONSO, María Victoria
"Ausencia." Mairena (3:7), p. 89.
"Disparo contra el mundo." Mairena (3:7), p. 89.
"Incendio en el alma." Mairena (3:7), p. 90.

al-QASIM, Sameeh
"Feast" (tr. by Sargon Boulus). Mund (12/13) 80-81, p. 22.

al-QASIM, Samih
"Songs of War." Stand (22:1) 80, p. 8.
"Travel Tickets." Stand (22:1) 80, p. 8.

al-SABUR, Salāh 'Abd
"On Repetition" (tr. by Muhammad Enani). Nimrod (24: 2) Spr/Sum 81,
pp. 124-125.
"Summing Up" (tr. by Muhammad Enani). Nimrod (24: 2) Spr /Sum 81, p. 123.
"That Evening" (tr. by Muhammad Enani). Nimrod (24: 2) Spr/Sum 81,
pp. 126-128.

ALSCHULER, Mari
"I Noticed Everything." Shen (32: 4) 81, p. 37.
"Still-Life with Mother and Vitamins." Shen (32: 4) 81, p. 36.

ALTHAUS, Keith
"The Feather." Agni (14) 81, pp. 89-90.
"First Memory." MissouriR (4:3) Sum 81, p. 26.
"The Lost." MissouriR (4:3) Sum 81, p. 24.
"Poem." Agni (14) 81, pp. 87-88.

ALURISTA
"¿Aztlán, quo vadis?" Maize (4:1/2) Aut-Wint 80-81, p. 64.
"Left just." Maize (4:3/4) Spr-Sum 81, p. 68.

ALVARADO TENORIO, Harold
Eight poems. RevI (10:3) Aut 80, pp. 409-413.

ALVAREZ, Griselda
"Arbol." RevI (10:2) Sum 80, p. 259.
"Decoy" (tr. by Elizabeth Bartlett). RevI (10:2) Sum 80, p. 262.
"Fruit" (tr. by Elizabeth Bartlett). RevI (10:2) Sum 80, p. 261.
"Fruto." RevI (10:2) Sum 80, p. 261.
"Hierba." RevI (10:2) Sum 80, p. 260.
"Pala." RevI (10:2) Sum 80, p. 263.
"Reclamo." RevI (10:2) Sum 80, p. 262.
"Shovel" (tr. by Elizabeth Bartlett). RevI (10:2) Sum 80, p. 263.
"Tree" (tr. by Elizabeth Bartlett). RevI (10:2) Sum 80, p. 259.
"Weeds" (tr. by Elizabeth Bartlett). RevI (10:2) Sum 80, p. 260.

ALVAREZ ROBLES, Tina
"City." Metam (3:2/4:1) 80-81, p. 25.
"So Often." Metam (3:2/4:1) 80-81, p. 25.

ALVEZ, Delia Cazarré de see CAZARRE de ALVEZ, Delia

ALWAN, Ameen
    "By the Sea." Mund (12/13) 80-81, p. 307.
    "A Tartness of My Anatomy." Mund (12/13) 80-81, p. 307.

AMESLEY, Cassandra
    "Heading for Shore." PoetryNW (22:2) Sum 81, pp. 32-33.

AMICHAI, Yehuda
    "Jacob and the Angel" (tr. by David Rosenberg). Nat (232:17) 2 My 81,
        p. 545.
    "A Meeting with My Father" (trans. by Tudor Parfitt and Glenda
        Abramson). Poetry (138:3) Je 81, p. 138.
    "Rain in a Foreign Land" (trans. by Tudor Parfitt and Glenda Abram-
        son). Poetry (138:3) Je 81, p. 139.
    "Songs for a Woman" (tr. by David Rosenberg). Nat (233:1) 4 Jl 81,
        p. 24.
    "Things That Have Been Lost" (trans. by Tudor Parfitt and Glenda
        Abramson). Poetry (138:3) Je 81, p. 137.
    "Tourist" (tr. by David Rosenberg). Nat (232:17) 2 My 81, p. 545.

AMMONS, A. R.
    "Spiritual Progress." YaleR (71: 1) Aut 81, p. 88.

AN, Min-yong
    "Return in Winter" (tr. by Graeme Wilson). WestHR (35:4) Wint 81, p.
        330.

ANDAY, Melih Cevdet
    "Chains" (tr. by Brian Swann and Talat S. Halman). WebR (6:1) Spr
        81, p. 18.
    "Copper Age" (tr. by Brian Swann and Talat S. Halman). LitR (24:3)
        Spr 81, p. 405-406.
    "Oblivion is Birds" (tr. by Talat S. Halman and Brian Swann). WebR
        (6:1) Spr 81, p. 15.
    "The Rowboat" (tr. by Talat S. Halman and Brian Swann). WebR (6:1)
        Spr 81, p. 17.
    "Sound" (tr. by Brian Swann and Talat S. Halman). WebR (6:1) Spr 81,
        p. 16.
    "Those Trees" ("Arama O Aglacari") (tr. by Ozcan Yalim, William A.
        Fielder, and Dionis Coffin Riggs). StoneC (8: 3) Spr 81, p. 31.

ANDERS, S.
    "She Said 'I Am Glad for Her.'" ChrC (98:33) 21 O 81, p. 1044.

ANDERSON, Barbara
    "Walking Out Into A Storm." Missouri R (4:2) Wint 81-82, p. 27.

ANDERSON, Claudia
    "The Ashes of Gramsci" (tr. of Pier Paolo Pasolini). SenR (12:1/2)
        81, pp. 143-55.
    "A Desperate Vitality" (tr. of Pier Paolo Pasolini). SenR (12:1/2) 81,
        pp. 157-67.
    "Testament Verses" (tr. of Pier Paolo Pasolini). SenR (12:1/2) 81,
        pp. 139-141.

ANDERSON, Erland
    "Esoteric icelandic bath 1241" (tr. of Lars Nordström).

PortR (27: 2) 81, p. 40.
"Sand Dunes." PortR (27: 2) 81, p. 16.
"Sibelius Museum, Turku, Suomi." PortR (27: 1) 81, p. 26.
"Smokey Bay" (tr. of Lars Nordstrom). PortR (27: 2) 81, p. 40.
"The hot water caves of Myvatn are they measured in meters or feet?"
    (tr. of Lars Nordström). PortR (27: 2) 81, p. 40.

ANDERSON, Jack
    "An Essay on Dance Criticism." Chelsea (39) 81, pp. 57-60.
    "The Guided Tour." PoetryE (6) Aut 81, pp. 65-66.
    "An Old Promise." PoNow (6:1 issue 31) 81, p. 16.
    "The Peaceable Kingdom." MinnR (17) Aut 81, p. 15.
    "A Poem of Tea." CharR (7:1) Spr 81, p. 23.
    "Their Work." MinnR (17) Aut 81, p. 14.

ANDERSON, James
    "Ballet at Nine Years Old." NowestR (19:3), p. 88.

ANDERSON, Jon
    "Sunlight/1944" (for J. L.). Antaeus (40/41) Wint-Spr 81, pp. 256-257.
    "The Time Machine" (for P. H.). Antaeus (40/41) Wint-Spr 81, pp.
    254-255.

ANDERSON, Kemmer
    "Jerusalem Ring." ChrC (98:7) 4 Mr 81, p. 232.

ANDERSON, Maggie
    "As Close." QW (12) Spr-Sum 81, p. 53.

ANDERSON, Michael
    "Cardiac Arrest." WormR (81/82) 81, p. 38.
    "Hens and Chicks, 1953." Hiram PoR (30) Spr-Sum 81, pp. 7-8.
    "Nursing Home Poetry Class." WormR (81/82) 81, p. 37.
    "Waterloo At Lithia Springs." WormR (81/82) 81, pp. 38-39.

ANDERSON, Nancy
    "Blue." BallSUF (22:2) Spr 81, p. 41.

ANDERSON, Sally
    "Raccoon." Aspect (77/79) 81, p. 8.

ANDERSON, Stanley P.
    "Faced with an Empty Bowl, the Weary Suburbanite Wishes He Could
    Create Sauerkraut Balls by Imitating God." KanQ (13:1) Wint 81, p.
    108.

ANDERSON, Susan
    "The Bay." AntR (39:2) Spr 81, pp. 200-201.

ANDERSON, Tom
    "Cuckold's Light." Aspect (77/79) 81, p. 7.

ANDERSSON, Claes
    "City" (tr. by Lennart Bruce). PoetryE (6) Aut 81, p. 9.
    "Dikter i Var Franvaro." SenR (12:1/2) 81, pp. 190, 192, 194.
    "Earthly Unearthly" (tr. by Lennart Bruce). PoetryE (6) Aut 81, pp.
    9-10.
    "Ensamheten är en pyramid staplad av mänska." SenR (12:1/2) 81, p.

188.
"The Falling in Love" (tr. by Lennart Bruce). SenR (12:1/2) 81, p. 185.
"Förälskelsen." SenR (12:1/2) 81, p. 184.
"Friendship" (tr. by Lennart Bruce). PoetryE (6) Aut 81, pp. 13-16.
"Loneliness is a pyramid, humans stacked" (tr. by Lennart Bruce). SenR (12:1/2) 81, p. 189.
"Mutters to Himself" (tr. by Rika Lesser). PoetryE (6) Aut 81, pp. 10-11.
"Nowadays there's much talk about identity" (tr. by Lennart Bruce). SenR (12:1/2) 81, p. 187.
"Nuförtiden talas mycket om identitet." SenR (12:1/2) 81, p. 186.
"Poems in Our Absence" (tr. by Lennart Bruce). SenR (12:1/2) 81, pp. 191, 193, 195.
"Some People" (tr. by Rika Lesser). PoetryE (6) Aut 81, pp. 12-13.

ANDRADE, Carlos Drummond de
    "E agora, José?" SenR (12:1/2) 81, pp. 88-90.
    "José" (tr. by Mark Strand). SenR (12:1/2) 81, pp. 89-91.
    "Moonlight in Any City" (tr. by Duane Ackerson and Ricardo da Silveira Lobo Sternberg). Mund (12/13) 80-81, p. 271.
    "The Onset of Love" (tr. by Mark Strand). NewYorker (57:28) 31 Ag 81, p. 40.
    "Sadness in Heaven" (tr. by Jack E. Tomlins). Mund (12/13) 80-81, p. 270.
    "Story of the Dress" (tr. by Mark Strand). Antaeus (40/41) Wint-Spr 81, pp. 276-281.
    "To Be." Mund (12/13) 80-81, pp. 270-271.

ANDRADE, Eugenio de
    "As Palavras." ModernPS (10:2/3), p. 190.
    "At that time, whoever followed the rough track" (tr. by Alexis Levitin). ModernPS (10:2/3), p. 193.
    "Ela ere a que parava no limiar um pouco." ModernPS (10:2/3), p. 192.
    "Nesse tempo, quem seguisse o." ModernPS (10:2/3), p. 192.
    "She was the one who stopped on the threshold" (tr. by Alexis Levitin). ModernPS (10:2/3), p. 193.
    "Vegetal And Alone" (tr. by Alexis Levitin). ModernPS (10:2/3), pp. 191-193.
    "Vegetal E Só." ModernPS (10:2/3), pp. 190, 192.
    "Words" (tr. by Alexis Levitin). ModernPS (10:2/3), p. 191.

ANDRE, Michael
    "Cowboy Boots." UnmOx (22) Wint 81, p. 52.

ANDREA, Marianne
    "Anatomy of Dreams." Vis (7) 81, n.p.
    "Angles and Shadows" (for W. S. Merwin). Wind (11:40) 81, pp. 2-3.
    "Beneath the Music from a Farther Room: T. S. Eliot...." Wind (11:40) 81, pp. 1-2.
    "Between 4 A.M. and Dawn." Wind (11:40) 81, p. 4.
    "Beyond the Cold." Wind (11:40) 81, p. 2.
    "Paintings by Chagall." Wind (11:40) 81, pp. 3-4.

ANDREJCAK, Dawna Maydak
    "It May Make You Forget." EngJ (70:5) S 81, p. 68.
    "So Many Boxes within Boxes." EngJ (70:4) Ap 81, p. 58.
    "Who Really Is a Gold Fish." EngJ (70:5) S 81, p. 82.

ANDRESEN, Sophia de Mello Breyner
 "The Small Square" (tr. by Alexis Levitin). <u>PoNow</u> (6:2 issue 32) 81,
  p. 41.

ANDRUS, David
 "The Hell-Box." <u>MalR</u> (58) Ap 81, p. 90.
 "Language." <u>MalR</u> (58) Ap 81, p. 91.

ANGEL, Ralph
 "Between Two Tracks." <u>NewYorker</u> (56:52) 16 F 81, p. 44.
 "Cyclone Off the Coast." <u>NewYorker</u> (57:10) 27 Ap 81, p. 145.
 "Ground Glass." <u>AmerPoR</u> (10:2) Mr-Ap 81, p. 29.
 "Home Poem." <u>AmerPoR</u> (10:2) Mr-Ap 81, p. 29.
 "Pas De Deux." <u>AmerPoR</u> (10:2) Mr-Ap 81, p. 29.

ANGELAKI-ROOKE, Katerina
 "Entrails and the Rest" (tr. by Kimon Friar). <u>PoNow</u> (5:6 issue 30)
  81, p. 4.
 "My Feet" (tr. by Kimon Friar). <u>PoNow</u> (5:6 issue 30) 81, p. 4.
 "Voyaging at Night" (tr. by Kimon Friar). <u>PoNow</u> (5:6 issue 30) 81,
  p. 4.

ANGELES RUANO, Isabel de los see RUANO, Isabel de los Angeles

ANGELIS, Milo De see DeANGELIS, Milo

ANGELL, Roger
 "Greetings, Friends!" <u>NewYorker</u> (57:45) 28 D 81, p. 41.

ANGLESEY, Zoe Rita
 "I Hear Music." <u>PortR</u> (27: 2) 81, p. 79.

ANGST, Bim
 "Drinking." <u>PoNow</u> (6:3 issue 33) 81, p. 2.
 "Farmer's Market." <u>PoNow</u> (6:3 issue 33) 81, p. 2.
 "Now I Have My Feet In." <u>CapeR</u> (16:2) Sum 81, p. 3.

ANONYMOUS
 "And life so." <u>UnmOx</u> (22) Wint 81, p. 8.
 "The Boyhood of Christ" (tr. by Thomas Kinsella). <u>ConcPo</u> (14:2) Aut
  81, p. 76.
 "Busco una pluma de tinta." <u>Claridad/En Roio</u> (22: 1488) 7-13 Ag 81,
  p. 12.
 "Créde's Lament for Dínertech." (tr. by Thomas Kinsella). <u>ConcPo</u>
  (14:2) Aut 81, p. 77.
 "Dornava Palace" (tr. by William McLaughlin). <u>DenQ</u> (16:1) Spr 81, p.
  78.
 "El Salvador: Interview With A Rebel" (hiding in Panama City when
  poem was written) (tr. by Tim Woodruff). <u>Sam</u> (116) 81, p. 56.
 "Epitaph of Dionysios of Tarsus." <u>SouthernR</u> (17:4) Aut 81, p. 999.
 "Fragment from an Anglo-Saxon Charm" (tr. by Ezra Pound). <u>Iowa</u>
  (12:1) Wint 81, p. 38.
 "I bring you news" (tr. by Thomas Kinsella). <u>ConcPo</u> (14:2) Aut 81, p.
  78.
 "I don't know who it is" (tr. by Thomas Kinsella). <u>ConcPo</u> (14:2) Aut
  81, p. 78.
 "Kisaeng Song" (after a translation by Peter H. Lee) (tr. by Michael
  Stephens). <u>Pequod</u> (13) 81, p. 67.

"On Beginning Chinese Studies" (for Edward Avak). SouthernR (17:4)
     Aut 81, p. 992.
"Several Paintings of the Middle Sung Period." SouthernR (17:4) Aut
     81, p. 993.
"Wang Hsi-chih Gazing at Geese." SouthernR (17:4) Aut 81, p. 992.

ANSON, Joan
     "Ajijac Before the Rains." Poem (43) Nov. 81, p. 8.
     "Doomsday." Poem (43) Nov. 81, p. 7.
     "The Plant Lady." Poem (43) Nov. 81, p. 6.

ANSON, John S.
     "To Music." ArizQ (37:3) Aut 81, p. 213.
     "The Whisperer." PoNow (6:1 issue 31) 81, p. 21.

ANTHONY, Alicia
     "Carmen the mulatto." Obs (7:1) Spr 81, p. 48.
     "Detroit visions (from 800 miles away)." Obs (7:1) Spr 81, pp. 49-51.
     "Pieces." Obs (7:1) Spr 81, pp. 51-53.
     "Socks and answers." Obs (7:1) Spr 81, pp. 54-55.

ANTHONY, George
     "The World Within a World." OP (31/32) Aut 81, pp. 96-97.

ANTHONY, Michael
     "At the Sundown Hour." Poem (43) Nov 81, pp. 44-46.

ANTONYCH, Bohdan
     "The End of the World" (tr. by Mark Rudman and Bohdan Boychuk).
          PoNow (6:1 issue 31) 81, p. 43.

ANZAI, Hitoshi
     "Other Men's Wives" (tr. by Graeme Wilson). DenQ (16:4) Wint 81, p.
          45.

APOLLINAIRE, Guillaume
     "Autumn" (tr. by Patricia O'Callaghan). PoNow (5:6 issue 30) 81, p. 5.
     "The Crocuses" (tr. by Patricia O'Callaghan). PoNow (5:6 issue 30)
          81, p. 5.
     "Marizibill" (tr. by Patricia O'Callaghan). PoNow (5:6 issue 30) 81, p.
          5.
     "Mirabeau Bridge" (tr. by Richard Wilbur). ParisR (23:81) Aut 81, p.
          110.

APONTE, René Rivera see RIVERA APONTE, René

APPLEGATE, Olive V.
     "Meditation." WorldO (15:3/4), p. 30.

APPLEMAN, Philip
     "The Voyage Home." Poetry (137:6) Mr 81, pp. 342-348.

APPLEWHITE, James
     "Notes from a Journal by the River." SouthernPR (21:2) Aut 81, p. 39.
     "Pamlico River." PoNow (6:1 issue 31) 81, p. 23.
     "Rosster's Station." PoNow (6:1 issue 31) 81, p. 23.
     "Science Fiction." Poetry (138:3) Je 81, p. 156.

AQUINO, Luis Hernández
"Ofertorio." Mairena (3:8) 81, p. 2.
Twelve poems. Mairena (3:8) 81, pp. 120-130.

ARCHER, Nuala
"Christmas in Dublin." CreamCR (6:2) 81, p. 11.
"Rocking for Mary L." CreamCR (7:1) 81, pp. 110-111.
"Whale on the Line." CreamCR (6:2) 81, pp. 9-10.
"Your Heart, a Sad Goldfish Bowl, Needs Some Flowers and an Alliga-
    tor or Two." CreamCR (6:2) 81, p. 12.

ARCHILLA, Graciany Miranda see MIRANDA ARCHILLA, Graciany

ARENAS, Bibi
"Milagro." Mairena (3:7) 81, p. 69.
"Poesía." Mairena (2:6) 81, p. 81.

ARENAS, Braulio
"Day to Day" (tr. by Mary Crow). PoNow (5:6 issue 30) 81, p. 5.

ARENAS, Rosa Maria
"Crystal City." 13thM (5:1/2) 80, pp. 20-21.

ARGUELLES, I.
"In a Forest of Windows...." Wind (10:39) 80, pp. 5-6.

ARGÜELLES, Iván
"Before Sleep." Kayak (56) 81, p. 27.
"The Book of Lucifer." PortR (27:2) 81, p. 84.
"Childhood: an August Night." Kayak (56) 81, p. 28.
"The Crashing of the City of the Sun." CreamCR (7:1) 81, p. 49.
"December." Os (13) Aut 81, p. 2.
"Dido." PortR (27: 2) 81, p. 84.
"End of the Horizon." CreamCR (7:1) 81, p. 50.
"Golden Age." Os (13) Aut 81, p. 3.
"In the Ascension the Descent By the Banks of the Meander: A Season
    in the Other Life." CreamCR (6:1) Aut 80, pp. 7-8.
"The land of Helen." PortR (27: 2) 81, p. 84.
"Poppies." Kayak (56) 81, p. 28.
"Remains of Flying." CreamCR (6:1) Aut 80, p. 9.
"Saint Petersburg." PortR (27: 2) 81, p. 84.

ARIDJIS, Homero
"Epitaph for a Poet" (tr. by John Frederick Nims). Mund (12/13) 80-
    81, p. 69.

ARISTEGUIETA, Jean
"Nocturno en la Piedra del Recuerdo." Puerto Wint 81, p. 17.

ARIZA, René
"Primer soneto a las chinches." Notarte (6:11) N 81, p. 7.
"Soneto." Notarte (6:11) N 81, p. 7.

ARMANTROUT, Rae
"Pending." PartR (48:2) 81, p. 260.

ARMITAGE, Barri
"Homecoming Bulletin." Wind (11:41) 81, p. 5.
"In Praise of Each Sparrow." ChrC (98:24) 29 Jl-5 Ag, 81, p. 769.

ARNADOTTIR, Nina Bjork
"Poem: It may well be" (tr. by Alan Boucher). Vis (5) 81, n. p.

ARRILLAGA, Francisco A.
"Yo voy por un camino solitario." Mairena (2:6), pp. 29-30.

ARRILLAGA, María
"A John Lennon en su muerte, y a Carlos Soto Arriví." Mairena (2:6)
81, p. 77.
"A Manuel Ramos Otero." Claridad/En Rojo (22:1461) 30 Ja-5 F 81,
p. 9.
"Ya pronto llegará mi hija." Mairena (2:6) 81, p. 76.

ARROWSMITH, William
"Bagni Di Lucca" (tr. of Eugenio Montale). AmerPoR (10:5) S-O 81,
p. 28.
"The Earrings" (tr. of Eugenio Montale). SenR (12:1/2) 81, p. 171.
"English Horn" (tr. of Eugenio Montale). AmerPoR (10:5) S-O 81, p.
28.
"In the Park at Caserta" (tr. of Eugenio Montale). SenR (12:1/2) 81,
p. 173.
"Lindau" (tr. of Eugenio Montale). AmerPoR (10:5) S-O 81, p. 28.
"Local Train" (tr. of Eugenio Montale). SenR (12:1/2) 81, p. 169.
"Motets" (tr. of Eugenio Montale). AmerPoR (10:5) S-O 81, pp. 28-
30.
Nine poems (tr. of Eugenio Montale). ParisR (23:81) Aut 81, pp. 42-
49.
"The Prisoner's Dream" (tr. of Eugenio Montale). NewYRB (28:6) 16
Ap 81, p. 19.
"Ten poems" (tr. of Eugenio Montale). Antaeus (40/41) Wint-Spr 81,
pp. 349-361.
"Voice that Came with the Coots" (tr. of Eugenio Montale). NewYRB
(28:6) 16 Ap 81, p. 20.
"You've Given My Name To A Tree?" (tr. of Eugenio Montale).
AmerPoR (10:5) S-O 81, p. 28.

ARTHUR, Robert P.
"Elegy to my Mother, the Poet." Poem (41) Mar 81, pp. 54-55.
"The Harbinger." Poem (41) Mar 81, p. 56.
"The Horn." Poem (41) Mar 81, p. 57.

ARVEY, Michael
"Transient." Wind (11:42) 81, p. 31.

ARZOLA BARRIS, Miguel
from Piedras de Este Tiempo: (III, IV, XVI). Mairena (3:7) 81, pp.
37-42.

ASHANTI, Asa Paschal
"Columbia" (for Natalie). Obs (6:1/2) Spr-Sum 80, p. 178.
"Haki at J. C. Smith." Obs (6:1/2) Spr-Sum 80, pp. 176-177.
"I Have This Friend" (for Ruby). Obs (6:1/2) Spr-Sum 80, p. 175.
"Karen M." Obs (6:1/2) Spr-Sum 80, p. 174.
"Marjorie Maxine Paschal (1930-1958)." Obs (6:1/2) Spr-Sum 80, p.
177.
"Texas." Obs (6:1/2) Spr-Sum 80, p. 174.

ASHBERY, John
"Caesura." NewYRB (28:4) 19 Mr 81, p. 42.

"Homesickness." ParisR (23:79) Spr 81, p. 72.
"Late Echo." Atl (247:2) F 81, p. 69.
"The Lonedale Operator." VirQR (57:3) Sum 81, pp. 454-455.
"The Pursuit of Happiness." NewYorker (57:1) 23 F 81, p. 46.
"Qualm." NewYRB (28:2) 19 F 81, p. 20.
"This Configuration." ParisR (23:79) Spr 81, p. 73.
"Untitled." Sulfur (1) 81, p. 56.
"Whatever It Is, Wherever You Are." Iowa (12:1) Wint 81, pp. 119-
   120.
"White Collar Crime." Sulfur (1) 81, p. 57.

ASPENSTRÖM, Werner
"The Cave" (tr. by Robin Fulton). Mund (12/13) 80-81, p. 354.
"The City" (tr. by Siv Cedering). PoNow (5:6 issue 30) 81, p. 5.
"In The Pizzeria" (tr. by Robin Fulton). Pequod (13) 81, p. 102.
"The Larks" (tr. by Robin Fulton). Pequod (13) 81, p. 103.
"The Sardine in the Subway" (tr. by Siv Cedering). PoNow (5:6 issue
   30) 81, p. 5.
"This Year Too" (tr. by Robin Fulton). Pequod (13) 81, p. 104.

ASPINWALL, Dorothy B.
"In Memory of Odilon-Jean Perier" (tr. of Jules Supervielle). WebR
   (6:2) 81, p. 20.
"Karma" (tr. of Yvan Goll). WebR (6:2) 81, p. 19.

ASTOR, Susan
"Alien Corn." PoNow (6:2 issue 32) 81, p. 23.
"Grandpa P." PoNow (6:2 issue 32) 81, p. 23.
"The Poem Queen." PoNow (6:2 issue 32) 81, p. 23.
"Withholding." PoNow (6:2 issue 32) 81, p. 23.

ASTRADA, Etelvina
"15" (tr. by Timothy J. Rogers). WebR (6:2) 81, p. 18.

ATHEARN, Hope
"All Small Creatures." Ploughs (7:1) 81, p. 152.

ATKINS, Kathleen
"Dame Alys." Atl (248:3) S 81, p. 78.
"Salvage." Wind (11:43) 81, pp. 4-5.

ATKINSON, Ron
"Baby Blue." AmerPoR (10:5) S-O 81, p. 11.

ATWOOD, Margaret
"Five Poems for Grandmothers." OP (31/32) Aut 81, pp. 123-127.
"Mushrooms." Atl (247:4) Ap 81, p. 37.

AUBERT, Jimmy
"Scene I, Liveoak Ridge." KanQ (13:2) Spr 81, p. 6.
"Yellow Grass." KanQ (13:2) Spr 81, p. 15.

AUDEN, W. H.
"Eleven poems: Lyrics for Man of La Mancha." Antaeus (40/41) Wint-
   Spr 81, pp. 11-30.
"With Old Eyes I Look Back" (tr. of Pär Lagerkvist, w/ Leif Sjörberg).
   Mund (12/13) 80-81, pp. 326-328.

AUSTIN, F. A.
"The Conquest of Space." Aspect (77/79) 81, p. 8.

AVILES CONCEPCION, Jorge Luis
"Mi sangre." Mairena (2:6), p. 30.
"Poeta." Mairena (2:6), p. 31.

AWAD, Joseph
"Gift." Wind (11:43) 81, p. 5.

AYALA, Elena
"Gran Finale." Puerto Wint 81, p. 18.

AZZOPARDI, Mario
"Jien Mitt Elf Mewta" (tr. by Grazio Falzon). PortR (27: 1) 81, p. 38.
"Paesagg 2" (tr. by Grazio Falzon). PortR (27: 1) 81, p. 37.
"Parabola" (tr. by Grazio Falzon). PortR (27: 2) 81, p. 34.
"Tonight the Moon is Cross-eyed" (tr. by Grazio Falzon). PortR (27: 2) 81, p. 34.
"Vizjoni 22X" (tr. by Grazio Falzon). PortR (27: 1) 81, p. 37.
"When the Light Is Dimmed" (tr. by Grazio Falzon). PortR (27: 2) 81, p. 34.

BAATZ, Ronald
"Red Sauce." WormR (84) 81, pp. 118-119.
"September Lines #4." WormR (84) 81, p. 119.

BABB, Sanora
"In a Field in Peloponesia." ArizQ (37:2) Sum 81, p. 126.
"Night Visit." SouthernR (17:3) Sum 81, p. 583.

BACOVIA, George
"Nocturna." SenR (12:1/2) 81, p. 128.
"Nocturne" (tr. by Peter Jay). SenR (12:1/2) 81, p. 129.

BADOR, Bernard
"Anabasis" (tr. by Clayton Eshleman). Kayak (57) 81, pp. 34-35.
"The Call of the Caverns." Sulfur (3) 82, pp. 21-22.
"End of the Walk." Sulfur (3) 82, pp. 24-25.
"Powerlessness." Sulfur (3) 82, p. 23.
"Progress" (tr. by Clayton Eshleman). Sulfur (3) 82, p. 20.

BAEHR, Ann-Ruth Ediger
"Agatha, at Ninety-Seven." Wind (10:39) 80, p. 7.

BAGWELL, J. Timothy
"History Lesson" (for Raoul). Poem (43) Nov 81, p. 65.

BAHATI, Amirh
"Lesson I: Memories & Illusions." Prima (6/7) 81, p. 11.

BAILIN, George
"Departures." WebR (6:2) 81, pp. 55-56.

BAILY, Robert
"Sonnet 11." PortR (27: 2) 81, p. 79.

BAINES, Bill
    "810331: For D.W." Meadows (2:1) 81, p. 59.
    "Go Noi Island: 1969." Meadows (2:1) 81, p. 32.

BAIRD, Andrew
    "November Wedding." NewYorker (57:39) 16 N 81, p. 54.

BAIRD, Ansie
    "Two Poets Talk of Dying." PoNow (6:3 issue 33) 81, p. 2.

BAKER, Beverly
    "The First Day." EngJ (70:7) N 81, p. 32.

BAKER, David
    "Antonyms: Morning and Afternoon Near the Osage River." CimR (55)
        Ap 81, pp. 48-49.
    "Caves." CharR (7:2) Aut 81, p. 16-17.
    "Front Porch." WestHR (35:4) Wint 81, p. 304.
    "Homeland." CapeR (16:2) Sum 81, p. 43.
    "How the Student Should Behave." PortR (27: 2) 81, p. 78.
    "Late: Missouri Farm Town." CapeR (16:2) Sum 81, p. 43.
    "Peabody #7 Strip Mine." PortR (27: 2) 81, p. 78.
    "Return to the Pond." CimR (55) Ap 81, p. 34.
    "Socks." PoNow (6:3 issue 33) 81, p. 3.
    "Utah: The Lava Caves." PoetryNW (22:3) Aut 81, p. 23.

BAKER, Donald
    "The Coffin." MinnR (17) Aut 81, pp. 16-17.

BAKER, Donald W.
    "Advising." ColEng (43:3) Mr 81, pp. 259-260.

BAKER, James T.
    "Tehran Farewell." ChrC (98:7) 4 Mr 81, p. 223.

BAKER, Leon
    "From The Moment Of Motion" (for Marlene Preby). StoneC (9: 1-2)
        Aut-Wint 81/82, p. 41.
    "Human Right!" BallSUF (22:3) Sum 81, p. 79.

BAKER, Lois
    "Sky Jump." PoNow (6:3 issue 33) 81, p. 3.

BAKER, Mary
    "The Quail." StoneC (8: 3) Spr 81, p. 26.

BAKKEN, Dick
    "Priest of the Bees." PoNow (6:1 issue 31) 81, p. 10.

BALABAN, John
    "All Souls' Night Romania." SouthernR (17:3) Sum 81, pp. 574-576.
    "Dr. Alice Magheru's Room." SewanR (89:1) Wint 81, pp. 25-26.
    "Harper's Ferry." SewanR (89:1) Wint 81, pp. 24-25.
    "Prince Buu-Hoi's Watch." Nat (233:3) 25 Jl-1 Ag 81, p. 86.
    "Rhonda." PoNow (6:1 issue 31) 81, p. 37.

BALAKIAN, Peter
    "Clamming." LitR (24:3) Spr 81, p. 408.
    "Thoreau at Nauset." CarolQ (33:1) Wint 81, pp. 10-18.

BALAZS, Mary
   "Dark Blood." Wind (11:42) 81, p. 3.
   "Dead of Winter." WebR (6:2) 81, p. 71.
   "Mojave Desert: A Self-Portrait." SmPd (18:1) Wint 81, p. 28.
   "No Lions." CapeR (16:2) Sum 81, p. 19.
   "No Turning Back." Prima (6/7) 81, p. 20.
   "Son, On His Father's Most-Recent Divorce." WebR (6:2) 81, p. 70.
   "Splendor: A Fantasy." Wind (11:42) 81, p. 4.

BALES, Eugene H.
   "There's a Little Friend Inside of Me." KanQ (13:3/4) Sum-Aut 81, p.
    50.

BALL, Angela
   "Agoraphobia." LittleR (7:1, issue 15) 81, p. 8.
   "The Cabin." LittleR (7:1, issue 15) 81, p. 8.
   "The Lake in the Woods." LittleR (7:1, issue 15) 81, p. 8.
   "Learning to Sew." LittleR (7:1, issue 15) 81, p. 7.
   "Writing Letters of Courtesy" (Found Poem). LittleR (7:1, issue 15)
    81, p. 7.

BALL, Thomas
   "The 20th Horror." Tele (17) 81, pp. 136-137.

BALLENTINE, Lee
   "Nalo." PortR (27: 2) 81, p. 65-67.

BALLIETT, Whitney
   "9 P.M." NewYorker (57:10) 27 Ap 81, p. 154.

BANANI, Amin
   "The Gift" (tr. of Forugh Farrokhzad, w/ Jascha Kessler). PoNow
    (5:6 issue 30) 81, p. 15.

BANERGI, Debashish
   "Yamini Krishnamurti seen dancing the Dasavatara." Os (12) Spr 81,
    p. 8.

BANSET, Elizabeth
   "Lullaby." Peb (21) 81, p. 81.

BARAKA, Amiri
   "Pres Spoke in a Language." ParisR (23:79) Spr 81, p. 74.

BARANOW, Heather Joan
   "Full Moon." HolCrit (18:3) Je 81, p. 12.

BARBER, Dave
   "Early Fogs." Poem (42) Jul 81, p. 47.
   "Elements." CapeR (16:2) Sum 81, p. 5.
   "Pastoral." Poem (42) Jul 81, p. 48.

BARBOUR, Douglas
   "City." PortR (27: 2) 81, p. 68.

BARCIA, Hugo
   "Versos para tu vientre (Albergas)." Mairena (2:6), p. 65.

BARCIAUSKAS, Jonas
  "Nothing Now." KanQ (13:1) Wint 81, p. 156.
  "On the Boat to Corinth." KanQ (13:1) Wint 81, p. 55.
  "Three Deer." HolCrit (17:6 [i.e. 18:1?]) F 81, pp. 18-19.

BARGEN, Walter
  "Closing the Circle." Wind (10:39) 80, p. 8.
  "Drifting." Wind (10:39) 80, p. 8.
  "Revelations." WebR (6:2) 81, p. 47.
  "Route 2." WebR (6:2) 81, p. 48.
  "Signs of Life in the Skaggs Employee's Bathroom." WebR (6:2) 81, p.
    46.
  "Wintered." KanQ (13:3/4) Sum-Aut 81, p. 75.

BARKER, David
  "Borges Was In The Morning Papers." WormR (84) 81, p. 110.
  "Cold Duck." WormR (84) 81, pp. 108-109.
  "Fire In The Hills." WormR (84) 81, p. 106.
  "I Like Sunday Nights." WormR (84) 81, p. 111.
  "Ode For The Very Separate." WormR (84) 81, p. 109.
  "Smogged Out." WormR (84) 81, p. 107.
  "Yellow Kitchens." WormR (84) 81, p. 112.

BARKER, Lucile Angela Morreale
  "Sunday Night Pops." WindO (38) Spr-Sum 81, p. 23.

BARKER, Wendy
  "Drive to the Pig Farm." PoNow (6:3 issue 33) 81, p. 3.
  "Exorcism of a Nightmare." Poetry (138:6) S 81, p. 333.
  "Grandfather." CalQ (18/19) 81, p. 45.
  "New Talk" (for my sister). CalQ (18/19) 81, p. 44.
  "Schönbrunn Yellow." AmerS (50:4) Aut 81, p. 450.

BARLOW, George
  "Eulogy: Adiós Adiós" (for A. M. R.). Antaeus (40/41) Wint-Spr 81, pp.
    258-261.

BARNARD, Jane
  "Adventures of a Toe" (tr. of Benjamin Péret, with A. F. Moritz).
    Bound (9:2) Wint 81, p. 249.
  "A Bunch of Carrots" (tr. of Benjamin Péret, with A. F. Moritz).
    Bound (9:2) Wint 81, p. 249.
  "The Farthest Face" (tr. of Benjamin Péret, with A. F. Moritz).
    Bound (9:2) Wint 81, p. 251.
  "Laughing Stock" (tr. of Benjamin Péret, with A. F. Moritz). Bound
    (9:2) Wint 81, p. 251.
  "Samson" (tr. of Benjamin Péret, with A. F. Moritz). Bound (9:2)
    Wint 81, pp. 251-255.

BARNES, Dick
  "Ballad." Tele (17) 81, p. 84.
  "Chuang Tzu And Hui Tzu." Tele (17) 81, p. 85.
  "Doctor Knows Best." Tele (17) 81, p. 84.

BARNES, Jane
  "Letter to My Father." Aspect (77/79) 81, p. 9.

BARNES, Jim
  "Book of the Dead, American Style." Tendril (11) Sum 81, p. 11.

"5-Ring Circus at Season's End" (Carson & Barnes).   CimR (55) Ap
    81, p. 18.
"Heartland."   GeoR (35:1) Spr 81, p. 64.
"Riding through Wyoming."   Aspect (77/79) 81, p. 10.
"Twister."   Aspect (77/79) 81, p. 10.

BARNES, Mike
    "Two Poems on Praise."   Northeast (3:11) Sum 81, p. 37.

BARNET, Miguel
    "Envio para Lourdes Casal."   Areito (7: 25) 81, front cover verso.

BARNSTONE, Aliki
    "Vanishing Point."   PoNow (6:2 issue 32) 81, p. 20.

BARNSTONE, Willis
    "The Adolescent" (tr. of José Angel Valente).   Mund (12/13) 80-81, p.
        146.
    "Ash Fruit" (tr. with the author, of Matei Calinescu).   SenR (12:1/2)
        81, p. 131.
    "The Bet" (tr. of José Angel Valente).   Mund (12/13) 80-81, p. 146.
    "Circling into Rainy Dawn."   LitR (24:3) Spr 81, p. 402.
    "The Domination of Miracle."   LitR (24:3) Spr 81, p. 401.
    "Forever" (tr. of Luis Beltrán).   SenR (12:1/2) 81, p. 93.
    "The garden entered the sea" (tr. of Odysseus Elytis).   PoNow (6:2
        issue 32) 81, p. 40.
    "God."   LitR (24:3) Spr 81, p. 402.
    "The Great Theater for the World."   SouthernR (17:2) Spr 81, p. 399.
    "The house I loved" (tr. of Antonio Machado).   PoNow (5:6 issue 30)
        81, p. 28.
    "Lazy Time, I Am Growing Old" (tr. with the author, of Matei Calines-
        cu).   SenR (12:1/2) 81, p. 133.
    "My Books" (tr. of Jorge Luis Borges).   DenQ (16:1) Spr 81, p. 54.
    "My Voice" (tr. of Vicente Aleixandre).   Mund (12/13) 80-81, p. 403.
    "I never looked for glory" (tr. of Antonio Machado).   PoNow (5:6 issue
        30) 81, p. 28.
    "The Nightingale" (tr. of Jorge Luis Borges).   DenQ (16:1) Spr 81, p.
        56.
    "Over the Limit" (tr. of Alfredo Silva Estrada).   Mund (12/13) 80-81,
        pp. 124-125.
    "The Panther."   Im (7:2) 1981, p. 12.
    "Pear."   LitR (24:3) Spr 81, p. 401.
    "Prohibition of Incest" (tr. of José Angel Valente).   Mund (12/13) 80-81,
        p. 147.
    "The red fire of a violet twilight" (tr. of Antonio Machado).   PoNow
        (5:6 issue 30) 81, p. 28.
    "That Nothing is Known" (tr. of Jorge Luis Borges).   DenQ (16:1) Spr
        81, p. 55.
    from "To Die of Another Dream" (tr. of Reynaldo Pérez Só).   Mund
        (12/13) 80-81, pp. 100-102.
    "Twilight."   SouthernR (17:2) Spr 81, p. 400.

BARR, John
    "Corpus."   WestHR (35:2) Sum 81, pp. 143-144.

BARRACK, Jack
    "Margins."   Epoch (30:3) Spr-Sum 81, p. 202.

BARRAS-ABNEY, Jonetta
"Even the flies are dying. " Obs (6:1/2) Spr-Sum 80, p. 167.
"Someone could get killed. " Obs (6:1/2) Spr-Sum 80, p. 166.

BARRAX, Gerald W.
"Big Bang. " PoNow (6:1 issue 31) 81, p. 23.
"The Buffalo Ghosts. " PoNow (6:1 issue 31) 81, p. 23.
"The Evolution. " PoNow (6:1 issue 31) 81, p. 23.
"There Was a Song. " PoNow (6:1 issue 31) 81, p. 23.

BARRETT, Carol
"The visitor is quieted against her will. " Prima (6/7) 81, p. 22.

BARRETT, Gloria
"Ali to Annie. " PottPort (3) 81, p. 52.

BARRETT, Joseph
"Night Errand. " Wind (11:42) 81, p. 5.
"A View From the Bridge. " SouthernHR (15:2) Spr 81, p. 152.

BARRIS, Miguel Arzola see ARZOLA BARRIS, Miguel

BARROWS, Brenda
"Dream of a Perfect Place. " PoetryNW (22:1) Spr 81, pp. 30-31.
"Moving Day in May. " PoetryNW (22:1) Spr 81, pp. 31-32.
"On the Ridgepole. " PoetryNW (22:1) Spr 81, pp. 29-30.

BARTH, R. L.
"from Vietnam Letters. " SouthernHR (15:1) Wint 81, p. 73.
"Letter from a Ward. " FourQt (31:1) Aut 81, p. 20.

BARTKOWECH, R.
"If the Train Will Arrive on Time. " PikeR (2) Sum 81, pp. 30-31.

BARTLETT, Elizabeth
"Decoy" (tr. of Griselda Alvarez). RevI (10:2) Sum 80, p. 262.
"Fruit" (tr. of Griselda Alvarez). RevI (10:2) Sum 80, p. 261.
"Shovel" (tr. of Griselda Alvarez). RevI (10:2) Sum 80, p. 263.
"Tree" (tr. of Griselda Alvarez). RevI (10:2) Sum 80, p. 259.
"Weeds" (tr. of Griselda Alvarez). RevI (10:2) Sum 80, p. 260.

BARTLETT, Lee
"Fishbones. " Poetry (138:2) My 81, pp. 100-101.

BARTMANN, Susanna
"Die/a/Log. " CreamCR (7:1) 81, pp. 8-34.

BARTON, David
"The bulls have turned...." ColEng (43:3) Mr 81, pp. 257-258.
"Santa Cruz. " ColEng (43:3) Mr 81, pp. 258-259.
"Totem. " CarolQ (34:1) Sum 81, p. 21.

BARTON, Fred
"Running. " Wind (11:43) 81, p. 8.

BASCIANO, Irma Trotta de see TROTTA de BASCIANO, Irma

BASIC, Husein
"Meeting" (tr. by Stephen Stepanchev). PoNow (5:6 issue 30) 81, p. 7.

BASS, Dorothy Ossery
"The Blue Straw." HolCrit (18:3 [i.e. 4]) O 81, p. 16.

BASS, Madeline Tiger
"From Areopagus Hill." Im (7:2) 1981, p. 8.

BASSETT, Lee
"Buffalo Jump." QW (13) Aut/Wint 81/82, p. 96.
"Fences." QW (13) Aut/Wint 81/82, p. 97.

BASSI, María Susana Caprara see CAPRARA BASSI, María Susana

BASTING, Alan
"Approaching Blindness." HiramPoR (29) Aut-Wint 81, p. 8.

BATES, Peter
"Jack Pepper, Junk Shop Owner." Aspect (77/79) 81, pp. 11-12.

BATES, Randolph
"The Mockbee House" (for Norman and Margaret). CreamCR (6:1) Aut
  80, pp. 34-35.

BATKI, John
"Szindbad and Sleeping Women" (tr. of Gyula Krudy). WebR (6:2) 81,
  p. 34.
"(Szindbad and) The Bishop's Niece" (tr. of Gyula Krudy). WebR (6:2)
  81, p. 35.

BATTIN, Wendy
"Cape Cod" (in memory, E. B.). PoetryNW (22:1) Spr 81, pp. 11-12.
"The Lighthouse Has No Keeper." PoetryNW (22:1) Spr 81, pp. 10-11.

BAUDELAIRE, Charles
Nineteen poems (tr. by Richard Howard). ParisR (23:82) Wint 81, pp.
  23-43.

BAUER, Grace
"The Day the Moose Died." PoNow (6:3 issue 33) 81, p. 3.

BAUER, Steven
"Between Two Oceans." MassR (22:2) Sum 81, p. 243.
"House on the Opposite Hill." CharR (7:1) Spr 81, p. 10.
"In Chekhov." MassR (22:2) Sum 81, p. 244.
"Marconi Station, South Wellfleet." MassR (22:2) Sum 81, p. 242.
"Ring-Necked Pheasant." PoNow (6:3 issue 33) 81, p. 4.

BAUSCH, Victor H.
"The Ides." PoNow (6:3 issue 33) 81, p. 4.

BAXTER, Charles
"Amnesia." NowestR (19:3) 81, p. 91.
"Astrological Guide." PraS (55:3) Aut 81, p. 93.
"Imaginary Paintings: Boredom of Dogs." CarolQ (34:1) Sum 81, p.
  35.
"Imaginary Paintings: Fleetwood Cafe." CarolQ (34:1) Sum 81, p. 34.
"Imaginary Painting: Harvest Home." AntR (39:3) Sum 81, p. 340.
"Imaginary Paintings: Jesus and the Stone." CarolQ (34:1) Sum 81, p.
  33.

BAZHAN, Mykola
"The Blood of Captive Women" (tr. by Mark Rudman and Bohdan Boychuk). PoNow (5:6 issue 30) 81, p. 6.
"Prince Igor's Campaign" (tr. by Mark Rudman and Bohdan Boychuk). PoNow (5:6 issue 30) 81, p. 6.
"The Road" (tr. by Mark Rudman and Bohdan Boychuk). PoNow (5:6 issue 30) 81, p. 6.

BBB
"Darkness Falls: Darkness Does Not Rise." Wind (11:42) 81, pp. 1-2.

BEAKE, Fred
"An Elegy" (tr. of Alcuin). Stand (22: 4) 81, p. 47.

BEAM, Jeffery
"Coming Home." PoNow (6:3 issue 33) 81, p. 4.

BEAM, Patricia S.
"Watercolor." CapeR (16:2) Sum 81, p. 14.

BEARD, Michael
"The Genie of the Beach" (tr. of Khalil Hāwi, w/ Adnan Haydar). Nimrod (24: 2) Spr/Sum 81, pp. 101-103.
"A Gift" (tr. of Fu'ād Rifqa, w/ Adnan Haydar). Nimrod (24: 2) Spr/Sum 81, p. 36.
"God of Time" (tr. of Fu'ād Rifqa, w/ Adnan Haydar). Nimrod (24: 2) Spr/Sum 81, p. 37.
"Jerusalem" (tr. of Muzaffar al-Nawwab, w/ Andy Tenner). Nimrod (24: 2) Spr/Sum 81, pp. 135-138.
"My beloved says" (tr. of Fu'ād Rifqa, w/ Adnan Haydar). Nimrod (24: 2) Spr/Sum 81, p. 38.
"Smoke" (tr. of Fu'ād Rifqa, w/ Adnan Haydar). Nimrod (24: 2) Spr/Sum 81, p. 35.
"A Tale" (tr. of Fu'ād Rifqa, w/ Adnan Haydar). Nimrod (24: 2) Spr/Sum 81, p. 37.
"Verdura" (tr. of Fu'ād Rifqa, w/ Adnan Haydar). Nimrod (24: 2) Spr/Sum 81, p. 38.

BEASLEY, Bruce
"Amen." CutB (17) Aut-Wint 81, p. 46.
"The Crucifixion." CutB (17) Aut-Wint 81, p. 45.
"Talking To My Parents." QW (12) Spr-Sum 81, p. 46.

BEASLEY, Sherry
"This Is a Circus and the Horse Is Dead." HiramPoR (29) Aut-Wint 81, p. 9.

BECK, D. H.
"Destinations." PottPort (3) 81, p. 15.

BECK, John P.
"The Zealous Dentist." WindO (38) Spr-Sum 81, p. 45.

BECKER, Robin
"A Long Distance" (for L.). Aspect (77/79) 81, p. 15.
"The Plan" (for J.G. and M.G.). Aspect (77/79) 81, p. 13.
"Policy." Aspect (77/79) 81, p. 14.
"The Sketchbook" (for Kate). CarolQ (34:2) Aut 81, p. 69.

BECKETT, Tom
  "Stanzas." SunM (11) Spr 81, pp. 50-57.

BEDELL, Betty
  "The Way It Is." Tele (17) 81, p. 79.

BEDELL, Sean
  "Orchard of Apples." WindO (39) Wint 81/82, p. 21.
  "We Must Kill The Dragon." WindO (39) Wint 81/82, p. 22.

BEELER, Janet
  "Small Dead Animals." AmerPoR (10:4) Jl-Ag 81, p. 37.
  "The Tightrope Walker." OP (31/32) Aut 81, pp. 144-145.

BEHM, Richard
  "A Death in the Family." MidwQ (22:3) Spr 81, pp. 255-6.
  "A Dream of Woman." Northeast (3:11) Sum 81, p. 30.
  "Geographies of Loss (for Fred Eckman)." Northeast (3:11) Sum 81,
     p. 31.
  "Good Friday at the Laundromat." MidwQ (22:3) Spr 81, p. 257.
  "The Hunchback Dancers." CapeR (16:2) Sum 81, p. 16.
  "Jacob." CapeR (17:1) Wint 81, p. 6.
  "A Night of Animal Logic." KanQ (13:3/4) Sum-Aut 81, p. 16.
  "Nightpoem IV." KanQ (13:3/4) Sum-Aut 81, p. 17.

BEHRENDT, Lynn
  "1. Rome." Sulfur (1) 81, pp. 98-99.
  "2. Assisi." Sulfur (1) 81, pp. 100-101.
  "3. Rome." Sulfur (1) 81, pp. 102-103.

BEHRENDT, Stephen C.
  "Not Dragon's Teeth, But." SouthernPR (21: 1) Spr 81, p. 32.

BEINING, Guy
  "The Eclipse of Road, Town, and Self." EnPas (12), 81, p. 22.
  "Stoma 676. (section XIX--Artmous) unfound history." Tele (17) 81,
     p. 139.
  "Stoma 677." Tele (17) 81, p. 140.
  "Stoma 678." Tele (17) 81, p. 140.
  "Stoma 679." Tele (17) 81, p. 141.

BEISSEL, Henry
  "November" (tr. of Peter Huchel). Mund (12/13) 80-81, p. 32.
  "Verona" (tr. of Peter Huchel). Mund (12/13) 80-81, p. 33.

BEJEL, Emilio
  "A José J. Arrom." Areito (27: 28) 81, p. 36.

BELITT, Ben
  "Amores: Matilde" (tr. of Pablo Neruda). Mund (12/13) 80-81, pp.
     370-373.
  "Carol Adler" (tr. of Lucia Ungaro de Fox). Mund (12/13) 80-81, p.
     114.
  "For Whom I Write" (tr. of Vicente Aleixandre). Mund (12/13) 80-81,
     pp. 395-396.
  "Graffiti." GeoR (35:3) Aut 81, pp. 608-609.
  "I Know Nothing At All" (tr. of Pablo Neruda). Mund (12/13) 80-81, p.
     374.

"Necropolis and Perspectives" (tr. of Lucia Ungaro de Fox).   Mund
     (12/13) 80-81, p. 113.
"Poet" (tr. of Vicente Aleixandre).   Mund (12/13) 80-81, pp. 400-401.
"They Who Dance Are Consumed" (tr. of Vicente Aleixandre).   Mund
     (12/13) 80-81, pp. 398-399.

BELL, Marvin
     "Birds Who Nest in the Garage."   Ploughs (6:4) 81, pp. 17-20.
     "The Canal At Rye."   Ploughs (6:4) 81, pp. 21-22.
     "A Correspondence In Poetry" (w/ William Stafford) (24, 28, 30, 32,
          38, 40, 42).   AmerPoR (10:6) N-D 81, pp. 4-7.
     "During the War."   Atl (248:2) Ag 81, p. 28.
     "Eight poems."   AmerPoR (10:2) Mr-Ap 81, pp. 9-12.
     "Fighting November."   Nat (232:18) 9 My 81, p. 574.
     "Haleakala Crater, Maui."   Antaeus (40/41) Wint-Spr 81, pp. 266-267.
     "The Hedgeapple."   Antaeus (40/41) Wint-Spr 81, pp. 264-65.
     "Italian."   VirQR (57:3) Sum 81, pp. 466-467.
     "Late Naps."   Antaeus (40/41) Wint-Spr 81, pp. 262-263.
     "Little Story."   Ploughs (6:4) 81, p. 23.
     "A Motor."   NewYorker (57:15) 1 Je 81, p. 44.
     "Teaching Shriek."   Ploughs (6:4) 81, p. 24.
     "These Green-Going-to-Yellow."   Iowa (12:1) Wint 81, p. 1.
     "To an Adolescent Weeping Willow."   VirQR (57:3) Sum 81, pp. 464-
          465.
     "You Thought So Far."   GeoR (35:4) Wint 81, p. 872.

BELL, Robyn
     "Beginner."   ThRiPo (17/18) 81, p. 58.

BELLA, Joachim Du see Du BELLA, Joachim

BELLI, Carlos
     "Cien mil gracias."   SenR (12:1/2) 81, p. 110.
     "A Hundred Thousand Thanks" (tr. by Ken Weisner).   SenR (12:1/2) 81,
          p. 111.

BELLI, Giuseppe
     "A Rare Fish" (tr. by Robert Garioch w/ Antonia Stott).   Stand (22: 4)
          81, p. 4.
     "The Vou" (tr. by Robert Garioch w/ Antonia Stott).   Stand (22: 4) 81,
          p. 5.
     "The Wee Thief's Mither" (tr. by Robert Garioch w/ Antonia Stott).
          Stand (22: 4) 81, p. 4.

BELTRAN, Luis
     "Forever" (tr. by Willis Barnstone).   SenR (12:1/2) 81, p. 93.
     "Para toda la vida."   SenR (12:1/2) 81, p. 92.

BENAJOUN, Robert
     "Perception of the Right Line" (tr. by Elton Glaser and Janice Fritsch).
          ChiR (32:2) Aut 80, p. 29.
     "Ravishing" (tr. by Elton Glaser and Janice Fritsch).   ChiR (32:2) Aut
          80, p. 28.

BENBOW, Margaret
     "Cooking Lesson."   Poetry (137:5) F 81, p. 262.
     "Crazy Arms: Earlene Remembers."   Poetry (139:1) O 81, p. 9.
     "Hard Freeze."   Poetry (137:5) F 81, pp. 260-261.

"Laura's Visit to Aunt Lucrece." Poetry (139:1) O 81, pp. 8-9.
"The Queen of Everything." Poetry (137:5) F 81, p. 258-259.
"Racine 1950." Poetry (137:5) F 81, p. 263-264.
"Rose's Farm." Poetry (139:1) O 81, pp. 10-11.

BENDER, Sheila
"Burying the Dead Fish." PoetryNW (22:2) Sum 81, p. 23.

BENEDETTI, Mario
"Semántica." Calib (3:2) Aut-Wint 80, pp. 88-90.
"Semantics" (tr. by D. A. McMurray). Calib (3:2) Aut-Wint 80, pp. 89-91.

BENEDICT, Elinor
"Red-Tailed Hawk Over Stonington." SouthernHR (15:2) Spr 81, p. 130.

BENEDIKT, Michael
"The Beloved" (tr. of Paul Eluard). UnmOx (22) Wint 81, p. 37.
"The Dangerous Word Dude." SenR (10:2/11:1) 79-80, pp. 63-68.
"Fixing Her Little Red Wagon." UnmOx (22) Wint 81, pp. 38-39.
"How in Boston One Sunny Afternoon in June Psychology & Politics Fail the Literal But Poetry Helps" (for Z.). Aspect (77/79) 81, pp. 16-17.
"Mighty Talky Letter To Grace Schulman." Agni (14) 81, pp. 91-95.
"St. Rafael's Lament." ParisR (23:79) Spr 81, p. 75.
"A Vision" (tr. of Gérard de Nerval). SenR (12:1/2) 81, p. 51.

BENESA, Leonidas V.
"Meta Phora Jakarta." PortR (27: 2) 81, p. 37.
"Song to Deirdre." PortR (27: 2) 81, p. 37.
"Stigmata." PortR (27: 2) 81, p. 37.
"The Unholy Tooth." PortR (27: 2) 81, p. 37.

BENN, Gottfried
"Appendix" (tr. by Graeme Wilson). WestHR (35:3) Aut 81, pp. 216-17.
"I have met persons who" (tr. by Francis Golffing). PoNow (5:6 issue 30) 81, p. 7.

BENNETT, Beth
"First Snow." EngJ (70:5) S 81, p. 89.

BENNETT, Bruce
"At the Border." PoNow (6:2 issue 32) 81, p. 13.
"The Bone." Vis (7) 81, n. p.
"Rebellion." PoNow (6:3 issue 33) 81, p. 4.
"The Story-Teller." Vis (7) 81, n. p.
"The Unseen Hand." PoNow (6:2 issue 32) 81, p. 13.

BENNETT, Maria
"After Roses, Anaesthesia." SmPd (18:1) Wint 81, p. 24.

BEN-SHA'UL, Moseh
"You Wove Me A Long Blanket" (tr. by Bernhard Frank). PoNow (5:6 issue 30) 81, p. 7.

BENSHEIMER, Virginia
"A Portrait." LittleM (13:1/2) Spr-Sum 79, c1981, p. 109.

BENSKO, John
"A Guide To Trusting The Natives." Shen (32:2) 81, p. 84.
"A Last Look in the Sambre Canal" (for Wilfred Owen). PoNow (6:3 issue 33) 81, p. 21.
"The Trout Stream." PoetryNW (22:1) Spr 81, pp. 42-43.
"Uncle Robert's Peanut Vending Machines." PoNow (6:3 issue 33) 81, p. 21.

BENTLEY, Beth
"Bedtime." PoNow (6:2 issue 32) 81, p. 6.
"Lies, All Lies." PoetryNW (22:3) Aut 81, pp. 26-27.
"The Mechanism." PoNow (6:2 issue 32) 81, p. 6.
"Unnumbered Grandmother Song." StoneC (8: 3) Spr 81, pp. 10-11.
"Unnumbered Grandmother Song." StoneC (9: 1-2) Aut-Wint 81/82, pp. 78-79.

BENTLEY, Sean
"Bookmobile Crosses the Siskiyous." PoNow (6:3 issue 33) 81, p. 5.
"The Boy Who Was the Suitor of Electricity." PoNow (6:3 issue 33) 81, p. 5.
"Not a True Story." PoNow (6:3 issue 33) 81, p. 5.

BEN-TOV, S.
"Beginning Changes" (for AML). SouthernPR (21:2) Aut 81, pp. 61-62.
"The Biosphere of Knowledge." Ploughs (6:4) 81, pp. 27-29.
"Communication Theory." Ploughs (6:4) 81, p. 26.

BEN-TOV, Sharona
"My Old Friend Writes" (to Sarah). Tendril (10) Wint 81, p. 11.

BENVENUTO, Joyce
"The Raven's Fee." KanQ (13:1) Wint 81, p. 93.

BERG, Kimberly
"Until a Creature Stirs." Vis (7) 81, n.p.

BERG, Stephen
"And the Scream." Antaeus (40/41) Wint-Spr 81, pp. 273-274.
"Gratitude." Antaeus (40/41) Wint-Spr 81, pp. 268-269.
"In It." Antaeus (40/41) Wint-Spr 81, pp. 270-272.
"Late Spring." Iowa (11:2/3) Spr-Sum 80, pp. 83-84.

BERGE, Carol
"A Source of Light." UnmOx (22) Wint 81, p. 71.

BERGER, Suzanne
"Myth." Tendril (11) Sum 81, p. 12.

BERGER, Suzanne E.
"Over Chicago." Ploughs (7:1) 81, pp. 96-97.
"The Sister-Fish." MassR (22:3) Aut 81, pp. 446-447.

BERGMAN, David
"The Laying on of Hands." Shen (31:4) 80, pp. 12-13.

BERKE, Judith
"The Box." Pequod (13) 81, p. 18.
"The Jester." WormR (81/82) 81, pp. 9-10.

"A Knight." WormR (81/82) 81, pp. 7-8.
"Mermaid." StoneC (9: 1-2) Aut-Wint 81/82, p. 43.
"Mona Lisa." SouthernHR (15:3) Sum 81, p. 218.
"A Parrot." WormR (81/82) 81, p. 10.
"A Princess." WormR (81/82) 81, pp. 8-9.

BERKLEY, Rosalie Bay
    "Each Grabs for Breath." WebR (6:2) 81, p. 62.
    "William and Catherine Blake." WebR (6:2) 81, p. 61.

BERLIND, Bruce
    "The Geyser" (tr. of Agnes Nemes Nagy). PoNow (5:6 issue 30) 81, p.
    24.
    "The Scene" (tr. of Agnes Nemes Nagy). PoNow (5:6 issue 30) 81, p.
    24.

BERMAN, Ruth
    "Bedrock, Northern Minnesota." Im (7:3) 81, p. 8.
    "Dyed Garden." KanQ (13:3/4) Sum-Aut 81, p. 46.

BERMUDEZ, Ariel Santiago see SANTIAGO BERMUDEZ, Ariel

BERNAL, Juan Manuel
    "Cheech and Chong together." Maize (4:3/4) Spr-Sum 81, p. 78.
    "It took ten powerful trucks to haul." Maize (4:3/4) Spr-Sum 81, p. 80.
    "La vida fascinante de un individuo trivial." Maize (4:3/4) Spr-Sum
    81, p. 78.
    "Monólogo congruente." Maize (4:3/4) Spr-Sum 81, p. 80.
    "Oda a García Lorca." Maize (4:3/4) Spr-Sum 81, p. 79.
    "Quiero jugar bebeleche y la cebolla." Maize (4:3/4) Spr-Sum 81, p.
    79.

BERNAUER, Carol
    "Grim's Fairy Tale." Sam (117) 81, p. 50.
    "Manic." Sam (116) 81, p. 55.

BERNSTEIN, Charles
    "Island Life." SunM (11) Spr 81, pp. 95-101.
    "Islets/Irritations." SunM (11) Spr 81, pp. 92-94.

BERNSTEIN, Susan Naomi
    "Every so often." PortR (27: 2) 81, p. 93.

BERRIOS, Juan José
    "Elegía del trabajador." Caribe (2: 2/3) 80/81, p. 64.

BERROCAL, Beatriz
    "Elegía para Adolfina." Mairena (2:5) Aut 80, p. 4.

BERRY, Donald L.
    "The Secret of the Redeemed." ChrC (98:26) 26 Ag-2 S, 81, p. 832.

BERRYMAN, Jill E.
    "Grampa." Meadows (2:1) 81, p. 59.

BERTAGNOLLI, Olivia
    "Journey." SouthernPR (21:2) Aut 81, p. 24.
    "Kingman, Kansas." SouthernPR (21:1) Spr 81, p. 59.

BERTOLINO, James
   "The Big Rig." PoNow (6:2 issue 32) 81, p. 23.
   "The Fruit Vendor." PoNow (6:1 issue 31) 81, p. 22.
   "The Pear Orchard." PoNow (6:1 issue 31) 81, p. 22.
   "The Professional." PoNow (6:2 issue 32) 81, p. 23.
   "Turtle Song." PoNow (6:2 issue 32) 81, p. 23.
   "Winter Spiders." PoNow (6:1 issue 31) 81, p. 22.

BERTOLUCCI, Attilio
   "Giovanni Diodati" (tr. by Charles Tomlinson). Stand (22: 3) 81, p. 21.

BERTRAND, Kate
   "Riptide." HiramPoR (30) Spr-Sum 81, p. 9.

BETANCES, Ramón Emeterio
   "El antillano proscrito." Claridad/En Rojo (22: 1472) 17-23 Ap 81, p.
      11.

BETT, Stephen
   "Preparation for a Gift" (for Pam). Chelsea (40) 81, pp. 96-97.

BETTS, Chris
   "Rats at a Duel." HangL (40) Aut 81, p. 61.
   "Sunset." HangL (40) Aut 81, p. 62.

BETZ, Daniel R.
   "Aborted Lives: Irony in Three Parts." Sam (106) 81, pp. 48-49.

BEVOISE, Arlene De see DeBEVOISE, Arlene

BIAMONTE, Edgar L.
   "About the Edge of Rain." RevI (10:1) Spr 80, p. 119.
   "The After of a Rose." RevI (10:1) Spr 80, p. 119.
   "Toward a Monarch's Wings." RevI (10:1) Spr 80, p. 120.

BIASIO, Rodolfo Di see DiBIASIO, Rodolfo

BIDART, Frank
   "The War of Vaslav Nijinsky." ParisR (23:80) Sum 81, pp. 26-55.

BIENEK, Horst
   "Bakunin: Or the Anarchy of Words" (tr. by Ralph Read). NewOR
      (8:3) Aut 81, pp. 236-7.

BIERDS, Linda
   "Cicadas." QW (12) Spr-Sum 81, pp. 66-7.
   "Diver." EnPas (12), 81, p. 34.
   "Guide in a Glowworm Cave." Hudson (34:3) Aut 81, p. 387.
   "Heat Wave." CutB (17) Aut-Wint 81, p. 5.

BIGUENET, John
   "Aspects of the Knife." Mund (12/13) 80-81, p. 308.
   "A Short History of Barbed Wire." GeoR (35:2) Sum 81, p. 340.
   "A Song." Mund (12/13) 80-81, p. 308.

BIJOU, Rachelle
   "The Store That's Worth The Trip Downtown." Tele (17) 81, pp. 8-10.

BILICKE, Tom
  "The fall of grief." Wind (11:40) 81, p. 31.

BILL, Jim
  "The Migrant." PoetryNW (22:2) Sum 81, pp. 30-31.

BILLET, Bonnie
  "Twelve Moons." Poetry (138:5) Ag 81, pp. 271-274.
  "The Vanishing Species." Poetry (138:5) Ag 81, p. 275.

BILLINGS, Philip
  "A Runner's Morning Song." StoneC (9: 1-2) Aut-Wint 81/82, p. 61.

BILLINGS, Robert
  "Just After Dark." Chelsea (40) 81, pp. 118-119.
  "Song of the Open Eyes." Chelsea (40) 81, p. 118.
  "This Time, Iran." Chelsea (40) 81, pp. 119-120.

BISHOP, Wendy
  "Going Along Rivers." CreamCR (6:1) Aut 80, p. 45.
  "Last Letter to Peru." CreamCR (6:1) Aut 80, pp. 47-48.
  "Veteran." CreamCR (6:1) Aut 80, p. 46.

BISSERT, Ellen Marie
  "Outside my Window." 13thM (5:1/2) 80, pp. 23-26.

BIZZARD, Patrick
  "Caution Light" (for Susan). HiramPoR (30) Spr-Sum 81, p. 10.

BJØRNVIG, Thorkild
  "The Dolphin" (tr. by William Jay Smith and Leif Sjöberg). PoetryE
    (6) Aut 81, pp. 77-88.

BLACK, Candace
  "Homestead Family." QW (12) Spr-Sum 81, p. 47.
  "On A Footbridge." QW (12) Spr-Sum 81, p. 49.
  "Wedding Portrait: The Mother Of The Bride." QW (12) Spr-Sum 81,
    p. 48.

BLACK, Harold
  "For rag pickers who scratch in the rubbish..." (tr. of Itzik Manger).
    Vis (5) 81, n. p.
  "Let Us Sing" (tr. of Itzik Manger). Vis (5) 81, n. p.
  "Night Life of the Plants." Vis (7) 81, n. p.

BLACKBURN, Paul
  "Blackberry Bush" (tr. of Federico García Lorca). PoNow (5:6 issue
    30) 81, p. 23.
  "The Four Muleteers" (tr. of Federico García Lorca). PoNow (5:6 is-
    sue 30) 81, p. 23.
  "Kings in the Deck" (tr. of Federico García Lorca). PoNow (5:6 issue
    30) 81, p. 23.
  "Sevilla Slumber Song" (tr. of Federico García Lorca). PoNow (5:6 is-
    sue 30) 81, p. 23.
  "The Term." Sulfur (1) 81, p. 169.
  "Wind from All Compass Points" (tr. of Octavio Paz). Mund (12/13)
    80-81, pp. 1-6.

BLACKWELL, Marian W.
  "Holy Week." ChrC (98:13) 15 Ap 81, p. 414.

BLADES, Joe
  "Sawtooth Roads." PottPort (3) 81, p. 27.

BLAEUER, M. W.
  "Inventory." HiramPoR (30) Spr-Sum 81, p. 11.

BLANK, Alan R.
  "Pondering Canadian Vacations" (for Jim Hazard). Wind (11:42) 81,
    pp. 6-7.

BLASSING, Randy
  "Glimpse." PoNow (6:1 issue 31) 81, p. 40.
  from Things I Didn't Know I Loved: (5, 13) (tr. of Nazin Hikmet, w/
    Motlu Konuk). AmerPoR (10:3) My-Je 81, p. 6.

BLAUNER, Laurie
  "The Blue Distance of Night." QW (13) Aut/Wint 81/82, p. 50.

BLAZEK, Douglas
  "Of you Secretly in my Forgetting" (for Alta). WebR (6:2) 81, p. 83.
  "A Photograph by Wilhelm Hester: Under the Rigging." NewL (48:1)
    Aut 81, pp. 54-55.
  "Photograph of a Kentucky Auto Assembly Plant October 30, 1925."
    NewL (48:1) Aut 81, pp. 55-56.
  "Thinking." Ploughs (7:1) 81, p. 153.

BLESSING, Richard
  "Callahan Park Field, Bradford, Pa." PoetryNW (22:1) Spr 81, pp. 27-
    28.
  "Hawk-Man." PoetryNW (22:2) Sum 81, pp. 44-45.
  "Homecoming." PoetryNW (22:2) Sum 81, p. 47.
  "Late News." PoetryNW (22:1) Spr 81, pp. 28-29.
  "Scott" (for Eileen Cody, R.N.). PoetryNW (22:2) Sum 81, p. 46.
  "Seizure" (for Rick Rapport, M.D.). PoetryNW (22:2) Sum 81, pp. 41-
    42.
  "Sundowner." PoetryNW (22:2) Sum 81, pp. 43-44.
  "Tumor" (for Lisa Arrivey, R.N.). PoetryNW (22:2) Sum 81, pp. 42-
    43.

BLESSINGTON, Francis
  "Ad Patrem." StoneC (8: 3) Spr 81, p. 11.

BLESZ, Lynne
  "the moon's crescent." Tele (17) 81, p. 67.

BLEYTHING, Dennis
  "Three Crows." PortR (27: 2) 81, p. 23.

BLISS, S. W.
  "In the wind." Im (7:2) 81, p. 11.

BLOOM, Janet
  "Presence." PoNow (6:3 issue 33) 81, p. 5.

BLOSSOM, Lavina
  "Second Cutting." KanQ (13:1) Wint 81, p. 10.

BLUE-ZWARTS, Janice
"Two Women on Ward 2B." MalR (59) Jl 81, pp. 160-161.

BLUME, Burt
"Pearl-Handled Revolver." Vis (6) 81, n. p.

BLUMENTHAL, Michael
"The Bitter Truth." Nimrod (25:1) Aut-Wint 81, pp. 27-28.
"Corn Silk." SouthernPR (21: 1) Spr 81, p. 27.
"A Cure for Cancer." Nimrod (25:1) Aut-Wint 81, p. 26.
"Days We Would Rather Know." Poetry (138:4) Jl 81, p. 203.
"Freudian Slip." Ploughs (6:4) 81, p. 52.
"Last Supper" (for John McNally & Kelly Kellog). SouthernPR (21: 1)
    Spr 81, p. 26.
"A Man Lost By a River." Tendril (11) Sum 81, p. 13.
"What I Believe." Kayak (56) 81, p. 54.
"Wishes That Could Last a Lifetime." Kayak (56) 81, p. 55.
"The Woman Inside." MissouriR (4:3) Sum 81, p. 19.

BLUMENTHAL, Michael C.
"Debevoise, Plimpton, Lyons & Gates." HolCrit (17:6 [i. e. 18:1?]) F
    81, pp. 17-18.
"Half-Life." MichQR (20:3) Sum 81, p. 239.
"Seven O'Clock Muse." MichQR (20:3) Sum 81, p. 238.

BLY, Robert
"After a Long Dry Spell" (tr. of Tomas Tranströmer). Pequod (12) 81,
    p. 93.
"At Funchal" (tr. of Tomas Tranströmer). Pequod (12) 81, p. 91.
"At Midocean." Im (7:3) 81, p. 3.
"The Black Mountain" (tr. of Tomas Tranströmer). Pequod (12) 81, p.
    92.
"The Casks of Wine." Iowa (11:2/3) Spr-Sum 80, p. 209.
"Creation Night" (tr. of Harry Martinson). Mund (12/13) 80-81, p. 111.
"Fox Fire" (tr. of Rainer Maria Rilke). PoetryE (4/5) Spr-Sum 81, p.
    27.
"From the Winter of 1947" (tr. of Tomas Tranströmer). PoNow (5:6
    issue 30) 81, p. 26.
"Here Is What I Experienced." Ploughs (7:1) 81, p. 47.
"Herons." Poetry (138:5) Ag 81, p. 284.
"Imaginary Biography" (tr. of Rainer Maria Rilke). PoetryE (4/5)
    Spr-Sum 81, p. 26.
"Just As the Winged Energy of Delight" (tr. of Rainer Maria Rilke).
    PoetryE (4/5) Spr-Sum 81, p. 28.
"Kneeling Down to Look into a Culvert." Atl (248:3) S 81, p. 25.
"March Evening" (tr. of Harry Martinson). Mund (12/13) 80-81, p.
    112.
"The Moose." Poetry (138:5) Ag 81, p. 284.
"Mourning" (tr. of Rainer Maria Rilke). PoetryE (4/5) Spr-Sum 81, p.
    25.
"Old Farmhouse" (tr. of Harry Martinson). Mund (12/13) 80-81, p. 111.
"Poem on Sleep." NewYorker (57:29) 7 S 81, p. 36.
"The Prodigal Son." NewRep (184:5) 31 Ja 81, p. 28.
"A Ramage for Awakening Sorrow." Poetry (138:5) Ag 81, p. 283.
"A Ramage for the Star Man, Mourning." Poetry (138:5) Ag 81, p.
    283.
"The Scattered Congregation" (tr. of Tomas Tranströmer). Mund
    (12/13) 80-81, p. 90.
"Street Crossing" (tr. of Tomas Tranströmer). PoetryE (4/5) Spr-Sum

81, p. 233.
"Street Crossing" (tr. of Tomas Tranströmer). PoNow (5:6 issue 30)
    81, p. 26.
Ten poems. PoetryE (4/5) Spr-Sum 81, pp. 10-24.

BOBES LEON, Marilyn
    "Triste oficio." Areito (7: 27) 81, p. 23.

BOBROWSKI, Johannes
    "Holdering in Tubingen" (tr. by Francis Golffing). PoNow (5:6 issue
        30) 81, p. 8.
    "Plain" (tr. by Juliette Victor-Rood). DenQ (16:1) Spr 81, p. 67.
    "Recovery" (tr. by Francis Golffing). PoNow (5:6 issue 30) 81, p. 8.
    "Tale" (tr. by Juliette Victor-Rood). DenQ (16:1) Spr 81, p. 64.
    "Unsaid" (tr. by Juliette Victor-Rood). DenQ (16:1) Spr 81, p. 65.
    "The Wanderer" (tr. by Francis Golffing). PoNow (5:6 issue 30) 81,
        p. 8.
    "The Wanderer" (tr. by Juliette Victor-Rood). DenQ (16:1) Spr 81, p.
        66.

BOBYSHEV, Dmitry
    "Any Excuse (Venus in a Puddle)" (tr. by Olga Bobyshev and Elizabeth
        Williams). CreamCR (6:2) 81, p. 16.
    "The Claw" (tr. by Olga Bobyshev and Elizabeth Williams). CreamCR
        (6:2) 81, pp. 14-15.

BOBYSHEV, Olga
    "Any Excuse (Venus in a Puddle)" (tr. with Elizabeth Williams of
        Dmitry Bobyshev). CreamCR (6:2) 81, p. 16.
    "The Claw" (tr. with Elizabeth Williams of Dmitry Bobyshev).
        CreamCR (6:2) 81, pp. 14-15.

BOCK, Frederick
    "Stock." Poetry (138:1) Ap 81, p. 19.

BODINI, Vittorio
    "Brindisi" (tr. by Ruth Feldman and Brian Swann). PoNow (5:6 issue
        30) 81, p. 9.
    "But in the Hour" (tr. by Ruth Feldman and Brian Swann). PoNow (5:6
        issue 30) 81, p. 9.
    from Tabacco Leaves 1945-1947 (1-12) (tr. by Ruth Feldman and Brian
        Swann). PoNow (5:6 issue 30) 81, pp. 9-10.

BODVARSSON, Gudmundur
    "Brother" (tr. by Alan Boucher). Vis (5) 81, n. p.

BOE, Deborah
    "Daughter." US1 (14/15) Aut/Wint 81, p. 3.
    "Last Light." US1 (14/15) Aut/Wint 81, p. 2.
    "A Princess" (after the fairy tale). US1 (14/15) Aut/Wint 81, p. 2.
    "My Sister of the Horses." US1 (14/15) Aut/Wint 81, p. 2.

BOEBEL, Charles
    "Easter Eve." ChrC (98:12) 8 Ap 81, p. 384.

BOEHM, Susan
    "For Raphael." HiramPoR (29) Aut-Wint 81, p. 10.
    "The House." StoneC (9: 1-2) Aut-Wint 81/82, pp. 26-27.

BOGEN, Don
    "The All-Night Rumba." SouthernPR (21:2) Aut 81, p. 26.
    "Family Album." NoAmR (266:3) S 81, p. 63.
    "Klumb's Rise." Thrpny (7) Aut 81, p. 21.

BOGIN, George
    "Alone in the House." PoNow (6:3 issue 33) 81, p. 22.
    "The Canoes." PoNow (6:3 issue 33) 81, p. 22.
    "Champs Elysées" (tr. of Jules Supervielle). AmerPoR (10:4) Jl-Ag 81,
        p. 48.
    "The Drop of Rain (God Speaks)" (tr. of Jules Supervielle). ChiR (33:
        1) Sum 81, p. 83.
    "The Haircut." PoNow (6:3 issue 33) 81, p. 22.

BOISSEAU, Michelle
    "Twelve poems." ArkRiv (5:1) 81, pp. 8-21.

BOISVERT, P. W.
    "Christmas Cards From Home" (for Jane Schaefer). Tendril (10) Wint
        81, pp. 12-16.

BOLLS, Imogene L.
    "After the Breakdown" (For My Brothers). Nimrod (25:1) Aut-Wint 81,
        p. 55.

BOLT, William Walter De see De BOLT, William Walter

BONAZZI, Robert
    "Forgotten Dialogue." Chelsea (40) 81, p. 125.
    "Living with Plants and Animals." Chelsea (40) 81, p. 124.
    "On Hearing in Silence a Passage from Memory." Chelsea (40) 81, p.
        124.

BOND, Alec
    "Ginkgo Biloba." Northeast (3:11) Sum 81, p. 32.
    "Hilary Descending." Northeast (3:11) Sum 81, p. 33.

BOND, Harold
    "Her Eyes." Aspect (77/79) 81, p. 18.

BOND, Pearl
    "Street Person." PoNow (6:2 issue 32) 81, p. 35.

BONENFANT, Joseph
    "Vie courante." Os (13) Aut 81, p. 25.

BONILLA, Ronald
    "The Lone Children" (tr. by George McWhirter). Mund (12/13) 80-81,
        p. 292.

BONILLA, Sixto Méndez see MENDEZ BONILLA, Sixto

BONNEFOY, Yves
    "The Dialogue of Anguish and Desire" (tr. by Anthony Rudolf). Mund
        (12/13) 80-81, pp. 218-220.
    "Du signifiant." SenR (10:2/11:1) 79-80, p. 102.
    "Les feux." SenR (10:2/11:1) 79-80, p. 100.
    "The Fires" (tr. by Linda Orr). SenR (10:2/11:1) 79-80, p. 101.
    "On the Signifier" (tr. by Linda Orr). SenR (10:2/11:1) 79-80, p. 103.

BONNELL, Paula
  "Sunday Sensualist: Matins and Lauds." HiramPoR (30) Spr-Sum 81,
    p. 12.

BONOMO, Jacquelyn
  "Old Friend." MassR (22:2) Sum 81, p. 224.
  "Patience in the Endless Rain." MassR (22:2) Sum 81, p. 223.

BOOK, M. K.
  "Old." WormR (84) 81, p. 102.
  "Stein." WormR (84) 81, p. 102.

BORAWSKI, Walta
  "Wool-gathering." Aspect (77/79) 81, pp. 19-20.

BORCHERS, Elisabeth
  "The Head" (tr. by Gudrun Mouw). WebR (6:2) 81, p. 37.
  "It Is" (tr. by Gudrun Mouw). CharR (7:1) Spr 81, pp. 52-53.
  "On a Hero" (tr. by Gudrun Mouw). WebR (6:2) 81, p. 36.

BORENSTEIN, Emily
  "Burned Out." Vis (6) 81, n. p.
  "Change." Mund (12/13) 80-81, p. 300.
  "How as a Child." WebR (6:2) 81, p. 102.
  "Is Everybody Dead?" Tele (17) 81, p. 15.
  "Metric Pissoir & Ready For War." Tele (17) 81, p. 15.
  "Nothing Drops into a Void." WebR (6:2) 81, p. 103.

BORGES, Jorge Luis
  "My Books" (tr. by Willis Barnstone). DenQ (16:1) Spr 81, p. 54.
  "The Nightingale" (tr. by Willis Barnstone). DenQ (16:1) Spr 81, p.
    56.
  "That Nothing is Known" (tr. by Willis Barnstone). DenQ (16:1) Spr
    81, p. 55.

BORN, Bertran De see DE BORN, Bertran

BORNSTEIN, Miriam
  "Nicaragua." Areito (7: 25) 81, p. 52.
  "La señora del aseo de la biblioteca." Areito (7: 25) 81, p. 52.
  "El Templo Mayor." Areito (7: 25) 81, p. 52.

BOROWSKI, Tadeusz
  "And you stayed that way..." (tr. by Addison Bross). WebR (6:1) Spr
    81, p. 19.
  "Auschwitz Sun" (tr. by Addison Bross). WebR (6:1) 81, p. 20.

BORSON, Roo
  "Rain." AmerPoR (10:5) S/O 81, p. 39.
  "Spring." AmerPoR (10:5) S/O 81, p. 39.

BORUCH, Marianne
  "Secrets." NewL (47:4) Sum 81, p. 73.

BOSE, Harry
  "H-R Diagram." PortR (27: 2) 81, p. 50.
  "Milky Way." PortR (27: 2) 81, p. 50.
  "Moon Eclipses." PortR (27: 2) 81, p. 50.
  "M 13." PortR (27: 2) 81, p. 50.

BOSQUET, Alain
    "Earth Writes the Earth (Poems for a painter)" (tr. by Wallace Fowlie).
        Mund (12/13) 80-81, pp. 385-388.

BOSWORTH, Martha
    "A Troubling of Wings." ChrC (98:4) 4-11 F 81, p. 106.

BOTELHO, Eugene G. E.
    "Two Melodies for Lennart." PoNow (6:3 issue 33) 81, p. 6.

BOTTOMS, David
    "Fog on Kennesaw." Iowa (12:1) Wint 81, p. 117.
    "Hiking Toward Laughing Gull Point." VirQR (57:4) Aut 81, pp. 638-
        639.
    "A Home Buyer Watches the Moon." Poetry (137:5) F 81, p. 257.
    "Hurricane." Poetry (137:5) F 81, pp. 255-256.
    "The Husks." GeoR (35:4) Wint 81, p. 852.
    "In a U-Haul North of Damascus." Poetry (137:5) F 81, pp. 251-253.
    "In the Wilderness Motel." Poetry (138:5) Ag 81, pp. 263-264.
    "Rest at the Mercy House." Poetry (137:5) F 81, p. 254.
    "Turning the Double Play" (for Doug Fowler). VirQR (57:4) Aut 81, pp.
        639-640.

BOTTRALL, Ronald
    "Norma Departed." Stand (22: 4) 81, p. 54.

BOUCHER, Alan
    "As the train passes" (tr. of Thuridur Gudmundsdottir). Vis (5) 81,
        n. p.
    "Brother" (tr. of Gudmundur Bodvarsson). Vis (5) 81, n. p.
    "Child" (tr. of Thuridur Gudmundsdottir). Vis (5) 81, n. p.
    "The city laughed" (tr. of Matthias Johannessen). Vis (5) 81, n. p.
    "Poem: It may well be" (tr. of Nina Bjork Arnadottir). Vis (5) 81,
        n. p.
    "You are the day that vanished" (tr. of Matthias Johannessen). Vis
        (5) 81, n. p.

BOULLATA, Issa J.
    "Don't Sleep" (tr. of Mahmud Darwish). Mund (12/13) 80-81, pp. 258-
        259.

BOULUS, Sargon
    "Feast" (tr. of Sameeh al-Qasim). Mund (12/13) 80-81, p. 22.
    "Is This You or the Tale?" (tr. of Unsi al-Haj). Mund (12/13) 80-81,
        pp. 166-167.
    "Let others have" (tr. of Jabra Ibrahim Jabra). Mund (12/13) 80-81,
        p. 353.
    "Masks collapsed, and" (tr. of Jabra Ibrahim Jabra). Mund (12/13) 80-
        81, p. 352.
    "No, And Why" (tr. of Tawfig Sayegh). Mund (12/13) 80-81, p. 302.
    "A Stone" (tr. of Yusif Sa'di). Mund (12/13) 80-81, p. 31.

BOURNE, Daniel
    "Exposed." WindO (38) Spr-Sum 81, p. 37.
    "On Ancient Species." WindO (38) Spr-Sum 81, p. 36.

BOURNE, Louis
    "The Boy and the Stone" (tr. of Justo Jorge Padron). Stand (22: 2)
        81, p. 48.

BOURNE, Louis M.
  "Idea" (tr. of Vicente Aleixandre).   Mund (12/13) 80-81, p. 404.

BOUVARD, Marguerite G.
  "Hands."   LitR (24:3) Spr 81, p. 382.

BOUVARD, Marguerite Guzman
  "The Reunion."   Northeast (3:10) Wint 81, p. 33.
  "Strata."   Ploughs (6:4) 81, p. 173.

BOWDEN, Michael
  "The Diary of Crows."   CharR (7:1) Spr 81, p. 48.

BOWEN, James K.
  "Night Window."   AmerS (50:1) Wint 80-81, p. 90.

BOWERING, George
  "Uncle Louis."   Epoch (30:3) Spr-Sum 81, pp. 161-174.

BOWERING, Marilyn
  "Middle Estuary."   Stand (22: 4) 81, p. 23.

BOWERS, Edgar
  "Witnesses."   SouthernR (17:1) Wint 81, pp. 175-7.

BOWERS, Neal
  "Beginnings."   CimR (54) Ja 81, p. 38.
  "Farmer."   NewL (47:4) Sum 81, p. 100.
  "For My Brother."   BallSUF (22:2) Spr 81, p. 53.
  "Getting Mad."   KanQ (13:1) Wint 81, p. 155.
  "Intruder."   PoNow (6:2 issue 32) 81, p. 47.
  "Looking in."   HiramPoR (30) Spr-Sum 81, p. 13.
  "Ritual."   KanQ (13:1) Wint 81, p. 155.
  "The Secret" (for Linda).   HiramPoR (30) Spr-Sum 81, p. 13.
  "Sketching Audubon."   SouthernPR (21:2) Aut 81, p. 72.
  "The Truth About the Universe" (for Nancy).   SouthernPR (21: 1) Spr
      81, p. 28.
  "What Dying Must Be Like."   CimR (54) Ja 81, p. 38.

BOWIE, Robert
  "Assuming."   NewRena (14) Spr 81, pp. 81-82.

BOWIE, Robert B.
  "Limb."   ArizQ (37:4) Wint 81, p. 316.

BOWMAN, P. C.
  "An Atlas of Genetic Syndrome."   SouthernHR (15:3) Sum 81, p. 229.
  "Voyeur."   SouthernHR (15:1) Wint 81, p. 52.

BOXER, Ray
  "The Man in the Doorway."   SouthwR (68:1) Wint 81, p. 40.

BOYCHUK, Bohdan
  "An Even More Sultry Dawn" (tr. of Boris Pasternak, w/ Mark Rud-
      man).   AmerPoR (10:4) Jl-Ag 81, p. 38.
  "Balashov" (tr. of Boris Pasternak, w/ Mark Rudman).   AmerPoR (10:
      4) Jl-Ag 81, p. 39.
  "The Blood of Captive Women" (tr. of Mykola Bazhan, w/ Mark Rud-

man). PoNow (5:6 issue 30) 81, p. 6.
"Concerning These Poems" (tr. of Boris Pasternak, w/ Mark Rudman).
    PoNow (5:5 issue 30) 81, p. 35.
"Darling--the terror! It comes back!" (tr. of Boris Pasternak, w/
    Mark Rudman). PoNow (5:6 issue 30) 81, p. 34.
"The End of the World" (tr. of Bohdan Antonych, w/ Mark Rudman).
    PoNow (6:1 issue 31) 81, p. 43.
"Our Thunderstorm" (tr. of Boris Pasternak, w/ Mark Rudman).
    PoNow (5:6 issue 30) 81, p. 34.
"The Picture" (tr. of Boris Pasternak, w/ Mark Rudman). PoNow
    (5:6 issue 30) 81, p. 35.
"Prince Igor's Campaign" (tr. of Mykola Bazhan, w/ Mark Rudman).
    PoNow (5:6 issue 30) 81, p. 6.
"Rain" (tr. of Boris Pasternak, w/ Mark Rudman). AmerPoR (10:4)
    Jl-Ag 81, p. 39.
"The Road" (tr. of Mykola Bazhan, w/ Mark Rudman). PoNow (5:6
    issue 30) 81, p. 6.
"The Substitute" (tr. of Boris Pasternak, w/ Mark Rudman). AmerPoR
    (10:4) Jl-Ag 81, p. 38.
"A Sultry Night" (tr. of Boris Pasternak, w/ Mark Rudman). PoNow
    (5:6 issue 30) 81, pp. 34-35.

BOYD, Charley A.
    "God's Codpiece." Sam (16) 81, p. 30.

BOYER, Charles
    "Scholar in an Interior." CreamCR (7:1) 81, pp. 79-80.

BOZANIC, Nick
    "Fishing the Deadstream" (for Jack and Scott). SouthernPR (21:2) Aut
        81, p. 29.
    "Into Evening." CimR (57) O 81, pp. 61-62.

BRACKER, Jon
    "One-Night Stand." PoNow (6:3 issue 33) 81, p. 6.
    "Scene." PoNow (6:3 issue 33) 81, p. 6.

BRADFORD, Lisa
    "Answer of the Dervish" (tr. of Ida Vitale). Mund (12/13) 80-81, p. 103.
        103.
    "The City And The Striking Of A Match" (tr. of Ricardo Lindo). Mund
        (12/13) 80-81, p. 309.
    "Our Lady Of The Clock" (tr. of Ricardo Lindo). Mund (12/13) 80-81,
        p. 309.
    "Silence" (tr. of Juan Liscano). Mund (12/13) 80-81, p. 296.
    "Sinister Ants" (tr. of Ricardo Lindo). Mund (12/13) 80-81, p. 309.

BRADLEY, George
    "In the Himalayas." Shen (31:4) 80, pp. 48-49.

BRADLEY, Jerry
    "Estrangement." ModernPS (10:2/3) 81, p. 95.
    "Pickings." ModernPS (10:2/3) 81, pp. 93-94.
    "Strike at Salmon Time." ModernPS (10:2/3) 81, p. 92.
    "When the Continent Divided." ModernPS (10:2/3) 81, pp. 92-93.

BRADLEY, Sam
    "Cage-Sailing (The fantastic idea that slavery goes on & on...)." KanQ

(13:3/4) Sum-Aut 81, pp. 30-32.
"God-Spell of a Tree." Poem (41) Mar 81, p. 12.
"Head of Family." KanQ (13:1) Wint 81, p. 137.
"Shall We Look So Far And No Farther?" Poem (41) Mar 81, p. 11.

BRAGI, Einar
"Summer Song." Vis (6) 81, n. p.

BRAINARD, Joe
"The Outer Banks." ParisR (23:79) Spr 81, pp. 76-77.

BRAND, Helena
"A Passing Death." ChrC (98:6) 25 F 81, p. 200.

BRANDI, John
"Poem Reflecting World Events Written to the Beat of a Waterwheel
While Meditating on Shakyamuni's Ashes Circling the Sun." Chelsea
(40) 81, pp. 121-123.

BRANDT, Daryl S.
"Michael The Memnist." WindO (38) Spr-Sum 81, p. 7.

BRANIN, Jeff
"The Rose Garden." Wind (11:43) 81, pp. 6-7.

BRASFIELD, James
"Passage." Antaeus (43) Aut 81, p. 89.

BRASH, Edward
"Some Feast." Poetry (137:4) Ja 81, p. 201.
"The China Closet Neuron Loss." Poetry (137:4) Ja 81, pp. 199-200.

BRATOSEVICH, Nicolás A. S.
Nine poems. Mairena (3:7), pp. 13-17.

BRATOSEVICH (son), Nicolás
"Cuando se acaben los gigantes." Mairena (3:7), p. 60.
"Esta batalla de anaqueles y estantes." Mairena (3:7), pp. 61-62.
"Si supieras de todas esas noches." Mairena (3:7), pp. 63-64.
"Sumerges tu mano en la dicha de pájaros." Mairena (3:7), p. 61.
"Y todo esto sabemos...." Mairena (3:7), pp. 62-63.

BRAUDE, Michael
"Scarecrows." PartR (48:3) 81, p. 602.

BRAZIL, Brenda
"The Past" ('forget about it' for S. who said so). ThRiPo (17/18) 81,
p. 42.

BRECHT, Bertolt
"Against Bullshit" (tr. by Ed Ochester). MinnR (17) Aut 81, p. 9.
"The Burning of Books" (tr. by John Pauker). PoNow (5:6 issue 30)
81, p. 8.
"On the Infanticide Marie Farrar" (tr. by Ed Ochester). MinnR (17)
Aut 81, pp. 10-12.

BREHM, Gregory
"The Tides of Day and Night (for Octavio Paz)" (with Harry Haskell).
Mund (12/13) 80-81, pp. 310-313.

BREHM, John
"How I Spent My Summer Vacation As Told to Me by Someone Else."
    Peb (21) 81, p. 20.

BREITSPRECHER, Nancy
"January Prayer." ChrC (98:2) 21 Ja 81, p. 37.

BREM, Ilse
"Being" (tr. by Herbert Kuhner). PortR (27: 2) 81, p. 35.

BRENNAN, Matthew
"Anecdote for Fathers." WebR (6:1) 81, p. 79.
"In Memory of My Grandfather." WebR (6:1) 81, p. 78.

BRENNER, Sidney
"Resurrection." BelPoJ (31:4) Sum 81, pp. 4-5.
"From The Old Man and the Girl." BelPoJ (31:4) Sum 81, pp. 5-6.

BRESCIA, B. A.
"A Woman's Spring Prayer." Ploughs (7:1) 81, p. 145.

BRESLIN, Paul
"Two Sections from Elijah." Ploughs (7:2) 81, pp. 105-107.

BRETT, Peter
"The Hunger." PikeR (2) Sum 81, p. 8.
"seasons." PikeR (2) Sum 81, p. 7.

BRIEFS, Elinor
"Pathetique" (tr. of Anna, Comtess de Noailles). Vis (5) 81, n. p.

BRIGGS, Edwin
"Kokovoko." Tendril (10) Wint 81, p. 17.

BRIGHAM, Besmilr
"Before Stars Have Come Out." OP (31/32) Aut 81, pp. 120-121.
"In War, They Defoliate the Trees." OP (31/32) Aut 81, p. 78.
"The Wedding Party." SouthwR (66:1) Wint 81, pp. 18-20.

BRIGNONI, Yanina
"Alma de antaño." Mairena (2:6), p. 74.
"Pueblo natal." Mairena (2:6), p. 74.

BRILLIANT, Alan
"Come, Come Always" (tr. of Vicente Aleixandre). Mund (12/13) 80-81,
    pp. 402-403.

BRINGHURST, Robert
"Portrait in Blood." Mund (12/13) 80-81, pp. 116-118.

BRINSON-PINEDA, Barbara
"Love Song." Metam (3:2/4:1) 80-81, p. 46.
"South Chicago." Metam (3:2/4:1) 80-81, p. 46.

BRISTOW, Angela
"Plums." Aspect (77/79) 81, p. 22.

BROCK-BROIDO, Lucie
   "What the Whales Sound Like in Manhattan." SouthernPR (21:2) Aut 81,
      pp. 27-29.

BROCKLEY, Michael
   "Clowns." Wind (11:40) 81, p. 13.
   "White River in Spring." BallSUF (22:2) Spr 81, p. 2.

BRODINE, Karen
   "Woman Sitting at the Machine, Thinking." HangL (40) Aut 81, pp. 4-
      7.

BRODKEY, Harold
   "Sea Noise." NewYorker (57:33) 5 O 81, p. 50.

BRODSKY, Joseph
   "The Berlin Wall Tune" (for Peter Viereck). NewYRB (28:20) 17 D 81,
      p. 12.
   "Roman Elegy." NewYorker (57:21) 13 Jl 81, p. 30.
   "A Season." NewYRB (28:1) 5 F 81, p. 11.
   "Verses on the Winter Campaign 1980" (tr. by Alan Myers). NewYRB
      (28:14) 24 S 81, p. 8.

BRODSKY, Louis Daniel
   "Catching Fireflies." CapeR (16:2) Sum 81, p. 28.
   "Tortoise & Hare." BallSUR (22:4) Aut 81, p. 17.
   "Waving Good-Bye" (for J. F.). CapeR (17:1) Wint 81, p. 18.

BROF, Janet
   "To Cacho, A Note." StoneC (9: 1-2) Aut-Wint 81/82, p. 49.

BROMLEY, Anne
   "Banks Close Too Early for Painters." Kayak (56) 81, p. 58.
   "Intersection at Zero Hour." Kayak (56) 81, p. 56.
   "Da Vinci Crashes In Joy Dawson's Hog Farm." MassR (22:4) Wint 81,
      pp. 633-634.
   "Sleepwalking." Kayak (56) 81, p. 57.
   "Slow Men Working In Trees." MassR (22:4) Wint 81, p. 633.
   "White Cat in the Shell, Moon on the Wane." Kayak (56) 81, p. 59.

BROMWICH, David
   "On a Picture of Echo and Narcissus." Hudson (34:3) Aut 81, p. 386.

BROOKS, Phyllis
   "Man in a Mobile Home." OP (31/32) Aut 81, pp. 67-68.

BROOKS, Randy
   "all tongue." Northeast (3:11) Sum 81, p. 48.
   "dream apples." Northeast (3:11) Sum 81, p. 48.
   "ground picked clean." Northeast (3:11) Sum 81, p. 48.
   "leftovers." Northeast (3:11) Sum 81, p. 48.

BROOKS, Robert A.
   "Intravenous Trip." Atl (247:6) Je 81, p. 41.

BROOKS, Yvonne
   "Chalumeau." StoneC (8: 3) Spr 81, p. 13.

BROSS, Addison
    "And you stayed that way..." (tr. of Tadeusz Borowski). WebR (6:1)
      Spr 81, p. 19.
    "Auschwitz Sun" (tr. of Tadeusz Borowski). WebR (6:1) Spr 81, p. 20.

BROSTOWIN, P. R.
    "Grading Papers, Holistically." WindO (38) Spr-Sum 81, p. 24.
    "Hanging On." KanQ (13:1) Wint 81, p. 92.
    "A Teacher's Advice to His Students." RevI (9:4) Wint 79-80, p. 625.
    "The Verdict." KanQ (13:1) Wint 81, pp. 92-93.

BROUGHTON, T. Alan
    "Fall Games." Confr (22) Sum 81, p. 14.
    "Hazards." Poetry (138:6) S 81, p. 335.
    "Image." Confr (22) Sum 81, p. 14.
    "Landscape with Vanishing Point." Poetry (138:6) S 81, p. 334.
    "Partial Correspondence." BelPoJ (32:2) Wint 81-82, pp. 18-21.

BROVKA, Petrus
    "Life's Beginning" (tr. by Olga Shartse). PoNow (5:6 issue 30) 81, p.
      11.

BROWER, Gary
    "Calambur" (tr. of Angel González). Mund (12/13) 80-81, pp. 222-223.
    "Counterorder" (tr. of Angel González). Mund (12/13) 80-81, p. 222.
    "Everything Is Clear Now" (tr. of Angel González). Mund (12/13) 80-
      81, p. 223.
    "Order" (tr. of Angel González). Mund (12/13) 80-81, p. 221.
    "Poetics" (tr. of Angel González). Mund (12/13) 80-81, p. 221.

BROWN, Beth
    "Ancestors." Obs (6:1/2) Spr-Sum 80, p. 206.
    "House Arrest." Obs (6:1/2) Spr-Sum 80, p. 205.
    "Winter's End." Obs (6:1/2) Spr-Sum 80, p. 204.

BROWN, Elizabeth
    "On the Floor Plain." Wind (11:41) 81, p. 8.

BROWN, Harry
    "Barn Swallows." BallSUF (22:4) Aut 81, p. 30.
    "You Can Tell a Tree by its Fruit. Sometimes. But ... Are Potatoes
      Fruit?" Wind (10:39) 80, p. 9.

BROWN, Rebecca
    "Time For Power In The Desert." Tele (17) 81, p. 54.
    "Women's Work II." Tele (17) 81, p. 55.

BROWN, Steven Ford
    "An Explanation of the Prose Poem or the Prose Poem as Silent Movie."
      PoNow (6:1 issue 31) 81, p. 12.
    "Someone Moving in the Dark." Vis (7) 81, n.p.

BROWN, Thelma
    "Dear Harry." PortR (27: 2) 81, p. 96.
    "Yurako." PortR (27: 2) 81, p. 96.

BROWNE, Michael Dennis
    "Thanksgiving Day." Kayak (56) 81, pp. 43-47.

BROWNSTEIN, Michael
"Dinner Music." UnmOx (22) Wint 81, pp. 17-19.
from Oracle Night, a Love Poem: "A singing in the ears." SunM (11)
Spr 81, pp. 129-139.

BRUCE, Debra
"Brief." OhioR (26) pp. 122-123.
"Divorce: A Poem for Women." MissR (10:1) Spr-Sum 81, p. 167.
"Fasting." MissR (10:1) Spr-Sum 81, p. 166.

BRUCE, Lennart
"A long farewell, like looking" (tr. of Tua Forsström). SenR (12:1/2)
81, p. 201.
"Besvärjelser." SenR (12:1/2) 81, pp. 196-98.
"City" (tr. of Claes Andersson). PoetryE (6) Aut 81, p. 9.
"The Condition" (tr. of Edith Södergran). PoNow (5:6 issue 30) 81, p.
43.
"Earthly Unearthly" (tr. of Claes Andersson). PoetryE (6) Aut 81, pp.
9-10.
"The Falling in Love" (tr. of Claes Andersson). SenR (12:1/2) 81, p.
185.
"Friendship" (tr. of Claes Andersson). PoetryE (6) Aut 81, pp. 13-16.
"The Foreign Lands" (tr. of Edith Södergran). PoNow (5:6 issue 30)
81, p. 43.
"Gallup" (tr. of Tua Forsström). SenR (12:1/2) 81, pp. 205-207.
"Loneliness is a pyramid, humans Stacked" (tr. of Claes Andersson).
SenR (12:1/2) 81, p. 189.
"Nowadays there's much talk about identity" (tr. of Claes Andersson).
SenR (12:1/2) 81, p. 187.
"Poems in Our Absence" (tr. of Claes Andersson). SenR (12:1/2) 81,
pp. 191, 193, 195.
"Spells" (tr. by the author). SenR (12:1/2) 81, pp. 197-99.
"Tantalus, Fill Your Goblet" (tr. of Edith Södergran). PoNow (5:6 is-
sue 30) 81, p. 43.
"We live like words just begun" (tr. of Tua Forsström). SenR (12:1/2)
81, p. 203.
"Which Is My Homeland" (tr. of Edith Södergran). PoNow (5:6 issue
30) 81, p. 43.

BRUCHAC, Joseph
"Smoke." Aspect (77/79) 81, p. 21.

BRUMMELS, J. V.
"Amos." Peb (21) 81, pp. 95-96.
"A Man Alone in His Kitchen." QW (12) Spr-Sum 81, pp. 92-3.
"Evening Meal." Peb (21) 81, pp. 97-98.
"Lost Summer." QW (13) Aut/Wint 81/82, pp. 99-101.
"Viken Park" (for Lin). Peb (21) 81, p. 99.

BRUNER, Mark
"Sparagmos." Vis (6) 81, n. p.

BRUNET, David P.
"Love Song." BelPoJ (31:4) Sum 81, pp. 29-30.
"Northern Minnesota, Armistice Day, 1940." BelPoJ (31:4) Sum 81, pp.
31-33.

BRUNT, H. L. van see VAN BRUNT, H. L.

BRUSH, Thomas
  "Full Moon." QW (13) Aut/Wint 81/82, p. 45.
  "Muse." QW (13) Aut/Wint 81/82, p. 44.
  "Old Friends." PoetryNW (22:2) Sum 81, p. 34.
  "The Summer Poems." PoetryNW (22:4) Wint 81-82, p. 23.

BRUTTIN, Norman A.
  "After Visiting the Dakotas Again." BallSUF (22:4) Aut 81, pp. 32-33.

BRUTUS, Dennis
  "Pray if you believe in prayer." Mund (12/13) 80-81, pp. 181-182.

BRYAN, Sharon
  "One Basket." Iowa (11:2/3) Spr-Sum 80, pp. 109-110.

BUCHANAN, Carl
  "Dear Vincent." KanQ (13:3/4) Sum-Aut 81, p. 18.
  "Memoir of a Demolished Castle in Canterbury." KanQ (13:1) Wint 81,
      p. 27.
  "Waiting for the Hangman." KanQ (13:3/4) Sum-Aut 81, p. 17.
  "Works and Days." CapeR (16:2) Sum 81, p. 10.

BUCKINGHAM, Christina
  "Grandfather." PortR (27: 2) 81, p. 45.
  "Portrait of an Old Man." PortR (27: 2) 81, p. 45.
  "To My Grandfather" (written while he was still living). PortR (27: 2)
      81, p. 45.
  "Untitled." PortR (27: 2) 81, p. 45.
  "The Wet Black Bough." PortR (27: 2) 81, p. 45.

BUCKLEY, Christopher
  "Dust Light, Leaves." GeoR (35:3) Aut 81, pp. 594-595.
  "Equinox." QW (12) Spr-Sum 81, p. 75.
  "The Last I Remember." QW (13) Aut/Wint 81/82, p. 42.
  "Light Coming on the Plains." Nimrod (25:1) Aut-Wint 81, p. 25.
  "Misgivings." QW (12) Spr-Sum 81, pp. 16-7.
  "Red Poppy." Nimrod (25:1) Aut-Wint 81, p. 30.
  "Shells: A Cycle of Poems on the Paintings of Georgia O'Keeffe: Lad-
      der to the Moon." CharR (7:2) Aut 81, p. 21.
  "Shells: A Cycle of Poems ...: Black and White Photo on the Cover
      of the Penguine Edition of the Paintings." CharR (7:2) Aut 81, pp.
      21-22.
  "Shells: A Cycle of Poems ...: Lake George With Crows/Black Holly-
      hock, Blue Larkspur/the Lawrence Tree." CharR (7:2) Aut 81, p.
      23.
  "Summer Days/Ram's Head with Hollyhock." Nimrod (25:1) Aut-Wint
      81, p. 29.
  "Summer: From the San Joaquin." NewEngR (3:4) Sum 81, pp. 575-6.
  "To a Cold East." Thrpny (4) Wint 81, p. 4.
  "Traveling Light." MissouriR (4:3) Sum 81, p. 27.
  "Two Jimsonweeds." Antaeus (40/41) Wint-Spr 81, p. 275.
  "Watering (for Douglas Albert Salem [1947-79])." NewEngR (3:4) Sum
      81, pp. 576-7.
  "White." QW (13) Aut/Wint 81/82, pp. 40-41.
  "Young Girls Playing Catch in the Street Just Into Dark." NewYorker
      (57:24) 3 Ag 81, p. 32.
  "Your Life." MissouriR (4:3) Sum 81, p. 28.

BUCKLEY, M. T.
    "Safeway." Aspect (77/79) 81, p. 23.

BUDY, Andrea Hollander
    "The Mistress." SouthernPR (21: 1) Spr 81, p. 15.

BUELL, Tom
    "At Mizenhead." PortR (27: 2) 81, p. 22.

BUGEJA, Michael J.
    "The Bottom." SmPd (18:3) Aut 81, pp. 21-22.
    "Denny's Dog." SmPd (18:1) Wint 81, p. 32.
    "Mistaking A Beggar At The Open Market." Sam (116) 81, p. 35.

BUKOWSKI, Charles
    "Be Angry At San Pedro." WormR (84) 81, p. 124.
    "Love and Courage." PoNow (6:1 issue 31) 81, p. 11.
    "A Loser." WormR (84) 81, p. 125.
    "The Princess Tina." PoNow (6:2 issue 32) 81, p. 8.
    "smooth." Tendril (11) Sum 81, pp. 14-15.
    Thirteen Poems. WormR (81/82) 81, pp. 15-34.

BULLARD, G. L.
    "The Dogs of Mossy, West Virginia." Wind (11:41) 81, p. 7.

BULLIS, Jerald
    "Attention." BelPoJ (31:4) Sum 81, p. 36.
    "Recompense." BelPoJ (31:4) Sum 81, pp. 35-36.

BULLOCK, Michael
    "Childhood" (tr. of Karl Krolow). Mund (12/13) 80-81, p. 64.
    "Closeness" (tr. of Karl Krolow). Mund (12/13) 80-81, p. 61.
    "Shadows In The Air" (tr. of Karl Krolow). Mund (12/13) 80-81, p. 62.
    "Sick Weather" (tr. of Karl Krolow). Mund (12/13) 80-81, p. 63.

BURBANK, Jim
    "Lines: the first part." Bound (9:1) Aut 80, pp. 176-182.
    "October 18, 1973." Bound (9:1) Aut 80, p. 175.

BURCIAGA, José Antonio
    "For Emmy." DenQ (16:3) Aut 81, p. 94.
    "It's the Same Guy." Areito (7: 25) 81, p. 46.
    "Pasatiempos." Areito (7: 25) 81, p. 47.
    "To Mexico with Love." Areito (7: 25) 81, p. 47.
    "Valentine's Day 1980." Metam (3:2/4:1) 80-81, p. 26.

BURGESON, Bonnie
    "'77 State Fair at Lincoln." Peb (21) 81, pp. 73-77.
    "Songs without words villanelle." Peb (21) 81, p. 78.

BURIAN, Peter
    "In Memory of Delio Tessa" (tr. of Giorgio Mannacio). PoNow (5:6
        issue 30) 81, p. 29.
    "Some Praises of Wine" (tr. of Giorgio Mannacio). PoNow (5:6 issue
        30) 81, p. 29.

BURKARD, Michael
    "The Absolute." AmerPoR (10:3) My-Je 81, p. 42.

BURKE, France
    "Be." SouthwR (66:1) Wint 81, p. 82.

BURKE, Jeffrey
    "Celebrity Fare: The Namedroppers' Ball." Harp (262:1568) Ja 81,
        pp. 83-85.

BURKHARDT, Marilyn
    "To Mary." NowestR (19:3), p. 87.

BURLINGAME, Robert
    "A Woman." SouthwR (66:3) Sum 81, p. 313.

BURNES, Carol
    "Small." 13thM (5:1/2) 80, p. 123.

BURNHAM, Deborah
    "School Fire Kills 91, Six Nuns." BelPoJ (32:1) Aut 81, pp. 38-39.
    "Walking the Trestle." PoetryNW (22:4) Wint 81-82, pp. 38-39.

BURNS, Gerald
    "A Book of Spells." Sulfur (3) 82, pp. 37-39.

BURNS, Ralph
    "The Barrens of Washington County." ColEng (43:7) N 81, p. 681.
    "Fireflies." QW (13) Aut/Wint 81/82, p. 46.
    "A Game of Burnout." QW (12) Spr-Sum 81, p. 74.
    "Home Town." ColEng (43:7) N 81, p. 680.
    "Love Poem." ColEng (43:7) N 81, p. 681.

BURR, Gray
    "Storm's End." PoNow (6:2 issue 32) 81, p. 6.

BURSK, C.
    "Good As New." PartR (48:2) 81, p. 258.

BURSK, Chris
    "The Cellar Stairs." Im (7:2) 1981, p. 7.
    "Handpuppets." VirQR (57:2) Spr 81, pp. 274-275.
    "My Father's Timepieces." Im (7:3) 81, p. 8.
    "Parts of the Body." Im (7:3) 81, p. 8.
    "Undressing in My Father's Office." Im (7:2) 1981, p. 7.

BURSK, Christopher
    "Raising Money." AmerPoR (10:5) S-O 81, p. 48.
    "Visiting Schools." ColEng (43:2) F 81, p. 167.

BURT, John
    "Aboard the Californian." WebR (6:2) 81, p. 88.
    "Indian Summer." WebR (6:2) 81, pp. 87-88.
    "Lecture on the Moral Sentiment." WebR (6:2) 81, p. 88.

BUSCH, Trent
    "The Great Plateau." BelPoJ (32:1) Aut 81, p. 33.

BUSSEY, Elmira
    "Wedgwood Vase." Aspect (77/79) 81, p. 24.

BUSSY, Jacques
  "Didyme." Os (13) Aut 81, pp. 4-6.

BUSTA, Christine
  "Gedichte." Mund (11:2) 79, p. 72.
  "Poems" (tr. by Herbert Kuhner). Mund (11:2) 79, p. 73.

BUTKIE, Joseph D.
  "David." PoNow (6:3 issue 33) 81, p. 6.
  "A Marine." PoNow (6:2 issue 32) 81, p. 36.
  "A Poem for Francis." PoNow (6:2 issue 32) 81, p. 36.
  "In Praise of a Gay Marine." PoNow (6:3 issue 33) 81, p. 6.
  "A Sailor with Fourteen Tattoos." PoNow (6:3 issue 33) 81, p. 6.

BUTLER, Jack
  "Correcting Selectric" (for JPJ). PoetryNW (22:3) Aut 81, pp. 44-45.

BUTLER-KNIGHT, Marie
  "Canis Lupus." CalQ (18/19) 81, p. 77.

BUTRICK, L. H.
  "The Hitch Hiker." PoNow (6:3 issue 33) 81, p. 7.
  "Nan." PoNow (6:3 issue 33) 81, p. 7.

BUXO, Joaquín
  "En Una Escuela de Párvulos." Puerto Wint 81, p. 19.

BYRNE, Edward
  "The Withdrawal Of The Season." QW (12) Spr-Sum 81, p. 16.

BYRNE, Vincent
  "Nell" (For Neil McCabe, 1 day old). Confr (22) Sum 81, p. 55.

CABALLERO, Raúl
  "Festival a puertas abiertas." Maize (4:3/4) Spr-Sum 81, p. 83.
  "El jazz del vagabundo." Maize (4:3/4) Spr-Sum 81, p. 82.
  "Parque de diversiones." Maize (4:3/4) Spr-Sum 81, p. 81.

CABRAL, Manuel del
  "The Buried One" (tr. by Donald D. Walsh). DenQ (16:1) Spr 81, p.
    63.
  "To a Newborn Child" (tr. by Donald D. Walsh). DenQ (16:1) Spr 81,
    p. 62.
  "Word" (tr. by Donald Walsh). AmerPoR (10:3) My-Je 81, p. 34.

CABRAL DE MELO NETO, João see MELO NETO, João Cabral de

CACHO, Manuel Joglar see JOGLAR CACHO, Manuel

CADENAS, Rafael
  "Defeat" (tr. by Elinor Randell). Mund (12/13) 80-81, pp. 138-140.

CADNUM, Michael
  "The Doctors." KanQ (13:1) Wint 81, pp. 164-165.

CAGE, John
  "Three Mesostics." Chelsea (39) 81, pp. 117-119.

CAHILL, Patricia
    "Toward the End." WebR (6:2) 81, p. 67.

CAHN, Cynthia
    "Swimming Out Too Far." SouthernHR (15:3) Sum 81, p. 242.

CAIN, Michael Scott
    "Space Song." PoNow (6:3 issue 33) 81, p. 7.

CAIRNS, Scott C.
    "Waking Here" (for Kathleen and Zap). QW (13) Aut/Wint 81/82, p.
    47.

CALANDRO, Ann
    "Contour Drawing" (for D.). WebR (6:2) 81, p. 72.
    "Verbal Silences" (for M.). WebR (6:2) 81, p. 72.

CALENDA, Eleanor Davidson
    "In the City." Wind (11:40) 81, p. 38.

CALINESCU, Matei
    "Ash Fruit" (tr. by Willis Barnstone and the author). SenR (12:1/2)
    81, p. 131.
    "Fruct de cenusa." SenR (12:1/2) 81, p. 130.
    "In lenea timpului imbatrinesc." SenR (12:1/2) 81, p. 132.
    "Lazy Time, I Am Growing Old" (tr. by Willis Barnstone and the au-
    thor). SenR (12:1/2) 81, p. 133.

CALISCH, Richard
    "To Cathy, Sleeping in My Second Hour Class--Hamlet." EngJ (70:7)
    N 81, p. 99.
    "To Mr. Calisch, Putting Me to Sleep in Second Hour Class--Ophelia."
    EngJ (70:7) N 81, p. 99.

CALLAGHAN, Barry
    "Amputation." OntR (15) Aut-Wint 81-82, p. 39.
    "The Astoria Hotel." OntR (15) Aut-Wint 81-82, p. 46.
    "Café Society." OntR (15) Aut-Wint 81-82, p. 41.
    "Cradle Song." OntR (15) Aut-Wint 81-82, p. 45.
    "Ice Fishing." OntR (15) Aut-Wint 81-82, p. 38.
    "In Moulten Light." OntR (15) Aut-Wint 81-82, pp. 42-44.
    "Stones." OntR (15) Aut-Wint 81-82, p. 40.

CALLANAN, Deirdre G.
    "All Flesh is Grass." BelPoJ (32:2) Wint 81-82, pp. 15-17.
    "Viva James Dean." Iowa (11:4) Aut 80, p. 67.

CALLAWAY, Kathy
    "The Lodge." Iowa (11:4) Aut 80, p. 68.

CAMACHO ILARRAZA, Carmen
    "A Jabnia." Mairena (2:6) 81, p. 91.
    "Soy." Mairena (2:6) 81, p. 91.

CAMMACK, Bruce
    "My Friends Make Decisions Without Consulting Me and I Do Too."
    Peb (21) 81, p. 62.

CAMOES, Luis de
"Nostalgia de Coimbra." Mairena (2:6) 81, p. 97.

CAMP, James
"After the Philharmonic." OP (31/32) Aut 81, p. 122.
"The Alleged Perpetrators." OP (31/32) Aut 81, pp. 165-166.
"For Alyssa about to Enter Wonderland." OP (31/32) Aut 81, p. 34.
"Song: The Figure in the Carpet." OP (31/32) Aut 81, pp. 51-52.

CAMPANA, Conni
"Putting Out the Light." ThRiPo (17/18) 81, p. 21.

CAMPBELL, Rick
"Ode to Crow Island." CreamCR (6:2) 81, p. 52.

CAMPBELL, Roy
"The Pilgrim Woos a Cowgirl." KanQ (13:2) Spr 81, p. 16.

CAMPBELL, Virginia
"The Coast At Mazatlan." AmerPoR (10:2) Mr-Ap 81, p. 28.
"Mariposa Avenue." AmerPoR (10:2) Mr-Ap 81, p. 28.
"Night In Echo Park." AmerPoR (10:2) Mr-Ap 81, p. 28.

CAMPBELL-KEASE, John
"Footpath." Wind (11:41) 81, pp. 9-10.
"Highland Scene." Wind (11:41) 81, p. 9.

CAMPION, Thomas
"Epitaph: On Nicholas Breton." SouthernR (17:4) Aut 81, p. 999.

CAMPOS, Hector
"Objetos." Mester (10:1/2) 81, p. 67.
"Oda." Mester (10:1/2) 81, p. 66.
"Poesía." Mester (10:1/2) 81, pp. 66-7.

CAMPOS, Marco Antonio
"My Brothers Left Little by Little" (tr. by Linda Scheer). PoNow (6:1 issue 31) 81, p. 42.

CANALE, Aurelio González
"Cuando otoño." Puerto Wint 81, p. 24.

CANAN, Janine
"Childhood." Cond (7) Spr 81, pp. 47-49.

CANDULO, Judith
"It Was Yesterday My Sorrows" (tr. of Antonio Machado, w/ Robert L. Smith). StoneC (9: 1-2) Aut-Wint 81/82, p. 57.

CANIZARO, Vincent, Jr.
"Blue-Eyed." StoneC (9: 1-2) Aut-Wint 81/82, p. 74.

CANSEVER, Edip
"Eyes" (tr. by Talat Sait Halman). Mund (12/13) 80-81, p. 354.

CANTRELL, Charles
"Deciduous." SouthernPR (21: 1) Spr 81, p. 39.
"Denying Plato." PoetryNW (22:3) Aut 81, pp. 30-31.

"Meditation on 54's Graphics." Kayak (56) 81, pp. 15-16.
"Nursing the Moon." CreamCR (6:1) Aut 80, p. 101.
"Winter Flashback." PoetryNW (22:3) Aut 81, pp. 31-32.

CAPONEGRO, Mary
    "Three pieces from Microfictions." Sulfur (1) 81, p. 192.

CAPRARA BASSI, María Susana
    "Mi ventana." Mairena (3:7), p. 99.
    "Nostalgia." Mairena (3:7), p. 99.
    "Payaso." Mairena (3:7), pp. 98-99.
    "Retorno." Mairena (3:7), p. 98.

CARAION, Ion
    "Tomorrow the Past Comes" (tr. by Marguerite Dorian and Elliot Ur-
        dang). Mund (12/13) 80-81, p. 305.
    "Unornamentation." Mund (12/13) 80-81, p. 306.

CARAM, Richard
    "1939." OP (31/32) Aut 81, pp. 106-107.

CARDENAL, Ernesto
    "A Ernesto Castillo mi sobrino." Areito (7: 26) 81, p. 57.
    "Epigram" (tr. by Steve Kowit). PoNow (5:6 issue 30) 81, p. 12.
    "La llegada." Areito (7: 26) 81, p. 56.
    "Otra llegada." Areito (7: 26) 81, p. 57.

CARDENAS, Margarita Cota see COTA CARDENAS, Margarita

CARÊME, Maurice
    "Gathering Pine-Cones" (tr. by Norma Farber). PoNow (5:6 issue 30)
        81, p. 11.
    "Stay as Simple..." (tr. by Norma Farber). PoNow (5:6 issue 30) 81,
        p. 11.
    "The Sun-Bathed Garden" (tr. by Norma Farber). PoNow (5:6 issue 30)
        81, p. 11.

CAREW, Jan
    "Exile." Carib (3:2) Aut-Wint 80, pp. 63-64.

CAREY, Michael A.
    "In Gratitude To My Hat." StoneC (9: 1-2) Aut-Wint 81/82, pp. 76-77.

CARISIO, Justin
    "Of Refraining to Kill Swallows." FourQt (31:1) Aut 81, p. 34.

CARLISLE, Thomas John
    "Flight to Freedom." ChrC (98:5) 18 F 81, p. 169.
    "Job's Messengers." ChrC (98:43) 30 D 81, p. 1359.
    "Match." ChrC (98:19) 27 My 81, p. 615.

CARLSEN, Ioanna
    "In a Manner of Speaking." Hudson (34:1) Spr 81, pp. 74-75.

CARLSON, Doug
    "The Disappearance." SouthernPR (21:2) Aut 81, p. 17.

CARMI, T.
    "Judgement" (tr. by Grace Schulman). Pequod (13) 81, p. 1.

"Miracles" (tr. by Grace Schulman). Pequod (13) 81, p. 3.
"This Sunset" (tr. by Grace Schulman). Pequod (13) 81, p. 2.

CARMONA, Neli Jo
  "Para otro siglo." Claridad/En Rojo (22: 1479) 5-11 Je 81, p. 12.

CARO PAZ, Lydia
  "Volveremos." Claridad/En Rojo (22: 1507) 18-23 D 81, p. 10.

CARPENTER, Lucas
  "January Sunday." KanQ (13:3/4) Sum-Aut 81, p. 76.

CARPENTER, William
  "Night Fishing." Poetry (138:5) Ag 81, pp. 259-260.

CARPINISAN, Mariana
  "The Ghost" (tr. with Mark Irwin of Nichita Stanescu). SenR (12:1/2)
    81, p. 137.
  "Marina" (tr. with Mark Irwin of Nichita Stanescu). SenR (12:1/2) 81,
    p. 135.

CARR, John
  "Figures by Giorgione." HolCrit (18:3 [i. e. 4]) O 81, pp. 19-20.

CARRANZA, María Mercedes
  "Never is Late" (tr. by Mary Crow). PoNow (5:6 issue 30) 81, p. 13.

CARREGA, Gordon
  "He Said." HangL (39) Wint 80-81, p. 2.

CARREL, Ann
  "The Upward Tending." QW (12) Spr-Sum 81, p. 10.
  "The Way To Go." QW (12) Spr-Sum 81, pp. 8-9.

CARRERA, Calixto
  "A pleno sol." Mairena (3:7), pp. 84-85.
  "Viento luminoso." Mairena (3:7), p. 84.
  "Yo vi pasar el viento." Mairena (3:7), p. 85.

CARRIER, Constance
  "The Girls, Salem, Massachusetts, 1692." ConcPo (14:1) Spr 81, pp.
    11-12.
  "Salem Massachusetts 1692: Dorcas Good, Her Daughter." Ploughs
    (6:4) 81, pp. 156-157.
  "Salem Massachusetts 1692: The Girls." Ploughs (6:4) 81, pp. 152-
    153.
  "Salem Massachusetts 1692: Sarah Good." Ploughs (6:4) 81, pp. 154-
    155.

CARRIER, Lois
  "Winter Dream II." BallSUF (21:4) Aut 80, p. 79.

CARRUTH, Hayden
  "Forever In That Year." AmerPoR (10:5) S-O 81, p. 10.
  "Judith's Garden, Late May." AmerPoR (10:5) S-O 81, p. 11.
  "Little Ode: The Snow At Saratoga." AmerPoR (10:5) S-O 81, p. 10.
  "Who I Am." Sulfur (1) 81, pp. 64-69.

CARSON, R. Dale
"The Seventh Son." ThRiPo (17/18) 81, p. 51.

CARTER, Jared
"At the Bass Historical Photo Archive." Im (7:3) 81, p. 4.
"Ginseng." Poetry (137:5) F 81, pp. 274-276.
"Glacier." NewYorker (56:47) 12 Ja 81, p. 82.
"The Oddfellows' Waiting-Room at Glencove Cemetery." Wind (10:39)
    80, p. 10.
"The Purpose of Poetry." Im (7:3) 81, p. 4.
"The Questioning." Stand (22: 3) 81, p. 44.
"Roadside Marker." Wind (10:39) 80, pp. 10-11.
"Shaking the Peonies" (for Effie). Poetry (137:5) F 81, pp. 272-273.
"Television." ColEng (43:1) Ja 81, p. 27.
"Wasps' Nests." ColEng (43:1) Ja 81, p. 27.

CARVALHO, Raul de
"Vivan Los Caballos!" (tr. by Alexis Levitan). ModernPS (10:2/3), p.
    90.

CARVER, Raymond
"The Mailman As Cancer Patient." Tendril (11) Sum 81, p. 16.
"Poem for Karl Wallenda, Aerialist Supreme." Kayak (57) 81, p. 27.

CASAL, Lourdes
"Ano VII." Areito (27: 28) 81, p. 48.
"Domingo." Areito (7: 26) 81, p. 10.
"Hay noches como estas." Areito (7: 26) 81, p. 10.
"La Habana 1968." Areito (7: 26) 81, p. 10.
"Para Ana Velfort." Areito (7: 26) 81, p. 9.
"Vivo en Cuba." Areito (7: 26) 81, p. 10.

CASAUS, Victor
"Oncimedia pe eme." Areito (27: 28) 81, p. 49.

CASE, Sandra
"Elegy for a Lost Poem." CapeR (17:1) Wint 81, p. 44.
"Hilda Latta." CapeR (17:1) Wint 81, p. 45.

CASEY, Michael
"Drive-in Movie." KanQ (13:1) Wint 81, p. 107.

CASH, Grace
"Tanka." WindO (39) Wint 81/82. On calendar.

CASO, José "Pepe"
"Carta elegíaca" (a Adolfina Villanueva). Claridad/En Rojo (22: 1502)
    13-19 N 81, p. 12.
"Carta iracunda a Adolfina Villanueva." Claridad/En Rojo (22: 1502)
    13-19 N 81, p. 12.

CASSIAN, Nina
"Knowledge." Mund (12/13) 80-81, p. 347.
"Quarrel With Chaos" (tr. by Michael Impey and Brian Swann). Mund
    (12/13) 80-81, p. 347.

CASSITY, Turner
"Ghosts." Poetry (138:4) Jl 81, p. 197.

"Hurricane Lamp." ChiR (33:1) Sum 81, p. 45.
"A Salutation to the Moons of Saturn." ChiR (33:1) Sum 81, p. 44.

CASTAN, Miguel Luesma see LUESMA CASTAN, Miguel

CASTAÑA, Luis
  "Acuarela en tres tiempos." Claridad/En Rojo (22: 1480) 12-18 Je 81,
    p. 12.

CASTILLO, Otto René
  "Apolitical Intellectuals" (tr. by Margaret Randall). Sam (109) 81, p.
    52.
  "Revolución." Areito (27: 28) 81, p. backcover.

CASTRO, Michael
  "Fool Poem #1" (for poets). Tele (17) 81, p. 101.
  "Two Views Of The World Via Hemp." Tele (17) 81, p. 101.

CASTRO RIOS, Andrés
  "Epitafio para un presidente, mayordomo de la injusticia." Claridad/En
    Rojo (22: 1477) 22-28 My 81, p. 12.
  "Glosa I." Mairena (2:6), pp. 31-2.
  "Luz desde tu cuerpo." Claridad/En Rojo (22: 1465) 27 F-Mr 5 81, p.
    12.

CASTRO Y CASTRO, Antonio
  "Cuando Llegue." Puerto Wint 81, p. 25.

CATALA, Rafael
  "Estampa de Union Township" (tr. by Pedro Mir). Calib (3:2) Aut-Wint
    80, p. 54.
  "Landscape Union Township." Calib (3:2) Aut-Wint 80, p. 55.
  "Landscape--Union Township." New York Times Sunday, 30 S 79, Sec-
    tion 11, p. 26.
  "Un Personaje Se Defiende." Lugar (1:1) 79, p. 4.
  "Mi Rostro." Lugar (1:1) 79, p. 4.

CATALDO, Susan
  "Them little ants. All those pants." Tele (17) 81, p. 25.
  "Arkansas, Are you ready to die?)." Tele (17) 81, p. 25.
  "Ah Thawt Ah'd Lett Yew Do." Tele (17) 81, p. 24.
  "So, How Did Francois Villon Do It?" Tele (17) 81, p. 24.

CATINA, Ray
  "Helicopters." Sam (116) 81, p. 57.
  "Southeast Asian Chess." Sam (116) 81, p. 57.
  "Viet Cong Mortar Round." Sam (117) 81, p. 16.

CATTAFI, Bartolo
  "Baedeker" (tr. by Ruth Feldman and Brian Swann). PoNow (5:6 issue
    30) 81, p. 12.
  "Cloth" (tr. by Ruth Feldman and Brian Swann). Mund (12/13) 80-81,
    p. 346.
  "Like A Blade." Mund (12/13) 80-81, p. 346.
  "No Pasaran" (tr. by Ruth Feldman and Brian Swann). PoNow (5:6 is-
    sue 30) 81, p. 12.
  "The Package" (tr. by Ruth Feldman and Brian Swann). PoNow (5:6
    issue 30) 81, p. 12.

"Toward Bastions and Warriors" (tr. by Ruth Feldman and Brian
  Swann). PoNow (5:6 issue 30) 81, p. 12.

CATULLUS
  "11" (tr. by Lisa Dickler).   ChiR (32:4) Spr 81, p. 90.
  "58" (tr. by Lisa Dickler).   ChiR (32:4) Spr 81, p. 91.

CATZ, Justin
  "In The Bitterness of January." StoneC (9: 1-2) Aut-Wint 81/82, p. 60.

CAVALCANTI, Guido
  "Gianni Quel Guido Salute" (tr. by Ezra Pound). Iowa (12:1) Wint 81,
    p. 45.
  "Noi Sian le Triste Penne Isbigotite" (tr. by Ezra Pound). Iowa (12:1)
    Wint 81, p. 47.

CAVALLARO, Carol
  "Visited." Chelsea (40) 81, pp. 131-133.

CAZARRE de ALVEZ, Delia
  "Dualidad." LetFem (7:2) Aut 81, p. 62.

CECIL, Richard
  "After the Funeral, Reading Hobbes." SouthernPR (21:2) Aut 81, pp.
    34-36.
  "Threnody For Sunrise." AmerPoR (10:6) N-D 81, p. 12.
  "Threnody For Sunset." AmerPoR (10:6) N-D 81, p. 12.

CEDERING, Siv
  "April Fool." GeoR (35:2) Sum 81, p. 400.
  "The City" (tr. of Werner Aspenström). PoNow (5:6 issue 30) 81, p.
    5.
  "In the Land of Shinar." PartR (48:3) 81, p. 599.
  "The Ring." Confr (22) Sum 81, p. 13.
  "The Sardine in the Subway" (tr. of Werner Aspenström). PoNow (5:6
    issue 30) 81, p. 5.
  "Ukiyo-e." Harp (263:1576) S 81, p. 80.

CEDRINS, Inara
  "In the evening forest a bird sings..." (tr. of Astrid Ivask). PoNow
    (5:6 issue 30) 81, p. 19.
  "Spring." PoNow (6:2 issue 32) 81, p. 43.
  "That evening the stars' quicksilver" (tr. of Astrid Ivask). PoNow (5:6
    issue 30) 81, p. 19.

CELAN, Paul
  "Conversation in the Mountains" (tr. by Katharine Washburn and Mar-
    garet Guillemin). ParisR (23:80) Sum 81, pp. 215-220.

CERNIGLIA, Alice
  "On the Line." Meadows (2:1) 81, p. 49.
  "Petals." Meadows (2:1) 81, p. 30.
  "Waiting." Meadows (2:1) 81, p. 36.

CERNUDA, Luis
  "Child Behind Glass" (tr. by Stephen Kessler). Thrpny (5) Spr 81, p.
    21.
  "Dostoyevsky and Physical Beauty" (tr. by David Unger). PoNow (5:6

issue 30) 81, p. 13.
"Seagulls in the Parks" (tr. by David Unger). PoNow (5:6 issue 30) 81,
   p. 13.

CERVANTES, James
   "The Sun Intent Upon this Earth." Ploughs (6:4) 81, pp. 160-161.

CERVANTES, Lorna Dee
   "The Anthill." PoNow (6:1 issue 31) 81, p. 28.
   "The Anthill." PoNow (6:3 issue 33) 81, p. 22.
   "The Body As Braille." Sam (109) 81, p. 53.
   "Cannery Town in August." PoNow (6:3 issue 33) 81, p. 22.
   "Emplumada." PoNow (6:1 issue 31) 81, p. 28.
   "For Virginia Chavez." PoNow (6:1 issue 31) 81, p. 28.
   "Meeting Mescalito at Oak Hill Cemetery." PoNow (6:3 issue 33) 81,
      p. 22.
   "Poem For The Young White Man Who Asked Me How I, An Intelligent,
      Well-Read Person Could Believe In The War Between Races." Sam
      (109) 81, pp. 22-23.

CERVERA, Juan
   "Siempre Vuelvo a la Tierra." Puerto Wint 81, p. 21.

CERVO, Nathan
   "Nocturne." EnPas (12), 81, p. 33.

CESAIRE, Aimé
   "Batoque" (tr. by Clayton Eshleman and Annette Smith). Sulfur (1) 81,
      pp. 212-218.

CEVDET ANDAY, Melih see ANDAY, Melih Cevdet

CHACON, Genoveva
   "Dejo de llamarle árbol al árbol." Metam (3:2/4:1) 80-81, p. 58.

CHAET, Eric
   "A Man Swerves His Car." Northeast (3:11) Sum 81, p. 3.

CHAFFIN, Lillie D.
   "The Tar Baby." Wind (11:41) 81, p. 4.

CHAFIN, Shirley R.
   "Too Late." Wind (11:42) 81, p. 8.

CHAMBERLAIN, Karen
   "Yerokastrinos." DenQ (16:2) Sum 81, p. 19.

CHAMBERLAIN, Marisha
   "Horse and Rider." PraS (55:3) Aut 81, p. 72.
   "Winter, Washday." PraS (55:3) Aut 81, p. 71.

CHAMBERLAIN, Stephen R.
   "The Water's Edge." ChrC (98:20) 3-10 Je 81, p. 631.

CHAMBERLAIN, William
   "How To Pan For Gold." PoetryNW (22:2) Sum 81, pp. 18-19.
   "The Lost Journal of Meriwether Lewis." CutB (16) Spr-Sum 81, pp.
      19-20.

CHAMBERS, Craig
 "Coming of Age." LittleR (7:1, issue 15) 81, p. 11.
 "Lives." LittleR (7:1, issue 15) 81, p. 11.
 "Locomotion." LittleR (7:1, issue 15) 81, p. 9.
 "Love Poem." LittleR (7:1, issue 15) 81, p. 11.
 "Meditations." LittleR (7:1, issue 15) 81, p. 10.
 "Mysteries." LittleR (7:1, issue 15) 81, p. 11.
 "The New Place." LittleR (7:1, issue 15) 81, p. 9.
 "The Parting." LittleR (7:1, issue 15) 81, p. 11.
 "Voices" (for Mac Bennett). LittleR (7:1, issue 15) 81, p. 9.

CHAMBERS, Douglas
 "Father and Son." Thrpny (7) Aut 81, p. 18.

CHAMBERS, Leland H.
 "Cornered" (tr. of Ramiro Valdez). DenQ (16:3) Aut 81, p. 96.
 "Stones" (tr. of Ramiro Valdez). DenQ (16:3) Aut 81, p. 95.

CHANDLER, Michael
 "Darkness." PortR (27: 2) 81, p. 95.
 "Quiero." PortR (27: 2) 81, p. 95.
 "Smells of the Universe." PoNow (6:3 issue 33) 81, p. 7.

CHANG, Chiu-ling
 "Gazing at the Moon and Longing for One Far Away" (tr. by C. H.
   Kwan). MalR (58) Ap 81, p. 36.

CHANG, Diana
 "A Dialogue with My Own Temperament." Confr (21) Wint 81, p. 13.
 "Naming." Confr (21) Wint 81, p. 14.

CHAPPEL, Allen H.
 "Glimpse from the Past" (tr. of Ilse Aichinger). NewOR (8:2) Sum 81,
   p. 189.
 "A Subject for Writing" (tr. of Gabriele Wohmann). NewOR (8:2) Sum
   81, p. 134.

CHAPPELL, Fred
 "The Homunculus." SouthernPR (21: 1) Spr 81, pp. 70-71.
 "Scarecrow Colloquy." VirQR (57:4) Aut 81, pp. 640-641.

CHAR, René
 "The Death Mask" (tr. by Carolyn Steiner and Franz Wright). SenR
   (12:1/2) 81, p. 47.
 "La Dot de Maubergeonne." SenR (12:1/2) 81, p. 48.
 "The Dowry of Maubergeonne" (tr. by Carolyn Steiner and Franz
   Wright). SenR (12:1/2) 81, p. 49.
 "Fastes." SenR (12:1/2) 81, p. 44.
 "Fastes" (tr. by Carolyn Steiner and Franz Wright). SenR (12:1/2) 81,
   p. 45.
 "Ligne de foi." SenR (12:1/2) 81, p. 44.
 "Line of Faith" (tr. by Carolyn Steiner and Franz Wright). SenR (12:
   1/2) 81, p. 45.
 "La masque funebre." SenR (12:1/2) 81, p. 46.
 "La Rainette." SenR (12:1/2) 81, p. 48.
 "The Tree Frog" (tr. by Carolyn Steiner and Franz Wright). SenR
   (12:1/2) 81, p. 49.

CHARIARSE, Leopoldo
"Paisaje de China." Lugar (1:1) 79, p. 5.
"El Pasado." Lugar (1:1) 79, p. 4.
"Los Poemas" (a Enrique Verastegui). Lugar (1:1) 79, p. 5.

CHASE, Alfonso
"Solar Music" (tr. by Harry Haskell). Mund (12/13) 80-81, pp. 238-
242.

CHASE, Josiah
"One-Hundred Miles from Nowhere." Wind (11:43) 81, p. 7.

CHASE, Karen
"The Pond Poem." SouthernPR (21: 1) Spr 81, pp. 53-54.

CHASE, Naomi F.
"Memento Mori." HolCrit (18:5) D 81, p. 13.

CHASE, Naomi Feigelson
"Me, Too, Andrew Marvell." HolCrit (18:3) Je 81, p. 19.

CHASE, Peter S.
"The Immigrants." Aspect (77/79) 81, p. 27.

CHASIN, Helen
"Trust." ThRiPo (17/18) 81, p. 8.

CHÂTILLON, Pierre
"Amoureuses." Os (12) Spr 81, pp. 12-13.

CHEDID, Andrée
"The Naked Face." Mund (12/13) 80-81, p. 329.
"Who Remains Standing?" (tr. by Samuel Hazo and Mirene Ghossein).
Mund (12/13) 80-81, p. 329.

CHEEVER, Mary
"Views of the Hudson: Bridging." LitR (24:3) Spr 81, pp. 411-412.

CHERNER, Ann
"Lavender." NewEngR (3:3) Spr 81, p. 410.
"Lullaby (for Ellen)." NewEngR (3:3) Spr 81, p. 411.
"Passenger." PoNow (6:3 issue 33) 81, p. 8.
"Reunion (for Joni)." NewEngR (3:3) Spr 81, p. 412.

CHERNICOFF, Billie
"Corona." Sulfur (1) 81, pp. 208-211.

CHERNOFF, Maxine
"Animal Magnetism." PoNow (6:1 issue 31) 81, p. 14.

CHERRY, Kelly
"At Night Your Mouth." OP (31/32) Aut 81, pp. 163-164.
"Hunting: A Story." MidwQ (22:2) Wint 81, pp. 126-131.

CHEVREMONT, Evaristo Ribera see RIBERA CHEVREMONT, Evaristo

CHEZIA, Brenda Thompson
"La Danse" (For Tereza Baptiste--Home from the Wars). Obs (6:1/2)

Spr-Sum 80, pp. 224-225.

"La Fleur Haitienne" (for Diane Sandaker).   Obs (6:1/2) Spr-Sum 80,
   p. 227.

"Parterres" (For Madame Marie Laveau).   Obs (6:1/2) Spr-Sum 80, pp.
   221-223.

CHIKOVANI, Simon
   "Haymaking" (tr. by Louis Zellikoff).   PoNow (5:6 issue 30) 81, p. 13.

CHILDS, John Steven
   "Days that Beat."   CapeR (17:1) Wint 81, p. 2.
   "The Girl in the Spee-Dee Mart Outside Manhattan, Kansas."   CapR
      (16:2) Sum 81, p. 17.
   "Search and Destroy."   CapeR (16:2) Sum 81, p. 18.

CHIN, Marilyn
   "Coal's Reply" (tr. of Ai Qing).   Iowa (12:1) Wint 81, p. 92.
   "The North" (tr. of Ai Qing).   Iowa (12:1) Wint 81, pp. 89-91.
   "Snow Falls on China" (tr. of Ai Qing).   SenR (12:1/2) 81, pp. 114-16.
   "Sun" (tr. of Ai Qing).   Iowa (12:1) Wint 81, p. 93.

CHIPASULA, Frank Mkalawile
   "Because the Wind Remembers."   Obs (7:1) Spr 81, p. 14.
   "The Hangman."   Obs (7:1) Spr 81, p. 18.
   "Message Man: Sterling A. Brown."   Obs (7:1) Spr 81, p. 15.
   "Satchmo and Trane."   Obs (7:1) Spr 81, p. 17.
   "A Small Black Bird Singing (for Letty Mbulu)."   Obs (7:1) Spr 81, pp.
      16-17.
   "Waposa."   Obs (7:1) Spr 81, pp. 13-14.

CHITWOOD, Michael
   "Sleeping in the Cemetery."   Wind (10:39) 80, pp. 12-13.

CHONG-CHOL
   "A Passing Woman" (tr. by Michael Stephens).   Pequod (13) 81, p. 68.

CHOYCE, Lesley
   "When the Kissing Stops."   PottPort (3) 81, p. 52.
   "Higher Math."   PottPort (3) 81, p. 33.
   "Editors in the Night."   PottPort (3) 81, p. 50.

CHRISTENSEN, Erleen
   "Night Song."   Meadows (2:1) 81, p. 56.
   "North by Northwest."   Meadows (2:1) 81, p. 18.
   "Prayer to a Grey Sky."   Meadows (2:1) 81, p. 56.
   "Time and Utah."   Meadows (2:1) 81, p. 18.

CHRISTENSEN, Erleen J.
   "Male and Female Created He Them."   KanQ (13:3/4) Sum-Aut 81, p.
      28.

CHRISTENSEN, Nadia
   "Bonjour Monsieur Gaugin" (tr. of Astrid Tollefsen).   PoNow (5:6 issue
      30) 81, p. 45.
   "Departure" (tr. of Tove Ditlevsen).   PoNow (5:6 issue 30) 81, p. 14.
   "The Eye of the Hurricane."   PoNow (6:1 issue 31) 81, p. 36.
   "Fyodor Dostoyevsky" (tr. of Ase-Marie Nesse).   PoNow (5:6 issue 30)
      81, p. 33.

"It's Fall. It's Raining in the Woods" (tr. of Kirsten Thorup, w/
Alexander Taylor). PoNow (5:6 issue 30) 81, p. 26.
"Magic" (tr. of Kate Naess). PoNow (5:6 issue 30) 81, p. 31.
"37° C" (tr. of Kirsten Thorup, w/ Alexander Taylor). PoNow (5:6
issue 30) 81, p. 26.
"Time" (tr. of Tove Ditlevsen). PoNow (5:6 issue 30) 81, p. 14.
"Trieste II" (tr. of Kirsten Thorup, w/ Alexander Taylor). PoNow (5:6
issue 30) 81, p. 26.

CHRISTIAN, Paula
"Haiku of Neonatals." Poem (43) Nov 81, p. 18.
"It's Nest Time, Daddy." Poem (43) Nov 81, p. 15.
"Old Gertrude's Gravid." Poem (43) Nov 81, p. 17.
"The Ku Klux Klan in Collinwood." Sam (109) 81, p. 23.
"Today." Poem (43) Nov 81, p. 16.

CHRISTINA, Martha
"Solace." PoNow (6:3 issue 33) 81, p. 8.

CHRISTMAN, Berniece Bunn
"Early Morning Jogger." Comm (108:4) 27 F 81, p. 126.

CHRISTOPHER, Nicholas
"The Driver in Italy." Ascent (6:2) 81, p. 17.
"The Road From Pisa to Florence." NewYRB (28:14) 24 S 81, p. 30.
"Room 10." Ascent (6:2) 81, p. 18-19.
"The Track." NewYorker (56:51) 9 F 81, p. 112.

CHUILLEANAIN, Eiléan Ní
"Light glancing along a public-house table." ConcPo (14:2) Aut 81, pp.
114-115.
"She is fifty, and missing the breast." ConcPo (14:2) Aut 81, p. 115.
"When she opened the egg the wise woman had given her." ConcPo
(14:2) Aut 81, p. 114.

CHUKWUDI, Obioma
"The Trophy." Obs (6:1/2) Spr-Sum 80, p. 198.

CHUNG, Ling see LING, Chung

CHURCHILL, Sauci
"Road closed from 5 a.m. to 7 p.m. after which traffic may resume."
Prima (6/7) 81, p. 58.

CHUTE, Robert M.
"After An Ice Storm." BelPoJ (31:4) Sum 81, p. 37.
"Burning Brush In Winter." BelPoJ (31:4) Sum 81, pp. 37-38.
"The Night after Christmas." SmPd (18:2) Spr 81, p. 25.

CICCO, Pier Giorgio di see DiCICCO, Pier Giorgio

CINTROL MARCANO, Luis A.
"Ninos (a todos los niños del mundo). Claridad/En Rojo (22:1460) 23-29
Ja 81, p. 12.

CIORDIA, Javier
"Cronos." Mairena (2:6) 80, pp. 56-8.

CISNEROS, Antonio
  "En la Puerta de Mi Casa." Inti (9) Spr 79, p. 97.
  "Para Soledad Cevallos (6 Agosto 78)." Inti (9) Spr 79, p. 98.

CITINO, David
  "After Cities." SoDakR (19:3) Aut 81, pp. 24-25.
  "Coming Home Again." PoNow (6:1 issue 31) 81, p. 44.
  "A Composite Life of the American Poet: an Experiment." HiramPoR
    (30) Spr-Sum 81, pp. 3-6.
  "Dust, Ash and Pine, and Dust Again." CentR (25:4) Aut 81, p. 380.
  "The Farmer." PoNow (6:3 issue 33) 81, p. 23.
  "Father Coughlin." ModernPS (10:2/3) 81, p. 120.
  "Francis Meets a Leper." LitR (24:3) Spr 81, pp. 379-380.
  "Herb Doctor." HiramPoR (29) Aut-Wint 81, p. 11.
  "In the Same Place, at the Same Time." PoetryNW (22:2) Sum 81, pp.
    36-37.
  "Lament of the Old Monk." Wind (11:40) 81, p. 5.
  "Meditation on the Skeleton of a Prehistoric Indian at the Ohio Histori-
    cal Center." SoDakR (19:3) Aut 81, p. 26.
  "Notes for a One-Act Play: The Chase." HiramPoR (30) Spr-Sum 81,
    p. 14.
  "Oldsmobiles: Before 1974." Confr (22) Sum 81, p. 106.
  "The Retired Pastor's Commentary on the Hymn 'Amazing Grace'."
    SouthernHR (15:4) Aut 81, p. 306.
  "The Retired Preacher Preaches on Revenge." HolCrit (18:2) Ap 81, p.
    12.
  "Ritual: on Leaving." Wind (11:40) 81, pp. 6-7.
  "The Savor of Words, the Bite of Love." CharR (7:1) Spr 81, p. 31.
  "Shortstop." PikeR (2) Sum 81, p. 28.
  "Sister Mary Appassionata's Lecture to the Eighth Grade Boys and
    Girls on the Things of this World, the Things of the Other." BelPoJ
    (32:2) Wint 81-82, pp. 2-5.
  "Sitting Next to the Father of the Quarterback at the Harding High
    School Homecoming Game." PoNow (6:2 issue 32) 81, p. 17.
  "Telling the Bees." LitR (24:3) Spr 81, p. 379.
  "The Thing." PoNow (6:3 issue 33) 81, p. 23.
  "The Three Winning Entries in the 1980 Forbidden Fantasy Contest."
    SouthernPR (21: 1) Spr 81, pp. 65-66.
  "Visiting My Father In Florida." MinnR (17) Aut 81, p. 45.

CLAMPITT, Amy
  "Amaranth and Moly." MassR (22:2) Sum 81, pp. 321-2.
  "Beethoven, Opus III." NewYorker (57:14) 25 My 81, p. 41.
  "Burial in Cypress Hills" (for B. and L. B.). Antaeus (43) Aut 81, pp.
    85-86.
  "Camouflage." NewYorker (56:47) 12 Ja 81, p. 40.
  "Gooseberry Fool." Poetry (139:3) D 81, pp. 144-145.
  "The Hickory Grove." Poetry (139:3) D 81, pp. 142-143.
  "Letters from Jerusalem." YaleR (71: 1) Aut 81, pp. 92-93.
  "Lindenbloom." NewYorker (57:12) 11 My 81, p. 135.
  "A Procession at Candlemas." NewEngR (4:2) Wint 81, pp. 185-9.
  "The Quarry." NewYorker (57:28) 31 Ag 81, p. 32.
  "Salvage." NewYorker (56:50) 2 F 81, p. 72.
  "Scavenging." Chelsea (40) 81, p. 130.
  "Slow Motion." Atl (248:2) Ag 81, p. 54.
  "Sunday Music." PoetryNW (22:3) Aut 81, pp. 41-42.
  "Times Square Water Music." NewYorker (57:26) 17 Ag 81, p. 34.

CLARE, Josephine
"Outside the Führerbunker." Ploughs (6:4) 81, pp. 74-77.

CLARK, Carl D.
"Domino Waltz" (Construction for John Cage). Aspect (77/79) 81, p. 31.

CLARK, Constance
"Sin." ChrC (98:18) 20 My 81, p. 576.

CLARK, Kevin
"Autumn, 1830. Her Letter to the Dead." CalQ (18/19) 81, pp. 41-43.
"Clarence King Names Mt. Tyndall" (1864, for Dave Robertson). CutB (16) Spr-Sum 81, pp. 49-50.
"The Grapes" (for Sandra Gilbert). SoCaR (13: 2) Spr 81, p. 56.
"In Your Backyard." CalQ (18/19) 81, pp. 39-40.
"Separation." CalQ (18/19) 81, pp. 38-39.
"The Walnut Tree: on turning thirty" (for C.). BelPoJ (31:3) Spr 81, pp. 4-7.

CLARK, Naomi
"Angel of the Dark Wings." CalQ (18/19) 81, p. 139.

CLARK, Tom
"Crisis On The Savannah." ParisR (23:79) Spr 81, p. 78.

CLARKE, Cecilia Cobb
"Asleep." LittleM (13:1/2) Spr-Sum 79, c1981, p. 121.

CLARKE, Gillian
"Buzzard." Pequod (13) 81, p. 38.
"Font de Gaume." Pequod (13) 81, p. 39.
"Plums." Pequod (13) 81, p. 40.
"Ram." Pequod (13) 81, p. 41.

CLARKE, Terence
"Intertidal Areas." PoNow (6:2 issue 32) 81, p. 20.

CLARY, Killarney
"A church made entirely of salt--in a mine." AmerPoR (10:2) Mr-Ap 81, p. 32.
"Easy as an arm moving over water, a slight wind on the bay." AmerPoR (10:2) Mr-Ap 81, p. 32.
"No more cicacas winding the evening into a single, small fist." AmerPoR (10:2) Mr-Ap 81, p. 32.

CLAUDEL, Alice Moser
"Midwestern Tutoring." Vis (6) 81, n.p.
"Rich Land, Thin Much Desired." CharR (7:1) Spr 81, p. 17.

CLEARY, Suzanne
"Taking Count." AmerPoR (10:4) Jl-Ag 81, p. 37.

CLEMENT, Jean-Baptiste
"El tiempo de cerezas" (a la valiente ciudadana Lousie, la ambulanciera de la calle Fontaine-au-Roi, ..." Claridad/En Rojo (22: 1472) 17-23 Ap 81, p. 5.

CLIFF, William
    "Mr. X, Doctor of Laws" (tr. by Maxine Kumin and Judith Kumin).
      PoNow (5:6 issue 30) 81, p. 14.

CLIFTON, Charles H.
    "A Certain Squint." Ploughs (6:4) 81, p. 50.
    "Reading Dante." Ploughs (6:4) 81, p. 49.

CLIFTON, Lucille
    "In Salem (to Jeanette)." Mund (12/13) 80-81, p. 184.
    "New Bones." Mund (12/13) 80-81, p. 184.

CLIFTON, Merritt
    "Bleeding Ulcer." Sam (116) 81, p. 56.
    "Green Mountain Grade." Sam (117) 81, p. 2.
    "The Last Warrior-Hero." Sam (117) 81, p. 7.
    "The Madman's Second Thoughts." Sam (106) 81, p. 26.
    "Trinity: Digital Clock." Sam (109) 81, p. 15.
    "Trinity: Judgement." Sam (109) 81, p. 19.
    "Trinity: The Big Bang Theory." Sam (109) 81, pp. 16-18.

CLOUTIER, David
    "Immaculate." Aspect (77/79) 81, p. 37.
    "Night has a hand." Aspect (77/79) 81, p. 37.

CLOUTIER, Sylvie
    "Saparine." Os (12) Spr 81, p. 24.

COAKLEY, William Leo
    "Changing Bodies." Confr (22) Sum 81, p. 26.
    "Family Burial." Confr (22) Sum 81, p. 26.

COBEAN, C. S.
    "Name That Time." Outbr (6/7) Aut 80-Spr 81, pp. 19-21.
    "Sunset/July/Alabama." Outbr (6/7) Aut 80-Spr 81, pp. 16-18.

COBIAN, Ricardo
    "Caminante adjunto." Areito (27: 28) 81, p. 50.
    "Carlos Muñiz Varela." Areito (7: 27) 81, p. backcover.
    "Después del sueño." Maize (4:3/4) Spr-Sum 81, pp. 66-7.
    "Ocurre a veces, que no quepo en mi dolor." Maize (4:3/4) Spr-Sum
      81, pp. 64-5.
    "Saludo a mi vecino." Maize (4:3/4) Spr-Sum 81, p. 65.

COBIN, Susan
    "After Three Years." Im (7:2) 1981, p. 12.
    "In the Dream You Were Wearing." Kayak (56) 81, p. 34.
    "In Your Dream the Dead." Kayak (56) 81, p. 35.

COCHRAN, Jo
    "Coyote and River." MalR (60) O 81, pp. 148-149.
    "The Hunt." MalR (60) O 81, p. 149.
    "Letter to Kieffer from Orcas Island." MalR (60) O 81, pp. 150-151.
    "The Old Friend Arriving." MalR (60) O 81, p. 147.
    "Poem at Winter Solstice." MalR (60) O 81, p. 146.
    "The Rough Hewn Walls." MalR (60) O 81, p. 152.
    "Through the Night." MalR (60) O 81, pp. 145-146.

COCHRANE, Guy R.
  "Common Sense." WormR (81/82) 81, p. 36.
  "Formality." WormR (81/82) 81, p. 37.
  "Short Story." WormR (81/82) 81, p. 37.
  "Three Women." WormR (81/82) 81, p. 36.

CODINA, Norberto
  "Un poema de amor, según datos demográficos." Areito (7: 27) 81, p.
  21.

COE, Dina
  "Beaching." US1 (14/15) Aut/Wint 81, p. 20.
  "On Her First Trip, An Airline Stewardess Steps Out on a Balcony."
    US1 (14/15) Aut/Wint 81, p. 20.
  "On Her First Trip, an Airline Stewardess Steps out on a Balcony."
    CutB (17) Aut-Wint 81, p. 47.
  "Sitting Down in the Midst of a Hot Spell, May 20." US1 (14/15) Aut/
    Wint 81, p. 20.

COFFIN, Lyn
  "Bedtime." PortR (27: 2) 81, p. 14.
  "Crossing the Bridge." KanQ (13:3/4) Sum-Aut 81, p. 76.
  "The Dark Facts, The Marriage Fable." PortR (27: 2) 81, p. 15.
  "A Day on the Pavement." PortR (27: 2) 81, p. 14.
  "Emily Dickinson Meets Ogden Nash." PortR (27: 2) 81, p. 15.
  "A Life." SouthwR (66:2) Spr 81, p. 157.
  "Mirror Women." Northeast (3:10) Wint 81, p. 9.
  "Numbs." HolCrit (18:3 [i. e. 4]) O 81, p. 17.
  "The Stone Boat." HolCrit (18:5) D 81, p. 19.

COGSWELL, Fred
  "Aesthete." PottPort (3) 81, p. 50.
  "Could I...." PottPort (3) 81, p. 16.

COHEN, Gerald
  "Racing the Flow." CapeR (17:1) Wint 81, p. 27.

COHEN, Helen Degen
  "In an Age of Relationships." KanQ (13:3/4) Sum-Aut 81, p. 213.

COHEN, Marc
  "Cento From Delmore." Tele (17) 81, p. 87.

COLAMECO, Andy
  "Indian Summer Nightfall." Nimrod (25:1) Aut-Wint 81, p. 97.

COLBIN, Annemarie
  "Guru" (tr. of Sergio Mondragón). Mund (12/13) 80-81, p. 305.
  "November" (tr. of Sergio Mondragón). Mund (12/13) 80-81, p. 304.

COLBY, Joan
  "Abandoned Woman." Im (7:3) 81, p. 11.
  "Beheaded." CreamCR (7:1) 81, p. 112.
  "The Deep End." Im (7:2) 1981, p. 11.
  "Disguises." CreamCR (6:2) 81, pp. 26-27.
  "Divorce." MinnR (17) Aut 81, pp. 18-19.
  "Homage to Apollonaire." StoneC (9: 1-2) Aut-Wint 81/82, p. 19.
  "Lollipops." KanQ (13:3/4) Sum-Aut 81, p. 176.

"Squirrel on the Highway." Tendril (10) Wint 81, p. 18.
"The Street of the Cultist." Ascent (7:1) 81, p. 44.
"What Happens to the Land." Tendril (10) Wint 81, p. 19.

COLE, Henri
    "Picking Blackberries for Twelve Days in Vermont." CreamCR (6:2)
        81, pp. 17-18.
    "Runner of Bradford Beach, Milwaukee." PoNow (6:1 issue 31) 81, p.
        47.

COLE, James
    "Europe, 1961" (to RHM). PraS (55:1/2) Spr-Sum 81, p. 126.

COLE, Jeremy
    "Pink Flamingo." HangL (40) Aut 81, p. 63.
    "The Sharp Blade." HangL (40) Aut 81, p. 63.

COLE, Peter
    "Apology For Loneliness." Ploughs (6:4) 81, p. 51.

COLE, Richard
    "Aubade." Hudson (34:3) Aut 81, p. 383.
    "Recovering in the Sandwich Islands." Hudson (34:3) Aut 81, pp. 382-
        383.

COLEMAN, Wanda
    "Beneath the Rubble." Obs (6:1/2) Spr-Sum 80, pp. 229-233.

COLES, Katharine
    "Climbing Lesson." PoetryNW (22:1) Spr 81, pp. 26-27.

COLLIER, Michael
    "Bay Lands." ThRiPo (17/18) 81, pp. 45-46.
    "In Khabarovsk." Nat (232:20) 23 My 81, p. 636.

COLLINS, Billy
    "The Wedding." PoNow (6:2 issue 32) 81, p. 32.

COLLINS, Denise A.
    "The Ad." US1 (14/15) Aut/Wint 81, p. 18.

COLLINS, Martha
    "The Blue Room." VirQR (57:4) Aut 81, pp. 629-630.
    "Depression." NewEngR (3:3) Spr 81, p. 368.
    "The Farm." AmerPoR (10:3) My-Je 81, p. 7.
    "More About the Bear." VirQR (57:4) Aut 81, pp. 628-629.
    "Snow." PraS (55:4) Wint 81-82, p. 82.

COLLINS, Pat Lowery
    "Drift Tree." SmPd (18:2) Spr 81, p. 31.
    "To Mother, Who Sewed." Prima (6/7) 81, p. 80.

COLLINS, Robert
    "Epiphany." HiramPoR (29) Aut-Wint 81, p. 12.

COLLOM, Jack
    "awoke at six feeling blue." Peb (21) 81, pp. 21-22.

COLOMBO, Silvia N. Giménez Giorio de see GIMENEZ GIORIO de
COLOMBO, Silvia N.

COLON RUIZ, José O.
  "Sueño de mayo." Mairena (2:6) 81, p. 35.

COMAN, Brad
  "Caught in a Storm." CalQ (18/19) 81, p. 140.

COMBS, Bruce
  "Farewell" (for my son Malcolm). Wind (11:43) 81, p. 9.
  "Progress." Sam (106) 81, p. 23.

COMITE PRO DEFENSA DE LA CULTURA
  "El Gobierno Araña." Claridad/En Rojo (22:1461) 30 Ja-5 F 81, p. 12.

CONARD, Audrey
  "Northern Lake." MichQR (20:2) Spr 81, p. 95.
  "Whale." MichQR (20:2) Spr 81, pp. 94-95.

CONCEPCION, Jorge Luis Avilés see AVILES CONCEPCION, Jorge Luis

CONDRY, Dorothea
  Corporate Security. Sam (121) 81, Entire issue.
  The Sign. Sam (108) 81, Entire issue.

CONGDON, Kirby
  "At twelve, in rage or for spite, one of the Caswell brothers...."
    PoNow (6:1 issue 31) 81, p. 15.
  "Big Mrs. Watrous hung her key on the rosebush, ..." PoNow (6:1
    issue 31) 81, p. 15.
  "He was the handsomest boy in school...." PoNow (6:1 issue 31) 81,
    p. 15.
  "When the cattle, the horses, and the farm were auctioned off...."
    PoNow (6:1 issue 31) 81, p. 15.

CONNELL, Kim
  "Poem to a Retired Whore." CimR (54) Ja 81, p. 51.
  "In Response to My Mother's Request for a Poem on My Father's Fifti-
    eth Birthday." SouthernR (17:2) Spr 81, p. 401.

CONNOR, Tony
  "An Old Acquaintance." PoetryNW (22:4) Wint 81-82, pp. 10-11.
  "Reminiscences Remembered." Poetry (138:4) Jl 81, pp. 198-202.

CONOLEY, Gillian
  "Death, As Described By The Living." MassR (22:4) Wint 81, p. 819.
  "Lust." MassR (22:4) Wint 81, p. 818.

CONROY, Carol
  "The Jewish Furrier Explains The Search For Beauty." ParisR (23:80)
    Sum 81, p. 138.

CONROY, James V.
  "A Distance in the Dark." Vis (5) 81, n.p.

CONTOSKI, Victor
  "The First Time." ThRiPo (17/18) 81, p. 10.

"Golden Mountains" (tr. of Tadeusz Rozewicz). PoNow (5:6 issue 30)
    81, p. 25.
"In Haste" (tr. of Tadeusz Rozewicz). PoNow (5:6 issue 30) 81, p. 25.
"The Last Time." PoNow (6:2 issue 32) 81, p. 7.
"To the Heart" (tr. of Tadeusz Rozewicz). PoNow (5:6 issue 30) 81, p.
    25.

CONTRAIRE, A. U.
    "The cold rain bumbles." WindO (39) Wint 81/82. On calendar.
    "Dry forsythia." WindO (39) Wint 81/82. On calendar.
    "Tracks." WindO (39) Wint 81/82. On calendar.
    "Zen in haiku?" WindO (39) Wint 81/82. On calendar.

COOK, Paul
    "In The Park." QW (13) Aut/Wint 81/82, pp. 28-29.

COOK, Paul H.
    "For a Friend Going Home" (for Dan). GeoR (35:1) Spr 81, pp. 158-
    159.

COOK, R. L.
    "Leaves Among the Snow." MalR (57) Ja 81, p. 107.
    "Reply To An Epitaph." MalR (57) Ja 81, p. 107.

COOLEY, Peter
    "Before the Summer is Over." MidwQ (23:1) Aut 81, p. 51.
    "The Lizard." MidwQ (23:1) Aut 81, p. 52.
    "Omar Says." MissR (10:1) Spr-Sum 81, p. 117.
    "The Night Season." MissR (10:1) Spr-Sum 81, pp. 115-116.
    "No One." PoNow (6:2 issue 32) 81, p. 32.

COONS, Alice
    "I found an eagle." Meadows (2:1) 81, p. 65.

COOPER, Bernard
    "Believe it or not." CarolQ (34:2) Aut 81, p. 27.

COOPER, Dennis
    "Reddest Lips to Our Hearts." PoNow (6:2 issue 32) 81, p. 36.

COOPER, Wyn
    "The Other Side." QW (12) Spr-Sum 81, p. 89.

CORBETT, William
    "Marie's irises." Aspect (77/79) 81, p. 38.

CORDING, Robert
    "Bats in the House." AmerS (50:4) Aut 81, p. 518.
    "Bittern." SouthernR (17:3) Sum 81, pp. 580-1.
    "Blossoms." QW (13) Aut/Wint 81/82, p. 22.
    "Fabre Works Through The Night." CarolQ (34:1) Sum 81, pp. 68-69.
    "The Horses." NewEngR (4:1) Aut 81, pp. 98-9.
    "Liljefors Makes a Rough Sketch for 'Living Peace'." NewEngR (4:1)
    Aut 81, pp. 97-8.
    "Looking at Photographs: New Year's Eve." SouthernPR (21: 1) Spr
    81, p. 49.
    "Shelley's Death." NewEngR (3:4) Sum 81, pp. 533-6.

COREY, Stephen
  "Confederates, 1978" (to Allen Tate, 1899-1979). SoCaR (14: 1) Aut
      81, p. 35.
  from Craftsmen: "Carpenter: Of His Pleasures." GeoR (35:1) Spr 81,
      p. 37.
  from Craftsmen: "Potter." GeoR (35:1) Spr 81, p. 35.
  from Craftsmen: "Quilts." GeoR (35:1) Spr 81, pp. 36-37.
  from Craftsmen: "Smith." GeoR (35:1) Spr 81, p. 34.
  from Craftsmen: "State Craft Fair: Berea, Kentucky." GeoR (35:1)
      Spr 81, p. 38.
  from Craftsmen: "Whittler to His Lover." GeoR (35:1) Spr 81, p. 35.
  "Deaf and Mute." SouthernPR (21:2) Aut 81, p. 25.
  "Divorce." CalQ (18/19) 81, pp. 88-89.
  "How Poets Would Have Us Know Them." BelPoJ (32:1) Aut 81, p. 15.
  "Migration." SouthernPR (21: 1) Spr 81, p. 54.
  "Sandlappers." BelPoJ (32:1) Aut 81, p. 16.
  "The Taxidermy Shop." CalQ (18/19) 81, p. 87.

CORKERY, Christopher Jane
  "Letter From Marcellus, Maker of Fountains, to Cominia His Mother."
      Tendril (10) Wint 81, pp. 20-22.

CORLEY, Elisabeth Lewis
  "Letting Go." CarolQ (33:1) Wint 81, p. 88.

CORMIER-SHEKERJIAN, Regina de see DeCORMIER-SHEKERJIAN, Regina

CORN, Alfred
  "Maple Canon." Ploughs (7:2) 81, p. 40.
  "Naskeag." NewYorker (57:24) 3 Ag 81, p. 36.
  "Trout and Mole." Ploughs (7:2) 81, pp. 41-42.

CORNBERG, David
  "A Grilled Cheese Holiday." StoneC (8: 3) Spr 81, p. 40.
  "Visitation." StoneC (8: 3) Spr 81, p. 41.

CORPI, Lucha
  "Ambito y jornada." Metam (3:2/4:1) 80-81, pp. 109-10.

CORRIGAN, Michael T.
  "College Girl." Wind (11:43) 81, p. 10.
  "Her Sixth Anniversary." Wind (11:43) 81, p. 10.

CORSERI, Gary Steven
  "The Cathedral Beaten By Rain" (tr. with Tsuyoshi Itoh of Kotaroh
      Takamura). WebR (6:2) 81, pp. 21-24.

CORSO, Gregory
  "Poets Are People And People Are Quite Often Unreliable." UnmOx
      (22) Wint 81, p. 5.
  Thirteen poems. UnmOx (22) Wint 81, pp. 103-122.

CORTEZ, Jayne
  "I Am New York City." Mund (12/13) 80-81, pp. 174-175.
  "Phraseology." Mund (12/13) 80-81, p. 173.

CORTEZ, Manuella
  "Still, It Is A Good Thing." MissR (10:1) Spr-Sum 81, pp. 174-175.

COSIER, Tony
  "Meng." Im (7:3) 81, p. 8.
  "Now That You Are Coming In A Week. " CapeR (17:1) Wint 81, p. 36.

COSS, José T.
  "Mamá-Unica. " Claridad/En Rojo (22:1475) 8-14 My 81, p. 12.

COSTA, Marithelma
  "Podría escribir la palabra. " Mairena (2:6) 81, p. 60.
  "Poema 0. " Mairena (3:7), p. 29.
  "Poema 4. " Mairena (3:7), pp. 29-31.
  "Poema 5. " Mairena (3:7), p. 31.
  "Teníamos una casa blanca de paredes redondas. " Mairena (2:6) 81, p.
    61.

COSTANZO, Gerald
  "Jeane Dixon's America. " NoAmR (266:3) S 81, p. 56.
  "Nobody Lives on Arthur Godfrey Boulevard. " GeoR (35:1) Spr 81, pp.
    62-63.
  "The Seventies. " MinnR (17) Aut 81, p. 13.

COSTELLO, James
  "The Admiral Byrd Poem. " EnPas (12), 81, pp. 24-26.
  "Father, Son, and Daughter. " Wind (10:39) 80, p. 14.

COSTLEY, Bill
  "War Stories: Soldiers (2) 09/29/75. " Aspect (77/79) 81, p. 39.
  "War Stories: Soldiers (6) 11/06/75. " Aspect (77/79) 81, p. 40.

COTA CARDENAS, Margarita
  "To a Young Son. " Areito (7: 25) 81, p. 44.

COTTERILL, Sarah
  "Poem Written After Seeing the Lennart Nilsson Photographs of Life
    Before Birth. " WebR (6:2) 81, pp. 57-58.

COTTON, Christine
  "Blood darkens the packaged fingers" (tr. of Kamal Ibrahim). Mund
    (12/13) 80-81, p. 291.
  "And I in ruins of Order" (tr. of Kamal Ibrahim). Mund (12/13) 80-81,
    p. 291.
  "If you love the desert" (tr. of Kamal Ibrahim). Mund (12/13) 80-81,
    p. 291.

COTTONWOOD, Sally
  "Choices. " Peb (21) 81, p. 103.
  "Like Lot's Wife. " Peb (21) 81, p. 102.

COUCH, Larry
  "A Blue Wind, A Calm Wave" (tr. of Yves Martin). Vis (5) 81, n. p.
  "Dada Dog. " Vis (7) 81, n. p.
  "Flowers. " Vis (6) 81, n. p.
  "Forest (His Memory of Existence)" (tr. of Mick Trean). Vis (5) 81,
    n. p.
  "Memories" (tr. of Yves Martin). Vis (5) 81, n. p.
  "Memory" (tr. of Gill Jouanard). Vis (5) 81, n. p.
  "Morning. " Vis (7) 81, n. p.
  "Songs" (tr. of Gill Jouanard). Vis (5) 81, n. p.
  "Summer Storm. " Vis (6) 81, n. p.

COURT, Wesli
"White for Weather Words" (in memoriam: d. a. levy). Wind (10:39)
  80, p. 4.

COURTOT, Martha
"The Freed Woman." Cond (7) Spr 81, pp. 57-58.
"The Rain Questions." Prima (6/7) 81, p. 51.

COUZYN, Jeni
"Life By Drowning." MalR (57) Ja 81, pp. 9-32.

COVINO, Michael
"Accessory after the Fact." PoNow (6:3 issue 33) 81, p. 8.

COX, C. B.
"After the War." Hudson (34:2) Sum 81, pp. 224-225.
"Anniversary." Hudson (34:2) Sum 81, pp. 225-226.
"Tiger Hill." Hudson (34:2) Sum 81, p. 223.

COX, Joel
"One Bird Song." PoNow (6:3 issue 33) 81, p. 8.

COX, Terrance
"Simony." MalR (58) Ap 81, pp. 98-99.
"Under New Management." MalR (58) Ap 81, p. 97.
"Arab Car." MalR (58) Ap 81, p. 96.

COX, Terrence
"I remember hot angry nights." Sam (109) 81, p. 47.

CRAIG, Barbara
"Cecilia's Portrait." Peb (21) 81, pp. 100-101.

CRAMER, Steven
"Bitter Exercise." Iowa (11:2/3) Spr-Sum 80, p. 190.

CRAWFORD, Jack, Jr.
"The Sailor Who Fell From Grace." PoNow (6:2 issue 32) 81, p. 30.
"Smooth as Baby Skin." PoNow (6:2 issue 32) 81, p. 30.

CREELEY, Robert
"For John Duff." ParisR (23:79) Spr 81, pp. 79-82.
"How that fact of." Mund (12/13) 80-81, pp. 266-267.

CRENSHAW, Brad
"Sarah Elam Imagines Her Death." ChiR (32:2) Aut 80, pp. 58-59.
"Sarah's Strawberries." ChiR (32:2) Aut 80, pp. 56-57.
"Sarah's Strawberries" (corrected version from 32:2, p. 56). ChiR
  (33:1) Sum 81, pp. 117-118.

CRESCENTIS, James de
"After Reading Neruda's Memoirs." NewL (48:1) Aut 81, p. 56.

CREWE, Jennifer
"The Fall of the Sparrow." AmerS (50:4) Aut 81, p. 498.

CREWS, Jacqueline
"The Spring at Diana, Tennessee." Tendril (11) Sum 81, pp. 17-21.

CREWS, John
"Bread and Wine." ChrC (98:5) 18 F 81, p. 157.

CREWS, Judson
"A Girl." PoNow (6:1 issue 31) 81, p. 40.
"If I: 79 Poems." WormR (83) 81, pp. 49-88.   Entire issue.
"Though the water." Wind (11:42) 81, p. 10.
"An un-." Wind (11:42) 81, pp. 9-10.
"Without imp-." Wind (11:42) 81, pp. 9-10.

CRIADO, Yolanda Gracia de see GRACIA de CRIADO, Yolanda

CROOKER, Barbara
"Appointed Rounds." Tele (17) 81, p. 111.
"Woman: Runner." Tele (17) 81, p. 111.

CROSS, John of the, Saint see CRUZ, Juan de la, San

CROW, Mary
"Day to Day" (tr. of Braulio Arenas). PoNow (5:6 issue 30) 81, p. 5.
"Idle Afternoon." ThRiPo (17/18) 81, p. 27.
"Never is Late" (tr. of Maria Mercedes Carranza). PoNow (5:6 issue
    30) 81, p. 13.

CRUM, Robert
"The Forest." NowestR (19:3), p. 19.

CRUZ, Isabel Zenón see ZENON CRUZ, Isabel

CRUZ, Iván de la
"Requiem a Curucho (Félix Monclova)." Mairena (2:5) Aut 80, p. 77.

CRUZ, Juan de la, San
"The Fountain" (version for Karin Lessing, tr. by Eliot Weinberger).
    Sulfur (3) 82, pp. 87-89.

CRUZADO, Nydia Rojas see ROJAS CRUZADO, Nydia

CSOORI, Sándor
"At the Bank of the River Tisza, Near Csongrad" (tr. by Nicholas Kol-
    umban). SenR (12:1/2) 81, pp. 119-121.
"Bölsohelyem, Esoben." SenR (12:1/2) 81, pp. 122-24.
"Combing Her Hair" (tr. by Nicholas Kolumban). CharR (7:2) Aut 81,
    p. 31.
"A Csongrádi Tiszaparton." SenR (12:1/2) 81, pp. 118-120.
"The Echo Of Vast Hollows" (tr. by Nicholas Kolumban). QW (13)
    Aut/Wint 81/82, p. 51.
"A Hobo's Elegy" (tr. by Nicholas Kolumban). CharR (7:2) Aut 81, p.
    37.
"In a Sickbed" (tr. by Nicholas Kolumban). Chelsea (40) 81, pp. 56-57.
"A Late Demonstration in a French Mining Town" (tr. by Nicholas
    Kolumban). CharR (7:2) Aut 81, p. 32.
"Memory of Snow" (tr. by Nicholas Kolumban). CharR (7:1) Spr 81, p.
    54.
"My Birthplace in the Rain" (tr. by Nicholas Kolumban). SenR (12:1/2)
    81, pp. 123-25.
"My Town in the Fall" (tr. by Nicholas Kolumban). Chelsea (40) 81,

pp. 55-56.
"Napi Halálommal." SenR (12:1/2) 81, p. 126.
"On the Third Day" (tr. by Nicholas Kolumban). DenQ (16:1) Spr 81,
    p. 74.
"The Poppy Heads Rattle" (tr. by Nicholas Kolumban). CharR (7:2) Aut
    81, p. 30.
"The Wait" (tr. by Nicholas Kolumban). CharR (7:2) Aut 81, p. 29.
"With My Daily Death" (tr. by Nicholas Kolumban). SenR (12:1/2) 81,
    p. 127.

CUADRA, Angel
    "Colloquy of Sadness" (Variation on text by Kathleen Agena; tr. by
        Donald Walsh). PartR (48:4) 81, pp. 595-6.
    "Police Efficiency" (Variation on text by Kathleen Agena; tr. by Donald
        Walsh). PartR (48:4) 81, p. 596.
    "Vision of the Keys" (Variation on text by Kathleen Agena; tr. by Donald
        Walsh). PartR (48:4) 81, p. 597.

CUADRA, Pablo Antonio
    "The Drowned Horse" (tr. by Steven White). NewOR (8:3) Aut 81, p.
        250.

CUDDIHY, Michael
    "Harvest" (for Robert Bly). PoetryE (4/5) Spr-Sum 81, p. 139.
    "Lake Ampersand." ThRiPo (17/18) 81, p. 12.

CUESTA, Francisco Ruiz de la see RUIZ de la CUESTA, Francisco

CUEVAS, Clara
    "Azul total." Mairena (2:6), p. 78.
    "Navegante sin barco." Mairena (2:6), p. 78.
    "Sin Rumbo." Mairena (2:6), p. 78.

CULLEN, John C.
    "A Good Camping Spot." PoNow (6:2 issue 32) 81, p. 46.

CUMMINS, James
    "From The Perry Mason Sestinas." Shen (32:1) 80, pp. 106-107.

CUNNINGHAM, Terrence
    "Still-Life." Confr (21) Wint 81, p. 118.

CURBELO, Silvia
    "The Strangler." SouthernPR (21: 1) Spr 81, p. 17.

CURBELO, Sylvia
    "One Day It Happens." Tendril (11) Sum 81, p. 22.

CURRIE, John
    "At the Ruins of the Old Fortress" (tr. of Jarkko Laine, w/ Stephen A.
        Kuusisto and Allan Kuusisto). SenR (12:1/2) 81, p. 209.
    "Gift of the Poem" (tr. of Stéphane Mallarmé). SenR (12:1/2) 81, p.
        39.
    "God Bless Finland" (tr. of Jarkko Laine, w/ Stephen A. Kuusisto and
        Allan Kuusisto). SenR (12:1/2) 81, pp. 217, 219.
    "I: The thewed horses slept" (tr. of Erik Akerlund w/ Leif Sjoberg).
        SenR (12:1/2) 81, p. 182.
    "II: They don't carry away much" (tr. with Leif Sjoberg of Erik Aker-

lund). SenR (12:1/2) 81, p. 183.
"The Last Judgment" (tr. of Jarkko Laine, w/ Stephen A. Kuusisto and
    Allan Kuusisto). SenR (12:1/2) 81, p. 211.
"Poem Written by the Number 5." SenR (10:2/11:1) 79-80, pp. 69-70.
"Tomb" (tr. of Stéphane Mallarmé). SenR (12:1/2) 81, p. 43.
"When the Shadow Threatened" (tr. of Stéphane Mallarmé). SenR (12:
    1/2) 81, p. 41.
"Yesterday" (tr. of Jarkko Laine, w/ Stephen A. Kuusisto and Allan
    Kuusisto). SenR (12:1/2) 81, pp. 213-215.

CURTIS, Tony
    "The Freezer." Kayak (57) 81, p. 32.
    "Land Army Photographs." NewYorker (57:32) 28 S 81, p. 54.

CURTIS, Walt
    "Chicken Plant." PortR (27: 2) 81, p. 21.
    "Chicken Tracks." PortR (27: 2) 81, p. 21.
    "Death" (for Isidoro de Blas) (tr. of Federico Garcia Lorca). PortR
        (27: 2) 81, p. 42.
    "I am the Chicken." PortR (27: 2) 81, p. 20.
    "The Miracle of John the Chicken Prince." PortR (27: 2) 81, p. 20.
    "Ode To The Sea Light" (tr. of Pablo Neruda). PortR (27: 2) 81, p.
        39.
    "A Pocketful on Ice." PortR (27: 2) 81, p. 21.
    "Romance of the Black Pain" (tr. of Federico Garcia Lorca). PortR
        (27: 2) 81, p. 42.
    "Saint Gabriel" (tr. of Federico Garcia Lorca). PortR (27: 2) 81, p.
        42.
    "Sexual Water" (tr. of Pablo Neruda). PortR (27: 2) 81, p. 38.
    "To the Wildest Bastard in the Country." PortR (27: 2) 81, p. 20.
    "The United Fruit Company" (tr. of Pablo Neruda). PortR (27: 2) 81,
        p. 39.
    "Walking Around" (tr. of Pablo Neruda). PortR (27: 2) 81, p. 38.

CUSACK, Anne E.
    "Et Puis au Jardin Publique." Prima (6/7) 81, p. 19.

CZAPLA, Cathy Young
    "Borderlands." Sam (117) 81, p. 12.
    "Genetic Memories." Sam (116) 81, p. 16.
    "Heirloom." Sam (112) 81, Entire issue.
    "Late Summer." Sam (117) 81, p. 10.
    "Nuclear Waste Disposal Site #2." Sam (109) 81, p. 64.
    "Twelve Years Later" (for Geoff Kline). Sam (106) 81, p. 44.

DACEY, Philip
    "Essays in Criticism: From the Lost Journal of Gerard Manley Hop-
        kins." KanQ (13:1) Wint 81, pp. 8-10.
    "Lines." Vis (6) 81, n. p.
    "Quicksong." Tendril (11) Sum 81, p. 23.
    "Sympathy Letter" (to Barton Sutter). Tendril (11) Sum 81, p. 24.

DAILEY, Joel
    "After Ever." PoNow (6:3 issue 33) 81, p. 8.
    "A Moment, 1950 (in memory of Cesare Pavese)." NewOR (8:2) Sum
        81, p. 158.
    "The Difference Between Poetry And Poultry." WormR (81/82) 81, p.
        2.

"Night Shift." WormR (81/82) 81, p. 2.
"Tuna" (for Jim Cloonan). WormR (81/82) 81, p. 1.

DALTON, Dorothy
"The White Blood." StoneC (8: 3) Spr 81, p. 27.

DALY, Christopher
"After One Too Many Samaritans." WormR (84) 81, p. 116.
"The Idea of Order At Biscayne Bay." WormR (84) 81, p. 115.

DALY, Daniel
"City Aunt." CapeR (17:1) Wint 81, p. 22.
"Exodus." CapeR (17:1) Wint 81, p. 19.
"Foule." CapeR (17:1) Wint 81, p. 21.
"The Tumbler Returns." CapeR (17:1) Wint 81, p. 20.

DAMROW, William J.
"Sacrament at Graymoor." ChrC (98:3) 28 Ja 81, p. 79.

DANA, Robert
"Key West: Looking for Hemingway." PoNow (6:2 issue 32) 81, p. 19.
"Notre Dame De Paris, 1974." AmerPoR (10:1) Ja-F 81, p. 6.
"Ordinary." NewOR (8:1) Wint 81, p. 41.
"0-21210 on seeing 'The Nazi Drawings'." PoNow (6:1 issue 31) 81, p. 27.

DANIEL, Arnaut
"Ans Quel Cim Reston de Branchas" (tr. by Ezra Pound). Iowa (12:1) Wint 81, pp. 41-42.
"Lo Ferm Voler Qu'el Cor M'Intra" (tr. by Ezra Pound). Iowa (12:1) Wint 81, pp. 43-44.

DANIEL, Marky
"Fall River Song for Spring." PoetryNW (22:1) Spr 81, pp. 41-42.

DANIELS, Jim
"After Practice" (for Rick). PoNow (6:2 issue 32) 81, p. 17.
"Delivery Man." PoNow (6:3 issue 33) 81, p. 9.
"Digger Goes On Vacation." NewL (47:4) Sam 81, pp. 67-70.
"Driving in the Midwest." Northeast (3:11) Sum 81, p. 7.
"Places Everyone." CimR (54) Ja 81, p. 52.
"Short-Order Cook." PoNow (6:3 issue 33) 81, p. 9.

DANIELS, Kate
"On the River." MassR (22:1) Spr 81, p. 40.
"Pyracantha." PoNow (6:3 issue 33) 81, p. 10.
"Sometimes When I'm Singing." NewEngR (4:2) Wint 81, p. 245.

DANIELS, M. Cortney
"The Blue Nash." PoNow (6:3 issue 33) 81, p. 9.

DANIELS, Steve
"The Country of Sleep." CarolQ (33:1) Wint 81, p. 48.
"The Dream." CarolQ (33:1) Wint 81, p. 47.

DANKLEFF, Richard
"As for Scalp Shirts." ColEng (43:5) S 81, p. 490.
"Ben Hodges, Colored." PoetryNW (22:4) Wint 81-82, p. 18.
"Flight." ColEng (43:5) S 81, p. 491.

DANTE
"Al poco giorno e al gran cerchio d'ombra." SenR (12:1/2) 81, pp. 34-6.
"The Sestina on the Lady Pietra" (tr. by Michael Stanford). SenR (12: 1/2) 81, pp. 35-7.

DANTE, Robert
"Intensive Care." EnPas (12) 81, pp. 16-17.

D'ANTIN, Carolina
"Eyes" (tr. by Patricia Schor). LetFem (7:2) Aut 81, p. 64.

DARIO, Rubén
"Los motivos del lobo." Notarte (6:1) Ja 81, p. 14.

DARLINGTON, Andrew
"Exiled into Babylon." Vis (6) 81, n. p.
"The Ghost in the Machine." CreamCR (7:1) 81, pp. 83-84.
"Guns of Brixton/Atavistic Logics." CreamCR (7:1) 81, p. 85.
"Incident From a Class War." Vis (6) 81, n. p.

D'ARPINO, Tony
"Cosmology." Tele (17) 81, p. 107.
"Mozart." Tele (17) 81, p. 108.

DARR, Ann
"But You Can't Say That." Agni (14) 81, pp. 64-65.
"Time Zones on the Rivers." Agni (15) 81, pp. 55-56.

DARUWALLA, Keki N.
"The Mistress." Stand (22: 4) 81, p. 53.
"You, Slipping Past." Stand (22: 4) 81, p. 52.

DARWISH, Mahmūd
"Cadenzas on Water" (tr. by Adnan Haydar). Nimrod (24: 2) Spr/Sum 81, pp. 78-79.
"The day my poems." Stand (22: 1) 80, p. 9.
"Don't Sleep" (tr. by Issa J. Boullata). Mund (12/13) 80-81, pp. 258-259.
"Last Evening In Paris" (to the memory of Izzeddin Qalaq) (tr. by Rana Kabbanī). Nimrod (24: 2) Spr/Sum 81, pp. 74-77.
"The Occupied City." Stand (22: 1) 80, p. 9.

DAUENHAUER, Richard
from This Life Is So Fast: "Everything's already said, written" (tr. of Pertti Nieminen). PoetryE (6) Aut 81, p. 34.
from Wine, Writing: "I'm not accusing you" (tr. of Paavo Haavikko). PoetryE (6) Aut 81, pp. 17-18.

DAUNT, Jon
"The Wind That Hunts Walking." Wind (11:43) 81, p. 11.

DAVID, Almitra
"Medusa." 13thM (5:1/2) 80, p. 104.

DAVIDSON, David
"Objet Trouve." Tele (17) 81, pp. 116-117.

DAVIDSON, Michael
"The Landing of Rochambeau." Sulfur (2) 81, pp. 197-200.
"The Letter on Injustice." Pequod (12) 81, p. 79.

DAVIE, Donald
"At the Café Parnasse." ParisR (23:79) Spr 81, pp. 83-84.
"Sorting Old Papers." AmerS (50:3) Sum 81, p. 312.

DAVIES, Nancy
"Next Time Send for Me." HiramPoR (30) Spr-Sum 81, p. 15.

DAVILA, Marcos F. Reyes see REYES DAVILA, Marcos F.

DAVIS, Duane
"She Wanted To Know What Had Happened." Sam (116) 81, p. 37.
"Winning." Sam (117) 81, pp. 42-44.

DAVIS, Ed
"Hostages." Sam (116) 81, p. 25.

DAVIS, Glover
"The Apparition." Shen (31:4) 80, p. 30.
"Lost Moments." Shen (31:4) 80, p. 31.
"The Wedding Feast." Shen (32:2) 81, p. 17.

DAVIS, Helene
"Weather: Chance of Snow." Ploughs (7:1) 81, p. 144.

DAVIS, Jon
"Perfect Landscapes, Rich Branches of Blossom." CutB (17) Aut-Wint
    81, pp. 48-49.

DAVIS, Lydia
"The Knight of the Trepan" (tr. of Danielle Serréra). ParisR (23:81)
    Aut 81, pp. 106-109.

DAVIS, Walter
"Illustrations: nine poems." Bound (9:2) Wint 81, pp. 267-270.

DAVIS, William Virgil
"An Afternoon Walk." Poem (43) Nov 81, p. 10.
"The Apple Tree (for my brothers)." NoAmR (266:1) Mr 81, p. 7.
"The Beat." Im (7:3) 81, p. 9.
"Celebration of a Worn-Out Shirt." CharR (7:1) Spr 81, p. 8.
"The Death of a Hawk." WebR (6:2) 81, p. 68.
"Driftwood Summer." MidwQ (23:1) Aut 81, p. 54.
"Early One Morning." MidwQ (23:1) Aut 81, p. 53.
"The Empty Room." ArizQ (37:4) Wint 81, p. 370.
"Encounter." Wind (11:41) 81, p. 12.
"The Flow." Im (7:3) 81, p. 9.
"Having Its Own." Im (7:3) 81, p. 9.
"I would step out." Wind (11:41) 81, p. 11.
"Let the Dead." CharR (7:1) Spr 81, pp. 8-9.
"The Map." ChrC (98:16) 6 My 81, p. 507.
"Night Light." Poem (43) Nov 81, p. 9.
"A Place by the Side of the Road." HiramPoR (29) Aut-Wint 81, p. 13.
"The Poems of the Blood." Im (7:3) 81, p. 9.
"No Time for Welcome." CharR (7:2) Aut 81, p. 11.

"The Tombs." PoNow (6:2 issue 32) 81, p. 36.
"The Turn." Im (7:3) 81, p. 9.
"Where I am Going." Wind (11:41) 81, pp. 11-12.
"The Wound." Im (7:3) 81, p. 9.

DAVISON, Peter
"Atmospheres." Pequod (12) 81, pp. 22-25.
"Fawn." AmerS (50:3) Sum 81, p. 326.
"Gross National Product." PoetryNW (22:1) Spr 81, pp. 21-22.
"The Laughter of Women." Atl (247:1) Ja 81, p. 59.
"The Transvestite's Dream." PoetryNW (22:1) Spr 81, p. 22.

DAVREU, Robert
"Le ciel solide où ricochent en étoiles." SenR (10:2/11:1) 79-80, p.
     144.
"Comme à l'autre fou des poussières." SenR (10:2/11:1) 79-80, p.
     138.
"Connue comme la pluie de septembre sur." SenR (10:2/11:1) 79-80,
     p. 140.
"Did she vacillate" (tr. by Linda Orr). SenR (10:2/11:1) 79-80, p. 147.
"Dirigible silences in the blue and round" (tr. by Linda Orr). SenR
     (10:2/11:1) 79-80, p. 143.
"Known like September rain on" (tr. by Linda Orr). SenR (10:2/11:1)
     79-80, p. 141.
"Like to the other fool for dust" (tr. by Linda Orr). SenR (10:2/11:1)
     79-80, p. 139.
"Que loin des harmonies." SenR (10:2/11:1) 79-80, p. 140.
"Silence made-bleu the words of the façade" (tr. by Linda Orr). SenR
     (10:2/11:1) 79-80, p. 137.
"Le silence a bleui les mots de la façade." SenR (10:2/11:1) 79-80, p.
     136.
"Silences dirigeables dans le peuple bleu." SenR (10:2/11:1) 79-80, p.
     142.
"So that far from the plumbed" (tr. by Linda Orr). SenR (10:2/11:1)
     79-80, p. 141.
"The solid sky where ricochet in stars" (tr. by Linda Orr). SenR (10:
     2/11:1) 79-80, p. 145.
"Vacillait-elle." SenR (10:2/11:1) 79-80, p. 146.

DAWE, Tom
"A Communion." PottPort (3) 81, p. 15.

DAWSON, Hester Jewell
"A Conversation." StoneC (9: 1-2) Aut-Wint 81/82, pp. 33-35.

DAY, Lucille
"Applying for AFDC." Hudson (34:3) Aut 81, p. 368.
"King of the Mountain." Hudson (34:3) Aut 81, p. 367.
"Neurochemist." Hudson (34:3) Aut 81, p. 369.

DAYTON, Irene
"Images-Opus 1." StoneC (9: 1-2) Aut-Wint 81/82, p. 40.
"The Feud." Wind (11:42) 81, pp. 11-12.
"Opus-3." Wind (11:42) 81, p. 11.

DEAL, Susan
"Daguerreotype VI--Drought." EnPas (12), 81, p. 30.
"Not So Sad." EnPas (12) 81, p. 31.

DEAL, Susan Strayer
"And What If You've Read." Poem (41) Mar 81, p. 62.
"Do Not Expect to be Rescued." Poem (41) Mar 81, p. 63.

De ALVEZ, Delia Cazarre see CAZARRE de ALVEZ, Delia

De ANDRADE, Carlos Drummond see ANDRADE, Carlos Drummond de

De ANDRADE, Eugenio see ANDRADE, Eugenio de

De ANGELIS, Milo
"Becoming." PartR (48:2) 81, p. 261.
"The Central Idea." PartR (48:2) 81, p. 261.

DeBEVOISE, Arlene
"Cancer Clinic." BallSUF (22:2) Spr 81, p. 59.
"Just Reward." BallSUF (21:4) Aut 80, p. 78.
"A Sort of Creed." ChrC (98:9) 18 Mr 81, p. 292.

De BOLT, William Walter
"Discrimination." ChrC (98:23) 15-22 Jl 81, p. 727.
"Greed." ChrC (98:12) 8 Ap 81, p. 373.
"Two Maps." ChrC (98:22) 1-8 Jl 81, p. 701.
"Why?" ChrC (98:29) 23 S 81, p. 933.

DE BORN, Bertran
"Un Sirventes on Motz no Falh" (tr. by Ezra Pound). Iowa (12:1) Wint
81, pp. 39-40.

De CAMOES, Luis see CAMOES, Luis de

De CARVALHO, Raul see CARVALHO, Raul de

DECAVALLES, Andonis
"Robert Trail Spence Lowell" (tr. by Kimon Friar). Poetry (139:2) N
81, pp. 79-80.

DeCORMIER-SHEKERJIAN, Regina
"The Czar." LittleM (13:1/2) Spr-Sum 79, c1981, pp. 48-49.
"Letter from Sophia." LittleM (13:1/2) Spr-Sum 79, c1981, pp. 46-47.
"Michel Writes from Roven." NowestR (19:1/2), pp. 62-4.

De DIEGO, Eliseo Alberto see DIEGO, Eliseo Alberto de

DEEN, Rosemary
"Keeping the Spider Awake." LittleM (13:1/2) Spr-Sum 79, c1981, pp.
68-69.

DeFOE, Mark
"Harvest." BallSUF (22:3) Sum 81, pp. 2-3.
"Story." NoAmR (266:2) Je 81, p. 35.
"West Virginia: Driving the Gauley River, Listening to the Radio."
MinnR (17) Aut 81, pp. 37-38.

De FOX, Lucia Ungaro see FOX, Lucia Ungaro de

DeFREES, Madeline
"Imaginary Ancestors: Eminent Victorians." AmerPoR (10:6) N-D 81,

p. 18.
"New England Interlude." Ploughs (6:4) 81, pp. 193-194.
"Variations On The Edible Tuber." MassR (22:4) Wint 81, pp. 804-806.

DeGENOVA, Albert
"Warm Fingers." Os (12) Spr 81, p. 11.

de GRAVELLES, Charles
"Nightwalk" (for Meg). ThRiPo (17/18) 81, p. 25.

DEGUY, Michel
"I Call Muse..." (tr. by Clayton Eshleman). Sulfur (3) 82, pp. 65-67.
"Interlude" (tr. by Linda Orr). SenR (10:2/11:1) 79-80, p. 107.
"Interlude." SenR (10:2/11:1) 79-80, p. 106.
"Le fard." SenR (10:2/11:1) 79-80, p. 104.
"Make-up" (tr. by Linda Orr). SenR (10:2/11:1) 79-80, p. 105.
"To Forget the Image." Sulfur (3) 82, pp. 68-70.

DEKIN, Thimothy
"Moving In." ChiR (32:4) Spr 81, p. 30.
"The Professor." ChiR (32:4) Spr 81, pp. 27-29.
"Winter Fruit." ChiR (32:4) Spr 81, p. 31.

De la CRUZ, Iván see CRUZ, Iván de la

De la CRUZ, Juan, San see CRUZ, Juan de la, San

DELAHAYE, Alain
"Le Feuillage en Exemple." SenR (10:2/11:1) 79-80, p. 118.
"The Folliage as Example" (tr. by Linda Orr). SenR (10:2/11:1) 79-80, p. 119.
"Le Jeu Des Branches." SenR (10:2/11:1) 79-80, p. 116.
"Liens." SenR (10:2/11:1) 79-80, p. 118.
"L'Orbe." SenR (10:2/11:1) 79-80, p. 120.
"The Orbit" (tr. by Linda Orr). SenR (10:2/11:1) 79-80, p. 121.
"The Play of Branches" (tr. by Linda Orr). SenR (10:2/11:1) 79-80, p. 117.
"Ties" (tr. by Linda Orr). SenR (10:2/11:1) 79-80, p. 119.
"Toward Beauty" (tr. by Linda Orr). SenR (10:2/11:1) 79-80, p. 117.
"Vers la Beauté." SenR (10:2/11:1) 79-80, p. 116.

DELANEY, John
"Overcast." SouthernHR (15:1) Wint 81, p. 18.
"Portrait of a Teacher." Confr (22) Sum 81, p. 119.
"Scuba: Self-Contained Underwater Breathing Apparatus." BelPoJ (32:1) Aut 81, p. 9.

del CABRAL, Manuel see CABRAL, Manuel del

De LESCOET, Henri
"No Existen Caminos" (A Jean Cocteau). Puerto Wint 81, p. 22.

DELISLE, Pierre
"Chacun: Nine Poems from 'Dialogues pour la nuit.'" (tr. by Geoffrey Gardner). Bound (9:2) Wint 81, pp. 257-265.

De LOACH, Nancy E.
"Pan." Wind (11:41) 81, p. 13.
"Sea Scape." Wind (11:41) 81, p. 13.

de LONGCHAMPS, Joanne
"Becoming Crippled." Meadows (2:1) 81, p. 20.
"Picnic." Meadows (2:1) 81, p. 15.

de los ANGELES RUANO, Isabel see RUANO, Isabel de los Angeles

DELP, Michael
"Catalogue." PoNow (6:2 issue 32) 81, p. 15.

del UCAR, Gina see UCAR, Gina del

Del VECCHIO, Gloria
"The Pink Aftergrowth of Jesus." StoneC (9: 1-2) Aut-Wint 81/82, p. 67.

DeMOTT, Robert
"The Burden of Walking Erect." OntR (15) Aut-Wint 81-82, pp. 20-21.
"The Naming: for My Grandfather." OntR (15) Aut-Wint 81-82, pp. 22-3.

DEMPSEY, Ivy
"Lost at an Early Age in Russell County, Kansas." CharR (7:1) Spr 81, p. 22.

DeNAGY, Francis B.
"Sign on the Door." Poem (42) Jul 81, p. 56.
"The Swan." Poem (42) Jul 81, p. 57.

De NAPOUT, Lilian see NAPOUT, Lilian de

DENBERG, Kenneth
"Dead Man's Flies." CimR (55) Ap 81, p. 50.

DENIS, Philippe
"In the Thickness/Dans l'epaisseur." (tr. by Susanna Lang). ChiR (32: 2) Aut 80, pp. 95-107.
"Moored to your blood" (tr. by Mark Irwin). Mund (12/13) 80-81, p. 348.
"To live as to breathe" (tr. by Mark Irwin). Mund (12/13) 80-81, p. 348.

DENIZE, Donna
"Toward the Silence." WorldO (16:1), pp. 35-36.

DENNING, Steve
"In Vietnam." PortR (27: 1) 81, p. 19.
"Mother Remembers the Birth of Her Fourth Child." PortR (27: 2) 81, p. 97.

DENNIS, Carl
"Clara Hopes for a Lie." Poetry (137:5) F 81, p. 265.
"The Descent." VirQR (57:3) Sum 81, pp. 463-464.
"The Man on My Porch Makes Me an Offer." GeoR (35:4) Wint 81, p. 806.
"News From Cleveland." Poetry (137:5) F 81, pp. 267-268.
"The Rabbi of Ellicottville." PoetryNW (22:1) Spr 81, pp. 25-26.
"The Sweetness of the Law." Poetry (137:5) F 81, p. 266.

DENNISON, George
"The Animals in Winter." Harp (262:1572) My 81, p. 79.

De NOAILLES, Anna, Comtesse see NOAILLES, Anna, Comtesse de

De OCA, Marco Antonio Montes see MONTES DE OCA, Marco Antonio

De ORAA, Pedro see ORAA, Pedro de

De PALCHI, Alfredo
"Ashamed of myself?" (tr. by Sonia Raiziss). Mund (12/13) 80-81, p.
349.
"Existence--solitary habit--" (tr. of Sonia Raiziss). Mund (12/13) 80-
81, p. 349.

DEPESTRE, René
"The Luminous Point" (for Roque Dalton and Enrique Lihn) (tr. by D.
A. McMurray and G. M. Lang). Calib (3:2) Aut-Wint 80, p. 93.
"Le Point Lumineux" (A Roque Dalton et Enrique Lihn). Calib (3:2)
Aut-Wint 80, p. 92.

De QUEVEDO, Francisco see QUEVEDO, Francisco de

Der HOVANESSIAN, Diana
"James Audubon Comes to Louisiana." LitR (24:3) Spr 81, p. 387.
"Solution." LitR (24:3) Spr 81, p. 388.
"Some Lullabies." PoNow (6:2 issue 32) 81, p. 33.
"Trying to Remember." PoNow (6:2 issue 32) 81, p. 33.

DERISH, Gary
"My Grandfather's Funeral." Wind (11:43) 81, p. 12.

De RONSARD, Pierre
"Ah, longues nuits d'hiver." SouthernR (17:4) Aut 81, p. 996.

DERR, Mark B.
"In the Hall of Mirrors." KanQ (13:1) Wint 81, p. 128.

DERRICOTTE, Toi
"For Sandra Maria Esteves." 13thM (5:1/2) 80, p. 19.

De SENA, Jorge see SENA, Jorge de

DESNOS, Robert
Eight poems (four tr. by James McCorkle). SenR (12:1/2) 81, pp. 72-
79.
"Last Poem" (tr. by Jim Kates). Stand (22: 4) 81, p. 30.

DESSI, Gigi
"Affogato." StoneC (8: 3) Spr 81, p. 20.
"Inquieti." StoneC (8: 3) Spr 81, p. 21.
"Stifled" (tr. by Dominick Lepore). StoneC (8: 3) Spr 81, p. 20.
"Worried" (tr. by Dominick Lepore). StoneC (8: 3) Spr 81, p. 21.

DESY, Peter
"Poem at Forty-Five: To My Father." PoNow (6:3 issue 33) 81, p.
10.

DEUTSCH, Babette
"The Photographs." Comm (108:11) 5 Je 81, p. 342.

De VAUL, Diane
"Boy-God." Vis (7) 81, n. p.

De VIAU, Théophile
"A Special Preference." SouthernR (17:4) Aut 81, p. 1000.

De VILMORIN, Louise see VILMORIN, Louise de

DeYOUNG, Robert
"The Seconds Between the Hours." SouthernHR (15:2) Spr 81, p. 128.
"Slow Motion." SouthernPR (21: 1) Spr 81, pp. 67-68.

DHIKTEOS, Aris
"St. Mark" (tr. by Kimon Friar). Poetry (139:2) N 81, pp. 77-78.

DHIMOULAS, Athos
"Sic Transit" (tr. by Kimon Friar). Poetry (139:2) N 81, p. 82.

DHOUKARIS, Dhimitris
"The Grammar of the Body" (tr. by Kimon Friar). Poetry (139:2) N
81, p. 94.

DIAKHATE, Lamine
"Five from Sixth Day Priorities" (tr. by Jan Pallister). EnPas (12) 81,
pp. 8-9.

DIAZ, Luis
"Canto mío de amor." Areito (7: 27) 81, p. 20.

DIAZ-DIOCARRETZ, Myriam
"Encadenada." LetFem (7:2) Aut 81, pp. 48-49.

DIAZ MARRERO, Andrés
"Agenda." Claridad/En Rojo (22:1458) 9-15 Ja 81, p. 12.
"La Masacre de Loiza." Claridad/En Rojo (22:1458) 9-15 Ja 81, p. 12.

Di BIASIO, Rodolfo
"Winter Returns" (tr. by Frank Judge). PoNow (6:2 issue 32) 81, p. 41.

DiCICCO, Pier Giorgio
"The Man with No Arms." SouthwR (66:1) Wint 81, p. 72.
"Permutations." MalR (58) Ap 81, p. 124.

DICKEY, James
"Five poems from Puella." Poetry (137:6) Mr 81, pp. 313-20.
"The Lyric Beasts." ParisR (23:79) Spr 81, pp. 165-166.

DICKEY, William
"Avalanche." CarolQ (34:2) Aut 81, pp. 86-87.
"Grown Men." NewEngR (3:3) Spr 81, p. 367.
"Here There are Three of Us Driving South in this Expensive Car."
NewEngR (3:3) Spr 81, p. 365.
"January White Sale." NewEngR (3:3) Spr 81, pp. 365-6.
"Opera." PoNow (6:2 issue 32) 81, p. 45.

DICKLER, Lisa
"11" (tr. of Catullus).   ChiR (32:4) Spr 81, p. 90.
"58" (tr. of Catullus).   ChiR (32:4) Spr 81, p. 91.

DICKSON, John
"Feeding the Neighbor's Cat." Poetry (139:1) O 81, pp. 12-13.
"The Runaway." Poetry (139:1) O 81, pp. 14-15.

DIEGO, Eliseo Alberto de
"Sinónimos." Areito (7: 27) 81, p. 23.

DIGGS, Lucy
"To Carin Who Was a Cook." SmPd (18:2) Spr 81, p. 29.
"Hymn to Us." SmPd (18:1) Wint 81, p. 13.
"Vita." SmPd (18:1) Wint 81, pp. 11-12.

DILLARD, Emil L.
"Filing." KanQ (13:3/4) Sum-Aut 81, p. 48.

DILSAVER, Paul
"Veteran as Schizophrenic." Northeast (3:11) Sum 81, p. 44.

Di MICHELE, Mary
"Charting Inner Space." MalR (59) Jl 81, p. 157.

DINWOODIE, Nielsen
"Seven Days in Moglos, Crete." NewOR (8:3) Aut 81, pp. 278-80.

DIORIO, Margaret T.
"Graduation." CentR (25:2) Spr 81, p. 164.
"Housewife." CentR (25:2) Spr 81, p. 165.

DiPALMA, Ray
"January Zero." SunM (11) Spr 81, pp. 149-151.

DiPASQUALE, E.
"Squirrel and Hawk." New York Times, 30 S 79, Section 11, p. 26.

DiPASQUALE, Emanuel
Eight Poems. Poem (41) Mar 81, pp. 25-34.

Di PIERO, W. S.
"The Bell's Clanging at the End of the Line" (tr. of Leonardo Sinisgal-
   li). Pequod (12) 81, p. 27.
"Cities." SewanR (89:2) Ap-Je 81, p. 181.
"Concentric Circles" (tr. of Leonardo Sinisgalli). PoNow (5:6 issue 30)
   81, p. 43.
"Early Light." YaleR (71: 1) Aut 81, pp. 90-91.
"Easter 1952" (tr. of Leonardo Sinisgalli). Agni (14) 81, pp. 15-16.
"Fourteen Poems" (tr. of Sandro Penna). PoNow (5:6 issue 30) 81, pp.
   36-37.
"Freightyard at Narni-Amelia" (tr. of Leonardo Sinisgalli). Pequod (12)
   81, p. 26.
"Endymion." SewanR (89:2) Ap-Je 81, p. 179.
"Given." SewanR (89:2) Ap-Je 81, p. 181.
"Holly Saturday in Manfredonia" (tr. of Leonardo Sinisgalli). Agni (14)
   81, p. 14.
"In Our Room." SewanR (89:2) Ap-Je 81, p. 180.

"The Journey" (tr. of Sandro Penna). PoNow (6:1 issue 31) 81, p. 43.
"Modern Love." SouthernR (17:2) Spr 81, pp. 366-372.
"Reliquary" (tr. of Leonardo Sinisgalli). PoNow (5:6 issue 30) 81, p.
    43.
"Smoke" (for Peppino). Ploughs (7:1) 81, p. 94.
"The Snow Owl" (tr. of Leonardo Sinisgalli). PoNow (6:2 issue 32) 81,
    p. 41.
"Sown Men." NewEngR (3:3) Spr 81, pp. 387-8.
"Spring News" (tr. of Sandro Penna). PoNow (6:1 issue 31) 81, p. 43.
"Techniques" (tr. of Leonardo Sinisgalli). PoNow (5:6 issue 30) 81, p.
    43.
"Triangulations" (tr. of Leonardo Sinisgalli). PoNow (5:6 issue 30) 81,
    p. 43.
"Untitled." PartR (48:2) 81, p. 249.
"The Valley" (tr. of Leonardo Sinisgalli). PoNow (5:6 issue 30) 81, p.
    43.

DiPRISCO, Joseph
    "The Day I Devoured the White Wolf." MidwQ (22:2) Wint 81, pp. 133-
        34.
    "Occam Shaving with his Razor." MidwQ (22:2) Wint 81, p. 132.
    "Some Alarming, Some Statistics." Kayak (57) 81, pp. 28-31.

DIRI, Phyl
    "A Child of the Eisenhower Years Dreams of Becoming a Dummy."
        OP (31/32) Aut 81, p. 81.

DISCH, Thomas M.
    "Cosmology And Us." MichQR (20:3) Sum 81, pp. 236-237.

DISCH, Tom
    "The Forbidden Children." OP (31/32) Aut 81, p. 140.
    "The Goldberg Variations." OP (31/32) Aut 81, p. 57.
    "The Prospect Behind Us" (for John Berger). Chelsea (40) 81, pp. 138-
        139.

DISCHELL, Stuart
    "Azan." Agni (15) 81, p. 49.
    "'Because Sorrow is What We Own.'" Agni (15) 81, p. 50.
    "The Scholar." Iowa (11:2/3) Spr-Sum 80, p. 198.
    "The Supplicant." Iowa (11:2/3) Spr-Sum 80, p. 197.

DISHKIN, Lahna
    "Prayer: Goodbye, Hello." CEAFor (12:2) D 81, p. 3.
    "Returning to the Scene." EngJ (70:3) Mr 81, p. 70.

DITLEVSEN, Tove
    "Departure" (tr. by Nadia Christensen). PoNow (5:6 issue 30) 81, p.
        14.
    "Time" (tr. by Nadia Christensen). PoNow (5:6 issue 30) 81, p. 14.

DITSKY, John
    "Hot Goods." OntR (14) Spr-Sum 81, p. 54.
    "I'm Sorry, Your Allusions Are too Remote." Wind (11:43) 81, pp. 13-
        14.
    "Keystone." Wind (11:43) 81, p. 13.
    "Rage, Rage." OntR (14) Spr-Sum 81, p. 56.
    "A Steal." OntR (14) Spr-Sum 81, p. 55.
    "The Texture of America." HolCrit (17:6 [i.e. 18:1?]) F 81, p. 16.

DITTA, Joseph M.
   "The Book of Friends #1 (H. F.)." SouthernHR (15:3) Sum 81, p. 255.
   "March Morning." CharR (7:1) Spr 81, pp. 38-40.

DIXON, Alan
   "Taking Leave." Poetry (138:6) S 81, p. 336.
   "What Dignity is Not." Poetry (138:6) S 81, p. 336.

DIXON, Melvin
   "Voodoo Mambo: To The Tourists" (for Catuxo Badillo, Port-au-
      Prince, Haiti). Calib (3:2) Aut-Wint 80, pp. 101-102.

DOBBERSTEIN, Michael
   "China Nights." QW (13) Aut/Wint 81/82, pp. 73-77.
   "The House." SouthernPR (21: 1) Spr 81, p. 51.
   "Nightwatch: The Carrier, The Sea." CimR (54) Ja 81, p. 28.
   "Roses." WestHR (35:3) Aut 81, p. 218.

DOBBS, Jeannine
   "You Remember What It's Like There." MidwQ (22:3) Spr 81, pp. 258-
      9.

DOBLER, Patricia
   "August." OhioR (26), p. 96.
   "Family Dream." PoNow (6:3 issue 33) 81, p. 10.
   "Jealous Wife." OhioR (26), p. 97.

DOBSON, Joanne A.
   "Feasting." Tendril (11) Sum 81, p. 25.

DOBYNS, Stephen
   "The Children." Pequod (13) 81, pp. 25-26.
   "Farmyard at Chassy" (after Bathus). Antaeus (43) Aut 81, p. 36.
   Five Poems After Balthus 1. "Larchant." Pequod (13) 81, p. 23.
   2. "The Moth." Pequod (13) 81, p. 24.
   3. "The Children." Pequod (13) 81, pp. 25-26.
   4. "Nude in Profile." Pequod (13) 81, p. 27.
   5. "Nude Resting." Pequod (13) 81, pp. 28-29.
   "Getting Up." NewYorker (57:36) 26 O 81, p. 54.
   "Japanese Girl with Red Table." NoAmR (266:4) D 81, p. 43.
   "Landscape with Oxen" (after Balthus). Antaeus (43) Aut 81, p. 37.
   "Larchant." Pequod (13) 81, p. 23.
   "The Moth." Pequod (13) 81, p. 24.
   "Nude in Profile." Pequod (13) 81, p. 27.
   "Nude Resting." Pequod (13) 81, pp. 28-29.
   "Six Poems After Balthus." Poetry (138:4) Jl 81, pp. 187-193.
   "Six Poems After Balthus." Poetry (139:1) O 81, pp. 1-7.
   "The White Skirt" (after Balthus). Antaeus (43) pp. 38-39.
   "The Window." NewYorker (57:36) 26 O 81, p. 54.

DODD, Wayne
   "Of Butterflies." GeoR (35:2) Sum 81, pp. 338-339.

DOEZEMA, Herman P.
   "All is Not a Dream" (tr. of Francisco Pérez Perdomo). Mund (12/13)
      80-81, p. 145.

DOLCI, Danilo
   "non di una maschera" (tr. by Justin Vitiello). PortR (27: 2) 81,

p. 35.
"Ti affascina" (tr. by Justin Vitiello).   PortR (27: 2) 81, p. 35.

DOLMATZ, Steven
    "Vachel Lindsay Considers Kansas. "   CutB (17) Aut-Wint 81, p. 52.

DONEGAN, Nancy
    "Aeneas Remembering Dido. "   Tendril (10) Wint 81, p. 49.
    "The Gargoyles in the Garden. "   Tendril (10) Wint 81, p. 48.
    "Gravity. "   Tendril (10) Wint 81, p. 50.
    "How Nimble Are the Goats. "   Tendril (10) Wint 81, pp. 52-53.
    "Treeman. "   Tendril (10) Wint 81, p. 47.
    "Windfall. "   Tendril (10) Wint 81, p. 51.

DONELAN, Steve
    "From the start we were caught up in the measure of the poem. "
        HangL (39) Wint 80-81, p. 11.

DONNELLY, Dorothy
    "Quid Est?"   ChrC (98:6) 25 F 81, p. 189.

DONOVAN, Gregory
    "The Boys Invent Religion. "   CimR (57) O 81, pp. 23-24.
    "The Firebombers. "   CimR (57) O 81, p. 53.

DONOVAN, Laurence
    "Netting Crabs. "   NewEngR (4:1) Aut 81, pp. 55-6.

DONOVAN, Rhoda
    "Full Moon in Scorpio: a Love Poem. "   KanQ (13:3/4) Sum-Aut 81, p.
        29.

DORCAS, Gazella
    "The Gazelle" (tr. by Bernhard Frank).   WebR (6:2) 81, p. 29.

DORESKI, William
    "Somerville Junction. "   Aspect (77/79) 81, pp. 53-54.
    "Speechless Highways. "   Tendril (10) Wint 81, p. 23.

DORIAN, Marguerite
    "Tomorrow the Past Comes" (tr. of Ion Caraion, w/ Elliott Urdang).
        Mund (12/13) 80-81, p. 305.
    "Unornamentation" (tr. of Ion Caraion, w/ Elliott Urdang).   Mund (12/
        13) 80-81, p. 306.

DORMAN, Sonya
    "Kasvin Rug. "   OP (31/32) Aut 81, p. 94.
    "Love in the North. "   OP (31/32) Aut 81, p. 76.
    "On a Kayak Rejection Slip. "   Kayak (57) 81, p. 40.
    "Woman, with Elms. "   PoNow (6:1 issue 31) 81, p. 10.
DORNEY, Dennis M.
    "Canter the Awkward Body. "   CutB (17) Aut-Wint 81, p. 9.
    "Cape Cod's Angel. "   CapeR (17:1) Wint 81, p. 7.
    "Old Neighborhood. "   CapeR (16:2) Sum 81, p. 30.
    "Those Cases of Rebirth in Managua. "   CapeR (16:2) Sum 81, p. 31.
    "Wedding Anniversary with Fish. "   CutB (17) Aut-Wint 81, p. 10.

DORSET, Gerald
"Confession of a Suburbanite." Tele (17) 81, p. 109.

DOSS, James
"I Want to Talk of Hope." PoetryE (6) Aut 81, p. 49.
"The Wound." PoetryE (6) Aut 81, p. 48.

DOTY, M. R.
"Bois De Rose." Tendril (11) Sum 81, p. 26.
"La Casa de Las Maderistas." CreamCR (6:1) Aut 80, p. 23.
"Credo." Tendril (10) Wint 81, p. 24.
"A Death in Fall." CreamCR (6:1) Aut 80, pp. 24-25.

DOTY, Mark
"1980." NewEngR (4:2) Wint 81, p. 190.

DOUBIAGO, Sharon
"Huron." Sam (116) 81, p. 52.

DOUGLAS, Prentice
"Roadside Mourner." ChrC (98:41) 16 D 81, p. 1312.

DOUSKEY, Franz
"Inventions." Chelsea (40) 81, p. 129.
"Rowing Across the Dark." NewYorker (56:49) 26 Ja 81, p. 105.

DOVE, Rita
"Agosta the Winged Man and Rasha the Black Dove." Poetry (139:2)
    N 81, pp. 64-65.
"The Ants of Argos." Nat (233:21) 19 D 81, p. 664.
"Dusting." Poetry (139:2) N 81, pp. 66-67.
"Geometry." PoNow (6:1 issue 31) 81, p. 24.
"The Hill Has Something to Say." GeoR (35:3) Aut 81, pp. 554-555.
"Nexus." PoNow (6:1 issue 31) 81, p. 24.
"November for Beginners." Poetry (139:2) N 81, p. 63.
"Small Town." PoNow (6:1 issue 31) 81, p. 24.

DOWD, Jeanne
"The Hunter." ThRiPo (17/18) 81, p. 19.

DOXEY, W. S.
"Another June." Nimrod (25:1) Aut-Wint 81, p. 99.
"Grace." Nimrod (25:1) Aut-Wint 81, p. 99.

DOXEY, William S.
"The Star Poem." PortR (27: 2) 81, p. 57.

DOYLE, Lynne
"My Mother in Majorca." Shen (32:1) 80, pp. 104-105.

DRABIK, Grazyna
"Any Case" (tr. of Wisaw Szymborska w/ Sharon Olds). Pequod (12)
    81, p. 1.
"The Number Pi" (tr. of Wislawa Szymborska, w/ Sharon Olds). AntR
    (39:1) Wint 81, p. 77.
"Wolfang Lefevre" (tr. of Julian Kornhauser, w/ Austin Flint). PoNow
    (5:6 issue 30) 81, p. 22.

DRAKE, Albert
"Eden." PoNow (6:2 issue 32) 81, p. 10.
"Old Car Haters." OP (31/32) Aut 81, pp. 74-75.

DRAKE, Barbara
"The Photograph." PoNow (6:2 issue 32) 81, p. 18.

DREW, George
"Either You Fall in the River of Despair or You Walk on the Water Like
    Christ." AntR (39:2) Spr 81, pp. 198-199.

DRINNAN, Marjorie
"If the Hook Were Only in My Head." PottPort (3) 81, p. 51.

DRISCOLL, Jack
"First Kiss" (with William Meissner). NowestR (19:1/2), p. 87.
"Fishing the Backwash." Antaeus (43) Aut 81, p. 40.
"The Funeral." SouthernPR (21:2) Aut 81, p. 16.
"Hunting Coyote." PoetryNW (22:2) Sum 81, pp. 25-26.
"Keeping in Touch" (with William Meissner). NowestR (19:1/2), p. 86.
"Part of the Waking" (with William Meissner). NowestR (19:1/2), p. 85.
"The Mill" (Worthington, Massachusetts-1958). QW (12) Spr-Sum 81,
    pp. 90-1.
"The Somnambulist's Music" (w/ William Meissner). Chelsea (40) 81,
    p. 149.
"Taking What is Mine." CutB (17) Aut-Wint 81, p. 50.

DRISKELL, Leon
"Letter from Cape Town." Wind (10:39) 80, pp. 15-17.

DROUGHT, Rodney
"Closing Night." Sam (116) 81, p. 62.

DRUMMOND DE ANDRANDE, Carlos see ANDRADE, Carlos Drummond de

DRURY, John
"Construction Site." PoNow (6:3 issue 33) 81, p. 10.
"Fire in the Wax Museum." PoNow (6:2 issue 32) 81, p. 35.
"Publication of the Bride Sheets." Shen (31:4) 80, pp. 50-53.

Du BELLAY, Joachim
"Rome." SouthernR (17:4) Aut 81, p. 994.
"La terre est fertile, amples les édifices." SouthernR (17:4) Aut 81,
    p. 995.

DUBIE, Norman
"Grandmother." Ploughs (6:4) 81, p. 59.
"To a Young Woman Dying at Weir." NewYorker (57:34) 12 O 81, p.
    46.

DUBIE, William
"The Slow One." PoNow (6:3 issue 33) 81, p. 10.

DUCHESNE WINTER, Griselle
"Carnaval." Claridad/En Rojo (22:1459) 16-22 Ja 81, p. 12.
"Libertad." Claridad/En Rojo (22:1459) 16-22 Ja 81, p. 12.
"El Salvador." Claridad/En Rojo (22:1459) 16-22 Ja 81, p. 12.

DUDDY, Patrick
"Chamberlain at Little Round Top." NewEngR (3:3) Spr 81, pp. 3 85-6.

DUEMER, Joseph
"The Animals in Her Dream." PoNow (6:3 issue 33) 81, p. 11.
"Note." PoNow (6:3 issue 33) 81, p. 11.
"The Second Person as Muse." PoetryNW (22:1) Spr 81, pp. 20-21.

DUFAULT, Peter Kane
"April Hemlocks." NewYorker (57:7) 6 Ap 81, p. 42.
"Small Wild Creatures Along a Road at Night." NewYorker (57:29) 7 S
81, p. 32.

DUFFY, John Kasten
"Dream of My Father in Old Age, Mastering the Violin." Tendril (10)
Wint 81, p. 25.

DUFFY, Maureen Nevin
"For Nancy On The Stage in Plainfield." US1 (14/15) Aut/Wint 81, p.
8.

DUGAN, Alan
"On Shields. Against World War III. (for Paul Bowen)." MassR (22:
2) Sum 81, p.285.
"Untitled Poem." Atl (247:2) F 81, p. 64.

DUGAN, Marianne
"Suspended." Wind (11:41) 81, p. 14.

DUGGAN, Lilvia
"Nostradamus" (tr. of Pedro Lastra). Mund (12/13) 80-81, p. 118.

DUHAMEL, Vaughn
"The Sinking (for Carolyn)." NewOR (8:2) Sum 81, pp. 202-3.

DUNBAR, Paul
"Tuesday." Stand (22: 4) 81, pp. 10-12.

DUNCAN, Robert
"In Blood's Domaine." Sulfur (3) 82, pp. 4-5.

DUNMORE, Helen
"In Rodmell Garden." Stand (22: 2) 81, p. 32.

DUNN, Ann
"I am the Sweet Gum tree...." CarolQ (34:2) Aut 81, p. 44.
"This big old hoary pine cone is more like it." CarolQ (34:2) Aut 81,
p. 45.

DUNN, Douglas
"An Address To The Destitution Of Scotland." Stand (22: 1) 80, p. 51.

DUNN, Robert
"A Ghost." Aspect (77/79) 81, p. 57.

DUNN, Stephen
"Coming On" (for Joe Gillon). GeoR (35:1) Spr 81, p. 16.
"Deer Hunting." PoetryNW (22:2) Sum 81, p. 10.

"Elementary Poem." Poetry (138:1) Ap 81, pp. 37-38.
"The End of the World." Poetry (139:3) D 81, pp. 163-164.
"Essay to a Friend in Love with the Wrong Man Again." AmerS (50:4)
     Aut 81, p. 464.
"Fairy Tale." Poetry (138:1) Ap 81, p. 35.
"Fishing." PoetryNW (22:2) Sum 81, pp. 10-11.
"In the Blowdown Zone." Poetry (139:3) D 81, p. 161.
"In the San Bernardinos." Antaeus (40/41) Wint-Spr 81, pp. 282-283.
"Instructions for the Next Century." Iowa (11:4) Aut 80, p. 92.
"Not Even Half Way Home" (after Cheever). ThRiPo (17/18) 81, p. 15.
"The Rain Falling Now." OhioR (26), pp. 26-27.
"Silence." Chelsea (40) 81, p. 147.
"The Snow Leopard." Poetry (139:3) D 81, p. 162.
"The Universe Is Too Big to Love." GeoR (35:3) Aut 81, p. 646.
"Workers." Poetry (138:1) Ap 81, p. 36.

DUNNE, Carol
"Just to Give Something Away." Antaeus (40/41) Wint-Spr 81, p. 287.
"Resolve in the City." Antaeus (40/41) Wint-Spr 81, p. 286.
"Tornado Watch." Antaeus (40/41) Wint-Spr 81, p. 284.
"The Twice Sad Man." Antaeus (40/41) Wint-Spr 81, p. 285.

DUNNING, Stephen
"Invention." HiramPoR (29) Aut-Wint 81, p. 14.
"The men raking the boulevard." Tendril (11) Sum 81, p. 28.
"To know how the very old feel." Tendril (11) Sum 81, p. 27.

DuPLESSIS, Nancy
"Forecast: Ambivalent." Tele (17) 81, p. 120.
"Freelance Thoughts." Tele (17) 81, p. 118.
"Okay Punka" (to A. A. with love and affection). Tele (17) 81, p. 119.

DuPLESSIS, Rachel Blau
"Eclogue." Sulfur (1) 81, pp. 204-205.
"Killing Me." Sulfur (1) 81, pp. 206-207.
"Ode." Sulfur (3) 82, pp. 15-18.

DUPREE, Edison
"Breakfast with News of a Shipping Accident." LitR (24:3) Spr 81, p.
     400.
"Monster Movie." Iowa (11:4) Aut 80, p. 78.
"Report from April." Confr (22) Sum 81, p. 142.

DUPUIS, Gilbert
"A Propos de L'écriture I." Os (12) Spr 81, p. 22.
"A Propos de L'écriture II." Os (12) Spr 81, p. 23.

DUTTON, Mike
"I Wish...." EngJ (70:2) F 81, p. 47.

DUVAL, Quinton
"Autumn River." CimR (56) Jl 81, p. 4.
"Feet" (for all the others). CutB (17) Aut-Wint 81, p. 41.
"For You ... Winter Dancing." CimR (56) Jl 81, p. 60.
"Heaven." QW (13) Aut/Wint 81/82, p. 27.

DUYN, Mona van see VAN DUYN, Mona

DWYER, David
    "Diamond Head: instead of another day." Agni (15) 81, pp. 14-15.

DWYER, Deirdre
    "Closing the Eye." PottPort (3) 81, p. 31.
    "For Jeanne Robinson." PottPort (3) 81, p. 32.

DWYER, Frank
    "Autumn." KanQ (13:1) Wint 81, p. 69.
    "Dover." LittleM (13:1/2) Spr-Sum 79, c1981, p. 84.
    "Falcon." AmerPoR (10:2) Mr-Ap 81, p. 22.
    "A Lullaby for Mother's Day." KanQ (13:2) Spr 81, p. 44.

DYBEK, Stuart
    "Bastille Day on 25th St." SenR (10:2/11:1) 79-80, p. 53.
    "Brass Knuckles." SenR (10:2/11:1) 79-80, pp. 56-57.
    "Electrostatic." SenR (10:2/11:1) 79-80, p. 54.
    "Luncheonette: West Branch, Iowa." PoNow (6:2 issue 32) 81, p. 19.
    "The Rape of Persephone." SenR (10:2/11:1) 79-80, pp. 58-61.
    "Vivaldi." SenR (10:2/11:1) 79-80, p. 55.
    "Writing at Night." PoNow (6:1 issue 31) 81, p. 35.

DYER, Dan
    "October Legend." StoneC (9: 1-2) Aut-Wint 81/82, p. 15.
    "Saint Cicada Sings Forever Without Doubt." StoneC (9: 1-2) Aut-Wint
        81/82, p. 14.

EACKER, Sandra
    "Reductions." PortR (27: 2) 81, p. 91.

EAKINS, Patricia
    "Cup." OP (31/32) Aut 81, p. 128.
    "Lamp." OP (31/32) Aut 81, p. 128.

EARLE, Jean
    "A Neighbour's House." Stand (22: 4) 81, p. 22.
    "A Wood Behind the Sea." Stand (22: 4) 81, p. 21.

EASTMAN, Bruce
    "The Sky Snakes." Nat (233:14) 31 O 81, p. 448.
    "Ward of the Bunker" (Myo-Chemul). CharR (7:2) Aut 81, pp. 14-15.

EATON, Charles Edward
    "A Day In The Life of a Magpie." ModernPS (10:2/3), p. 173.
    "The Amazon." PoNow (6:2 issue 32) 81, p. 24.
    "The Cave Painting." SouthernHR (15:3) Sum 81, p. 208.
    "The Circular Staircase." AntR (39:2) Spr 81, p. 209.
    "Collector's Items." PoNow (6:2 issue 32) 81, p. 24.
    "Cuff Links." PoNow (6:2 issue 32) 81, p. 29.
    "El Dorado." ConcPo (14:1) Spr 81, p. 14.
    "The Hanging Gardens." ColEng (43:1) Ja 81, p. 28.
    "Haruspex of the Happy Country." HolCrit (17:6 [i. e. 18:1?]) F 81, p.
        15.
    "The Haystack." SouthwR (66:3) Sum 81, p. 267.
    "The Kiss." Confr (21) Wint 81, p. 94.
    "The Muscle." ConcPo (14:1) Spr 81, p. 13.
    "Needlepoint In Autumn." MassR (22:3) Aut 81, p. 448.
    "The Palm Voyeur." SoCaR (13: 2) Spr 81, p. 55.

"Paracelsus in Puerto Rico." HolCrit (18:3 [i.e. 4]) O 81, p. 10.
"Red Snapper." KanQ (13:3/4) Sum-Aut 81, p. 56.
"Suit of Lights." MidwQ (22:3) Spr 81, p. 260.

EATON, Philip
   "For My Student Who is a Christian." PoNow (6:1 issue 31) 81, p. 20.

EBERHARDT, Janis Herring
   "Grandmother." Wind (10:39) 80, p. 11.

EBERHART, Richard
   "Cutting Back." Mund (12/13) 80-81, p. 345.
   "A Dream." NewEngR (3:3) Spr 81, pp. 342-3.
   "Half Way Measure." Mund (12/13) 80-81, p. 345.
   "Target." Ploughs (7:1) 81, pp. 40-41.
   "Transformation." NewEngR (3:3) Spr 81, pp. 343-4.

EBERLY, David
   "Renewal" (in memory of H. R. Hays). Kayak (57) 81, p. 26.

ECELBERGER, Dana
   "Between the Lines." HolCrit (18:2) Ap 81, pp. 18-19.

ECHEVERRI MEJIA, Oscar
   "Eres Como la Ola." Puerto Wint 81, p. 26.

ECONOMOU, George
   from Amerpikh Two: "The mothers through whom I fell." Pequod
      (12) 81, pp. 8-10.

EDDY, Darlene Mathis
   "Blossom and Cloud." HiramPoR (29) Aut-Wint 81, p. 15.

EDDY, Gary
   "On the Banks of the Rio Grande." PoNow (6:1 issue 31) 81, p. 29.

EDDY, Jennifer
   "Heloise Refuses to Repent." Peb (21) 81, p. 104.

EDIGER, Peter J.
   "Hostage." ChrC (98:5) 18 F 81, p. 168.

EDKINS, Anthony
   "Cezanne" (tr. of Xavier Villaurrutia). Chelsea (40) 81, p. 87.
   "Death--Is It Shipwreck?" (tr. of Leon Felipe). Chelsea (40) 81, p. 83.
   From Dutch Week: "Friday" (tr. of Carlos Pellicer). Chelsea (40) 81,
      p. 82.
   From Dutch Week: "Tuesday-Rembrandt" (tr. of Carlos Pellicer).
      Chelsea (40) 81, p. 82.
   "A moment in an eighteenth-century day immobilized by a Japanese
      painter" (tr. of Isabel Fraire). Chelsea (40) 81, p. 86.
   "Turner's Landscape" (tr. of José Emilio Pacheco). Chelsea (40) 81,
      p. 85.
   "Venice" (tr. of José Emilio Pacheco). Chelsea (40) 81, p. 84.

EDSON, Russell
   "Charity." MassR (22:4) Wint 81, p. 628.
   "A Dog's Tail." MassR (22:4) Wint 81, p. 629.

"Elephant Tears." MassR (22:4) Wint 81, pp. 628-629.
"The Amateur." Field (25) Aut 81, p. 59.
"The Dark Side of the Moon." Field (25) Aut 81, p. 58.
"The Dynamite Quartet." PoNow (6:2 issue 32) 81, p. 12.
"The Fat Woman." PoNow (6:1 issue 31) 81, p. 13.
"The Hallway Closet." UnmOx (22) Wint 81, p. 53.
"The Park Bench." MassR (22:4) Wint 81, p. 630.
"The Restaurant Explosions." MassR (22:4) Wint 81, p. 630.
"The Slaughterhouse Dance." PoNow (6:2 issue 32) 81, p. 12.
"What Sara Jean Enjoys." PoNow (6:1 issue 31) 81, p. 13.
"Why It Is Better to Be Married." Iowa (11:2/3) Spr-Sum 80, p. 200.
"A Zoography." Field (25) Aut 81, p. 57.

EDWARDS, Duane
"An Autumn Fire." Confr (21) Wint 81, p. 124.

EFTHIMIDES, Emil
"Marauder." KanQ (13:1) Wint 81, p. 56.

EHRHART, W. D.
"Driving into the Future." Wind (11:43) 81, p. 15.
"Pagan." Sam (116) 81, p. 53.
"Sound Advice." PoetryE (6) Aut 81, pp. 72-73.
"The Vision." PoetryE (6) Aut 81, pp. 70-71.
"What Went Wrong." Sam (117) 81, p. 13.

EICH, Günter
"A Moment in June" (tr. by Francis Golffing). PoNow (5:6 issue 30)
    81, p. 15.
"West Wind" (tr. by Francis Golffing). PoNow (5:6 issue 30) 81, p. 15.

EIGNER, Larry
"Cars making someplace up." SunM (11) Spr 81, p. 58.
"a late hour...." Sulfur (3) 82, pp. 71-74.
"The lifespan life life." SunM (11) Spr 81, p. 61.
"No flies in the doorway." SunM (11) Spr 81, p. 59.
"Rocks brought indoors." SunM (11) Spr 81, p. 62.
"Witnuts breakfast." SunM (11) Spr 81, p. 60.

EISEMINGER, Skip
"A Monday Morning, the Twelfth Year." PoNow (6:2 issue 32) 81, p.
    47.

ELDER, Karl
"Catoptrophobia." CalQ (18/19) 81, p. 83.
"Yet such is detail." StoneC (9: 1-2) Aut-Wint 81/82, p. 63.

ELEKTOROWICZ, Leszek
"An Everyday Psalm" (tr. with Frederic Will of Tadeusz Nowak). SenR
    (12:1/2) 81, p. 113.

ELGIN, Suzette Haden
"Happyvalentine." PortR (27: 2) 81, p. 54.

el-HAGE, G. N.
"Chariot of Light" (tr. by D. Malouf). Nimrod (24: 2) Spr/Sum 81, pp.
    105-107.
"Exile" (tr. by D. Malouf). Nimrod (24: 2) Spr/Sum 81, p. 107.
"Sufiyya" (tr. by D. Malouf). Nimrod (24: 2) Spr/Sum 81, p. 105.

ELLIOT, William D.
  "Field on Monday." PoNow (6:1 issue 31) 81, p. 18.

ELLIOTT, David L.
  "August Heat." PikeR (2) Sum 81, p. 24.
  "Hands." PikeR (2) Sum 81, p. 21.
  "Worn Smooth." PikeR (2) Sum 81, pp. 22-23.

ELLIS, Edward
  "The Hum of Gypsy Rosaries." Wind (10:39) 80, p. 18.

ELLIS, Kate
  "Maiden Aunt." 13thM (5:1/2) 80, pp. 52-53.

ELLIS, Mary Anne
  "The Rattlesnake." Poem (42) Jul 81, pp. 30-31.
  "The Shooting." Poem (42) Jul 81, p. 32.

ELLIS, Noreen
  "To Sally Thomas." HangL (39) Wint 80-81, pp. 59-60.

ELLISON, Jessie T.
  "California Coastline." WindO (38) Spr-Sum 81, p. 10.
  "Departures." WindO (38) Spr-Sum 81, p. 9.
  "Something About How Trees Accept Light*" (*Richard Shelton). WindO
     (38) Spr-Sum 81, p. 8.

EL MAR, Yekhi
  "Days" (tr. by Bernhard Frank). PoNow (5:6 issue 30) 81, p. 29.

ELMSLIE, Kenward
  "August." ParisR (23:79) Spr 81, pp. 167-168.

ELSON, Virginia
  "Hunt." PoNow (6:2 issue 32) 81, p. 35.
  "Runaways in a Winter Thaw." LitR (24:3) Spr 81, p. 375.
  "Small-Town Laundromat." LitR (24:3) Spr 81, p. 375.
  "Touching Moons." PoetryNW (22:3) Aut 81, p. 43.

ELUARD, Paul
  "The Beloved" (tr. by Michael Benedikt). UnmOx (22) Wint 81, p. 37.
  "The Face of Peace" (tr. by Don Wilson). PoetryE (6) Aut 81, pp. 89-
     92.

ELYTIS, Odysseus
  "Adolescence of Day" (tr. by Edmund Keeley and Philip Sherrard).
     MalR (57) Ja 81, p. 143.
  "The Age of Blue Memory" (tr. by Edmund Keeley and Philip Sherrard).
     MalR (57) Ja 81, pp. 143-144.
  "Burnished Day, Conch of the Voice" (tr. by Edmund Keeley and Philip
     Sherrard). MalR (57) Ja 81, p. 144.
  "The garden entered the sea" (tr. by Willis Barnstone). PoNow (6:2
     issue 32) 81, p. 40.
  "Laconic" (tr. by Edmund Keeley and Philip Sherrard). MalR (57) Ja
     81, p. 146.
  "Seven Days for Eternity" (tr. by Kimon Friar). Mund (12/13) 80-81,
     p. 269.
  "Seven Days for Eternity" (tr. by Edmund Keeley and Philip Sherrard).

MalR (57) Ja 81, p. 147.
"Seven Nocturnals" (tr. by Edmund Keeley and Philip Sherrard). MalR
    (57) Ja 81, pp. 141-142.
"The Sleep of the Brave" (tr. by Edmund Keeley and Philip Sherrard).
    MalR (57) Ja 81, p. 145.
"Sleep of the Valiant" (tr. by Kimon Friar). Mund (12/13) 80-81, pp.
    268-269.

EMANS, Elaine V.
    "For William Butler Yeats." CentR (25:2) Spr 81, p. 162.
    "Talking to My Cells." PikeR (2) Sum 81, p. 19.

EMERSON, Dorothy
    "Down Sleep's Dark Bank We Sink" (typographical errors in Aut 80 is-
        sue). YaleR (70: 3) Spr 81, p. 480.
    "Lake Ainslee" (typographical errors in Aut 80 issue). YaleR (70: 3)
        Spr 81, p. 480.

EMERY, Michael J.
    "Doing the Dishes." WindO (39) Wint 81/82, p. 10.

ENANI, Muhammad
    "On Repetition" (tr. of Salāh 'Abd al-Sabūr). Nimrod (24: 2) Spr/Sum
        81, pp. 124-125.
    "Summing Up" (tr. of Salāh 'Abd al-Sabūr). Nimrod (24: 2) Spr/Sum
        81, p. 123.
    "That Evening" (tr. of Salāh 'Abd al-Sabūr). Nimrod (24: 2) Spr/Sum
        81, pp. 126-128.

ENCARNACION, Angel M.
    "Allá en Atlanta los ríos...." Claridad/En Rojo (22: 1495) 25 S-1 O
        81, p. 12.
    "Una historia de niños para adultos (A todos los niños en el Año Inter-
        nacional del Niño. A Manolito)." Mairena (2:6), pp. 35-6.

ENDREZZE-DANIELSON, Anita
    "The Courtship of Sun and Moon." MalR (60) O 81, p. 98.
    "Message from a Ponca Woman to her friends, the Omahas, 1877, dur-
        ing the first removal." MalR (60) O 81, p. 94.
    "Naming the Sun." MalR (60) O 81, pp. 96-97.
    "Shaman/Bear." MalR (60) O 81, p. 95.
    "The Solid Beasts." ThRiPo (17/18) 81, pp. 71-72.
    "They say the earth is slowing down." MalR (60) O 81, p. 99.
    "Wind-changers." MalR (60) O 81, p. 100.

ENEKWE, Ossie Onuora
    "The Joker." Mund (12/13) 80-81, p. 180.

ENGELS, John
    "The Cold in This Place." NewYorker (57:10) 27 Ap 81, pp. 44-5.
    "The Disconnections." Harp (262:1568) Ja 81, pp. 44-45.
    "Flying over Illinois at Sunset." GeoR (35:4) Wint 81, p. 847.
    "For Mozart, from the Beginning." Harp (262:1570) Mr 81, p. 70.
    "The Word '...Love?' Spoken to the Fifth Floor." Antaeus (40/41)
        Wint-Spr 81, pp. 288-289.

ENGLE, Ed, Jr.
    "Snakehandlers" (for John Douglas). StoneC (9: 1-2) Aut-Wint 81/82,

p. 71.
"Snowshoe Rabbit." Sam (116) 81, p. 19.

ENGLE, Paul
"Images of China." Poetry (138:5) Ag 81, pp. 291-296.

ENGLER, Robert Klein
"The Love of Leaden Gold." Poem (43) Nov 81, p. 20.
"A Little Uneasy." Poem (43) Nov 81, p. 19.
"Poor Apology." Tendril (11) Sum 81, p. 29.

ENGMAN, John
"Keeping Still Mountain." MissouriR (4:3) Sum 81, p. 16.
"The Late Show." PoetryNW (22:4) Wint 81-82, pp. 33-34.
"Sandcastles." PoetryNW (23:4) Wint 81-82, pp. 32-33.

ENGONOPOULOS, Nikos
"News of the Death of the Spanish Poet Federico García Lorca on August
    19, 1936, in a Ditch at Camino de la Fuente" (tr. by Yannis Gow-
    mas). Mund (12/13) 80-81, p. 185.

ENLOE, Glen
"Homicide #126 on the year." Wind (11:43) 81, p. 16.

ENSLIN, Theodore
"Axes 26." Sulfur (2) 81, pp. 30-38.
"A Paper for G. D., Who Said: 'It is right for me to live here now.
    It would not have been right to live in the country, twenty years ago,
    when I was a young man.'" UnmOx (22) Wint 81, pp. 26-27.

EPELBAUM, Susana
"The Drunken Girl" (tr. of Efraín Huerta). PoNow (5:6 issue 30) 81,
    p. 18.

EPSTEIN, Daniel Mark
"Fortune." MichQR (20:2) Spr 81, pp. 20-21.
"How Shall We Dress for Heaven?" Agni (15) 81, pp. 5-6.
"Lafayette Square." VirQR (57:1) Wint 81, pp. 62-69.
"Mannequins." AmerS (50:2) Spr 81, pp. 211-12.
"The Royal Hotel in Pisa." PraS (55:3) Aut 81, p. 91.

EPSTEIN, Elaine
"Letter to Sea, Sky, and Earth." Pequod (12) 81, pp. 28-29.
"They Said." Pequod (12) 81, pp. 30-31.

EPSTEIN, Susan
"To My Friends on the Surface." Aspect (77/79) 81, p. 60.

ERBA, Luciano
"Transfer" (tr. by RoseAnna M. Mueller). PoNow (5:6 issue 30) 81, p.
    15.

ERICKSON, Jon
"In Every Moment of Crisis." CreamCR (7:1) 81, pp. 40-41.

ERICKSON, Thomas
"American Platitudes." WindO (39) Wint 81/82, p. 19.
"Picking Up Garbage on Tuesday Morning in the Summer." WindO (39)
    Wint 81/82, p. 20.

ERLICH, Shelley
"Shower." Northeast (3:11) Sum 81, p. 26.

ERNST, David
"Steps" (tr. by Herbert Kuhner). Mund (11:2) 79, p. 73.
"Stufen." Mund (11:2) 79, p. 72.

ESCOBAR, Jaime Ruiz see RUIZ ESCOBAR, Jaime

ESHLEMAN, Clayton
"Anabasis" (tr. of Bernard Bador). Kayak (57) 81, pp. 34-35.
"Batoque" (tr. of Aimé Césaire, w/ Annette Smith). Sulfur (1) 81, pp. 212-218.
"The Death of Bill Evans." Ploughs (7:2) 81, pp. 70-71.
"The Distance from St.-Cirq to Caravaggio." SenR (11:2) 81, pp. 69-70.
"Equal Time." PartR (48:1) 81, p. 130.
"I call muse..." (tr. of Michel Deguy). Sulfur (3) 82, pp. 65-67.
"Interior Deposition." SenR (11:2) 81, pp. 73-75.
"The Loaded Sleeve of Hades." Sulfur (1) 81, pp. 182-185.
"Permanent Shadow." SenR (11:2) 81, pp. 71-72.
"Progress" (tr. of Bernard Bador). Sulfur (3) 82, p. 20.
"Saturos." Ploughs (7:2) 81, p. 68.
"A Small Cave." Ploughs (7:2) 81, p. 69.
"Sound Grottos" (for Bernad Heidsieck). SenR (11:2) 81, pp. 76-77.

ESPINO, Federico Lisci, Jr.
"The Recrucifixion at Mt. Banahaw." PortR (27: 2) 81, p. 36.
"To the First Woman." PortR (27: 2) 81, p. 36.
"U.F.O." PortR (27: 2) 81, p. 36.

ESPOSITO, Nancy
"Gotham Sometime Later." Tendril (10) Wint 81, pp. 26-27.
"The woman in Translation." SouthernPR (21:2) Aut 81, p. 48.

ESRIG, Mark
"Soundings." ConcPo (14:1) Spr 81, p. 58.

ESTEBAN, Claude
"Glance that the morning invades" (tr. by Rainer Schulte). Mund (12/13) 80-81, p. 92.
"No one yet against the sky." Mund (12/13) 80-81, p. 92.
"With each stone." Mund (12/13) 80-81, pp. 92-93.

ESTENSSORO, Hugo
"Elegía Paceña." Lugar (1:1) 79, pp. 6-7.

ESTRADA, Alfredo Silva see SILVA ESTRADA, Alfredo

ETTER, Dave
"Friendly Persuasion." PoNow (6:2 issue 32) 81, p. 34.
"Ghester Greene: Taking the Census." PoNow (6:1 issue 31) 81, p. 24.
"Perry Meek: Wife Killer." PoNow (6:1 issue 31) 81, p. 24.
"Ruby Kimble: Homecoming Game." PoNow (6:1 issue 31) 81, p. 24.

EUGSTER, Carla
"Black Jews." Sam (106) 81, p. 2.

Rural Water. Sam (104) 81, Entire issue.
"Stopped Clock." Sam (109) 81, p. 2.

EULBERG, Mary Thomas
"Annunciation." ChrC (98:41) 16 D 81, p. 1302.
"Pre-Vatican II." ChrC (98:11) 1 Ap 81, p. 343.

EUSEBIO, Enrique
"Compañera." Caribe (2: 2/3) 80/81, p. 66.
"Diálogo con Pedro Mir." Caribe (2: 2/3) 80/81, p. 65.

EVANS, Bill
"Eighth Elegy" (w/ Andrew Gent). HangL (40) Aut 81, pp. 10-12.
"Sixth Elegy" (w/ Andrew Gent). HangL (40) Aut 81, pp. 8-9.

EVANS, David
"Girls Working in Drive-up Banks." HiramPoR (29) Aut-Wint 81, p.
    16.
"Uncle Elmer." Northeast (3:11) Sum 81, p. 34.

EVANS, David Allan
"A Blossom." PoNow (6:2 issue 32) 81, p. 21.

EVARTS, Prescott, Jr.
"Mark It Down." KanQ (13:3/4) Sum-Aut 81, p. 55.

EVE, Barbara
"Dark Side of the Moon." VirQR (57:1) Wint 81, p. 74.

FABIAN, R. Gerry
A Fallen Woman. Sam (114) 81, Entire issue.

FABRIS, Dino
"Lion." PoNow (6:1 issue 31) 81, p. 47.

FAHEY, W. A.
"The Blanket." Confr (22) Sum 81, p. 83.
"Psalm II." WebR (6:2) 81, pp. 52-53.
"Shovels." WebR (6:2) 81, p. 54.

FAHEY, William A.
"The Artichoke." WormR (84) 81, p. 90.
"The Cauliflower." WormR (84) 81, p. 91.
"The Eggplant." WormR (84) 81, p. 90.
"Potatoes." WormR (84) 81, p. 91.

FAIRCHILD, B. H.
"Black Bear Creek." Outbr (6/7) Aut 80-Spr 81, p. 37.
"C & W Machine Works." HiramPoR (29) Aut-Wint 81, p. 17.
"The Dance." Outbr (6/7) Aut 80-Spr 81, p. 36.

FALCONE, James
"Friends at the Bar." PottPort (3) 81, p. 39.

FALKENBERG, Betty
"Revenge" (tr. of Else Lasker-Schuler). PoNow (6:2 issue 32) 81, p.
    41.
"Suicide" (tr. of Else Lasker-Schuler). PoNow (6:2 issue 32) 81, p. 41

FALZON, Grazio
    "I Died A Thousand Deaths" (tr. of Mario Azzopardi).   PortR (27: 1)
        81, p. 38.
    "Landscape 2" (tr. of Mario Azzopardi).   PortR (27: 1) 81, p. 37.
    "Parabola" (tr. by Grazio Falzon).   PortR (27: 2) 81, p. 34.
    "Tonight the Moon is Cross-eyed" (tr. by Grazio Falzon).   PortR (27:
        2) 81, p. 34.
    "Vision 22X" (tr. of Mario Azzopardi).   PortR (27: 1) 81, p. 37.
    "When the Light Is Dimmed" (tr. by Grazio Falzon).   PortR (27: 2) 81,
        p. 34.

FANDEL, John
    "Houses. " Confr (21) Wint 81, p. 26.
    "Snow Storm. " HolCrit (18:3 [i. e. 4]) O 81, p. 9.

FARBER, Norma
    "Age of Heroes. " Wind (11:43) 81, p. 18.
    "Gathering Pine-Cones" (tr. of Maurice Carême).   PoNow (5:6 issue 30)
        81, p. 11.
    "High-Rise. " Wind (11:43) 81, p. 17.
    "I Came Like Water. " Wind (11:43) 81, pp. 17-18.
    "Let Them In!"   ChrC (98:41) 16 D 81, p. 1303.
    "On Reflection. " CentR (25:1) Wint 81, pp. 46-47.
    "Stay as Simple..." (tr. of Maurice Carême).   PoNow (5:6 issue 30)
        81, p. 11.
    "The Sun-Bathed Garden" (tr. of Maurice Carême).   PoNow (5:6 issue
        30) 81, p. 11.

FAREWELL, Patricia
    "The Roofers. " AmerPoR (10:2) Mr-Ap 81, p. 34.
    "Runaways. " AmerPoR (10:2) Mr-Ap 81, p. 34.
    "Working Around Words. " AmerPoR (10:2) Mr-Ap 81, p. 34.

FARINELLA, Salvatore
    "Each Day. " Aspect (77/79) 81, p. 61.

FARLEY, Michael
    "Sea Knot. " Pequod (13) 81, p. 42.
    "There Is Nothing Given" (Gipsy Castle Earthwork, Spring).   Pequod
        (13) 81, p. 43.

FARMER, Frank
    "In Other Moments. " Wind (11:42) 81, p. 35.

FARNSWORTH, Robert
    "Music for Piano and Electrical Storm. " Poetry (139:3) D 81, pp. 135-
        136.
    "Natural History. " CarolQ (34:1) Sum 81, pp. 11-12.
    "Pegasus. " ThRiPo (17/18) 81, p. 23.
    "Poem Timed to an Egg. " CarolQ (34:1) Sum 81, p. 10.
    "Sampler. " Poetry (139:3) D 81, pp. 137-138.

FARRANT, Elizabeth
    "Complexities of the Fact. " Poem (41) Mar 81, p. 65.
    "The Light House Keepers. " Poem (41) Mar 81, p. 64.

FARRELL, Katy
    "Bourbon Street Jazz on Acadian Lines Bus. " PottPort (3) 81, p. 32.
    "married. " PottPort (3) 81, p. 37.

FARROKHZAD, Forugh
   "From Darkness" (tr. by Jascha Kessler with Amin Banani). VirQR
     (57:2) Spr 81, pp. 270-271.
   "The Gift" (tr. by Jascha Kessler and Amin Banani). PoNow (5:6 issue
     30) 81, p. 15.
   "Leaving: the Poem" (tr. by Jascha Kessler with Amin Banani).
     VirQR (57:2) Spr 81, pp. 271-272.

FASEL, Ida
   "At Dini's: A Boston Legend." Vis (7) 81, n. p.

FAUCHER, Real
   "A Stranger Mourns A Dead Man." Sam (116) 81, p. 62.
   "Victory Dance." Wind (11:40) 81, p. 7.

FAULKNER, Leigh
   "Images of Love." PottPort (3) 81, p. 41.

FAULKNER, Margherita
   "For Mother." BallSUF (22:4) Aut 81, p. 51.
   "Request." BallSUF (22:3) Sum 81, p. 74.
   "The Visit." Wind (10:39) 80, p. 13.

FAUTEUX, Bob
   "Stranger" (for Susan Talanda). FourQt (31:1) Aut 81, p. 12.

FAWCETT, Susan
   "Partial Likeness." Prima (6/7) 81, p. 5.

FEDO, David
   "Home." KanQ (13:3/4) Sum-Aut 81, p. 182.
   "Towers." HiramPoR (29) Aut-Wint 81, pp. 18-19.
   "Winter Gull." CapeR (17:1) Wint 81, p. 17.

FEDOR, Michael
   "Sympathy." ChrC (98:25) 12-19 Ag 81, p. 789.

FEE, Dan
   "A Memory of Joel." KanQ (13:3/4) Sum-Aut 81, p. 82.

FEENY, Thomas
   "Leaving." CapeR (17:1) Wint 81, p. 46.
   "A Much-Married King" (for ep). HiramPoR (30) Spr-Sum 81, p. 16.

FEINSTEIN, Elaine
   "from An England Sequence." ParisR (23:79) Spr 81, p. 169.

FEIRSTEIN, Frederick
   "Divorced." OntR (15) Aut-Wint 81-82, p. 66.
   "The Old Neighborhood." OntR (15) Aut-Wint 81-82, p. 67.
   "The Pilot." OntR (15) Aut-Wint 81-82, pp. 70-71.
   "What the Police Report Said." OntR (15) Aut-Wint 81-82, p. 72.
   "The Widow." OntR (15) Aut-Wint 81-82, pp. 68-69.

FELDMAN, Alan
   "At the Barbeque." Ploughs (6:4) 81, pp. 45-46.
   "One of My Daughter's Drawings." Ploughs (6:4) 81, p. 47.

FELDMAN, Irving
  "Homeric Simile: The All-Stars." Shen (31:3) 80, p. 24.
  "Millions of Strange Shadows." Shen (31:3) 80, p. 25.
  "Read to the Animals, or Orpheus at the SPCA." Shen (32:4) 81, pp.
    18-21.
  "Social Constructions of Reality at Coney Island." Poetry (138:4) Jl 81,
    pp. 227-230.

FELDMAN, Ruth
  "Baedeker" (tr. of Bartolo Cattafi, w/ Brian Swann). PoNow (5:6 issue
    30) 81, p. 12.
  "Brindisi" (tr. of Vittorio Bodini, w/ Brian Swann). PoNow (5:6 issue
    30) 81, p. 9.
  "But in the Hour" (tr. of Vittorio Bodini, w/ Brian Swann). PoNow
    (5:6 issue 30) 81, p. 9.
  "Charity of my Village?" (tr. of Rocco Scotellaro, w/ Brian Swann).
    PoNow (5:6 issue 30) 81, p. 41.
  "The City Sweetheart" (tr. of Rocco Scotellaro, w/ Brian Swann).
    PoNow (5:6 issue 30) 81, p. 41.
  "Cloth" (tr. of Bartolo Cattafi, w/ Brian Swann). Mund (12/13) 80-81,
    p. 346.
  "The Dawn is Always New" (tr. of Rocco Scotellaro, w/ Brian Swann).
    PoNow (5:6 issue 30) 81, p. 25.
  "The Grain of the Sepulchre" (tr. of Rocco Scotellaro, w/ Brian Swann).
    PoNow (5:6 issue 30) 81, p. 41.
  from Holland: "Amsterdam" (tr. of Vittorio Sereni, w/ Brian Swann).
    PoNow (5:6 issue 30) 81, p. 42.
  from Holland: "The Interpreter" (tr. of Vittorio Sereni, w/ Brian
    Swann). PoNow (5:6 issue 30) 81, p. 42.
  from Holland: "Volendam" (tr. of Vittorio Sereni, w/ Brian Swann).
    PoNow (5:6 issue 30) 81, p. 42.
  "Journeys" (tr. of Rocco Scotellaro, w/ Brian Swann). PoNow (5:6
    issue 30) 81, p. 25.
  "The Mad Mother" (tr. of Margherita Guidacci). PortR (27: 1) 81, p.
    38.
  "No Pasaran" (tr. of Bartolo Cattafi, w/ Brian Swann). PoNow (5:6
    issue 30) 81, p. 12.
  "Now that July Rules" (tr. of Rocco Scotellaro, w/ Brian Swann).
    PoNow (5:6 issue 30) 81, p. 25.
  "The Package" (tr. of Bartolo Cattafi, w/ Brian Swann). PoNow (5:6
    issue 30) 81, p. 12.
  "Rainbow" (tr. of Rocco Scotellaro, w/ Brian Swann). PoNow (5:6 is-
    sue 30) 81, p. 41.
  "The Rule" (tr. of Rocco Scotellaro, w/ Brian Swann). PoNow (5:6 is-
    sue 30) 81, p. 41.
  from Tabacco Leaves 1945-1947 (tr. of Vittorio Bodini). PoNow (5:6
    issue 30) 81, pp. 9-10.
  "Toward Bastions and Warriors" (tr. of Bartolo Cattafi, w/ Brian
    Swann). PoNow (5:6 issue 30) 81, p. 12.
  "Vico Tapera" (tr. of Rocco Scotellaro, w/ Brian Swann). PoNow (5:6
    issue 30) 81, p. 25.

FELDMAN, Susan
  "American Gothic." Aspect (77/79) 81, p. 62.

FELICIANO MENDOZA, Ester
  "De ausubo y cielo." Mairena (2:6), p. 59.

"Hallazgo." Mairena (2:6), p. 59.
"Querencia." Mairena (2:6), p. 59.

FELIPE, León
  "Death--Is It Shipwreck?" (tr. by Anthony Edkins). Chelsea (40) 81, p.
  83.

FENSTERMAKER, Vesle
  "Appetite." KanQ (13:1) Wint 81, pp. 156-157.
  "Talk Show." KanQ (13:1) Wint 81, p. 157.

FENTON, Elizabeth
  "The Typing Test." Aspect (77/79) 81, pp. 63-64.

FENTON, Kevin
  "Several Minutes in the Life of (Dry Cleaner)." BelPoJ (31:3) Spr 81,
  p. 9.

FEREN, David
  "Defiance." KanQ (13:1) Wint 81, p. 114.
  "The Hardest Season." KanQ (13:1) Wint 81, p. 113.

FERGUSON, Gordon
  "Loki I." ThRiPo (17/18) 81, pp. 76-77.

FERICANO, Paul
  "Jimmy Durante Is Dead." WormR (84) 81, pp. 96-97.
  "High Wire Act Over California." WormR (84) 81, pp. 95-96.
  "Thank You Elizabeth Taylor." WormR (84) 81, p. 95.

FERLINGHETTI, Lawrence
  "Tall Tale of the Tall Cowboy." Harp (262:1573) Je 81, p. 55.

FERNANDEZ IGLESIAS, Roberto
  "In some far-off place" (tr. by Donald Walsh). Mund (12/13) 80-81, p.
  331.
  "You saw her growing." Mund (12/13) 80-81, p. 331.

FERNANDEZ MEJIA, Abel
  "Amor." Caribe (2: 2/3) 80/81, p. 70.
  "Este es un diálogo no estrictamente patriótico." Caribe (2: 2/3) 80/81,
  p. 71-73.

FERNANDEZ SANZ, Yolanda
  "Sudar la patria." Claridad/En Rojo (22: 1468) 20-26 Mr 81, p. 12.

FERNOS MALDONADO, Gonzalo
  "A la vieja ciudad de San Juan." Mairena (2:6), p. 79.

FERRANDEZ, Vicente Rincón see RINCON FERRANDEZ, Vicente

FERRARI, Mary
  "Train Poem." Tele (17) 81, p. 1.

FERREIRA, José Gômes see GOMES FERREIRA, José

FERRY, David
  "A Tomb at Tarquinia." NewRep (184:4) 24 Ja 81, p. 28.

FERSCH, Peter Paul
  "Hidden Behind Flowers." Mund (12/13) 80-81, p. 123.
  "Winterscape" (tr. by Derek Wynand). Mund (12/13) 80-81, p. 123.

FERSTER, Judith
  "Java." GeoR (35:1) Spr 81, p. 77.

FEWELL, Carol
  "People of the Sea, Tierra del Fuego." Prima (6/7) 81, p. 18.

FIALKOWSKI, Barbara
  "My Brother" (for Tony). WindO (38) Spr-Sum 81, p. 20.

FICKERT, Kurt J.
  "Foolish Consistency." Wind (11:40) 81, p. 8.
  "Visitation Hour." Wind (11:40) 81, pp. 8-9.

FIELDER, William A.
  "This Beautiful Weather" (tr. of Orhan Veli, w/ Ozcan Yalim and Dionis
    Coffin Riggs). StoneC (8: 3) Spr 81, p. 31.
  "Those Trees" (tr. of Melih Cevdet Anday, w/ Ozcan Yalim and Dionis
    Coffin Riggs). StoneC (8: 3) Spr 81, p. 31.
  "Swallows" (tr. of Oktay Rifat, w/ Ozcan Rifat and Dionis Coffin Riggs).
    StoneC (8: 3) Spr 81, p. 30.
  "Umbrella" (tr. of Oktay Rifat, w/ Ozcan Rifat and Dionis Coffin Riggs).
    StoneC (8: 3) Spr 81, p. 30.

FIFER, Elizabeth
  "Dancers: The Greek Islands." NewL (48:1) Aut 81, pp. 52-53.

FIFER, Ken
  "Cronology." CharR (7:1) Spr 81, pp. 17-18.
  "Locomotive." PoNow (6:1 issue 31) 81, p. 33.

FIGMAN, Elliot
  "Giving In." Confr (22) Sum 81, p. 95.

FINALE, Frank
  "Exorcism." Wind (11:41) 81, p. 15.

FINCH, Casey
  "Elegy" (for Bonnie Taylor). PoNow (6:3 issue 33) 81, p. 11.

FINCH, Roger
  "A Fish Print." BelPoJ (31:4) Sum 81, p. 25.
  "Hualross." MichQR (20:3) Sum 81, p. 240.
  "Ringing the Well." WebR (6:2) 81, pp. 50-51.
  "The Time Came When There Was a Birthday." CreamCR (6:2) 81, p.
    127.

FINCKE, Gary
  "At the Nursing Home the Former Novelist Writes Again." WebR (6:2)
    81, p. 73.
  "Before Sleep." OntR (14) Spr-Sum 81, p. 61.
  "Chamberlain." SouthernPR (21: 1) Spr 81, p. 16.
  "Home Run." PoNow (6:2 issue 32) 81, p. 17.
  "Humid Poem." OntR (14) Spr-Sum 81, p. 63.
  "The Imaginary Fear." ArizQ (37:1) Spr 81, p. 58.

"Mothman." PoNow (6:1 issue 31) 81, p. 15.
"The Owner of Regret." WebR (6:2) 81, p. 74.
"Place of Places." PoNow (6:1 issue 31) 81, p. 15.
"Tennis Lesson." EnPas (12), 81, p. 32.
"The Theater With No Seats Together." WebR (6:2) 81, p. 73.
"Thirty-five." OntR (14) Spr-Sum 81, p. 62.
"Weeding by Hand." OntR (14) Spr-Sum 81, p. 64.

FINE, Warren
    "Diabetic." Peb (21) 81, pp. 27-30.

FINK, Robert A.
    "The Warning." SouthwR (66:1) Wint 81, pp. 39-40.

FINKEL, Donald
    "Simeon." SenR (11:2) 81, pp. 35-59.

FINKELSTEIN, Caroline
    "Seeing the Light." Poetry (138:2) My 81, p. 89.
    "Stories of Houses." Poetry (138:2) My 81, p. 90.

FINLEY, C. Stephen
    "Journey." CarolQ (33:1) Wint 81, p. 49.
    "South of Galveston" (for Gordon). HiramPoR (30) Spr-Sum 81, p. 17.

FINLEY, Michael
    "Beer Joint." KanQ (13:1) Wint 81, p. 91.

FINLEY, Mike
    "How Old Man Stone Entered Into Heaven." PoNow (6:2 issue 32) 81,
        p. 38.

FINNEL, Dennis
    "Saturday Night." CharR (7:1) Spr 81, p. 11.

FISCHLEIN, Linda Synovec
    "Grandparents." Wind (11:41) 81, p. 10.

FISET, Joan
    "Opposed to Darkness." PoetryNW (22:2) Sum 81, pp. 22-23.

FISHER, Allen
    "The artist's third monologue." Sulfur (3) 82, pp. 9-14.

FISHER, David
    "Death of Rimbaud." Kayak (57) 81, p. 13.

FISHER, Gordon
    "Alphabituary." HiramPoR (30) Spr-Sum 81, p. 18.
    "Letter Fragment [World War II]." PoNow (6:3 issue 33) 81, p. 11.
    "War Story." PoNow (6:3 issue 33) 81, p. 11.

FISHER, Nancy M.
    "First Raking." Wind (10:39) 80, p. 19.
    "Lighting the Fire." Wind (10:39) 80, p. 19.

FISHER, Sally
    "Annunciation Ghazal." Field (25) Aut 81, p. 45.

FISHMAN, Charles
    "The Image." PoNow (6:2 issue 32) 81, p. 15.
    "War Babies." NewEngR (4:1) Aut 81, p. 92.

FITZGERALD, C. M.
    "Duo Diablo." Peb (21) 81, p. 51.

FITZGERALD, Robert
    "The westering moon has gone" (tr. of Sappho).   SenR (12:1/2) 81, p. 3.

FITZPATRICK, Jean A.
    "In the Window." HiramPoR (30) Spr-Sum 81, p. 19.

FITZSIMMONS, Thomas
    "Howrah Sta. (Calcutta)." PortR (27: 2) 81, p. 88.
    "T." PortR (27: 2) 81, p. 73.
    "Talk talk." PortR (27: 2) 81, p. 73.

FIXEL, Lawrence
    "The Leopards/The Temple" (1-5). PoNow (6:1 issue 31) 81, p. 14.

FLAMM, Matthew
    "Weekday." PoetryE (6) Aut 81, p. 55.

FLANDERS, Jane
    "Peacetime." Wind (11:41) 81, pp. 16-17.
    "The Portrait." MassR (22:2) Sum 81, p. 334.
    "Snowbirds." NewEngR (4:1) Aut 81, pp. 34-5.

FLAVIN, Jack
    "After the Ice Storm." MidwQ (22:2) Wint 81, p. 135.
    "An Interview With The Oracle." MassR (22:4) Wint 81, p. 660.
    "Easter." MidwQ (22:3) Spr 81, p. 262.
    "Out of This." MidwQ (22:3) Spr 81, p. 261.
    "Two Poems from the Greek Anthology." MidwQ (22:3) Spr 81, p. 263.

FLEISHER, Bernice
    "Bosc Pear." Vis (7) 81, n. p.

FLEMING, Gerald
    "On the Photograph 'A Jewish Giant at Home with His Parents in the
        Bronx, New York' by Diane Arbus." PoNow (6:3 issue 33) 81, p.
        12.

FLEMING, Harold
    "Lights of Ben Franklin." ConcPo (14:1) Spr 81, p. 28.
    "Nothing's Alone." Wind (11:42) 81, p. 24.
    "Oxfordshire Spring." KanQ (13:3/4) Sum-Aut 81, p. 92.
    "So On And On And On." StoneC (8: 3) Spr 81, p. 37.
    "These Young Trees." StoneC (8: 3) Spr 81, p. 36.

FLEMMING, Susan
    "Marsh Song." PottPort (3) 81, p. 27.

FLEU, Richard
    "The Karnak Stele." StoneC (9: 1-2) Aut-Wint 81/82, p. 38.

FLINT, Aili
    "Birth and Death" (tr. of Veijo Meri, w/ Austin Flint). PoetryE (6)

Aut 81, p. 32.

"Blue Eve" (tr. of Arto Melleri, w/ Austin Flint). PoetryE (6) Aut 81,
p. 28.

"Epitaph" (tr. of Arto Melleri, w/ Austin Flint). PoetryE (6) Aut 81,
p. 29.

"Mother Tongues" (tr. of Kirsti Simonsuuri, w/ Austin Flint).
PoetryE (6) Aut 81, p. 6.

"On the Contrary" (tr. of Veijo Meri, w/ Austin Flint). PoetryE (6)
Aut 81, p. 33.

"Storm" (tr. of Veijo Meri, w/ Austin Flint). PoetryE (6) Aut 81, p.
33.

"The Word" (tr. of Arto Melleri, w/ Austin Flint). PoetryE (6) Aut
81, pp. 30-31.

FLINT, Austin

"Birth and Death" (tr. of Veijo Meri, w/ Aili Flint). PoetryE (6) Aut
81, p. 32.

"Blue Eve" (tr. of Arto Melleri, w/ Aili Flint). PoetryE (6) Aut 81,
p. 28.

"Epitaph" (tr. of Arto Melleri, w/ Aili Flint). PoetryE (6) Aut 81, p.
29.

"Mother Tongues" (tr. of Kirsti Simonsuuri, w/ Aili Flint). PoetryE
(6) Aut 81, p. 6.

"On the Contrary" (tr. of Veijo Meri, w/ Aili Flint). PoetryE (6) Aut
81, p. 33.

"Pyres" (tr. of Arto Melleri, w/ Sanna Tolsa). PoetryE (6) Aut 81,
pp. 29-30.

"Storm" (tr. of Veijo Meri, w/ Aili Flint). PoetryE (6) Aut 81, p. 33.

"Wolfang Lefevre" (tr. of Julian Kornhauser, w/ Grazyna Drabik).
PoNow (5:6 issue 30) 81, p. 22.

"The Word" (tr. of Arto Melleri, w/ Aili Flint). PoetryE (6) Aut 81,
pp. 30-31.

FLOOD, Jean Garis
"Trauma." ChrC (98:37) 18 N 81, p. 1181.

FLOOK, Maria

"The Childlike Lives of the Sweep Second Hand and the Single Mother."
Agni (14) 81, p. 59.

"The Late-Shift Comptroller." Poetry (138:2) My 81, pp. 98-99.

"Missing from Home." Iowa (11:4) Aut 80, pp. 69-70.

"Strangers: Many Perfect Examples." Poetry (138:2) My 81, pp. 96-
97.

FLORENTINO NUÑEZ, Oscar

"Datos de curriculum." Mairena (3:7) 81, pp. 93-94.

"El poema olvidado." Mairena (3:7) 81, p. 95.

"Qué es felicidad." Mairena (3:7) 81, pp. 94-95.

FLYNN, Gale
"Co-Workers." EnPas (12) 81, p. 20.

FOE, Mark De see DeFOE, Mark

FOLEY, M. J.
"Rabbit." FourQt (30:2) Wint 81, p. 22.

FOLLAIN, Jean
"Basically" (tr. by Heather McHugh). NewYorker (57:7) 6 Ap 81, p.

123.
"Event" (tr. by Heather McHugh). NewYorker (57:7) 6 Ap 81, p. 123.
"Faces" (tr. by Heather McHugh). NewYorker (57:7) 6 Ap 81, p. 123.

FONTENOT, Ken
"Hoping to Make No More Mistakes." WebR (6:2) 81, pp. 76-77.
"To Lorraine." WebR (6:2) 81, pp. 75-76.

FORCHE, Carolyn
"Ourselves Or Nothing" (for T. D. P.). AmerPoR (10:4) Jl-Ag 81, p.
    7-8.

FORD, R. A. D.
"The English Cemetery, Bogota." MalR (58) Ap 81, p. 125.

FOREST, Mark
"The Two Poets." PortR (27: 2) 81, p. 79.

FORESTA, De
"Corner of Cedar and N. 2nd." Im (7:3) 81, p. 3.

FORSSTROM, Tua
"Gallup." SenR (12:1/2) 81, pp. 204-206.
"Gallup" (tr. by Lennart Bruce). SenR (12:1/2) 81, p. 205-207.
"Vi lever som påbörjade ord." SenR (12:1/2) 81, p. 202.
"We live like words just begun" (tr. by Lennart Bruce). SenR (12:1/2)
    81, p. 203.
"Ett långt farväl, som att." SenR (12:1/2) 81, p. 200.
"A long farewell, like looking" (tr. by Lennart Bruce). SenR (12:1/2)
    81, p. 201.

FOSTER, Don
"And then there is preparation." Aspect (77/79) 81, p. 67.

FOSTER, Ruel
"Palm Sunday and the Drunken Poet." KanQ (13:3/4) Sum-Aut 81, pp.
    49-50.

FOURTOUNI, Eleni
"The Return." EnPas (12) 81, p. 11.
"Taygetos." EnPas (12) 81, p. 10.

FOWLIE, Wallace
"Earth Writes the Earth (Poems for a painter)" (tr. of Alain Bosquet).
    Mund (12/13) 80-81, pp. 385-388.

FOX, Connie
Blood Cocoon. Zahir (11) 80, Entire issue.

FOX, Janet
"Notes on The Man Who Fell to Earth." PortR (27: 2) 81, p. 62.

FOX, Lucia Ungaro de see UNGARO de FOX, Lucia

FOX, Robert
"Dinner at a Chain Steakhouse." PoNow (6:3 issue 33) 81, p. 12.

FOX, Susan
"Rotfoot Runs the Subways" (for Kay). PoNow (6:3 issue 33) 81, p. 12.

FOX, William L.
"California Gold Miner, circa 1975, 'leaving the mine.'" Meadows
(2:1) 81, pp. 21-3.

FRAIRE, Isabel
"a moment in an eighteenth-century day immobilized by a Japanese
painter" (tr. by Anthony Edkins). Chelsea (40) 81, p. 86.
"Noon" (tr. by Thomas Hoeksema). Mund (12/13) 80-81, p. 91.
"Ontology, Epistemology, Literature... (for Juan García Ponce)" (tr.
by Thomas Hoeksema). NewOR (8:1) Wint 81, p. 59.

FRANCE, Peter
"The Old Park" (tr. of Boris Pasternak, w/ Jon Stallworthy). Hudson
(34:4) Wint 81, pp. 550-551.
"Winter approaches" (tr. of Boris Pasternak, w/ Jon Stallworthy).
Hudson (34:4) Wint 81, p. 549.

FRANCIS, Pat Therese
"The Garden." CapeR (17:1) Wint 81, p. 14.
"Husband." ColEng (43:8) D 81, pp. 790-791.
"Thunder." Prima (6/7) 81, p. 77.

FRANCIS, Robert
"Bravura." Field (25) Aut 81, pp. 31-32.
"Excellence." Field (25) Aut 81, p. 15.
"Bluejay." Field (25) Aut 81, p. 8.
"His Running My Running." Field (25) Aut 81, p. 12.
"If Heaven at All." Field (25) Aut 81, p. 34.
"Manifesto of the Simple." Field (25) Aut 81, p. 35.
"The Mockery of Great Music." Field (25) Aut 81, p. 33.
"Remind Me of Apples." Field (25) Aut 81, p. 27.
"Sheep." Field (25) Aut 81, p. 23.
"Silent Poem." Field (25) Aut 81, p. 19.

FRANCO OPPENHEIMER, Félix
"Cantador en timbre vario." Mairena (2:6), p. 36.

FRANGOPOULOS, T. D.
"Death of the Solitary Man" (tr. by Kimon Friar). Poetry (139:2) N 81,
pp. 90-91.

FRANK, Bernhard
"And That's How He Knew Your Face" (for the poet Yokheved Bat-
Miriam) (tr. of Abba Kovner). PoNow (5:6 issue 30) 81, p. 27.
"The Angels" (tr. of Rainer Maria Rilke). WebR (6:2) 81, p. 28.
"At the Wind's Mercy" (tr. of Abba Kovner). PoNow (5:6 issue 30) 81,
p. 27.
"A Bird Beloved and Strange" (tr. of Eli Netser). PoNow (5:6 issue
30) 81, p. 33.
"Days" (tr. of Yekhi'el Mar). PoNow (5:6 issue 30) 81, p. 29.
"Fall" (tr. of M. Winkler). PoNow (5:6 issue 30) 81, p. 47.
"The Flamingos" (tr. of Rainer Maria Rilke). WebR (6:2) 81, p. 28.
"The Gazelle" (tr. of Gazella Dorcas). WebR (6:2) 81, p. 29.
"I Don't Know Whether Mt. Zion" (tr. of Abba Kovner). PoNow (5:6
issue 30) 81, p. 27.
"My Child" (tr. of Rinah Shney). PoNow (5:6 issue 30) 81, p. 42.
"Near Morning" (tr. of Me'ir Wieseltier). PoNow (5:6 issue 30) 81, p.
47.

131   FRATE

"Observation of a Young Man Running Across the Street After Parking
   Jeep in a No-Parking Zone" (tr. of Abba Kovner). PoNow (5:6 issue
   30) 81, p. 27.
"Observation on the Sea's Edge at Natanya, with Flashback" (tr. of Abba
   Kovner). PoNow (5:6 issue 30) 81, p. 27.
"'Our Piss,' She Said" (tr. of Me'ir Wieseltier). PoNow (5:6 issue 30)
   81, p. 47.
"The Panther" (tr. of Rainer Maria Rilke). WebR (6:2) 81, p. 29.
"Père David's Deer." HiramPoR (29) Aut-Wint 81, p. 20.
"Sadness Pursues Me" (tr. of Me'ir Wieseltier). PoNow (5:6 issue 30)
   81, p. 47.
"The Toads" (for Leah Goldberg) (tr. of Daliah Rabikovich). PoNow
   (5:6 issue 30) 81, p. 40.
two garden poems: "Giants" (tr. of Daliah Rabikovich). PoNow (5:6
   issue 30) 81, p. 40.
two garden poems: "They All Grow" (tr. of Daliah Rabikovich).
   PoNow (5:6 issue 30) 81, p. 40.
"You Wove Me A Long Blanket" (tr. of Moseh Ben-Sha'ul). PoNow
   (5:6 issue 30) 81, p. 7.
"Your white breasts" (tr. of M. Winkler). PoNow (5:6 issue 30) 81, p.
   47.

FRATE, Frank
   Investigations. Sam (107) 81, Entire issue.
   Investigations Two. Sam (119) 81, Entire issue.

FRAZEE, C. Mann
   "Kate at Forty." Wind (11:42) 81, p. 39.

FRAZEE, James
   "Becoming a Son." PoNow (6:3 issue 33) 81, p. 12.
   "Boccaccio's Garden." NoAmR (266:3) S 81, p. 75.
   "The House Where Stevens Died." VirQR (57:4) Aut 81, pp. 642-643.
   "Night Harvest." SouthernPR (21: 1) Spr 81, pp. 10-11.
   "Thug." VirQR (57:4) Aut 81, pp. 641-642.
   "When I Walked in Alicante." SouthernPR (21: 1) Spr 81, p. 9.

FRAZIER, Robert
   "Nightwalk." PortR (27: 1) 81, p. 36.
   "The Starfarers" (1-4) (w/ Gene Van Troyer). PortR (27: 2) 81, pp.
   70-72.

FRAZIER, Tom
   "The Timeless Revel." Wind (10:39) 80, p. 20.

FREEMAN, William T.
   Ten poems. Obs (6:1/2) Spr-Sum 80, pp. 156-165.

FREES, Madeline De see DeFREES, Madeline

FRENCH, Donna
   "We are Naked." AntR (39: 1) Wint 81, p. 67.
   "My Boyhood." AntR (39:1) Wint 81, p. 68.

FRESE, Marcos Rodríguez see RODRIGUEZ FRESE, Marcos

FREYTAG-LORINGHOVEN, Elsa von
   "Perspective." SunM (11) Spr 81, p. 75.

FRIAR, Kimon
"Ablutions" (tr. of Yannis Ritsos). PoNow (6:2 issue 32) 81, p. 40.
"After a Settlement of Debts" (tr. of Yannis Ritsos, w/ Kostas Myrsiades). PoNow (5:6 issue 30) 81, p. 24.
"Announcement" (tr. of Yannis Ritsos, w/ Kostas Myrsiades). Hudson (34:2) Sum 81, p. 171.
"Cartoon Classics" (tr. of Jenny Mastoraki). PoNow (5:6 issue 30) 81, p. 30.
"Crane and Vulture" (tr. of Nikos Phocas). PoNow (5:6 issue 30) 81, p. 37.
"Danger Outstripped" (tr. of Yannis Ritsos). Mund (12/13) 80-81, p. 356.
"The Dark Shop" (tr. of Yannis Ritsos, w/ Kostas Myrsiades). PoNow (5:6 issue 30) 81, p. 24.
"Dilettantism" (tr. of Yannis Ritsos, with Kostas Myrsiades). Ploughs (6:4) 81, pp. 198-199.
"Entrails and the Rest" (tr. of Katerina Angelaki-Rooke). PoNow (5:6 issue 30) 81, p. 4.
"The Episodes" (tr. of Jenny Mastoraki). PoNow (5:6 issue 30) 81, p. 30.
"The Excursion" (tr. of Yánnis Kondós). PoNow (5:6 issue 30) 81, p. 22.
"False Discoveries" (tr. of Yannis Ritsos w/ Kostas Myrsiades). ArizQ (37:3) Aut 81, p. 244.
"The Get-Away" (tr. of Yannis Ritsos, w/ Kostas Myrsiades). PoNow (5:6 issue 30) 81, p. 24.
"Graduate Excercises" (tr. of Jenny Mastoraki). PoNow (5:6 issue 30) 81, p. 30.
"The Hill" (tr. of Yannis Ritsos). PoNow (6:2 issue 32) 81, p. 40.
"I Can Still Talk with You" (tr. of Yannis Patilis). PoNow (5:6 issue 30) 81, p. 33.
"Improvised Achievement" (tr. of Yannis Ritsos, with Kostas Myrsiades). Ploughs (6:4) 81, p. 199.
"The Iron Mosaic" (tr. of Yannis Ritsos, with Kostas Myrsiades). Ploughs (6:4) 81, p. 196.
"Level Duration" (tr. of Yannis Ritsos, w/ Kostas Myrsiades). Hudson (34:2) Sum 81, p. 169.
"Life Traces" (tr. of Yannis Patilis). PoNow (5:6 issue 30) 81, p. 33.
"Like Travelers" (tr. of Yannis Ritsos, w/ Kostas Myrsiades). Hudson (34:2) Sum 81, p. 170.
"The Mirror" (tr. of Lefteris Paulios). PoNow (5:6 issue 30) 81, p. 39.
"My Feet" (tr. of Katerina Angelaki-Rooke). PoNow (5:6 issue 30) 81, p. 4.
"Perpetual" (tr. of Yannis Ritsos, w/ Kostas Myrsiades). Hudson (34:2) Sum 81, p. 169.
"A Poet" (tr. of Lefteris Paulios). PoNow (5:6 issue 30) 81, p. 39.
"Remembrances" (tr. of Yannis Ritsos, w/ Kostas Myrsiades). Hudson (34:2) Sum 81, p. 172.
"The Roots" (tr. of Yannis Ritsos, w/ Kostas Myrsiades). Hudson (34:2) Sum 81, pp. 170-171.
"The Scarecrow" (tr. of Yannis Ritsos, with Kostas Myrsiades). Ploughs (6:4) 81, p. 197.
"Seven Days for Eternity" (tr. of Odysseus Elytis). Mund (12/13) 80-81, p. 269.
"Sleep of the Valiant" (tr. of Odysseus Elýtis). Mund (12/13) 80-81, pp. 268-269.
"The Sower of the Year" (tr. of Lefteris Paulios). PoNow (5:6 issue

30) 81, p. 39.

"There's Oil Somewhere" (tr. of Yánnis Kondŏs). PoNow (5:6 issue 30) 81, p. 22.

"Timetable for Fairview" (tr. of Nikos Phocas). PoNow (5:6 issue 30) 81, p. 37.

"Traces" (tr. of Yannis Ritsos, w/ Kostas Myrsiades). Hudson (34:2) Sum 81, p. 172.

"The Transistor's Loneliness" (tr. of Yánnis Kondŏs). PoNow (5:6 issue 30) 81, p. 22.

Twenty Translations of Greek Poets. Poetry (139:2) N 81, pp. 76-98.

"Voyaging at Night" (tr. of Katerina Angelaki-Rooke). PoNow (5:6 issue 30) 81, p. 4.

"Waiting Room" (tr. of Takis Sinopoulos). Mund (12/13) 80-81, pp. 254-255.

"Winter Approaches" (tr. of Yannis Ritsos). PoNow (6:2 issue 32) 81, p. 40.

FRIEBERT, Stuart

"Forever" (tr. of Karl Krolow). PoNow (6:1 issue 31) 81, p. 42.

"Like a Man." CentR (25:3) Sum 81, pp. 262-263.

"Little Comedy" (tr. of Giovanni Raboni, w/ Vinio Rossi). Field (24) Spr 81, p. 11.

"Magdalen's Fears" (tr. of Giovanni Raboni, w/ Vinio Rossi). Field (24) Spr 81, p. 12.

"Mr. Cogito on Virtue" (tr. of Herbert Zbigniew). PoNow (5:6 issue 30) 81, p. 17.

"Old View" (tr. of Ilse Aichinger). Field (25) Aut 81, p. 65.

"On Smoking Things Out" (tr. of Herbert Zbigniew). PoNow (5:6 issue 30) 81, p. 17.

"On the Death of a Younger Brother." CimR (54) Ja 81, p. 62.

"Subtracted" (tr. of Ilse Aichinger). Field (25) Aut 81, p. 64.

"Teeth" (tr. of Miroslav Holub, w/ Miroslav Holub). Field (24) Spr 81, p. 41.

"This and That" (tr. of Karl Krolow). PoNow (6:1 issue 31) 81, p. 42.

"This Is the Catalogue" (tr. of Giovanni Raboni, w/ Vinio Rossi). Field (24) Spr 81, p. 10.

"Timely Advice" (tr. of Ilse Aichinger). Field (25) Aut 81, p. 63.

"Zurich." MissouriR (4:2) Wint 81-82, p. 26.

FRIED, Erich

"Speechless" (tr. by Herbert Kuhner). Mund (11:2) 79, p. 79.

"Sprachlos." Mund (11:2) 79, p. 78.

FRIEDMAN, Racelle

"She pulls down her pants." Ploughs (7:1) 81, p. 151.

FRITSCH, Janice

"Perception of the Right Line" (tr. of Robert Benajoun, w/ Elton Glaser). ChiR (32:2) Aut 80, p. 29.

"Ravishing" (tr. of Robert Benajoun, w/ Elton Glaser). ChiR (32:2) Aut 80, p. 28.

"Times Square" (tr. of Lorand Gaspar, with Elton Glaser). CharR (7:1) Spr 81, p. 53.

FROST, Carol

"The Beautiful islands." PraS (55:3) Aut 81, p. 35.

"The Fearful Child." VirQR (57:4) Aut 81, pp. 631-632.

"Hands." PoNow (6:2 issue 32) 81, p. 42.

"The Light Asks." PraS (55:3) Aut 81, p. 36-7.
"Packing Mother's Things." NewEngR (3:4) Sum 81, p. 579.
"Rain." PoNow (6:2 issue 32) 81, p. 42.
"She." NewL (47:4) Sum 81, p. 62.

FROST, Kenneth
"The Telephone." Wind (10:39) 80, pp. 21-22.

FROST, Richard
"Line of Sight." Shen (31:4) 80, p. 32.

FRUMKIN, Gene
"Another Life." SoDakR (19:3) Aut 81, p. 93.
"Badlands." SoDakR (19:3) Aut 81, p. 92.
"Reaching." SoDakR (19:3) Aut 81, p. 94.
"A Uniform Solution." Kayak (56) 81, p. 51.

FUCHS, Jurgen
"Always I See You in Prison" (tr. by Wayne Kvam). CentR (25:4) Aut
    81, pp. 381-382.
"The Bad Part" (tr. by Wayne Kvam). CentR (25:4) Aut 81, p. 382.
"Maybe" (tr. by Wayne Kvam). CentR (25:4) Aut 81, p. 381.

FUERTES, Gloria
"The Final Visit" (tr. by Dorothy Scott Loos). PoNow (5:6 issue 30)
    81, p. 16.
"The Rag Vendor--Or The Luckless Poet" (tr. by Dorothy Scott Loos).
    PoNow (5:6 issue 30) 81, p. 16.
"To a Dead Raccoon on the Highway" (tr. by Dorothy Scott Loos).
    PoNow (5:6 issue 30) 81, p. 16.

FULLEN, George
"The Agnostic." Wind (10:39) 80, p. 6.

FULTON, Alice
"My Diamond Stud." BelPoJ (31:4) Sum 81, p. 7.

FULTON, Robin
"Answers to Letters" (tr. of Tomas Tranströmer). Pequod (13) 81, p.
    107.
"Brief Pause in the Organ Recital" (tr. of Tomas Tranströmer).
    Pequod (13) 81, pp. 108-09.
"The Cave" (tr. of Werner Aspenström). Mund (12/13) 80-81, p. 354.
"Clearness" (tr. of Göran Sonnevi). Mund (12/13) 80-81, p. 107.
"Cloth" (tr. of Bartolo Cattafi, w/ Brian Swann). Mund (12/13) 80-81,
    p. 346.
"Ground" (tr. of Göran Sonnevi). Mund (12/13) 80-81, p. 107.
"The Larks" (tr. of Werner Aspenström). Pequod (13) 81, p. 103.
"I Pass the Arctic Circle" (tr. of Olav Hauge). Pequod (13) 81, p. 111.
"In the Pizzeria" (tr. of Werner Aspenström). Pequod (13) 81, p. 102.
"Like A Blade" (tr. of Bartolo Cattafi, w/ Brian Swann). Mund (12/13)
    80-81, p. 346.
"Mountains No Longer Entice Me" (tr. of Olav Hauge). Pequod (13) 81,
    p. 112.
from Starnberger See: "Black Square White Square Black" (tr. of
    Gunnar Harding). Pequod (13) 81, pp. 105-106.
"This Year Too" (tr. of Werner Aspenström). Pequod (13) 81, p. 104.
"Winter's Gaze" (tr. of Tomas Tranströmer). Pequod (13) 81, p. 110.

FUMIO, Uda
"Fireplace." PortR (27: 1) 81, p. 38.

FUNKHOUSER, Erica
"Three Feathers." Tendril (10) Wint 81, p. 28.
"Three Postcards And A Seed." Ploughs (7:1) 81, pp. 91-92.
"The Women Who Clean Fish." Ploughs (7:1) 81, p. 93.

FUSSENEGGER, Gertrud
"The Word--This Boat" (tr. by Herbert Kuhner). Mund (11:2) 79, p.
    81.
"Das Wort--Den Kahn." Mund (11:2) 79, p. 80.

GACH, Gary
"The Difference." Tele (17) 81, p. 48.

GAIK, Frank
"Boat." CreamCR (6:2) 81, p. 54.
"My Father Sits on the Toilet Again." HolCrit (18:3 [i. e. 4]) O 81, p.
    16.

GALASSI, Jonathan
"Elms" (to a teacher). ParisR (23:80) Sum 81, p. 84.
"The Intellectual" (tr. of Eugenio Montale). Antaeus (43) Aut 81, pp.
    130-132.

GALE, Susan
"Staying Faithful." Sam (106) 81, p. 60.

GALIANO, Alina
"Casi por Convicción." Lugar (1:1) 79, p. 8.
"Diálogo." Lugar (1:1) 79, p. 8.
"Pronóstico." Lugar (1:1) 79, p. 9.

GALLAGHER, Tess
"The Calm." OP (31/32) Aut 81, p. 100.
"Crepes Flambeau." OP (31/32) Aut 81, pp. 153-154.
"Skin Graft." Mund (12/13) 80-81, p. 330.

GALLEGO, Laura
"Como volar palomas." Mairena (2:6), p. 37.

GALLER, David
"L'Inconnu." Confr (22) Sum 81, p. 25.

GALT, Tom
"Leaping the Gap." Poem (42) Jul 81, p. 5.
"Noise." Poem (42) Jul 81, p. 8.
"Returning." Poem (42) Jul 81, p. 7.
"A Pretty Face." Poem (42) Jul 81, p. 6.

GALVIN, Brendan
"August." Ascent (6:2) 81, pp. 31-33.
"Explaining a Fiend to My Daughter." PoetryNW (22:1) Spr 81, pp. 5-6.
"Horse Killer's Daughter." Tendril (11) Sum 81, p. 30.
"The Last Open Air Concert." NewEngR (4:2) Wint 81, pp. 217-18.
"Listening By a Woodpile, Night of Moon After Snow." NewYorker (57:
    5) 23 Mr 81, p. 36.

"Lost Countrymen." SewanR (89:2) Ap-Je 81, p. 182.
"Lying to Fall Warblers." NewEngR (4:2) Wint 81, pp. 215-16.
"Marsh." PoetryNW (22:1) Spr 81, pp. 3-4.
"Nose." NewRep (184:3) 17 Ja 81, p. 24.
"The Renting Coloratura." PoetryNW (22:1) Spr 81, pp. 4-5.
"Winter Oysters." ThRiPo (17/18) 81, p. 18.

GALVIN, James
    "Drift Fence." NewYorker (57:6) 30 Mr 81, p. 107.
    "Explication of an Imaginary Text." NewEngR (4:1) Aut 81, p. 79.
    "The Last Man's Club." Antaeus (40/41) Wint-Spr 81, pp. 290-291.
    "Rainshadow." PoNow (6:3 issue 33) 81, p. 23.
    "Sara" (-SDL, 1922-57). QW (12) Spr-Sum 81, p. 56.
    "Scrimshaw." QW (12) Spr-Sum 81, p. 57.
    "The Stone's Throw." PoNow (6:3 issue 33) 81, p. 23.
    "Water Table." AntR (39:3) Sum 81, pp. 333-335.

GALVIN, Martin
    "For taking Leave." Wind (11:41) 81, p. 18.
    "Georges Bank." Poem (41) Mar 81, p. 61.
    "Job Transfer." Poem (41) Mar 81, p. 60.

GARCIA, Adolfo
    "A Yoruba." Claridad (22: 1467) 13-19 Mr 81, p. 13.
    "A Yoruba." Claridad/En Rojo (22: 1471) 10-16 Ap 81, p. 5.
    "Al emplazado" (a mi cuñado Norberto Cruz). Claridad (22: 1467) 13-
        19 Mr 81, p. 12.
    "Al emplazado" (a mi cuñado Norberto Cruz). Claridad/En Rojo (22:
        1471) 10-16 Ap 81, p. 5.
    "Ausencia." Claridad (22: 1467) 13-19 Mr 81, p. 12.
    "Ausencia." Claridad/En Rojo (22: 1471) 10-16 Ap 81, p. 4.
    "Memorias de un viaje." Claridad/En Rojo (22: 1471) 10-16 Ap 81, p.
        5.
    "Para tu viaje al agua." Claridad/En Rojo (22: 1471) 10-16 Ap 81, p.
        4.
    "Pensando en tu voz." Claridad/En Rojo (22: 1471) 10-16 Ap 81, p. 4.
    "Rostro que tuvo que perderse." Claridad (22: 1467) 13-19 Mr 81, p.
        12.
    "Rostro que tuvo que perderse." Claridad/En Rojo (22: 1471) 10-16 Ap
        81, p. 5.
    "6 de noviembre en Nueva York." Claridad/En Rojo (22: 1471) 10-16
        Ap 81, p. 5.

GARCIA LORCA, Federico
    "Blackberry Bush" (tr. by Paul Blackburn). PoNow (5:6 issue 30) 81,
        p. 23.
    "Death" (for Isidoro de Blas) (tr. by Walt Curtis). PortR (27: 2) 81,
        p. 42.
    "The Four Muleteers" (tr. by Paul Blackburn). PoNow (5:6 issue 30)
        81, p. 23.
    "Kings in the Deck" (tr. by Paul Blackburn). PoNow (5:6 issue 30) 81,
        p. 23.
    "Preguntas." SenR (12:1/2) 81, p. 94.
    "Questions" (tr. by Burton Raffel). SenR (12:1/2) 81, p. 95.
    "Romance of the Black Pain" (tr. by Walt Curtis). PortR (27: 2) 81,
        p. 42.
    "Saint Gabriel" (tr. by Walt Curtis). PortR (27: 2) 81, p. 42.
    "Sevilla Slumber Song" (tr by Paul Blackburn). PoNow (5:6 issue 30)
        81, p. 23.

GARCIA MARRUZ, Fina
  "En la muerte de una heroína de la Patria." Areito (7: 27) 81, p.
    frontcover.

GARCIA ORTEGA, Adolfo
  "En defensa propia." Mairena (3:7), p. 48.
  "Hermetismo del ropaje." Mairena (3:7), p. 48.
  "Hundimiento al sueño." Mairena (3:7), p. 47.
  "Tabulario XII." Mairena (3:7), p. 47.

GARCIA RAMOS, Reinaldo
  "Como un romántico" (para G. O.). Notarte (6:11) N 81, p. 13.
  "La mejor travesía." Notarte (6:11) N 81, p. 13.

GARCIA-RODRIGUEZ, José María
  "Soneto de la libelula elusiva y deleitosa." Mairena (3:7), p. 92.
  "Soneto del pajarillo enamorado." Mairena (3:7), p. 91.
  "Soneto de la sensualidad o de las uñas carniceras." Mairena (3:7), p.
    92.

GARDINER, Elaine
  "Exile" (tr. of Nadia Tuéni). Mund (12/13) 80-81, p. 253.
  "Inventory" (tr. of Nadia Tuéni). Mund (12/13) 80-81, p. 253.

GARDNER, Geoffrey
  "Chacun: Nine Poems from 'Dialogues pour la nuit'" (tr. of Pierre
    Delisle). Bound (9:2) Wint 81, pp. 257-265.

GARDNER, Isabella
  "Eros in May at MacDowell." Confr (21) Wint 81, p. 12.
  "Knowing." UnmOx (22) Wint 81, p. 41.
  "One Sunday in 1966." Confr (21) Wint 81, pp. 11-12.

GARDNER, Stephen
  "2 A. M. , incense, a quart of gin, my dog with a bone" (for Jim Peter-
    son). SouthernR (17:3) Sum 81, p. 579.

GARIOCH, Robert
  "A Rare Fish" (tr. of Giuseppe Belli, w/ Antonia Stott). Stand (22: 4)
    81, p. 4.
  "The Vou" (tr. of Giuseppe Belli, w/ Antonia Stott). Stand (22: 4) 81,
    p. 5.
  "The Wee Thief's Mither" (tr. of Giuseppe Belli, w/ Antonia Stott).
    Stand (22: 4) 81, p. 4.

GARLAND, Max
  "Current Events." PoNow (6:3 issue 33) 81, p. 13.
  "Complaint." PoNow (6:3 issue 33) 81, p. 13.

GARMON, John
  "Deliberate Weddings." SouthernHR (15:2) Spr 81, p. 151.

GARRETT, Charlotte
  "You Used To Pass By." SouthernR (17:2) Spr 81, p. 386.
  "Not To Look Back is the Rule." SouthernR (17:2) Spr 81, pp. 384-5.

GARRISON, Joseph
  "Thieves." PoetryNW (22:1) Spr 81, pp. 33-34.

GARRISON, Peggy
   "Gone." Tele (17) 81, p. 77.
   "Tud." Tele (17) 81, p. 77.

GARSON, Karl
   "Hemlocks." Northeast (3:10) Wint 81, p. 32.

GARTON, Victoria
   "Granfather's Niche." Prima (6/7) 81, p. 79.
   "New Winter Wheat." QW (12) Spr-Sum 81, p. 11.
   "Roofer on the Courthouse Spire." CapeR (17:1) Wint 81, p. 32.
   "We Pick The Bittersweet." CapeR (17:1) Wint 81, p. 31.

GASCOT, Gladys E.
   "Paso a la libertad." Claridad/En Rojo (22: 1504) 27 N-D 3 81, p. 12.

GASPAR, Frank
   "Getting Back." CimR (57) O 81, p. 36.

GASPAR, Lorand
   "Times Square" (tr. by Elton Glaser and Janice Fritsch). CharR (7:1)
      Spr 81, p. 53.

GATENBY, Greg
   "At the Beach" (tr. of Kolyo Sevov, w/ Dobrina Nikolava). PortR (27:
      1) 81, p. 14.
   "Beside Rhodes" (tr. of Kolyo Sevov, w/ Dobrina Nikolava). PortR
      (27: 1) 81, p. 14.
   "The Dolphin" (tr. of Vanja Petkova, w/ Dobrina Nikolava). PortR (27:
      1) 81, p. 14.
   "The Marvellous Mistress." MalR (57) Ja 81, pp. 108-109.

GATEWOOD, Arthur S.
   "On Saplings." ChrC (98:4) 4-11 F 81, p. 102.

GAU, Juh
   "Ching Ming Festival" (tr. by C. H. Kwan). MalR (58) Ap 81, p. 36.

GAUER, Jim
   "This Feeds on the Light." Poetry (138:1) Ap 81, p. 14.
   "How Strange the Words Sound after She's Gone." Iowa (11:4) Aut 80,
      pp. 81-82.
   "Measuring the Distance." Poetry (138:1) Ap 81, p. 13.
   "The Train Problem." Iowa (11:4) Aut 80, pp. 79-80.

GEBHARD, Christine
   "After Wishing Me Luck." OhioR (26), p. 63.

GEHRING, Wes D.
   "A Chaplin Celebration." BallSUF (22:4) Aut 81, p. 46.

GEIER, Joan Austin
   "Lovers in a Row House Landscape." CapeR (16:2) Sum 81, p. 15.

GEIGER, Geoff
   "The Promise." Sam (109) 81, pp. 28-30.

GENEGA, Paul
   "Dear Son." NowestR (19:1/2), pp. 79-81.

"The Life at Miss Edith's." Vis (7) 81, n.p.
"Scavenging." LitR (24:3) Spr 81, pp. 349-350.

GENOVA, Albert De see DeGENOVA, Albert

GENT, Andrew
    "Eighth Elegy" (w/ Bill Evans). HangL (40) Aut 81, pp. 10-12.
    "Sixth Elegy" (w/ Bill Evans). HangL (40) Aut 81, pp. 8-9.

GENTILE DE MORAT, Angela
    "El cambio del ángel." Mairena (3:7), pp. 57-58.
    "Hijo de la pradera." Mairena (3:7), p. 57.
    "Lluviosas lilas de junio." Mairena (3:7), pp. 58-59.
    "Minutos de atardecer." Mairena (3:7), p. 58.

GENTRY, Jane
    "Swallows." Wind (11:41) 81, p. 19.

GEORGE, Alice Rose
    "Correspondence." NewEngR (3:4) Sum 81, pp. 546-7.

GEORGE, Emery
    "Appetite of the Sea" (tr. of Lajos Kassák). PoNow (5:6 issue 30) 81,
        p. 20.
    "Auntie" (tr. of Lajos Kassák). PoNow (5:6 issue 30) 81, p. 20.
    "Chaos of the Night" (tr. of Lajos Kassák). PoNow (5:6 issue 30) 81,
        p. 20.
    "Elysium in November" (tr. of Janos Pilinszky). PoNow (5:6 issue 30)
        81, p. 38.
    "Evening, Woman, Child on Her Back" (for Karoly Hilbert) (tr. of
        Miklós Radnóti). Pequod (12) 81, p. 84.
    "In Venice" (tr. of Gyula Illyés). DenQ (16:1) Spr 81, pp. 75-76.
    "Introit" (tr. of Janos Pilinszky). PoNow (5:6 issue 30) 81, p. 38.
    "Magdalene" (tr. of Agnes Gergely). DenQ (16:1) Spr 81, p. 77.
    "Passion" (tr. of Janos Pilinszky). PoNow (5:6 issue 30) 81, p. 38.
    "Ravensbruck Passion" (tr. of Janos Pilinszky). PoNow (5:6 issue 30)
        81, p. 38.
    "Van Gogh" (tr. of Janos Pilinszky). PoNow (5:6 issue 30) 81, p. 38.
    "Self-Portrait" (tr. of Sandor Weöres). PoNow (5:6 issue 30) 81, p.
        47.
    "Song with Drinks" (tr. of Miklós Radnóti). Pequod (12) 81, p. 85.
    "Variations on Luck" (tr. of Lajos Kassák). PoNow (5:6 issue 30) 81,
        p. 20.

GEORGE, Stefan
    "Anniversary" (tr. by Peter Viereck). PoNow (5:6 issue 30) 81,
        p. 16.
    "Guardianship" (tr. by Peter Viereck). PoNow (5:6 issue 30) 81,
        p. 16.

GERARD, Jim
    "The Spelunkers." Wind (11:41) 81, p. 15.

GERBER, Dan
    "First Love." PoNow (6:2 issue 32) 81, p. 32.

GERGELY, Agnes
    "Magdalene" (tr. by Emery George). DenQ (16:1) Spr 81, p. 77.

GERITZ, Micka Lynn
"Metamorphosis." CalQ (18/19) 81, pp. 123-124.
"Young Girl Entering a Boat." CalQ (18/19) 81, pp. 124-125.

GERNES, Sonia
"The Deaf Girl's Love Child." PoetryNW (22:1) Spr 81, pp. 38-39.

GERRARD, Jill
"Journey." QW (12) Spr-Sum 81, pp. 70-1.
"The Loss." QW (12) Spr-Sum 81, p. 69.

GERY, John
"Charlemagne's Third Daughter." LitR (24:3) Spr 81, p. 392.
"The Daughter of Desiderius." LitR (24:3) Spr 81, p. 391.
"For Sally Ann, Wherever She Is, in Alabama." Outbr (6/7) Aut 80-
    Spr 81, p. 57.

GETSI, John
"In nameless signs" (tr. of Serge Meurant, w/ Lucia Getsi). Mund (12/
    13) 80-81, p. 99.
"Sometimes form explodes" (tr. of Serge Meurant, w/ Lucia Getsi).
    Mund (12/13) 80-81, p. 99.

GETSI, Lucia
"In nameless signs" (tr. of Serge Meurant, w/ John Getsi). Mund (12/
    13) 80-81, p. 99.
"Lullaby." Mund (12/13) 80-81, p. 314.
"Mother." Mund (12/13) 80-81, p. 314.
"Sometimes form explodes" (tr. of Serge Meurant, w/ John Getsi).
    Mund (12/13) 80-81, p. 99.

GETTY, Sarah
"Cleaning The Storm Windows." BelPoJ (32:1) Aut 81, pp. 4-5.
"How They Sleep." BelPoJ (32:1) Aut 81, pp. 5-6.
"Troupers." Shen (32:2) 81, pp. 82-83.

GHIGNA, Charles
"The Ballet of a Boxing Fan." PoNow (6:1 issue 31) 81, p. 30.
"The Tennis Pro." PoNow (6:2 issue 32) 81, p. 16.

GHISELIN, Brewster
"Semblance on Semblance." Poetry (137:5) F 81, p. 284.
"Theft." Poetry (137:5) F 81, p. 285.

GHITELMAN, David
"Young Woman Approaching Blindness." Iowa (11:2/3) Spr-Sum 80, p.
    99.

GHOSSEIN, Mirene
"A river races its own course" (tr. of Salim Nakad). Nimrod (24: 2)
    Spr/Sum 81, p. 48.
"The Naked Face" (tr. of Andrée Chedid, w/ Samuel Hazo). Mund (12/
    13) 80-81, p. 329.
"Who Remains Standing?" (tr. of Andrée Chedid, w/ Samuel Hazo).
    Mund (12/13) 80-81, p. 329.

GIACOMELLI, Eloah F.
"Nocturne" (tr. of João Cabral de Melo Neto). Mund (12/13) 81, p. 11.

"The Seasons" (tr. of João Cabral de Melo Neto). Mund (12/13) 80-81,
    pp. 10-11.

GIANOLI, Paul
    "Daughter. " WebR (6:2) 81, p. 80.

GIBB, Robert
    "Bows and Arrows. " Wind (11:42) 81, p. 14.
    "Doublings. " EnPas (12), 81, p. 23.
    "The Dawning of Birds. " Tendril (11) Sum 81, p. 31.
    "Elegy for the Dead. " PoetryNW (22:3) Aut 81, pp. 37-38.
    "For Now. " CharR (7:2) Aut 81, pp. 19-20.
    "16th Street. " Wind (11:42) 81, pp. 13-14.
    "Waiting for the Snow. " PoetryNW (22:3) Aut 81, pp. 38-39.

GIBBENS, John
    "The Farrier. " Stand (22: 4) 81, p. 24.
    "Rhys. " Stand (22: 4) 81, p. 25.

GIBBONS, Reginald
    "Affidavit. " ParisR (23:80) Sum 81, pp. 136-137.
    "Here Everything" (tr. of Laureano Albán). Mund (12/13) 80-81, p.
        293.
    "The Letter. " SewanR (89:1) Wint 81, pp. 27-28.
    "Questions and Answers" (tr. of Luis Suardíaz). Mund (12/13) 80-81,
        p. 104.
    "Small Elegy. " Stand (22: 2) 81, p. 47.

GIBBS, Robert
    "Saskatoon, May 1980" (for Eddie and Catherine Buckaway). PottPort
        (3) 81, p. 15.

GIBSON, Kim
    "A Kind of Apron Strings. " Obs (7:1) Spr 81, p. 57.
    "Hazards of the Shy. " Obs (7:1) Spr 81, pp. 58-59.
    "It's a Melon. " Obs (7:1) Spr 81, p. 56.
    "The Nightgown Brigade. " Obs (7:1) Spr 81, p. 58.
    "Obsession. " Obs (7:1) Spr 81, p. 59.
    "The Social Worker. " Obs (7:1) Spr 81, p. 60.

GIBSON, Stephen M.
    "The Body in the Bog. " PoNow (6:3 issue 33) 81, p. 13.
    "The Geography of Haraldsjaer Bog. " KanQ (13:1) Wint 81, p. 128.

GILBERT, Celia
    "Clyde. " Ploughs (6:4) 81, pp. 136-137.
    "The Cow. " Ploughs (6:4) 81, p. 135.
    "Moving In. " Ploughs (6:4) 81, p. 138.

GILBERT, Chris
    "she (for Carolyn Grace). " Obs (7:1) Spr 81, p. 47.
    "theory of curve. " Obs (7:1) Spr 81, p. 46.

GILBERT, Christopher
    "Blue. " Tendril (11) Sum 81, p. 32.
    "Kite-flying. " Tendril (11) Sum 81, p. 33.

GILBERT, Sandra
    "The Language Of Flowers" (1-7). AmerPoR (10:5) S-O 81, p. 9.

GILBERT, Sandra M.
  "A Year Later." BelPoJ (32:1) Aut 81, pp. 6-7.
  "The Brussels Sprouts." BelPoJ (32:1) Aut 81, p. 8.
  "The Emily Dickinson Black Cake Walk." PoetryNW (22:3) Aut 81, pp.
    9-10.
  "Five Potatoes." PoNow (6:1 issue 31) 81, p. 14.
  "On the Train." PraS (55:4) Wint 81-82, pp. 26-7.
  "Phaeton." PoetryNW (22:1) Spr 81, pp. 24-25.
  "This is not...." PoetryNW (22:4) Wint 81-82, pp. 36-37.
  "The Three Sisters." PraS (55:4) Wint 81-82, pp. 27-30.

GILBERT, Virginia
  "Blackbird Winter." PoNow (6:2 issue 32) 81, p. 20.
  "The Study." PoNow (6:2 issue 32) 81, p. 20.

GILCH, Diane
  "Huswifery." LitR (24:3) Spr 81, p. 404.

GILDNER, Gary
  "Carmina Explains to Jabón." Tendril (11) Sum 81, pp. 35-36.
  "Jabón and the Pill Hawker." NoAmR (266:1) Mr 81, p. 19.
  "Jabón Blesses El Baso." Tendril (11) Sum 81, pp. 36-37.
  "A Letter From My Good Hand." NowestR (19:1/2), pp. 71-3.
  "Santos Reyes." PoetryNW (22:1) Spr 81, pp. 18-19.
  "Uncle George at the Home." Shen (32:2) 81, p. 24.
  "Wheat." GeoR (35:2) Sum 81, pp. 408-410.
  "Where Jabón Came From." Tendril (11) Sum 81, pp. 34-35.

GILL, James D.
  "Intruders." Poem (43) Nov 81, p. 47.
  "October." Poem (43) Nov 81, p. 48.

GILROY, James P.
  "Mazurka" (tr. of Louise de Vilmorin). DenQ (16:1) Spr 81, p. 79.
  "Postlude: Polonaise" (tr. of Louise de Vilmorin). DenQ (16:1) Spr 81,
    p. 80.

GIMELSON, Deborah
  "July Fourth: The Lake." PoNow (6:3 issue 33) 81, p. 14.
  "Where I Am Now." Nat (233:18) 28 N 81, p. 584.

GIMENEZ GIORIO de COLOMBO, Silvia N.
  "Amanecer misionero." LetFem (7:2) Aut 81, pp. 58-59.

GINGERICH, Willard
  "Maple (for John Ashbery)." NewEngR (4:1) Aut 81, pp. 6-9.

GIOIA, Dana
  "An Elegy for Vladimir de Pachmann." Hudson (34:3) Aut 81, pp.
    332-333.
  "God Only Knows." Hudson (34:3) Aut 81, p. 333.
  "Lives of the Great Composers." Hudson (34:3) Aut 81, pp. 334-335.
  "Photograph of My Mother as a Young Girl." Hudson (34:3) Aut 81, p.
    335.
  "View from the Second Story." Hudson (34:3) Aut 81, p. 336.

GIORIO de COLOMBO, Silvia N. Giménez see GIMENEZ GIORIO de
COLOMBO, Silvia N.

GIRARD, Linda Walvoord
 "Anniversary Near the Dunes." Ascent (7:1) 81, p. 39.
 "Foxy Loxy." Ascent (7:1) 81, p. 38.
 "Peter." Ascent (6:2) 81, pp. 29-30.

GITIN, Maria
 "Baile de Amor." Tele (17) 81, p. 39.
 "Otro para Edgardo." Tele (17) 81, p. 41.
 "Pensamientos" (Para Edgardo). Tele (17) 81, p. 38.
 "Walk Away." Tele (17) 81, p. 40.

GITLIN, Todd
 "What To Do In Doubt." MichQR (20:3) Sum 81, p. 263.

GIULIANI, Alfredo
 "Resurrection After the Rain" (tr. by Lawrence R. Smith). PoNow (5:6
    issue 30) 81, p. 16.

GLADDING, Jody
 "The Mutant." SouthernPR (21:2) Aut 81, p. 51.

GLANCY, Diane
 "Arkansas." StoneC (9: 1-2) Aut-Wint 81/82, p. 69.
 "The Schoolhouse." CapeR (17:1) Wint 81, p. 43.

GLASER, Elton
 "Baudelaire on the Rue de Babylone." CharR (7:2) Aut 81, p. 15.
 "The Desert Mothers." CharR (7:1) Spr 81, pp. 26-27.
 "Doctor Snow." PoNow (6:1 issue 31) 81, p. 21.
 "Dolls Divided." PoNow (6:2 issue 32) 81, p. 15.
 "Perception of the Right Line" (tr. of Robert Benajoun, w/ Janice
    Fritsch). ChiR (32:2) Aut 80, p. 29.
 "Le Piano Introspectif." PoetryNW (22:3) Aut 81, pp. 34-35.
 "Ravishing" (tr. of Robert Benajoun, w/ Janice Fritsch). ChiR (32:2)
    Aut 80, p. 28.
 "Some Nights." ChiR (33:1) Sum 81, p. 39.
 "Times Square" (tr. of Lorand Gaspar, with Janice Fritsch). CharR
    (7:1) Spr 81, p. 53.

GLASER, Michael S.
 "Monument." ChrC (98:27) 9 S 81, p. 863.

GLASS, Jesse
 "Post-Modernistic Triptych." CreamCR (6:2) 81, pp. 128-130.

GLASS, Judith
 "My sister is my muse." Tele (17) 81, p. 83.

GLASS, Malcolm
 "Getting There." BallSUF (22:4) Aut 81, p. 58.
 "Hitting the Deer" (for Dave Till). Outbr (6/7) Aut 80-Spr 81, p. 56.
 "Sky-Diving." SewanR (89:2) Ap-Je 81, p. 183.

GLAZE, Andrew
 "Dog Dancing." SouthernPR (21: 1) Spr 81, pp. 45-46.
 "76th Street." SouthernPR (21: 1) Spr 81, p. 44.
 "Wizard." PoNow (6:1 issue 31) 81, p. 11.

GLEN, Emilie
   "Apple Head." Wind (11:40) 81, p. 10.
   "Balls." Tele (17) 81, p. 123.
   "Moon Empty." SouthwR (66:1) Wint 81, p. 38.
   "My Grand." Aspect (77/79) 81, pp. 73-74.
   "Remains." Tele (17) 81, p. 124.
   "Sunred River." Wind (11:40) 81, pp. 10-11.
   "Technique." Tele (17) 81, p. 124.

GLENN, Karen
   "The Naming of Wolves." HiramPoR (30) Spr-Sum 81, p. 20.

GLENN, Laura
   "Trying to Relax." PoNow (6:3 issue 33) 81, p. 13.

GLOVER, Jon
   "Pure." Stand (22: 2) 81, p. 59.

GLOWNEY, John
   "Solstice." Northeast (3:10) Wint 81, p. 22.
   "The Way Out." OhioR (26), p. 28.

GLÜCK, Louise
   "Brooding Likeness." NewYorker (57:9) 20 Ap 81, p. 40.
   "Horse." Antaeus (40/41) Wint-Spr 81, p. 292.

GOAD, Craig M.
   "First Year." Wind (11:42) 81, pp. 15-16.
   "From Memory." HiramPoR (29) Aut-Wint 81, p. 21.
   "In Autumn." Wind (11:42) 81, p. 16.
   "Porky Battles the Bolts on an Exhaust Manifold and Contemplates God."
      NewL (47:4) Sum 81, pp. 94-95.
   "Summer Lessons." NewL (47:4) Sum 81, p. 93.

GODINEZ, Art
   "Slight Victory." DenQ (16:3) Aut 81, p. 61.

GOEDICKE, Patricia
   "Entering the Garden." CutB (17) Aut-Wint 81, pp. 12-14.
   "That Fall" (for Petra Cabot). SouthernR (17:2) Spr 81, pp. 397-8.
   "Letter from D.S." NowestR (19:1/2), pp. 91-2.
   "Mahler in the Living Room." NewYorker (57:37) 2 N 81, pp. 50-1.
   "The Man In The Wet Suit." StoneC (9: 1-2) Aut-Wint 81/82, pp. 16-
      18.
   "The Odor of Sanctity (for Lou Catching)." NowestR (19:3), pp. 11-12.
   "The Only Issue." PoetryNW (22:2) Sum 81, pp. 24-25.
   "Privileged." PoetryE (6) Aut 81, pp. 67-68.
   "The Structures We Love." MassR (22:3) Aut 81, pp. 470-476.
   "Wherever You Thought to Retreat." OP (31/32) Aut 81, p. 103.

GOETHE
   "Amor Als Landschaftsmaler." SenR (12:1/2) 81, pp. 8-12.

GOETTE, Ann
   "The George Prince." Outbr (6/7) Aut 80-Spr 81, pp. 70-71.

GOLD, Herman
   "Cindy-Lu." PoNow (6:2 issue 32) 81, p. 43.

GOLDBARTH, Albert
  "All-Nite Donuts." OntR (14) Spr-Sum 81, pp. 44-45.
  "Astronomy/Myth: A Seminar." Shen (32:2) 81, pp. 44-45.
  "Before." Poetry (138:6) S 81, pp. 342-343.
  "Blue Flowers." Poetry (138:6) S 81, pp. 338-339.
  "By the 20s, they'd all left home." SenR (10:2/11:1) 79-80, pp. 18-21.
  "A Charm." SouthwR (66:4) Aut 81, p. 376.
  "The Day I turned 33 1/3." SouthernPR (21: 1) Spr 81, p. 40.
  "Dr. Paul Walker...." SenR (10:2/11:1) 79-80, pp. 29-30.
  "First Ride & First Walk." CalQ (18/19) 81, p. 92.
  "Gleanings from the Diary of Henry David Tarot: 4 Suit Cards & a
    Reading." LittleM (13:1/2) Spr-Sum 79, c1981, pp. 24-26.
  "Hey Sweetie." Poetry (137:5) F 81, p. 281.
  "A History of Civilization." Agni (14) 81, p. 17.
  "I quote near-verbatim...." SenR (10:2/11:1) 79-80, pp. 22-23.
  "Jan. 31st--31 Yrs." VirQR (57:2) Spr 81, pp. 281-283.
  "Mackerel, bedbug, pig-on-wheels." SenR (10:2/11:1) 79-80, pp. 24-26.
  "Meaning Distance." OntR (14) Spr-Sum 81, p. 46.
  "Of this Gold." BelPoJ (32:2) Wint 81-82, pp. 32-41.
  "Please to Eat It With Fingers." Confr (21) Wint 81, p. 89.
  "Pleasures." Poetry (138:6) S 81, pp. 340-341.
  "Poem: Because they're stupid." Kayak (57) 81, p. 59.
  "The Rest of My Life." CutB (17) Aut-Wint 81, p. 44.
  "Roof & Writing." VirQR (57:2) Spr 81, pp. 283-285.
  "Saucer Station, Monday-Friday." LittleM (13:1/2) Spr-Sum 79, c1981,
    pp. 27-29.
  "Sympathetic Magic." Poetry (137:5) F 81, p. 282.
  "35,000 Feet/The Lanterns." NowestR (19:3), pp. 95-8.
  "Vacation: an extended postcard." OntR (14) Spr-Sum 81, pp. 42-43.
  "Weave." Poetry (137:5) F 81, pp. 280-281.
  "Why the Gypsy Can't Go Wrong." SouthernHR (15:2) Spr 81, p. 118.
  "Yarmulke." SouthernHR (15:2) Spr 81, p. 165.
  "You add on your hands...." SenR (10:2/11:1) 79-80, pp. 27-28.

GOLDENSHON, Lorrie
  "Cello." Ploughs (6:4) 81, p. 195.
  "Preparation for the Wedding." YaleR (70: 3) Spr 81, pp. 413-414.
  "Quotation." YaleR (70: 3) Spr 81, p. 415.
  "The Tether." YaleR (70: 3) Spr 81, pp. 414-415.

GOLDMAN, Beate
  "Woman in the Windows in the Hague." ConcPo (14:1) Spr 81, p. 27.

GOLDMAN, Maximilian
  "No. 2 Line, Pelham Parkway, December." LittleM (13:1/2) Spr-Sum
    79, c1981, p. 85.

GOLDSBERRY, Steven
  "Colder." NewYorker (57:45) 28 D 81, p. 51.

GOLDSTEIN, Laurence
  "In the San Clemente Hills After the Jonestown Murders. " OntR (14) Spr-
    Sum 81, p. 51.
  "Long Beach, Long Neglected." OntR (14) Spr-Sum 81, pp. 52-53.

GOLDWITZ, Susan
  "Inside the Still Life." Tendril (10) Wint 81, p. 29.

GOLEMBIEWSKI, Alison
"The Gold Pistol." Poetry (138:6) S 81, p. 317.
"The Rapture Is Coming." GeoR (35:3) Aut 81, p. 610.

GOLFFING, Francis
"Declension" (tr. of Georg Frankl). PoNow (6:1 issue 31) 81, p. 43.
"Holdering in Tubingen" (tr. of Johannes Bobrowki). PoNow (5:6 issue 30) 81, p. 8.
"I have met persons who" (tr. of Gottfried Benn). PoNow (5:6 issue 30) 81, p. 7.
"A Moment in June" (tr. of Günter Eich). PoNow (5:6 issue 30) 81, p. 15.
"Recovery" (tr. of Johannes Bobrowki). PoNow (5:6 issue 30) 81, p. 8.
"Towards Evening" (tr. of Oskar Loerke). ChiR (32:4) Spr 81, p. 89.
"Troubled Hour" (tr. of Ernst Stadler). PoNow (5:6 issue 30) 81, p. 44.
"The Wanderer" (tr. of Johannes Bobrowki). PoNow (5:6 issue 30) 81, p. 44.
"West Wind" (tr. of Günter Eich). PoNow (5:6 issue 30) 81, p. 15.
"Why do you come so often to visit me" (tr. of Georg Heym). PoNow (5:6 issue 30) 81, p. 17.

GOLL, Yvan
"Karma" (tr. by Dorothy B. Aspinwall). WebR (6:2) 81, p. 19.

GOMBAR, Richard
"I swung my yellow giant." Aspect (77/79) 81, pp. 75-76.

GOMES FERREIRA, José
from "Melody" (I & II) (tr. by Alexis Levitin). PortR (27: 2) 81, p. 31.

GOMEZ, Alexis
"Paul Giudicelli." Lugar (1:1) 79, p. 10.

GOMEZ, Cristina
"Desempleo." Maize (4:1/2) Aut-Wint 80-81, p. 60.
"Exilio (para Enrique)." Maize (4:1/2) Aut-Wint 80-81, p. 59.
"Sin que nadie la vea... (a Jorge Sanabria)." Maize (4:1/2) Aut-Wint 80-81, p. 61.

GONGORA, Helcías Martán see MARTAN GONGORA, Helcías

GONTAREK, Leonard
"Monet Walking Back Through Halflight." NewEngR (3:3) Spr 81, p. 429.

GONZALEZ, Angel
"Everything is Clear Now." Mund (12/13) 80-81, p. 223.
"Calambur." Mund (12/13) 80-81, pp. 222-223.
"Counterorder." Mund (12/13) 80-81, p. 222.
"Order." Mund (12/13) 80-81, p. 221.
"Poetics" (tr. by Gary Brower). Mund (12/13) 80-81, p. 221.

GONZALEZ, Graciano Peraita see PERAITA GONZALEZ, Graciano

GONZALEZ, Josemilio
"Betances." Claridad/En Rojo (22: 1494) 18-24 S 81, p. 12.
"Los hombres del 23." Claridad/En Rojo (22: 1494) 18-24 S 81, p. 12.
"Mañana." Claridad/En Rojo (22: 1468) 20-26 Mr 81, p. 12.
"Meditación." Claridad/En Rojo (22: 1468) 20-26 Mr 81, p. 12.

GONZALEZ, Miguel
"Te regalo." Mairena (3:7), p. 81.
"Las petunias los pasados los presentes." Mairena (3:7), p. 81.
"Es mejor, sí, muchacha, mejor y más feliz." Mairena (3:7), p. 78.
"Buenas noches, Ofelia." Mairena (3:7), p. 77.
"Buenos días, Ofelia." Mairena (3:7), pp. 76-77.

GONZALEZ, Oquendo Medina see MEDINA GONZALEZ, Oquendo

GONZALEZ, Rafael Jesús
"A mis estudiantes." Metam (3:2/4:1) 80-81, p. 48.
"For San Rafael Arcángel." Metam (3:2/4:1) 80-81, p. 47.
"October Poem in the Style of Yuan Chen." Metam (3:2/4:1) 80-81, p. 47.
"A Sunday Morning." Metam (3:2/4:1) 80-81, p. 48.

GONZALEZ, Ray
"How Far Back?" DenQ (16:3) Aut 81, p. 48.
"Someone." DenQ (16:3) Aut 81, p. 49.
"Through the Creek, Cloride, New Mexico." DenQ (16:3) Aut 81, pp. 50-51.

GONZALEZ CANALE, Aurelio
"Cuando Otoño." Puerto Wint 81, p. 24.

GOOD, Ruth
"Catherine the Great, Empress of Russia." LitR (24:3) Spr 81, pp. 371-372.
"A Refusal." LitR (24:3) Spr 81, pp. 372-374.
"The Sadness of Fathers." CharR (7:1) Spr 81, pp. 46-47.

GOODELL, Larry
"contemporary modern." Tele (17) 81, p. 106.
"Dogs & Cats." Tele (17) 81, p. 107.
"The Story of Football." Tele (17) 81, p. 106.

GOODENBERGER, Dan
"To Judge a Book." EngJ (70:5) S 81, p. 56.

GOODENOUGH, J. B.
"Death of a Maiden Aunt." DenQ (16:1) Spr 81, p. 39.
"Early Gifts." DenQ (16:1) Spr 81, p. 38.
"Excursion." Hudson (34:3) Aut 81, p. 384.
"For Luck." Ascent (6:3) 81, pp. 40-41.
"In the Castle." Ascent (6:3) 81, p. 41.
"Night Guests." Ascent (6:3) 81, p. 40.
"Time Before." ArizQ (37:3) Aut 81, p. 274.
"Up Country." StoneC (9: 1-2) Aut-Wint 81/82, p. 65.

GOODFELLOW, Robin
"Tracking Down Faces." Nimrod (25:1) Aut-Wint 81, pp. 72-73.

GOODMAN, Diane
"When My Grandmother Died." StoneC (8: 3) Spr 81, p. 45.

GOODMAN, Larry
"In A Nice Restaurant." ThRiPo (17/18) 81, pp. 79-80.

GOODMAN, Miriam
"Industrial Park from the Air." Aspect (77/79) 81, pp. 76-77.

GOODMAN, Ryah Tumarkin
"The Door." Poem (41) Mar 81, p. 9.
"The End." Poem (41) Mar 81, p. 10.

GOODWIN, Sister
"Centennial Year for the Spirits." MalR (60) O 81, pp. 78-81.

GORDETT, Marea
"When I Was Young." PartR (48:2) 81, p. 247.

GORDON, Bonnie
"Biography." VirQR (57:3) Sum 81, pp. 460-461.
"A Childhood in Reno." VirQR (57:3) Sum 81, p. 461.

GORDON, Coco
"Tracking Down that Marmora Mine with Prospects for Restoration."
    Im (7:2) 1981, p. 10.

GORDON, Dane R.
"The Kindergarten Generation at Worship." ChrC (98:17) 13 My 81, p.
    546.

GORDON, Jaimy
"Brief Lives." OP (31/32) Aut 81, p. 172.
"The Time." Aspect (77/79) 81, pp. 78-81.

GORDON, Kirpal
"On His Thirty-fifth Birthday, Holden Caulfield Writes J. D. Salinger."
    PoetryE (6) Aut 81, pp. 57-58.

GORDON, Mary
"Poem for the End of the Year." NewYRB (28:20) 17 D 81, p. 46.

GOREN, Judith
"Trading Movie Stars." PoNow (6:3 issue 33) 81, p. 14.

GOREY, Edward
"Q. E. Stramash." WormR (84) 81, p. 101.

GORLIN, Debra
"In Bold Relief." Poetry (138:2) My 81, pp. 77-78.
"Parents." Poetry (138:2) My 81, p. 78.

GORMAZ, José Verón see VERON GORMAZ, José

GOROSTIZA, José
"Prelude" (tr. by Laura Villaseñor). Mund (12/13) 80-81, pp. 375-377.

GOTTSCHALK, Felix C.
"Light-Years." PortR (27: 2) 81, p. 63-64.

GOULD, Charles
"Spring Geese." Peb (21) 81, p. 36.

GOUMAS, Yannis
"News of the Death of the Spanish Poet Federico García Lorca on Au-

gust 19, 1936, in a Ditch at Camino de la Fuente" (tr. of Nikos
Engonopoulos). Mund (12/13) 80-81, p. 185.
"On the Tip of the Tongue. " Mund (12/13) 80-81, p. 105.

GOVAN, Rosetta
  "Niggers for Days. " WindO (39) Wint 81/82, p. 17.

GRABER, John
  "Late Passover Afternoon. " ChrC (98:12) 8 Ap 81, p. 384.

GRABILL, James
  "Dusk on the Oregon Coast. " PoNow (6:1 issue 31) 81, p. 19.
  "To the Golden Flower. " Kayak (56) 81, p. 53.

GRACIA de CRIADO, Yolanda
  "Me voy haciendo caminos. " Mairena (2:6), p. 88.

GRAF, Roger
  "Redeemer. " Meadows (2:1) 81, p. 29.
  "Secular Scenes. " Meadows (2:1) 81, p. 50.

GRAFENAUER, Niko
  "Silence" (tr. by Jose Lazar). Mund (12/13) 80-81, p. 93.

GRAHAM, David
  "Father Movies. " NewEngR (4:2) Wint 81, pp. 221-2.

GRAHAM, Jorie
  "The Daffodil. " Antaeus (40/41) Wint-Spr 81, pp. 295-296.
  "For John Keats. " MissouriR (4:3) Sum 81, p. 30.
  "Haying. " GeoR (35:2) Sum 81, p. 318.
  "I Watched a Snake. " Iowa (11:2/3) Spr-Sum 80, pp. 217-218.
  "Kimono. " Ploughs (6:4) 81, pp. 171-172.
  "Mimosa Blossoming Over the Pond. " PoetryNW (22:1) Spr 81, p. 7.
  "Mist. " Iowa (11:2/3) Spr-Sum 80, pp. 219-220.
  "My Garden, My Daylight. " NewEngR (4:1) Aut 81, pp. 20-21.
  "Piano Lessons. " PoetryNW (22:1) Spr 81, pp. 8-9.
  "Poem in a Windstorm. " PoetryNW (22:1) Spr 81, pp. 9-10.
  "San Sepolcro. " Antaeus (40/41) Wint-Spr 81, pp. 293-294.
  Ten poems. AmerPoR (10:5) S-O 81, pp. 3-7.
  "Two Paintings By Gustav Klimt. " AmerPoR (10:3) My-Je 81, p. 48.

GRAHAM, W. S.
  From: "Implements in Their Places. " NowestR (19:3), p. 1.

GRANT, Victoria Mary
  "Euless, Texas:" CapeR (16:2) Sum 81, p. 42.

GRAPENTINE, Rachel
  "Encounter. " HiramPoR (29) Aut-Wint 81, p. 22.

GRASS, Günter
  "Cherries" (tr. by Lane Jennings). Vis (6) 81, n. p.
  "Placed Amid Old Men" (tr. by Michael Hamburger). Mund (12/13) 80-
    81, p. 316.

GRAVELLES, Charles de see de GRAVELLES, Charles

GRAY, Patrick Worth
    "Arnett, Oklahoma in Summer." PoNow (6:2 issue 32) 81, p. 19.
    "Closing Hour on Farnam Street." KanQ (13:2) Spr 81, p. 26.
    "End of Beginnings." Focus (14:89) N 80, p. 10.
    "Friday the Thirteenth." ChrC (98:8) 8 Mr 81, p. 262.
    "Leaving." PoNow (6:1 issue 31) 81, p. 29.
    "Mortality Report." Poem (42) Jul 81, pp. 2-3.
    "Movie." ColEng (43:5) S 81, p. 492.
    "Parlor." HiramPoR (30) Spr-Sum 81, p. 21.
    "The Passing of my Father." ConcPo (14:1) Spr 81, p. 30.
    "Rain." ConcPo (14:1) Spr 81, pp. 29-30.
    "Snapshot with Mongrel in Foreground." Poem (42) Jul 81, p. 1.

GRAY, Stephen
    "From Jarenda: Falling In Time." Wind (11:41) 81, p. 20.

GRAZIANO, Frank
    "Homage to Marcus Aurelius." NewEngR (3:4) Sum 81, pp. 592-3.
    "Puno." CharR (7:1) Spr 81, pp. 15-16.

GRAZNAK, Lynn
    "Bob Payne and Otis West." OP (31/32) Aut 81, p. 72.

GREENBERG, Alvin
    "i am aware that i am, therefore i must be thinking, i suppose."
        OhioR (26), p. 124.

GREENBERG, Barbara L.
    "Stammerer." PoNow (6:1 issue 31) 81, p. 33.

GREENWAY, William
    "Heir Apparent." Wind (11:42) 81, p. 17.

GREGER, Debora
    "Camera Obscura." PoetryNW (22:3) Aut 81, pp. 33-34.
    "The Difference Between Novels and Life." Iowa (11:2/3) Spr-Sum 80,
        p. 199.
    "A Hermitage." MissouriR (4:2) Wint 81-82, p. 19.
    "Leavings." Agni (15) 81, p. 54.
    "Love Poem." MissouriR (4:2) Wint 81-82, p. 18.
    "99 South." Agni (15) 81, pp. 52-53.
    "Open Window." PoetryNW (22:3) Aut 81, pp. 32-33.
    "321 Normal Street." MissouriR (4:2) Wint 81-82, p. 20.

GREGERSON, Linda
    "Egress." PoNow (6:3 issue 33) 81, p. 14.
    "Neck Verse." PoNow (6:3 issue 33) 81, p. 14.
    "The Weather." PoNow (6:3 issue 33) 81, p. 14.
    "To Albert Speer." Iowa (11:2/3) Spr-Sum 80, p. 191.

GREGG, Linda
    "At the Shore." Pequod (13) 81, p. 21.
    "Birds and in Their Wake Gods Wander." Pequod (13) 81, p. 22.
    Nine poems. Tendril (11) Sum 81, pp. 81-89.
    "Now Destroyed." Pequod (13) 81, p. 19.
    "The Small Lizard." Pequod (13) 81, p. 20.
    "Trouble In the Portable Marriage." Ploughs (6:4) 81, p. 25.

GREGOR, Arthur
  "Die Liebe Liebt Das Wandern." PoNow (6:1 issue 31) 81, p. 7.
  "The Shaper of Words on his Instruction." PoNow (6:1 issue 31) 81, p. 7.

GREGORY, Horace
  "A Hansel of Horatian Odes." NewL (47:4) Sum 81, pp. 53-57.
  "Nature & the Architect." Poetry (139:3) D 81, pp. 133-134.

GREGORY, R. D.
  "Lullaby." Mund (12/13) 80-81, p. 105.

GREGSON, Ian
  "The Vicar and the Rag-and-Bone Man." Stand (22: 2) 81, p. 72.

GREIG, Andrew
  "The Glove." Stand (22: 1) 80, p. 40.

GRENNAN, Eamon
  "In the National Library." OP (31/32) Aut 81, p. 129.

GREY, Robert
  "Revere Beach." KanQ (13:1) Wint 81, p. 127.

GRIECO, Joseph
  "Stories at the Kitchen Table." SmPd (18:2) Spr 81, p. 34.

GRIFFIN, Gail
  "That Was a House." Prima (6/7) 81, p. 79.

GRIFFITH, Jonathan
  "Steve Keltner/A Letter." KanQ (13:3/4) Sum-Aut 81, p. 55.

GRIFFITH, Margaret
  "Oh My Young Poet." Wind (11:40) 81, pp. 12-13.

GRIGSBY, Gordon
  "Released from Sleep." Vis (6) 81, n. p.

GRINDE, Olav
  "Atnenna Forest" (tr. by Rolf Jacobsen). CalQ (18/19) 81, p. 127.
  "Asphalt" (tr. by Rolf Jacobsen). CalQ (18/19) 81, p. 126.

GROFF, David
  "The Memory." PoetryNW (22:4) Wint 81-82, p. 39.

GROLMES, Sam
  "A Distant Land" (tr. of Ruichi Tamura, w/ Yumiko Tsumura). Mund (12/13) 80-81, pp. 34-35.
  "October Poem" (tr. of Ruichi Tamura, w/ Yumiko Tsumura). Mund (12/13) 80-81, p. 35.
  "The Withered Leaves" (tr. of Ruichi Tamura, w/ Yumiko Tsumura). Mund (12/13) 80-81, p. 34.

GRONOWICZ, Antoni
  "night." Wind (10:39) 80, p. 22.
  "Purgatory" (tr. of Tadeusz Rozewicz). WebR (6:2) 81, p. 33.

GROSHOLZ, Emily
"The Return." NewEngR (4:1) Aut 81, pp. 57-8.

GROSS, T. A.
"Sunday Night." KanQ (13:1) Wint 81, p. 164.

GROSSMAN, Allen
"Bow Spirit." ParisR (23:79) Spr 81, pp. 170-176.
"Of the Great House." Ploughs (7:2) 81, pp. 11-23.

GROSSMAN, Florence
"Alpine Museum." GeoR (35:1) Spr 81, p. 91.
"Below Zero." Chelsea (40) 81, p. 152.
"Keeping a Secret." Chelsea (40) 81, p. 153.

GROSSMAN, Richard
"Blind Salamander." SouthernR (17:2) Spr 81, p. 405.
"Film." PortR (27: 1) 81, p. 27.
"Ostrich." NewL (47:4) Sum 81, p. 92.
"Stalemate." PortR (27: 1) 81, p. 27.

GROVER, Dorys C.
"Naias." BallSUF (22:4) Aut 81, p. 36.

GRYPHIUS, Andreas
"Sestina: Denial of the World." SouthernR (17:4) Aut 81, pp. 997-8.

GUDMUNDSDOTTIR, Thuridur
"As the train passes" (tr. by Alan Boucher). Vis (5) 81, n. p.
"Child" (tr. by Alan Boucher). Vis (5) 81, n. p.

GUEREÑA, Jacinto-Luis
"Caminos de la palabra." Os (13) Aut 81, p. 26.
"Diálogo entre pintura y poesía." Os (12) Spr 81, pp. 30-31.
"Jeunes et Vieilles Empreintes." Os (12) Spr 81, pp. 2-5.

GUERNELLI, Adelaide Lugo see LUGO-GUERNELLI, Adelaide

GUERNSEY, Bruce
"The Chopping Block." BelPoJ (32:1) Aut 81, p. 13.
"The Coop." BelPoJ (32:1) Aut 81, pp. 14-15.
"The Icehouse." Nat (233:6) 5 S 81, p. 185.
"Stray." ColEng (43:2) F 81, pp. 165-166.
"The Tongue." Ascent (6:2) 81, p. 20.
"A Winter Without Snow." ColEng (43:2) F 81, p. 165.

GUIDACCI, Margherita
"The Mad Mother" (tr. by Ruth Feldman). PortR (27: 1) 81, p. 38.
"Three Images From the Plitvice Lakes" (tr. by Renata Treitel and
    Manly Johnson). WebR (6:2) 81, pp. 25-26.

GUILLEMIN, Margaret
"Conversation in the Mountains" (tr. with Katharine Washburn of Paul
    Celan). ParisR (23:80) Sum 81, pp. 215-220.

GUILLEN, Nicolás
"I Got" (tr. by Donald Walsh). AmerPoR (10:3) My-Je 81, p. 34.

GUILLEN, Pablo
"Qué puedo darte...." Maize (4:1/2) Aut-Wint 80-81, p. 49.
"Volver a empezar." Maize (4:1/2) Aut-Wint 80-81, p. 52.
"Voy a denunciar al silencio." Maize (4:1/2) Aut-Wint 80-81, pp. 50-51.

GUILLEVIC, Eugène
"Rocks" (tr. by Teo Savory). Mund (12/13) 80-81, pp. 234-236.

GUILLORY, Daniel
"The Cabbage." Aspect (77/79) 81, p. 90.

GUISCAFRE, Marilyn R. Ramírez see RAMIREZ GUISCAFRE, Marilyn R.

GUITART, Jorge
"Four Poems: The Bottom of the Bowl." (tr. of José Kózer).
   ModernPS (10:2/3), pp. 96-97.

GULLBERG, Hjalmar
"The Lilies of the Field" (tr. by Judith Moffett). PoNow (5:6 issue 30)
   81, p. 23.
"Non-Occurring Thud" (tr. by Judith Moffett). PoNow (5:6 issue 30) 81,
   p. 23.
"Put the Photographs Away" (tr. by Judith Moffett). PoNow (5:6 issue
   30) 81, p. 23.

GULLETTE, David
"Angling." Ploughs (7:1) 81, pp. 98-99.

GUNDERSON, Andreus
"Extraordinary Encounter." Sam (109) 81, p. 21.

GUNN, Thom
"Crosswords." SouthernR (17:4) Aut 81, pp. 985-6.
"Delayed Preface." SouthernR (17:4) Aut 81, pp. 987-8.
"A Drive to Los Alamos." Thrpny (4) Wint 81, p. 3.
"Selves." ParisR (23:79) Spr 81, pp. 190-191.
"Slow Waker." NewYRB (28:4) 19 Mr 81, p. 8.

GURNIS, Peter
"There Is Only One." Ploughs (7:1) 81, p. 156.

GUSTAFSSON, Lars
"Elegy for a Dead Labrador" (tr. by Yvonne L. Sandstroem).
   NewYorker (57:27) 24 Ag 81, p. 34.
"Lines for the Count of Venosa" (tr. by Yvonne L. Sandstroem). Mund
   (12/13) 80-81, pp. 94-98.

GUTIERREZ, Guillermo
"Montaña y mar (secuencias) (A Manuel de la Puebla)." Mairena (2:5)
   Aut 80, pp. 70-71.

GUTIERREZ, Houle
"Cult." Poem (43) Nov 81, p. 51.
"July." Poem (43) Nov 81, p. 49.
"Legacy." Poem (43) Nov 81, p. 50.

GUTIERREZ-REVUELTA, Pedro
"A Marilyn con unas violetas." Maize (4:3/4) Spr-Sum 81, pp. 47-50.

HAAVIKKO, Paavo
from Wine, Writing: "I'm not accusing you" (tr. by Richard Dauen-
hauer). PoetryE (6) Aut 81, pp. 17-18.

HACKENBRUCH, Carol R.
"To the High Places." Im (7:3) 81, p. 11.

HACKER, Marilyn
"Gerda in the Eyrie." Poetry (138:4) Jl 81, pp. 204-207.
"Little Green-Eyed Suite." OP (31/32) Aut 81, pp. 157-160.
"Pantoum." 13thM (5:1/2) 80, pp. 101-103.
"Prayer for My Daughter." OP (31/32) Aut 81, p. 135.
"Towards Autumn." MissouriR (4:2) Wint 81-82, p. 32.

HADAS, Pamela White
"Father Doctor Handy Man." NewEngR (3:3) Spr 81, p. 432.
from: "The Bandit Queen's Abandonment: Belle Starr Remembering."
Poetry (137:4) Ja 81, pp. 217-219.
"Seein This Heap of Writin On My Table." AmerPoR (10:1) Ja-F 81,
p. 32.
"Yet Another Unanswered Letter." AmerPoR (10:1) Ja-F 81, p. 32.

HADAS, Rachel
"Around an August Silence." DenQ (16:2) Sum 81, pp. 26-27.
"Five September Hours." Ploughs (7:2) 81, pp. 43-46.
"Four Dreams About the Same Fortress." Pequod (13) 81, pp. 13-14.
"Hanum in Caledonia County." Pequod (13) 81, p. 15.
"Honeymoon." DenQ (16:2) Sum 81, p. 25.
"Island Noons." DenQ (16:2) Sum 81, pp. 20-21.
"Island Self." DenQ (16:2) Sum 81, pp. 22-23.
"Kaleidoscope." DenQ (16:2) Sum 81, p. 28.
"Letter to a Niece" (for D. H.). Agni (15) 81, p. 51.
"Marriage Rhapsody" (to G.). Agni (14) 81, pp. 55-57.
"Triptych." DenQ (16:2) Sum 81, p. 24.

HAFELI, Bernie
"Snow Covers the Dead." HiramPoR (30) Spr-Sum 81, p. 22.

HAGIWARA, Sakutaro
"Sickroom" (tr. by Graeme Wilson). DenQ (16:4) Wint 81, p. 34.

HAHN, Oscar
"Fotografia." StoneC (9: 1-2) Aut-Wint 81/82, p. 36.
"Photography." (tr. by James Hoggard). StoneC (9: 1-2) Aut-Wint 81/
82, p. 36.

HAIGHT, Robert
"The Salmon Are Barking." HiramPoR (29) Aut-Wint 81, p. 23.

HAINES, John
"Death and the Miser (after Bosch)." NewEngR (4:1) Aut 81, pp. 125-7.
"Homage to David Smith." NewEngR (4:1) Aut 81, p. 128.
"Mothball Fleet: Benicia, California." NewEngR (4:1) Aut 81, p. 129.

HAINES, Jonathan
"And I Didn't." LittleM (13:1/2) Spr-Sum 79, c1981, pp. 40-41.

HAJNAL, Gabor
  "Consolation" (tr. by Herbert Kuhner).   WebR (6:2) 81, p. 39.

HALE, Frances
  "David."   MalR (57) Ja 81, p. 130.
  "Eurydice's Song."   MalR (57) Ja 81, p. 132.
  "Independence."   MalR (57) Ja 81, p. 131.

HALES, Corrinne
  "Great Salt Lake: July, 1955."   CimR (57) O 81, pp. 54-55.

HALEY, Richard
  "To My Son at Fourteen."   GeoR (35:1) Spr 81, p. 80.

HALL, David
  "Coming Out."   SouthwR (66:2) Spr 81, p. 140.
  "Fever."   SouthwR (66:4) Aut 81, p. 350.

HALL, Donald
  "Illustration."   ParisR (23:79) Spr 81, p. 192.
  "A Novel in Two Volumes."   Antaeus (40/41) Wint-Spr 81, p. 297.

HALL, Frances
  "Skeptic."   SouthwR (66:3) Sum 81, p. 292.

HALL, James B.
  "Bad Habits (Or, Scoring Sunshine)."   SouthwR (66:4) Aut 81, p. 360.

HALL, James Baker
  "A Love Poem."   PoNow (6:2 issue 32) 81, p. 43.
  "The First Winter Light."   NewYorker (57:45) 28 D 81, p. 46.
  "In the Exit Lane."   ThRiPo (17/18) 81, p. 20.

HALL, Jim
  "My Acceptance Speech."   PoNow (6:1 issue 31) 81, p. 45.

HALL, Joan Joffe
  "The Red Moon."   GeoR (35:1) Spr 81, pp. 107-110.

HALL, Judith
  "The Book of Joanna 2."   Nimrod (25:1) Aut-Wint 81, pp. 60-61.
  "The Book of Joanna 1."   Nimrod (25:1) Aut-Wint 81, pp. 59-60.

HALL, Vickie
  "The Writer."   Wind (11:42) 81, p. 19.

HALLEY, Anne
  "In Kingston: Hope's Rumor."   Ploughs (6:4) 81, pp. 162-163.
  "Rumors of the Turning Wheel."   Ploughs (6:4) 81, pp. 164-165.

HALLIDAY, Mark
  "Describers."   Ploughs (7:2) 81, pp. 144-149.
  "New York Breeze."   NewRep (184:6) 7 F 81, p. 26.

HALMAN, Talat
  "Chains" (tr. of Melih Cevdet Anday, w/ Brian Swann).   WebR (6: 1)
    Spr 81, p. 18.
  "Copper Age" (tr. of Melih Cevdet Anday, w/ Brian Swann).   LitR (24:

3) Spr 81, p. 405-406.
"Eyes" (tr. of Edip Cansever). Mund (12/13) 80-81, p. 354.
"Laughing Stock" (tr. of Gulten Akin, w/ Brian Swann). PoNow (5:6
   issue 30) 81, p. 2.
"Oblivion is Birds" (tr. of Melih Cevdet Anday, w/ Brian Swann).
   WebR (6: 1) Spr 81, p. 15.
"The Rowboat" (tr. of Melih Cevdet Anday, w/ Brian Swann). WebR
   (6: 1) Spr 81, p. 17.
"Sound" (tr. of Melih Cevdet Anday, w/ Brian Swann). WebR (6: 1)
   Spr 81, p. 16.

HALPERN, Daniel
"The Corpse of the Insensitive." NewYorker (57:17) 15 Je 81, p. 44.
"Dead Fish." Iowa (11:2/3) Spr-Sum 80, pp. 214-215.
"Defensive Epigram." ThRiPo (17/18) 81, p. 22.
"Elegies for Careless Love." Iowa (11:2/3) Spr-Sum 80, pp. 210-213.
"Night Scene" (for Bill). VirQR (57:2) Spr 81, pp. 277-278.
"Sunday Avenue." VirQR (57:2) Spr 81, p. 276.
"This Time of the Year." NewYorker (57:11) 4 My 81, p. 42.

HALTRICH, Josef
"The Sick Gypsy Boy" (tr. by Ann J. Toumi). Northeast (3:10) Wint
   81, p. 31.

HAMBLIN, Robert W.
"First Snowfall, Thanksgiving, 1980." CapeR (17:1) Wint 81, p. 10.
"The Lovers." CapeR (16:2) Sum 81, p. 15.

HAMBRICK, Brenda
"Topaz Lady." BlackALF (15:2) Sum 81, p. 72.

HAMBURGER, Michael
"Placed Amid Old Men" (tr. of Günter Grass). Mund (12/13) 80-81, p.
   316.
"Variations: In Suffolk." Stand (22: 1) 80, pp. 28-29.

HAMILTON, Alfred Starr
"City." PoNow (6:2 issue 32) 81, p. 31.
"The Gold Dust Twins." PoNow (6:2 issue 32) 81, p. 31.
"Lake Erie." PoNow (6:2 issue 32) 81, p. 31.
"Rainbow." PoNow (6:2 issue 32) 81, p. 31.

HAMILTON, Carol
"The Mimosas Do Their Part As I Do Mine." WindO (38) Spr-Sum 81,
   pp. 35-36.
"Passing By." CapeR (16:2) Sum 81, p. 6.

HAMILTON, David
"The Blue He Seized." HolCrit (18:3) Je 81, pp. 19-20.

HAMILTON, Elissa
"Cooking Demons." Sam (106) 81, pp. 27-29.

HAMILTON, Elissa L. A.
"The Lunar Year Ends With A Fright." PortR (27: 2) 81, p. 96.

HAMILTON, Horace
"Learning Arithmetic." SouthernR (17:2) Spr 81, pp. 382-3.
"A Return and Two Farewells." SouthernR (17:2) Spr 81, p. 381.

HAMMER, Langdon
"Chenega Island." YaleR (70: 3) Spr 81, p. 409-410.
"Detail From 'The Assassination of Khosrow Parviz.'" Ploughs (7:2)
    81, pp. 95-96.

HAMMOND, Ann B.
"Waiting for the Word." ChrC (98:27) 9 S 81, p. 856.

HAMMOND, Karla M.
"To a Child." Im (7:3) 81, p. 11.

HANDLIN, Jim
"Akbar's Algebra." Poetry (138:2) My 81, p. 75.
"Remnants." Poetry (138:2) My 81, p. 76.

HANDY, Ellen
"Epithalamium." Iowa (12:1) Wint 81, p. 107.

HANDY, Nixeon Civille
"Coldwater Flat." CharR (7:1) Spr 81, p. 43.

HANKLA, Cathryn
"Answering the Past." Outbr (6/7) Aut 80-Spr 81, p. 106.
"Firefly." Outbr (6/7) Aut 80-Spr 81, pp. 104-105.
"Mockingbird." QW (13) Aut/Wint 81/82, p. 94.
"A Moment of Violence." Outbr (6/7) Aut 80-Spr 81, p. 103.

HANLEY, Katherine
"Ark Dark." ChrC (98:19) 27 My 81, p. 606.
"Parable." ChrC (98:13) 22 Ap 81, p. 437.

HANNERS, LaVerne
"Death and the Dissertation." BallSUF (22:4) Aut 81, p. 31.
"Death of an Antique Lady." BallSUF (22:3) Sum 81, p. 24.

HANSEN, Betty
"Geneology." Poem (41) Mar 81, pp. 52-53.

HANSEN, Matthew
"Four Letters from the End of Summer." CutB (16) Spr-Sum 81, pp.
    117-118.

HANSEN, Tom
"Another Country." VirQR (57:2) Spr 81, pp. 279-280.
"At Home in the Lost Hotel." PoetryNW (22:3) Aut 81, pp. 39-40.
"Found Poem." Kayak (57) 81, pp. 38-39.
"How it Happens." CEACritic (44:1) N 81, p. 34.
"The Land of Watery Dark." CEACritic (44:1) N 81, p. 35.
"Leaving the House." CEACritic (44:1) N 81, p. 34.
"What They Said." CEACritic (44:1) N 81, p. 33.
"The Women Who Fell in Love with Water." CEACritic (44:1) N 81,
    p. 35.
"The Woman Who Fell in Love with Water." PoetryNW (22:3) Aut 81,
    pp. 40-41.

HANSON, Alice Taylor
"On Writing." EngJ (70:7) N 81, p. 86.

HANSON, Charles
    "Elegy to a Stove." WindO (38) Spr-Sum 81, p. 44.
    "The Meek Again." CentR (25:2) Spr 81, p. 166.
    "The Taste of Salt." Wind (10:39) 80, p. 23.
    "Under Scorpio." CentR (25:2) Spr 81, pp. 165-166.

HANSON, Howard G.
    "Cornflowers." BallSUF (22:4) Aut 81, p. 3.
    "The Mystery of Pots." ArizQ (37:4) Wint 81, p. 361.
    "October." ArizQ (37:3) Aut 81, p. 255.
    "On Meeting Images." BallSUF (22:2) Spr 81, p. 10.

HANSON, Kenneth O.
    "Greek Coffee." NowestR (19:3), pp. 6-7.
    "Lighting the Night Sky." NowestR (19:3), pp. 8-10.

HANZLICEK, C. G.
    "Portrait of a Laugh." CimR (55) Ap 81, p. 56.
    "Two Faces: A Fable." CimR (55) Ap 81, p. 17.

HARALSON, Carol
    "Mockingbird." Nimrod (25:1) Aut-Wint 81, p. 71.

HARDING, Gunnar
    From "Starnberger See" (tr. by Robin Fulton). Pequod (13) 81, pp.
      105-106.

HARDY, Catherine
    "The New Dress." PoNow (6:2 issue 32) 81, p. 28.
    "Real Estate." Wind (11:43) 81, p. 19.

HARJO, Joy
    "Leaving." Cond (7) Spr 81, p. 19.
    "September Moo." Cond (7) Spr 81, p. 24.
    "Talking to the Moon No. 002." Cond (7) Spr 81, p. 22.
    "Talking to the Moon No. 003." Cond (7) Spr 81, pp. 22-23.
    "White Bear." Cond (7) Spr 81, pp. 20-21.

HARLOW, Terry
    "In Chicago I saw." Aspect (77/79) 81, p. 100.

HARMON, William
    "A Crapulist Manifesto." CarolQ (34:2) Aut 81, pp. 46-52.
    "Two Artifacts, Two Metamorphoses." Agni (15) 81, pp. 16-17.

HARMSEL, Larry Ten
    "Double Metamorphosis" (tr. of Lucebert). Mund (12/13) 80-81, p. 37.
    "Harvest" (tr. of Lucebert). Mund (12/13) 80-81, p. 37.

HARPER, Elizabeth
    "Fermata." PottPort (3) 81, p. 39.

HARPER, Michael S.
    "Chief." Ploughs (7:1) 81, pp. 30-31.
    "Dear Old Stockholm" (for Miles Davis). GeoR (35:1) Spr 81, pp. 140-
      141.
    "The Drowning of the Facts of a Life." Ploughs (7:1) 81, pp. 36-38.
    "Elegy for a Metaphor: Dogwood/Pear" (for Robert Hayden and James

Wright). Iowa (12:1) Wint 81, pp. 108-109.
"Hooking" (for Ellen 'Nellie' Shannon). Field (25) Aut 81, pp. 41-42.
"Myrdal's Sacred Flame." Ploughs (7:1) 81, pp. 32-35.
"The Negatives." Mund (12/13) 80-81, p. 171.
"Photographs: Negatives: History as Apple Tree." Mund (12/13) 80-
    81, p. 171.
"Strands." Ploughs (7:1) 81, pp. 28-29.
"Utility Room." Mund (12/13) 80-81, p. 172.

HARRAL, Warren
"The Caravan Motel." PoNow (6:3 issue 33) 81, p. 15.
"Collage." PoNow (6:3 issue 33) 81, p. 15.

HARRIS, Alan
"Away from Home." Stand (22: 2) 81, p. 61.

HARRIS, Jana
"Lipstick." Tele (17) 81, p. 87.
"This Is How Men Get Hard And Callous." Tele (17) 81, p. 86.

HARRIS, Michael
"Art." Atl (247:2) F 81, p. 39.

HARRIS, Michael D.
"Country Lady." Obs (6:1/2) Spr-Sum 80, pp. 199-200.
"The One Still Standing (Notes on a Lecture by Dick Gregory)." Obs
    (6:1 /2) Spr-Sum 80, p. 201.

HARRIS, Norman
"A Dream." Obs (7:1) Spr 81, p. 77.
"Friends and Lovers." Obs (7:1) Spr 81, p. 76.
"I Don't Like Your Poetry." Obs (7:1) Spr 81, pp. 73-75.
"Work." Obs (7:1) Spr 81, p. 75.

HARRIS, Peter
"Commercial Curses." Obs (6:1/2) Spr-Sum 80, p. 236.
"More Souls Lost." Obs (6:1/2) Spr-Sum 80, pp. 235-236.
"A Rotting Loincloth." Obs (6:1/2) Spr-Sum 80, pp. 237-238.
"Words to Offer Lost Respect." Obs (6:1/2) Spr-Sum 80, p. 234.

HARRIS, William J.
"My Hero." PoNow (6:2 issue 32) 81, p. 29.
"Yesterday My Pig Died." PoNow (6:2 issue 32) 81, p. 29.

HARRISON, Keith
"Otters at Battle Lake" (for Jake and Catherine Barner). HiramPoR
    (29) Aut-Wint 81, p. 7.

HARRISON, Pamela
"South Rim. November." NewEngR (4:2) Wint 81, pp. 278-9.

HARROLD, William
"The Himalayas of the Mind." CreamCR (6:2) 81, pp. 7-8.

HARSHMAN, Marc
"Beside County 303." QW (13) Aut/Wint 81/82, p. 43.
"Checking the Spring" (for Steve & Chris Paull). PoNow (6:1 issue 31)
    81, p. 40.

HART, Henry
　　"Delos." CharR (7:1) Spr 81, p. 49.
　　"Thorns." Stand (22: 4) 81, pp. 34-35.

HARTMAN, Charles O.
　　"Catching A Ray." Ploughs (6:4) 81, pp. 182-184.
　　"Gravitation." CarolQ (34:1) Sum 81, pp. 49-52.
　　"Homage to Jay Silverheels." CarolQ (34:2) Aut 81, p. 7.
　　"Not Oscar Wilde in Duluth." Poetry (138:5) Ag 81, p. 265.
　　"Terzanelle." Poetry (138:5) Ag 81, p. 266.

HARVEY, Gail Ellen
　　"Dark slalom" (after a news report on handicapped skiers). PortR (27:
　　　2) 81, p. 93.
　　"Road Climbing Through Long Grass--Renoir." PortR (27: 2) 81, p. 93.

HARVEY, Gayle Elen
　　"Dog days--tight shoes." WindO (38) Spr-Sum 81, p. 12.
　　"August 27th." CapeR (16:2) Sum 81, p. 50.
　　"Thunder storm." WindO (38) Spr-Sum 81, p. 12.
　　"Trick-or-treat." CapeR (17:1) Wint 81, p. 15.
　　"trick-or-treat." Wind (11:42) 81, p. 18.

HARVEY, Helen
　　"Poetry vs. Profanity." Wind (10:39) 80, p. 24.

HASAN, Rabiul
　　"The Little Bighorn, Montana, 1980." Maize (4:1/2) Aut-Wint 80-81, p.
　　　72.
　　"Report from the Delta: Central Mississippi." Maize (4:1/2) Aut-Wint
　　　80-81, p. 73.
　　"To Rima." Wind (11:43) 81, p. 20.
　　"Snowfall in Columbus: Mississippi." Vis (7) 81, n. p.

HASKELL, Harry
　　"Affirmation of the Word" (tr. of Pedro de Oraa). Mund (12/13) 80-81,
　　　p. 301.
　　"Solar Music" (tr. of Alfonso Chase). Mund (12/13) 80-81, pp. 238-242.
　　"The Tides of Day and Night (for Octavio Paz)" (with Gregory Brehm).
　　　Mund (12/13) 80-81, pp. 310-313.

HASKINS, Lola
　　"Julia, Fort Lauderdale, Early." BelPoJ (32:1) Aut 81, pp. 20-32.
　　"Persistence: The Will of Jeremy Bentham" (for Ger). SouthernPR
　　　(21:2) Aut 81, p. 12.

HASS, Robert
　　"The Harbor at Seattle." NewRep (184:9) 28 F 81, p. 26.
　　"Late Spring." Antaeus (40/41) Wint-Spr 81, pp. 302-303.
　　"Museum." Antaeus (40/41) Wint-Spr 81, p. 304.
　　"Novella." Antaeus (40/41) Wint-Spr 81, p. 305.
　　"Old Dominion." Thrpny (5) Spr 81, p. 7.
　　"Rusia en 1931." Antaeus (40/41) Wint-Spr 81, pp. 298-299.
　　"Vintage." Antaeus (40/41) Wint-Spr 81, pp. 300-301.

HASSE, Margaret
　　"The Shy Girl, Melinda." Prima (6/7) 81, p. 77.

HASTY, Palmer
"The Scalpel and the Spider." Confr (21) Wint 81, p. 103.

HATHAWAY, Dev
"Asseteague Refuge." QW (12) Spr-Sum 81, p. 113.

HATHAWAY, Jeanine
"Mercy As the Constant." Northeast (3:10) Wint 81, pp. 20-21.
"The Name of God Is Simple." GeoR (35:2) Sum 81, p. 257.
"Poem for Christmas." OhioR (26), p. 121.
"Something the Woman Dreams." Northeast (3:10) Wint 81, p. 21.

HATHAWAY, William
"Escape from Angola Prison." Im (7:2) 1981, p. 9.
"Halfway House." Northeast (3:10) Wint 81, p. 7.
"Prose Poem about a Horse." PoetryE (6) Aut 81, pp. 62-63.
"The Souls of Dolphins." Northeast (3:10) Wint 81, p. 6.
"Sunshine, L. A.: A Pastoral." ThRiPo (17/18) 81, p. 24.

HAUG, James
"First Flight." PoNow (6:3 issue 33) 81, p. 15.

HAUGE, Olav
"I Pass the Arctic Circle" (tr. by Robin Fulton). Pequod (13) 81, p.
    111.
"Mountains No Longer Entice Me" (tr. by Robin Fulton). Pequod (13)
    81, p. 112.

HAUPTMAN, Robert
"Three Poems" (tr. of Nelly Sachs). WebR (6:2) 81, p. 104.

HAUPTMAN, Terry
"Crazed." SouthernR (17:2) Spr 81, p. 390.
"The Edger of the Inner Circle." SouthernR (17:2) Spr 81, pp. 387-8.
"Ice." SouthernR (17:2) Spr 81, p. 392.
"Fearful Symmetry." SouthernR (17:2) Spr 81, p. 391.
"The Needle's Eye." SouthernR (17:2) Spr 81, p. 393.
"Point of Departure." SouthernR (17:2) Spr 81, pp. 389-390.

HAUSMAN, Gerald
"The Runners." ArizQ (37:4) Wint 81, p. 292.

HAVEN, Richard
"In Sum." MalR (58) Ap 81, p. 50.
"Problem." MalR (58) Ap 81, p. 49.
"Relativity." MalR (58) Ap 81, p. 50.
"Sound." MalR (58) Ap 81, p. 51.
"Things." MalR (58) Ap 81, p. 49.

HĀWI, Khalil
"The Genie of the Beach" (tr. by Michael Beard and Adnan Haydar).
    Nimrod (24: 2) Spr/Sum 81, pp. 101-103.

HAY, John
"Sailing (for C. L. Barber 1913-1980)." NewEngR (4:1) Aut 81, p. 84.

HAYDAR, Adnan
"Cadenzas on Water" (tr. of Mahmūd Marwish). Nimrod (24: 2) Spr/

Sum 81, pp. 78-79.

"The Genie of the Beach" (tr. of Khalil Hāwi, w/ Michael Beard).
Nimrod (24: 2) Spr/Sum 81, pp. 101-103.

"A Gift" (tr. of Fu'ād Rifqa, w/ Michael Beard). Nimrod (24: 2) Spr/
Sum 81, p. 36.

"God of Time" (tr. of Fu'ād Rifqa, w/ Michael Beard). Nimrod (24: 2)
Spr/Sum 81, p. 37.

"My beloved says" (tr. of Fu'ād Rifqa, w/ Michael Beard). Nimrod (24:
2) Spr/Sum 81, p. 38.

"Smoke" (tr. of Fu'ād Rifqa, w/ Michael Beard). Nimrod (24: 2) Spr/
Sum 81, p. 35.

"A Tale" (tr. of Fu'ād Rifqa, w/ Michael Beard). Nimrod (24: 2) Spr/
Sum 81, p. 37.

"Verdura" (tr. of Fu'ād Rifqa, w/ Michael Beard). Nimrod (24: 2)
Spr/Sum 81, p. 38.

HAYN, Annette
"Colonial Dollhouse." Tele (17) 81, p. 110.

HAYNES, John
"Tailor." Stand (22: 2) 81, p. 50.

HAZARD, James
"The Cucumbers." CreamCR (6:2) 81, p. 109.
"8732 S. Harper Avenue." CreamCR (6:2) 81, p. 110.

HAZARD, John
"Percussion: Spring Concert at South High." PoetryNW (22:1) Spr 81,
pp. 19-20.

HAZO, Samuel
"The Day's Roulette." Mund (12/13) 80-81, pp. 294-295.
"A Dream for Any Man" (tr. of Adonis). Mund (12/13) 80-81, p. 31.
"Elegy in Exile" (tr. of Adonis). Mund (12/13) 80-81, pp. 28-30.
"The Naked Face" (tr. of Andrée Chedid, w/ Mirene Ghossein). Mund
(12/13) 80-81, p. 329.
"The Past" (tr. of Adonis). Mund (12/13) 80-81, p. 27.
"The Sleep of Hands" (tr. of Adonis). Mund (12/13) 80-81, p. 27.
"Who Remains Standing?" (tr. of Andrée Chedid, w/ Mirene Ghossein).
Mund (12/13) 80-81, p. 329.

HEAD, Gwen
"The Gardener's Daughter." PoetryNW (22:2) Sum 81, pp. 5-6.
"Hannah's Quilt." AntR (39: 1) Wint 81, pp. 70-72.
"Sestina: Seraphim." PoetryNW (22:2) Sum 81, pp. 8-9.
"Sleeping Alone." PoetryNW (22:2) Sum 81, pp. 6-7.
"Stone Speech." PoetryNW (22:2) Sum 81, pp. 7-8.
"Wreck." PoetryNW (22:2) Sum 81, pp. 3-4.

HEAD, Robert
I Once Was Alive. (To Darlene Fife). Sam (115) 81, Entire issue.

HEALY, Christine Kaczynski
"An Abortion." Comm (108:8) 24 Ap 81, p. 242.

HEALY, Howard
"The 1948 Plymouth." Comm (108:22) 4 D 81, p. 698.

HEALY, Ron
"Lace Curtains." Vis (6) 81, n. p.
"A Man at His Desk." Vis (5) 81, n. p.

HEARNE, Vicki
"The Claim of Speech." Poetry (138:5) Ag 81, pp. 257-258.
"On R. L. S. and Happiness." Poetry (138:5) Ag 81, pp. 255-256.

HEARST, James
"Bound to Happen." NewEngR (3:3) Spr 81, p. 369.
"Love Is Not Earned." Northeast (3:11) Sum 81, p. 5.
"Shy Breeder." PoNow (6:1 issue 31) 81, p. 16.
"A Small Matter." Northeast (3:11) Sum 81, p. 4.

HEBALD, Carol
"Child of the Ravenhair." Confr (21) Wint 81, p. 51.
"A Strange Flower." KanQ (13:1) Wint 81, p. 163.

HECHT, Anthony
"A Love for Four Voices: Homage to Franz Joseph Haydn" (for Frank
  and Ruth Glazer). Poetry (138:1) Ap 81, pp. 1-12.
"Murmur." NewYorker (57:4) 16 Mr 81, p. 46.

HEFFERNAN, Michael
"Squirrels Worshipping Crows." PoetryNW (22:2) Sum 81, p. 17.
"Ten Past Eleven." Poetry (137:5) F 81, p. 271.

HEJINIAN, Lyn
"The erosion of rocks blooms." SunM (11) Spr 81, p. 88.
"Counter Measure." Tele (17) 81, p. 26.
"Punctual 2" (for Henry Kaiser). Tele (17) 81, p. 27.
"Punctual 13" (for Henry Kaiser). Tele (17) 81, p. 27.

HEMSCHEMEYER, Judith
"Ah! You've Come Back" (tr. of Anna Akhmatova, w/ Anne Wilkinson).
  Hudson (34:4) Wint 81, pp. 553-554.
"Confession" (tr. of Anna Akhmatova, w/ Anne Wilkinson). PoNow (5:6
  issue 30) 81, p. 1.
"Epithalamion." PortR (27: 1) 81, p. 23.
"For Us to Lose Freshness" (tr. of Anna Akhmatova, w/ Anne Wilkin-
  son). Hudson (34:4) Wint 81, p. 553.
"I came as the poet's guest" (to Alexander Blok) (tr. of Anna Akhma-
  tova, w/ Anne Wilkinson). Stand (22: 2) 81, p. 4.
"I Dreamed that Dream." PortR (27: 1) 81, p. 21.
"Kiev" (tr. of Anna Akhmatova, w/ Anne Wilkinson). Hudson (34:4)
  Wint 81, pp. 552-553.
"Meine Heilige Einsamkeit." PortR (27: 1) 81, p. 23.
"My imagination obeys me" (tr. of Anna Akhmatova, w/ Anne Wilkinson).
  Stand (22: 2) 81, p. 4.
"On Being Expelled from Paradise." PortR (27: 1) 81, p. 21.
"One heart isn't chained to another" (tr. of Anna Akhmatova, w/ Anne
  Wilkinson). PoNow (5:6 issue 30) 81, p. 1.
"Song of Our Last Meeting" (tr. of Anna Akhmatova, w/ Anne Wilkin-
  son). PoNow (6:1 issue 31) 81, p. 43.
"The Twenty-First" (tr. of Anna Akhmatova, w/ Anne Wilkinson).
  Hudson (34:4) Wint 81, p. 554.
"They didn't bring me a letter today" (tr. of Anna Akhmatova, w/ Anne
  Wilkinson). PoNow (5:6 issue 30) 81, p. 1.

"Under the Icon" (tr. of Anna Akhmatova, w/ Anne Wilkinson). Hudson
(34:4) Wint 81, p. 552.
"Verses about Petersburg" (tr. of Anna Akhmatova, w/ Anne Wilkinson).
Stand (22: 2) 81, p. 3.
"We are drinkers and fornicators here, one and all" (tr. of Anna Akhma-
tova, w/ Anne Wilkinson). PoNow (5:6 issue 30) 81, p. 1.
"When you're drunk you're so much fun!" (tr. of Anna Akhmatova, w/
Anne Wilkinson). PoNow (5:6 issue 30) 81, p. 1.

HENDERSON, Jock
"Eurydice or Eve." Comm (108:8) 24 Ap 81, p. 242.

HENDLER, Earl
"Tattle." SouthernHR (15:3) Sum 81, p. 230.

HENLEY, Lloyd
"Recollections of Viewing a 600-pound Man at Ava, Missouri." KanQ
(13:2) Spr 81, p. 56.
"Routine Matters." CapeR (16:2) Sum 81, p. 37.
"Visual Aids for Telling News." CapeR (16:2) Sum 81, p. 36.

HENNESSEY, Michael F.
"The Young Seaman." PottPort (3) 81, p. 11.

HENNESSY, Madeleine
"The Christmas." 13thM (5:1/2) 80, p. 33.

HENRI, Raymond
"Choices." Confr (22) Sum 81, p. 65.

HENRY, Gerrit
"The Beloved Ingrate." AmerPoR (10:2) Mr-Ap 81, p. 30.
"Cole Porter's Son." AmerPoR (10:2) Mr-Ap 81, p. 30.
"Schools." AmerPoR (10:2) Mr-Ap 81, p. 30.

HENRY, Larry
"Jerry Silkwood Defends Himself." ThRiPo (17/18) 81, p. 93.

HENRY, Michael
"Praire Gold." Sam (109) 81, p. 31.

HENRY, Sarah
"At Last." SmPd (18:2) Spr 81, p. 17.
"Geography." SmPd (18:2) Spr 81, p. 18.

HENSHAW, Tyler
"Lost Cowboy." KanQ (13:2) Spr 81, p. 72.
"Navies Turn to Rust Having Gone Aground Wars Ago." KanQ (13:2)
Spr 81, p. 72.
"Watching Birds Fly into the Trees." KanQ (13:2) Spr 81, p. 72.

HENSON, David
"How Nessie Acquired Her Taste for Lamb." Im (7:3) 81, p. 11.
"Loch Ness Monster in the Rain at Night." Im (7:3) 81, p. 11.

HEPWORTH, James
"Emily Dickinson's Neighbor." Kayak (56) 81, pp. 62-63.
"A Psychiatrist Questions Louis Aragon." Kayak (56) 81, p. 63.

HERBERT, Zbigniew
  "Mr. Cogito on Virtue" (tr. by Stuart Friebert). PoNow (5:6 issue 30)
    81, p. 17.
  "On Smoking Things Out" (tr. by Stuart Friebert). PoNow (5:6 issue
    30) 81, p. 17.

HERHOLD, Robert
  "The Church." ChrC (98:43) 30 D 81, p. 1359.

HERNANDEZ, Orlando
  "3." Lugar (1:1) 79, p. 11.
  "13." Lugar (1:1) 79, p. 11.
  "22." Lugar (1:1) 79, p. 11.

HERNANDEZ, Orlando José
  "Un caballo de luz para montar el agua de los sueños" (a Clemente
    Soto Vélez). Claridad (22: 1465) 27 F-5 Mr 81, p. 15.

HERNANDEZ RODRIGUEZ, Rafael
  "Poema de amor." Areito (7: 27) 81, p. 21.

HERNICK, J.
  "From the Spillway." PoNow (6:3 issue 33) 81, p. 15.

HERRERA, Juan Felipe
  "Black Tenor on Powell Street." Metam (3:2/4:1) 80-81, p. 37.
  "Ferlinghetti on the North Side of San Francisco Poem." Metam (3:2/
    4:1) 80-81, p. 35.
  "La 24 y el otoño (para yvonne maría, arnoldo y el salvador)." Metam
    (3:2/4:1) 80-81, p. 36.
  "The Waiters." DenQ (16:3) Aut 81, pp. 62-63.

HERRERA SOBEK, María
  "No supimos amarnos." Maize (4:3/4) Spr-Sum 81, p. 85.
  "Noches perdidas." Maize (4:3/4) Spr-Sum 81, p. 86.
  "Tomate rojo." Maize (4:3/4) Spr-Sum 81, p. 87.

HERRINGTON, Neva
  "According to Aristotle." SouthwR (66:2) Spr 81, p. 139.
  "The Drinker's Christmas." Ascent (7:1) 81, p. 30.
  "Lilacs." Ascent (7:1) 81, p. 31.

HERRSTROM, David
  "The Deadline, A Parable." US1 (14/15) Aut/Wint 81, p. 8.

HERSHON, Robert
  "After the War with Paraguay." PoNow (6:2 issue 32) 81, p. 24.
  "The Bank of Tokyo." PoNow (6:2 issue 32) 81, p. 24.
  "Miniature Armies." Tele (17) 81, p. 96.
  "The People On The Platform." Tele (17) 81, p. 97.
  "The Public Hug." PoNow (6:2 issue 32) 81, p. 24.
  "Spitting on Ira Rosenblatt." PoNow (6:2 issue 32) 81, p. 24.
  "Still Life." Tele (17) 81, p. 96.

HERTLE, Frank
  "Faces of Diana." Poem (43) Nov 81, p. 58.
  "Out of the Corner of My Eye." Poem (43) Nov 81, p. 60.
  "Starfish." Poem (43) Nov 81, p. 59.

HERZIG, Jack
"The Samurai." HolCrit (18:3) Je 81, p. 11.

HESTER, M. L.
"Teaching the Child." Northeast (3:10) Wint 81, p. 14.
"The Victim of the Beautiful Bandit." AmerS (50:3) Sum 81, p. 388.

HETTICH, Michael
"Hands." KanQ (13:1) Wint 81, p. 37.

HEWITT, Geof
"The Hello of Horrors." PoNow (6:1 issue 31) 81, p. 31.
"January." PoNow (6:1 issue 31) 81, p. 31.
"Vision." PoNow (6:1 issue 31) 81, p. 31.

HEY, Phil
"Why Can't We Get a Baler, Dad?" PoNow (6:2 issue 32) 81, p. 9.

HEYEN, William
"Arrows." Poetry (138:1) Ap 81, p. 25.
"The Berries." Poetry (139:3) D 81, p. 160.
"Catbird." Poetry (138:1) Ap 81, p. 26.
"A New Bible." PoetryE (6) Aut 81, p. 47.
"The Oregon Coast at Seal Rock: Thinking of Wallace Stevens at
    Seventy." Poetry (139:3) D 81, pp. 158-159.
"Post Mortem: Literary Criticism." Poetry (138:1) Ap 81, p. 27.
"Ram Time." Poetry (138:1) Ap 81, pp. 22-24.
"Released from Dachau, 1939." PoetryE (6) Aut 81, p. 46.
"The Snow Hen (1-7)." OntR (14) Spr-Sum 81, pp. 15-30.
"Yellowthroats." GeoR (35:4) Wint 81, pp. 802-803.

HEYM, Georg
"Why do you come so often to visit me" (tr. by Francis Golffing).
    PoNow (5:6 issue 30) 81, p. 17.

HEYMANN, John
"Spring Cat." OP (31/32) Aut 81, p. 119.

HEYNEN, Jim
"Dinner Music." CutB (17) Aut-Wint 81, p. 43.
"Uncle Jack and Miss Paraffin." PoNow (6:2 issue 32) 81, p. 14.
"Uncle Jack and the Beautiful School Teacher." PoNow (6:2 issue 32)
    81, pp. 14-15.

HEYTT, Barbara Helfgott
"The Bath." Prima (6/7) 81, p. 10.

HICKS, John V.
"Cauchemar." MalR (59) Jl 81, p. 163.

HIGGINS, Frank
"Behind the Corn." PoNow (6:3 issue 33) 81, p. 16.
"Caught by Whim I close the Window on a Wasp." KanQ (13:1) Wint 81,
    p. 40.
"The Eyes of Abraham Lincoln." KanQ (13:1) Wint 81, p. 40.
"Things to Do and See." PoNow (6:1 issue 31) 81, p. 31.

HIGLEY, Jerry
"Ammons Talks to the Motions." PortR (27: 2) 81, p. 16.

"Hemophilic" (for Charlene Lowry). PortR (27: 2) 81, p. 19.
"Kiss Me Simply." PortR (27: 2) 81, p. 16.
"Sax." PortR (27: 2) 81, p. 16.

HIKMET, Nazin
    from Things I Didn't Know I Loved: (5, 13) (tr. by Randy Blasing and
        Motlu Konuk). AmerPoR (10:3) My-Je 81, p. 6.

HILBERRY, Conrad
    "Letter to the North." MichQR (20:4) Aut 81, pp. 376-377.
    "The Birdwatcher and the Heron." MichQR (20:4) Aut 81, pp. 374-375.

HILDEBIDLE, John
    "For Harriet Quimby, Aviatrix: July 1, 1912." PoNow (6:3 issue 33)
        81, p. 24.
    "Monet at Giverny." LittleM (13:1/2) Spr-Sum 79, c1981, p. 108.
    "Relics." PoNow (6:3 issue 33) 81, p. 24.
    "The Supplication of Dorothy Bradford." Aspect (77/79) 81, pp. 101-
        102.

HILL, Claudia Weber
    "Love." Sam (117) 81, p. 25.
    "One Touch." Sam (117) 81, p. 26.
    "She Waits." Sam (117) 81, p. 25.

HILL, Jane Bowers
    "Yet Again They've Missed the Point." KanQ (13:3/4) Sum-Aut 81, pp.
        47-48.

HILL, Meg
    "Listening Back." ChrC (98:4) 4-11 F 81, p. 107.

HILL, Nellie
    "Black and White Ectogram." CentR (25:4) Aut 81, pp. 387-388.

HILL, Norah
    "Awaiting Poetry: For The Re-Maker On Receiving A Gift Of Transla-
        tions." Stand (22: 2) 81, p. 71.

HILL, Robert W.
    "Chicago: Lake Shore and Twenty-third." Ascent (6:2) 81, p. 48.
    "Reading the Lines." Ascent (6:2) 81, p. 49.
    "Whole Thought." Shen (31:4) 80, pp. 76-77.

HILLMAN, Brenda
    "Birth." AmerPoR (10:4) Jl-Ag 81, p. 11.
    "Driving." Field (25) Aut 81, p. 37.
    "Ellipsis." Field (25) Aut 81, p. 36.
    "Invisible Corral" (for S. H.). AntR (39:3) Sum 81, p. 336.
    "Kilauea." Thrpny (7) Aut 81, p. 7.
    "Tenant." AmerPoR (10:4) Jl-Ag 81, p. 11.

HILTON, William C.
    "Coleridge, Sleep Yet Gently." BallSUF (22:1) Wint 81, p. 2.
    "The Enemies of Time." BallSUF (22:4) Aut 81, p. 37.
    "Woman on a Plane." BallSUF (22:3) Sum 81, p. 70.

HILTY, Peter
    "Sunday Night Visit at the Retirement Home." CapeR (17:1) Wint 81, p. 16.

HIMMIRSKY, Krassin
"Drawing on an Ancient Vase" (tr. by Elisavietta Ritchie and Krassin Himmirsky). PoNow (5:6 issue 30) 81, p. 18.
"Elegy from Vesletza (To my mother)" (tr. by the author with Elisavietta Ritchie). Vis (5) 81, n. p.
"Fire" (tr. by the author with Elisavietta Ritchie). Vis (5) 81, n. p.
"Krali Marko (The Giant hero of old Bulgarian epic)" (tr. by the author with Elisavietta Ritchie). Vis (5) 81, n. p.
"Masks" (tr. by Elisavietta Ritchie and Krassin Himmirsky). PoNow (5:6 issue 30) 81, p. 18.
"Night Skyscrapers" (tr. by the author with Elisavietta Ritchie). Vis (5) 81, n. p.

HINDLEY, Norman
"Getaway." StoneC (8: 3) Spr 81, pp. 46-47.
"Red is a Hard Rose." ThRiPo (17/18) 81, p. 86.

HINE, Daryl
"Rigor Mortis, Rigor Amoris." YaleR (70: 3) Spr 81, p. 413.
"Vivid Season of Decay." Poetry (138:6) S 81, pp. 315-316.

HINOJOSA, Rolando
"Retaguardia en noviembre which means: the 219th isn't doing well at all." Maize (4:3/4) Spr-Sum 81, pp. 61-63.

HIRSCH, Edward
"Dino Campana and the Bear." Nat (233:18) 28 N 81, p. 582.
"I Need Help." NewYorker (57:33) 5 O 81, p. 169.
"Postcard to Tristan Tzara." Kayak (56) 81, p. 3.
"Sleepwatch." Kayak (56) 81, pp. 4-5.

HIRSCHFIELD, Ted
"Conversations." CapeR (16:2) Sum 81, p. 48.
"Emblem." CapeR (16:2) Sum 81, p. 47.
"Learning Distances." CapeR (16:2) Sum 81, p. 49.
"Reburial." CapeR (16:2) Sum 81, p. 45.
"Sunday." CapeR (16:2) Sum 81, p. 47.
"What Animals Dream." CapeR (16:2) Sum 81, p. 46.

HIRSH, Linda Blaker
"Making archaic forms." Outbr (6/7) Aut 80-Spr 81, pp. 47-48.

HIRSHFIELD, Jane
"The Conquerors Of Troy." CalQ (18/19) 81, p. 84.
"A Continuous Embroidery." CalQ (18/19) 81, p. 85.
"How To Give." CalQ (18/19) 81, p. 86.

HOAG, Ronald Wesley
"Noiselessly as Time." ConcPo (14:1) Spr 81, p. 57.

HOBEN, Sandra
"Earrings." ThRiPo (17/18) 81, p. 38.

HOCKING, Beverly
"Instructions." MalR (58) Ap 81, p. 111.

HOCQUARD, Emmanuel
Eight poems (four tr. by Jane Staw). SenR (12:1/2) 81, pp. 62-69.

HODGE, Marion
    "Pond."   Wind (11:41) 81, pp. 22-23.
    "Yearbook."   Wind (11:41) 81, pp. 21-22.

HODGEN, John
    "For the Breasts of the Unattractive Girl."   Tendril (11) Sum 81, p.
      38.

HOEFT, Robert D.
    "Dead Bird on the Path."   Poem (41) Mar 81, p. 6.
    "Spring."   Poem (41) Mar 81, p. 4.
    "A Stand of Ferns."   Wind (11:42) 81, p. 19.
    "Summer."   Poem (41) Mar 81, p. 5.

HOEKSEMA, Thomas
    "Always" (tr. of Luis García Morales).   Mund (12/13) 80-81, p. 122.
    "Like A Hollow Snail" (tr. of Bertalicia Peralta).   Mund (12/13) 80-81,
      p. 237.
    "Noon" (tr. of Isabel Fraire).   Mund (12/13) 80-81, p. 91.
    "Ontology, Epistemology, Literature... (for Juan García Ponce)" (tr. of
      Isabel Fraire).   NewOR (8:1) Wint 81, p. 59.
    "Silence" (tr. of Bertalicia Peralta).   Mund (12/13) 80-81, p. 237.

HOFER, Mariann
    "Abandoned Launderette."   StoneC (9: 1-2) Aut-Wint 81/82, p. 50.
    "Without Apologies."   StoneC (9: 1-2) Aut-Wint 81/82, p. 51.

HOFFMAN, Daniel
    "A Barn Built in Ohio."   NewEngR (4:2) Wint 81, pp. 274-7.
    "Scrolls from the Dead."   Shen (32: 4) 81, p. 17.

HOGAN, Linda
    "Bright Wings, Daybreak."   Prima (6/7) 81, p. 49.

HOGAN, Mary Ann
    "Recognition."   PottPort (3) 81, p. 10.

HOGAN, Michael
    "Uncharted."   PoNow (6:2 issue 32) 81, p. 6.
    "Verde que te quiero verde" (--García Lorca).   Aspect (77/79) 81, p.
      103.

HOGG, Robert
    "Heat Lightning."   Bound (9:2) Wint 81, pp. 275-276.
    "Three Rooms."   Bound (9:2) Wint 81, pp. 271-275.

HOGGARD, James
    "Nightwraithing."   Tele (17) 81, p. 93.
    "Photography" (tr. of Oscar Hahn).   StoneC (9: 1-2) Aut-Wint 81/82, p.
      36.

HOGUE, Cynthia
    "After the Great Rain."   CutB (17) Aut-Wint 81, p. 42.
    "an untitled poem" (tr. of Göran Sonnevi, w/ Jan Karlsson).   AmerPoR
      (10:6) N-D 81, p. 32.

HOLBROOK, John
    "Chester, Montana: All the Windrows One Way."   CutB (16) Spr-Sum
      81, pp. 110-111.

HOLDEN, Jonathan
   "Afterward." CalQ (18/19) 81, pp. 93-94.
   "The Edge." CalQ (18/19) 81, pp. 94-95.
   "Elizabeth." GeoR (35:1) Spr 81, pp. 138-139.
   "Framing." QW (12) Spr-Sum 81, p. 88.
   "The History of the Moon." Ascent (6:3) 81, pp. 33-34.
   "Making Things Grow." OP (31/32) Aut 81, p. 93.
   "Monday Morning." Ascent (6:3) 81, pp. 34-36.
   "On a Mild October Evening." QW (12) Spr-Sum 81, pp. 86-7.
   "Piece-work." CimR (56) Jl 81, pp. 21-22.
   "Pin Oak." CimR (56) Jl 81, pp. 62-63.
   "A Poem Against Daylight Savings." NewEngR (3:3) Spr 81, pp. 433-4.
   "A Poem for Ed 'Whitey' Ford." Ascent (6:3) 81, pp. 32-33.
   "Three Mile Island." StoneC (9: 1-2) Aut-Wint 81/82, p. 30.

HOLLAMAN, Keith
   "A Couple of Words" (tr. of Benjamin Peret). SenR (12:1/2) 81, p. 53.
   "There Is Only One Wonder on Earth" (tr. of Benjamin Peret). SenR
     (12:1/2) 81, p. 55.

HOLLAND, Barbara
   "A Covering Letter." Aspect (77/79) 81, p. 104.
   "Moon Drinker." Aspect (77/79) 81, p. 105.
   "Partial Evolution." Aspect (77/79) 81, p. 105.

HOLLAND, Barbara A.
   "Caught Unprepared for May." Wind (10:39) 80, p. 25.

HOLLAND, David
   "The heron's scream." PortR (27: 1) 81, p. 7.
   "Who's singing that song." PortR (27: 1) 81, p. 33.

HOLLAND, John
   "Texts for Speaking Voice." Agni (15) 81, pp. 124-129.

HOLLANDER, Jean
   "Complaint." Confr (21) Wint 81, p. 33.

HOLLANDER, John
   "All Our Poems of Death Are Juvenilia." ParisR (23:79) Spr 81, pp.
     193-194.
   "A Garden in Pasadena." YaleR (70: 3) Spr 81, pp. 406-407.
   "Grounds and Beliefs." Nat (233:1) 4 Jl 81, p. 22.
   "Looking Ahead." NewYorker (56:48) 19 Ja 81, p. 40.
   "The Meaning of It." YaleR (70: 3) Spr 81, pp. 407-408.
   "Our Dominion." Stand (22: 4) 81, p. 6.
   "Songs and Sonnets." GeoR (35:2) Sum 81, pp. 273-274.
   "Thirteens." Poetry (138:3) Je 81, pp. 125-131.
   "A Time of Year." NewRep (184:8) 21 F 81, p. 34.
   "A Walk with You." NewYRB (28:5) 2 Ap 81, p. 30.

HOLLANDER, Robert
   "Audiences." AmerS (50:1) Wint 80-81, p. 72.
   "The Lecturer's One Thought." SouthernR (17:2) Spr 81, p. 402.

HOLLINS, Walter H.
   "Grandpa Said." Obs (7:1) Spr 81, p. 34.
   "Papa." Obs (7:1) Spr 81, p. 35.

"ROOM." Obs (7:1) Spr 81, p. 34.
"Understand the Flower Song." Obs (7:1) Spr 81, p. 35.

HOLLIS, Ena
"Each Time I Return To You" (tr. of Cintio Vitier). Mund (12/13) 80-81, pp. 21-22.
"The Word" (tr. of Cintio Vitier). Mund (12/13) 80-81, p. 21.

HOLLO, Anselm
from The Dance-Floor on the Mountain: "Today, I walk another way" (tr. of Pentti Saarikoski). PoetryE (6) Aut 81, pp. 38-40.

HOLM, Bill
"A Circle of Pitchforks." Nat (233:7) 12 S 81, p. 212.

HOLMES, Charlotte
"Leaving Home." SouthernR (17:3) Sum 81, p. 561.

HOLT, Nancy
"Disconsolate Etalosnocsid." Chelsea (39) 81, p. 175.
"Hammond, 1969." Chelsea (39) 81, p. 174.
"Making Waves." Chelsea (39) 81, p. 176.
"New Years" (Second version). Chelsea (39) 81, pp. 177-179.

HOLUB, Miroslav
"Teeth" (tr. by Miroslav Holub and Stuart Friebert). Field (24) Spr 81, p. 41.

HOMER, Art
"Tour of Pittock Mansion." QW (12) Spr-Sum 81, pp. 94-5.

HONGNANG
"Breaking the Branch" (tr. by Michael Stephens). Pequod (13) 81, p. 69.

HONGO, Garrett Kaoru
"A Restless Night" (for Cynthia). PoetryNW (22:2) Sum 81, pp. 13-14.
"Evacuation." Nat (232:20) 23 My 81, p. 636.
"Off from Swing Shift." Kayak (57) 81, pp. 24-26.
"On The Last Performance Of Musume Dojoji At The Niroon-kan Of The Astor Hotel, Seattle, Washington." MissouriR (4:2) Wint 80-81, p. 11.
"Preaching the Blues." Kayak (57) 81, pp. 22-24.

HONIG, Edwin
"The Abstract Man Encounters the Adjutant." Im (7:3) 81, pp. 6-7.
"Volcano." PoNow (6:1 issue 31) 81, p. 7.

HOOKER, Jeremy
"Sycamore Buds." Pequod (13) 81, p. 44.

HOOPER, Patricia
"My Mother, Long-Distance." CentR (25:3) Sum 81, p. 261.
"The Park." CentR (25:3) Sum 81, p. 262.

HOOVER, Paul
"The Blue Cliff Records." MissR (10:1) Spr-Sum 81, pp. 157-158.
"The Critical Vocabulary." MissR (10:1) Spr-Sum 81, pp. 155-156.

"The Eagerness." SunM (11) Spr 81, p. 155.
"Five Minutes Worth of Writing." SunM (11) Spr 81, pp. 156-157.
"Just Plain Beauty." Chelsea (40) 81, p. 95.
"The Longest Distance Between Two Points." MissR (10:1) Spr-Sum 81,
    pp. 151-154.
"Thirty-Three." LittleM (13:1/2) Spr-Sum 79, c1981, pp. 122-123.

HOPES, David
    "Calling Dance." StoneC (9: 1-2) Aut-Wint 81/82, p. 32.
    "The Knot." PikeR (2) Sum 81, p. 18.

HOPKINS, Bill
    "Kyriolexy" (for W. C. W.). CapeR (16:2) Sum 81, p. 23.

HOPPER, Paul Thorfinn
    "Muse" (tr. of Anna Akhmatova). Vis (5) 81, n. p.
    "To Build a Tower" (tr. of Tor Jonsson). Vis (5) 81, n. p.
    "Tunnel" (tr. of Tor Jonsson). Vis (5) 81, n. p.

HORACE (HORATIUS)
    "Carminum, Liber I. 9. " SenR (12:1/2) 81, p. 30.
    "Odes, Book I. v." SenR (12:1/2) 81, p. 32.
    "Odes, Book I. v" (tr. by Stephen Sandy). SenR (12:1/2) 81, p. 33.
    "Odes I. 9" (tr. by Frank J. Nisetich). SenR (12:1/2) 81, p. 31.

HORIGUCHI, Daigaku
    "National Flag of the Sky" (tr. by Graeme Wilson). DenQ (16:4) Wint
    81, p. 37.

HORNE, Lewis
    "Kite and Self." OntR (15) Aut-Wint 81-82, p. 88.
    "Morning in a New House." KanQ (13:1) Wint 81, p. 27.
    "Summer Wish." OntR (15) Aut-Wint 81-82, p. 90.
    "Watching My Daughters Drive off for University." OntR (15) Aut-Wint
    81-82, p. 89.

HOROWITZ, Shel
    "Dead Wrong." Sam (106) 81, p. 13.

HORSTING, Eric
    "Coal Miners and Other People." DenQ (16:1) Spr 81, p. 99.
    "Sunday Morning In Columbus." NewL (47:4) Sum 81, pp. 88-89.
    "To Give, To Take, To Be Taken." NewL (47:4) Sum 81, p. 89.

HORVATH, Lou
    "The Cultural Necessity of Slapping New-Borns." Poem (42) Jul 81, pp.
    20-21.
    "Naming A New Son For The Dead Son." Poem (42) Jul 81, p. 22.
    "Kapital Versus I. " SunM (11) Spr 81, pp. 6-7.

HOTCHKISS, Bill
    "White World." Poetry (137:4) Ja 81, pp. 189-191.

HOTCHKISS, Marina
    "Stew." BelPoJ (31:4) Sum 81, p. 39.

HOUGHTON, Tim
    "The Boulevard Turned Back From the Woods." Wind (11:42) 81, p. 20.
    "Fishing." ArizQ (37:1) Spr 81, p. 74.

HOUSE, Tom
    "The Finale." Wind (11:43) 81, p. 21.
    "Juke House Jive." Sam (106) 81, p. 60.
    "Kathy's Admirer." Sam (109) 81, p. 33.

HOUSTON, Peyton
    "The Death of the Minotaur." OP (31/32) Aut 81, p. 134.
    "Fox Matters." OP (31/32) Aut 81, pp. 54-55.
    "The Tricks of the Magician." OP (31/32) Aut 81, p. 77.

HOVANESSIAN, Diana der see DER HOVANESSIAN, Diana

HOWARD, Ben
    "Departure." Iowa (11:2/3) Spr-Sum 80, p. 104.
    "Vocation." Iowa (11:2/3) Spr-Sum 80, p. 103.

HOWARD, Maureen
    "Plagiarism (For My Students in Writing 210)." NewYorker (57:41) 30
        N 81, p. 50.

HOWARD, Richard
    "Eugene Delacroix" (the portrait by Nadar). Salm (52/53) Spr/Sum 81,
        pp. 57-58.
    "Jean-Francois Millet" (the portrait by Nadar). Salm (52/53) Spr/Sum
        81, pp. 59-60.
    Nineteen poems (tr. of Charles Baudelaire). ParisR (23:82) Wint 81,
        pp. 23-43.
    "With A Potpourri From Down Under." ParisR (23:79) Spr 81, pp. 195-
        196.

HOWE, Fanny
    from "On The Meaning Of Life." Tele (17) 81, pp. 74-76.

HOWE, Susan
    from "Pythagorean Silence." Tele (17) 81, pp. 16-22.
    "Pythagorean Silence." Sulfur (3) 82, pp. 57-64.

HOWELL, Christopher
    "Enough." MassR (22:1) Spr 81, pp. 203-4.
    "Keeping Watch under a Lamppost in the Deep Wood I Experience the
        Caress of the Other World." ChiR (32:2) Aut 80, pp. 48-49.
    "Seascape." ChiR (32:2) Aut 80, p. 50.

HOY, Ruby
    "Greenland Gap." HiramPoR (29) Aut-Wint 81, p. 24.
    "Greenland Gap." PoNow (6:3 issue 33) 81, p. 46.

HSIN, Ch'i-chi
    "At Home in the Village" (tr. by C. H. Kwan). MalR (58) Ap 81, p.
        40.

HUA JUI, Lady
    "Life In The Palace" (tr. by Kennoth Rexroth and Ling Chung). UnmOx
        (22) Wint 81, pp. 15-16.

HUANG, Ting-jian
    "Late Spring" (tr. by C. H. Kwan). MalR (58) Ap 81, p. 41.

HUASI, Julio
"Defeats" (tr. by Roberto Márquez). Calib (3:2) Aut-Wint 80, p. 95.
"Derrotas." Calib (3:2) Aut-Wint 80, p. 94.

HUCHEL, Peter
"November" (tr. by Henry Beissel). Mund (12/13) 80-81, p. 32.
"Verona" (tr. by Henry Beissel). Mund (12/13) 80-81, p. 33.

HUDDLE, David
"Cousin." LittleR (7:1, issue 15) 81, p. 3.
"The Field." Agni (14) 81, p. 63.
"George." LittleR (7:1, issue 15) 81, p. 4.
"Nerves." LittleR (7:1, issue 15) 81, p. 4.
"Revelation." LittleR (7:1, issue 15) 81, p. 4.
"Short." LittleR (7:1, issue 15) 81, p. 3.
"Smoke." LittleR (7:1, issue 15) 81, p. 4.
"Transfer." LittleR (7:1, issue 15) 81, p. 3.

HUDGINS, Andrew
"After Grace." SouthernHR (15:3) Sum 81, p. 256.
"At Chancellorville: The Battle of the Wilderness." SouthernR (17:2)
    Spr 81, p. 377.
"At Chancellorsville: The Battle of the Wilderness." Bound (9:2) Wint
    81, p. 150.
"Bull Against a Black Rock." Confr (21) Wint 81, p. 42.
"Magnolias." NoAmR (266:4) D 81, p. 40.
"My Father's House." MassR (22:3) Aut 81, p. 573.
"A Rapproachement with Death." Bound (9:2) Wint 81, pp. 149-150.
"Serenades in Virginia: Summer, 1863." MissouriR (4:3) Sum 81, p.
    37.
"Sidney Lanier in Montgomery: August, 1866." SouthernR (17:2) Spr
    81, pp. 373-6.
"Sidney Lanier in Montgomery: August, 1866." Bound (9:6) Wint 81,
    pp. 152-155.
"Touching Jonathan." AntR (39:4) Aut 81, pp. 444-445.

HUDSON, Frederick B.
"Sunday for Art." Obs (6:1/2) Spr-Sum 80, pp. 202-203.

HUDSON, Marc
"By La Push (for Pablo Neruda)." MalR (57) Ja 81, pp. 112-113.
"Reading Chretien by Hood Canal (for David Fowler)." NewEngR (3:4)
    Sum 81, pp. 511-15.

HUDSPITH, Vicki
"I Like My Fingernails Painted." Pequod (12) 81, p. 21.
"New Year's Eve." SunM (11) Spr 81, pp. 152-153.
"Sixth Avenue." SunM (11) Spr 81, p. 154.

HUERTA, Efraín
"The Drunken Girl" (tr. by Susana Epelbaum). PoNow (5:6 issue 30)
    81, p. 18.

HUETER, Diane
"First Thunder Storm." KanQ (13:1) Wint 81, p. 166.
"For A Girl Holding Eggs With Her Eyes Closed." ThRiPo (17/18) 81,
    p. 11.
"Josie's Poem." PoNow (6:3 issue 33) 81, p. 16.

HUFFSTICKLER, Albert
  "Credo." Nimrod (25:1) Aut-Wint 81, p. 105.
  "Stone Hymn." Nimrod (25:1) Aut-Wint 81, p. 104.

HUGHES, Beverlee
  "Going Home." 13thM (5:1/2) 80, p. 32.

HUGHES, Sophie
  "Farmer's Daughter." Confr (21) Wint 81, p. 53.

HUGO, Richard
  "Death in the Aquarium." Antaeus (40/41) Wint-Spr 81, pp. 306-307.
  "Letter to Bly from La Push." PoetryE (4/5) Spr-Sum 81, p. 85.

HUIDOBRO, Vicente
  "Altazor, or Journey by Parachute" (tr. by Richard Lebovitz). Mund
    (12/13) 80-81, pp. 380-384.

HULBERT, Gary
  "The Point of it All." BelPoJ (31:4) Sum 81, p. 24.

HULDEN, Lars
  "Advice to Happy Folk" (tr. by George Schoolfield). PoetryE (6) Aut
    81, p. 27.
  "Bulletin from Staff-Headquarters" (tr. by George Schoolfield). PoetryE
    (6) Aut 81, pp. 21-22.
  "Countryside Organizations" (tr. by George Schoolfield). PoetryE (6)
    Aut 81, pp. 22-23.
  "Like a Cautious Flier" (tr. by George Schoolfield). PoetryE (6) Aut
    81, p. 25.
  "Once, Long Ago" (tr. by Rika Lesser). PoetryE (6) Aut 81, pp. 20-
    21.
  "The Book of Finland-Swedish Poems" (tr. by Rika Lesser). PoetryE
    (6) Aut 81, pp. 19-20.
  "The Children Were Packed Off" (tr. by George Schoolfield). PoetryE
    (6) Aut 81, pp. 23-24.
  "Today God" (tr. by George Schoolfield). PoetryE (6) Aut 81, p. 26.
  "When the Church Burned" (tr. by George Schoolfield). PoetryE (6)
    Aut 81, p. 24.

HULL, Barbara
  "This House She Dreams In." CalQ (18/19) 81, pp. 134-135.

HUMES, Harry
  "A Cold Condition." Comm (108:11) 5 Je 81, p. 342.
  "Hawk over a Friend's Meadow." LittleM (13:1/2) Spr-Sum 79, c1981,
    p. 72.
  "It Could Be." PoetryNW (22:1) Spr 81, p. 46.
  "Legend For A June Morning." PoetryNW (22:1) Spr 81, pp. 44-45.
  "A New Description." LittleM (13:1/2) Spr-Sum 79, c1981, p. 70.
  "The Rain Walkers." PoetryNW (22:1) Spr 81, p. 44.
  "The Return from Argentina." Kayak (56) 81, p. 66.
  "Swimming with Foxes." LittleM (13:1/2) Spr-Sum 79, c1981, p. 71.
  "There Is No End to It." HiramPoR (29) Aut-Wint 81, p. 25.
  "Touching There and There." Kayak (56) 81, p. 6.
  "Winter Weeds." StoneC (9: 1-2) Aut-Wint 81/82, p. 24-25.

HUMFLEET, Melanie
  "The Red Canoe." ConcPo (14:1) Spr 81, p. 59.

HUMMA, John
"Mother, 71; Berchie, 93." Comm (108:11) 5 Je 81, p. 342.

HUMMER, T. R.
"The Age before Passion: A Vision." NewEngR (3:4) Sum 81, pp. 537-9.
"Dawn: What I Might Have Dreamed." NewYorker (57:38) 9 N 81, p. 54.
"Flight (for Brooke Hopkins)." NewEngR (4:1) Aut 81, pp. 36-39.
"Love Poem: The Possessed." NewEngR (4:1) Aut 81, pp. 39-40.
"The passion of the Right-Angled Man." Ascent (6:3) 81, p. 24.
"Where You Go When She Sleeps." Ascent (6:3) 81, p. 25.

HURLOW, Marcia L.
"Gambling Bone Game." KanQ (13:3/4) Sum-Aut 81, p. 94.
"The House." KanQ (13:3/4) Sum-Aut 81, p. 93.
"Postcard." BallSUF (22:1) Wint 81, p. 78.

HUSS, Steven W.
"Anger." Wind (11:43) 81, p. 27.

HUSTED, Chris
"Turning the Worm Beds." Vis (7) 81, n. p.

HUSTVEDT, Siri
"Weather Markings." ParisR (23:81) Aut 81, pp. 136-137.

HUTCHINSON, Joseph
"Dream During Bach's Violin Sonatas." PortR (27: 2) 81, p. 94.
"Elegy for Michael, a Friend, Killed in His Car." DenQ (16:2) Sum 81, pp. 56-57.
"A Natural History." PortR (27: 2) 81, p. 94.
"The Next Room." OhioR (26), p. 64.

HUTTEN, Katrine von
"The Fat Years" (tr. by Norbert Krapf). PoNow (5:6 issue 30) 81, p. 46.
"Memory of" (tr. by Norbert Krapf). PoNow (5:6 issue 30) 81, p. 46.
"Statement of Place" (tr. by Norbert Krapf). PoNow (5:6 issue 30) 81, p. 46.
"When I Was Little" (tr. by Norbert Krapf). PoNow (5:6 issue 30) 81, p. 46.

HWANG-CHINI
"What Is A Girl To Do?" (tr. by Michael Stephens). Pequod (13) 81, p. 70.

HYDE, Lewis
"It's Not Possible Now" (tr. of Vicente Aleixandre, w/ David Unger). PoNow (5:6 issue 30) 81, p. 3.
"Love's Cutting Edge" (tr. of Vicente Aleixandre, w/ David Unger). PoNow (5:6 issue 30) 81, p. 3.
"No Man's Land" (tr. of Vicente Aleixandre, w/ David Unger). PoNow (5:6 issue 30) 81, p. 3.
"Street Money & Music." Thrpny (4) Wint 81, p. 17.
"The Wealth of Metals." Thrpny (5) Spr 81, p. 8.

HYLAND, Paul
"Shepstor" (for Bob Groves). Pequod (13) 81, pp. 45-46.

HYMAN, Lateifa-Ramona L.
    "Silhouettes from the Street." Obs (6: 1/2) Spr-Sum 80, p. 228.

IACOBACCI, Nicola
    "Shipwreck" (tr. by Lawrence Venuti). Chelsea (40) 81, p. 49.
    "Sleep Is the Death of the Aged" (tr. by Lawrence Venuti). Chelsea
        (40) 81, p. 48.

IBAÑEZ, Jorge J.
    "Poética." Mairena (2:6), pp. 37-8.

IBARAGI, Noriko
    "Running" (tr. by Graeme Wilson). DenQ (16:4) Wint 81, p. 49.

IBARRA, Graciela Paterno see PATERNO IBARRA, Graciela

IBRAHIM, Kamal
    "And I in ruins of Order" (tr. by Christine Cotton). Mund (12/13) 80-81,
        p. 291.
    "Blood darkens the packaged fingers" (tr. by Christine Cotton). Mund
        (12/13) 80-81, p. 291.
    "If you love the desert" (tr. by Christine Cotton). Mund (12/13) 80-81,
        p. 291.

IGLESIAS, Roberto Fernández see FERNANDEZ IGLESIAS, Roberto

IGNATOW, David
    "After my first meeting with Williams...." UnmOx (22) Wint 81, pp.
        68-69.
    "Behind His Eyes." NewL (47:4) Sum 81, p. 64.
    "A Cloud Creates." Poetry (137:5) F 81, p. 277.
    "Entrance to a tunnel underneath the hill." UnmOx (22) Wint 81, p. 67.
    "A Fable." Harp (263:1574) Jl 81, p. 24.
    "The Garden and the Store." ThRiPo (17/18) 81, p. 26.
    "I Am." NewL (47:4) Sum 81, p. 65.
    "I am like a scrap of paper stuck...." UnmOx (22) Wint 81, p. 66.
    "I have enemies among the leaves." UnmOx (22) Wint 81, p. 66.
    "I'm sure trees are depressed also...." UnmOx (22) Wint 81, p. 65.
    "In the Garden." GeoR (35:3) Aut 81, p. 556.
    "Of That Fire." NewL (47:4) Sum 81, p. 63.
    "On Going to the Movies." NewL (47:4) Sum 81, p. 65.
    "A Requiem." NewL (47:4) Sum 81, p. 66.
    "Street Scene." NewL (47:4) Sum 81, p. 64.
    "Survivors." PoetryE (6) Aut 81, p. 76.
    "To Oneself." GeoR (35:3) Aut 81, p. 556.
    "To the President." PoetryE (6) Aut 81, p. 75.
    "The Window." NewL (47:4) Sum 81, p. 63.

IKAN, Ron
    "And a Box of White Owl Cigars." CapeR (17:1) Wint 81, p. 49.
    "Good Packing." FourQt (30:2) Wint 81, p. 31.

IKKYU, The Abbot
    "Pleasing Oneself" (tr. by Graeme Wilson). WestHR (35:1) Spr 81, p.
        58.

ILARRAZA, Carmen Camacho see CAMACHO ILARRAZA, Carmen

ILLYES, Gyula
  "In Venice" (tr. by Emery George). DenQ (16:1) Spr 81, pp. 75-76.

IMPEY, Michael
  "Knowledge" (tr. of Nina Cassian, w/ Brian Swann). Mund (12/13) 80-
    81, p. 347.
  "Quarrel With Chaos" (tr. of Nina Cassian, w/ Brian Swann). Mund
    (12/13) 80-81, p. 347.

INEZ, Colette
  "Animal Nature." VirQR (57:4) Aut 81, pp. 644-645.
  "Apothegms and Counsels." OP (31/32) Aut 81, p. 91.
  "Better to See the Face than to Hear the Name." PortR (27: 2) 81, p.
    85.
  "Blue and Silver Spectrum Jazz Trio." PoNow (6:1 issue 31) 81, p. 10.
  "Erin's Days." PortR (27: 2) 81, p. 85.
  "Lost Daughters at School." Conf (22) Sum 81, pp. 94-95.
  "Out of the Frame and Into this Blue Dream." CalQ (18/19) 81, pp.
    82-83.
  "Plane Tree Dance Sequences." VirQR (57:4) Aut 81, pp. 643-644.
  "A Quarrel Put to Rest." PoNow (6:1 issue 31) 81, p. 10.
  "Untitled." PartR (48:2) 81, p. 251.
  "Wichita Ruby." PortR (27: 2) 81, p. 85.

INGALLS, Jeremy
  "Prayer To The Third Angel." MichQR (20:4) Aut 81, p. 422.

IRBY, James E.
  "Ten Prose Poems" (tr. of José Lezama Lima). Sulfur (3) 82, pp. 40-
    51.

IRION, Mary Jean
  "Curves and Movements." ChrC (98:9) 18 Mr 81, p. 297.
  "Gardener in Early Spring." ChrC (98:11) 1 Ap 81, p. 354.

IRWIN, Mark
  "The Cemetery At Lakeview." ThRiPo (17/18) 81, pp. 82-83.
  "The Distance of Flesh." Antaeus (43) Aut 81, pp. 87-88.
  "The Ghost" (tr. with Mariana Carpinisan of Nichita Stanescu). SenR
    (12:1/2) 81, p. 137.
  "Integrity." AntR (39:2) Spr 81, p. 204.
  "Marina" (tr. with Mariana Carpinisan of Nichita Stanescu). SenR (12:
    1/2) 81, p. 135.
  "Moored to your blood" (tr. of Philippe Denis). Mund (12/13) 80-81,
    p. 348.
  "Rue Saint Denis." AntR (39:2) Spr 81, p. 205.
  "Stars and Trees." MalR (58) Ap 81, p. 123.
  "To live as to breathe" (tr. of Philippe Denis). Mund (12/13) 80-81,
    p. 348.
  "Vermeer." Atl (248:3) S 81, p. 79.
  "Wild Strawberries." PoNow (6:2 issue 32) 81, p. 47.

ISHIKAWA, Takuboku
  "Old Man" (tr. by Graeme Wilson). DenQ (16:4) Wint 81, p. 32.

ISSENHUTH, Jean-Pierre
  "La mine." Os (13) Aut 81, p. 11.

ITOH, Tsuyoshi
"The Cathedral Beaten By Rain" (tr. with Gary Steven Corseri of Kotaroh Takamura). WebR (6:2) 81, pp. 21-24.

IVANISEVIC, Drago
"Games at the European Masked Ball" (tr. by Vasa D. Mihailovich). Mund (12/13) 80-81, p. 153.

IVASK, Astrid
"In the evening forest a bird sings, ... " (tr. by Inara Cedrins). PoNow (5:6 issue 30) 81, p. 19.
"That evening the stars' quicksilver" (tr. by Inara Cedrins). PoNow (5:6 issue 30) 81, p. 19.

JABRA, Jabra Ibrahim
"Let others have" (tr. by Sargon Boulus). Mund (12/13) 80-81, p. 353.
"Masks collapsed, and" (tr. by Sargon Boulus). Mund (12/13) 80-81, p. 352.

JACHOWSKI, Elsie Schmidt
"And I Awaken into Nothingness" (tr. of Gabino Coria Penaloza). Vis (5) 81, n. p.

JACKSON, Angela
"The leaves listen to aretha sing." Prima (6/7) 81, p. 68.

JACKSON, Fleda Brown
"Edward Hopper's Woman." BelPoJ (31:3) Spr 81, p. 1.
"To Mark, My Retarded Brother, Who Lived 20 Years and Learned to Speak 300 Words." SouthernHR (15:4) Aut 81, pp. 344-345.

JACKSON, Haywood
"Amtrack Heading East." StoneC (8: 3) Spr 81, p. 32.
"Celebrating the Fall." PikeR (2) Sum 81, p. 3.
"Fellow Travelers." Sam (105) 81, Entire issue.
"On Being Here Today, And...." AmerPoR (10:1) Ja-F 81, p. 18.
"On Reading a Billboard at 500 Paces." LittleM (13:1/2) Spr-Sum 79, c1981, pp. 86-87.
"Trouble In The Family." Sam (116) 81, p. 64.

JACKSON, Patti-Gayle
"ancient physic." Obs (7:1) Spr 81, p. 45.
"edfu." Obs (7:1) Spr 81, p. 45.
"these loves: revolution." Obs (7:1) Spr 81, p. 44.
"what do you dream of." BlackALF (15:1) Spr 81, p. 30.

JACKSON, Richard
"The Changes." ConcPo (14:1) Spr 81, p. 74.
"The Pilgrim Soul." ConcPo (14:1) Spr 81, p. 73.
"Poem for My Father at the Death of His Father." SouthernPR (21: 1) Spr 81, p. 41.

JACOBIK, Gray
"At the Supper Hour." CreamCR (6:2) 81, p. 53.

JACOBOWITZ, Judah L.
"From The Window." WindO (39) Wint 81/82, p. 8.

"A Loser." WindO (39) Wint 81/82, p. 6.
"Operation." WindO (39) Wint 81/82, p. 7.
"Redbird, Lost." CreamCR (7:1) 81, pp. 6-7.

JACOBS, Teresa
"Ara." Maize (4:1/2) Aut-Wint 80-81, p. 43.
"At my bedroom window." Maize (4:1/2) Aut-Wint 80-81, p. 43.
"Ceremonies." Maize (4:1/2) Aut-Wint 80-81, p. 42.
"Metamorfose." Maize (4:1/2) Aut-Wint 80-81, p. 41.

JACOBSEN, Joanne
"A Pennsylvania Hill Cemetery." QW (12) Spr-Sum 81, p. 17.

JACOBSEN, Josephine
"Distance." Comm (108:19) 23 O 81, p. 602.
"The Monosyllable." Poetry (139:1) O 81, p. 16.
"Reading Aloud at Dusk in Spring." SouthernPR (21: 1) Spr 81, p. 43.
"Tears." Nat (232:13) 4 Ap 81, p. 410.

JACOBSEN, Rolf
"Antenna Forest" (tr. of Olav Grinde). CalQ (18/19) 81, p. 127.
"Asphalt" (tr. of Olav Grinde). CalQ (18/19) 81, p. 126.

JACOBSON, Dale
"Loneliness." Northeast (3:11) Sum 81, p. 39.
"Quiet Poem." Northeast (3:11) Sum 81, p. 38.
"Song." Northeast (3:11) Sum 81, p. 39.
"Upon Revisiting My Home Town." Northeast (3:11) Sum 81, p. 38.

JACOBSON, Seesler Dawn
"Her Rubbings." QW (12) Spr-Sum 81, p. 73.

JACOBY, Stan
"The Lost Calf." LittleM (13:1/2) Spr-Sum 79, c1981, p. 97.

JAFRATE, Keith
"Work." Pequod (13) 81, pp. 47-48.

JAGODZINSKE, Marcia
"The Electrician." Sam (117) 81, p. 27.
"Oedipus Rex & The Freud Complex." Sam (116) 81, p. 21.

JALLAIS, Denise
"Maturity" (tr. by Maxine Kumin and Judith Kumin). PoNow (5:6 issue
    30) 81, p. 19.

JAMES, David
"Eyes" (for Lance Gravette). WormR (84) 81, p. 113.
"Going There." WormR (84) 81, pp. 114-115.
"Hair." WormR (84) 81, p. 114.
"Harvest." QW (13) Aut/Wint 81/82, p. 48.
"Kissing the Earth." KanQ (13:3/4) Sum-Aut 81, p. 130.
"Mouth." WormR (84) 81, p. 113.
"Snapshots." CimR (54) Ja 81, pp. 26-27.
"Three From An Anatomy." WormR (84) 81, p. 113.

JAMES, Elizabeth Ann
"Edgar Degas and His Coryphées." NewEngR (4:1) Aut 81, p. 83.

JAMES, Percy
  "A Vision." PottPort (3) 81, p. 45.

JAMES, Sibyl
  "The Beach at Moclips" (for Barbara). Tendril (10) Wint 81, p. 54.
  "Crying Wolf" (for Nick). Tendril (10) Wint 81, p. 61.
  "Going Places." Tendril (10) Wint 81, p. 55.
  "The Grand Piano Range." Tendril (10) Wint 81, p. 60.
  "Interior Points of Reference." Tendril (10) Wint 81, pp. 62-63.
  "June in New York" (for Belinoff). Tendril (10) Wint 81, pp. 58-59.
  "Twisp, Washington." Tendril (10) Wint 81, pp. 56-57.

JAMMES, Francis
  "As I Dreamed..." (tr. by Antony Oldknow). AntR (39:3) Sum 81, p.
    338.
  "I Took the Train to Lourdes" (tr. by Antony Oldknow). WebR (6:2)
    81, pp. 31-32.
  "See in the Months of Autumn..." (for F.V.G.) (tr. by Antony Oldknow).
    AntR (39:3) Sum 81, p. 337.
  "When I'm Dead" (tr. by Antony Oldknow). WebR (6:2) 81, p. 30.

JANDL, Ernst
  "Outpouring" (tr. by Lane Jennings). Vis (5) 81, n.p.

JANDL, Hermann
  "Aren't to Blame" (tr. by Herbert Kuhner). Mund (11:2) 79, p. 81.
  "Können Nichts Dafür." Mund (11:2) 79, p. 80.

JANETSCHEK, Albert
  "End Phase" (tr. by Herbert Kuhner). Mund (11:2) 79, p. 83.
  "Endphase." Mund (11:2) 79, p. 82.

JANEY, Peggy
  "Black Churches Hold Us Weeping." Obs (7:1) Spr 81, p. 80.
  "E. A. POE." Obs (7:1) Spr 81, p. 78.
  "Going Through Some Changes." Obs (7:1) Spr 81, p. 79.
  "Leave Them to the Missionaries." Obs (7:1) Spr 81, p. 78.
  "Marlon, Honey." Obs (7:1) Spr 81, p. 80.
  "Matrilineal Depression." Obs (7:1) Spr 81, p. 79.
  "Woman Will Cherish and Weep." Obs (7:1) Spr 81, p. 81.

JANIK, Phyllis
  "From Mexico." PraS (55:3) Aut 81, p. 48.
  "Knots." NewRena (14) Spr 81, pp. 64-65.
  "Over Water, For Fire." StoneC (9: 1-2) Aut-Wint 81/82, p. 77.
  "Piece VIII." NewRena (14) Spr 81, pp. 67-68.
  "Still Life." NewRena (14) Spr 81, pp. 66-67.

JANOWITZ, Phyllis
  "Waiting for Father in Pawling, N.Y." NewYorker (57:34) 12 O 81, p.
    163.

JANOWS, Jill
  "Improvisations After Chardin." Tendril (10) Wint 81, pp. 30-31.
  "The Recluse." Tendril (10) Wint 81, p. 32.

JAQUISH, Karen
  "Flying to Milwaukee." Im (7:2) 1981, p. 8.

JARDINE, Mary
    "The Pasture." Meadows (2:1) 81, p. 68.

JARMAN, Mark
    "A Mackerel Sky." Pequod (12) 81, p. 83.
    "The Rote Walker." Pequod (12) 81, pp. 80-82.
    "The Supremes." NewYorker (57:25) 10 Ag 81, p. 34.
    "What Child Is This?" Field (24) Spr 81, p. 38.

JASON, Kathrine
    "On the Jetty (from Works by Edvard Munch)." NewYorker (57:9) 20
        Ap 81, p. 36.

JASON, Philip K.
    "Bedtime Story." CentR (25:2) Spr 81, p. 167.
    "Bus Number One." WebR (6:1) 81, p. 57.
    "Change." WebR (6:1) 81, p. 60.
    "The Dead Sea." WebR (6:1) 81, p. 59.
    "Lines on Lines." CimR (57) O 81, p. 31.
    "The Old Place." CentR (25:2) Spr 81, p. 168.
    "The Price of Survival." WebR (6:1) 81, p. 58.
    "The Red Sea." WebR (6:1) 81, p. 61.

JAY, Peter
    "At the Florist's" (tr. of Jacques Prévert). SenR (12:1/2) 81, p. 71.
    "Nocturne" (tr. of George Bacovia). SenR (12:1/2) 81, p. 129.

JEFFERIES, David
    "The Visible Man." NewEngR (3:4) Sum 81, p. 578.
    "Winter Drought." KanQ (13:1) Wint 81, p. 113.

JELLEMA, Rod
    "Some Aches Are Good." PoNow (6:2 issue 32) 81, p. 28.

JENEAULT, Jeanette
    "Father." Sam (116) 81, pp. 36-37.

JENNINGS, Kate
    "Lullaby." SouthernHR (15:4) Aut 81, p. 336.
    "She Explains Why She Likes the Moon." SouthernHR (15:4) Aut 81, p.
        336.

JENNINGS, Lane
    "Cherries" (tr. of Günter Grass). Vis (6) 81, n.p.
    "Outpouring" (tr. of Ernst Jandl). Vis (5) 81, n.p.

JENNINGS, Michael
    "Along the Avenue of Dead Gestures." GeoR (35:3) Aut 81, p. 627.

JENSEN, Dana Christian
    "I Seek More Than Friendship." Northeast (3:11) Sum 81, p. 36.
    "Unemployed." Northeast (3:11) Sum 81, p. 36.

JENSEN, Laura
    "To Anne Henson." AntR (39:1) Wint 81, p. 73.
    The Crow is Mischief. OP (31/32) Aut 81, p. 108.
    "Window Views." PoetryNW (22:4) Wint 81-82, pp. 26-30.

JENTZSCH, Bernd
  "Meine Mutter." SenR (12:1/2) 81, p. 14.
  "My Mother" (tr. by Frederic Will). SenR (12:1/2) 81, p. 15.

JEROME, Judson
  "Encounters Of Kind." AmerPoR (10:5) S-O 81, p. 40.

JIMENEZ, Juan Ramón
  "Tenebrae" (tr. by Jan Pallister). PoNow (5:6 issue 30) 81, p. 19.

JNANA
  "Circus Death." Tele (17) 81, p. 80.
  "Horowitz." Tele (17) 81, p. 81.
  "In Blue Sky." Tele (17) 81, p. 81.
  "Like The Baths." Tele (17) 81, p. 80.

JOENS, Harley
  "Burnt Meat." Northeast (3:10) Wint 81, p. 26.
  "Girls." Northeast (3:10) Wint 81, p. 25.
  "The Jasmine Days." Northeast (3:10) Wint 81, p. 23.
  "Solitary Morning." Northeast (3:10) Wint 81, p. 23.
  "Van Gogh's Self Portrait." Northeast (3:10) Wint 81, p. 24.

JOGLAR CACHO, Manuel
  "A Luis Hernández Aquino (Entre la elegía y el requiem)." Mairena
    (3:8) 81, p. 117.

JOHANNESSEN, Matthias
  "The city laughed" (tr. by Alan Boucher). Vis (5) 81, n. p.
  "You are the day that vanished" (tr. by Alan Boucher). Vis (5) 81,
    n. p.

JOHANSSON-IRWIN, Monica
  "The Waterman." Vis (7) 81, n. p.

JOHN OF THE CROSS, Saint see CRUZ, Juan de la, San

JOHNSON, Denis
  "The Incognito Lounge." Antaeus (40/41) Wint-Spr 81, pp. 308-312.

JOHNSON, Don
  "The Sergeant" (For my father). Poetry (137:4) Ja 81, pp. 210-212.

JOHNSON, Donald R.
  "The Colonel (Ret.)." PraS (55:3) Aut 81, pp. 93-4.

JOHNSON, Greg
  "Eye of the Storm." Poem (42) Jul 81, p. 13.
  "Lovers in Autumn." Poem (42) Jul 81, pp. 14-15.
  "Oates." KanQ (13:3/4) Sum-Aut 81, p. 93.
  "Room 13." KanQ (13:3/4) Sum-Aut 81, p. 92.
  "This Voice." Poem (42) Jul 81, p. 16.
  "Virginia Woolf." Poem (42) Jul 81, p. 17.

JOHNSON, Joan
  "Forgive Me, Sweetheart, For Talking Tough." StoneC (8: 3) Spr 81,
    p. 16.
  "She Dreams His Suicide." StoneC (8: 3) Spr 81, p. 17.

JOHNSON, Kathleen J.
"Gap Fence." SmPd (18:1) Wint 81, p. 23.

JOHNSON, Linnea
"One More David." BelPoJ (32:2) Wint 81-82, pp. 22-23.

JOHNSON, Manly
"Three Images From the Plitvice Lakes" (tr. of Margherita Guidacci,
    w/ Renata Treitel). WebR (6:2) 81, pp. 25-26.

JOHNSON, Michael L.
"On the Royal Lady of the Han Dynasty Exhumed Near Ch'angsha."
    KanQ (13:3/4) Sum-Aut 81, p. 144.
"Puberty." Sam (116) 81, p. 40.

JOHNSON, Nick
"Here." Shen (32:2) 81, p. 104.
"In the Dark." Epoch (30:3) Spr-Sum 81, p. 190.

JOHNSON, Paulette S.
"Summer Thursday" (Epitaph for Mellow--1978). Obs (6:1/2) Spr-Sum
    80, pp. 154-155.

JOHNSON, Ronald
"Ark 35." Sulfur (2) 81, pp. 27-29.

JOHNSON, Thomas
"Ohio." PoNow (6:2 issue 32) 81, p. 28.

JOLLIE, Karen
"Comfort, Comfort Ye." PortR (27: 2) 81, p. 73.

JONES, Andrea E.
"The Burning." Obs (7:1) Spr 81, p. 25.
"Moments." Obs (7:1) Spr 81, p. 24.

JONES, Courtney
"I Hear Horses in Their Grazing." US1 (14/15) Aut/Wint 81, p. 9.

JONES, Daryl
"The Tiger." SewanR (89:1) Wint 81, p. 29.

JONES, Freida
"Lucky Strikes Legacy: A Texture." Obs (6:1/2) Spr-Sum 80, pp. 195-
    196.
"Man and Madness Chant." Obs (6:1/2) Spr-Sum 80, p. 197.

JONES, Patricia Thuner
"Fruition." MalR (57) Ja 81, p. 165.
"Interval." MalR (57) Ja 81, p. 163.
"Still-Life." MalR (57) Ja 81, p. 164.

JONES, Paul
"Not the Moon." SouthernPR (21:2) Aut 81, p. 50.

JONES, Paula
"Litany." HiramPoR (30) Spr-Sum 81, p. 23.

JONES, Robert C.
"Three Chinese Paintings." CharR (7:1) Spr 81, pp. 40-41.

JONES, Tom
"Hymn to the Sun." Wind (11:40) 81, pp. 15-16.
"Let's Pretend." Wind (11:40) 81, pp. 14-15.

JONSSON, Tor
"To Build a Tower" (tr. by Paul Thorfinn Hopper). Vis (5) 81, n. p.
"Tunnel" (tr. by Paul Thorfinn Hopper). Vis (5) 81, n. p.

JORDAN, June
"Addenda to the Papal Bull" (for Nicanor Parra). 13thM (5:1/2) 80, p. 18.
"Taking Care." LittleM (13:1/2) Spr-Sum 79, c1981, pp. 30-3.

JORDAN, Pierrette
"Hello." Aspect (77/79) 81, p. 112.

JORIS, Pierre
"The Broken Glass." Sulfur (2) 81, pp. 53-56.

JORON, Andrew
"The Tetrahedron Letters." PortR (27: 2) 81, p. 51.

JORVA, Manuel
"No tengo mano de hilo tenso." RevI (9:4) Wint 79-80, p. 626.

JOSELOW, Beth
"On the Boards." AmerPoR (10:4) Jl-Ag 81, p. 35.
"Soon I Will Begin My New Life" (for E.). AmerPoR (10:4) Jl-Ag 81, p. 35.

JOSEPH, Lawrence
"Even the Idiot Makes Deals." NewL (47:4) Sum 81, p. 91.

JOSEPHS, Laurence
"Hawks." SouthernR (17:3) Sum 81, p. 567.
"Indian Pipe." SouthernR (17:3) Sum 81, p. 568.
"Winter as a Japanese Drawing." SouthernR (17:3) Sum 81, p. 569.

JOUANARD, Gill
"Memory" (tr. by Larry Couch). Vis (5) 81, n. p.
"Songs" (tr. by Larry Couch). Vis (5) 81, n. p.

JOYCE, William
"Class Reunion." KanQ (13:1) Wint 81, p. 94.
"For the Toes, For the Last Braille." (for V.) Agni (14) 81, p. 62.
"The Poet In The Public School." WormR (81/82) 81, p. 36.
"Stillbirth" (for Emily). Chelsea (40) 81, pp. 74-77.
"Waiting For The Mailman." WormR (81 /82) 81, p. 35.

JUAN DE LA CRUZ, San see CRUZ, Juan de la, San

JUARROZ, Roberto
"Death no longer faces mirrors." Mund (12/13) 80-81, p. 24.
"I think that in this moment." Mund (12/13) 80-81, p. 24.
"Man, the puppet of the night." Mund (12/13) 80-81, p. 23.

"One day I will find a word" (tr. by Sergio Mondragón and Rainer
Schulte). Mund (12/13) 80-81, p. 23.

JUDGE, Frank
"Winter Returns" (tr. of Rodolfo Di Biasio). PoNow (6:2 issue 32) 81,
p. 41.

JUDSON, John
"Mobile Oil." BelPoJ (32:2) Wint 81-82, p. 1.
"Morning on the Desert." NoAmR (266:1) Mr 81, p. 7.

JUI, Hua, Lady see HUA JUI, Lady

JUNKINS, Donald
"Robert Lowell: The Church of The Advent, Boston September 1977."
AmerPoR (10:4) Jl-Ag 81, pp. 8-10.

JURADO MORALES, José
"Riotinto y las Minas." Puerto Wint 81, p. 27.

JURD, Allan
"Roy." WormR (81/82) 81, pp. 39-41.

JUSTICE, Donald
"Lines at the New Year." Antaeus (40/41) Wint-Spr 81, p. 314.
"Mule Team and Poster." Antaeus (40/41) Wint-Spr 81, p. 313.

KABBANI, Rana
"Aisha." Nimrod (24: 2) Spr/Sum 81, p. 34.
"Last Evening In Paris" (to the memory of Izzeddin Qalaq) (tr. of Mah-
mūd Darwish). Nimrod (24: 2) Spr/Sum 81, pp. 74-77.
"Woman." Nimrod (24: 2) Spr/Sum 81, p. 33.

KAHN, Paul
"The sun takes a slow warm slide thru Virgo." Aspect (77/79) 81, pp.
120-121.

KALIKOFF, Beth
"Dr. Cliff Notes Reads Pamela." ColEng (43:6) O 81, p. 579.
"We do it Aloft." BelPoJ (31:3) Spr 81, pp. 10-11.

KALLAS, Anthony
"And Though He Fought Like a Tiger He Went Down--He Went Down."
CreamCR (6:2) 81, p. 13.

KALLET, Marilyn
"Ah! For you with what pleasure I'd bend" (tr. of Jules Laforgue).
SenR (12:1/2) 81, p. 61.
"Sundays" (tr. of Jules Laforgue). SenR (12:1/2) 81, pp. 57-9.
"Thirst." NewL (47:4) Sum 81, p. 75.
"To Break the Hold." NewL (47:4) Sum 81, p. 76.

KAMENETZ, Rodger
"American Express." Tele (17) 81, p. 7.
"Lullaby." HangL (40) Aut 81, p. 26.
"Nympholepsy." Shen (32: 4) 81, p. 70.
"Southern Crescent." Shen (32: 4) 81, pp. 70-71.

KANE, Katherine
"Unreturned Love." Chelsea (40) 81, pp. 134-135.

KANE, T. Paul
"Lady With a Falcon Sitting in a Flower Grove, a Tapestry." Shen
(32:1) 80, p. 59.
"Rooms." Shen (32: 4) 81, pp. 68-69.

KANFER, Allen
"My Father and the Mississippi." SouthernHR (15:1) Wint 81, p. 17.

KANI, Ntshona
"Finggering the Why." Obs (7:1) Spr 81, pp. 39-41.

KANTER, Mark
"The Camel" (tr. of Rajzel Zichlinsky). PortR (27: 1) 81, p. 25.

KAPLAN, Carla
"What he calls disagreement." Prima (6/7) 81, p. 38.

KAPLAN, David Michael
"Shady Groves." Outbr (6/7) Aut 80-Spr 81, pp. 49-50.

KAPLAN, Edward
"Hunter's Moon." StoneC (9: 1-2) Aut-Wint 81/82, p. 39.

KAPLAN, Howard
"Holiday." Bound (9:2) Wint 81, p. 156.

KAPTER, Kap
"Suicide." Northeast (3:11) Sum 81, p. 40.

KARLINS, Mark
"the farmyard is infested with rivers." Sulfur (3) 82, p. 115.
"Perry." Sulfur (3) 82, pp. 114-115.
"Snow White." Sulfur (3) 82, p. 113.

KARLSSON, Jan
"an untitled poem" (tr. of Göran Sonnevi, w/ Cynthia Hogue). AmerPoR
(10:6) N-D 81, p. 32.

KAROUZOS, Nikos
"Misery in the Chest" (tr. by Kimon Friar). Poetry (139:2) N 81, pp.
95-96.

KARP, Vickie
"Still-Life in the Coat-Factory Office." NewYorker (57:40) 23 N 81, p.
60.

KARPOWICZ, Tymoteusz
"Critically Ill" (tr. by Herbert Kuhner). WebR (6:2) 81, p. 38.

KARR, Mary
"Diogenes Goes to the Laundromat." Tendril (11) Sum 81, p. 40.
"Diogenes Tries to Forget." Poetry (138:3) Je 81, p. 133.
"The Double Helix." Tendril (11) Sum 81, p. 39.
"The Last Paris Poem." Poetry (138:3) Je 81, p. 132.
"Lipstick." Poetry (138:3) Je 81, p. 136.

"My New Diet." Poetry (138:3) Je 81, p. 135.
"The New Year." Poetry (138:3) Je 81, p. 134.

KASS, Jerry
"The Dancers." Poem (43) Nov 81, p. 2.
"Encore." Poem (43) Nov 81, p. 3.
"For Young Readers." KanQ (13:3/4) Sum-Aut 81, p. 112.
"In Late December." KanQ (13:3/4) Sum-Aut 81, p. 111.
"Poetic License." Poem (43) Nov 81, p. 1.
"The Pool." Poem (43) Nov 81, p. 4.
"Seascape." Poem (43) Nov 81, p. 5.

KASSAK, Lajos
"Appetite of the Sea" (tr. by Emery George). PoNow (5:6 issue 30) 81,
   p. 20.
"Auntie" (tr. by Emery George). PoNow (5:6 issue 30) 81, p. 20.
"Chaos of the Night" (tr. by Emery George). PoNow (5:6 issue 30) 81,
   p. 20.
"Somebody Stabbed A Girl" (tr. of Nicholas Kolumban). CalQ (18/19)
   81, p. 128.
"Variations on Luck" (tr. by Emery George). PoNow (5:6 issue 30) 81,
   p. 20.

KATES, J.
"Murphy's Lament." Tendril (11) Sum 81, p. 41.

KATES, Robert
"Last Poem" (tr. of Robert Desnos). Stand (22: 4) 81, p. 30.

KATZ, Jeffrey
"The Bomb People." Aspect (77/79) 81, p. 123.
"Eskimo Piety." Aspect (77/79) 81, p. 122.
"He Looks for A Window in the World" (for my father). Aspect (77/79)
   81, p. 123.

KATZ, Lisa
"Transsexual Operation." Shen (32: 4) 81, p. 54.

KAUFFMAN, Janet
"Appetizer, for You." PoNow (6:3 issue 33) 81, p. 24.
"Fall Plowing." PoNow (6:1 issue 31) 81, p. 33.
"Hunting." NewRep (184:12) 21 Mr 81, p. 38.
"Mennonite Farm Wife." PoNow (6:3 issue 33) 81, p. 24.
"Midlands Michigan Prison." AmerPoR (10:6) N-D 81, p. 48.
"The Monkey Man." AmerPoR (10:6) N-D 81, p. 48.
"Rally." PoNow (6:3 issue 33) 81, p. 24.
"Round Lake." NewL (47:4) Sum 81, pp. 96-97.
"Wild Asparagus." AmerPoR (10:6) N-D 81, p. 48.

KAUFMAN, Ellen
"Anaphase." CarolQ (34:1) Sum 81, pp. 40-41.

KAUFMAN, Shirley
"Acupuncture." Kayak (56) 81, p. 61.
"On a Photograph of Herself as Grandmother." PoetryNW (22:3) Aut 81,
   pp. 28-29.
"Mother." PoetryNW (22:3) Aut 81, p. 29.
"Need." PoetryNW (22:3) Aut 81, pp. 27-28.

KAUFMAN, Stuart
"But Not For." PartR (48:1) 81, p. 138.

KAVEN, Bob
"The Art of the Circle." GeoR (35:2) Sum 81, p. 296.

KAZEMEK, Francis E.
"Appalachian Coal Haul Trucks." Wind (11:41) 81, p. 24.

KAZIN, Cathrael
"Anima Poetarum." MassR (22:3) Aut 81, p. 575.
"Hoping These Letter Reach You." MassR (22:3) Aut 81, p. 574.

KEARNEY, Lawrence
"Elegy." Poetry (137:6) Mr 81, p. 330.
"Portrait of the Artist as a Nice Guy." Poetry (137:6) Mr 81, pp. 328-
330.

KEARNEY, Sally
"Dominique." Iowa (11:4) Aut 80, p. 85.

KEATS, Eleanor
"Playing Chess." DenQ (16:2) Sum 81, p. 58.

KEELER, Greg
"Boseman Creek." CutB (16) Spr-Sum 81, pp. 115-116.

KEELEY, Edmund
"At Least" (tr. of Yannis Ritsos). Antaeus (40/41) Wint-Spr 81, p.
376.
"Continued Waiting" (tr. of Yannis Ritsos). Antaeus (40/41) Wint-Spr
81, p. 378.
"Eight poems" (tr. of Yannis Ritsos). AmerPoR (10:4) Jl-Ag 81, p. 22.
"Elation" (tr. of Yannis Ritsos). OntR (14) Spr-Sum 81, p. 49.
"Elegy" (tr. of Yannis Ritsos). OntR (14) Spr-Sum 81, p. 47.
"Eleven poems" (tr. of Yannis Ritsos). Chelsea (40) 81, pp. 38-45.
"Enlightenment" (tr. of Yannis Ritsos). OntR (14) Spr-Sum 81, p. 50.
"Fragmented" (tr. of Yannis Ritsos). Antaeus (40/41) Wint-Spr 81, p.
376.
"Limits" (tr. of Yannis Ritsos). Antaeus (40/41) Wint-Spr 81.
"Narrowness" (tr. of Yannis Ritsos). OntR (14) Spr-Sum 81, p. 48.
"Our Land" (tr. of Yannis Ritsos). Antaeus (40/41) Wint-Spr 81, p. 377.
375.
"Return" (tr. of Yannis Ritsos). NewYRB (28:17) 5 N 81, p. 18.
"Silent Message" (tr. of Yannis Ritsos). SenR (12:1/2) 81, p. 21.
"Startled" (tr. of Yannis Ritsos). Antaeus (40/41) Wint-Spr 81, p. 377.
"Untitled Events" (tr. of Yannis Ritsos). Antaeus (40/41) Wint-Spr 81,
p. 377.

KEENAN, Deborah
"The Country Poet." KanQ (13:1) Wint 81, pp. 76-77.

KEENER, LuAnn
"Cambodia, October 1979." CharR (7:1) Spr 81, p. 50.
"Cutting Bulls." PoNow (6:3 issue 33) 81, p. 16.

KEITHLEY, George
"Ceremony." PoNow (6:2 issue 32) 81, p. 8.
"The Child." Iowa (11:2/3) Spr-Sum 80, pp. 105-106.

"If April." ThRiPo (17/18) 81, p. 28.
"These Small Songs." Iowa (11:2/3) Spr-Sum 80, pp. 107-108.

KELLER, David
"After the Movie (for Robert Hass)." NewEngR (4:2) Wint 81, pp. 254-5.
"Beauty, in the Present Sense." NewEngR (4:2) Wint 81, pp. 256-7.
"The Crank." US1 (14/15) Aut/Wint 81, p. 15.
"The Discovery of March." US1 (14/15) Aut/Wint 81, p. 14.
"How the Sioux Invented Cold." US1 (14/15) Aut/Wint 81, p. 15.
"Lessons." PoNow (6:3 issue 33) 81, p. 17.
"Looking for the Summer." PoNow (6:3 issue 33) 81, p. 17.
"One of the Old Songs." US1 (14/15) Aut/Wint 81, p. 15.
"Sumac." PoNow (6:3 issue 33) 81, p. 17.
"A Trombone." NewEngR (4:2) Wint 81, pp. 255-6.

KELLY, Robert
"The Burgundian Version." UnmOx (22) Wint 81, pp. 20-23.
"they came out of the Curragh." Tele (17) 81, p. 23.
"Postcards from the Underworld" (for L.K.). Sulfur (1) 81, pp. 78-95.

KEMMETT, Bill
"The Closet." Sam (116) 81, p. 35.
"Faith Of Stone." Sam (117) 81, p. 29.
"Seven Haiku." StoneC (9: 1-2) Aut-Wint 81/82, p. 64.

KEMNITZ, Charles
"Bog Dance." KanQ (13:3/4) Sum-Aut 81, p. 74.
from "Distances" (tr. of Susana Thénon, w/ Renata Treitel). NewOR (8:1) Wint 81, p. 37.
"Medea" (tr. of Susana Thenon, w/ Renata Trietel). PoNow (5:6 issue 30) 81, p. 45.
"Midwinter Calligraphy." KanQ (13:3/4) Sum-Aut 81, p. 75.
"Untitled." KanQ (13:3/4) Sum-Aut 81, p. 74.
"The woman of many names will return" (tr. of Susana Thenon, w/ Renata Trietel). PoNow (5:6 issue 30) 81, p. 45.

KEMPHER, Ruth Moon
"Found Poem: My Mother, The Typist, Practices After the Stroke." WindO (39) Wint 81/82, p. 5.
"Hilda Halfheart's Notes to the Milkman: #4." Tele (17) 81, p. 131.
"The Letters from Prattsburg, The Seventh Letter, Saturday." Tele (17) 81, pp. 132-133.
"Watching the House Burn." HiramPoR (29) Aut-Wint 81, p. 26.

KENNEDY, Jo
"Amish Woman." CapeR (17:1) Wint 81, p. 41.
"The Quickening." CapeR (17:1) Wint 81, p. 42.

KENNEDY, Morris
"Saigon Memento." Sam (106) 81, pp. 46-47.

KENNEDY, Terry
"Father's Day." Confr (21) Wint 81, p. 87.
"The Asylum Gardener." BallSUF (22:4) Aut 81, p. 38.
"Recovery." BallSUF (22:3) Sum 81, p. 80.

KENNEDY, X. J.
"Acumen." MassR (22:4) Wint 81, p. 780.

"Coinland--Gold Bought Here. " MassR (22:4) Wint 81, p. 780.
"The Death of Professor Backwards. " ParisR (23:79) Spr 81, p. 197.
"Ool's Parable. " SenR (10:2/11:1) 79-80, p. 32.
"Reading Trip. " OP (31/32) Aut 81, pp. 38-40.
"Similes. " SenR (10:2/11:1) 79-80, p. 31.

KENNY, Adele
    "Changes. " Wind (11:41) 81, p. 2-5.
    "Shadows: Seeley Road Cemetery. " Wind (11:41) 81, pp. 25-26.

KENT, Rolly
    "After the Stormy Night. " SenR (10:2/11:1) 79-80, p. 37.
    "Dust, Snow, Cold-Eureka, Nevada. " SenR (10:2/11:1) 79-80, p. 38.
    "Ice. " SenR (10:2/11:1) 79-80, pp. 33-36.

KEPLINGER, Carrie
    "Boredom is medium gray with grayed edges. " EngJ (70:5) S 81, p.
        66.

KERLIKOWSKE, Elizabeth
    "Elopement. " HiramPoR (30) Spr-Sum 81, p. 24.
    "Humming. " CentR (25:3) Sum 81, pp. 263-264.
    "Pickerel Fishing" (Currier and Ives, 1872). CentR (25:3) Sum 81, pp.
        264-265.

KERR, Kathryn
    "Plums. " Ascent (7:1) 81, p. 19.

KERSHNER, Brandon
    "Dredging. " Poetry (138:6) S 81, p. 326.

KERSLAKE, Susan
    "Litter. " PottPort (3) 81, p. 16.
    "A woman. " PottPort (3) 81, p. 51.

KERTESZ, Louise
    "Settlement. " Im (7:2) 1981, p. 11.

KESSLER, Jascha
    "Anacreontics" (tr. of Istvan Vas). Confr (21) Wint 81, p. 23.
    "From Darkness" (tr. of Forugh Farrokhzad, w/ Amin Banani).
        VirQR (57:2) Spr 81, pp. 270-271.
    "The Gift" (tr. of Forugh Farrokhzad, w/ Amin Banani). PoNow (5:6
        issue 30) 81, p. 15.
    "Leaving: the Poem" (tr. of Forugh Farrokhzad, w/ Amin Banani).
        VirQR (57:2) Spr 81, pp. 271-272.
    "Your Right Arm Beneath My Neck" (tr. of Miklos Radnoti). PoNow
        (5:6 issue 30) 81, p. 39.

KESSLER, Stephen
    "Child Behind Glass" (tr. of Luis Cernuda). Thrpny (5) Spr 81, p. 21.

KEYISHIAN, Marjorie Deiter
    "Argument. " LitR (24:3) Spr 81, p. 397.
    "Persephone. " LitR (24:3) Spr 81, p. 397.

KHAN, Louis I.
    "Silence and Light. " Chelsea (39) 81, p. 151.

KHOURY, Alexis
     "For Kamal Jiries Khoury." Bound (9:2) Wint 81, pp. 161-162.

KICH, Martin
     "Poem for Charlie." CapeR (16:2) Sum 81, p. 33.

KICKNOSWAY, Faye
     "The Horse." Nimrod (25:1) Aut-Wint 81, pp. 100-102.

KIKEL, Rudy
     "Autographs, 1955." MassR (22:2) Sum 81, pp. 273-284.
     "Miss Gottschee." Shen (32: 4) 81, pp. 86-97.

KIM, Chong-Sik see KIM, Sowol

KIM, Sowol
     "Azaleas" (tr. by Michael Stephens). Pequod (13) 81, p. 71.
     "Budding" (tr. by Michael Stephens). Pequod (13) 81, p. 72.
     "O Mother O Sisters" (tr. by Michael Stephens). Pequod (13) 81, p.
     73.

KIMM, R. E.
     "I Swear It's Getting Rough out Here" (a note to Plato). HiramPoR (30)
     Spr-Sum 81, p. 25.

KING, Betty
     "Poem for Good Friday and After." ChrC (98:13) 15 Ap 81, p. 421.

KING, Cynthia
     "Low Pressure into Hurricanes." Prima (6/7) 81, p. 61.
     "Signals." Prima (6/7) 81, p. 63.

KING, Harley
     "Haiku." WorldO (15:1 /2) 81, p. 46.

KING, Martha
     "Ailanthus songs." Chelsea (40) 81, pp. 154-158.

KING, Pat
     "Confessions of a Poet-Voyeur." Wind (11:42) 81, p. 12.
     "When You Touch Me It's Like." SmPd (18:2) Spr 81, p. 31.

KING, Robert S.
     "Orphans Adopting Themselves." WindO (38) Spr-Sum 81, p. 19.

KING, Rosie
     "After Breaking the Butter Dish." CalQ (18/19) 81, pp. 80-81.
     "The Young Bougainvillea." CalQ (18/19) 81, p. 81.

KINNELL, Galway
     "Memory of Wilmington." ThRiPo (17 /18) 81, pp. 30-31.
     "The Milk Bottle." ParisR (23:79) Spr 81, pp. 198-199.

KINSELLA, Thomas
     "The Boyhood of Christ" (tr. of Anonymous). ConcPo (14:2) Aut 81, p.
     76.
     "Crêde's Lament for Dínertech" (tr. of Anonymous). ConcPo (14:2) Aut
     81, p. 77.

"I bring you news" (tr. of Anonymous). ConcPo (14:2) Aut 81, p. 78.
"I don't know who it is" (tr. of Anonymous). ConcPo (14:2) Aut 81, p.
   78.

KINSMAN, Joan
   "If looks could kill. " EngJ (70:6) O 81, p. 66.

KIRBY, David
   "Lowell Wunstel. " SouthernPR (21:2) Aut 81, pp. 73-74.
   "In the Dark There Are Shapes Everywhere. " SouthernPR (21: 1) Spr
      81, pp. 20-21.
   "The Woman in the Tub. " CarolQ (34:2) Aut 81, p. 71.

KIRCHNER, Pamela
   "Feeding the Dead. " GeoR (35:1) Spr 81, pp. 92-93.

KIRKPATRICK, Patricia
   "The Room Was Candles. " HangL (40) Aut 81, p. 29.
   "The Twenty-Ninth Dream. " HangL (40) Aut 81, pp. 27-28.
   "Too Light to Be Seen. " HangL (40) Aut 81, p. 30.

KIRKUP, James
   "Dead Sun" (tr. of Chimako Tada). Mund (12/13) 80-81, p. 141.
   "Seal" (tr. of Kaneko Mitsuharu). Mund (12/13) 80-81, pp. 298-300.

KIRKWOOD, Judith
   "How to Fly. " KanQ (13:1) Wint 81, p. 75.

KIRSCH, Sarah
   "At the White Pansy Bed" (tr. by Agnes Stein). PoNow (5:6 issue 30)
      81, p. 21.
   Eight poems (In German). Mund (11:2) 79, pp. 24-30.
   Eight poems (tr. by Almut McAuley). Mund (11:2) 79, pp. 25-31.
   "I'm to Go Into an Airplane" (tr. by Agnes Stein). PoNow (5:6 issue 30)
      81, p. 21.
   "Letter" (tr. by Wayne Kvam). DenQ (16:1) Spr 81, p. 70.
   "Long Journey" (tr. by Agnes Stein). PoNow (5:6 issue 30) 81, p. 21.
   "Music on the Water" (tr. by Agnes Stein). PoNow (5:6 issue 30) 81,
      p. 21.
   "Renting a Small Room" (tr. by Wayne Kvam). DenQ (16:1) Spr 81, p.
      71.
   "The Rest of the String" (tr. by Wayne Kvam). DenQ (16:1) Spr 81, p.
      72.

KITAHARA, Hakashu
   "Tea Master" (tr. by Graeme Wilson). DenQ (16:4) Wint 81, p. 33.

KITCHEN, Judith
   "Focus. " GeoR (35:1) Spr 81, p. 28.
   "Lines Not Meant to Be Written. " GeoR (35:4) Wint 81, p. 848.
   "Photograph. " SouthernPR (21: 1) Spr 81, p. 48.
   "Settling for the Obvious. " SouthernPR (21: 1) Spr 81, p. 47.
   "Walking on Ice. " SouthernPR (21: 1) Spr 81, p. 46.
   "War Stories. " OhioR (26), pp. 32-33.

KIZER, Carolyn
   "Threatening Letter. " OP (31/32) Aut 81, pp. 151-152.
   "The Unbelievers. " NewYorker (57:5) 23 Mr 81, p. 127.

KLAPPERICH, Barbara
"It's Been a Very Long Summer." SmPd (18:1) Wint 81, p. 33.

KLAPPERT, Peter
"If Innocent." Ploughs (7:2) 81, pp. 108-116.
"Low Sunday." Agni (15) 81, pp. 7-13.
"That Must Have Been the Place" (for M. C.). Antaeus (40/41) Wint-
   Spr 81, pp. 315-318.

KLAUCK, D. L.
"Childhood." PoNow (6:1 issue 31) 81, p. 47.
"Dirty Joke." NewEngR (4:1) Aut 81, p. 101.
"Fame." NewEngR (4:1) Aut 81, pp. 100-1.

KLEINZAHLER, August
"Dejection Between Foot and Brow." Sulfur (3) 82, p. 119.
"86." Sulfur (3) 82, p. 121.
"The Interior Decorator on Sunday." Sulfur (3) 82, p. 118.
"Relaxing in California." Sulfur (3) 82, pp. 116-117.
"Song." Sulfur (3) 82, p. 120.

KLOEFKORN, William
"After the Ball Game." CapeR (16:2) Sum 81, p. 35.
"And Now the Milkcow." CutB (17) Aut-Wint 81, pp. 6-7.
"Flickinger." CapeR (16:2) Sum 81, p. 34.
from Honeymoon: "I advise Doris never to wake me." KanQ (13:3/4)
   Sum-Aut 81, p. 73.
from "Platte Valley Homestead." BelPoJ (31:4) Sum 81, pp. 11-17.
from "Platte Valley Homestead." MidwQ (22:4) Sum 81, pp. 361-367.
"The Wild Ducks Floating." CutB (17) Aut-Wint 81, p. 8.

KLUTZ, Larry
"Waiting." Wind (11:43) 81, p. 14.

KNEIPP, Janet
"Address Book." Poem (41) Mar 81, p. 3.
"Choice." Poem (41) Mar 81, p. 2.
"Of Seeming and Being." Poem (41) Mar 81, p. 1.

KNIGHT, Arthur Winfield
"A Game for Children." ColEng (43:2) F 81, p. 166.

KNIGHT, Etheridge
"Cell Song." HolCrit (18:5) D 81, pp. 1-2.

KNOELLER, Christian
"A Choice." SouthernPR (21: 1) Spr 81, p. 30.

KNOTT, Bill
"The Problem." MissouriR (4:3) Sum 81, p. 40.

KNOWLES, Peter
"Or Not." StoneC (9: 1-2) Aut-Wint 81/82, p. 66.

KNOX, Caroline
"The Houseparty." AmerS (50:3) Sum 81, p. 368.
"Louie." AmerS (50:1) Wint 80-81, p. 14.

KOCH, Claude
"Altarpieces." FourQt (30:3) Spr 81, p. 64.
"Boy Bicycling." FourQt (30:3) Spr 81, p. 81.
"Carlo Crivelli's 'Annunciation'." FourQt (30:3) Spr 81, pp. 62-63.
"The Germantown Road." FourQt (30:3) Spr 81, p. 71.
"The Gallery" (for M. P. K.). FourQt (30:3) Spr 81, p. 60.
"Late Autumn." FourQt (30:3) Spr 81, p. 55.
"The Laundress." FourQt (30:3) Spr 81, p. 61.
"Morning Thoughts." FourQt (30:3) Spr 81, p. 38.
"Once." FourQt (30:3) Spr 81, p. 58.
"Pieter Bruegel at Imhof's Restaurant." FourQt (30:3) Spr 81, pp. 61-62.
"Sea Change." FourQt (30:3) Spr 81, p. 19.
"Seascape." FourQt (30:3) Spr 81, p. 20.
"Springs." FourQt (30:3) Spr 81, p. 92.
"Summer Houses." FourQt (30:3) Spr 81, p. 28.
"That Other Fleet." FourQt (30:3) Spr 81, p. 59.
"The Women." FourQt (30:3) Spr 81, p. 45.

KOCH, Kenneth
"Best Wishes." ParisR (23:79) Spr 81, pp. 220-222.

KOCH, Tom
Playboy's Christmas Cards: "To a Diet Faddist"; "To America's Auto Makers"; "To Major-League Baseball"; "To Public Television"; "To Alexander Haig." Playb (28:12) 81, pp. 204-5.

KOEHN, Lala
"My New Wax Fingertips." MalR (59) Jl 81, pp. 44-45.
"They Readied The House Before I Woke." MalR (59) Jl 81, pp. 46-47.

KOENIG, Rachel
"Weekend in L. A." Kayak (56) 81, pp. 8-9.

KOERTGE, Ronald
"The John Deere Letter." PoNow (6:2 issue 32) 81, p. 15.
"Playing Doctor." PoNow (6:2 issue 32) 81, p. 15.
"Teenager Hit By Car." PoNow (6:1 issue 31) 81, p. 21.

KOESTENBAUM, Phyllis
"Harmony." NowestR (19:1/2), p. 65.
"Picking the Movies." NowestR (19:1/2), p. 66.

KOETHE, John
"Another Kind of Love." CreamCR (6:1) Aut 80, p. 49.
"A Sunny Day." CreamCR (6:1) Aut 80, pp. 50-51.

KOHL, Susan
"The Bound Foot of a Chinese Lady." PikeR (2) Sum 81, p. 4.

KOHLER, Sandra
"A Father and Mother." PoNow (6:3 issue 33) 81, p. 18.
"Moorefield, West Virginia." PoNow (6:3 issue 33) 81, pp. 18-19.

KOLUMBAN, Nicholas
"A Hungarian Nurse Lands At Kennedy." PikeR (2) Sum 81, p. 35.
"At the Bank of the River Tisza, Near Csongrad" (tr. of Sándor Csoóri). SenR (12:1/2) 81, pp. 119-121.

"Cloudy Sky" (tr. of Miklós Radnóti). Chelsea (40) 81, pp. 54-55.
"Combing Her Hair" (tr. of Sandor Csoori). CharR (7:2) Aut 81, p. 31.
"The Echo Of Vast Hollows" (tr. of Sandor Csoori). QW (13) Aut/Wint 81/82, p. 51.
"A Hobo's Elegy" (tr. of Sandor Csoori). CharR (7:2) Aut 81, p. 37.
"In a Sickbed" (tr. of Sándor Csoóri). Chelsea (40) 81, pp. 56-57.
"A Late Demonstration in a French Mining Town" (tr. of Sandor Csoori). CharR (7:2) Aut 81, p. 32.
"Memory of Snow" (tr. of Sandor Csoori). CharR (7:1) Spr 81, p. 54.
"My Birthplace in the Rain" (tr. of Sándor Csoóri). SenR (12:1/2) 81, pp. 123-25.
"My Town in the Fall" (tr. of Sándor Csoóri). Chelsea (40) 81, pp. 55-56.
"On the Third Day" (tr. of Sándor Csoóri). DenQ (16:1) Spr 81, p. 74.
"Poem: I watch Anne hanging out the wash." PikeR (2) Sum 81, p. 36.
"Somebody Stabbed A Girl" (tr. by Lajos Kassak). CalQ (18/19) 81, p. 128.
"The Poppy Heads Rattle" (tr. of Sandor Csoori). CharR (7:2) Aut 81, p. 30.
"Trees" (tr. of Agnes Nemes Nagy). DenQ (16:1) Spr 81, p. 73.
"The Wait" (tr. of Sandor Csoori). CharR (7:2) Aut 81, p. 29.
"With My Daily Death" (tr. of Sándor Csoóri). SenR (12:1/2) 81, p. 127.

KOMINARS, Sheppard B.
"Bliss." RevI (9:4) Wint 79-80, p. 623.
"Her Laughter." RevI (9:4) Wint 79-80, p. 623.
"Triangle." RevI (9:4) Wint 79-80, p. 623.

KOMUNYAKAA, Yusef
"Dreambook Bestiary." NoAmR (266:4) D 81, p. 25.

KONCEL, Mary A.
"Doing The Town In Cleveland, Ohio." MassR (22:4) Wint 81, p. 679.
"Ho-Hum." MassR (22:4) Wint 81, p. 680.

KONDOS, Yǎnnis
"The Excursion" (tr. by Kimon Friar). PoNow (5:6 issue 30) 81, p. 22.
"The Transistor's Loneliness" (tr. by Kimon Friar). PoNow (5:6 issue 30) 81, p. 22.
"There's Oil Somewhere" (tr. by Kimon Friar). PoNow (5:6 issue 30) 81, p. 22.

KONECKY, Edith
"Between Commas." OP (31/32) Aut 81, p. 95.

KÖNIG, Fritz H.
"Ad" (tr. of Günter Kunert). Mund (11:2) 79, pp. 21, 23.
"Ideogram" (tr. of Günter Kunert). Mund (11:2) 79, p. 19.
"Railways" (tr. of Günter Kunert). Mund (11:2) 79, pp. 19, 21.
"Statue" (tr. of Günter Kunert). Mund (11:2) 79, p. 23.

KONUK, Motlu
from Things I Didn't Know I Loved: (5, 13) (tr. of Nazin Hikmet, w/ Randy Blasing). AmerPoR (10:3) My-Je 81, p. 6.

KOOSER, Ted
    "After the Windstorm." SouthernPR (21: 1) Spr 81, p. 6.
    "At the Office Early." SouthernPR (21: 1) Spr 81, p. 5.
    "Book Club." ThRiPo (17/18) 81, p. 33.
    "Carmen Miranda." PoNow (6:1 issue 31) 81, p. 25.
    "Friday Noon." Agni (14) 81, p. 67.
    "Image at Thirty." PoNow (6:1 issue 31) 81, p. 25.
    "A Letter." CutB (17) Aut-Wint 81, p. 11.
    "A Monday in May." Agni (14) 81, p. 68.
    "Sister Mary Mercy." PoNow (6:1 issue 31) 81, p. 25.
    "Stealing Grapes." Agni (14) 81, p. 66.
    "Tillage Marks." SouthernPR (21: 1) Spr 81, p. 6.

KOPP, Karl
    "Thorndyke Ponders the Current Meaning of the Word 'Lust' and How It
        Got That Way." CharR (7:2) Aut 81, pp. 24-25.

KORNEGAY, Burt
    "Arah's Song." Poem (42) Jul 81, p. 49.
    "Primitive Baptist." HiramPoR (29) Aut-Wint 81, p. 27.
    "The Return." Poem (42) Jul 81, p. 51.
    "The Stuck Window." Poem (42) Jul 81, p. 50.

KORNHAUSER, Julian
    "Wolfang Lefevre" (tr. by Grazyna Drabik and Austin Flint). PoNow
        (5:6 issue 30) 81, p. 22.

KOSER, José
    "La Bella & el Muerto." Lugar (1:1) 79, p. 10.

KOSMICKI, Greg
    "Belly Button." PoNow (6:1 issue 31) 81, p. 20.
    "Changing a Diaper." Peb (21) 81, p. 15.
    "Changing a Diaper." PoNow (6:1 issue 31) 81, p. 20.
    "August Nineteenth." Peb (21) 81, p. 14.
    "To My Sister." Peb (21) 81, pp. 11-13.
    "Sunday Afternoon and Night." Peb (21) 81, pp. 8-10.
    "Under the Flyway." PoNow (6:1 issue 31) 81, p. 20.

KOSTELANETZ, Richard
    "Epiphanies." Confr (22) Sum 81, p. 42.
    "Turfs." SenR (11:2) 81, pp. 27-31.

KOTANSKY, Robert
    "Diving Beyond the Reef." Poem (43) Nov 81, p. 63.
    "Harvest." Poem (43) Nov 81, p. 64.

KOTSIUMBAS, Helen
    "pared down to a feel." Tele (17) 81, p. 85.

KOVNER, Abba
    "And That's How He Knew Your Face" (for the poet Yokheved Bat-
        Miriam) (tr. by Bernhard Frank). PoNow (5:6 issue 30) 81, p. 27.
    "At the Wind's Mercy" (tr. by Bernhard Frank). PoNow (5:6 issue 30)
        81, p. 27.
    "I Don't Know Whether Mt. Zion" (tr. by Bernhard Frank). PoNow (5:6
        issue 30) 81, p. 27.
    "Observation of a Young Man Running Across the Street After Parking

His Jeep in a No-Parking Zone" (tr. by Bernhard Frank). PoNow
(5:6 issue 30) 81, p. 27.
"Observation on the Sea's Edge at Natanya, with Flashback" (tr. by
Bernhard Frank). PoNow (5:6 issue 30) 81, p. 27.

KOWIT, Steve
"A Most Peculiar Girl" (tr. of Luis Suardiaz). PoNow (5:6 issue 30)
81, p. 44.
"Epigram" (tr. of Ernesto Cardenal). PoNow (5:6 issue 30) 81, p. 12.
"Witness for the Prosecution" (to Jorge and Noel Navarro) (tr. of Luis
Suardiaz). PoNow (5:6 issue 30) 81, p. 44.

KOZBERG, Donna Walters
"Beachside Park." Wind (11:40) 81, p. 17.

KOZER, José
"Four Poems: The Bottom of the Bowl" (tr. by Jorge Guitart).
ModernPS (10:2/3), pp. 96-97.

KRAMER, Aaron
"Feeding." NewEngR (3:4) Sum 81, p. 541.
"In the Shop" (tr. of Louis Miller). Vis (5) 81, n.p.
"Local." NewEngR (3:4) Sum 81, p. 542.
"Old Tunes." NewEngR (3:4) Sum 81, p. 542.
"The Visit." NewEngR (3:4) Sum 81, p. 541.
"Two Visits." Confr (21) Wint 81, p. 117.

KRAMER, Elizabeth
"From Boston to L. A." NewRena (14) Spr 81, p. 63.

KRAMER, Lawrence
"Four-Color Prints." NewEngR (3:3) Spr 81, pp. 370-1.

KRANZ, Judith
"The Field." Wind (11:43) 81, p. 25.

KRAPF, Norbert
"Durer Dreams of Animals." Confr (21) Wint 81, p. 34.
"Fall" (tr. of Rainer Maria Rilke). PoNow (5:6 issue 30) 81, p. 40.
"The Fat Years" (tr. of Katrine von Hutten). PoNow (5:6 issue 30) 81,
p. 46.
"Memory of" (tr. of Katrine von Hutten). PoNow (5:6 issue 30) 81, p.
46.
"Pin Oak." Confr (21) Wint 81, p. 35.
"Statement of Place" (tr. of Katrine von Hutten). PoNow (5:6 issue 30)
81, p. 46.
"When I Was Little" (tr. of Katrine von Hutten). PoNow (5:6 issue 30)
81, p. 46.

KRATT, Mary
"Bach in the Afternoon." SoCaR (14: 1) Aut 81, p. 126.

KRAUSE, Richard
"The advantage of being a thinker." PortR (27: 1) 81, p. 19.
"Epigrams." PortR (27: 1) 81, p. 39.
"Liking, Liking." PortR (27: 1) 81, p. 7.
"People don't want to see...." PortR (27: 1) 81, p. 14.
"You imagine a dwarf has to love...." PortR (27: 1) 81, p. 17.

KRAUSS, Ruth
    "Lullabye." PoNow (6:2 issue 32) 81, p. 11.

KRESH, David
    "Blue Shift." CharR (7:2) Aut 81, pp. 9-11.
    "Private Collection." KanQ (13:1) Wint 81, p. 158.
    "Sleeping Muse." SouthernPR (21: 1) Spr 81, p. 24.
    "Studies: Five Mornings." LitR (24:3) Spr 81, pp. 351-353.
    "The." Poetry (138:2) My 81, p. 92.

KRIEGER, Ted
    "Mama Nicks on Pershing." Wind (11:41) 81, p. 27.

KRISTOFCO, John P.
    "The Darkness Drops Again...." CapeR (17:1) Wint 81, p. 5.

KROK, Peter
    "Just Amazed." Poem (41) Mar 81, p. 49.
    "The Nightmare and the Frog." Poem (41) Mar 81, p. 48.
    "The Power." Poem (41) Mar 81, p. 50.

KROLL, Ernest
    "Atavism." WebR (6:2) 81, p. 49.
    "The Boy In The Gazebo" (Sutro Heights, San Francisco). Tele (17) 81,
        p. 67.
    "Brooklyn Bridge." HolCrit (18:2) Ap 81, p. 18.
    "Conversation." Poem (41) Mar 81, p. 58.
    "Departure." PoNow (6:1 issue 31) 81, p. 19.
    "Divisions of Labor." Poem (41) Mar 81, p. 59.
    "Tidewater Rag." FourQt (30:4) Sum 81, p. 14.

KROLL, Judith
    "Climacteric." Poetry (137:4) Ja 81, pp. 204-206.

KROLOW, Karl
    "Arid Breeze." LittleR (7:1, issue 15) 81, p. 5.
    "Autumn on the Lande." LittleR (7:1, issue 15) 81, p. 6.
    "Forever" (tr. by Stuart Friebert). PoNow (6:1 issue 31) 81, p. 42.
    "Funeral." LittleR (7:1, issue 15) 81, p. 6.
    "Keeping On Going" (tr. by Stuart Friebert). MassR (22:3) Aut 81, p.
        551.
    "Postcard of Autumn." LittleR (7:1, issue 15) 81, p. 5.
    "Rain." LittleR (7:1, issue 15) 81, p. 5.
    "The Secret." LittleR (7:1, issue 15) 81, p. 5.
    Ten poems. Mund (12/13) 80-81, pp. 57-64.
    "This and That" (tr. by Stuart Friebert). PoNow (6:1 issue 31) 81, p.
        42.
    "To a Musical Piece by Vivaldi." LittleR (7:1, issue 15) 81, p. 6.
    "Together" (tr. by Stuart Friebert). MassR (22:3) Aut 81, p. 552.
    "Words in Winter" (tr. by David Neal Miller). Aspect (77/79) 81, p.
        134.

KRUDY, Gyula
    "(Szindbad and) The Bishop's Niece" (tr. by John Batki). WebR (6:2) 81,
        p. 35.
    "Szindbad and Sleeping Women" (tr. by John Batki). WebR (6:2) 81, p.
        34.

KRÜGER, Michael
"Additional poem" (tr. by Von Underwood).   Mund (11:2) 79, p. 33.
"Gedicht Über Einen Spaziergang Am Stausee Und Über Gedichte. "
    Mund (11:2) 79, pp. 34-6.
"Nachgedicht. "   Mund (11:2) 79, p. 32.
"Poem About a Walk By the Reservoir and About Poems" (tr. by Von
    Underwood).   Mund (11:2) 79, pp. 35-37.

KRUMHOLZ, Allyn
"Daylight Savings Time. "   Northeast (3:10) Wint 81, p. 5.

KRUPA, Warren C.
"Bathers, Coney Island, 1939" (for Milton Avery).   PortR (27: 2) 81, p.
    91.

KRUSOE, James
"Letter to Kirchner. "   Aspect (77/79) 81, p. 135.
"Two Hurt Ones" (1. A Face, 2. The Giant).   PoNow (6:2 issue 32) 81,
    p. 38.
"Two Poems with My Father in Them" (1. Stuart, 2. A Story).   PoNow
    (6:2 issue 32) 81, p. 38.

KRYSL, Marilyn
"Mother and Child. "   LittleM (13:1/2) Spr-Sum 79, c1981, p. 58.
"Sestina Extolling the Pleasure of Creation. "   LittleM (13:1/2) Spr-Sum
    79, c1981, pp. 56-57.

KUBASAK, Sharon
"At the Memory Trial. "   Kayak (56) 81, p. 29.

KUCHINSKY, Walter
"Inez. "   StoneC (9: 1-2) Aut-Wint 81/82, p. 70.

KUHNER, Herbert
"The Animal" (tr. of Heidi Pataki).   Mund (11:2) 79, p. 75.
"Aren't to Blame" (tr. of Hermann Jandl).   Mund (11:2) 79, p. 81.
"Being" (tr. of Ilse Brem).   PortR (27: 2) 81, p. 35.
"Consolation" (tr. of Gabor Hajnal).   WebR (6:2) 81, p. 39.
"Critically Ill" (tr. of Tymoteusz Karpowicz).   WebR (6:2) 81, p. 38.
"End" (tr. of Peter Paul Wiplinger).   PortR (27: 2) 81, p. 35.
"End Phase" (tr. of Albert Janetscheck).   Mund (11:2) 79, p. 83.
"Everything is Only" (tr. of Ernst Schenwiese).   Mund (11:2) 79, p. 77.
"Legends" (tr. of Peter Paul Wiplinger).   PortR (27: 2) 81, p. 35.
"Note" (tr. of Helmut Zenker).   Mund (11:2) 79, p. 79.
"Poems" (tr. of Christine Busta).   Mund (11:2) 79, p. 73.
"Reflection" (tr. of Franz Storch).   WebR (6:2) 81, p. 37.
"Speechless" (tr. of Erich Fried).   Mund (11:2) 79, p. 79.
"Steps" (tr. of Ernst David).   Mund (11:2) 79, p. 73.
"Without Thinking" (tr. of Ernst Nowak).   Mund (11:2) 79, p. 75.
"The Word--This Boat" (tr. of Gertrud Fussenegger).   Mund (11:2) 79,
    p. 81.
"Words Between You and Me" (tr. of Helmult H. Stradal).   Mund (11:2)
    79, p. 77.

KULKARNI, Venkatesh Srinivas
"Calamus. "   PikeR (2) Sum 81, p. 28.

KULYCKY, Michael
"The Wanderer. "   KanQ (13:3/4) Sum-Aut 81, p. 212.

KUMIN, Judith
    "Maturity" (tr. of Denise Jallais, w/ Maxine Kumin). PoNow (5:6 issue
        30) 81, p. 19.
    "Mr. X, Doctor of Laws" (tr. of William Cliff, w/ Maxine Kumin).
        PoNow (5:6 issue 30) 81, p. 14.

KUMIN, Maxine
    "Anger." MissouriR (4:2) Wint 81-82, p. 23.
    "Going to Jerusalem." ParisR (23:79) Spr 81, p. 223.
    "Maturity" (tr. of Denise Jallais, w/ Judith Kumin). PoNow (5:6 issue
        30) 81, p. 19.
    "Mr. X, Doctor of Laws" (tr. of William Cliff, w/ Judith Kumin).
        PoNow (5:6 issue 30) 81, p. 14.
    "The Poets Observe The Absence Of God From The St. Louis Zoo."
        MissouriR (4:2) Wint 81-82, p. 24.

KUNENE, Daniel P.
    "Coalescence." Mund (12/13) 80-81, pp. 182-183.

KUNERT, Günter
    "Ad" (tr. by Fritz H. König). Mund (11:2) 79, pp. 21, 23.
    "Anzeige." Mund (11:2) 79, pp. 20, 22.
    "Denkmal." Mund (11:2) 79, p. 22.
    "Eisenbahnen." Mund (11:2) 79, pp. 18, 20.
    "Ideogram" (tr. by Fritz H. König). Mund (11:2) 79, p. 19.
    "Ideogramm." Mund (11:2) 79, p. 18.
    "Railways" (tr. by Fritz H. König). Mund (11:2) 79, pp. 19, 21.
    "Statue" (tr. by Fritz H. König). Mund (11:2) 79, p. 23.

KUNITZ, Stanley
    "The Snakes of September." Antaeus (40/41) Wint-Spr 81, p. 319.
    "The Wellfleet Whale." Atl (248:5) N 81, pp. 68-69.

KURIBAYASHI, Laurie
    "Ele 'Ele." ThRiPo (17/18) 81, p. 32.

KUUSISTO, Allan
    "At the Ruins of the Old Fortress" (tr. of Jarkko Laine, w/ Stephen A.
        Kuusisto and John Currie). SenR (12:1/2) 81, p. 209.
    "God Bless Finland" (tr. of Jarkko Laine, w/ Stephen A. Kuusisto and
        John Currie). SenR (12:1/2) 81, pp. 217, 219.
    "The Last Judgment" (tr. of Jarkko Laine, w/ Stephen A. Kuusisto and
        John Currie). SenR (12:1/2) 81, p. 211.
    "Yesterday" (tr. of Jarkko Laine, w/ Stephen A. Kuusisto and John
        Currie). SenR (12:1/2) 81, pp. 213, 215.

KUUSISTO, Stephen A.
    "At the Ruins of the Old Fortress" (tr. of Jarkko Laine, w/ Allan
        Kuusisto & John Currie). SenR (12:1/2) 81, p. 209.
    "God Bless Finland" (tr. of Jarkko Laine, w/ Allan Kuusisto & John
        Currie). SenR (12:1/2) 81, pp. 217, 219.
    "The Last Judgment" (tr. of Jarkko Laine, w/ Allan Kuusisto & John
        Currie). SenR (12:1/2) 81, p. 211.
    "Yesterday" (tr. of Jarkko Laine, w/ Allan Kuusisto & John Currie).
        SenR (12:1/2) 81, pp. 213, 215.

KUZMA, Greg
    "Apology." PraS (55:3) Aut 81, p. 54.

"Childhood." PraS (55:3) Aut 81, p. 55.
"The Coffee Room of the Department of Art and Literature." PraS (55:
      3) Aut 81, pp. 61-4.
"Crocus." PraS (55:3) Aut 81, p. 51.
"Dry Winter." PraS (55:3) Aut 81, pp. 59-60.
"The Face." PraS (55:3) Aut 81, p. 53.
"For My Brother." PoetryE (6) Aut 81, p. 59.
"The Fruit Trees." Peb (21) 81, pp. 82-85.
"The Great Poems." GeoR (35:1) Spr 81, p. 61.
"The Island." Ploughs (6:4) 81, pp. 60-66.
"It." MidwQ (22:4) Sum 81, p. 369.
"It Was At Midnight." Peb (21) 81, p. 89.
"Love Poem." MidwQ (23:1) Aut 81, p. 55.
"The Muskrat." PraS (55:3) Aut 81, p. 55.
"Sometimes." PraS (55:3) Aut 81, pp. 57-8.
"Street Scene." PraS (55:3) Aut 81, p. 53.
"The Tree." Peb (21) 81, pp. 86-88.
"Turning." PraS (55:3) Aut 81, p. 56.
"Two AM, January." Hudson (34:4) Wint 81, p. 561.
"The Vision." PraS (55:3) Aut 81, p. 60.
"Vita Sheet (for George P. Elliott)." MidwQ (23:1) Aut 81, p. 57.
"For Weldon Kees." MidwQ (22:4) Sum 81, p. 368.
"Winter." PraS (55:3) Aut 81, p. 52.
"Yes." MidwQ (23:1) Aut 81, pp. 55-6.

KVAM, W.
"The Road to Gospic (Yugoslavia)." Im (7:3) 81, p. 11.

KVAM, Wayne
"Always I See You in Prison" (tr. of Jurgen Fuchs). CentR (25:2) Aut
      81, pp. 381-382.
"The Bad Part" (tr. of Jurgen Fuchs). CentR (25:2) Aut 81, p. 382.
"Letter" (tr. of Sarah Kirsch). DenQ (16:1) Spr 81, p. 70.
"Maybe" (tr. of Jurgen Fuchs). CentR (25:2) Aut 81, p. 381.
"Renting a Small Room" (tr. of Sarah Kirsch). DenQ (16:1) Spr 81, p.
      71.
"The Rest of the String" (tr. of Sarah Kirsch). DenQ (16:1) Spr 81, p.
      72.
"This October Afternoon." WindO (38) Spr-Sum 81, p. 19.

KWAIN, Constance Anna
"When Hunger Strikes." Tele (17) 81, p. 114.

KWAN, C. H.
"An Inscription on the Buddhist Retreat of Master Yi" (tr. of Meng Hao-
      jan). MalR (58) Ap 81, p. 39.
"At Home in the Village" (tr. of Hsin Ch'i-chi). MalR (58) Ap 81, p.
      40.
"Autumn Evening" (tr. of Tu Mu). MalR (58) Ap 81, p. 37.
"The Beautiful Regions South of the Yangtse River" (tr. of Wei Chuang).
      MalR (58) Ap 81, p. 37.
"Ching Ming Festival" (tr. of Gau Juh). MalR (58) Ap 81, p. 36.
"The Chung Yang Festival" (tr. of Li Ching-chao). MalR (58) Ap 81,
      p. 39.
"Climbing the Lo-Yu Plateau" (tr. of Li Shang-yin). MalR (58) Ap 81,
      p. 39.
"Hibiscus" (tr. of Wang An-shih). MalR (58) Ap 81, p. 37.
"Gazing at the Moon and Longing for One Far Away" (tr. of Chang

Chiu-ling). MalR (58) Ap 81, p. 36.
"Keeping Watch in Vain by a Flowing River" (tr. of Wen Ting-yun).
    MalR (58) Ap 81, p. 40.
"Late Spring" (tr. of Huang Ting-jian). MalR (58) Ap 81, p. 41.
"Snow on the River" (tr. of Liu Chang-yuan). MalR (58) Ap 81, p. 38.
"To Visit all Famous Gardens in Flowering Time" (tr. of Lu Yu).
    MalR (58) Ap 81, p. 41.
"The Winding River" (tr. of Tu Fu). MalR (58) Ap 81, p. 38.

LaBARE, M.
"Teeth." Aspect (77/79) 81, pp. 136-137.

LABE, Louise
"Elegy xxii." SouthernR (17:4) Aut 81, p. 995.

LAFFEY, Tim
"And Your Car Will Run." Sam (116) 81, p. 61.

LaFOLLETE, Melvin Walker
"The Maiden and The Unicorn." SoCaR (14: 1) Aut 81, p. 50.
"Pen Ghu: A Vision of Islands." SoCaR (14: 1) Aut 81, p. 49.

LAFORGUE, Jules
"Ah! For you with what pleasure I'd bend" (tr. by Marilyn Kallet).
    SenR (12:1/2) 81, p. 61.
"Ah! que je te les tordrais avec plaisir." SenR (12:1/2) 81, p. 60.
"Dimanches." SenR (12:1/2) 81, pp. 56-8.
"Sundays" (tr. by Marilyn Kallet). SenR (12:1/2) 81, pp. 57-9.

LaGATTUTA, Margo
"Dry Skin on the Sheets." LittleM (13:1/2) Spr-Sum 79, c1981, pp. 82-
    83.

LAGERKVIST, Pär
"With Old Eyes I Look Back" (tr. by W. H. Auden and Leif Sjöberg).
    Mund (12/13) 80-81, pp. 326-328.

LAINE, Jarkko
"At the Ruins of the Old Fortress" (tr. by Stephen A. Kuusisto, Allan
    Kuusisto and John Currie). SenR (12:1/2) 81, p. 209.
"Eilispäivä." SenR (12:1/2) 81, pp. 212, 214.
"God Bless Finland" (tr. by Stephen A. Kuusisto, Allan Kuusisto and
    John Currie). SenR (12:1/2) 81, pp. 217, 219.
"The Last Judgment" (tr. by Stephen A. Kuusisto, Allan Kuusisto and
    John Currie). SenR (12:1/2) 81, p. 211.
"Siunaa Jumala Suomea." SenR (12:1/2) 81, pp. 216, 218.
"Vanhan Linnan Raunioilla." SenR (12:1/2) 81, p. 208.
"Viimeinen Tuomio." SenR (12:1/2) 81, p. 210.
"Yesterday" (tr. by Stephen A. Kuusisto, Allan Kuusisto and John Cur-
    rie). SenR (12:1/2) 81, pp. 213, 215.

LAKE, Kathleen
"What Happens To Animals In Whom The Touch Instinct is Kindled."
    Ploughs (7:1) 81, pp. 146-147.

LAKE, Paul
"Along the Pacific." Thrpny (5) Spr 81, p. 8.
"The Classics Station: This Is Just a Test." Thrpny (7) Aut 81, p.
    22.

LALIC, Ivan V.
"Voices of the Dead" (tr. by Charles Simic). Mund (12/13) 80-81, pp. 350-351.

LALLY, Michael
"The Definite Article, the Indefinite Article, and the Genuine Article" (for Terence Winch). HangL (40) Aut 81, pp. 31-34.
"Just Cooling." HangL (40) Aut 81, p. 36.
"This Is Me Speaking." HangL (40) Aut 81, pp. 34-35.

LAMON, Laurie
"Last Gray Scene." CutB (16) Spr-Sum 81, pp. 103-104.
"Leaving Emelia." CutB (16) Spr-Sum 81, pp. 101-102.

LAMORTE, Pat
"Gypsy." PoNow (6:3 issue 33) 81, p. 19.

LANDERS, Jonathan
"Almost Too Much to Bear Today Father." PoetryE (6) Aut 81, p. 56.

LANE, Gary
"William Bronk to the Muse." BelPoJ (31:3) Spr 81, p. 7.

LANE, Mary
"I feel like a have-not country...." OP (31/32) Aut 81, pp. 98-99.

LANE, William
"The Apple Priest." HangL (40) Aut 81, pp. 37-38.
"Charlie." PoNow (6:3 issue 33) 81, p. 25.
"Pickens, W. Va." PoNow (6:3 issue 33) 81, p. 25.

LANG, G. M.
"The Luminous Point" (for Roque Dalton and Enrique Lihn) (tr. of René Depestre, w/ D. A. McMurray). Calib (3:2) Aut-Wint 80, p. 93.

LANG, Stephen
"Morning Song." Poem (42) Jul 81, p. 60.
"A Picture of Harry O'More, With Friend." Poem (42) Jul 81, p. 58.
"Tremor." Poem (42) Jul 81, p. 59.

LANG, Susanna
"In the Thickness/Dans l'epaisseur." (tr. of Philippe Denis). ChiR (32:2) Aut 80, pp. 95-107.

LANGENBERG, Chris
"Creative Black." Peb (21) 81, pp. 34-35.
"In Cognito." Peb (21) 81, p. 33.
"Mental Vehicle Homicide." Peb (21) 81, p. 31.
"A Picture Taken." Peb (21) 81, p. 32.

LANGLAND, Joseph
"A Bare Portrait For My Friend, Aslak, In Lappland." Ploughs (6:4) 81, pp. 180-181.
"One Foreign Road." Ploughs (6:4) 81, pp. 179-180.

LANGTON, Daniel J.
"Admonition." CharR (7:2) Aut 81, p. 7.

LANIK, Glenda
"I gave it to you--do you remember me?" Peb (21) 81, pp. 52-54.

LANSING, Gerrit
"Olana (or The Shark of Craving)." Sulfur (1) 81, pp. 186-191.

LANTEIGNE, M. P.
"My Sister Giving Birth." PottPort (3) 81, p. 34.
"Picking Cranberries." PottPort (3) 81, p. 41.

LANTER, Wayne
"Spring Planting." PoNow (6:3 issue 33) 81, p. 19.

LAPE, Walter
"The Fisherman's Phoenix." EngJ (70:8) D 81, p. 69.

LAPIDUS, Jacqueline
"Penelope." HangL (40) Aut 81, pp. 42-44.
"Privileged Resident." HangL (40) Aut 81, p. 45.
From Voyage to Lesbos: "Athens." Cond (7) Spr 81, p. 91.
From Voyage to Lesbos: "Eressos." Cond (7) Spr 81, pp. 95-96.
From Voyage to Lesbos: "Mytilene." Cond (7) Spr 81, p. 92.
From Voyage to Lesbos: "Plomari." Cond (7) Spr 81, p. 93.
From Voyage to Lesbos: "Site of the Petrified Forest." Cond (7) Spr
    81, p. 94.

LAPPIN, Linda
"Letter from the Taverna on the Edge of Desire." Kayak (57) 81, pp.
    11-12.
"Sleepwalking to Trastevere." Kayak (57) 81, p. 10.

LARDAS, Konstantinos
"Aegean." SouthernPR (21: 1) Spr 81, p. 63.
"War." Wind (11:41) 81, p. 28.
"Startled." Wind (11:41) 81, pp. 28-29.
"Testament." Wind (11:41) 81, p. 29.

LARKIN, Mary Ann
"The Silence of the Birds." HiramPoR (29) Aut-Wint 81, p. 28.

LARRAHONA K., Alfonso
"Una Redoma" (A Pedro Paredes, poeta venezolano). Puerto Wint 81,
    p. 28.

LARREA, Juan
"A Color Used to Call Him Juan (To the Memory of Juan Gris)" (tr. by
    Ana Waisman). DenQ (16:1) Spr 81, p. 59.
"Occupied" (tr. by Ana Waisman). DenQ (16:1) Spr 81, p. 57.
"Provisional Spring" (tr. by Ana Waisman). DenQ (16:1) Spr 81, p. 58.

LARSON, Kris
"South Addison." Wind (11:43) 81, p. 22.

LARSON, R. A.
"Maps." PoNow (6:3 issue 33) 81, p. 19.
"312 West Third." PoNow (6:3 issue 33) 81, p. 19.

LaSALLE, Peter
"Topolobampo." SoCaR (14: 1) Aut 81, p. 121.

LASH, Kenneth
"In Iowa." Ploughs (6:4) 81, p. 43.

LASHER, Darlene
"Domesticated Gypsy." CalQ (18/19) 81, p. 91.

LASKER-SCHÜLER, Else
"Revenge" (tr. by Betty Falkenberg). PoNow (6:2 issue 32) 81, p. 41.
"Suicide" (tr. by Betty Falkenberg). PoNow (6:2 issue 32) 81, p. 41.
"To God" (tr. by James Liddy and Ruth Schwertfeger). DenQ (16:1)
    Spr 81, p. 69.

LASKEY, Karen
"Riders." MidwQ (22:4) Sum 81, pp. 370-1.

LASTRA, Pedro
"Brief Account" (tr. by Lilvia Duggan). Mund (12/13) 80-81, p. 118.
"Diario de Viaje." Inti (9) Spr 79, p. 99.
"Fascinacion del Vacio." Inti (9) Spr 79, p. 100.
"Nostradamus" (tr. by Lilvia Duggan). Mund (12/13) 80-81, p. 118.
"El Sueño de Graciela Coulson." Inti (9) Spr 79, p. 99.

LATTA, Richard
"Flower Pot." Aspect (77/79) 81, p. 138.

LATTIMORE, Richmond
"Aspects of Time." Hudson (34:1) Spr 81, pp. 58-59.
"Bone Structure." Poetry (138:3) Je 81, p. 150.
"Flesh Tones." Poetry (138:3) Je 81, p. 149.
"Home." Hudson (34:1) Spr 81, p. 59.
"Shanhaikuan." Hudson (34:1) Spr 81, p. 57.
"They Used to Have a Homecoming Day." Hudson (34:1) Spr 81, p. 58.

LAUBER, Peg
"Song III." Wind (11:41) 81, p. 31.
"Where They Go." Wind (11:41) 81, p. 30.

LAURENCE, Michael
"Murder Mystery" (to Stuart Allingham). WormR (84) 81, pp. 97-99.
"Religious Instructions." Tele (17) 81, p. 100.

LAUTERBACH, Ann
"Second Descent: 1980." PartR (48:2) 81, p. 250.

LAUTERMILCH, Steven
"The Buddha in Glory" (tr. of Rainer Maria Rilke). LitR (24:4) Sum
    81, p. 518.
"Buddha" (tr. of Rainer Maria Rilke). LitR (24:4) Sum 81, p. 517.
"Dear Neighbor God" (tr. of Rainer Maria Rilke). LitR (24:4) Sum 81,
    p. 516.
"I Keep Finding You" (tr. of Rainer Maria Rilke). LitR (24:4) Sum 81,
    p. 517.
"Sonnets to Orpheus" (tr. of Rainer Maria Rilke). LitR (24:4) Sum 81,
    pp. 514-515.

LAVAZZI, Thomas
"The Imaginary Tree." EnPas (12) 81, pp. 14-15.

LAVENDER, William
"Forgotten Moment." NewOR (8:2) Sum 81, p. 166.

LAVORGNA, Linda E.
"The Collector." SmPd (18:1) Wint 81, p. 19.
"They Tell Me." SmPd (18:1) Wint 81, p. 18.
"They Tell Me" (corrected version of 18:1, Wint 81, p. 18). SmPd
    (18:3) Aut 81, p. 33.

LAWDER, Donald
"In Poetry, Everything Is Permitted (responding to a student's poem
    beginning 'I feel horny tonight')." KanQ (13:3/4) Sum-Aut 81, pp.
    15-16.

LAWDER, Douglas
"Convenant." SouthernPR (21:2) Aut 81, p. 40.

LAWLER, Patrick
"Studio Cards." Shen (31:3) 80, p. 73.

LAWNER, Lynne
"Sorceress." Poetry (137:5) F 81, pp. 269-270.

LAWRY, Mercedes
"Rapunzel, Rapunzel." Vis (7) 81, n. p.

LAWS, David
from The Myerson Poems (I-VI, IX, X, XII, XVII). Epoch (30:1) Aut
    80, pp. 16-21.

LAX, Robert
"A thin white line." HangL (40) Aut 81, pp. 46-47.
"While raining here." HangL (40) Aut 81, p. 48.

LAYTON, Irving
"The Black Thread." PottPort (3) 81, p. 37.
"Modern Poet." UnmOx (22) Wint 81, p. 24.
"Poetry Conference." PottPort (3) 81, p. 5.
"The Tower." UnmOx (22) Wint 81, p. 25.
"Tristessa." PottPort (3) 81, p. 9.
"Waterfront." PottPort (3) 81, p. 26.

LAZAR, Jos̆e
"Silence" (tr. of Niko Grafenauer). Mund (12/13) 80-81, p. 93.

LAZARD, Naomi
"The Secret Life Of Ghosts." PartR (48:4) 81, p. 598.

LEA, Sydney
"At Hardscrabble: Face to the Moon." Hudson (34:2) Sum 81, pp. 219-
    222.
"Bernie's Quick-Shave (1968)." NewYorker (57:2) 2 Mr 82, p. 36.
"Battle." PraS (55:3) Aut 81, pp. 33-4.
"Reaching Over." Hudson (34:2) Sum 81, pp. 218-219.
"To a Surgeon." Iowa (11:2/3) Spr-Sum 80, pp. 138-140.
"Toward Silhouette: December." Antaeus (43) Aut 81, pp. 90-91.

LEAKE, Brent T.
"Mexico By Friday." Wind (10:39) 80, p. 26.
"Vina." Wind (10:39) 80, p. 26.

LEAMON, Marlene
"Happy Ending." GeoR (35:3) Aut 81, p. 645.

LEARD, Lonnie
"Fatherhood." PoNow (6:3 issue 33) 81, p. 19.

LEBOVITZ, Richard
"Altazor, or Journey by Parachute" (tr. of Vicente Huidobro).   Mund
      (12/13) 80-81, pp. 380-384.

LeCOMPTE, Kendall
"Calenture." HiramPoR (30) Spr-Sum 81, p. 26.
"Night Dive." HiramPoR (30) Spr-Sum 81, p. 27.

LeCOMTE, Serge
"A L'équateur." Os (12) Spr 81, p. 25.

LEDERMAN, Sherri
"Madeleine de Demandolx (1593-1670, France)." 13thM (5:1/2) 80, pp.
      97-98.
"Elizabeth Clark (d. 1645, England)." 13thM (5:1/2) 80, p. 95.
"Sarah Good (d. 1692, Salem)." 13thM (5:1/2) 80, p. 99.

LEE, Li-Young
"Persimmons." AmerPoR (10:6) N-D 81, p. 46.
"Water." AmerPoR (10:6) N-D 81, p. 47.

LEE, Pete
"Love Song." SmPd (18:2) Spr 81, p. 5.
"My Half." SmPd (18:2) Spr 81, p. 5.

LEEDER, Ken
"February." Atl (247:2) F 81, p. 71.

LEET, Judith
"Early Friday Evening Observations." Poetry (139:1) O 81, pp. 17-18.

LEFCOWITZ, Barbara F.
"Choice." PoNow (6:2 issue 32) 81, p. 32.
"Driving Before Dawn." Aspect (77/79) 81, p. 139.
"Fog." CapeR (17:1) Wint 81, p. 24.
"November Dance." Aspect (77/79) 81, p. 139.
"Sisyphus's Reprieve." PraS (55:3) Aut 81, pp. 91-2.
"Words for Scattered Ancestors." WebR (6:1) 81, pp. 62-66.

LeFORGE, P. V.
"The Secret Life of Moles." LittleM (13:1/2) Spr-Sum 79, c1981, pp.
      94-95.

LEFTWITCH, Joseph
"On Sunny Days" (tr. of Rajzel Zichlinsky). PortR (27: 1) 81, p. 25.

LEGGET, Lee
"Bread" (tr. of Michel Butor). Mund (12/13) 80-81, p. 155.

"The Insect" (tr. of Michel Butor).   Mund (12/13) 80-81, pp. 154-155.
"The Roof" (tr. of Michel Butor).   Mund (12/13) 80-81, p. 154.
"The Ruin" (tr. of Michel Butor).   Mund (12/13) 80-81, p. 155.
"Sleep" (tr. of Michel Butor).   Mund (12/13) 80-81, p. 154.

LEGLER, Philip
   "Eggs."   PraS (55:4) Wint 81-82, pp. 80-81.

Le GUIN, Ursula K.
   "Hard Words."   PortR (27: 1) 81, p. 17.
   "More Useful Truths."   PortR (27: 1) 81, p. 17.
   "Walking Through Cornwall."   PortR (27: 1) 81, pp. 15-16.

LEHMAN, David
   "An Alternative to Speech."   Shen (31:3) 80, p. 49.
   "Beginning of Terror."   Epoch (30:3) Spr-Sum 81, pp. 214-215.
   "Shake the Superflux!"   Epoch (30:3) Spr-Sum 81, pp. 216-217.

LEHMANN, Wilhelm
   "Belated Festival" (tr. by Rodney Nelson).   EnPas (12) 81, p. 4.
   "Final Evening" (tr. by Rodney Nelson).   EnPas (12) 81, p. 6.
   "The Magpie" (tr. by Rodney Nelson).   EnPas (12) 81, p. 5.
   "In Solothurn" (tr. by Rodney Nelson).   EnPas (12) 81, p. 7.

LEIGHTTY, David
   "Shelbyville Road."   Wind (11:40) 81, p. 18.

LEIPER, Esther M.
   "Blue Bottle Glass."   Nimrod (25:1) Aut-Wint 81, pp. 75-76.

LEISER, Dorothy
   "Campground in Yosemite."   ChrC (98:23) 15-22 Jl 81, p. 737.

LEITHAUSER, Brad
   "Additional Bats."   PartR (48:2) 81, p. 248.
   "A Needle Bed."   Atl (247:2) F 81, p. 71.
   "Law Clerk, 1979."   NewEngR (4:2) Wint 81, pp. 223-7.

LEIVA, Angel
   "Seasons" (tr. by Carolyne Wright).   DenQ (16:1) Spr 81, p. 61.
   "Zone" (tr. by Carolyne Wright).   DenQ (16:1) Spr 81, p. 60.

LEMBKE, Janet
   "Lessons in Prison."   BelPoJ (31:4) Sum 81, pp. 8-11.

Le MIEUX, Dotty
   "Lines."   Tele (17) 81, pp. 142-143.

LEMM, Richard
   "Border Crossing" (or The Great Bulldozer Chase).   PottPort (3) 81, p.
       14.
   "Little Spirit."   MalR (58) Ap 81, p. 129.
   "Love Canal."   PottPort (3) 81, p. 13.
   "Somebody Else's Luck."   PottPort (3) 81, p. 5.

LENBENTRITT, Julia
   "White Sister."   Tele (17) 81, p. 122.
   "Your landlady."   Tele (17) 81, p. 121.

LENSON, David
"Hopkins: The Bedspring." MassR (22:4) Wint 81, p. 782.
"Wordsworth: The Moose-Flayer." MassR (22:4) Wint 81, p. 782.

LENTON, Scott
"The Musician At His Wedding." WindO (38) Spr-Sum 81, p. 40.

LEON, Armando Rojo see ROJO LEON, Armando

LEON, Marilyn Bobes see BOBES LEON, Marilyn

LEOPARDI, Giacomo
"To Himself (A Se Stesso)" (tr. by Burton Raffel). LitR (24:3) Spr 81,
   p. 381.

LEPORE, Dominick
"Stifled" (tr. of Gigi Dessi). StoneC (8: 3) Spr 81, p. 20.
"Worried" (tr. of Gigi Dessi). StoneC (8: 3) Spr 81, p. 21.

LEPORE, Dominick J.
"Atlantis." ArizQ (37:2) Sum 81, p. 148.

LEPSON, Ruth
"In the Garden." PoNow (6:3 issue 33) 81, p. 25.
"July Morning." PoNow (6:3 issue 33) 81, p. 25.
"Skywriting." PoNow (6:3 issue 33) 81, p. 25.

Le RIVEREND, Pablo
"Destierro." Puerto Wint 81, p. 29.

LERNER, Linda
"The Mistletoe Girl." CentR (25:1) Wint 81, p. 44.
"The One." ConcPo (14:1) Spr 81, p. 72.
"Wanting." CentR (25:1) Wint 81, pp. 44-45.

LESCOET, Henri de see De LESCOET, Henri

LESHER, Fred
"Capacity." Northeast (3:11) Sum 81, p. 9.
"February Lark." Northeast (3:11) Sum 81, p. 8.
"No Title." Northeast (3:11) Sum 81, p. 8.

LESNIAK, Rose
"Night of the 24th." Tele (17) 81, p. 66.
"Smashed on the IRT no. 1." Tele (17) 81, pp. 65-66.
"Some Cows." Tele (17) 81, p. 64.

LESSER, Rika
"Autumn's Final Flower" (tr. of Edith Södergran). PoetryE (6) Aut 81,
   pp. 42-43.
"The Book of Finland-Swedish Poems" (tr. of Lars Huldén). PoetryE
   (6) Aut 81, pp. 19-20.
"The Day Cools" (tr. of Edith Södergran). PoetryE (6) Aut 81, pp. 41-
   42.
"Hand to Hand." Shen (32:1) 80, pp. 102-103.
"The Land That Is Not" (tr. of Edith Södergran). PoetryE (6) Aut 81,
   p. 43.
"Mutters to Himself" (tr. of Claes Andersson). PoetryE (6) Aut 81,

pp. 10-11.
"Northern Spring" (tr. of Edith Södergran). PoetryE (6) Aut 81, p. 41.
"Once, Long Ago" (tr. of Lars Huldén). PoetryE (6) Aut 81, pp. 20-21.
"Some People" (tr. of Claes Andersson). PoetryE (6) Aut 81, pp. 12-13.

LESSING, Karin
    "Primavera." Sulfur (3) 82, p. 32.
    "Sea-Foam." Sulfur (1) 81, pp. 60-61.
    "September-Wings." Sulfur (1) 81, pp. 62-63.
    "Shadows, Firstcomers...." Sulfur (3) 82, p. 36.
    "stood here." Sulfur (1) 81, p. 58.
    "Terra Cotta Figures, Villa Guilia" (in memoriam D. H. Lawrence).
        Sulfur (3) 82, pp. 33-34.
    "Vigil." Sulfur (3) 82, p. 35.
    "What it Wants." Sulfur (1) 81, p. 59.

LEVENDOSKY, Charles
    "4.16.78. (Macon, Georgia)." NowestR (19:1/2), pp. 69-70.
    "The boys pock highways signs." PoNow (6:2 issue 32) 81, p. 44.

LEVERING, Donald
    "Cocteau's Orpheus." Wind (11:40) 81, pp. 19-20.
    "A Leak in the Gas Line." Wind (11:43) 81, pp. 24-25.
    "Love at the County Fair" (for Janice). Wind (11:40) 81, p. 19.
    "Paper, Scissors, & Stone." Wind (11:43) 81, pp. 23-24.

LEVERTOV, Denise
    "For the Blind." Mund (12/13) 80-81, p. 295.
    "The Heart." OP (31/32) Aut 81, p. 33.
    "Rain Spirit Passing." PoetryE (6) Aut 81, p. 52.
    "Sound of the Axe." ParisR (23:79) Spr 81, p. 224.
    "Vocation." PoetryE (6) Aut 81, pp. 50-51.

LEVICH, Christine
    "Generations." ConcPo (14:1) Spr 81, pp. 15-16.

LEVIN, Arthur
    "The Eminent Journalist Lies Near Death." Confr (21) Wint 81, pp.
        104-105.

LEVIN, John
    "Blew it." Tele (17) 81, p. 126.
    "Click." Tele (17) 81, p. 128.
    "Rowena." Tele (17) 81, pp. 129-130.
    "Things." Tele (17) 81, p. 126.
    "Two associations." Tele (17) 81, p. 127.

LEVIN, Phillis
    "Citizens & Sky." Pequod (12) 81, p. 77.
    "The Way to Mount Aetna." Pequod (12) 81, pp. 75-76.

LEVINE, Anne-Marie
    "Two Part Invention." BelPoJ (31:4) Sum 81, pp. 21-24.

LEVINE, Ellen
    "Chateau D'if." CutB (17) Aut-Wint 81, p. 4.

LEVINE, Miriam
"More Than My Hands." 13thM (5:1/2) 80, pp. 121-122.

LEVINE, Philip
"Above Jazz." NewEngR (3:3) Spr 81, pp. 335-6.
"Another Song." NewYorker (56:49) 26 Ja 81, p. 39.
"Ascension." NewYorker (56:49) 26 Ja 81, p. 39.
"Belief." NewEngR (3:3) Spr 81, pp. 333-5.
"The Conductor of Nothing." Antaeus (40/41) Wint-Spr 81, pp. 322-323.
"Depot Bay." MissouriR (4:2) Wint 80-81, p. 9.
"Elements." CarolQ (33:1) Wint 81, pp. 106-107.
"I Remember Clifford." NewYorker (56:49) 26 Ja 81, p. 39.
"I Sing the Body Electric." Antaeus (40/41) Wint-Spr 81, pp. 320-321.
"I Wanted You To Know." MissouriR (4:2) Wint 80-81, p. 7.
"Illinois." CarolQ (33:1) Wint 81, p. 105.
"Invitation to the Dance." Antaeus (40/41) Wint-Spr 81, pp. 324-325.
"Plea from the Angel of Good Luck." Hudson (34:1) Spr 81, pp. 35-36.
"Roofs." Hudson (34:1) Spr 81, pp. 34-35.
"A Sign." ParisR (23:79) Spr 81, p. 225.
"Sources." NewYorker (56:49) 26 Ja 81, p. 39.
"A Spirit." PartR (48:1) 81, p. 134.
"Those Were the Days." NewYorker (57:16) 8 Je 81, p. 44.
"To a New Mother" (for Marcia). Hudson (34:1) Spr 81, pp. 36-37.
"The Window." Hudson (34:1) Spr 81, pp. 37-38.

LEVINE, R. S.
"Ishmael, Tell Us: What Was Ahab Really Like?" PartR (48:4) 81, p.
601.

LEVIS, Larry
"The Double." OP (31/32) Aut 81, pp. 104-105.
"Edward Hopper, Hotel Room, 1931." Antaeus (40/41) Wint-Spr 81, pp.
326-327.
"Ice." Antaeus (40/41) Wint-Spr 81, pp. 330-331.
"Magnolia." Antaeus (40/41) Wint-Spr 81, pp. 328-329.

LEVITIN, Alexis
"At that time, whoever followed the rough track" (tr. of Eugenio de
Andrade). ModernPS (10:2/3), p. 193.
"Dead Star" (tr. of Augusto Frederico Schmidt). PortR (27: 2) 81, p.
31.
"The Hanged" (tr. of Alexandre O'Neill). PortR (27: 2) 81, p. 31.
"In this morning Silence..." (tr. of Jorge de Sena). PortR (27: 2) 81,
p. 31.
"Last Request" (tr. of Jorge de Sena). Im (7:2) 1981, p. 10.
from "Melody" (I & II) (tr. of Jose Gomes Ferreira). PortR (27: 2)
81, p. 31.
"Muddling Lullabye" (tr. of Alexandre O'Neill). PortR (27: 2) 81, p.
31.
"Seven Poem" (tr. of Joaquim Manuel Magalhaes). ModernPS (10:2/3),
pp. 195-201.
from Seven Poems (II, VI) (tr. of Joaquin Manuel Magalhães). PoNow
(5:6 issue 30) 81, p. 29.
"She was the one who stopped on the threshold" (tr. of Eugenio de
Andrade). ModernPS (10:2/3), p. 193.
"The Small Square" (tr. of Sophia de Mello Breyner Andresen). PoNow
(6:2 issue 32) 81, p. 41.
"Vegetal And Alone" (tr. of Eugenio de Andrade). ModernPS (10:2/3),

pp. 191-193.
"Vivan Los Caballos!" (tr. of Raul de Carvalho). ModernPS (10:2/3),
   p. 90.
"Who Polluted, Who Ripped My Linen Sheets" (tr. of Camilo Pessanha).
   ModernPS (10:2/3), p. 91.
"Words" (tr. of Eugenio de Andrade). ModernPS (10:2/3), p. 191.

LEVITT, Peter
   "Remembering a Dream" (tr. of Li Qingzhao, w/ Jean Sutherland).
   SenR (12:1/2) 81, p. 117.

LEVY, D. A.
   "Marealien 1." UnmOx (22) Wint 81, pp. 29-30.
   "Marealien 2." UnmOx (22) Wint 81, p. 31.
   "Marealien 3." UnmOx (22) Wint 81, pp. 32-33.

LEVY, Robert J.
   "Bishop Berkeley Writes a Love Poem." Kayak (57) 81, p. 53.
   "A Concise History of Art." Kayak (57) 81, p. 54.
   "The Don of Toast." Kayak (57) 81, p. 52.
   "King Kong, Married." Kayak (57) 81, p. 50.
   "To a Fly Trapped in Amber." Kayak (57) 81, p. 51.

LEWIS, J. Patrick
   "The Roosevelt Avenue Grin." HiramPoR (30) Spr-Sum 81, p. 28.

LEWIS, Joel
   "Anxiety Management." Tele (17) 81, pp. 6-7.
   "Clear Spot." Tele (17) 81, p. 5.
   "Immediate Curtain." Tele (17) 81, p. 5.
   "Was rush hour on the PATH train." Tele (17) 81, pp. 2-4.

LEWISOHN, James
   "Grief Revisited." NewYorker (57:31) 21 S 81, p. 44.

LEYVA PORTAL, Waldo
   "Desde el este de Angola." Areito (7: 27) 81, p. 23.

LEZAMA LIMA, José
   "Los fragmentos de la noche." Notarte (6:3) Mr 81, p. 9.
   "Ten Prose Poems" (tr. by James E. Irby). Sulfur (3) 82, pp. 40-51.

LI, Ching-chao
   "The Chung Yang Festival" (tr. by C. H. Kwan). MalR (58) Ap 81, pp.
   39-40.

LI, Qingzhao
   "Remembering a Dream" (tr. by Joan Sutherland and Peter Levitt).
   SenR (12:1/2) 81, p. 117.

LI, Shang-yin
   "Climbing The Lo-Yu Plateau" (tr. by C. H. Kwan). MalR (58) Ap 81,
   p. 39.

LIBBEY, Elizabeth
   "Apparent Horizon." Poetry (137:4) Ja 81, pp. 195-196.
   "Juncture." Ploughs (6:4) 81, pp. 54-55.
   "Late One Night" (for Ida Elizabeth Boggs). Poetry (137:4) Ja 81, pp.

192-193.
"Themselves." Poetry (137:4) Ja 81, p. 194.

LIBERA, Sharon
  "Circe." Ploughs (6:4) 81, p. 31.
  "How You Were Born." Ploughs (6:4) 81, pp. 32-33.
  "News From Home." Ploughs (6:4) 81, p. 30.

LICHTER, Alan
  "A Song." KanQ (13:1) Wint 81, pp. 126-127.

LIDDY, James
  "from After Grodek." CreamCR (6:1) Aut 80, p. 104.
  "Factory Streets by Day" (tr. of Paul Zech, w/ Ruth Schwertfeger).
    DenQ (16:1) Spr 81, p. 68.
  "To God" (tr. of Else Lasker-Schüler, w/ Ruth Schwertfeger). DenQ
    (16:1) Spr 81, p. 69.

LIEBERMAN, David
  "My Night Ship." KanQ (13:3/4) Sum-Aut 81, p. 197.

LIEBERMAN, Laurence
  "Purgatory: The Anticraft Screen." SewanR (89:3) Sum 81, p. 401.
  "Worming into the Boulder Caves." ChiR (33:1) Sum 81, pp. 13-15.

LIETZ, Robert
  "After Rain" (for Adam Vroman). Pequod (12) 81, p. 68.
  "First Confessions." QW (13) Aut/Wint 81/82, pp. 20-21.
  "A Grandfather Considers His Granddaughter Old" (for my great-
    grandfather and my mother). CarolQ (33:1) Wint 81, p. 87.
  "The Lindbergh Half-Century." LitR (24:3) Spr 81, pp. 398-400.
  "The Man who Loves Rain." SouthernHR (15:1) Wint 81, p. 32.
  "The Neighborhood, Dusk: 1961." SouthernHR (15:1) Wint 81, p. 33.

LIEURANCE, Chuck
  "my mother and her brother." Peb (21) 81, pp. 42-43.

LIFSHIN, Lyn
  "Alone the Weekend Her Bone Madonna." Confr (22) Sum 81, p. 81.
  "An Absence of Man." HangL (40) Aut 81, pp. 49-51.
  "Anger." PoNow (6:1 issue 31) 81, p. 38.
  "Crystal Night." CentR (25:4) Aut 81, pp. 386-387.
  "Barns." PoNow (6:1 issue 31) 81, p. 38.
  "Cat Callahan." PoNow (6:1 issue 31) 81, p. 38.
  "Crystal Night." ColEng (43:1) Ja 81, p. 29.
  "Deer." US1 (14/15) Aut/Wint 81, p. 3.
  "Divorce Dumplings." PoNow (6:1 issue 31) 81, p. 38.
  "The Dream of Turquoise." WebR (6:2) 81, p. 81.
  "Editing The Anthology." SoCaR (13: 2) Spr 81, p. 106.
  "Falling Thru White Trees, Maine." PoNow (6:1 issue 31) 81, p. 38.
  "Five O'Clock Wind the Amber Beads Burning." CapeR (17:1) Wint 81,
    p. 9.
  "Georgia O'Keeffe." MichQR (20:2) Spr 81, p. 74.
  "Georgia O'Keefe." PoNow (6:2 issue 32) 81, p. 11.
  "Goldy Locks Madonna." WormR (81/82) 81, pp. 10-12.
  "Guerrilla." CentR (25:4) Aut 81, p. 386.
  "Guerilla." MichQR (20:2) Spr 81, pp. 74-75.
  "Howland House." NowestR (19:1/2), pp. 76-7.

"I Should Have Known When He Ate the One Provolone Sandwich."
    HangL (40) Aut 81, pp. 52-53.
"In Thailand In Malaysia." 13thM (5:1/2) 80, p. 17.
"In This House." SoCaR (14: 1) Aut 81, pp. 99-100.
"In Those Ten Years." SoCaR (14: 1) Aut 81, p. 100.
"It Happened the Way." PoNow (6:1 issue 31) 81, p. 38.
"The Librarian Who Couldn't." PoNow (6:2 issue 32) 81, p. 11.
"The Man in the Boiler Room Is." PoNow (6:1 issue 31) 81, p. 38.
"Maryland Film Censor." LittleM (13:1/2) Spr-Sum 79, c1981, p. 44.
"Middle of the Nightmare." PoNow (6:1 issue 31) 81, p. 38.
"Now With The Weather Getting Warmer." WindO (38) Spr-Sum 81, pp.
    3-4.
"Outsider Outsider Madonna." Confr (22) Sum 81, p. 81.
"Poetry Reading Benefit." SoCaR (13: 2) Spr 81, pp. 104-105.
"Ramona Weeks." CentR (25:4) Aut 81, p. 385.
"Raven's Black." 13thM (5:1/2) 80, p. 15.
"Reading." SoCaR (13: 2) Spr 81, pp. 107-108.
"Saturday Ballet Matinee Saratoga." Wind (11:42) 81, p. 7.
"She Said in My Family." HiramPoR (29) Aut-Wint 81, p. 29.
Twenty-one poems. PoNow (6:1 issue 31) 81, pp. 2-6.
"With the Bluest Eyes." MidwQ (22:3) Spr 81, p. 264.
"With The Bluest Eyes." SoCaR (13: 2) Spr 81, p. 105.
"You're Like." Vis (6) 81, n. p.
"Your Next Lover." SoCaR (14: 1) Aut 81, p. 101.

LIFSON, Martha R.
    "The Balcony By Manet." MassR (22:3) Aut 81, p. 538.
    "By the Practice Rooms: To a Young Musician." PoetryNW (22:2) Sum
        81, pp. 35-36.
    "Moss." MassR (22:3) Aut 81, p. 537.
    "Vermont Cemetery" (for Joe Eck). PoetryNW (22:2) Sum 81, p. 35.

LIHN, Enrique
    "Marta Kuhn-Weber" (tr. by David Unger). PoNow (5:6 issue 30) 81,
        p. 28.
    "Olana 1." Os (13) Aut 81, p. 27.
    "Olana 2." Os (13) Aut 81, pp. 28-30.

LIKOWSKI, Alice
    "Medicine Woman." AntR (39:3) Sum 81, p. 331.
    "Whether Peacocks Exist." AntR (39:3) Sum 81, p. 330.

LILLARD, Charles
    "Alaska off Whidbey Island." MalR (60) O 81, p. 153.
    "Potlatch." MalR (60) O 81, pp. 156-157.
    "Winter Brothers." MalR (60) O 81, pp. 154-155.

LILLYWHITE, Harvey
    "Cape Breton." MissouriR (4:3) Sum 81, p. 33.
    "Recovery." Ploughs (6:4) 81, p. 44.
    "Rooting." MissouriR (4:3) Sum 81, p. 36.
    "Photographs." MissouriR (4:3) Sum 81, p. 34.
    "Tides." Tele (17) 81, p. 11.
    "Walking." Tele (17) 81, p. 11.

LIMA, José Lezama see LEZAMA LIMA, José

LIMA, Robert
  "Obscenities to Perform at Home" (tr. of Mauricio Marquina).   Mund
    (12/13) 80-81, p. 297.

LINDEMAN, Mitch
  "Institution."   Peb (21) 81, p. 69.

LINDNER, Carl
  "Earthworm."   SouthernPR (21: 1) Spr 81, p. 36.
  "Landfill."   SouthernPR (21:2) Aut 81, p. 53.
  "Trying to Open a Door."   SouthwR (66:1) Wint 81, p. 71.

LINDO, Ricardo
  "The City and the Striking of a Match."   Mund (12/13) 80-81, p. 309.
  "Our Lady of the Clock."   Mund (12/13) 80-81, p. 309.
  "Sinister Ants" (tr. by Lisa Bradford).   Mund (12/13) 80-81, p. 309.

LINDSAY, Fran
  "It Is Possible."   PoetryNW (22:2) Sum 81, pp. 27-28.
  "The Kiss on the Ferris Wheel."   PoetryNW (22:2) Sum 81, pp. 26-27.
  "Quarry."   Atl (247:2) F 81, p. 70.

LINDSAY, Frannie
  "For Someone Sitting Still."   Agni (15) 81, p. 62.
  "The Limit."   Agni (15) 81, p. 58.
  "The Loser's Filly."   Agni (15) 81, p. 68.
  "Plum Island."   Agni (15) 81, pp. 60-61.
  "Relic."   Agni (15) 81, p. 63.
  "Saying Enough."   AmerPoR (10:5) S-O 81, p. 30.
  "Summer House."   Agni (15) 81, pp. 64-65.
  "The Tango is Indifference."   Shen (31:4) 80, p. 54.
  "The Third Floor."   Sam (116) 81, p. 63.
  "Timer."   Agni (15) 81, p. 59.
  "Wet on Wet."   AmerPoR (10:5) S-O 81, p. 30.
  "The Women With Strange Names."   Agni (15) 81, pp. 66-67.

LINDSTRON, Naomi
  "I Always Thought a Walk in the Dark" (tr. of Jaime Sabines).   CharR
    (7:1) Spr 81, p. 52.

LINEHAN, Don
  "God Save Our Queen."   PottPort (3) 81, p. 33.
  "I'm ready to split wood."   PottPort (3) 81, p. 30.
  "It tickles my mind to see."   PottPort (3) 81, p. 14.
  "Untitled."   PottPort (3) 81, p. 14.

LING, Chung
  "Life In The Palace" (tr. of Lady Hua Jui, w/ Kennoth Rexroth).
    UnmOx (22) Wint 81, pp. 15-16.

LINTHICUM, John
  "The Big Game."   Bound (9:2) Wint 81, pp. 142-145.
  "Horizon."   Bound (9:2) Wint 81, pp. 140-141.
  "Second Anniversary Of A Drowning."   Bound (9:2) Wint 81, pp. 139-
    140.
  "Sedentary Ode."   Bound (9:2) Wint 81, p. 138.

LIPSCOMB, James
  "The Ring in Lyra."   PortR (27: 2) 81, p. 62.

LIPSINER, Sue
  "His Turning." Ploughs (6:4) 81, p. 151.

LISCANO, Juan
  "Silence" (tr. by Lisa Bradford). Mund (12/13) 80-81, p. 296.

LISOWSKI, Joseph
  "Crows." Vis (5) 81, n. p.

LITT, Iris
  "After You Moved out of the Upstairs Apartment." PoNow (6:3 issue
  33) 81, p. 20.

LITTLE, Geraldine
  "Diptych." Shen (32:1) 80, pp. 60-62.

LIU, Chung-yuan
  "Snow on the River" (tr. by C. H. Kwan). MalR (58) Ap 81, p. 38.

LIU, Stephen Shu Ning
  "My Father's Martial Art." AntR (39:3) Sum 81, p. 332.

LIVADHITIS, Tasos
  "Craft" (tr. by Kimon Friar). Poetry (139:2) N 81, p. 92.
  "It Has Been Written..." (tr. by Kimon Friar). Poetry (139:2) N 81,
  p. 93.
  "The Juggler with the Oranges" (tr. by Kimon Friar). Poetry (139:2)
  N 81, p. 93.

LLOYD, Roseann
  "My Mother's Body." 13thM (5:1/2) 80, p. 27.

LLUCH MORA, Francisco
  "A Mi Esposa." Puerto Wint 81, p. 31.

LOACH, Nancy E. de see De LOACH, Nancy E.

LOBERTO, Ordenio
  "Feast Day" (tr. by Lawrence Venuti). Chelsea (40) 81, p. 51.

LOCKE, Karen Colyear
  "My Mother Cries Out in Her Sleep" (for Mother). 13thM (5:1/2) 80, p.
  35.

LOCKLING, Gerald
  "Back From Vacation." WormR (84) 81, p. 123.
  "A Colonist." WormR (81/82) 81, pp. 43-44.
  "Found Poem." PoNow (6:1 issue 31) 81, p. 17.
  "I Don't Think She Was Putting Me On." Wind (10:39) 80, p. 27.
  "Her Friends Have A Certain Way Of Looking At Me." WormR (84) 81,
  p. 121.
  "joan of lorraine." Wind (10:39) 80, pp. 27-28.
  "Poem Shorter Than Its Epigraph." WormR (81/82) 81, p. 44.
  "The Russian Weightlifter." PoNow (6:2 issue 32) 81, p. 17.
  "Small-Time Financier." WormR (81/82) 81, p. 43.
  "Stalking Papa." WormR (84) 81, pp. 122-123.
  "They Don't Leave You Much." Wind (10:39) 80, p. 28.

LOCKWOOD, Margo
"Half Sun." Ploughs (7:2) 81, p. 97.
"Ulster Television." Ploughs (7:2) 81, p. 98.

LOERKE, Oskar
"Towards Evening" (tr. by Francis Golffing). ChiR (32:4) Spr 81, p. 89.

LOGAN, John
"Believe It" (for T.). Antaeus (43) Aut 81, p. 33.
"Cambridge Reverie." ThRiPo (17/18) 81, p. 35.
"Coming of Age (for David Logan)." NewL (47:4) Sum 81, p. 58.
"A Day in the Sun (for Stephen Logan)." NewL (47:4) Sum 81, p. 59.
"Medicine Bow." ParisR (23:79) Spr 81, p. 226.

LOGAN, William
"After Illness." SewanR (89:3) Sum 81, pp. 404-405.
"The Angels among the Liars." SewanR (89:2) Ap-Je 81, p. 185.
"The Bath." Tendril (11) Sum 81, p. 43.
"Cartography." Agni (15) 81, p. 45.
"The Country of the Imagination." Shen (31:3) 80, p. 78.
"The Dancer and the Bear." Tendril (11) Sum 81, p. 42.
"Hard Waters." Agni (15) 81, pp. 46-48.
"In The Himalayas." Ploughs (7:1) 81, p. 136.
"Jealousy." NewYorker (57:3) 9 Mr 81, p. 40.
"News of the Moon." SewanR (89:3) Sum 81, pp. 403-404.
"Questions of Waking." Iowa (11:2/3) Spr-Sum 80, p. 208.
"Sheep." SewanR (89:3) Sum 81, pp. 402-403.
"Tatiana Kalatschova." SewanR (89:2) Ap-Je 81, pp. 184-185.
"Travel Report." Nat (232:18) 9 My 81, p. 576.
"Violations of the Dream." SewanR (89:3) Sum 81, pp. 405-407.

LOGUE, Christopher
"Urbanal." ParisR (23:79) Spr 81, pp. 227-230.

LOMAS, Herbert
from Invitation to the Dance: (II, III, XXV, XXVII, XXX, XXXIV, XLVII, L, LIV, LVIII) (tr. of Pentti Saarikoski). PoetryE (6) Aut 81, pp. 35-38.

LONDON, Jonathan
"Brief Passage." Wind (11:40) 81, p. 22.
"Half Moon Spilling Over" (for Maureen). Wind (11:40) 81, p. 21.
"Keith Jarret." Wind (11:40) 81, p. 21.
"Passover: Silence in the Lonely House." CharR (7:1) Spr 81, p. 37.
"Song to the River." Wind (11:40) 81, pp. 21-22.

LONG, Robert
"In the Red." Poetry (138:4) Jl 81, p. 196.
"Leaving Vermont." Tendril (11) Sum 81, p. 44.
"Old Story" (for Ali Cole). Poetry (138:4) Jl 81, pp. 194-195.
"Strange Insects" (for Josh Dayton). Poetry (138:4) Jl 81, p. 195.

LONGCHAMPS, Joanne de see de LONGCHAMPS, Joanne

LOONEY, Jon
"March." ConcPo (14:1) Spr 81, pp. 49-50.

LOOS, Dorothy Scott
   "The Final Visit" (tr. of Gloria Fuertes). PoNow (5:6 issue 30) 81, p.
    16.
   "The Rag Vendor--Or The Luckless Poet" (tr. of Gloria Fuertes).
    PoNow (5:6 issue 30) 81, p. 16.
   "To a Dead Raccoon on the Highway" (tr. of Gloria Fuertes). PoNow
    (5:6 issue 30) 81, p. 16.

LOPEZ, Carlos A.
   "El Desalojo" (a Gerard Jean-Juste). Claridad/En Rojo (22: 1489) 14-20
    Ag 81, p. 12.

LOPEZ, Edith Tarrius see TARRIUS LOPEZ, Edith

LOPEZ, Emy A.
   "Igual que el resto." Metam (3:2/4:1) 80-81, p. 83.
   "Será...." Metam (3:2/4:1) 80-81, p. 83.

LOPEZ, Julio César
   "Desnudez." Mairena (2:6), p. 38.

LOPEZ SURIA, Violeta
   "Canto en perdón (A Carmen Quiroga Cebollero)." Mairena (2:5) Aut
    80, p. 69.

LORCA, Federico García see GARCIA LORCA, Federico

LORDE, Audre
   "Bazaar." DenQ (16:1) Spr 81, p. 35.
   "Between Ourselves." DenQ (16:1) Spr 81, pp. 29-31.
   "Chorus." DenQ (16:1) Spr 81, p. 28.
   "Contact Lenses." DenQ (16:1) Spr 81, p. 32.
   "The Evening News." DenQ (16:1) Spr 81, p. 34.
   "Timepiece." DenQ (16:1) Spr 81, p. 33.

LORENTE, Luis
   "Glosa." Areito (7: 27) 81, p. 19.

LORENZO, Rafael
   "'Muse' Etcetera." SunM (11) Spr 81, p. 48.
   "Revolutionary Songs." SunM (11) Spr 81, pp. 47-48.
   "U. S. O." SunM (11) Spr 81, p. 49.

LORR, Katharine
   "How the Elm Moved." Vis (6) 81, n. p.
   "Planting Bulbs with Benjamin New Years Day 1980." Vis (5) 81, n. p.
   "Song of a Woman in Waiting." Vis (6) 81, n. p.

LOTIERZO, Antonio
   "Luisa of the Slums, Demoiselle D'Avignon" (tr. by Lawrence Venuti).
    Chelsea (40) 81, p. 50.

LOUISE, Esther
   "jesus' song." Obs (6:1/2) Spr-Sum 80, p. 169.
   "on predestination." Obs (6:1/2) Spr-Sum 80, p. 169.
   "swinging doors of knocking-wood cowards." Obs (6:1/2) Spr-Sum 80,
    pp. 170-173.

LOURIE, Richard
    "The Ghost of Delmore Schwartz." Ploughs (7:1) 81, p. 102.

LOW, Denise
    "Mothers Day Drive." Focus (14:89) N 80, p. 10.
    "Two Gardens." KanQ (13:1) Wint 81, p. 37.

LOWELL, Robert
    "Bellosquardo" (tr. of Eugenio Montale). NewYRB (28:16) 22 O 81, p.
        10.
    "Boats on the Marne" (tr. of Eugenio Montale). NewYRB (28:16) 22 O
        81, p. 10.
    "Flux" (tr. of Eugenio Montale). NewYRB (28:16) 22 O 81, p. 10.

LOWENSTEIN, Robert
    "Sunset at Sounion." HiramPoR (30) Spr-Sum 81, p. 29.

LOWERY, Mike
    "Cancer." CapeR (16:2) Sum 81, p. 20.
    "The Divorce." PoNow (6:1 issue 31) 81, p. 40.

LOWRY, Betty
    "A Man Stranded on the Rocks in the Niagara River 1853." EnPas (12)
        81, p. 21.
    "Be Kind to Cats." Nimrod (25:1) Aut-Wint 81, p. 103.
    "Choosing the Poet." LittleM (13:1/2) Spr-Sum 79, c1981, p. 22.
    "Cotswald Passage." Nimrod (25:1) Aut-Wint 81, p. 103.
    "Oestrus." LittleM (13:1/2) Spr-Sum 79, c1981, p. 23.

LOWRY, John
    "Everything went swell today." PoNow (6:3 issue 33) 81, p. 20.
    "Freedom's Just Another Word." PoNow (6:3 issue 33) 81, p. 20.
    "My friend found this great restaurant in upstate New York." PoNow
        (6:3 issue 33) 81, p. 20.
    "Victorian Elegies." WormR (84) 81, pp. 92-94.
    "Yesterday, she said, she couldn't take it anymore." PoNow (6:3 issue
        33) 81, p. 20.

LOY, Mina
    Eight poems. Montra (8), pp. 119-146.

LOYD, Marianne
    "Letter to Thomas in Bangor, Wales." NewL (47:4) Sum 81, pp. 77-78.

LOYNAZ, Dulce María
    "Loves" (tr. by Pat Hollis Smith). LetFem (7:2) Aut 81, p. 65.

LU, Yu
    "To Visit All Famous Gardens in Flowering Time" (tr. by C. H. Kwan).
        MalR (58) Ap 81, p. 41.

LUCEBERT
    "Double Metamorphosis." Mund (12/13) 80-81, p. 37.
    "Harvest" (tr. by Larry Ten Harmsel). Mund (12/13) 80-81, p. 37.

LUCINA, Sister Mary
    "Adversity I and II." Wind (11:42) 81, pp. 23-24.
    "Breathing as Best you can" (for Susan). Wind (11:42) 81, p. 23.

"Clearing Maybe." FourQt (31:1) Aut 81, p. 11.
"Eddie's Fires." Wind (11:42) 81, p. 22.
"The Last Year of Myrtle." Wind (11:42) 81, p. 21.
"Moving Ahead." Wind (11:42) 81, p. 21.

LUCKEY, Jeffery
"The Last Dance." Obs (7:1) Spr 81, pp. 42-43.
"Plum Street." Obs (7:1) Spr 81, p. 43.
"The Teacher." Obs (7:1) Spr 81, p. 43.

LUDVIGSON, Susan
"The Crossing." Atl (248:4) O 81, p. 82.
"Fear in New Hampshire." SouthernR (17:3) Sum 81, p. 565.
"It Comes to This." PikeR (2) Sum 81, p. 2.
"Lesson." GeoR (35:3) Aut 81, p. 553.
"Listening." SouthernR (17:3) Sum 81, p. 566.
"There is Always Someone." SouthernPR (21:2) Aut 81, p. 36.
"The Woman Who Keeps Fish." PikeR (2) Sum 81, p. 1.

LUEDERS, Edward
"Rainscape With Children." ThRiPo (17/18) 81, p. 37.

LUESMA CASTAN, Miguel
"Espejo de Otras Vidas." Puerto Wint 81, p. 30.

LUGO, Carmen
"En el taller del pintor" (tr. of Robert Villanua). Claridad/En Rojo
    (22: 1470) 3-9 Ap 81, p. 11.
"Enrique" (tr. of Robert Villanua). Claridad/En Rojo (22: 1470) 3-9 Ap
    81, p. 10.
"El imperfecto que más" (tr. of Robert Villanua). Claridad/En Rojo
    (22: 1470) 3-9 Ap 81, p. 11.
"Lenguaje afectado" (tr. of Robert Villanua). Claridad/En Rojo (22:
    1470) 3-9 Ap 81, p. 10.
"Pointe-a-Pitre/Burdeos" (tr. of Robert Villanua). Claridad/En Rojo
    (22: 1470) 3-9 Ap 81, p. 10.
"Telegrama" (tr. of Robert Villanua). Claridad/En Rojo (22: 1470) 3-9
    Ap 81, p. 11.
"El tulipán africano" (tr. of Robert Villanua). Claridad/En Rojo (22:
    1470) 3-9 Ap 81, p. 10.

LUGO-GUERNELLI, Adelaide
"A Luciano Pavarotti (En Nueva York, 14 de enero de 1980)." Mairena
    (2:6), p. 70.

LUHRMANN, Tom
"The Good Old Summertime." Confr (22) Sum 81, p. 56.

LUIS, Leopoldo de
"Los prismáticos." Os (13) Aut 81, p. 18.

LUKE, Hugh
"Bequest." Peb (21) 81, pp. 70-71.

LUNDE, David
"The Darkness." Chelsea (40) 81, p. 117.
"The Darkness." PortR (27: 2) 81, p. 99.
"Illegal Tender." PortR (27: 2) 81, p. 99.

"In Paradoxical Light." Chelsea (40) 81, p. 117.
"In Paradoxical Light." PortR (27: 2) 81, p. 99.
"Symbionts." PortR (27: 2) 81, p. 99.

LUNDKVIST, Artur
  "The American Woman" (tr. by Diana W. Wormuth). LitR (24:4) Sum
    81, pp. 543-44.
  "Demon and the Bible" (tr. by Diana W. Wormuth). LitR (24:4) Sum
    81, p. 546.
  "Tigers" (tr. by Diana W. Wormuth). LitR (24:4) Sum 81, p. 547.
  "You Met A Beggar" (tr. by Diana W. Wormuth). LitR (24:4) Sum 81,
    pp. 544-545.

LUNDQUIST, Robert
  "Breach." PoNow (6:3 issue 33) 81, p. 20.
  "I Have Been Expecting Them for Almost a Week." PoNow (6:3 issue
    33) 81, p. 20.

LUNN, Jenni
  "Atlantic Low." PottPort (3) 81, p. 51.

LURIA-SUKENICK, Lynn
  "Beatrice Reveals a Dream about the Future, about the Ones Who Will
    Not Escape." Pequod (12) 81, p. 74.
  "Bess Tells Him." OP (31/32) Aut 81, p. 141.

LUSK, Daniel
  "Tangents." NewRena (14) Spr 81, pp. 90-91.

LUTERMAN, Alison
  "Poem For A Refrigerator Door." MassR (22:4) Wint 81, pp. 734-735.

LUTHER, Susan
  "The Guests." ConcPo (14:1) Spr 81, pp. 105-106.
  "Revolution: Flashback." MalR (59) Jl 81, pp. 158-159.

LUX, Thomas
  "A Lit Match Is Dropped in a Saucer." Pequod (12) 81, p. 5.
  "Early on, This Decade's Light Smelled." Pequod (12) 81, p. 2.
  "Hospital View." Ploughs (7:1) 81, p. 48.
  "If I Die Before I Wake." Pequod (12) 81, p. 4.
  "It Must Be the Monk in Me." Pequod (12) 81, p. 3.
  "On Resumption of the Military Draft." Ploughs (7:1) 81, p. 49.

LUZI, Mario
  "Las Animas" (tr. by I. L. Salomon). Mund (12/13) 80-81, pp. 232-
    233.

LYLE, Curtis
  "Tampa Red's Contemporary Blues." Mund (12/13) 80-81, pp. 176-177.

LYLE, Peggy Willis
  "After the wind storm." Northeast (3:10) Wint 81, p. 36.

LYNCH, Thomas P.
  "A Death." Poetry (138:6) S 81, p. 327.
  "The Old Dilemma." Poetry (138:6) S 81, p. 328.

LYNE, Sandford
    "The Invention of Dragons." VirQR (57:4) Aut 81, pp. 632-633.
    "Separation: November." VirQR (57:4) Aut 81, pp. 633-634.

LYNSKEY, Edward
    "Teeth Of The Hydra." AmerPoR (10:1) Ja-F 81, p. 30.
    "Unearthed Visions." AmerPoR (10:1) Ja-F 81, p. 30.

LYNSKEY, Edward C.
    "Blue Becomes Janet." PoNow (6:3 issue 33) 81, p. 29.
    "Do You Have the Time." Vis (6) 81, n. p.
    "Exposing the Mystic." PoNow (6:3 issue 33) 81, p. 29.
    "L'Enfant's Town." StoneC (8: 3) Spr 81, p. 32.

LYON, George Ella
    "Final Exam." PoetryNW (22:1) Spr 81, pp. 39-40.
    "Rings." ColEng (43:4) Ap 81, p. 373.

LYON, Paul
    "Excerpt from Whispering Beans." Meadows (2:1) 81, pp. 38-9.

LYONS, Kimberly
    "Variations." Sulfur (1) 81, pp. 28-32.

McAFEE, Thomas
    "The Lesson of Shih Huang-Ti." MidwQ (22:2) Wint 81, p. 136.
    "The Unconscionable Waving Flag." CharR (7:1) Spr 81, p. 51.

McAFEE, Tom
    "Trains." OP (31/32) Aut 81, p. 41.

McALEAVY, David
    "The Fort." PoNow (6:1 issue 31) 81, p. 22.
    "Hammock" (for Hugh Walthall). Epoch (30:2) Wint-Spr 81, pp. 130-
        131.
    "Reading Mark Trail." Poetry (138:3) Je 81, pp. 160-162.
    "Starship." VirQR (57:3) Sum 81, p. 459.
    "Supposing the Ocean." VirQR (57:3) Sum 81, pp. 459-460.

McALLISTER, B. L.
    "The day the top blew off Mount Arak-tala." Poem (42) Jul 81, p. 65.
    "Kind Month." Poem (42) Jul 81, p. 66.

McAULEY, Almut
    Eight poems (tr. of Sarah Kirsch). Mund (11:2) 79, pp. 25-31.

McBRIDE, Ann
    from "The Fleeing And The Permanent" (tr. of Juan Sánchez Peláez,
        w/ Mary McBride). Mund (12/13) 80-81, pp. 106-107.

McBRIDE, Mary
    from "The Fleeing And The Permanent" (tr. of Juan Sánchez Peláez,
        w/ Ann McBride). Mund (12/13) 80-81, pp. 106-107.

McBRIDE, Mekeel
    "Aubade." Poetry (137:6) Mr 81, p. 341.

"A Blessing." NewYorker (57:14) 25 My 81, p. 116.
"One River Story." Tendril (10) Wint 81, p. 33.
"Or Failing." Poetry (137:6) Mr 81, pp. 340-341.
"Over the Phone." NewYorker (56:52) 16 F 81, p. 38.
"Reversals on a Day That Begins With Rain." Poetry (137:6) Mr 81,
    pp. 338-339.
"People Who Deserve to Live in Light." Aspect (77/79) 81, p. 150.
"The Pharmacist Goest Cloud Bathing" (for R.D.). Ascent (77/79) 81,
    pp. 148-149.
"Whether or Not." Tendril (10) Wint 81, pp. 34-35.

McCAFFREY, Phillip
    "Thalia ('Bloom')." SouthernHR (15:1) Wint 81, p. 52.

McCANN, Janet
    "The Choice of Life." Tendril (11) Sum 81, p. 47.
    "Commuter." CEACritic (43:4) My 81, p. 16.
    "Every Morning." CEACritic (43:4) My 81, p. 17.
    "The Housewife's Dream." CEACritic (43:4) My 81, p. 16.
    "Merlin." CEACritic (43:4) My 81, p. 15.
    "Statues." HiramPoR (29) Aut-Wint 81, p. 31.
    "Suburbia." CEACritic (43:4) My 81, p. 17.
    "The Trip." CEACritic (43:4) My 81, p. 17.
    "Van Gogh: 'Outdoor Cafe at Night.'" CEACritic (43:4) My 81, p. 15.
    "Visiting the Farm." Confr (21) Wint 81, p. 52.

McCARRISTON, Linda
    "Second Marriage." NewEngR (4:1) Aut 81, p. 22.

McCARTHY, Rebecca Roberts
    "Marlboro Street." KanQ (13:3/4) Sum-Aut 81, p. 190.

McCARTIN, James T.
    "Aunt Kate." Comm (108:22) 4 D 81, p. 698.

McCLANE, Kenneth
    "Winter." StoneC (8: 3) Spr 81, p. 29.
    "Winterland." StoneC (8: 3) Spr 81, pp. 28-29.

McCLANE, Kenneth A.
    "Ali." Obs (6:1/2) Spr-Sum 80, pp. 212-213.
    "Cantata." Obs (6:1/2) Spr-Sum 80, p. 216.
    "Family." BlackALF (15:1) Spr 81, pp. 29-30.
    "From a Silent Center." Obs (6:1/2) Spr-Sum 80, pp. 214-215.
    "The Owls." CapeR (16:2) Sum 81, p. 44.
    "Song: A Chant for Michael S. Harper." BlackALF (15:1) Spr 81, p.
    29.
    "A Tree Beyond Telling" (for Gwendolyn Brooks). Obs (6:1/2) Spr-
    Sum 80, p. 211.

McCLATCHY, J. D.
    "The Halt." Ploughs (7:2) 81, p. 137.

McCLEERY, David
    "One Sparrow." Peb (21) 81, pp. 18-19.

McCLEERY, Nancy
    "The Coral Reefs We Rest On, Caves of Abandoned Hydrozoans." Peb

(21) 81, p. 91.
"Night Muse." Peb (21) 81, pp. 92-93.

McCLELLAND, Bruce
  "[Polis]." Sulfur (1) 81, pp. 19-20.

McCLOSKEY, Mark
  "Advice to the Cowboys." MidwQ (22:3) Spr 81, p. 265.
  "The Annual Salmon Bake." PoetryNW (22:2) Sum 81, pp. 14-15.
  "I Will Go Away." PoetryNW (22:4) Wint 81-82, p. 21.
  "The Queen of the Cowgirls Kept Her Babies." MidwQ (22:3) Spr 81,
    pp. 267-8.
  "The Seamstress." MidwQ (22:3) Spr 81, p. 266.
  "There's a New Bar in Town." MinnR (17) Aut 81, pp. 41-42.

McCLURE, Barbara
  "Approaching the End of March." KanQ (13:1) Wint 81, p. 165.

McCLURE, Michael
  "On an Imaginary Etching by Samuel Palmer." Kayak (56) 81, p. 41.

McCORD, Andrew
  "Ocean of Fire--In Rivers a Snake-King." Epoch (30:1) Aut 80, pp.
    62-63.

McCORD, Howard
  "Fatherhood." PoNow (6:1 issue 31) 81, p. 35.
  "Home Surveying." PoNow (6:2 issue 32) 81, p. 7.
  "Hunting Canaries with Robert Bly." PoetryE (4/5) Spr-Sum 81, p.
    216.
  "Three Unforgetable Sights." PoNow (6:2 issue 32) 81, p. 21.

McCORKLE, James
  "The Epitaph" (tr. of Robert Desnos). SenR (12:1/2) 81, p. 75.
  "The Hill" (tr. of Robert Desnos). SenR (12:1/2) 81, p. 79.
  "The House" (tr. of Robert Desnos). SenR (12:1/2) 81, p. 77.
  "The Voice" (tr. of Robert Desnos). SenR (12:1/2) 81, p. 73.

McCULLOUGH, Lisa
  "Note in a Bottle." PoNow (6:3 issue 33) 81, p. 30.

McCULLOUGH, Lisa J.
  "January in Woodstock, Maryland: Coming Home." BelPoJ (32:2) Wint
    81-82, pp. 29-30.
  "The Winter Kite" (for v.f.). BelPoJ (32:2) Wint 81-82, pp. 30-31.

McCURDY, Harold
  "Blast-off." ChrC (98:1) 7-14 Ja 81, p. 11.
  "The Wat'ry Shore." Wind (11:40) 81, p. 24.
  "Zagreb." ChrC (98:14) 29 Ap 81, p. 477.

McDANIEL, Wilma Elizabeth
  "A Gift." HangL (39) Wint 80-81, p. 12.
  "After Easter." WormR (81/82) 81, p. 3.
  "Grandpa Recalled." HangL (39) Wint 80-81, p. 12.
  "Insight." WormR (81/82) 81, p. 3.
  "Sleuthing In New Mexico." WormR (81/82) 81, p. 4.
  "Tears of Joy." CimR (54) Ja 81, p. 44.
  "Wisdom." StoneC (8: 3) Spr 81, p. 44.

McDONALD, Agnes
  "Winter Psalm: Toward a Time of Darkness." SouthernPR (21:2) Aut
      81, pp. 70-71.

McDONALD, Barry
  "Neighbor." Peb (21) 81, p. 94.

McDONALD, Ellie
  "Fairins." Pequod (13) 81, p. 49.

McDONALD, L. M.
  "Two Deaf-Mutes In Halifax Bus Terminal." PottPort (3) 81, p. 37.

McDONALD, Walter
  "On the Great Plains." PoNow (6:1 issue 31) 81, p. 46.
  "Reminders." PoNow (6:1 issue 31) 81, p. 46.
  "You Can't Teach an Old Dog New Tricks." PoNow (6:1 issue 31) 81,
      p. 46.

McDONOUGH, Robert E.
  "At the Natural History Museum." WindO (39) Wint 81/82, p. 3.

McDONOUGH, Thomas
  "The Misfit." SmPd (18:2) Spr 81, p. 27.

McDOUGAL, Dianne
  "Incest." CalQ (18/19) 81, p. 132.
  "Separation." CalQ (18/19) 81, p. 133.
  "Waiting Up for Your Daughters" (for G. M.). CalQ (18/19) 81, p. 131.

McDOWELL, Robert
  "Poppies" (for Dana Gerhardt and Steve Hagel, and for Patti). Hudson
      (34:2) Sum 81, p. 244.

McDUFF, David
  "Nel mezzo del cammin di nostra vita" (to the memory of Konstantin
      Bogatyrev) (tr. of Tomas Venclova). Stand (22: 2) 81, p. 15.
  "The Trip Back." Stand (22: 4) 81, p. 48.
  "Villanella" (tr. of Tomas Venclova). Stand (22: 2) 81, p. 14.

McELROY, Colleen J.
  "Etymologies." PortR (27: 2) 81, p. 25.
  "Lie and Say You Love M." PortR (27: 2) 81, p. 26.
  "Looking Into the Eyes." PortR (27: 2) 81, p. 27.
  "While Poets Are Watching" (for Quincy Troupe). Ploughs (7:1) 81, pp.
      88-90.

McERMOTT, John
  "In The Movies." US1 (14/15) Aut/Wint 81, p. 3.

McEUEN, James
  "Ghosts." PoetryNW (22:3) Aut 81, pp. 46-47.
  "Twister (Western Ohio)." PoetryNW (22:3) Aut 81, p. 47.

McFALL, Gardner
  "Complaint." Ploughs (6:4) 81, p. 140.
  "Facts" (for my father). Ploughs (6:4) 81, pp. 139-140.
  "Shadowlawn." GeoR (35:2) Sum 81, p. 364.

McFARLAND, Ron
    "Asotin Girl Still Lost." Confr (22) Sum 81, p. 93.
    "Funeral at Bethel Baptist Church." Outbr (6/7) Aut 80-Spr 81, p. 69.
    "Gardening." PoetryNW (22:3) Aut 81, pp. 11-12.
    "Hide-n-Seek." PoetryNW (22:3) Aut 81, pp. 10-11.
    "They Remain Quietly and Independently in the Vast Florida Everglades."
        Outbr (6/7) Aut 80-Spr 81, p. 68.

McFEE, Michael
    "Bluff." Ploughs (6:4) 81, pp. 41-42.
    "Buster Keaton." HolCrit (17:6 [i.e. 18:1?]) F 81, p. 16.
    "Dvořák In The Open Air." AmerPoR (10:3) My-Je 81, p. 35.
    "Holiday Around the House." SouthernPR (21:2) Aut 81, pp. 66-67.
    "The Okra Flower." GeoR (35:3) Aut 81, p. 571.
    "Retirement." PoNow (6:3 issue 33) 81, p. 30.

McFERREN, Martha
    "Going Public." PoNow (6:3 issue 33) 81, p. 30.
    "Mountain Soprano." GeoR (35:3) Aut 81, pp. 572-582.
    "To the Monstrous Regiment: A Love Song, 1914." GeoR (35:1) Spr
        81, pp. 78-79.
    "Vivienne." SouthernHR (15:4) Aut 81, p. 335.

McGARY, C. R.
    "Horsehawks." Wind (11:41) 81, p. 23.

McGARTY, Ray
    "The Interview as an Epigram." PoNow (6:3 issue 33) 81, p. 30.

McGOVERN, Robert
    "Joy to the World." ChrC (98:42) 23 D 81, p. 1338.

McGRATH, Thomas
    "Doper's Song at Little Ah Sid's" (from a play in progress). PoNow
        (6:1 issue 31) 81, p. 33.
    "Driving Toward Boston I Run Across One of Robert Bly's Old Poems."
        PoetryE (4/5) Spr-Sum 81, pp. 62-63.
    "Totems (I)." PoetryE (4/5) Spr-Sum 81, p. 61.

McHUGH, Heather
    "Acts of God." Poetry (137:5) F 81, p. 288.
    "Basically" (tr. of Jean Follain). NewYorker (57:7) 6 Ap 81, p. 123.
    "The Birds and the Bees and Your Commie Mommy." OP (31/32) Aut
        81, p. 84.
    "Damage." VirQR (57:1) Wint 81, p. 73.
    "Elevated." Poetry (137:5) F 81, p. 291.
    "Event" (tr. of Jean Follain). NewYorker (57:7) 6 Ap 81, p. 123.
    "Faces" (tr. of Jean Follain). NewYorker (57:7) 6 Ap 81, p. 123.
    "Impressionist." VirQR (57:1) Wint 81, pp. 72-73.
    "In Light of Time." ThRiPo (17/18) 81, p. 39.
    "Inside." ParisR (23:80) Sum 81, p. 135.
    "Intensive Care." ParisR (23:80) Sum 81, pp. 133-134.
    "Lines." Poetry (137:5) F 81, p. 286.
    "Mind." Poetry (137:5) F 81, p. 290.
    "North Island Song." ParisR (23:80) Sum 81, pp. 134-135.
    "Remains To Be Seen." Poetry (137:5) F 81, p. 289.
    "What the Old Women See." Poetry (137:5) F 81, p. 287.

McKAIN, Dave
"Days in the Sun." PoetryE (6) Aut 81, p. 54.

McKAY, Matthew
"I Got a Television He Said." Confr (21) Wint 81, p. 68.
"The Man Who Could Talk to Fish." Confr (22) Sum 81, p. 43.
"She Turns in Her Keys." BallSUF (22:4) Aut 81, pp. 50-51.

McKEAN, James
"Bus Ride, Pie de la Cuesta." Poetry (138:2) My 81, p. 91.
"Green Lake." NowestR (19:3), p. 92.

McKEE, Carrie
"Bride." Tele (17) 81, p. 94.
"Progress." Tele (17) 81, p. 95.

McKEE, Louis
"Final Exam." EngJ (70:7) N 81, p. 70.

McKEEVER, Julia
"Quilt." KanQ (13:3/4) Sum-Aut 81, p. 172.
"10 P.M." KanQ (13:3/4) Sum-Aut 81, p. 171.

McKENZIE-PORTER, Patricia
"Branches." PottPort (3) 81, p. 41.

McKEOWN, Tom
"For Paul Eluard." Kayak (56) 81, p. 64.
"Homage to André Breton." Kayak (56) 81, p. 65.
"Thresholds." CreamCR (6:1) Aut 80, p. 109.

McKERNAN, John
"Hot Fudge Sundae a Hersey with Almonds and a Large Pepsi to Go
    Please." Wind (11:43) 81, pp. 26-27.
"Red Cloud." PraS (55:1/2) Spr-Sum 81, p. 34.
"The Song of the Confined Man." SouthernPR (21: 1) Spr 81, p. 69.
"The Source." Tele (17) 81, p. 61.

McKINNEY, Irene
"Limited Access." NoAmR (266:3) S 81, p. 63.

McKINSEY, Martin
"Eight poems" (tr. of Yannis Ritsos). AmerPoR (10:4) Jl-Ag 81, pp.
    23-29.

McLAUGHLIN, Joe-Anne
"The Tent." ThRiPo (17/18) 81, pp. 16-17.

McLAUGHLIN, William
"Dornava Palace" (tr. of anonymous poem). DenQ (16:1) Spr 81, p.
    78.
"The Portage." StoneC (9: 1-2) Aut-Wint 81/82, p. 23.

McLAURIN, Ken
"Storm Pit." BelPoJ (32:2) Wint 81-82, p. 43.
"Taboos." BelPoJ (32:2) Wint 81-82, p. 42.

McLEAN, Sammy
"Respect" (tr. of Helga Novak). Mund (11:2) 79, pp. 39, 41.

"Reborn" (tr. of Helga Novak). Mund (11:2) 79, p. 41.
"A Shirt" (tr. of Helga Novak). Mund (11:2) 79, p. 39.

McMAHON, Lynne
"Prodigy." Atl (248:3) S 81, p. 80.

McMAHON, Michael
"Fishing For Horn Pout." Tendril (11) Sum 81, pp. 48-51.

McMAHON, Michael Beirne
"Something Belated" (for Peter). PoNow (6:3 issue 33) 81, p. 30.

McMICHAEL, James
"An Apple Fell in the Night and a Wagon Stopped." Ploughs (7:2) 81,
p. 141.

McMILLAN, Sam
"Taking Words As He Finds Them." Wind (10:39) 80, p. 29.

McMURRAY, D. A.
"The Luminous Point" (for Roque Dalton and Enrique Lihn) (tr. of René
Depestre, w/ G. M. Lang). Calib (3:2) Aut-Wint 80, p. 93.
"Semantics" (tr. of Mario Benedetti). Calib (3:2) Aut-Wint 80, pp. 89-
91.

McNAIR, Wesley
"The Fat Enter Heaven." Poetry (138:3) Je 81, p. 159.
"Hair on Television." Poetry (138:3) Je 81, pp. 157-158.
"Trees That Pass Us In Our Cars." Atl (248:3) S 81, p. 79.

McNAMAR, Hugh
"The Evidence at Camp O'Connell." Poem (42) Jul 81, pp. 36-37.

McNAMARA, Bob
"The Sideshow, the Fair." CharR (7:1) Spr 81, pp. 28-29.
"The Miner's Canary." PortR (27: 2) 81, p. 92.

McNAMARA, Ed
"The Eels." HiramPoR (29) Aut-Wint 81, p. 32.

McNAMEE, Thomas
"Landfall." GeoR (35:3) Aut 81, p. 644.

McNULTY, Tim
"Ohalet." MalR (60) O 81, p. 83.
"Song of the Northern Lights." MalR (60) O 81, p. 82.

McPHERSON, Sandra
"Diary--May 15, 1980--Twin Cities." Poetry (138:3) Je 81, pp. 167-
169.
"Discoveries, Mid-Letter." AmerPoR (10:5) S-O 81, p. 15.
"In Costume." AmerPoR (10:5) S-O 81, p. 14.
"Lavender Mist." Field (24) Spr 81, pp. 7-8.
"Living Glass." Poetry (138:3) Je 81, pp. 163-164.
"The Museum of the Second Creation." Field (24) Spr 81, pp. 5-6.
"Night Vision." ParisR (23:81) Aut 81, pp. 132-133.
"Precocity, November 24." AmerPoR (10:5) S-O 81, p. 14.
"Preparing the Will, Three Generations." Poetry (138:3) Je 81, p. 166.

"The Root Hunters." Iowa (11:2/3) Spr-Sum 80, p. 189.
"Russian Lyric." AmerPoR (10:5) S-O 81, p. 15.
"7, 22, 66." Antaeus (40/41) Wint-Spr 81, p. 344.
"Singing Teakettle." Poetry (138:3) Je 81, p. 165.
"To Mary Barnard." Iowa (11:2/3) Spr-Sum 80, p. 188.
"A Tracing." Antaeus (40/41) Wint-Spr 81, pp. 342-343.
"Two Anonymous Poems, Found in a Drawer, Dated 1979." Antaeus
(40/41) Wint-Spr 81, pp. 345-346.

McQUADE, Molly
"Mint Advent." Prima (6/7) 81, p. 49.

McQUILKIN, Rennie
"Hands." Poetry (138:2) My 81, pp. 86-87.
"The Other Woman." Poetry (138:2) My 81, p. 88.
"Sap Run." PoNow (6:3 issue 33) 81, p. 31.
"Signs." PoetryNW (22:4) Wint 81-82, pp. 15-16.

McWHIRTER, George
"As Water Over A Stone" (tr. of Alejandra Pizarnik). Mund (12/13)
80-81, p. 26.
"A Condition (Of Being)" (tr. of Alejandra Pizarnik). Mund (12/13) 80-
81, p. 25.
"A Dream Where Silence Is Made Of Gold" (tr. of Alejandra Pizarnik).
Mund (12/13) 80-81, p. 26.
"Contemplation" (tr. of Alejandra Pizarnik). Mund (12/13) 80-81, p.
25.
"The Lone Children" (tr. of Ronald Bonilla). Mund (12/13) 80-81, p.
292.
"Rescue" (for Octavio Paz) (tr. of Alejandra Pizarnik). Mund (12/13)
80-81, p. 26.
"Vertigo Or The Contemplation Of Something That Ends" (tr. of Alejan-
dra Pizarnik). Mund (12/13) 80-81, p. 25.

MacAFEE, Norman
"Old Men Tormented by Their Youth." PoNow (6:3 issue 33) 81, p.
29.

MacDONALD, Cynthia
"By the Sea." NewYorker (57:21) 13 Jl 81, p. 36.
"Degrees Of Pen/Man/Ship." MassR (22:4) Wint 81, p. 721.
"Postcard Of Child Peeking Out From Under Its Mother's Skirt."
MassR (22:4) Wint 81, pp. 718-719.
"Supplanting The Beloved." MassR (22:4) Wint 81, pp. 719-720.

MacDONALD, Kathryn
"Emmeline's Dream." PortR (27: 2) 81, p. 23.
"Thinking of Men, Emmeline Buys a Red Dress." PortR (27: 2) 81, p.
23.

MacDOUGALL, Judith
"Freyja." PottPort (3) 81, p. 40.

MacFADYEN, Janet
"Tarantelle." Atl (248:3) S 81, p. 79.

MacGUIRE, Deirdre
"Into Arizona." Aspect (77/79) 81, p. 144.

MACHADO, Antonio
"Caminante, Son Tus Huellas" (tr. by Robert L. Smith and Judith Can-
dullo). WebR (6:2) 81, p. 27.
"Eran Ayer Mis Dolores." StoneC (9: 1-2) Aut-Wint 81/82, p. 56.
"The house I loved" (tr. by Willis Barnstone). PoNow (5:6 issue 30)
81, p. 28.
"I never looked for glory" (tr. by Willis Barnstone). PoNow (5:6 issue
30) 81, p. 28.
"It Was Yesterday My Sorrows" (tr. by Robert L. Smith and Judith
Candulo). StoneC (9: 1-2) Aut-Wint 81/82, p. 57.
"The red fire of a violet twilight" (tr. by Willis Barnstone). PoNow
(5:6 issue 30) 81, p. 28.

MacINNES, Mairi
"The Moorland Road." OntR (14) Spr-Sum 81, p. 59.
"Luskentyre, Isle of Harris." OntR (14) Spr-Sum 81, p. 60.

MacKENZIE, Ginny
"Anonymous Collaboration." Iowa (11:2/3) Spr-Sum 80, p. 204.
"Lucia Drawn as Santa Zita by Francesca Alexander for The Roadside
Songs of Tuscany, 1883." Shen (31:4) 80, p. 78.
"Mary Magdalene at the House of Simon." Ploughs (6:4) 81, p. 141.
"Pentimento." Thrpny (5) Spr 81, p. 3.
"Tintoretto To His Apprentice." Thrpny (5) Spr 81, p. 3.

MACKEY, Nathaniel
"Grisgris Dancer." Iowa (11:4) Aut 80, pp. 76-77.
"Black Snake Visitation." Iowa (11:4) Aut 80, pp. 73-75.
"Tarot-Teller." Iowa (11:4) Aut 80, pp. 71-72.

MACKLIN, Elizabeth
"Brecht Backstage: The Good Master." NewYorker (57:7) 6 Ap 81, p.
46.

MacLAINE, Wendell
"Untitled." PottPort (3) 81, p. 10.

MacLEAN, Catharin
"Six Draught." PottPort (3) 81, p. 16.
"Sky Weaver." PottPort (3) 81, p. 31.

MacLENNAN, James
"In A Trucker's Cafe." PottPort (3) 81, p. 34.

MacLOW, Jackson
"A Vocabulary for Custer LaRue: First Realization--12/4/78." SunM
(11) Spr 81, p. 71.
"58th Light Poem: For Anne Tardos--19 March 1979." SunM (11) Spr
81, pp. 63-66.

MADDOCK, Jerome
"Problems of the Great Romantics." PoetryE (6) Aut 81, p. 69.

MADDOCK, Mary
"In a secret region for the intimate" (tr. of Anna Akhmatova). ChiR
(33:1) Sum 81, p. 80.
"My pillow is hot on both sides" (tr. of Anna Akhmatova). ChiR (33:1)
Sum 81, p. 81.

MADDOX, Everette
"Cruising Down the River." Kayak (57) 81, p. 49.
"Front Street, New Orleans." Kayak (57) 81, p. 48.
"September Sonnet." Kayak (57) 81, p. 49.
"Southern Eclogue." Kayak (57) 81, p. 48.

MADDOX, Marjorie
"Pregnant Woman at English Station." Confr (22) Sum 81, p. 42.

MADGETT, Naomi Long
"Black Poet" (In memory of Langston Hughes). Obs (7:1) Spr 81, p.
    36.
"The Sun Do Move." Obs (7:1) Spr 81, p. 37.
"TEN." Obs (7:1) Spr 81, p. 36.

MADSEN, Sven Age
"Schizophrenic Pictures" (tr. by Leonie A. Marx). Mund (12/13) 80-81,
    pp. 148-150.

MAGALHÃES, Joaquin Manuel
"Sete Poema." ModernPS (10:2/3), pp. 194-200.
"Seven Poem" (tr. by Alexis Levitin). ModernPS (10:2/3), pp. 195-
    201.
from Seven Poems (II, VI) (tr. by Alexis Levitin). PoNow (5:6 issue
    30) 81, p. 29.

MAGEE, Wes
"The Wolf Child." MichQR (20:4) Aut 81, pp. 421-422.

MAINO, Jeannette
"Blue Hope." CapeR (16:2) Sum 81, p. 39.
"Hiatus." SouthwR (66:4) Aut 81, p. 403.
"Honeysuckle." SouthwR (66:2) Spr 81, p. 184.

MAIZELL, Sylvia
"The Last Suburban Train" (tr. of Andrei Vosnesensky, w/ Robert L.
    Smith). StoneC (9: 1-2) Aut-Wint 81/82, pp. 11-12.

MAJOR, Clarence
"Marriage by Capture." Mund (12/13) 80-81, p. 179.
"So, Welcome." UnmOx (22) Wint 81, p. 45.

MAKUCK, Peter
"Letter Poem." Hudson (34:1) Spr 81, pp. 70-71.
"Players." Ploughs (6:4) 81, p. 35.
"Rerun Scene: You Rescue My Son." Ploughs (6:4) 81, p. 34.
"Teachers." CimR (57) O 81, p. 16.
"To the Snow-Walker." Hudson (34:1) Spr 81, pp. 71-72.
"Villages Perches." QW (13) Aut/Wint 81/82, p. 95.
"Wine Country Near Les Abymes." PraS (55:3) Aut 81, p. 32.

MALANGA, Gerard
"Sonnet VIII." NowestR (19:1/2), p. 84.

MALDONADO, Angel
"Escucha." Mairena (2:5) Aut 80, p. 65.
"Hábitos del poeta." Mairena (2:5) Aut 80, pp. 65-6.

MALDONADO, Gonzalo Fernos see FERNOS MALDONADO, Gonzalo

MALEC, Emily Keller
  "The Park At Dusk." CapeR (16:2) Sum 81, p. 7.
  "Snow Child." Im (7:3) 81, p. 4.

MALINOWITZ, Michael
  "Against Time." Tele (17) 81, p. 112.
  "Parody on the Letter E." Tele (17) 81, p. 113.

MALLARME, Stéphane
  "Don du poéme." SenR (12:1/2) 81, p. 38.
  "Gift of the Poem" (tr. by John Currie). SenR (12:1/2) 81, p. 39.
  "Miss Mallarme's Fan" (tr. by Ernest Smart). Stand (22: 1) 80, p. 38.
  "Quand l'ombre menaça...." SenR (12:1/2) 81, p. 40.
  "Tomb" (tr. by John Currie). SenR (12:1/2) 81, p. 43.
  "Tombeau." SenR (12:1/2) 81, p. 42.
  "When the Shadow Threatened" (tr. by John Currie). SenR (12:1/2) 81,
    p. 41.

MALONE, Talt, Jr.
  "American Dream #1." Obs (7:1) Spr 81, p. 72.
  "Chicago ... New York ... L. A. ... looking for love barmaid." Obs
    (7:1) Spr 81, p. 70.
  "Demons." Obs (7:11) Spr 81, p. 72.
  "Fantasies Across Tall Grassy Plains." Obs (7:1) Spr 81, p. 69.
  "His Life--Past and Future Tenses." Obs (7:1) Spr 81, p. 72.
  "Restraint." Obs (7:1) Spr 81, p. 71.

MALOUF, D.
  "Chariot of Light" (tr. of G. N. el-Hage). Nimrod (24: 2) Spr/Sum 81,
    pp. 105-107.
  "Exile" (tr. of G. N. el-Hage). Nimrod (24: 2) Spr/Sum 81, p. 107.
  "Sufiyya" (tr. of G. N. el-Hage). Nimrod (24: 2) Spr/Sum 81, p. 105.

MALPEZZI, Frances M.
  "Of Pumice and Chrysanthemums." SmPd (18:1) Wint 81, p. 26.

MA'LUF, Fawzi
  from On the Magic Carpet: "Canton 3: The Slave" (tr. by Michael
    Zwettler). Nimrod (24: 2) Spr/Sum 81, pp. 59-60.

MANCINELLI, Steve
  "Two Epigrams." HiramPoR (29) Aut-Wint 81, p. 30.

MANDELSTAM, Osip
  "Bessonnitsa Gomer." SenR (12:1/2) 81, p. 26.
  "Insomnia" (tr. by Michael Stanford). SenR (12:1/2) 81, p. 27.
  "To Olga Arbenina" (tr. by Michael Stanford). SenR (12:1/2) 81, p.
    29.
  "Za to, chto ia ruki tvoi ne sumel uderzhat." SenR (12:1/2) 81, p.
    28.

MANESS, Sandra
  "It's No Use, Mr. James." KanQ (13:1) Wint 81, p. 30.

MANGER, Itzik
  "For rag pickers who scratch in the rubbish..." (tr. by Harold Black).
    Vis (5) 81, n.p.
  "Let Us Sing" (tr. by Harold Black). Vis (5) 81, n.p.

MANJARREZ, Hector
Eight poems (tr. by Nathaniel Tarn). Sulfur (2) 81, pp. 59-64.

MANNACIO, Giorgio
"In Memory of Delio Tessa" (tr. by Peter Burian). PoNow (5:6 issue
30) 81, p. 29.
"Some Praises of Wine" (tr. by Peter Burian). PoNow (5:6 issue 30)
81, p. 29.

MANUS, Fay Whitman
"Neighbor." Confr (22) Sum 81, p. 82.

MANZANARES, Silvio
"Metamorfosis." Areito (27: 28) 81, p. 50.

MAR, Yekhi El see EL MAR, Yekhi

MARANO, Russell
"The Indian." PoNow (6:3 issue 33) 81, p. 29.

MARCANO, Luis A. Cintrón see CINTRON MARCANO, Luis A.

MARCANO MONTAÑEZ, Jaime
"A Luis Hernández Aquino." Mairena (3:8) 81, pp. 116-17.
"Búsqueda suprema." Mairena (3:7) 81, p. 21.
"Dación del verso." Mairena (3:7) 81, p. 18.
"Gozo de la espera." Mairena (3:7) 81, p. 21.
"Inmensidad feliz." Mairena (3:7) 81, p. 19.
"Misión del canto." Mairena (3:7) 81, pp. 18-19.
"Sol de mi existencia." Mairena (3:7) 81, pp. 19-20.
"Vida luminosa." Mairena (3:7) 81, p. 20.

MARCUS, Adrianne
"Directions." SouthernPR (21: 1) Spr 81, p. 18-19.

MARCUS, Mordecai
"Conventions." Im (7:2) 1981, p. 4.
"The Decline of Horses." Kayak (57) 81, p. 58.
"Girls on Summer Porches." CapeR (16:2) Sum 81, p. 13.
"Puritan Esthetics." Poem (43) Nov 81, p. 42.
"Reliquary Afternoons." Peb (21) 81, pp. 79-80.
"Renewals." Poem (43) Nov 81, p. 41.
"Talismans." Sparrow (41) 81, Entire issue.
"Traveler." Im (7:2) 1981, p. 4.
"A Woman Who Lives Alone." Poem (43) Nov 81, p. 43.

MARCUS, Morton
"Dust." Kayak (57) 81, pp. 36-37.

MARGOLIS, Gary
"Address." PoNow (6:2 issue 32) 81, p. 37.
"California." MinnR (17) Aut 81, p. 28.
"My Dear Helen." NewEngR (3:4) Sum 81, pp. 598-9.

MARIANI, Paul
"Early Autumn Song" (for Cathy O'Connell). Tendril (11) Sum 81, pp.
45-46.
"Fire in the Choir Loft." Agni (14) 81, pp. 12-13.

MARION, Jeff Daniel
"Thistles" (for Lynn Powell).   SouthernPR (21: 1) Spr 81, p. 34.

MARION, Paul
"Blood Alley, Fat City."   Aspect (77/79) 81, p. 145.

MARKERT, Lawrence
"A Study in Conception."   Wind (11:40) 81, p. 23.

MARKHAM, E. A.
"An Old Man Regrets."   Stand (22: 2) 81, p. 32.

MARKS, S. J.
"Overnight, 1961."   AmerPoR (10:1) Ja-F 81, p. 30.

MARLIS, Stefanie
"not lost and lost."   PortR (27: 1) 81, p. 39.
"This Parallel" (for Robert Huotari).   PortR (27: 2) 81, p. 22.
"Von Portheim."   CutB (17) Aut-Wint 81, p. 75.

MARQUEZ, Roberto
"Defeats" (tr. of Julio Huasi).   Calib (3:2) Aut-Wint 80, p. 95.

MARQUINA, Mauricio
"Obscenities to Perform at Home" (tr. by Robert Lima).   Mund (12/13)
    80-81, p. 297.

MARRERO, Andrés Díaz see DIAZ MARRERO, Andrés

MARRON, Mary Jo
"Postcard."   Wind (11:40) 81, p. 11.

MARRUZ, Fina García see GARCIA MARRUZ, Fina

MARSHALL, David
"Window."   MassR (22:3) Aut 81, p. 518.

MARSHALL, Gregory
"Winter Cure."   WindO (38) Spr-Sum 81, p. 27.

MARTAN GONGORA, Helcías
"Sabiduría."   Puerto Wint 81, p. 32.

MARTEAU, Robert
"from The Watch (Vigie)" (tr. by Anne Winters).   Ploughs (7:2) 81, p.
    60.

MARTIN, Charles
"To the Living Bait."   LittleM (13:1/2) Spr-Sum 79, c1981, pp. 42-43.

MARTIN, Charles Casey
"The Identity Property."   AntR (39:1) Wint 81, pp. 75-76.

MARTIN, Connie
"Seal."   SouthernPR (21:2) Aut 81, p. 30.

MARTIN, D. Roger
"Birth: 1961."   Sam (116) 81, pp. 38-39.
"Country Girl Wading."   SmPd (18:2) Spr 81, p. 24.

"First Love" (someone remembered). Sam (106) 81, pp. 38-39.
"Small Plane Down." Sam (109) 81, pp. 48-49.
Specimens. Sam (111) 81, Entire issue.

MARTIN, Jennifer
"Elementary." ThRiPo (17/18) 81, p. 48.

MARTIN, José Luis
"En el principio infinito de la vida." Mairena (2:6) 80, p. 43.

MARTIN, Philip
"Christmas Ghosts." Poetry (139:3) D 81, p. 149.
"Greek Migrant Goes Home." HiramPoR (29) Aut-Wint 81, p. 5.

MARTIN, Yves
"A Blue Wind, A Calm Wave" (tr. by Larry Couch). Vis (5) 81, n. p.
"Memories" (tr. by Larry Couch). Vis (5) 81, n. p.

MARTINEZ, Dionisio D.
"When You Visit My Father's Farm" (for Alicia). SouthernPR (21: 1)
    Spr 81, pp. 31-32.

MARTINEZ, Víctor
"My Uncle Rudolfo." Metam (3:2/4:1) 80-81, p. 92.

MARTINSON, Harry
"The Butterfly" (tr. by Yvonne L. Sandstroem). Mund (12/13) 80-81,
    p. 112.
"Creation Night" (tr. by Robert Bly). Mund (12/13) 80-81, p. 111.
"March Evening." Mund (12/13) 80-81, p. 112.
"Old Farmhouse." Mund (12/13) 80-81, p. 111.

MARTY, Miriam
"Portrait of Pertuiset, the Lion Hunter." HolCrit (18:3) Je 81, p. 12.

MARUYAMA, Kaoru
"Rhinoceros and Lion" (tr. by Graeme Wilson). DenQ (16:4) Wint 81,
    p. 38.

MARX, Leonie A.
"Schizophrenic Pictures" (tr. of Sven Age Madsen). Mund (12/13) 80-
    81, pp. 148-150.

MARZAN, Julio
"Epitafio." Mairena (2:6) 80, p. 42.

MASARIK, Al
"American Gothic." PoNow (6:1 issue 31) 81, p. 21.

MASKALERIS, Thanasis
"The Crows of Hakone." ThRiPo (17/18) 81, p. 41.
"Sun Moon Lake" (for Nina). ThRiPo (17/18) 81, p. 41.

MASTERSON, Dan
"Avalanche." PoetryNW (22:3) Aut 81, pp. 12-16.
"Safe Distance." Poetry (137:4) Ja 81, pp. 207-209.

MASTORAKI, Jenny
"Cartoon Classics" (tr. by Kimon Friar). PoNow (5:6 issue 30) 81,

p. 30.
"The Episodes" (tr. by Kimon Friar). PoNow (5:6 issue 30) 81, p. 30.
"Graduate Excercises" (tr. by Kimon Friar). PoNow (5:6 issue 30) 81,
    p. 30.

MATE, Sarah
    "I'd Never Carved a Pumpkin." PoNow (6:3 issue 33) 81, p. 29.

MATHIEU-GRACE, Lois
    "Dictum." PortR (27: 2) 81, p. 98.
    "Inscription." PortR (27: 2) 81, p. 98.
    "Pantoum For A Son With Sailors' Dreams." PortR (27: 2) 81, p. 98.
    "A Witch for Gemini" (for Beth). PortR (27: 2) 81, p. 98.

MATHIS, Cleopatra
    "Leaving." AmerPoR (10:2) Mr-Ap 81, p. 19.
    "The Moon over Crete, the Stars in the Sea." Antaeus (40/41) Wint-
        Spr 81, pp. 332-334.
    "Nemesis." MissouriR (4:2) Wint 81-82, p. 29.
    "To A Friend Who Has Difficulty Waking." AmerPoR (10:2) Mr-Ap 81,
        p. 19.

MATHIS-EDDY, Darlene
    "First Frosts" (In memory of N. M. R.). BallSUF (21:4) Aut 80, p. 1.
    "Fieldstone." BallSUF (22:4) Aut 81, p. 80.
    "Spring Snow." BallSUF (22:2) Spr 81, p. 80.

MATOS, Germán
    "Sucesos del 25 de noviembre de 1981, UPR-Río Piedras." Claridad/
        En Rojo (22: 1507) 18-23 D 81, p. 12.

MATOS PAOLI, Francisco
    "Al jardín de Borinquen." Mairena (2:6) 80, p. 41.
    "César Vallejo." Mairena (2:5) Aut 80, pp. 46-7.
    "El ser amenazado." Mairena (2:6) 80, pp. 71-3.
    "Homenaje lírico a Luis Hernández Aquino." Mairena (3:8) 81, pp.
        115-116.
    "La justificación del plan." Mairena (2:6) 80, p. 39.
    "Poética." Mairena (2:6) 80, pp. 39-40.

MATTESON, Fredric
    "The Fisherman." Aspect (77/79) 81, p. 146.

MATTHEWS, Jack
    "The Instant." Poetry (138:6) S 81, p. 324.
    "On the Etiology of Ghosts." Poetry (138:6) S 81, p. 325.
    "That Poems Should Be Printed on Recyclable Paper is Only Right."
        Poetry (138:6) S 81, p. 325.
    "Woman Sitting." Poetry (138:6) S 81, p. 324.

MATTHEWS, William
    "The Bay at Grand Case." PoNow (6:2 issue 32) 81, p. 45.
    "Bmp Bmp." NewEngR (4:1) Aut 81, pp. 18-19.
    "Burglary." Antaeus (40/41) Wint-Spr 81, pp. 335-336.
    "Bystanders." Ploughs (6:4) 81, pp. 70-71.
    "Depressive." Ploughs (6:4) 81, pp. 68-69.
    "Dog." PoNow (6:2 issue 32) 81, p. 10.
    "Dylan and the Band, Boston Gardens, 1974." PoNow (6:2 issue 32)

81, p. 10.
"Flood." Atl (248:1) Jl 81, p. 69.
"Flood." GeoR (35:2) Sum 81, pp. 294-295.
"Flood." NewEngR (4:1) Aut 81, p. 17.
"Flood." Pequod (13) 81, p. 11.
"Flood." Pequod (13) 81, p. 12.
"The Inventions of Memory." GeoR (35:4) Wint 81, p. 873.
"Manic." Ploughs (6:4) 81, p. 67.
"Nabokov's Death." Antaeus (40/41) Wint-Spr 81, pp. 338-339.
"Roman Stones in August." Antaeus (40/41) Wint-Spr 81, p. 337.
"Rosewood, Ohio." NewEngR (4:1) Aut 81, pp. 16-17.
"School Figures" (for S.). Antaeus (40/41) Wint-Spr 81, pp. 340-341.
"What's Wrong with This Picture?" PoNow (6:1 issue 31) 81, p. 8.

MATTHIAS, John
"Contemporary" (tr. of Jan Östergren, w/ Göran Printz-Pahlson).
    ChiR (32:2) Aut 80, pp. 44-47.
"Indian Summer I" (tr. of Jan Östergren, w/ Göran-Pahlson). ChiR
    (32:2) Aut 80, pp. 41-43.

MATTISON, Alice
"Germchild." Aspect (77/79) 81, p. 147.
"The Phone." Shen (32:2) 81, p. 81.

MAURA, Sister
"Near the School for Exceptional Children." SouthernHR (15:2) Spr 81,
    p. 129.
"On Teaching Katherine Anne Porter in Japan." SouthernHR (15:2) Spr
    81, p. 129.

MAXHAM, Catherine
"Separation." PottPort (3) 81, p. 16.

MAXSON, Gloria
"Agnostic." ChrC (98:40) 9 D 81, p. 1278.
"Defector." ChrC (98:19) 27 My 81, p. 605.
"Etiquette." ChrC (98:35) 4 N 81, p. 1148.
"Leah." ChrC (98:37) 18 N 81, p. 1190.
"Traditionalist." ChrC (98:42) 23 D 81, p. 1332.
"Weeder." ChrC (98:31) 7 O 81, p. 992.
"Winterset." ChrC (98:2) 21 Ja 81, p. 43.

MAXSON, H. A.
"Designing a Fist" (for Carrie). HolCrit (18:2) Ap 81, pp. 11-12.
"Discovering February." CimR (56) Jl 81, p. 50.
"Parts of You Just Keep Escaping." KanQ (13:3/4) Sum-Aut 81, p. 158.
"Who Comes." CimR (56) Jl 81, p. 32.
"A Woman Dressing in Early Morning Window Light." PoetryNW (22:2)
    Sum 81, pp. 17-18.

MAXWELL, Anna
"The betrayal." NewRena (14) Spr 81, p. 29.
"A Building of Arms." SmPd (18:2) Spr 81, p. 28.
"Migration." StoneC (8: 3) Spr 81, p. 37.
"Miscarriage." CalQ (18/19) 81, p. 90.
"Pieces." PortR (27: 1) 81, p. 11.
"A Place to Live." NewRena (14) Spr 81, p. 30.
"The Rehearsal." HolCrit (18:2) Ap 81, p. 20.
"The Wise Man Visits." PortR (27: 1) 81, p. 11.

MAY, Anna
    "Poem for Kathy." <u>Wind</u> (11:42) 81, p. 29.

MAYER, Jim
    "Gravel Ponds in Spring i. m. T. M. J. M." <u>Stand</u> (22: 1) 80, p. 27.
    "Norwood Place." <u>Stand</u> (22: 1) 80, p. 26.

MAYEWSKI, Pawel
    "The Survivor" (tr. of Tadeusz Rozewicz). <u>Mund</u> (12/13) 80-81, p.
      231.

MAYHALL, Jane
    "Antidotes." <u>Confr</u> (21) Wint 81, p. 22.
    "For Elizabeth Who Telephoned to Say She'd Washed Her Windows and
      Now Can See New Jersey's Coral Shores." <u>Hudson</u> (34:2) Sum 81,
      pp. 245-246.
    "On Burnett Avenue." Hudson (34:2) Sum 81, p. 245.
    "Rain on 67th." <u>NewYorker</u> (57:5) 23 Mr 81, p. 41.

MAYHEW, Jonathan
    "Approaching the Atocha Station." <u>CalQ</u> (18/19) 81, p. 122.

MAYNE, Seymour
    "For My Child" (tr. of Abraham Sutzkever). <u>Stand</u> (22: 3) 81, p. 6.
    "Mother" (tr. of Abraham Sutzkever). <u>Stand</u> (22: 3) 81, pp. 7-9.
    "Self-Portrait" (tr. of Abraham Sutzkever). <u>Stand</u> (22: 3) 81, pp. 4-5.

MAYO, E. L.
    Collected Poems. <u>NewL</u> (47:2/3) Wint-Spr 80-81. Entire issue, pp.
      1-268.

MAZUR, Gail
    "In the Garment District." <u>Ploughs</u> (7:2) 81, pp. 134-135.
    "Norumbega Park." <u>Ploughs</u> (7:1) 81, pp. 42-43.

MAZZOCCO, Robert
    "East of Eden." <u>NewYorker</u> (57:34) 12 O 81, p. 38.
    "Foyer Des Jeunes." <u>AmerPoR</u> (10:6) N-D 81, p. 33.
    "Muertes." <u>AmerPoR</u> (10:6) N-D 81, p. 34.
    "Steps." <u>AmerPoR</u> (10:6) N-D 81, p. 33.

MEADS, Kathy
    "Two Sides Of The Same Poem." <u>WormR</u> (81/82) 81, pp. 6-7.

MEDFORD, Floyd C.
    "Observation." <u>WebR</u> (6:1) 81, p. 77.
    "On Re-Reading The Sun Rising." <u>WebR</u> (6:1) 81, p. 77.

MEDINA, Jorge Luis
    "Balada para un niño." <u>Claridad/En Rojo</u> (22: 1491) 28 Ag-S 3 81, p.
      12.

MEDINA, Luis
    "Neptuno." <u>Mairena</u> (2:5) Aut 80, p. 72.
    "María Lionza." <u>Mairena</u> (2:5) Aut 80, p. 72.

MEDINA, Ramón Felipe
    "Asi fue la cosa" (a Carmín y Pedro Juan, fraternalmente). <u>Claridad/</u>
      <u>En Rojo</u> (22: 1487) 31 Jl-Ag 6 81, p. 12.

MEDINA, Rubén
"Angels of the City." Maize (4:1/2) Aut-Wint 80-81, p. 58.
"Clasificados (para David Sternbach)." Maize (4:1/2) Aut-Wint 80-81, pp. 56-57.
"Post card." Maize (4:1/2) Aut-Wint 80-81, p. 55.

MEDINA GONZALEZ, Oquendo
"Debo morir una tarde." Mairena (3:7) 81, p. 86.

MEEK, Jay
"Air Show." OP (31/32) Aut 81, pp. 111-112.

MEIER, Henrique
"A la Memoria de Antonio Echeverría Capriles." Puerto Wint 81, p. 33.

MEIER, Kay
"Last Rites." CapeR (17:1) Wint 81, p. 50.

MEINERS, R. K.
"OF ORIGAMI: Letter From Buffalo Creek to England." Wind (11:41) 81, pp. 32-35.

MEINERS, Roger
"Dried Pasqueflowers." Stand (22: 4) 81, pp. 36-37.

MEINKE, Peter
"Rage." NewYorker (57:44) 21 D 81, p. 99.

MEISNER, Sarah
"The Hit" (for R. C.). Ascent (77/79) 81, p. 152.

MEISSNER, Bill
"The Crippled Child." ColEng (43:6) O 81, p. 580.
"Letter from the Consumer." CharR (7:2) Aut 81, p. 27.
"Son of a Traveling Salesman." CharR (7:2) Aut 81, p. 28.
"The Voice Gymnast." CarolQ (34:2) Aut 81, p. 28.

MEISSNER, William
"End of the World: Hearing that Snow Had Collapsed the Alpine Cafe Roof (for Baraboo, Wis.)." Northeast (3:10) Wint 81, pp. 30-31.
"First Kiss" (with Jack Driscoll). NowestR (19:1/2), p. 87.
"Keeping in Touch" (with Jack Driscoll). NowestR (19:1/2), p. 86.
"Part of the Waking" (with Jack Driscoll). NowestR (19:1/2), p. 85.
"Poem for the Insect in Fall." Chelsea (40) 81, p. 148.
"The Psychometrist and His Woman." PoetryNW (22:3) Aut 81, pp. 42-43.
"The Somnambulist's Music" (w/ Jack Driscoll). Chelsea (40) 81, p. 149.
"The Water Tower Climbers." Northeast (3:10) Wint 81, p. 29.

MEJIA, Abel Fernández see FERNANDEZ MEJIA, Abel

MEJIA, Oscar Echeverri see ECHEVERRI MEJIA, Oscar

MELENDEZ, Carlos "La Sombra" Torres see TORRES MELENDEZ, Carlos "La Sombra"

MELENDEZ, Jesús Papoleto
"Antonia." Maize (4:1/2) Aut-Wint 80-81, pp. 66-7.
"Story from a Mountain." Maize (4:1/2) Aut-Wint 80-81, pp. 68-9.
"Who i am, who i touch." Maize (4:1/2) Aut-Wint 80-81, p. 70.

MELENDEZ, Joserramón
"A don Pedro Albizu Campos." Mairena (2:6) 80, p. 89.

MELLERI, Arto
"Blue Eve" (tr. by Aili Flint and Austin Flint). PoetryE (6) Aut 81,
    p. 28.
"Epitaph" (tr. by Aili Flint and Austin Flint). PoetryE (6) Aut 81, p.
    29.
"Pyres" (tr. by Sanna Tolsa and Austin Flint). PoetryE (6) Aut 81, pp.
    29-30.
"The Word" (tr. by Aili Flint and Austin Flint). PoetryE (6) Aut 81,
    pp. 30-31.

MELNYCZUK, Askold
"The Flower" (tr. of Mykola Rudenko). Agni (14) 81, p. 99.
"The King of Tasmania" (tr. of Mykola Rudenko). Agni (14) 81, pp.
    96-97.
"At Least, You" (tr. of Mykola Rudenko). Agni (14) 81, p. 98.
"Spring" (tr. of Mykola Rudenko). Agni (14) 81, p. 100.

MELO NETO, João Cabral de
"Nocturne." Mund (12/13) 80-81, p. 11.
"The Seasons" (tr. by Eloah F. Giacomelli). Mund (12/13) 80-81, pp.
    10-11.

MENDEZ, Roberto
"Las Abuelas." Areito (7: 27) 81, p. 19.

MENDEZ BONILLA, Sixto
"El maldito carbón" (décima). Claridad/En Rojo (22: 1484) 10-16 Jl 81,
    p. 12.

MENDOZA, Ester Feliciano see FELICIANO MENDOZA, Ester

MENDOZA, Ricardo
"Nana." Metam (3:2/4:1) 80-81, pp. 63-65.

MENEBROKER, Ann
"Love." PoNow (6:2 issue 32) 81, p. 43.

MENG, Hao-Jan
"An Inscription on the Buddhist Retreat of Master Yi" (tr. by C. H.
    Kwan). MalR (58) Ap 81, p. 39.

MENKITI, Ifeanyi
"Ezidimma." Ploughs (7:1) 81, p. 46.

MENTZER, Brett
"Hippos." HiramPoR (30) Spr-Sum 81, p. 30.

MERCADO, Karmen
"A las musas." Mairena (2:6) 80, p. 42.

MEREDITH, Joseph
"The Kid Poets" (for CFK). FourQt (30:3) Spr 81, p. 2.

MEREDITH, William
"In the Rif Mountains (Northern Morocco)." Shen (31:3) 80, p. 23.
"REM Sleep." ThRiPo (17/18) 81, pp. 43-44.

MERI, Veijo
"Birth and Death" (tr. by Aili Flint and Austin Flint). PoetryE (6) Aut
81, p. 32.
"On the Contrary" (tr. by Aili Flint and Austin Flint). PoetryE (6) Aut
81, p. 33.
"Storm" (tr. by Aili Flint and Austin Flint). PoetryE (6) Aut 81, p.
33.

MERNIT, Susan
"Dancing in the Kitchen with Long Tall Sally Beating on the Drums with
Miss Molly." Prima (6/7) 81, p. 66.
"Swan Moon." Confr (21) Wint 81, p. 93.

MERRIAM, Eve
"Beauty and The." PoNow (6:1 issue 31) 81, p. 36.
"Soap Opera." PoNow (6:1 issue 31) 81, p. 36.

MERRILL, James
"Clearing the Title." NewYorker (56:50) 2 F 81, pp. 36-37.
"A Look Askance." Antaeus (40/41) Wint-Spr 81, pp. 347-348.
"The Suppliant." NewYorker (57:19) 29 Je 81, p. 32.
"Trees Listening to Bach." Ploughs (7:2) 81, pp. 38-39.

MERROW, Jim
"Nights in Küstenja." Atl (248:3) S 81, p. 80.

MERWIN, W. S.
"The Arrival." Mund (12/13) 80-81, p. 15.
"The Drive Home." Mund (12/13) 80-81, p. 20.
"Migration." Mund (12/13) 80-81, p. 18.
"The Next Moon." Mund (12/13) 80-81, p. 17.
"The Snow." Mund (12/13) 80-81, p. 18.
"The Tree of the Heirs." Mund (12/13) 80-81, p. 16.
"Walls." Mund (12/13) 80-81, p. 19.

MESCHERY, Tom
"Base Camp." Meadows (2:1) 81, p. 65.
"Speed." Meadows (2:1) 81, p. 33.

MESSERLI, Douglas
"Actually Swallowed." MissR (10:1) Spr-Sum 81, p. 87.
"Beating the Sheep." MissR (10:1) Spr-Sum 81, p. 86.
"Swiss and German Matriarchs." MissR (10:1) Spr-Sum 81, p. 85.

MESZAROS, Robert
"The Turtles." EnPas (12), 81, p. 35.

METASTASIO
from "Nel comporre l'Olimpiade" (tr. by Anonymous). PortR (27: 1)
81, p. 15.

METRAS, Gary
    "Ducks." Sam (117) 81, p. 20.
    "The Mechanic As Metaphysician." Sam (116) 81, pp. 58-60.
    "Parable of the Fish." EnPas (12) 81, p. 12.

METZ, Roberta
    "After." Prima (6/7) 81, p. 54.
    "Evidence." Chelsea (40) 81, p. 150.
    "It Moves Nevertheless" (Galileo). Confr (21) Wint 81, p. 127.
    "Mondo Cane." CreamCR (6:1) Aut 80, pp. 10-11.
    "Witness." Chelsea (40) 81, p. 151.

MEURANT, Serge
    "in nameless signs" (tr. by John Getsi and Lucia Getsi). Mund (12/13)
        80-81, p. 99.
    "Sometimes form explodes" (tr. by John Getsi and Lucia Getsi). Mund
        (12/13) 80-81, p. 99.

MEYER, Tom
    "Fin de siècle." Sulfur (1) 81, p. 73.
    "The Labyrinth at Crete." Sulfur (1) 81, pp. 70-72.

MEZEY, Robert
    "In the Fields of the Dead." ParisR (23:79) Spr 81, pp. 244-245.

MICHELE, Mary di see Di MICHELE, Mary

MICHELINE, Jack
    "Louise." UnmOx (22) Wint 81, p. 28.

MICHELSON, Richard
    "Aunt Frieda in the Movies." PoetryNW (22:2) Sum 81, p. 30.

MICKA, Mary Virginia
    "The Dancer." SouthernPR (21: 1) Spr 81, p. 55.

MIDDLETON, Christopher
    "After a Noise in the Street." Poetry (139:2) N 81, pp. 74-75.
    "Amor As Landscape Painter (1787)" (tr. of Goethe). SenR (12:1/2) 81,
        pp. 9-13.

MIHAILOVICH, Vasa D.
    "Echoing" (tr. of Vasko Popa, w/ Ronald Moran). Mund (12/13) 80-81,
        p. 230.
    "The Game of the Ashes" (tr. of Vasko Popa). Mund (12/13) 80-81, p.
        229.
    "Games at the European Masked Ball" (tr. of Drago Ivanišević). Mund
        (12/13) 80-81, p. 153.

MIHAN, Elisabeth Louise
    "1938: Letter from Harlem." US1 (14/15) Aut/Wint 81, p. 3.

MIKLITSCH, Robert
    "The Imminence of Winter." CentR (25:1) Wint 81, pp. 42-43.
    "Manifesto of Pleasure in a Rainy Season." NewEngR (3:3) Spr 81, p.
        413.
    "Vision After the Sermon (or Jacob Wrestling with the Angel)."
        NewEngR (3:3) Spr 81, p. 414.

MILBURN, Michael
  "The Blind Student." Ploughs (7:1) 81, pp. 103-105.

MILES, Jeffrey
  "Birthsong" (for Gwen Shapard). QW (12) Spr-Sum 81, pp. 6-7.

MILES, Josephine
  "Balance." Poetry (139:1) O 81, p. 21.
  "Faces." Poetry (139:1) O 81, p. 22.
  "Sleep." Poetry (139:1) O 81, p. 22.
  "Vigils." Poetry (139:1) O 81, p. 21.

MILES, Sara
  "Heroes." HangL (39) Wint 80-81, p. 13.
  "I Forget." HangL (39) Wint 80-81, pp. 14-15.

MILIDRAGOVIC, Bazidar
  "Talk About Poetry" (tr. by Stephen Stepanchev). PoNow (5:6 issue 30)
      81, p. 31.

MILLER, David
  "Entrance." MalR (59) Jl 81, p. 20.
  "Freeze Up." MalR (59) Jl 81, p. 21.
  "Gesture." MalR (59) Jl 81, p. 22.
  "The Thin Grey Bitch." MalR (59) Jl 81, p. 23.

MILLER, David Neal
  "Words in Winter" (tr. of Karl Krolow). Aspect (77/79) 81, p. 134.

MILLER, E. S.
  "Shelley Set Right." OP (31/32) Aut 81, p. 92.

MILLER, J. L.
  "Poem Written While Crossing Kansas from Colorado to Missouri in
      June 1971." OP (31/32) Aut 81, pp. 58-63.

MILLER, Jacob
  "Words for Robert Hayden" (d. Feb. 1980). WorldO (15:1), p. 4.

MILLER, James A.
  "Memoriam, Jesse Owens." Comm (108:4) 27 F 81, p. 126.

MILLER, Jane
  "Anonymous Meditation" (for G. R.). AmerPoR (10:1) Ja-F 81, p. 7.
  "Black Tea." Tendril (11) Sum 81, pp. 52-53.
  "Graphic Meditation." VirQR (57:3) Sum 81, p. 458.
  "Green of Mildew and of Verdigris." VirQR (57:3) Sum 81, pp. 455-
      456.
  "Hanging Meditation." AmerPoR (10:1) Ja-F 81, p. 7.
  "Mind Form." VirQR (57:3) Sum 81, pp. 457-458.
  "The Stagger of the Wind That I Think Is Your Turning." GeoR (35:1)
      Spr 81, p. 47.
  "Steamy Meditation" (Maho Bay). AmerPoR (10:1) Ja-F 81, p. 7.
  "Three Secrets for Alexis." Iowa (11:2/3) Spr-Sum 80, pp. 194-196.

MILLER, John N.
  "Listening Now." Confr (22) Sum 81, p. 107.

MILLER, Leslie Adrienne
  "Pen Drawing for Harper's Young People." Tele (17) 81, pp. 138-139.

MILLER, Louis
  "In the Shop" (tr. by Aaron Kramer). Vis (5) 81, n. p.

MILLER, Margaret W.
  "This Trick" (for A. D.). HolCrit (18:5) D 81, pp. 12-13.

MILLER, Philip
  "Grandma Moses." KanQ (13:3/4) Sum-Aut 81, p. 56.

MILLER, Raeburn
  "For Donald Justice" (after Li Po). SouthernR (17:3) Sum 81, p. 560.
  "For Rachel Merker." SouthernR (17:3) Sum 81, p. 560.

MILLER, Vassar
  "Summation." PoNow (6:1 issue 31) 81, p. 36.

MILLER, Warren C.
  "The Gates Woman." Outbr (6/7) Aut 80-Spr 81, p. 7.

MILLER-DUGGAN, Devon
  "Horsefeathers." HiramPoR (30) Spr-Sum 81, p. 31.

MILLET, John
  "Heat." Sam (116) 81, p. 39.
  "Map." StoneC (9: 1-2) Aut-Wint 81/82, p. 21.

MILLIKEN, Patrick
  "To Welcome Us Back." GeoR (35:2) Sum 81, p. 399.

MILLIS, C.
  "Achilles." Nimrod (25:1) Aut-Wint 81, p. 88.
  "Chryse." Nimrod (25:1) Aut-Wint 81, p. 89.
  "Chryses' Prayer." Nimrod (25:1) Aut-Wint 81, p. 89.
  "Cyst." StoneC (9: 1-2) Aut-Wint 81/82, p. 68.

MILLS, Sparling
  "Being A Life Guard." PottPort (3) 81, p. 46.
  "Debussy." PottPort (3) 81, p. 9.

MILNER, Philip
  "The Itinerant Professor Shaves His Whiskers And Marvels At Life."
     PottPort (3) 81, p. 13.

MILOSZ, Czeslaw
  "Elegy For N. N." AmerPoR (10:1) Ja-F 81, p. 48.

MINER, Virginia Scott
  "Breakfast In New Orleans." WindO (38) Spr-Sum 81, p. 22.
  "Lakes Are Women." WindO (38) Spr-Sum 81, p. 21.
  "Photograph and Painting." KanQ (13:3/4) Sum-Aut 81, p. 204.

MINICH, Jan C.
  "The McClellan Farm." NowestR (19:3), pp. 89-90.

MINICK, Jeffrey
  "First Communion." Sam (116) 81, p. 2.

MINOR, James
"All leaves." Northeast (3:11) Sum 81, p. 9.
"Stealing time." Northeast (3:11) Sum 81, p. 9.
"Wintry night." Northeast (3:11) Sum 81, p. 9.

MINTON, Helena
"Artifacts." Poetry (138:2) My 81, p. 71.
"Balm." BelPoJ (31:3) Spr 81, p. 29.
"Bread." Poetry (138:2) My 81, p. 71.
"The Hunt." BelPoJ (31:3) Spr 81, p. 31.
"Letter From Shuyak Island, Alaska" (To my grandmother). Poetry
    (138:2) My 81, p. 72.
"Maps." BelPoJ (31:3) Spr 81, pp. 30-31.
"On The Tundra: Ursus." BelPoJ (31:3) Spr 81, p. 32.
"Raccoon Skeleton at Long Plain Creek." Ascent (77/79) 81, p. 150.

MINTY, Judith
"Conjoined." Mund (12/13) 80-81, p. 68.
"Women Poets." Mund (12/13) 80-81, pp. 66-68.

MIR, Francisco
"Laguna." Areito (7: 27) 81, p. 20.

MIR, Pedro
"Estampa de Union Township" (tr. of Rafael Catalá). Calib (3:2) Aut-
    Wint 80, p. 54.

MIRANDA, Gary
"Magician." Atl (247:1) Ja 81, p. 66.

MIRANDA ARCHILLA, Graciany
"Poema-8." Lugar (1:1) 79, p. 13.
"Poema-10." Lugar (1:1) 79, p. 13.
"Poema-12." Lugar (1:1) 79, p. 12.

MIRENBERG, Anita
"Ochre" (for F. B.). BelPoJ (32:1) Aut 81, pp. 10-12.

MISHKIN, Julia
"Confession" (for Yukio Mishima). Confr (22) Sum 81, pp. 48-49.
"Dust in Paradise." Pequod (12) 81, p. 19.
"Insomnia." GeoR (35:1) Spr 81, p. 126.
"The Lily Pond." Pequod (12) 81, pp. 15-16.
"Temptation in Museums." Confr (22) Sum 81, p. 49.
"For Your Discomfort." MissouriR Sum 81, p. 22.
"Waking: 3 A. M." Pequod (12) 81, pp. 17-18.

MISHLER, Richard M.
"Ceremony." BelPoJ (31:4) Sum 81, pp. 34-35.

MITCHELL, Karen L.
"Birmingham, Alabama, 1963." OP (31/32) Aut 81, pp. 136-137.
"My Mother Bakes Cookies." Obs (6: 1/2) Spr-Sum 80, p. 220.
"Visit." Obs (6: 1/2) Spr-Sum 80, pp. 218-219.
"Where Have the Black Sheep Gone? They Have Gone Grazing in the
    Fields" (for Toni Cade Bambara). Obs (6: 1/2) Spr-Sum 80, pp.
    216-217.

MITCHELL, Roger
    "All Hallow's Eve." NoAmR (266:3) S 81, p. 47.
    "For Courbet." Im (7:3) 81, p. 9.
    "These are the Ladies." ColEng (43:4) Ap 81, p. 371.
    "To Molly and Bridget, In a Bad Time." Im (7:2) 1981, p. 8.
    "Untitled." ThRiPo (17/18) 81, p. 47.

MITCHELL, Stephen
    Ten poems (tr. of Rainer Maria Rilke). ParisR (23:82) Wint 82, pp.
       111-128.

MITCHELL, Susan
    "Aubade." Nat (232:2) 17 Ja 81, p. 58.
    "Blackbirds." AmerPoR (10:2) Mr-Ap 81, p. 22.
    "The Mouse and The Clock." Agni (14) 81, pp. 69-70.
    "The Trowel." AmerPoR (10:2) Mr-Ap 81, p. 22.
    "When Grandfather Died." Nat (232:19) 16 My 81, p. 610.

MITSUHARU, Kaneko
    "Seal" (tr. by James Kirkup). Mund (12/13) 80-81, pp. 298-300.

MITSUNE, Oshikochi no see OSHIKOCHI no MITSUNE

MIYAZAWA, Kenji
    "Love and Fever" (tr. by Graeme Wilson). DenQ (16:4) Wint 81, p. 39.

MIYOSHI, Tatsuji
    "Stories" (tr. by Graeme Wilson). DenQ (16:4) Wint 81, p. 41.

MIZEJEWSKI, Linda
    "The Lover an Hour or More Late." PoNow (6:3 issue 33) 81, p. 31.
    "Stickshift." PoNow (6:3 issue 33) 81, p. 31.

MOE, Julia
    "Reflection of the Hawk." MalR (59) Jl 81, pp. 26-27.

MOE, Keith
    "Australian Snails." LittleM (13:1/2) Spr-Sum 79, c1981, p. 73.

MOFFEIT, Tony
    "outlaw." Obs (6: 1/2) Spr-Sum 80, p. 168.

MOFFETT, Judith
    "Canticle 2: The Cursing." LittleM (13:1/2) Spr-Sum 79, c1981, p.
       66.
    "Lucia Day." MissouriR (4:3) Sum 81, p. 7.
    "The Lilies of the Field" (tr. of Hjalmar Gullberg). PoNow (5:6 issue
       30) 81, p. 23.
    "Missing Person (for James Merrill)." NewEngR (3:4) Sum 81, pp.
       506-10.
    "The Old Country." MissouriR (4:3) Sum 81, p. 10.
    "Non-Occurring Thud" (tr. of Hjalmar Gullberg). PoNow (5:6 issue 30)
       81, p. 23.
    "Put the Photographs Away" (tr. of Hjalmar Gullberg). PoNow (5:6 is-
       sue 30) 81, p. 23.
    "Smoke." Iowa (11:2/3) Spr-Sum 80, pp. 88-89.

MOFFI, Larry
    "To the Preacher's Son, Paddled for Dropping His Pants in the Lunch-
    room. " PoNow (6:2 issue 32) 81, p. 45.

MOLE, John
    "The Mountain." Stand (22: 3) 81, p. 22.

MOLEN, Robert Vander see VANDER MOLEN, Robert

MOLINA, Teodosio Muñoz see MUÑOZ MOLINA, Teodosio

MOLTON, Warren Lane
    "On Easter Morning." ChrC (98:13) 15 Ap 81, p. 407.
    "On Good Friday." ChrC (98:13) 15 Ap 81, p. 407.
    "You Left Me Slowly Falling." ChrC (98:6) 25 F 81, p. 197.
    "The Jesus Walk." ChrC (98:12) 8 Ap 81, p. 384.

MOMBOURQUETTE, Jocelyn
    "Clearly." PottPort (3) 81, p. 32.
    "Inuit in snowmobile suits." PottPort (3) 81, p. 52.
    "Untitled." PottPort (3) 81, p. 31.

MONDRAGON, Sergio
    "Guru." Mund (12/13) 80-81, p. 305.
    "Death no longer faces mirrors" (tr. of Roberto Juarroz, w/ Rainer
      Schulte). Mund (12/13) 80-81, p. 24.
    "I think that in this moment" (tr. of Roberto Juarroz, w/ Rainer
      Schulte). Mund (12/13) 80-81, p. 24.
    "Man" (tr. of Roberto Juarroz, w/ Rainer Schulte). Mund (12/13) 80-
      81, p. 23.
    "One day I will find a word" (tr. of Roberto Juarróz, w/ Rainer
      Schulte). Mund (12/13) 80-81, p. 23.
    "November" (tr. by Annemarie Colbin). Mund (12/13) 80-81, p. 304.
    "Reverend Malthus On The Beach" (tr. of Gabriel Zaid, w/ Sandra
      Smith). Mund (12/13) 80-81, p. 156.
    "Thousand and One Nights" (tr. of Gabriel Zaid, w/ Sandra Smith).
      Mund (12/13) 80-81, p. 156.

MONTAG, Tom
    "Nightfall." Im (7:3) 81, p. 5.
    "The Plow." Im (7:3) 81, p. 5.
    "Poem Exhorting Its Own Publication." Aspect (77/79) 81, p. 151.
    "Summer's End." Im (7:3) 81, p. 5.
    "The Winter Barn." Im (7:3) 81, p. 5.

MONTAGUE, John
    "Northern Lights." ConcPo (14:2) Aut 81, pp. 24-26.
    "A Small Death." MalR (59) Jl 81, pp. 24-25.

MONTALE, Eugenio
    "Accelerato." SenR (12:1/2) 81, p. 168.
    "After Palio" (tr. by Luciano Rebay). NewYRB (28:1) 5 F 81, p. 23.
    "Bagni Di Lucca" (tr. by William Arrowsmith). AmerPoR (10:5) S-O
      81, p. 28.
    "Bellosquardo" (tr. by Robert Lowell). NewYRB (28:16) 22 O 81, p.
      10.
    "Boats on the Marne" (tr. by Robert Lowell). NewYRB (28:16) 22 O
      81, p. 10.

"The Earrings" (tr. by William Arrowsmith). SenR (12:1/2) 81, p. 171.
"English Horn" (tr. by William Arrowsmith). AmerPoR (10:5) S-O 81,
    p. 28.
"Flux" (tr. by Robert Lowell). NewYRB (28:16) 22 O 81, p. 10.
"Gli orecchini." SenR (12:1/2) 81, p. 170.
"In the Park at Caserta" (tr. by William Arrowsmith). SenR (12:1/2)
    81, p. 173.
"The Intellectual" (tr. by Jonathan Galassi). Antaeus (43) Aut 81, pp.
    130-132.
"Lindau" (tr. by William Arrowsmith). AmerPoR (10:5) S-O 81, p. 28.
"Local Train" (tr. by William Arrowsmith). SenR (12:1/2) 81, p. 169.
"Motets" (tr. by William Arrowsmith). AmerPoR (10:5) S-O 81, pp.
    28-30.
"Nel parco di Caserta." SenR (12:1/2) 81, p. 172.
Nine poems (tr. by William Arrowsmith). ParisR (23:81) Aut 81, pp.
    42-49.
"The Prisoner's Dream" (tr. by William Arrowsmith). NewYRB (28:6)
    16 Ap 81, p. 19.
"Ten poems" (tr. by William Arrowsmith). Antaeus (40/41) Wint-Spr
    81, pp. 349-361.
"Voice that Came with the Coots" (tr. by William Arrowsmith).
    NewYRB (28:6) 16 Ap 81, p. 20.
"You've Given My Name To A Tree?" (tr. by William Arrowsmith).
    AmerPoR (10:5) S-O 81, p. 28.

MONTAÑEZ, Jaime Marcano see MARCANO MONTAÑEZ, Jaime

MONTECINO A., Sonia
    "Tres poemas y una impresión etnográfica." Maize (4:3/4) Spr-Sum 81,
        pp. 70-73.

MONTERO, Alvaro
    "Canto a Ignacio Villa." Caribe (2: 2/3) 80/81, pp. 76-77.
    "Sale el Sol" (a Ismael Rivera). Caribe (2: 2/3) 80/81, pp. 74-75.

MONTES DE OCA, Marco Antonio
    "At Sea Level" (tr. by Laura Villaseñor). Mund (12/13) 80-81, pp.
        256-257.
    "Have You Noticed?" (tr. by Linda Scheer). PoNow (5:6 issue 30) 81,
        p. 31.
    "Light In Readiness." Mund (12/13) 80-81, p. 257.
    "Variations Without A Theme" (tr. by Linda Scheer). PoNow (5:6 issue
        30) 81, p. 31.

MONTGOMERY, Carol Artman
    "After His First Vacation, Bucky Hamilton." PoNow (6:3 issue 33) 81,
        p. 31.

MOODY, Rodger
    "I Could See Twin Falls, Idaho, in the Distance." PoNow (6:1 issue
        31) 81, p. 19.
    "The Name on the Moon." Wind (11:41) 81, p. 42.

MOODY, Shirley
    "Ritual to Catch Birds." SouthernPR (21:2) Aut 81, p. 41.

MOONEY, Kathleen Kirk
    "Variance." EngJ (70:5) S 81, p. 72.

MOORE, Barbara
  "Room by Moonlight." NoAmR (266:3) S 81, p. 59.

MOORE, Elizabeth
  "New Jerusalem Descending." Wind (10:39) 80, p. 42.

MOORE, Frank D.
  "Chair." FourQt (30:4) Sum 81, p. 2.

MOORE, George B.
  "The Rivers East of Here." ThRiPo (17/18) 81, p. 60.
  "The Statues of San Agustin." ThRiPo (17/18) 81, p. 61.

MOORE, James
  "Into the Circle of Death." AntR (39:1) Wint 81, p. 74.

MOORE, Laurie
  "Bugs." Wind (11:42) 81, p. 25.

MOORE, Richard
  "Friends." Poetry (138:1) Ap 81, p. 17.
  "The Mouse's Departure from the Pedagogical Rat." OntR (15) Aut-
    Wint 81-82, pp. 49-56.
  "On Coming to Nothing." Poetry (138:1) Ap 81, p. 18.
  "The Playground." Poetry (138:1) Ap 81, p. 16.

MOORHEAD, Andrea
  "August Days." Os (13) Aut 81, pp. 12-15.
  "Burning Snow." Os (12) Spr 81, p. 27.
  "Eros." Os (12) Spr 81, pp. 20-21.
  "Skin of Land and Water." Os (12) Spr 81, p. 29.
  "Snowing Across Light." Os (12) Spr 81, p. 28.

MORA, Francisco Lluch see LLUCH MORA, Francisco

MORA, Pablo
  "Probabilidad." Puerto Wint 81, p. 34.

MORAFF, Barbara
  "Desire." Sulfur (3) 82, p. 86.
  "For COCHISE in Brooklyn." Tele (17) 81, p. 92.
  "Going to Sleep." Sulfur (3) 82, p. 85.
  "Now." Sulfur (3) 82, pp. 82-83.
  "September Morn." Tele (17) 81, p. 90.
  "Upcountry Breakdown." Tele (17) 81, p. 91.
  "Vermont Farming." Sulfur (3) 82, p. 84.

MORAGA, Cherríe
  "Anatomy Lesson." Cond (7) Spr 81, p. 88.
  "For the Color of my Mother." Cond (7) Spr 81, pp. 89-90.

MORALES, José Jurado see JURADO MORALES, José

MORALES, Luis García
  "Always" (tr. by Thomas Hoeksema). Mund (12/13) 80-81, p. 122.

MORAN, Ronald
  "Echoing" (tr. of Vasko Popa, w/ Vassa D. Mihailovich). Mund (12/13)
    80-81, p. 230.

MORAT, Angela Gentile de see GENTILE DE MORAT, Angela

MOREIRA, Rubinstein
"Apuesta" (Al Dr. Emilio Uzcátegui, grande de Ecuador). Puerto Wint
    81, p. 35.

MOREJON, Nancy
"Obrera del tabaco. " Areito (27: 28) 81, p. 48.

MORELAND, Jane P.
"On Your Astonishment. " GeoR (35:2) Sum 81, p. 306.
"To Cousin Beth. " PoetryNW (22:3) Aut 81, pp. 22-23.

MORENO, Hilda Luz
"Rescato tu vuelo. " Mairena (2:6) 80, p. 81.

MORENO TORRES, Gerardo
"Dirán. " Mairena (3:7) 81, p. 88.
"Ocaso. " Mairena (3:7) 81, p. 88.
"Si al fin la última realidad. " Mairena (2:6) 80, p. 80.
"Tríptico. " Mairena (3:7) 81, p. 87.
"Ven pequeño. " Mairena (3:7) 81, p. 87.

MORETTI, Bruno
"Nipple" (tr. by Lawrence Venuti). Chelsea (40) 81, p. 51.

MORGAN, Colin
"Remembrance. " Stand (22: 2) 81, p. 60.

MORGAN, Frederick
"At the Hidden Springs" (for Rosemary Felton). Hudson (34:4) Wint 81,
    pp. 522-523.
"Castle Rock. " Harp (263:1579) D 81, p. 78.
"The Demonstration" (for Rosemary Felton). Hudson (34:4) Wint 81, pp.
    519-520.
"The Diagrams" (for Rosemary Felton). Hudson (34:4) Wint 81, pp.
    523-524.
"From the Terrace. " YaleR (70: 3) Spr 81, pp. 411-412.
"I Remember the Sea When I Was Six...." AmerS (50:1) Wint 80-81,
    p. 71.
"Landscape in a Mirror. " YaleR (70: 3) Spr 81, pp. 410-411.
"The Murder. " VirQR (57:2) Spr 81, pp. 278-279.
"Northbook. " SouthernR (17:1) Wint 81, pp. 178-189.
"The Reflection" (for Rosemary Felton). Hudson (34:4) Wint 81, pp.
    521-522.
"The Soldier. " Kayak (56) 81, pp. 48-49.
"Twelve Riddles. " NewEngR (3:3) Spr 81, pp. 337-41.
"Visitor" (for Rosemary Felton). Hudson (34:4) Wint 81, p. 520.

MORGAN, John
"The House Of Mirth. " AmerPoR (10:2) Mr-Ap 81, p. 8.
"I Paint My Face Blue. " PoetryNW (22:4) Wint 81-82, pp. 17-18.
"The Killing Of Anton Webern. " AmerPoR (10:2) Mr-Ap 81, p. 8.
"The Reef. " PoetryNW (22:2) Sum 81, pp. 31-32.

MORGAN, Robert
"Gap Trails. " Tendril (11) Sum 81, p. 54.
"Mistletoe. " PoNow (6:2 issue 32) 81, p. 5.
"Mowing. " Poetry (138:6) S 81, p. 313.

"Passenger Pigeons." Tendril (11) Sum 81, p. 55.
"Purple Asters." Poetry (138:6) S 81, p. 314.
"White Autumn." Poetry (138:6) S 81, pp. 311-312.

MORGAN, Robin
"The Fall Of A Sparrow." AmerPoR (10:3) My-Je 81, p. 4-6.
"Phobiphilia." 13thM (5:1/2) 80, pp. 5-7.

MORGAN, Tom
"Mea Culpa." CreamCR (6:2) 81, p. 102.

MORI, Kyoko
"Relics." WindO (38) Spr-Sum 81, p. 17.
"September." WindO (38) Spr-Sum 81, p. 18.

MORITZ, A. F.
"A Bunch of Carrots" (tr. of Benjamin Péret, with Jane Barnard).
    Bound (9:2) Wint 81, p. 249.
"Adventures of a Toe" (tr. of Benjamin Péret, with Jane Barnard).
    Bound (9:2) Wint 81, p. 249.
"The Farthese Face" (tr. of Benjamin Péret, with Jane Barnard).
    Bound (9:2) Wint 81, p. 251.
"Laughing Stock" (tr. of Benjamin Péret, with Jane Barnard). Bound
    (9:2) Wint 81, p. 251.
"Samson" (tr. of Benjamin Péret, with Jane Barnard). Bound (9:2)
    Wint 81, pp. 251-255.

MORLEY, Hilda
"After the Moon-Walk." NewL (47:4) Sum 81, p. 83.
"Duende (Homage to García Lorca)." NewL (47:4) Sum 81, pp. 80-81.
"Herbal." NewL (47:4) Sum 81, pp. 79-80.
"Narcissus in Georgia." NewL (47:4) Sum 81, p. 82.
"Times." NewL (47:4) Sum 81, pp. 84-85.
"The Tree." NewL (47:4) Sum 81, p. 83.
"Woods Hole." NewL (47:4) Sum 81, p. 79.

MORRIS, Herbert
"A Photograph By August Sander." Shen (32:1) 80, pp. 38-44.
"Praise for the Second Daughter." ParisR (23:79) Spr 81, pp. 246-247.
"River Road." NewEngR (3:4) Sum 81, pp. 580-2.
"South." Kayak (56) 81, pp. 38-40.
"South." Kayak (57) 81, pp. 65-67.
"Wallace Steven's Daughter." Shen (31:3) 80, p. 46.

MORRIS, John N.
"Boxtrap." Poetry (138:1) Ap 81, p. 43.
"The Cure." Poetry (138:1) Ap 81, p. 44.
"The Grand Birthday." Poetry (138:1) Ap 81, pp. 41-42.
"Grandfather's Picture." Poetry (138:1) Ap 81, pp. 39-40.
"In the Album." YaleR (71: 1) Aut 81, p. 89.
"A Schedule of Benefits." Poetry (138:1) Ap 81, p. 45.

MORRIS, Paul
"Evening in Lans" (tr. of Georg Trakl). PoNow (5:6 issue 30) 81, p.
    45.
"Landscape" (tr. of Georg Trakl). PoNow (5:6 issue 30) 81, p. 45.
"The Rats" (tr. of Georg Trakl). PoNow (5:6 issue 30) 81, p. 45.
"Stutter." Thrpny (7) Aut 81, p. 3.

MORRIS, Robert
"A Cenotaph For Air Crash Victims." Chelsea (39) 81, p. 106.
"A Cenotaph For Cancer." Chelsea (39) 81, p. 112.
"A Cenotaph For Flood Victims." Chelsea (39) 81, p. 111.
"A Final Tomb For Frank 'Jelly' Nash." Chelsea (39) 81, p. 107.
"Project For A Tomb--The Towers Of Silence." Chelsea (39) 81, p. 109.
"Roller Disco: Cenotaph For A Public Figure." Chelsea (39) 81, p. 105.
"Tomb For A Dismembered Body." Chelsea (39) 81, p. 110.
"A Tomb Garden Outside The City." Chelsea (39) 81, p. 108.

MORRIS, William L.
"Every Poem Is Perfect." Poetry (138:6) S 81, p. 337.

MORRISON, Lillian
"House Call." Confr (22) Sum 81, p. 129.

MORRISON, Mateo
"Las Camaradas." Caribe (2: 2/3) 80/81, p. 67.
"Poemas de Julio Agosto." Caribe (2: 2/3) 80/81, p. 68-69.

MORTIMER, Anthony
"Grace After Pears." Poetry (138:6) S 81, p. 332.
"Paraclausithyron." Poetry (138:6) S 81, p. 331.

MORTON, Bruce
"Le Cafe Ideal." KanQ (13:1) Wint 81, p. 154.

MORTON, Carlos
"Mayan Madness." Metam (3:2/4:1) 80-81, p. 94.
"Mummy de un Niño de Tres Años by the Name of Anoubias." Metam (3:2/4:1) 80-81, p. 93.

MOSBY, George, Jr.
"Entrance." HangL (39) Wint 80-81, p. 18.
"Escape to Freedom-land 2." Im (7:2) 1981, p. 9.
"I Remember Langston Hughes." HangL (39) Wint 80-81, p. 19.
"Locked at a Window inside a Fence." HangL (39) Wint 80-81, p. 20.
"On the Visit of Uncle Alfred." HangL (39) Wint 80-81, p. 17.
"The Love Song of Li Po (Who Fell From His Boat and Drowned While Trying to Embrace the Reflection of the Moon in the Sea)." Im (7:2) 1981, p. 9.
"The Matinee." HangL (39) Wint 80-81, p. 16.

MOSCA, Marcelene
"Versions of Zukofsky Song No. 28." SunM (11) Spr 81, pp. 76-78.

MOSCHES, Julio César
"¿Con Qué Algodón?" Puerto Wint 81, p. 36.

MOSES, Daniel David
"Panty Favour." MalR (57) Ja 81, pp. 110-111.

MOSES, Joseph
"Bar Ledge." NewYorker (57:17) 15 Je 81, p. 40.

MOSES, W. R.
"Outlines." Northeast (3:10) Wint 81, pp. 3-5.

"Snares." PoNow (6:2 issue 32) 81, p. 8.
"A Small Mansion." PoNow (6:2 issue 32) 81, p. 8.

MOSKIN, Ilene
"In Reply." OhioR (26), p. 53.
"Letter During a Separation (for Harry Kondoleon)." OhioR (26), pp.
    54-55.
"A View of Titian's Mary Magdalene." Iowa (12:1) Wint 81, p. 110.

MOSS, Greg
"Madonna with Child: Vietnam 1975." AmerS (50:2) Spr 81, p. 236.

MOSS, Howard
"In Umbria." NewYorker (57:6) 30 Mr 81, p. 42.
"News From The Border." ParisR (23:79) Spr 81, p. 248.
"No Harm." NewYorker (57:43) 14 D 81, p. 40.
"Tango: The South Bronx." Chelsea (39) 81, p. 79.
"Upstairs, Queens." Antaeus (40/41) Wint-Spr 81, pp. 362-363.
"Variation on a Theme by Kenneth Koch." Antaeus (40/41) Wint-Spr 81,
    p. 364.

MOSS, Stanley
"For James Wright 1927-1980." AmerPoR (10:6) N-D 81, p. 18.

MOTT, Robert De see De MOTT, Robert

MOUCHARD, Claude
From "Marriage" (tr. by Linda Orr). SenR (10:2/11:1) 79-80, pp. 133-
    135.
From "Perdre." SenR (10:2/11:1) 79-80, pp. 132-134.

MOULTON-BARRETT, Donalee
"One Word: Forever." PottPort (3) 81, p. 10.

MOUW, Gudrun
"The Head" (tr. of Elisabeth Borchers). WebR (6:2) 81, p. 36.
"It Is" (tr. of Elisabeth Borcher). CharR (7:1) Spr 81, pp. 52-53.
"On a Hero" (tr. of Elisabeth Borchers). WebR (6:2) 81, p. 36.

MOYLES, Lois
"The Prodigal Son." NewYorker (57:4) 16 Mr 81, p. 42.

MUELLER, Lisel
"Before the Credits Appear on the Screen." Poetry (139:3) D 81, p.
    129.
"Facets." GeoR (35:4) Wint 81, p. 759.
"Fugitive." Poetry (139:3) D 81, p. 127.
"Full Moon." Poetry (139:3) D 81, p. 130.
"Heard By Moonlight." Tendril (11) Sum 81, p. 56.
"Milkweed Pods in Winter." GeoR (35:4) Wint 81, p. 758.
"Southpaw." GeoR (35:2) Sum 81, p. 258.
"Stalking the Poem." Poetry (139:3) D 81, pp. 131-132.
"What is Left to Say." Poetry (139:3) D 81, p. 128.

MUELLER, Melinda
"Climbing a Mountain under the Ocean." Iowa (12:1) Wint 81, pp. 115-
    116.

MUELLER, RosseAnna M.
   "The New Doctor Livingstone" (tr. of Gianpiero Neri). PoNow (5:6 issue 30) 81, p. 31.
   "Transfer" (tr. of Luciano Erbb). PoNow (5:6 issue 30) 81, p. 15.

MUIR, Lloyd
   "Grandfather." PottPort (3) 81, p. 51.
   "Phylogeny II: Survival Traits." Harp (263:1577) O 81, p. 14.

MULDOON, Paul
   "Edward Kienholz The State Hospital." ConcPo (14:2) Aut 81, p. 46.
   "Mushrooms." ConcPo (14:2) Aut 81, pp. 44-45.

MULLEN, Harryette
   "Momma Sayings." OP (31/32) Aut 81, pp. 149-150.

MULLER, Erik
   "Poor Kids." Northeast (3:11) Sum 81, p. 35.

MULLIGAN, J. B.
   "Indian Summer." Wind (10:39) 80, p. 45.
   "Office Workers." Sam (106) 81, p. 59.

MULRANE, Scott H.
   "After Seeing Your Face on the News." Wind (11:41) 81, p. 36.

MUÑOZ MOLINA, Teodosio
   "Barrio Modelo." Mairena (2:5) Aut 80, p. 74.
   "Cambio de traje." Mairena (2:5) Aut 80, pp. 73-4.
   "Hijo." Mairena (2:6) 80, p. 52.
   "Vida burguesa (Carta a Manuel de la Puebla)." Mairena (2:6) 80, pp. 52-53.

MUNRO, Madeline
   "Afed." Stand (22: 2) 81, p. 70.

MURA, David
   "Baltimore." HiramPoR (30) Spr-Sum 81, p. 32.
   "Lan Nguyen: The Uniform Of Death (1971)." AmerPoR (10:1) Ja-F 81, p. 33.

MURAWSKI, Elisabeth
   "Firewatch." SouthernPR (21:2) Aut 81, p. 32.
   "Haze." PortR (27: 1) 81, p. 11.
   "Into Existence: To Wonder At." SouthernPR (21:2) Aut 81, p. 31.
   "Leap." PortR (27: 1) 81, p. 11.
   "On Garments of the Sea." SouthernHR (15:1) Wint 81, p. 31.
   "Painting Found in the Lap of a Poem." LitR (24:3) Spr 81, p. 386.
   "Quite without Reason." HolCrit (18:3) Je 81, p. 10.

MURDY, Anne Elizabeth
   "Bobolink." Prima (6/7) 81, p. 63.

MURFIN, Ross
   "Death of a Dog." LittleR (7:1, issue 15) 81, p. 18.

MURO, Saisei
"Summer Flower" (tr. by Graeme Wilson). DenQ (16:4) Wint 81, p. 35.

MURPHY, Earl Paulus
"Once Men Worked With Sod." Aspect (77/79) 81, p. 152.

MURPHY, Frank
"Crossing Over." HangL (39) Wint 80-81, p. 22.
"Everything should come easy." HangL (39) Wint 80-81, p. 21.

MURPHY, Mardy
"Cour de Bois." 13thM (5:1/2) 80, p. 11.
"Mary Jemison." 13thM (5:1/2) 80, p. 13.
"Seminole Legend About Corn." 13thM (5:1/2) 80, p. 14.
"They Are Also Called." 13thM (5:1/2) 80, p. 12.

MURPHY, Mary P.
"Exposure." CapeR (16:2) Sum 81, p. 12.
"Invitation." CapeR (16:2) Sum 81, p. 12.
"Spring Contagion." CapeR (16:2) Sum 81, p. 12.

MURPHY, Rich
"Deep Down We Are Still Fish." PoNow (6:3 issue 33) 81, p. 32.
"Fish Market." PoNow (6:3 issue 33) 81, p. 32.
"A Fox in Snow." PortR (27: 2) 81, p. 86.

MURPHY, Richard
"Dry Stonework." ConcPo (14:2) Aut 81, p. 4.
"Tony White at Inishbofin 1959." ConcPo (14:2) Aut 81, p. 58.

MURPHY, Sheila E.
"The News." Vis (7) 81, n. p.
"Recession." WindO (38) Spr-Sum 81, pp. 32-33.
"Tornado Warning." WindO (38) Spr-Sum 81, pp. 33-34.
"In Translation." Vis (7) 81, n. p.
"The Visiting Nurses' Book Sale." WindO (38) Spr-Sum 81, pp. 31-32.
"World's End." CapeR (16:2) Sum 81, p. 38.

MURRAY, Catherine
"Three Poems" (1, 2, 3). Tele (17) 81, pp. 98-100.

MURRAY, G. E.
"On the Train to Dubuque." CharR (7:1) Spr 81, p. 5.
"Swear to God: A Prologue from Memory." CharR (7:1) Spr 81, pp. 6-7.
"Winter Sermon: Northside Chicago." SouthernHR (15:1) Wint 81, p. 34.

MURRAY, Joan
"Twelve Bathing Suits." PoNow (6:3 issue 33) 81, p. 32.

MURRAY, Philip
"Confidences d'artiste." MichQR (20:2) Spr 81, pp. 72-73.
"The Tracks." Iowa (12:1) Wint 81, p. 106.

MURZI, Marco Ramírez see RAMIREZ MURZI, Marco

MUSGRAVE, Susan
"After the Battle." Mund (12/13) 80-81, p. 65.

MUSIL, Robert
"Sheep, Looked at Another Way" (tr. by E. M. Valk). Pequod (12) 81,
pp. 32-33.

MUSKE, Carol
"Friend on Stilts. " Ploughs (6:4) 81, p. 72.
"The Funeral. " Ploughs (6:4) 81, p. 73.

MUTIS, Alvaro
"Moirologhia. " SenR (12:1/2) 81, pp. 84-86.
"From Moirologhia" (tr. by Frederic Will). SenR (12:1/2) 81, pp. 85-
87.
"Una palabra. " SenR (12:1/2) 81, pp. 80-82.
"A Word" (tr. by Frederic Will). SenR (12:1/2) 81, pp. 81-83.

MYCUE, Edward
"What Is the Matter with Nijinsky?" Im (7:2) 1981, p. 12.

MYERS, Alan
"The Russian God" (tr. of Prince P. A. Vyazemsky). NewYRB (28:2)
19 F 81, p. 31.
"Verses on the Winter Campaign 1980" (tr. of Joseph Brodsky).
NewYRB (28:14) 24 S 81, p. 8.

MYERS, Douglas H.
"Survey Chief at Bigfork. " CutB (16) Spr-Sum 81, p. 21.

MYERS, Jack
"On Nights Like This. " CimR (54) Ja 81, p. 16.

MYERS, Joan Rohr
"Entering a Relationship. " PortR (27: 1) 81, p. 26.

MYERS, Marjorie A.
"Fairy Tales. " DenQ (16:3) Aut 81, p. 24.

MYERS, Neil
"Chicken Little. " CharR (7:1) Spr 81, pp. 41-42.
"My Brother's Woods. " CharR (7:1) Spr 81, pp. 42-43.

MYONG-OK
"If I Had Been As I Am Now" (tr. by Michael Stephens). Pequod (13)
81, p. 74.

MYRSIADES, Kostas
"After a Settlement of Debts" (tr. of Yannis Ritsos, w/ Kimon Friar).
PoNow (5:6 issue 30) 81, p. 24.
"Announcement" (tr. of Yannis Ritsos, w/ Kimon Friar). Hudson (34:2)
Sum 81, p. 171.
"The Dark Shop" (tr. of Yannis Ritsos, w/ Kimon Friar). PoNow (5:6
issue 30) 81, p. 24.
"Dilettantism" (tr. of Yannis Ritsos, with Kimon Friar). Ploughs (6:4)
81, pp. 198-199.
"False Discoveries" (tr. of Yannis Ritsos w/ Kimon Friar). ArizQ
(37:3) Aut 81, p. 244.
"The Get-Away" (tr. of Yannis Ritsos, w/ Kimon Friar). PoNow (5:6
issue 30) 81, p. 24.
"Improvised Achievement" (tr. of Yannis Ritsos, with Kimon Friar).

"Improvised Achievement" (tr. of Yannis Ritsos, with Kimon Friar).
   Ploughs (6:4) 81, p. 199.
"The Iron Mosaic" (tr. of Yannis Ritsos, with Kimon Friar).   Ploughs
   (6:4) 81, p. 196.
"The Laugh" (tr. of Yannis Ritsos).   SenR (12:1/2) 81, p. 23.
"Level Duration" (tr. of Yannis Ritsos, w/ Kimon Friar).   Hudson (34:
   2) Sum 81, p. 169.
"Like Travelers" (tr. of Yannis Ritsos, w/ Kimon Friar).   Hudson (34:
   2) Sum 81, p. 170.
"Multidimensional" (tr. of Yannis Ritsos).   SenR (12:1/2) 81, p. 25.
"Penelope's Despair" (tr. of Yannis Ritsos).   NewOR (8:1) Wint 81, p.
   14.
"Perpetual" (tr. of Yannis Ritsos, w/ Kimon Friar).   Hudson (34:2)
   Sum 81, p. 169.
"Remembrances" (tr. of Yannis Ritsos, w/ Kimon Friar).   Hudson (34:
   2) Sum 81, p. 172.
"The Roots" (tr. of Yannis Ritsos, w/ Kimon Friar).   Hudson (34:2)
   Sum 81, pp. 170-171.
"The Scarecrow" (tr. of Yannis Ritsos, with Kimon Friar).   Ploughs
   (6:4) 81, p. 197.
"Traces" (tr. of Yannis Ritsos, w/ Kimon Friar).   Hudson (34:2) Sum
   81, p. 172.

NADEL, Alan
   "To February."   NewEngR (3:3) Spr 81, p. 415.

NAESS, Kate
   "Magic" (tr. by Nadia Christensen).   PoNow (5:6 issue 30) 81, p. 31.

NAGY, Agnes Nemes
   "The Geyser" (tr. by Bruce Berlind).   PoNow (5:6 issue 30) 81, p. 24.
   "The Scene" (tr. by Bruce Berlind).   PoNow (5:6 issue 30) 81, p. 24.
   "Trees" (tr. by Nicholas Kolumban).   DenQ (16:1) Spr 81, p. 73.

NAGY, Francis B. De see De NAGY, Francis B.

NAKAD, Salim
   "A river races its own course" (tr. by Mirene Ghossein).   Nimrod (24:
   2) Spr/Sum 81, p. 48.

NAKAE, Toshio
   "Love Song" (tr. by Graeme Wilson).   DenQ (16:4) Wint 81, p. 52.

NAPIER, Alan
   "Address to Hart Crane."   LitR (24:3) Spr 81, p. 376.
   "An American Education."   FourQt (30:2) Wint 81, pp. 32-33.
   "The Walter Symphony."   AmerPoR (10:1) Ja-F 81, p. 37.

NAPOLEONE, Mary Ann
   "Curtains for the Mermaid."   Vis (7) 81, n. p.

NAPOUT, Lilian de
   "A veces."   LetFem (7:2) Aut 81, p. 53.
   "Ayer murió."   LetFem (7:2) Aut 81, p. 54.
   "Estás ya fuera."   LetFem (7:2) Aut 81, p. 53.
   "Puedo."   Puerto Wint 81, p. 23.
   "Puedo ponerle."   LetFem (7:2) Aut 81, p. 55.
   "Soy."   LetFem (7:2) Aut 81, p. 52.
   "Vivo por los espejos."   LetFem (7:2) Aut 81, p. 52.

NARANJO, Carmen
    "Listen" (tr. by Nicomedes Suarez). Mund (12/13) 80-81, p. 119.

NARVESON, Robert
    "Dream Poem." Peb (21) 81, p. 105.
    "Urban Night Pastoral." Peb (21) 81, p. 106.

NASH, Mildred J.
    "Hera, Elderly." Vis (7) 81, n. p.
    "A Muse from Miss Moore." BallSUF (22:4) Aut 81, p. 49.

NASIO, Brenda
    "Beyond Santa Fe." StoneC (8: 3) Spr 81, pp. 42-43.

NATAMBU, Kofi
    Eight poems. Obs (7:1) Spr 81, pp. 62-68.

NATELEGE, Schaarazetta
    "The Violin's Song." Obs (7:1) Spr 81, p. 61.

NATHAN, Leonard
    "Cold Snap." PraS (55:1/2) Spr-Sum 81, p. 296.
    "Confession." ThRiPo (17/18) 81, p. 49.
    "Hello Again." PraS (55:1/2) Spr-Sum 81, p. 295.
    "Portrait." PraS (55:1/2) Spr-Sum 81, p. 295.
    "The Reunion." PoNow (6:1 issue 31) 81, p. 16.
    "Wedding." PraS (55:1/2) Spr-Sum 81, p. 296.

NATHAN, Norman
    "Dinner at 'The Market Place' in Charleston." Poem (41) Mar 81, p.
    40.
    "Doubts." Poem (41) Mar 81, p. 38.
    "Elegy Written in a Hall of Fame." Poem (41) Mar 81, p. 41.
    "Frenzy." Poem (41) Mar 81, p. 37.
    "Love's Purity." Poem (41) Mar 81, p. 39.
    "Moses." SoCaR (14: 1) Aut 81, p. 72.
    "Till We Have Built Our Neighborhood in the World's Green and Pleas-
    ant Land." Poem (41) Mar 81, p. 42.

NATHANIEL, Isabel
    "Two Camelias in a Vase." Iowa (11:4) Aut 80, p. 83.

NATSUME, Soseki
    "Sickbed" (tr. by Graeme Wilson). DenQ (16:4) Wint 81, p. 26.

NAUEN, Elinor
    "American Sentiment" (w/ Rachel Walling). Tele (17) 81, p. 13.
    "Dinner With The Folks" (w/ Rachel Walling). Tele (17) 81, p. 13.
    "Maine." Tele (17) 81, p. 12.

NAVARRE, Jane Piirto
    "Lilac Time." PoNow (6:3 issue 33) 81, p. 32.

NEELON, Am
    "Canticle of the Surgeon as Lover." PoetryNW (22:2) Sum 81, pp. 28-
    29.

NELMS, Sheryl L.
    "Cumulus Clouds." PoNow (6:3 issue 33) 81, p. 32.

NELSON, Nils
   "Try Your Luck." ThRiPo (17/18) 81, pp. 13-14.

NELSON, Paul
   "Ash." Ploughs (6:4) 81, p. 134.
   "Bone Davening." DenQ (16:4) Wint 81, p. 78.
   "Cleaning the Outhouse." Ploughs (6:4) 81, p. 132.
   "Milking." Ploughs (6:4) 81, p. 131.
   "The Snake in the Spring-Box." Ploughs (6:4) 81, p. 133.
   "Reasons for a Pond." DenQ (16:4) Wint 81, p. 79.
   "Spring Deer." DenQ (16:4) Wint 81, p. 76.
   "Travelling with Animals." DenQ (16:4) Wint 81, p. 77.

NELSON, Rodney
   "Belated Festival" (tr. of Wilhelm Lehmann). EnPas (12) 81, p. 4.
   "Final Evening" (tr. of Wilhelm Lehmann). EnPas (12) 81, p. 6.
   "In Solothurn" (tr. of Wilhelm Lehmann). EnPas (12) 81, p. 7.
   "The Magpie" (tr. of Wilhelm Lehmann). EnPas (12) 81, p. 5.

NEMEROV, Howard
   "Achievement." MassR (22:1) Spr 81, p. 42.
   "Because You Asked about the Line between Prose and Poetry." PoNow
     (6:2 issue 32) 81, p. 25.
   "During a Solar Eclipse." PoNow (6:2 issue 32) 81, p. 25.
   "Innocence." MassR (22:1) Spr 81, p. 42.
   "Instant Replay." MassR (22:1) Spr 81, p. 41.
   "On Growth and Form." MassR (22:1) Spr 81, p. 41.
   "The Plain Fact." PoNow (6:2 issue 32) 81, p. 25.

NEMET-NEJAT, Murat
   "Come, when you can" (tr. of Feriha Aktan). Mund (12/13) 80-81, p.
     115.

NEMSER, Paul
   "Without a Whisper." Pequod (12) 81, p. 14.
   "It Would Be Better" (for Rebecca). Pequod (12) 81, pp. 12-13.

NEPO, Mark
   "At a Standstill." CharR (7:1) Spr 81, p. 47.
   "Cirrus." DenQ (16:4) Wint 81, p. 114.
   "The rusted Pail." EnPas (12), 81, p. 37.

NERI, Gianpiero
   "The New Doctor Livingstone" (tr. by RoseAnna M. Mueller). PoNow
     (5:6 issue 30) 81, p. 31.

NERUDA, Pablo
   "Amores: Matilde" (tr. by Ben Belitt). Mund (12/13) 80-81, pp. 370-
     373.
   "Goodness" (tr. by Margaret Sayers Peden). NewOR (8:1) Wint 81, p.
     6.
   "I Know Nothing At All" (tr. by Ben Belitt). Mund (12/13) 80-81, p.
     374.
   "Injustice" (tr. by Alastair Reid). Nat (232:12) 28 Mr 81, p. 376.
   "Nine poems" (tr. by Alastair Reid). AmerPoR (10:3) My-Je 81, pp.
     21-27.
   "Ode To The Sea Light" (tr. by Walt Curtis). PortR (27: 2) 81, p. 39.
   "Sexual Water" (tr. by Walt Curtis). PortR (27: 2) 81, p. 38.

"Smoke" (tr. by Margaret Sayers Peden). NewOR (8:1) Wint 81, pp.
   8-9.
"Stones of the Sky" (3, 10, 18, 21, 22, 24) (tr. by James Nolan).
   PoNow (5:6 issue 30) 81, pp. 32-33.
"The Struggle to Keep One's Memories" (tr. by Margaret Sayers Peden).
   NewOR (8:1) Wint 81, p. 7.
"Suddenly, A Ballad" (tr. by Alastair Reid). Nat (232:19) 16 My 81, p.
   606.
"The Tent" (tr. by Margaret Sayers Peden). NewOR (8:1) Wint 81, p.
   5.
"The United Fruit Company" (tr. by Walt Curtis). PortR (27: 2) 81, p.
   39.
"Walking Around" (tr. by Walt Curtis). PortR (27: 2) 81, p. 38.

NERVAL, Gérard de
   "Vision." SenR (12:1/2) 81, p. 50.
   "A Vision" (tr. by Michael Benedikt). SenR (12:1/2) 81, p. 51.

NESSE, Ase-Marie
   "Fyodor Dostoyevsky" (tr. by Nadia Christensen). PoNow (5:6 issue 30)
      81, p. 33.

NETSER, Eli
   "A Bird Beloved and Strange" (tr. by Bernhard Frank). PoNow (5:6
      issue 30) 81, p. 33.

NEWCOMER, Duncan D.
   "After She Did Not Make the Trip." KanQ (13:1) Wint 81, p. 114.

NEWMAN, Jerry
   "Premature Minutes." Wind (10:39) 80, pp. 30-31.

NEWMAN, P. B.
   "Cleaning Guns." Outbr (6/7) Aut 80-Spr 81, p. 5.
   "Frisbees." SouthernPR (21: 1) Spr 81, p. 66.
   "Mary Ball Washington." KanQ (13:1) Wint 81, pp. 38-39.
   "Mr. Cherry at Bat." Outbr (6/7) Aut 80-Spr 81, p. 6.
   "A Southern Story." Outbr (6/7) Aut 80-Spr 81, pp. 3-4.
   "Washington, Waiting for a Parley." KanQ (13:1) Wint 81, p. 38.
   "Wolf Rock Second Visit." KanQ (13:3/4) Sum-Aut 81, p. 189.

NIATUM, Duane
   "Cedar Man." MalR (60) O 81, pp. 20-21.
   "Journey to the Islands." MalR (60) O 81, p. 22.
   "The Realities of Autumn." MalR (60) O 81, p. 19.
   "The Waterfall Song." MalR (60) O 81, p. 18.

NICHOLAS, Christopher
   "Kansas: before the war." Ploughs (7:1) 81, pp. 50-51.

NICHOLS, Joye
   "My Special One." Meadows (2:1) 81, p. 71.

NICHOLS, Martha
   "Female Astronomy" (The Milky Way). Sam (116) 81, p. 31.
   "Running In The Rain." Sam (117) 81, p. 51.

NICHOLSON, Joseph
   "The Autopsy Man." PoNow (6:1 issue 31) 81, p. 12.

"The Giant Sour Gnat of Jupiter." PoNow (6:1 issue 31) 81, p. 12.
"A Solomonic Decision." PoNow (6:1 issue 31) 81, p. 12.

NIDITCH, B. Z.
"Emily Dickinson's Welcome House." HolCrit (18:3 [i. e. 4]) O 81, p. 18.
"Grandfather Mendes." StoneC (9: 1-2) Aut-Wint 81/82, p. 58.
"In Our Monstrous Infancy." WebR (6:2) 81, p. 78.
"Marc Chagall." Os (12) Spr 81, p. 10.
"Poet's Night." Os (13) Aut 81, p. 24.
"The Sink." WebR (6:2) 81, p. 79.
"Spanish Country." StoneC (9: 1-2) Aut-Wint 81/82, p. 59.
"Tree-House Poem." CapeR (16:2) Sum 81, p. 27.

NIEMINEN, Pertti
"from This Life Is So Fast: "Everything's already said, written" (tr. by Richard Dauenhauer). PoetryE (6) Aut 81, p. 34.

NIGGEMANN, Clara
"La Rosa Ha Dicho Ya Todos Sus Pétalos." Puerto Wint 81, p. 37.

NIKARCHOS
Epitaph: "On Markos, the Family Doctor." SouthernR (17:4) Aut 81, p. 999.

NIKOLAIDIS, Aristotle
"A Brief Code for Poets" (tr. by Kimon Friar). Poetry (139:2) N 81, p. 85.
"Views of an Ascetic" (tr. by Kimon Friar). Poetry (139:2) N 81, p. 86.
"Word" (tr. by Kimon Friar). Poetry (139:2) N 81, p. 84.

NIKOLAVA, Dobrina
"At the Beach" (tr. of Kolyo Sevov, w/ Greg Gatenby). PortR (27: 1) 81, p. 14.
"Beside Rhodes" (tr. of Kolyo Sevov, w/ Greg Gatenby). PortR (27: 1) 81, p. 14.
"The Dolphin" (tr. of Vanja Petkova, w/ Greg Gatenby). PortR (27: 1) 81, p. 14.

NIMNICHT, Nona
"The Loaned Child." CalQ (18/19) 81, pp. 138-139.

NIMS, John Frederick
"Epitaph for a Poet" (tr. of Homero Aridjis). Mund (12/13) 80-81, p. 69.
"Sonnet Almost Petrarchan." SewanR (89:4) Aut 81, p. 514.
"Yin and Yang." SewanR (89:4) Aut 81, p. 515.

NISETICH, Frank J.
"Odes I. 9" (tr. of Horace). SenR (12:1/2) 81, p. 31.

NIST, John
"Between Cockcrow and Heartbreak." Poem (43) Nov 81, p. 54.
"Dream and Wake." ArizQ (37:3) Aut 81, p. 264.
"Ecce Homo." Poem (43) Nov 81, p. 52.
"Negative Prayer For Lent." Poem (43) Nov 81, p. 53.
"Transition." ArizQ (37:4) Wint 81, p. 334.

NIXON, Colin
  "Passages of Time." ChrC (98:18) 20 My 81, p. 565.
  "Uprooted Tree." ChrC (98:36) 11 N 81, p. 1152.
  "Urban/Rural." ChrC (98:35) 4 N 81, p. 1116.

NOAILLES, Anna, Comtesse de
  "Pathetique" (tr. by Elinor Briefs). Vis (5) 81, n. p.

NOCERINO, Kathryn
  "Bride in the Bath." Tele (17) 81, p. 105.
  "Old Blood." Tele (17) 81, p. 104.

NOGG, Ozzie
  "Forecast." Wind (11:41) 81, p. 17.

NOGUERAS, Luis Rogelio
  "Materia de poesía." Areito (27: 28) 81, p. 50.

NOLAN, James
  "Italy, I want to Kiss." NewL (47:4) Sum 81, pp. 86-87.
  "Stones of the Sky" (3, 10, 18, 21, 22, 24) (tr. of Pablo Neruda).
    PoNow (5:6 issue 30) 81, pp. 32-33.

NOLL, Bink
  "Blue Thirst." NewEngR (4:2) Wint 81, pp. 250-1.
  "On Loving a One-Legged Man." NewEngR (4:2) Wint 81, p. 252.

NORDHAUS, Jean
  "The Death of an Immigrant Mother." Hudson (34:4) Wint 81, pp. 559-
    560.
  "My Father Blowing Smoke Rings." Hudson (34:4) Wint 81, p. 560.

NORDSTRÖM, Lars
  "Esoteric icelandic bath 1241" (tr. by Erland Anderson and the author).
    PortR (27: 2) 81, p. 40.
  "The hot water caves of Myvatn are they measured in meters or feet?"
    (tr. by Erland Anderson and the author). PortR (27: 2) 81, p. 40.
  "Smoky Bay" (tr. by Erland Anderson and the author). PortR (27: 2)
    81, p. 40.

NORRIS, Gunilla
  "Enough." SouthernPR (21: 1) Spr 81, p. 23.

NORSE, Harold
  "Once in La Linea." Os (12) Spr 81, p. 7.
  "The Relationship." PoNow (6:2 issue 32) 81, p. 7.

NORTH, Gloria
  "The Hypocrite." Sam (109) 81, p. 41.

NORTH, Michael
  "Mallory's Camera." CarolQ (34:2) Aut 81, p. 61.

NORTH, Susan
  "Encore." OP (31/32) Aut 81, p. 142.

NORTHSUN, Nila
  "Dirt on the move." Meadows (2:1) 81, p. 64.
  "I was thinking about death again." Meadows (2:1) 81, p. 63.

NORTON, Camille
"Felicani of Milk Street." Aspect (77/79) 81, p. 153.
from "Harrisburg Poem" (2, 3). Aspect (77/79) 81, pp. 154-155.

NOVACK, Robin K.
"Last Night We Lived." CalQ (18/19) 81, p. 50.
"The Sound." CalQ (18/19) 81, p. 51.

NOVAK, Helga
"Ein Hemd." Mund (11:2) 79, p. 38.
"Neu Geboren." Mund (11:2) 79, p. 40.
"Reborn" (tr. by Sammy McLean). Mund (11:2) 79, p. 41.
"Respect" (tr. by Sammy McLean). Mund (11:2) 79, pp. 39, 41.
"Respekt." Mund (11:2) 79, pp. 38, 40.
"A Shirt" (tr. by Sammy McLean). Mund (11:2) 79, p. 39.

NOVEMBER, Sharyn
"The Aquarium Caretaker." Shen (32:2) 81, p. 46.
"At the Eye Clinic." Poetry (138:3) Je 81, pp. 142-143.
"Travelling by Water." Poetry (138:3) Je 81, pp. 140-141.

NOWAK, Ernst
"Ohne Gedanken." Mund (11:2) 79, p. 74.
"Without Thinking" (tr. by Herbert Kuhner). Mund (11:2) 79, p. 75.

NOWAK, Tadeusz
"An Everyday Psalm" (tr. by Leszek Elektorowicz and Frederic Will).
SenR (12:1/2) 81, p. 113.
"Psalm Codzienny." SenR (12:1/2) 81, p. 112.

NOWLAN, Alden
"On the Road." PottPort (3) 81, p. 40.
"This is a Recording." PottPort (3) 81, p. 4.
"Visiting Friends" (for Jerry and Leta Clayden). PottPort (3) 81, p.
14.

NOWLAN, Michael O.
"Illusion." PottPort (3) 81, p. 26.
"Overtaken" (for my first girl friend). PottPort (3) 81, p. 9.

NUÑEZ, Carlos Hugo
"La Pena." Mairena (3:7) 81, pp. 49-50.
"Poema de Amor." Mairena (3:7) 81, p. 49.
"Primera persona." Mairena (3:7) 81, p. 51.
"Visión constante." Mairena (3:7) 81, pp. 50-51.

NUÑEZ, Oscar Florentino see FLORENTINO NUÑEZ, Oscar

NUÑEZ, Victor Rodríguez see RODRIGUEZ NUÑEZ, Victor

NURKSE, D.
"Travel by Night." HangL (40) Aut 81, p. 54.

NUWER, Hank
"Threesome: Four AM." Meadows (2:1) 81, p. 76.

OATES, Joyce Carol
"Another." Hudson (34:1) Spr 81, p. 62.

"Boredom." VirQR (57:4) Aut 81, pp. 636-637.
"First Dark." ParisR (23:80) Sum 81, p. 130.
"Forgetful America." Hudson (34:1) Spr 81, pp. 60-61.
"The Loss." VirQR (57:4) Aut 81, pp. 637-638.
"Luxury of Sin." GeoR (35:4) Wint 81, p. 805.
"The Magic Show." MalR (57) Ja 81, p. 124.
"Night Thoughts." CalQ (18/19) 81, pp. 78-79.
"The Proofs of God." Hudson (34:1) Spr 81, pp. 61-62.
"Small Miracles." ParisR (23:79) Spr 81, p. 249.
"The Stone Orchard." MalR (57) Ja 81, p. 125.
"Thimble-sized Soul." ParisR (23:80) Sum 81, p. 129.
"The Wasp." Atl (248:4) N 81, p. 28.

O'BRIEN, John
"American Scene." PoNow (6:3 issue 33) 81, p. 33.
"Black-Eyed Susan." PoNow (6:3 issue 33) 81, p. 33.
"Blue Heron." WindO (38) Spr-Sum 81, p. 6.
"Drunkwalk." PoNow (6:3 issue 33) 81, p. 33.
"Early Spring: Green Bank, West Virginia." WindO (38) Spr-Sum 81,
    p. 5.
"Mojo Poem." SouthernHR (15:4) Aut 81, p. 326.
"A Postcard To Gary Stein." StoneC (9: 1-2) Aut-Wint 81/82, p. 75.
"Summer Dusk on Mohawk Street." PoNow (6:3 issue 33) 81, p. 33.

O'BRIEN, William P.
"My Father's Shadow." KanQ (13:3/4) Sum-Aut 81, p. 8.

OBUCHOWSKI, Peter
"The Sting." KanQ (13:1) Wint 81, p. 138.

OCA, Marco Antonio Montes de see MONTES DE OCA, Marco Antonio

O'CALLAGHAN, Patricia
"Autumn" (tr. of Guillaume Apollinaire). PoNow (5:6 issue 30) 81, p.
    5.
"The Crocuses" (tr. of Guillaume Apollinaire). PoNow (5:6 issue 30)
    81, p. 5.
"Marizibill" (tr. of Guillaume Apollinaire). PoNow (5:6 issue 30) 81,
    p. 5.

OCHESTER, Ed
"Against Bullshit" (tr. from B. Brecht). MinnR (17) Aut 81, p. 9.
"Robert Bly Watched by Elves." OP (31/32) Aut 81, p. 50.
"This Poem Is for Margaret." GeoR (35:3) Aut 81, p. 643.

O'CONNOR, Michael Patrick
"The Soprano" (for Birgit Nilsson). Shen (31:3) 80, p. 48.

O'GRADY, Desmond
"Mistress Mine" (for Florence Tamburro). OP (31/32) Aut 81, pp. 45-
    48.
"Suburban Recluse." OP (31/32) Aut 81, p. 70.

O'HEHIR, Diana
"Body." Poetry (139:1) O 81, p. 24.
"The Dead Pull Us Toward Winter." Poetry (139:1) O 81, p. 26.
"Family Tragedy." MassR (22:2) Sum 81, p. 373.
"Firelight." PoetryNW (22:2) Sum 81, pp. 37-38.

"Fog." PoetryNW (22:2) Sum 81, p. 38.
"Our World Ends in Radioactive Fire." PoetryNW (22:2) Sum 81, pp.
   38-39.
"Private Song." Poetry (139:1) O 81, p. 23.
"Shore (for my Father)." MassR (22:2) Sum 81, p. 374.
"Snow." Poetry (139:1) O 81, p. 25.
"Television." PoNow (6:1 issue 31) 81, p. 9.

OHMAN, Anne C.
"Annie." BallSUF (22:4) Aut 81, p. 66.

ÖLJER, Bruno K.
"A Jack Daniel's in Tombstone." NewRena (14) Spr 81, p. 53.
"En Jack Daniel's I Tombstone." NewRena (14) Spr 81, p. 52.
"Gambler's Stone." NewRena (14) Spr 81, pp. 49, 51.
"Spelarens Sten." NewRena (14) Spr 81, pp. 48, 50.

OKTENBERG, Adrian
"Hokku." NewL (47:4) Sum 81, p. 98.
"She Pleads Guilty." NewL (47:4) Sum 81, p. 99.
"Summer Elegy." NewL (47:4) Sum 81, p. 98.

OLDKNOW, Anthony
"Anthem for Rusty Saw and Blue Sky." LitR (24:3) Spr 81, p. 377.
"As I Dreamed..." (tr. of Francis Jammes). AntR (39:3) Sum 81, p.
   338.
"At the Bar." CreamCR (6:1) Aut 80, p. 15.
"Barges...." CreamCR (6:1) Aut 80, pp. 12-13.
"Her Father." CreamCR (6:2) 81, pp. 28-30.
"I Think I Am Alone." KanQ (13:1) Wint 81, p. 69.
"I Took the Train to Lourdes" (tr. of Francis Jammes). WebR (6:2)
   81, pp. 31-32.
"In the Morning in the Room." KanQ (13:1) Wint 81, p. 70.
"Rain." CreamCR (6:1) Aut 80, p. 14.
"See in the Months of Autumn..." (for F.V.G.) (tr. of Francis
   Jammes). AntR (39:3) Sum 81, p. 337.
"Shot." CreamCR (6:2) 81, pp. 31-32.
"When I'm Dead" (tr. of Francis Jammes). WebR (6:2) 81, p. 30.

OLDS, Sharon
"Any Case" (tr. of Wisaw Szymborska w/ Grazyna Drabik). Pequod
   (12) 81, p. 1.
"Burn Center." Poetry (139:1) O 81, p. 34.
"Cambridge Elegy" (for Henry Avrell Gerry, 1941-1960). Poetry (139:1)
   O 81, pp. 32-33.
"The Ideal Father." PraS (55:4) Wint 81-82, pp. 64-5.
"Japanese Farmhouse, California (November 1942)." Pequod (12) 81,
   p. 78.
"The Moment." PraS (55:4) Wint 81-82, p. 64.
"The Number Pi" (tr. of Wislawa Szymborska, w/ Grazyna Drabik).
   AntR (39:1) Wint 81, p. 77.
"The Quest." Poetry (139:1) O 81, p. 31.
"The Shrink's Wife." Aspect (77/79) 81, p. 156.
"The Signal" (for Col. J. P. Phillips). Poetry (139:1) O 81, p. 30.
"Things That Are Worse Than Death (for Margaret Randall)." Nat
   (232:15) 18 Ap 81, p. 474.
"The Winter After Your Death." NewYorker (56:48) 19 Ja 81, p. 99.

OLES, Carole
    "Better Vision." Poetry (138:4) Jl 81, p. 226.
    "Like Musical Chairs." Poetry (138:4) Jl 81, p. 225.
    "Poem Found in an Ensign's Journal." Aspect (77/79) 81, p. 159.

OLIVA, Jorge
    "A la Sombra de los Portales" (a Borge). Lugar (1:1) 79, p. 15.
    "La Casa." Lugar (1:1) 79, p. 14.

OLIVER, Mary
    "First Snow." NewYorker (57:3) 9 Mr 81, p. 73.
    "The Gardens." GeoR (35:2) Sum 81, pp. 378-379.
    "A Poem for the Winter Nights." WestHR (35:4) Wint 81, pp. 344-45.
    "Rain in Ohio." Atl (247:4) Ap 81, p. 126.

OLIVER, Raymond
    "Aux Miens." SouthernR (17:4) Aut 81, p. 991.
    "Carcasonne." Ploughs (6:4) 81, p. 178.
    "Distance." SouthernR (17:4) Aut 81, p. 989.
    "To Fireflies in an Old Yard." SouthernR (17:4) Aut 81, p. 990.
    "Hobson's Choice." SouthernR (17:4) Aut 81, p. 991.
    "Moral Anecdote." SouthernR (17:4) Aut 81, p. 990-1.
    "Thinking About Jane Austen." Thrpny (5) Spr 81, p. 11.
    "Twenty Years After." SouthernR (17:4) Aut 81, p. 989.

OLMO OLMO, José R.
    "Las peras del olmo." Mairena (2:6) 80, pp. 82-83.

OLSEN, William
    "In Memory of Jean Rhys." Shen (32:1) 80, pp. 81-83.
    "To Darwin Reading the Bible." AntR (39:2) Spr 81, p. 202.

OLSON, Andrew
    "Ice Fishing." Peb (21) 81, p. 90.

OLSON, Elder
    "A Clock." NewYorker (57:2) 2 Mr 82, p. 42.

OLSON, Nancy A.
    "Thoroughbreds" (for Victor). Confr (22) Sum 81, p. 53.

OLSON, Toby
    "Standard --9, Just One (Some) Of Those Things." Bound (9:1) Aut 80,
        pp. 183-190.
    "Standard--11, Anything Goes (The Emerald City: a Key)." SunM (11)
        Spr 81, pp. 116-121.

O'MALLEY, Emanuela
    "The Keening." KanQ (13:1) Wint 81, p. 68.

O'NEILL, Alexandre
    "The Hanged" (tr. by Alexis Levitin). PortR (27: 2) 81, p. 31.
    "Muddling Lullabye" (tr. by Alexis Levitin). PortR (27: 2) 81, p. 31.

ONO, Tosaburo
    "Battleship" (tr. by Graeme Wilson). DenQ (16:4) Wint 81, p. 42.

OPALOV, Leonard
    "Laundry Room." Wind (10:39) 80, p. 34.

OPERE, Fernando
"De aquí a mil años" (A Mariano). RevI (9:4) Wint 79-80, p. 624.

OPITZ, Martin
"Epitaph for a Dog. " SouthernR (17:4) Aut 81, p. 1000.

OPPENHEIMER, Felix Franco see FRANCO OPPENHEIMER, Felix

ORAA, Pedro de
"Affirmation of the Word" (tr. by Harry Haskell). Mund (12/13) 80-81,
    p. 301.

ORE, Pam
"Migrating. " CreamCR (6:1) Aut 80, pp. 102-103.

OREL, Gwen
"Lapse. " HangL (40) Aut 81, p. 64.

ORESICK, Peter
"God Stunning Paradise. " Vis (7) 81, n. p.

ORR, Ed
"Toyonobu: Nakamura Kiyosaburō and Onoe Kikugorō as Lovers Playing
    a Samisen. " BallSUF (22:4) Aut 81, p. 48.

ORR, Gregory
"Pastoral: 'We Are Going Home.'" SenR (10:2/11:1) 79-80, p. 71.
"Sleep Song. " SenR (10:2/11:1) 79-80, p. 72.

ORR, Linda
"Bluish wolf" (tr. of Raymond Queneau). SenR (10:2/11:1) 79-80, p.
    95.
"The column spreads silence" (tr. of Charles Racine). SenR (10:2/11:1)
    79-80, p. 111.
"Cool suns whiten" (tr. of Charles Racine). SenR (10:2/11:1) 79-80, p.
    109.
"Did she vacillate" (tr. of Robert Davreau). SenR (10:2/11:1) 79-80,
    p. 147.
"Dirigible silences in the blue and round" (tr. of Robert Davreu).
    SenR (10:2/11:1) 79-80, p. 143.
"Effective in the long run..." (tr. of Judith Schlanger). SenR (10:2/
    11:1) 79-80, pp. 129-131.
"The feast over, the visitor walks away..." (tr. of Raymond Queneau).
    SenR (10:2/11:1) 79-80, p. 97.
"The Fires" (tr. of Yves Bonnefoy). SenR (10:2/11:1) 79-80, p. 101.
"The Folliage as Example" (tr. of Alain Delahaye). SenR (10:2/11:1)
    79-80, p. 119.
"I brake so suddenly..." (tr. of Jacques Réda). SenR (10:2/11:1) 79-
    80, p. 113.
"I write the third gospel..." (tr. of Danielle Sarréra). SenR (10:2/
    11:1) 79-80, p. 123.
"If we consider..." (tr. of Danielle Sarréra). SenR (10:2/11:1) 79-80,
    p. 125.
"Interlude" (tr. of Michel Deguy). SenR (10:2/11:1) 79-80, p. 107.
"It is from a single soul..." (tr. of Danielle Sarréra). SenR (10:2/
    11:1) 79-80, p. 127.
"Known like September rain" (tr. of Robert Davreu). SenR (10:2/11:1)
    79-80, p. 141.

"Like to the other fool for dust" (tr. of Robert Davreu). SenR (10:2/11:1) 79-80, p. 139.
"Make-Up" (tr. of Michel Deguy). SenR (10:2/11:1) 79-80, p. 105.
"Marriage: the pact is constantly present..." (tr. of Claude Mouchard). SenR (10:2/11:1) 79-80, pp. 133-135.
"On the Rue de Tournelles..." (tr. of Jacques Réda). SenR (10:2/11:1) 79-80, p. 115.
"On the Signifier" (tr. of Yves Bonnefoy). SenR (10:2/11:1) 79-80, p. 103.
"The Orbit" (tr. of Alain Delahaye). SenR (10:2/11:1) 79-80, p. 121.
"The Play of Branches" (tr. of Alain Delahaye). SenR (10:2/11:1) 79-80, p. 117.
"Silence made-blue the words of the façade" (tr. of Robert Davreu). SenR (10:2/11:1) 79-80, p. 137.
"So that far from the plumbed" (tr. of Robert Davreu). SenR (10:2/11:1) 79-80, p. 141.
"The solid sky where ricochet in stars" (tr. of Robert Davreu). SenR (10:2/11:1) 79-80, p. 145.
"These urges to live grabbing me" (tr. of Georges Perros). SenR (10:2/11:1) 79-80, p. 99.
"Ties" (tr. of Alain Delahaye). SenR (10:2/11:1) 79-80, p. 119.
"Toward Beauty" (tr. of Alain Delahaye). SenR (10:2/11:1) 79-80, p. 117.

ORTEGA, Adolfo García see GARCIA ORTEGA, Adolfo

ORTEGA, Julio
"Lección de la Naturaleza." Inti (9) Spr 79, p. 103.
"Libro del Alba." Inti (9) Spr 79, p. 103.
"Museo de Historia Peruana." Inti (9) Spr 79, p. 104.

ORTENBERG, Neil
"Lord Whiskey." PortR (27: 2) 81, p. 88.

ORTOLANI, Al
"Below the hospital bed." WindO (39) Wint 81/82. On calendar.
"Night Fall along the Big Piney River." MidwQ (22:4) Sum 81, p. 372.
"A Night of Lilac and Shadow." Wind (10:39) 80, p. 35.
"The Visitation." MidwQ (22:4) Sum 81, p. 373.

OSAKI, Mark
"My Father Holding Squash." ThRiPo (17/18) 81, p. 50.

OSBORN, Kelley
"Cello Woman" (for Nancy). Prima (6/7) 81, p. 37.

OSHIKOCHI no MITSUNE
From The Kokinshu: "Grebe" (tr. by Graeme Wilson). WestHR (35:4) Wint 81, p. 347.

OSING, Gordon
"Matinee" (for Tom Carlson). PoetryNW (22:4) Wint 81-82, p. 37.

OSKAR, Jón
"Flower-poem." Vis (6) 81, n. p.
"Friður." SenR (12:1/2) 81, pp. 176-78.
"Peace" (tr. by Frederic Will). SenR (12:1/2) 81, pp. 177-79.

OSTASZEWSKI, Krzysztof
"Opus 12, A Comedy" (tr. by Wojtek Stelmaszynski). MichQR (20:4)
Aut 81, p. 423.
"Opus 30" (tr. by Wojtek Stelmaszynski). MichQR (20:4) Aut 81, pp.
423-24.
"Opus 75" (tr. by Wojtek Stelmaszynski). MichQR (20:4) Aut 81, p.
424.

ÖSTERGREN, Jan
"Contemporary" (tr. by John Matthias and Göran Printz-Pahlson).
ChiR (32:2) Aut 80, pp. 44-47.
"Indian Summer I" (tr. by John Matthias and Göran Printz-Pahlson).
ChiR (32:2) Aut 80, pp. 41-43.

OSTRIKER, Alicia
"Message from the Sleeper at Hell's Mouth." US1 (14/15) Aut/Wint 81,
pp. 18-19.
"The Pure Unknown." Hudson (34:3) Aut 81, p. 381.

OTIS, Emily
"Letter to My Daughter." Wind (11:42) 81, pp. 27-28.
"On Reading a Book About Friends." Wind (11:42) 81, pp. 28-29.
"On the Ohio." Wind (11:42) 81, pp. 26-27.
"Return." Wind (11:42) 81, p. 26.

OTT, Gil
"Middle-Range Voice Parts for a Proposed Four-Voice Poem." SunM
(11) Spr 81, pp. 73-74.

OVERTON, Ron
"The Gunfighter." OP (31/32) Aut 81, pp. 79-80.
"The Motor Boys Under the Sea." PoetryNW (22:1) Spr 81, p. 47.

OWEN, Garnet
"De-cross Him." ChrC (98:12) 8 Ap 81, p. 376.

OWEN, Guy
"Commencement Day." SouthernPR (21:2) Aut 81, p. 7.
"For Dorothy" (Re-Dedication, April 6, 1981). SouthernPR (21:2) Aut
81, p. 7.
"My Son's Illness" (for Leslie). SouthernPR (21:2) Aut 81, p. 6.
"Stormbirth" (for Jimmy, March 5, 1956). SouthernPR (21:2) Aut 81,
p. 6.

OWEN, Maureen
"Frogs Ringing Gongs in a Skull." OP (31/32) Aut 81, p. 173.
"Novembers or Straight Life." SunM (11) Spr 81, p. 122.

OWEN, Sue
"The Spell." PoNow (6:3 issue 33) 81, p. 26.
"Two Wrongs." PoNow (6:3 issue 33) 81, p. 26.

OWENS, Don E.
"A Plowboy Dreams." Aspect (77/79) 81, p. 160.

OWENS, Rochelle
"American revolutionary." PoNow (6:1 issue 31) 81, p. 30.
"Eat Bookstore." UnmOx (22) Wint 81, pp. 46-51.
"The Raw Material of Dr. Williams' Love." Confr (21) Wint 81, p. 41.

"The sacred heart is American revolutionary." PoNow (6:1 issue 31)
    81, p. 30.

OWER, John
    "The Pit." Poem (42) Jul 81, p. 26.
    "Sow" (for C. A.). Poem (42) Jul 81, pp. 24-25.
    "The Wolf Child." Poem (42) Jul 81, p. 23.

OXENHORN, Harvey
    "Fall Colours." SouthernR (17:3) Sum 81, p. 578.
    "Time's Fool." SouthernR (17:3) Sum 81, p. 577.

OXHOLM, José M.
    "Vendimia." Puerto Wint 81, p. 38.

OYENARD, Sylvia Puentes de see PUENTES de OYENARD, Sylvia

PACERNICK, Gary
    "Poet of Silences." Im (7:3) 81, p. 12.

PACHECO, Javier
    "Califas Dreams." Metam (3:2/4:1) 80-81, p. 56.
    "Days Are Gone." Metam (3:2/4:1) 80-81, p. 57.

PACHECO, José Emilio
    "Bounds" (tr. by Elinor Randall). Mund (12/13) 80-81, p. 315.
    "Turner's Landscape" (tr. by Anthony Edkins). Chelsea (40) 81, p. 85.
    "Venice" (tr. by Anthony Edkins). Chelsea (40) 81, p. 84.

PACK, Robert
    "Going and Staying." NewEngR (4:2) Wint 81, pp. 280-1.
    "Making Her Will." Poetry (138:4) Jl 81, pp. 223-224.
    "Painter To Self-Portrait." Tendril (11) Sum 81, pp. 57-58.
    "Persuasion." PraS (55:1/2) Spr-Sum 81, pp. 122-3.
    "Secrets." PraS (55:1/2) Spr-Sum 81, pp. 124-5.
    "Sister To Sister." Tendril (11) Sum 81, pp. 59-60.
    "Trying to Separate." GeoR (35:2) Sum 81, pp. 362-363.

PADGETT, Ron
    "Poem." ParisR (23:79) Spr 81, p. 250.

PADILLA, Martha
    "El Brujulario." Mairena (3:7) 81, p. 73.
    "Poda imperativa." Mairena (3:7) 81, p. 74.
    "Tiempo ceñido." Mairena (3:7) 81, p. 75.
    "Visión del hielo." Mairena (3:7) 81, p. 74.

PADRON, Justo Jorge
    "The Boy and the Stone" (tr. by Louis Bourne). Stand (22: 2) 81, p.
    48.

PAGE, William
    "After the War." Wind (11:42) 81, p. 30.
    "From What I Remember." WindO (38) Spr-Sum 81, p. 29.
    "Hurt." WebR (6:2) 81, p. 82.
    "If the Bacon Takes Time." WindO (38) Spr-Sum 81, p. 28.
    "Neruda." Wind (11:42) 81, p. 31.
    "The Sickness." WindO (38) Spr-Sum 81, p. 30.
    "Spring Forward, Fall Back." CharR (7:1) Spr 81, p. 13.

PALADINO, Thomas
   "Last Garden at Giverny." AntR (39:3) Sum 81, p. 341.

PALCHI, Alfredo de see De PALCHI, Alfredo

PALLISTER, Jan
   "Five from Sixth Day Priorities" (tr. of Lamine Diakhatê). EnPas (12)
      81, pp. 8-9.
   "Tenebrae" (tr. of Juan Ramón Jiménez). PoNow (5:6 issue 30) 81, p.
      19.

PALMA, Marigloria
   "Alegría en la renuncia." Mairena (2:5) Aut 80, p. 18.
   "Espina y sombra." Mairena (2:5) Aut 80, p. 17.
   "Llanto por una ausência." Mairena (2:5) Aut 80, p. 17.
   "Reto." Mairena (2:5) Aut 80, p. 15.
   "Tono de convivencia." Mairena (2:5) Aut 80, p. 18.

PALMA, Michael
   "Cats." Northeast (3:10) Wint 81, p. 11.
   "The Flowers." Northeast (3:10) Wint 81, p. 10.
   "In the End." Northeast (3:10) Wint 81, p. 10.

PALMA, Ray di see DiPALMA, Ray

PALMER, Kathleen Olive
   "Baptismal: The Water Spirit Speaks." Poem (41) Mar 81, p. 22.
   "Clear Water, Fresh Fruit." Poem (41) Mar 81, p. 19.
   "Walking with the Bees in McGregor Park." Poem (41) Mar 81, pp.
      20-21.

PALMER, Michael
   "Echo (a commentary)." Sulfur (1) 81, pp. 179-181.
   "Echo (alternate text)." Sulfur (1) 81, pp. 176-178.
   "Echo (texte antiparallèle pour Pascal Quignard)." Sulfur (1) 81, pp.
      170-175.

PAOLI, Francisco Matos see MATOS PAOLI, Francisco

PAPADHITSAS, P. D.
   "Other Ways" (tr. by Kimon Friar). Poetry (139:2) N 81, p. 83.

PAPADHOPOULOS, Yannis
   "The Greek Colony in Alexandria" (tr. by Kimon Friar). Poetry (139:2)
      N 81, pp. 97-98.

PAPE, Greg
   "The Night: Ensenada." GeoR (35:3) Aut 81, pp. 628-629.
   "Notes from a Reunion" (for Lance and Margaret). OP (31/32) Aut 81,
      pp. 109-110.
   "Out Here the Weather." PoNow (6:1 issue 31) 81, p. 8.
   "Summer Storm." PoNow (6:1 issue 31) 81, p. 8.

PARENTI, Jane
   "Conversation/ Spring Piece" (for Virginia Blakelock). Im (7:2) 1981,
      p. 10.

PARFITT, Tudor
   "A Meeting with My Father" (tr. with Glenda Abramson of Yehuda

Amichai). Poetry (138:3) Je 81, p. 138.
"Rain in a Foreign Land" (tr. with Glenda Abramson of Yehuda Amichai).
    Poetry (138:3) Je 81, p. 139.
"Things That Have Been Lost" (tr. with Glenda Abramson of Yehuda
    Amichai). Poetry (138:3) Je 81, p. 137.

PARHAM, Robert
    "Dreams, Burning." WebR (6:1) 81, p. 80.

PARINI, Jay
    "The Miner's Wake." Ploughs (6:4) 81, p. 58.
    "The Sea Lily." Atl (247:3) Mr 81, p. 32.

PARISH, Barbara Shirk
    "A Woman Stays a Long Time Old." KanQ (13:3/4) Sum-Aut 81, p.
    202.

PARISH, Michael
    "First Daughter." Ploughs (7:2) 81, pp. 93-94.

PARKER, Martha
    "Noh Dancers." SoCaR (14: 1) Aut 81, p. 65.
    "Rubais and Fries." Wind (11:41) 81, p. 19.

PARKER, Mary
    "The Mother Lets Go" (for Susan Mickelberry). SouthernPR (21:2) Aut
    81, pp. 37-38.

PARKERSON, Michelle
    Nine poems. Obs (6: 1/2) Spr-Sum 80, pp. 186-194.

PARRAGUEZ, Eledino
    "If I Wanted to Explain my My Days" (tr. by Martha Wright). PortR
    (27: 2) 81, p. 94.

PARRATT, Ann
    "Absinthe." PortR (27: 2) 81, p. 29.
    "Altitude." PortR (27: 2) 81, p. 29.

PARRIS, Peggy
    "Olga Escapes, 1917." Tendril (10) Wint 81, p. 36.
    "Rimbaud." Kayak (56) 81, p. 50.

PARRY, Marian
    "Scythian Gold." Tendril (10) Wint 81, pp. 37-38.

PASOLINI, Pier Paolo
    "The Ashes of Gramsci" (tr. by Claudia Anderson). SenR (12:1/2) 81,
    pp. 143-55.
    "Le ceneri di Gramsci." SenR (12:1/2) 81, pp. 142-154.
    "A Desperate Vitality" (tr. by Claudia Anderson). SenR (12:1/2) 81,
    pp. 157-67.
    "Una disperata vitalità." SenR (12:1/2) 81, pp. 156-66.
    "Testament Verses" (tr. by Claudia Anderson). SenR (12:1/2) 81, pp.
    139-141.
    "Versi da testamento." SenR (12:1/2) 81, pp. 138-40.

PASQUALE, E. di see DiPASQUALE, E.

PASS, John
Ten poems. MalR (58) Ap 81, pp. 10-16.

PASTAN, Linda
"Ark" (for Stephen and Elizabeth). Field (24) Spr 81, pp. 39-40.
"Cold Front." ThRiPo (17/18) 81, pp. 52-53.
"Extremities." Poetry (138:6) S 81, p. 330.
"History." StoneC (9: 1-2) Aut-Wint 81/82, p. 47.
"I Am Learning to Abandon the World." Poetry (138:6) S 81, p. 329.
"In Spring" (for James Wright). StoneC (9: 1-2) Aut-Wint 81/82, p. 46.
"November." VirQR (57:1) Wint 81, p. 75.
"To a Friend Moving Away." PoNow (6:2 issue 32) 81, p. 22.
"We Come to Silence." GeoR (35:4) Wint 81, p. 762.
"Weather Forecast." Antaeus (40/41) Wint-Spr 81, p. 365.
"What I Learned Last Week" (for William Stafford). StoneC (9: 1-2)
    Aut-Wint 81/82, p. 48.
"What We Want." VirQR (57:1) Wint 81, pp. 75-76.

PASTAN, Rachel
"Apple." PoNow (6:3 issue 33) 81, p. 33.

PASTERNAK, Boris
"An Even More Sultry Dawn" (tr. by Mark Rudman and Bondan Boy-
    chuk). AmerPoR (10:4) Jl-Ag 81, p. 38.
"Balashov" (tr. by Mark Rudman and Bohdan Boychuk). AmerPoR (10:
    4) Jl-Ag 81, p. 39.
"Concerning These Poems" (tr. by Mark Rudman and Bohdan Boychuk).
    PoNow (5:6 issue 30) 81, p. 35.
"Darling--the terror! It comes back!" (tr. by Mark Rudman and Bohdan
    Boychuk). PoNow (5:6 issue 30) 81, p. 34.
"The Old Park" (tr. by Jon Stallworthy and Peter France). Hudson
    (34:4) Wint 81, pp. 550-551.
"Our Thunderstorm" (tr. by Mark Rudman and Bohdan Boychuk). PoNow
    (5:6 issue 30) 81, p. 34.
"The Picture" (tr. by Mark Rudman and Bohdan Boychuk). PoNow (5:6
    issue 30) 81, p. 35.
"Rain" (tr. by Mark Rudman and Bohdan Boychuk). AmerPoR (10:4) Jl-
    Ag 81, p. 39.
"The Substitute" (tr. by Mark Rudman and Bohdan Boychuk). AmerPoR
    (10:4) Jl-Ag 81, p. 38.
"A Sultry Night" (tr. by Mark Rudman and Bohdan Boychuk). PoNow
    (5:6 issue 30) 81, pp. 34-35.
"Winter Approaches" (tr. by Jon Stallworthy and Peter France). Hudson
    (34:4) Wint 81, p. 549.

PATAKI, Heidi
"The Animal" (tr. by Herbert Kuhner). Mund (11:2) 79, p. 75.
"Das Tier." Mund (11:2) 79, p. 74.

PATERNO IBARRA, Graciela
"Despertar María" (with Suzana Albornoz Stein). LetFem (7:1) Spr 81,
    pp. 90-91.

PATERSON, Evangeline
"Armaments Race." Pequod (13) 81, p. 50.
"Visitation." Pequod (13) 81, p. 51.

PATILIS, Yánnis
"I Can Still Talk with You" (tr. by Kimon Friar). PoNow (5:6 issue

30) 81, p. 33.
"Life Traces" (tr. by Kimon Friar). PoNow (5:6 issue 30) 81, p. 33.

PATTERSON, Caroline
  "From the Slimer." CutB (16) Spr-Sum 81, p. 51.
  "In Praise of Famous Men." CutB (16) Spr-Sum 81, pp. 52-53.

PATTON, Kimberly
  "Antiquities" (for Larry). Prima (6/7) 81, p. 37.

PAUKER, John
  "The Burning of Books" (tr. of Bertolt Brecht). PoNow (5:6 issue 30)
    81, p. 8.

PAUL, James
  "Hearken." Iowa (11:4) Aut 80, p. 84.

PAUL, Jay S.
  "Dishes Dried and Put Away." PoetryNW (22:1) Spr 81, pp. 36-37.
  "Orchard and Chicken Coop." CapeR (17:1) Wint 81, p. 3.
  "Right Before the Parade." CreamCR (6:2) 81, p. 111.
  "Round In An Inclement Season." StoneC (8: 3) Spr 81, p. 38.
  "U-Haul." PoetryNW (22:1) Spr 81, pp. 37-38.
  "Working My Way." CapeR (17:1) Wint 81, p. 4.

PAUL, John
  "Foot Prints 1980." Tele (17) 81, p. 82.
  "Natural Sewer Water." Tele (17) 81, p. 82.
  "Upper Crust." Tele (17) 81, p. 83.

PAULI, Ken
  "Old Jock." StoneC (9: 1-2) Aut-Wint 81/82, p. 55.

PAULIOS, Lefteris
  "A Poet" (tr. by Kimon Friar). PoNow (5:6 issue 30) 81, p. 39.
  "The Mirror" (tr. by Kimon Friar). PoNow (5:6 issue 30) 81, p. 39.
  "The Sower of the Year" (tr. by Kimon Friar). PoNow (5:6 issue 30)
    81, p. 39.

PAU-LLOSA, Ricardo
  "Carthage." KanQ (13:3/4) Sum-Aut 81, p. 203.
  "Knot." BelPoJ (31:3) Spr 81, p. 27.
  "Lille." EnPas (12), 81, p. 28.

PAVLICH, Walter
  "The Bridgetender" (for Verlena Richardson). PortR (27: 2) 81, p. 88.
  "Living North of Yachats, West of Friends" (for Melinda). CutB (17)
    Aut-Wint 81, p. 15.
  "The Room." PortR (27: 2) 81, p. 88.

PAVLOVIC, Miodrag
  "The Last Supper" (tr. by Alan Williamson). Ploughs (7:2) 81, pp. 64-
    65.
  "Nativity" (tr. by Richard Tillinghast). Ploughs (7:2) 81, p. 61.
  "The Transfiguration" (tr. by Alan Williamson). Ploughs (7:2) 81, pp.
    62-63.

PAVLOVSKI, Radovan
  "from Country of Lakes" (tr. by Eugene Prostov with Elisavietta

Ritchie). Vis (5) 81, n. p.

PAYACK, Peter
"The Final Resting Place for Lost Thoughts." Tele (17) 81, p. 134.
"20,000,001,980." Tele (17) 81, p. 135.

PAYNE, John Burnett
"Doubles" (for Eleanore Prokop). Wind (11:40) 81, pp. 25-26.

PAYNE, Nina
"Marriage." Ploughs (6:4) 81, pp. 145-146.

PAZ, Lydia Caro see CARO PAZ, Lydia

PAZ, Octavio
"Wind from All Compass Points" (tr. by Paul Blackburn). Mund (12/13)
80-81, pp. 1-6.

PEACOCK, Molly
"Hell, I'm Afraid." Shen (31:4) 80, pp. 28-29.
"Just About Asleep Together." NewL (47:4) Sum 81, p. 72.
"The Lull." NewL (47:4) Sum 81, p. 72.
"My Vast Presumption." NewL (47:4) Sum 81, p. 73.
"Old Roadside Resorts." Shen (31:4) 80, p. 29.
"So, When I Swim to the Shore." Shen (31:4) 80, p. 28.

PEARCE-LEWIS, Kathleen
"Cinderella." Vis (7) 81, n. p.

PEASE, Deborah
"Maintenance." Chelsea (40) 81, pp. 78-79.
"To Muffle the Grief of Revolution." Confr (21) Wint 81, p. 88.
"Refuge." CharR (7:1) Spr 81, p. 25.

PEASE, Roland
"Ant Anxiety." Confr (21) Wint 81, p. 70.
"Spring Fever # 1." Confr (21) Wint 81, p. 71.

PECK, Gail
"Leaving Home" (for my sister). Vis (6) 81, n. p.

PECK, John
"The Bloody Sark." Ploughs (7:2) 81, pp. 81-82.
"Passacaglias." Ploughs (6:4) 81, pp. 174-177.
"The Vigil of Parmenides." Ploughs (7:2) 81, p. 80.

PECKENPAUGH, Angela
"Ham Chamberlayne to His Mother from Camp Walker, Dec. 17, 1864
4½ Miles South of Petersburgh." NowestR (19:1/2), pp. 67-8.

PEDEN, Margaret Sayers
"Goodness" (tr. of Pablo Neruda). NewOR (8:1) Wint 81, p. 6.
"Smoke" (tr. of Pablo Neruda). NewOR (8:1) Wint 81, pp. 8-9.
"The Struggle to Keep One's Memories" (tr. of Pablo Neruda). NewOR
(8:1) Wint 81, p. 7.
"The Tent" (tr. of Pablo Neruda). NewOR (8:1) Wint 81, p. 5.

PEDERSON, Miriam
"Conversion." Prima (6/7) 81, p. 8.

PEECH, John
  "Arrival." ParisR (23:81) Aut 81, p. 61.
  "Old Man." ParisR (23:81) Aut 81, p. 60.
  "The River." ParisR (23:81) Aut 81, p. 58.
  "Sunday Mass." ParisR (23:81) Aut 81, pp. 57-58.
  "The Violinist." ParisR (23:81) Aut 81, p. 59.

PELAEZ, Juan Sánchez see SANCHEZ PELAEZ, Juan

PELL, Derek
  "Don't Wake Rimbaud." Tele (17) 81, pp. 58-61.

PELLETIER, G.
  "Marked for Cutting." CapeR (16:2) Sum 81, p. 21.

PELLETIER, Marianne
  "Autobiography." HangL (39) Wint 80-81, p. 65.

PELLICER, Carlos
  From Dutch Week: "Friday" (tr. by Anthony Edkins). Chelsea (40) 81,
    p. 82.
  From Dutch Week: "Tuesday-Rembrandt" (tr. by Anthony Edkins).
    Chelsea (40) 81, p. 82.

PENALOZA, Gabino Coria
  "And I Awaken into Nothingness" (tr. by Elsie Schmidt Jachowski).
    Vis (5) 81, n. p.

PENDLETON, Conrad
  "Morning Song of an Urban Student." KanQ (13:3/4) Sum-Aut 81, p.
    198.

PENNA, Sandro
  "Fourteen Poems" (tr. by W. S. Di Piero). PoNow (5:6 issue 30) 81, pp.
    36-37.
  "The Journey" (tr. by W. S. Di Piero). PoNow (6:1 issue 31) 81, p.
    43.
  "Spring News" (tr. by W. S. Di Piero). PoNow (6:1 issue 31) 81, p.
    43.

PENNANT, Edmund
  "Reprisals." Confr (21) Wint 81, p. 40.

PENNINGTON, Lee
  "Blackbird Fruit." Wind (10:39) 80, p. 32.

PENSAK, Susan
  Nine poems (tr. of Alejandra Pizarnik). 13thM (5: 1/2) 80, pp. 57-75.

PENZI, J.
  "Cyclone." Mund (12/13) 80-81, p. 126.
  "The Voice." Mund (12/13) 80-81, p. 126.

PERAITA GONZALEZ, Graciano
  "Tu, Por Aquí, Conmigo." Puerto Wint 81, p. 39.

PERALTA, Bertalicia
  "Like a Hollow Snail." Mund (12/13) 80-81, p. 237.
  "Silence" (tr. by Thomas Hoeksema). Mund (12/13) 80-81, p. 237.

PERCHIK, Simon
"*." NoAmR (266:4) D 81, p. 40.
"* A burial emptied this page." HiramPoR (30) Spr-Sum 81, p. 33.
"By height. Kids stripping the peak." Im (7:2) 1981, p. 7.
"Each raindrop, from behind." BelPoJ (32:1) Aut 81, pp. 34-35.
"I took friends." PoNow (6:1 issue 31) 81, p. 18.
"This hinge each night louder." BelPoJ (32:1) Aut 81, p. 35.
"You Added Shade." SouthwR (66:2) Spr 81, p. 185.

PERDOMO, Francisco Pérez see PEREZ PERDOMO, Francisco

PERELMAN, Bob
"3 Noises." Tele (17) 81, p. 33.

PERET, Benjamin
"Adventures of a Toe" (tr. by Jane Barnard and A. F. Moritz). Bound
(9:2) Wint 81, p. 249.
"Aventures d'un Orteil." Bound (9:2) Wint 81, p. 248.
"A Bunch of Carrots" (tr. by Jane Barnard and A. F. Moritz). Bound
(9:2) Wint 81, p. 249.
"A Couple of Words" (tr. by Keith Hollaman). SenR (12:1/2) 81, p. 53.
"Deux mots." SenR (12:1/2) 81, p. 52.
"The Farthese Face" (tr. by Jane Barnard and A. F. Moritz). Bound
(9:2) Wint 81, p. 251.
"Il n'y a qu'une merveille sur la terre." SenR (12:1/2) 81, p. 54.
"Laughing Stock" (tr. by Jane Barnard and A. F. Moritz). Bound (9:2)
Wint 81, p. 251.
"Le Plus Lointain Visage." Bound (9:2) Wint 81, p. 250.
"Samson." Bound (9:2) Wint 81, pp. 250-255.
"Samson" (tr. by Jane Barnard and A. F. Moritz). Bound (9:2) Wint
81, pp. 251-255.
"Souffre-Douleurs." Bound (9:2) Wint 81, p. 250.
"There Is Only One Wonder on Earth" (tr. by Keith Hollaman). SenR
(12:1/2) 81, p. 55.
"Une Botte de Carottes." Bound (9:2) Wint 81, p. 248.

PEREZ, Ilma Valenzuela de see VALENZUELA de PEREZ, Ilma

PEREZ, María de los Milagros
"Nana del borrachito." Mairena (2:6) 80, p. 87.

PEREZ, Nola
"Blountstown, 1938." Wind (11:41) 81, pp. 37-38.
"At Eleven, I Love a Boy Named Norman." Wind (11:41) 81, p. 37.

PEREZ PERDOMO, Francisco
"All is Not a Dream" (tr. by Herman P. Doezeima). Mund (12/13) 80-
81, p. 145.

PEREZ SO, Reynaldo
from "To Die of Another Dream" (tr. by Willis Barnstone). Mund
(12/13) 80-81, pp. 100-102.

PERLMAN, Anne S.
"At the Houghton Library" (for E.D.). CalQ (18/19) 81, p. 89.
"Housewife Riddle." SouthernR (17:3) Sum 81, p. 571.
"The Money." SouthernR (17:3) Sum 81, p. 570.

PERLMAN, John
"Geese crane long necks." PoNow (6:2 issue 32) 81, p. 35.
"Rain pudding." PoNow (6:2 issue 32) 81, p. 35.

PERRON, Lee
"My Love is Alive." CharR (7:1) Spr 81, pp. 14-15.

PERROS, George
"Ces envies de vivre qui me prennent." SenR (10:2/11:1) 79-80, p. 98.
"These urges to live grabbing me" (tr. by Linda Orr). SenR (10:2/11:1) 79-80, p. 99.

PERRUEL, Juan C.
"La Palabra." Puerto Wint 81, p. 6.

PERRY, John O.
"Munch's Voice" (Boston Museum of Fine Arts). StoneC (9: 1-2) Aut-Wint 81/82, p. 37.

PERRY, Richard
"A Short Marriage." CreamCR (6:2) 81, p. 112.

PERRY, Rick
"Kitchen Burning Down or How I Spend My Friday Evenings." WindO (38) Spr-Sum 81, p. 39.

PERRY, Ronald
"The Hollow White." Poetry (139:3) D 81, pp. 165-166.
"In the Smoke." Poetry (139:3) D 81, pp. 168-170.
"The Mirror Walk" (for Miles, recently turned six). Poetry (138:5) Ag 81, pp. 276-277.
"Portrait of a Tree." Poetry (139:3) D 81, p. 167.

PESEROFF, Joyce
"The Captive." Aspect (77/79) 81, p. 157.
"Florida." Aspect (77/79) 81, pp. 157-158.
"To the Skaters." Ploughs (7:2) 81, pp. 139-140.

PESSANHA, Camilo
"Who Polluted, Who Ripped My Linen Sheets" (tr. by Alexis Levitan). ModernPS (10:2,3), p. 91.

PETERNEL, Joan
"The Vigil." KanQ (13:3/4) Sum-Aut 81, p. 152.

PETERS, Nancy
"As I Shall Remember McCleery." Peb (21) 81, pp. 45-46.
"Death Scene, Highway 77." Peb (21) 81, pp. 47-48.
"Making a Hand for the Child." Peb (21) 81, pp. 49-50.
"Poem to Take Along." Peb (21) 81, p. 44.

PETERS, Robert
"Acrostic Poem, For Right and Left Eyes." CreamCR (6:1) Aut 80, p. 78.
"The 1930's." PoNow (6:2 issue 32) 81, p. 32.
"Prince Ludwig and the Drowned Gardner." CreamCR (6:1) Aut 80, pp. 76-77.
"So many steps to the mailbox." PoNow (6:1 issue 31) 81, p. 11.

"Walking back from town at dusk or dark." PoNow (6:1 issue 31) 81, p. 11.

PETERSON, Jim
"The Dock." Poem (42) Jul 81, p. 53.
"Here." Poem (42) Jul 81, p. 55.
"Keeping the Dream." Poem (42) Jul 81, p. 52.
"The Motel." CharR (7:2) Aut 81, pp. 17-18.
"Resistance." Poem (42) Jul 81, p. 54.
"A Son of Stone." CharR (7:2) Aut 81, pp. 18-19.

PETERSON, Karen
"Inheretance." Prima (6/7) 81, p. 7.

PETERSON, Perry
"Eraser" (for A.). CapeR (16:2) Sum 81, p. 41.

PETIT, Michael
"Without Fears." MissouriR (4:2) Wint 80-81, p. 13.

PETKOVA, Vanja
"The Dolphin" (tr. by Greg Gatenby and Dobrina Nikolava). PortR (27:1) 81, p. 14.

PETREMAN, David A.
"Looking for Cats." MalR (58) Ap 81, p. 100.

PETRIE, Paul
"Crows over Amsterdam." Comm (108:15) 28 Ag 81, p. 467.
"Florence Revisited." NewL (48:1) Aut 81, p. 51.
"Mine Song." NewL (48:1) Aut 81, p. 50.
"The Old Poet Looks at the Night Sky." ArizQ (37:2) Sum 81, p. 100.
"Rest Home." AmerS (50:4) Aut 81, p. 526.
"The Runners." Comm (108:4) 27 F 81, p. 126.

PETROSKY, Anthony
"Change." Iowa (12:1) Wint 81, p. 118.

PETROSKY, Tony
"My Father Is." Agni (14) 81, p. 61.

PETTINELLA, Dora
"Silence" (tr. of Giuseppe Ungaretti). Mund (12/13) 80-81, p. 377.
"The Seasons" (tr. of Giuseppe Ungaretti). Mund (12/13) 80-81, pp. 378-379.

PETTIT, Carolyn
"Nora's Mother" (whose baby has Down's Syndrome). CreamCR (7:1) 81, p. 51.

PETTY, Lyle
"Para Mi Viejo." StoneC (8: 3) Spr 81, p. 33.

PETURSSON, Hannes
"Old Storyteller." Vis (7) 81, n. p.

PEYCERE ROMAÑA, Valdir
"Canto al Río de la Plata." Puerto Wint 81, p. 40.

PFINGSTON, Roger
  "Broken Trust." NewL (48:1) Aut 81, p. 46.
  "Double Exposure." EnPas (12) 81, p. 18.
  "The Equestriennce." Im (7:3) 81, p. 12.
  "Goose Bones." Im (7:3) 81, p. 12.
  "An Indiana Poet Travels East to MacDowell with the Migrating Coyotes."
      MalR (58) Ap 81, p. 119.
  "Lantern Boxes." Im (7:2) 1981, p. 5.
  "The New Year." Im (7:2) 1981, p. 5.
  "A Rainy Day." MalR (58) Ap 81, p. 118.
  "Virtue." EnPas (12) 81, p. 19.

PHILBRICK, Stephen
  "Haylike and After." PoNow (6:1 issue 31) 81, p. 32.
  "Let It Fall On Me." NewL (47:4) Sum 81, pp. 74-75.
  "Untitled." ThRiPo (17/18) 81, p. 56.

PHILLIPS, Dennis
  "from: Two Cross." Sulfur (2) 81, pp. 188-190.

PHILLIPS, Dorrie
  "Red Flame." PottPort (3) 81, p. 25.

PHILLIPS, Jayne Anne
  "Sanitive." OP (31/32) Aut 81, p. 138.

PHILLIPS, Louis
  "Amatorio." Poem (43) Nov 81, p. 34.
  "As Ignorant as the Man in the Moon." Poem (43) Nov 81, p. 38.
  "Fingers." Poem (43) Nov 81, p. 39.
  "Lying In." BallSUF (22:3) Sum 81, p. 44.
  "Meteor Shower." Poem (43) Nov 81, p. 37.
  "Primary Worlds." Poem (43) Nov 81, pp. 35-36.
  "Sweaters." Poem (43) Nov 81, p. 40.

PHILLIPS, Robert
  "Figures of the Past." OntR (15) Aut-Wint 81-82, p. 28.
  "Flatworms." PoNow (6:2 issue 32) 81, p. 10.
  "A Model Education." PoNow (6:1 issue 31) 81, p. 18.
  "Promising." OntR (15) Aut-Wint 81-82, p. 29.
  "Sharks" (for Tom Baker). ThRiPo (17/18) 81, p. 55.
  "The Suit of Clothes." PoNow (6:2 issue 32) 81, p. 10.
  "Woodchuck Redux." OntR (15) Aut-Wint 81-82, p. 27.

PHILLIS, Yannis
  "Look at The Netherlands Sky." StoneC (8: 3) Spr 81, pp. 14-15.

PHINNEY, A. W.
  "The Need for a Morning Meal on the Shore of the Sea of Galilee."
      ChrC (98:35) 4 N 81, p. 1123.

PHOCAS, Nikos
  "Crane and Vulture" (tr. by Kimon Friar). PoNow (5:6 issue 30) 81,
      p. 37.
  "Timetable for Fairview" (tr. by Kimon Friar). PoNow (5:6 issue 30)
      81, p. 37.

PICANO, Felice
  "Five Posthumous Poems: In the Form of a Letter From Li Po to Tu
      Fu." CreamCR (7:1) 81, pp. 100-103.

PICARD, Maureen
  "Repeating Images." KanQ (13:1) Wint 81, p. 39.

PICHE, Alphonze
  "Brumes." HolCrit (18:5) D 81, p. 12.
  "Fog" (tr. by Gary Wilson). HolCrit (18:5) D 81, p. 12.

PICHON, Ulysses A.
  "All Fly Home" (a letter: staring at Al Jarreau's album cover). Tele
      (17) 81, pp. 50-53.

PICKETT, Thomas
  "Progressions." Wind (10:39) 80, pp. 33-34.

PIERCE, Pamela
  "Roberta." SoDakR (19:3) Aut 81, pp. 76-77.

PIERCY, Marge
  "The Annealing." PartR (48:1) 81, p. 125.
  "Cutting the Grapes Free." OP (31/32) Aut 81, pp. 155-156.
  "A Key To Common Lethal Fungi." Tendril (11) Sum 81, p. 61.
  "Morning Athletes" (For Gloria). OP (31/32) Aut 81, pp. 146-147.
  "Snow, Snow." OP (31/32) Aut 81, p. 171.
  "The Thrifty Lover." UnmOx (22) Wint 81, p. 70.
  "The Twelve-Spoked Wheel Flashing." OP (31/32) Aut 81, pp. 115-116.
  "The world comes back, like an old cat." Aspect (77/79) 81, p. 161.

PIERMAN, Carol
  "Bay of Angels." Tele (17) 81, p. 73.
  "Camp Discovery." Tele (17) 81, p. 73.
  "Listening Post." Tele (17) 81, p. 72.
  "MS Found in a Bottle." Tele (17) 81, p. 73.
  "Prophecy the Same as Fate." Tele (17) 81, p. 72.

PIERMAN, Carol J.
  "Eight Cows." CarolQ (34:1) Sum 81, p. 23.
  "The Shortest Night of the Year." SouthernPR (21:2) Aut 81, p. 49.

PIERO, W. S. di see DiPIERO, W. S.

PIERSON, Philip
  "The Apple." SouthwR (66:2) Spr 81, p. 209.

PIETRI, Pedro
  "Hoy Do Your Eggs Want You? Cont." Lugar (1:1) 79, p. 17.
  "The First Day Of Spring." Lugar (1:1) 79, p. 17.

PIJEWSKI, John
  "Hunting the Passive." NewYorker (57:13) 18 My 81, p. 48.
  "A Man Who Lost His Daughter" (after "Fragments" by S. Dobyns).
      QW (12) Spr-Sum 81, p. 54-5.
  "Short Portrait From Exeter." Tendril (11) Sum 81, p. 62.

PILIA, Guillermo Eduardo
  "Arsénico (I)." Mairena (2:5) Aut 80, p. 67.

"Arsénico (II)." Mairena (2:5) Aut 80, p. 67.
"Arsénico (VII)." Mairena (2:5) Aut 80, p. 67.
"Gaya Ciencia (III)." Mairena (2:5) Aut 80, p. 67.
"Melancolía." Mairena (2:5) Aut 80, p. 68.
"Nuestro Corazón." Mairena (2:5) Aut 80, p. 68.
"Punto Muerto." Mairena (2:5) Aut 80, p. 68.

PILINSZKY, Janos
"Elysium in November" (tr. by Emery George). PoNow (5:6 issue 30)
    81, p. 38.
"Introit" (tr. by Emery George). PoNow (5:6 issue 30) 81, p. 38.
"Passion" (tr. by Emery George). PoNow (5:6 issue 30) 81, p. 38.
"Ravensbruck Passion" (tr. by Emery George). PoNow (5:6 issue 30)
    81, p. 38.
"Van Gogh" (tr. by Emery George). PoNow (5:6 issue 30) 81, p. 38.

PILLIN, William
"Lilith." Kayak (56) 81, p. 68.
"The Waltz." Kayak (56) 81, p. 68.

PIMPL, Bill E.
"Dreams." Meadows (2:1) 81, p. 60.
"The Invisible Man." Meadows (2:1) 81, p. 16.
"My Life Is Like a Raindrop." Meadows (2:1) 81, p. 69.

PINKERTON, Helen
"Autumn Drought" (to the memory of A. Y. W.). SouthernR (17:4) Aut
    81, pp. 983-4.

PINSKY, Robert
"The Saving." ParisR (23:80) Sum 81, pp. 139-140.
"Three on Luck." Antaeus (40/41) Wint-Spr 81, pp. 366-368.

PITA, Juana Rosa
"Colores." Puerto Wint 81, p. 41.

PIZARNIK, Alejandra
"As Water Over a Stone." Mund (12/13) 80-81, p. 26.
"A Condition (Of Being)" (tr. by George McWhirter). Mund (12/13) 80-
    81, p. 25.
"Contemplation." Mund (12/13) 80-81, p. 25.
"A Dream Where Silence is Made of Gold." Mund (12/13) 80-81, p. 26.
Nine poems (tr. by Susan Pensak). 13thM (5:1/2) 80, pp. 57-75.
"Rescue" (for Octavio Paz). Mund (12/13) 80-81, p. 26.
"Vertigo or the Contemplation of Something That Ends." Mund (12/13)
    80-81, p. 25.

PLANZ, Allen
"Sailing to Ireland." OP (31/32) Aut 81, pp. 36-37.

PLATH, Sylvia
"Black Pine Tree In An Orange Light" AmerPoR (10:5) S-O 81, p. 8.
"Incommunicado." AmerPoR (10:5) S-O 81, p. 8.
"Morning In The Hospital Solarium." AmerPoR (10:5) S-O 81, p. 8.
"Rhyme." AmerPoR (10:5) S-O 81, p. 8.

PLESSIS, Nancy Du see DuPLESSIS, Nancy

PLESSIS, Rachel Blau Du see PLESSIS, Rachel Blau Du

PLIMPTON, Sarah
   "A shortened sky." <u>NewYRB</u> (28:11) 25 Je 81, p. 20.

PLUMLY, Stanley
   "After Whistler." <u>Antaeus</u> (43) Aut 81, pp. 34-35.
   from The Book of Poverty and Death: "There is the poverty of children
     shy with child." <u>Iowa</u> (11:2/3) Spr-Sum 80, p. 100.
   "Chertea." <u>GeoR</u> (35:4) Wint 81, pp. 790-791.
   "It seems we are asleep, blind at the bottom" (tr. of Rainer Maria
     Rilke). <u>SenR</u> (12:1/2) 81, p. 5.
   "Kittyhawks." <u>AmerPoR</u> (10:1) Ja-F 81, p. 6.
   "Lapsed Meadow" (for J.W.). <u>Antaeus</u> (40/41) Wint-Spr 81, pp. 371-
     372.
   "Nag's Head." <u>Antaeus</u> (40/41) Wint-Spr 81, pp. 369-370.

PLUMPP, Sterling
   "Behind the Rose" (for Lena Horne). <u>BlackALF</u> (15:2) Sum 81, p. 73.
   "In Remembrance of Fire" (for Hoyt W. Fuller). <u>BlackALF</u> (15:2) Sum
     81, p. 47.

PLYMELL, Charles
   "Cows." <u>Aspect</u> (77/79) 81, p. 167.

PO, Chu-I
   from "The Letter" (tr. by Arthur Waley). <u>NowestR</u> (19:1/2), p. i.

POBO, Kenneth
   "Vampire." <u>CapeR</u> (16:2) Sum 81, p. 32.

POLING, William
   "The Cave at Makapan." <u>PortR</u> (27: 1) 81, p. 32.

POLITO, Robert
   "Dead Cells." <u>Ploughs</u> (7:2) 81, p. 136.

POLLAK, Felix
   "Love Is a Present Tense Noun." <u>Northeast</u> (3:11) Sum 81, p. 6.
   "Weather Vane." <u>Northeast</u> (3:11) Sum 81, p. 6.

POLLENS, David
   "After Cleaning Out the Roof Gutters." <u>NewYorker</u> (57:22) 20 Jl 81, p.
     38.
   "Behind the House." <u>NewYorker</u> (57:22) 20 Jl 81, p. 38.
   "In the Woods." <u>NewRep</u> (184:1/2) 3-10 Ja 81, p. 26.
   "Watching June." <u>NewYorker</u> (57:22) 20 Jl 81, p. 38.

POLLET, Sylvester
   "Sestina for Terry Plunkett." <u>NewEngR</u> (4:1) Aut 81, pp. 102-3.

POLLITT, Katha
   "Archaeology." <u>NewYorker</u> (57:18) 22 Je 81, p. 35.
   "Failure." <u>NewYorker</u> (57:18) 22 Je 81, p. 35.
   "Metaphors of Women." <u>Atl</u> (247:2) F 81, p. 43.
   "Night Blooming Flowers." <u>Atl</u> (247:5) My 81, p. 69.
   "Parthians." <u>Antaeus</u> (40-41) Wint-Spr 81, pp. 373-374.
   "To an Antarctic Traveller." <u>NewYorker</u> (57:18) 22 Je 81, p. 35.
   "Turning Thirty." <u>Pequod</u> (12) 81, p. 11.

POLSTER, J. E.
    "Love Letters." Field (25) Aut 81, pp. 43-44.

PONSOT, Marie
    "Song, from Theophrastus." LittleM (13:1/2) Spr-Sum 79, c1981, p.
      51.

POPA, Vasko
    "Echoing" (tr. by Vasa D. Mihailovich and Ronald Moran). Mund (12/
      13) 80-81, p. 230.
    "The Game of the Ashes" (tr. by Vasa D. Mihailovich). Mund (12/13)
      80-81, p. 229.

POPE, Deborah
    "Preparation." Poem (42) Jul 81, p. 62.
    "Winter Afternoon." Poem (42) Jul 81, p. 61.

PORPETTA, Antonio
    "El Secreto." Os (13) Aut 81, p. 19.

PORTAL, Waldo Leyva see LEYVA PORTAL, Waldo

PORTER, Helen
    "Takeover." PottPort (3) 81, p. 44.

PORTEUS, Mark
    "Hymn." Bound (9:2) Wint 81, p. 148.
    "In Answer." Bound (9:2) Wint 81, pp. 148-149.
    "Untitled." Bound (9:2) Wint 81, p. 149.

PORTUGILL, Jestyn
    "Mekelle Road, 1974." Nat (233:3) 25 Jl- 1 Ag 81, p. 90.

POSNER, David
    "High Mass in Central Park" (for Tom Stacey). Kayak (57) 81, pp. 3-
      6.
    "Ode to Myself." Kayak (57) 81, p. 7.

POSTER, Carol
    "A Rarefied Atmosphere VI." KanQ (13:3/4) Sum-Aut 81, p. 152.

POTREBENKO, H.
    "Parking Lot." MalR (59) Jl 81, pp. 120-121.
    "They're Not Crazy, You Know." MalR (59) Jl 81, pp. 122-124.

POTTS, Charles
    "Feast of the Dead." PortR (27: 1) 81, p. 26.

POULIN, A., Jr.
    "Children In Fog (to Michael Waters)." NewL (47:4) Sum 81, pp. 60-61.

POUND, Ezra
    "Ans Quel Cim Reston de Branchas" (tr. of Arnaut Daniel). Iowa (12:1)
      Wint 81, pp. 41-42.
    "Fragment from an Anglo-Saxon Charm" (tr. of Anonymous). Iowa (12:
      1) Wint 81, p. 38.
    "From an Unpublished Draft of Canta LXXXIV." Sulfur (1) 81, pp. 6-
      10.

"Gianni Quel Guido Salute" (tr. of Guido Cavalcanti). Iowa (12:1) Wint
81, p. 45.
"Guido, Quel Gianni Ch'a Te Fu L'Altr' Ieri" (tr. of Gianni Alfani).
Iowa (12:1) Wint 81, p. 46.
"Künc Constantin de Gap sô Vil" (tr. of Walther von der Vogelweide).
Iowa (12:1) Wint 81, p. 49.
"Lo Ferm Voler Qu'el Cor M'Intra" (tr. of Arnaut Daniel). Iowa (12:1)
Wint 81, pp. 43-44.
"Noi Sian le Triste Penne Isbigotite" (tr. of Guido Cavalcanti). Iowa
(12:1) Wint 81, p. 47.
"Solt Ich den Pfaffen Râten an den Triuwen Mîn" (tr. of Walther von
der Vogelweide). Iowa (12:1) Wint 81, p. 48.
"Un Sirventes on Motz no Falh" (tr. of Bertran de Born). Iowa (12:1)
Wint 81, pp. 39-40.

POWELL, J. A.
"Send me a postcard from Paterson." ChiR (33:1) Sum 81, pp. 28-29.
"Against Annihilation." ChiR (33:1) Sum 81, pp. 30-31.

POWELL, James A.
"Labor Day." Thrpny (4) Wint 81, p. 17.

POWELL, Katherine
"Cracks and Springs" (tr. of Thor Sørheim). Field (25) Aut 81, p. 40.
"Pinetrees and Large Heavy Rowboats" (tr. of Thor Sørheim). Field
(25) Aut 81, p. 38.
"Rails, Poles and Barbed Wire" (tr. of Thor Sørheim). Field (25) Aut
81, p. 39.

POWERS, Jack
"Gregory Corso Shoot-Up." Sam (116) 81, p. 26.

POWERS, John Margaret
"Talking To Herself Again." Sam (117) 81, p. 26.

POWERS, Richard
"I Ate with the Dead Woman's Spoon." Poem (43) Nov 81, p. 61.
"The Old Daunce." Poem (43) Nov 81, p. 62.

POWERS, William
"First Light Took Us." Northeast (3:11) Sum 81, p. 12.
"New Ice." Northeast (3:11) Sum 81, p. 13.
"Returned to Cabin." Northeast (3:11) Sum 81, p. 14.

POWIS, Barbara
"The House." MalR (57) Ja 81, p. 148.

POYNER, Ken
"Fidelity." HiramPoR (30) Spr-Sum 81, p. 34.

PRADO, Holly
"Sky." Sulfur (3) 82, pp. 92-93.

PRATS, Delfin
"Lenguaje de mudos." Notarte (6:11) N 81, p. 17.

PRATT, Charles
"The Bliss of Bears" (for Cabot Lyford). LitR (24:3) Spr 81, p. 354.

PRESTON, D. S.
"Adolescence." ChrC (98:21) 17-24 Je 81, p. 660.

PRESTON, Eunice
"Progress." Peb (21) 81, p. 24.
"Regrets." Peb (21) 81, p. 26.
"A Snowstorm." Peb (21) 81, p. 25.

PREVERT, Jacques
"At the Florist's" (tr. by Peter Jay). SenR (12:1/2) 81, p. 71.
"Chez la fleuriste." SenR (12:1/2) 81, p. 70.
"Good Young Weather" (tr. by Harriet Zinnes). PoNow (6:1 issue 31)
      81, p. 42.
"The Key" (tr. by Harriet Zinnes). PoNow (6:1 issue 31) 81, p. 42.

PRICE, Reynolds
"Rescue." Poetry (138:3) Je 81, pp. 144-148.

PRIDA, Dolores
"Los niños de Truffaut." Areito (27: 28) 81, p. 49.

PRINTZ-PAHLSON, Göran
"Contemporary" (tr. of Jan Östergren, w/ John Matthias). ChiR (32:2)
      Aut 80, pp. 44-47.
"Indian Summer I" (tr. of Jan Östergren, w/ John Matthias). ChiR
      (32:2) Aut 80, pp. 41-43.

PRISCO, Joseph di see DiPRISCO, Joseph

PRIVETT, Katharine
"How is it with you, Borges?" CapeR (17:1) Wint 81, p. 40.
"Native Stone." Wind (11:42) 81, p. 32.
"School Girls" (for Jo and Mart and Til). HiramPoR (30) Spr-Sum 81,
      p. 35.
"A Softer Name." CapeR (17:1) Wint 81, p. 40.

PROPP, Karen
"The Gate." Ploughs (7:1) 81, p. 95.

PROPPER, Dan
"Last Beach in America." PoNow (6:1 issue 31) 81, p. 37.
"Report on the Progress of the Popular Front." PoNow (6:1 issue 31)
      81, p. 37.

PROSPERE, Susan
"Farm Life." NewYorker (57:8) 13 Ap 81, p. 42.
"Milliner." NewYorker (57:27) 24 Ag 81, p. 81.

PROSTOV, Eugene
"from Country of Lakes" (tr. with Elisavietta Ritchie of Radovan Pav-
      laski). Vis (5) 81, n. p.

PROTHRO, Nancy
"Eucalyptus." Vis (6) 81, n. p.

PROVOST, George
"Transitions." NewWR (49:1) Ja/F 81, p. 5.

PROVOST, Sarah
"Loup-Garou." PoNow (6:3 issue 33) 81, p. 33.
"Shirley, Good Mrs. Murphy." MassR (22:4) Wint 81, p. 781.

PRUNTY, Wyatt
"A Family Portrait for Our Daughter." CharR (7:1) Spr 81, p. 32.
"Our Tree of Opposites." GeoR (35:3) Aut 81, p. 630.

PRYTZ, Carl Frederik
"The Wind-Bent" (tr. by Martin S. Allwood). OntR (14) Spr-Sum 81,
pp. 57-58.

PUENTES de OYENARD, Sylvia
"Mi Pequeño País." Puerto Wint 81, p. 42.

PUGH, Sheenagh
"I Am Roerek." Pequod (13) 81, p. 52.
"Sailors." Pequod (13) 81, p. 53.

PUIGDOLLERS, Carmen
"Asisto al banquete para celebrar la parada puertorriqueña." Claridad/
En Rojo (22: 1478) 29 My-4 Je 81, p. 12.
"Asisto al banquete para celebrar la parada puertorriqueña." Claridad/
(22: 1478) 29 My-4 Je 81, p. 16.
"Noticias." Claridad (22: 1489) 14-20 Ag 81, p. 16.

PUSHKIN, Alexander
"For God's sake, let me not go mad." NewYRB (28:5) 2 Ap 81, p. 9.

PYBUS, Rodney
"Almanac of Herons." Stand (22: 3) 81, p. 71.
"Elterwater" (for Arthur Evans). Stand (22: 3) 81, p. 70.

QUENEAU, Raymond
"Bluish Wolf" (tr. by Linda Orr). SenR (10:2/11:1) 79-80, p. 95.
"The feast over" (tr. by Linda Orr). SenR (10:2/11:1) 79-80, p. 97.
"La fête finie." SenR (10:2/11:1) 79-80, p. 96.
"Loup blueté." SenR (10:2/11:1) 79-80, p. 94.

QUEVEDO, Francisco de
"Reloj de arena." Mairena (2:6) 80, p. 92.

QUILLMAN, Jane
"The Question." ColEng (43:4) Ap 81, pp. 371-372.

QUINN, John Robert
"Anna Elizabet Marsh." Wind (11:43) 81, p. 29.
"A Differing View." KanQ (13:3/4) Sum-Aut 81, p. 122.
"Glimpses of London." Wind (11:43) 81, p. 28.
"Indigo Bunting." ChrC (98:19) 27 My 81, p. 613.
"The Man Who Wanted to Grow Mushrooms." CutB (16) Spr-Sum 81,
p. 16.
"Picking Cherries." PoNow (6:1 issue 31) 81, p. 14.
"At Renishaw." PoNow (6:2 issue 32) 81, p. 42.
"Sonnet." Wind (11:43) 81, p. 29.
"Zinnias." ChrC (98:26) 26 Ag-2 S 81, p. 827.

QUINTANA, José
"Duerme, Mi Niño Poeta." Puerto Wint 81, p. 43.

QUIÑONES, Claraluz Vizcarrondo de see VIZCARRONDO de QUIÑONES,
Claraluz

RAAB, Lawrence
    "Afterwards." Poetry (137:5) F 81, p. 295.
    "As If." Iowa (11:2/3) Spr-Sum 80, p. 93.
    "Being Gone." Poetry (137:5) F 81, p. 293.
    "Coming Home." Poetry (137:5) F 81, p. 294.
    "For You." Poetry (137:5) F 81, p. 296.
    "This Day." Poetry (137:5) F 81, pp. 292-293.

RABIKOVICH, Daliah
    two garden poems: "Giants" (tr. by Bernhard Frank). PoNow (5:6
        issue 30) 81, p. 40.
    two garden poems: "They All Grow" (tr. by Bernhard Frank). PoNow
        (5:6 issue 30) 81, p. 40.
    "The Toads" (for Leah Goldberg) (tr. by Bernhard Frank). PoNow (5:6
        issue 30) 81, p. 40.

RABONI, Giovanni
    "Little Comedy" (tr. by Vinio Rossi and Stuart Friebert). Field (24)
        Spr 81, p. 11.
    "Magdalen's Fears" (tr. by Vinio Rossi and Stuart Friebert). Field
        (24) Spr 81, p. 12.
    "This Is the Catalogue" (tr. by Vinio Rossi and Stuart Friebert). Field
        (24) Spr 81, p. 10.

RABORG, Frederick A., Jr.
    "A Scapegoat Hurls Back His Stones." StoneC (8: 3) Spr 81, p. 25.

RACHEL, Naomi
    "All Work & No Play." WormR (81/82) 81, pp. 41-42.
    "Flood." SoCaR (13: 2) Spr 81, p. 60.
    "Detour." SoCaR (13: 2) Spr 81, p. 60.
    "Helpless in the Face of Poetry." MalR (58) Ap 81, p. 88.
    "Lone Stretch." MalR (58) Ap 81, p. 89.
    "Rat Race." SoCaR (13: 2) Spr 81, p. 61.
    "Simon The Super-Realist." WormR (81/82) 81, p. 42.

RACINE, Charles
    "La colonne répand le silence." SenR (10:2/11:1) 79-80, p. 110.
    "The column spreads silence" (tr. by Linda Orr). SenR (10:2/11:1)
        79-80, p. 111.
    "Cool Suns Whiten" (tr. by Linda Orr). SenR (10:2/11:1) 79-80, p.
        109.
    "Soleils frais blanchissent." SenR (10:2/11:1) 79-80, p. 108.

RADIN, Doris
    "The Gift." PoNow (6:2 issue 32) 81, p. 43.

RADNOTI, Miklós
    "Cloudy Sky" (tr. by Nicholas Kolumban). Chelsea (40) 81, pp. 54-55.
    "Evening, Woman, Child on Her Back" (for Károly Hilbert) (tr. by
        Emery George). Pequod (12) 81, p. 84.
    "Song with Drinks" (tr. by Emery George). Pequod (12) 81, p. 85.
    "Your Right Arm Beneath My Neck" (tr. by Jascha Kessler). PoNow
        (5:6 issue 30) 81, p. 39.

RADTKE, Rosetta
"Election Years." PoNow (6:3 issue 33) 81, p. 34.
"Touchstone." PoNow (6:3 issue 33) 81, p. 34.

RAFFA, J. L.
"Bowery Tourist Takes a Picture." CreamCR (6:2) 81, p. 55.

RAFFA, Joseph
"Academia: ground: in things begin responsibility." WindO (38) Spr-
Sum 81, pp. 34-35.

RAFFEL, Burton
"Questions" (tr. of Federico García Lorca). SenR (12:1/2) 81, p. 95.
"To Himself (A Se Stesso)" (tr. of Giacomo Leopardi). LitR (24:3)
Spr 81, p. 381.

RAIL, De Wayne
"Rolinda." PoNow (6:2 issue 32) 81, p. 33.

RAINES, Charlotte A.
"Taking the 1939 Jonathan Creek Road." BelPoJ (32:2) Wint 81-82, pp.
5-7.

RAISOR, Philip
"Foundation Building." SouthernPR (21: 1) Spr 81, pp. 35-36.

RAIZISS, Sonia
"Ashamed of myself? of this tree-" (tr. of Alfredo de Palchi). Mund
(12/13) 80-81, p. 349.
"Existence-solitary habit-" (tr. of Alfredo de Palchi). Mund (12/13)
80-81, p. 349.
"The Negative." PoNow (6:2 issue 32) 81, p. 27.

RAMANUJAN, A. K.
"Death and the Good Citizen." Poetry (139:2) N 81, pp. 70-71.
"Ecology." Poetry (139:2) N 81, pp. 68-69.

RAMIREZ, Joaquín
"Arlín." Mairena (2:6) 80, p. 44.

RAMIREZ, Marilyn
"UPR: Lucha Estudiantil a la altura de 1981." Claridad/En Rojo (22:
1507) 18-23 D 81, p. 11.

RAMIREZ, Orlando
"The Grey Ghost." Sam (109) 81, p. 31.

RAMIREZ GÜISCAFRE, Marilyn R.
"A Jorge Luis Borges" (Contestando y comentando entrevista a Borges
en 'El Mundo', 5 de junio de 1981). Claridad/En Rojo (22: 1482)
26 Je-2 Jl 81, p. 9.

RAMIREZ MURZI, Marco
"De Noche, Como el Río." Puerto Wint 81, p. 44.

RAMKE, Bin
"A Sense of Justice." Shen (32: 4) 81, p. 38.
"Sadness and Still Life." GeoR (35:4) Wint 81, p. 854.

RAMOS, Reinaldo García see GARCIA RAMOS, Reinaldo

RAMSEY, Jarold
"At Mesa Verde." NewEngR (3:4) Sum 81, pp. 594-5.
"Bringing Back the Dead." PoetryNW (22:4) Wint 81-82, pp. 34-35.
"Frost in Tibet." PoetryNW (22:4) Wint 81-82, p. 35.
"Jennie at Safeway." ConcPo (14:1) Spr 81, p. 60.
"The Last Gate." PoNow (6:1 issue 31) 81, p. 34.
"'Of the Making of Books....'" Chelsea (40) 81, p. 136.
"The Prayer of Those We Have Chosen to Die Last of Their Kind:
    Ishi of the Yahi, 'Tasmanian Annie,' 'Fuegia Basket'..." Chelsea
    (40) 81, p. 137.

RAMSEY, Paul
"The Flight of the Heart." SouthernR (17:3) Sum 81, pp. 555-7.

RAMSEY-PEREZ, Michael
"For the Jonestown Dead--November 18, 1978." Metam (3:2/4:1) 80-
    81, p. 9.
"Nurse." Metam (3:2/4:1) 80-81, p. 8.
"Pulling In." Metam (3:2/4:1) 80-81, p. 8.

RAND, Harry
"No one can say about animals." SunM (11) Spr 81, p. 161.

RANDALL, Belle
"Baptism." Thrpny (6) Sum 81, p. 16.
"The Death Car." Thrpny (7) Aut 81, p. 18.

RANDALL, David
"Homage to a Bottle of Chateau Lynch-Bages '69." HiramPoR (30)
    Spr-Sum 81, p. 36.

RANDALL, Dudley
"In Africa." Obs (6:1/2) Spr-Sum 80, p. 179.
"A Poet is Not a Jukebox." Obs (6:1/2) Spr-Sum 80, pp. 179-181.
"To an Old Man." Obs (7:1) Spr 81, p. 38.

RANDALL, Elinor
"Bounds" (tr. of José Emilio Pacheco). Mund (12/13) 80-81, p. 315.
"Defeat" (tr. of Rafael Cadenas). Mund (12/13) 80-81, pp. 138-140.

RANDALL, Margaret
"Apolitical Intellectuals" (tr. of Otto Rene Castillo). Sam (109) 81,
    p. 52.
"The Clockwise Dream." Metam (3:2/4:1) 80-81, p. 89.
"Our Own (for Saralee)." Metam (3:2/4:1) 80-81, p. 91.
"The Women: Mercedes." Metam (3:2/4:1) 80-81, p. 90.

RANDALL, Paula
"La Arborleda." StoneC (8: 3) Spr 81, p. 12.

RANDICH, Jean
"Possession." ThRiPo (17/18) 81, pp. 66-67.

RANDLE, Robert
"I Love the Bright Sun Light." LittleM (13:1/2) Spr-Sum 79, c1981,
    p. 92.

RANKIN, Paula
"Unreasonable Footprints." PoetryNW (22:2) Sum 81, pp. 33-34.

RANKIN, Robert J.
"The Birthday Party." MalR (59) Jl 81, p. 162.

RANKIN, Rush
"Brazil." Stand (22: 2) 81, p. 49.

RANSDELL, Emily
"Stories." CutB (17) Aut-Wint 81, pp. 73-74.

RANSON, Wm.
"Dream: A Picture Postcard to Linda." PortR (27: 2) 81, p. 83.
"Facing Winter." PortR (27: 2) 81, p. 83.
"Gathering Bones." PortR (27: 2) 81, p. 83.
"Map of the Last Long Night." PortR (27: 2) 81, p. 83.

RANTALA, Kathryn
"After Silence the First Sound." PortR (27: 1) 81, p. 12.
"Dreams of Victoria." PortR (27: 1) 81, p. 12.
"The Gargoyle." PortR (27: 2) 81, p. 55.
"Noah at Sea." PortR (27: 2) 81, p. 63.
"Rain." PortR (27: 2) 81, p. 55.
"Returning." PortR (27: 2) 81, p. 55.
"Tristes Tropique." PortR (27: 1) 81, p. 12.
"The Visionary." PortR (27: 1) 81, p. 12.

RASULA, Jed
"Four Poems." Sulfur (1) 81, pp. 199-201.
"Kirke." Sulfur (1) 81, pp. 202-203.

RATNER, Rochelle
"Case History." PoNow (6:1 issue 31) 81, p. 9.
"A Note on Our Life Here: September 24, 1980." Pequod (12) 81, p.
   20.

RATTRAY, David
"A red-framed print of the Summer Palace." Sulfur (3) 82, p. 56.

RAUTMAN, Linda
"Aunt Wilma." Peb (21) 81, p. 17.

RAWLING, Tom
"Grandmother." Pequod (13) 81, pp. 54-55.
"Rootcutter." Pequod (13) 81, p. 56.

RAWLINGS, Doug
"On The No Vote" (Nov. 23, 1980, the people of Maine voted 'no' to a
   proposal aimed at preventing nuclear power plant proliferation).
   Sam (106) 81, p. 16.
Survivor's Manual. Sam (120) 81, Entire issue.
"A Veteran's Survival Manual." Sam (106) 81, p. 47.

RAY, David
"After Mayakovsky." Iowa (11:2/3) Spr-Sum 80, p. 193.
"After Watching a Film about El Salvador." PoetryE (6) Aut 81, p.
   74.

"An Old Man Who Had Read Dorian Gray." PoNow (6:2 issue 32) 81,
  p. 28.
"In the Money" (for Robert Bly). PoetryE (4/5) Spr-Sum 81, p. 195.
"The Lady Guard." CharR (7:1) Spr 81, p. 44.
"The Mountain Speaks Anew." Iowa (11:2/3) Spr-Sum 80, p. 192.
"The Old Man with the Shopping Cart." NewEngR (3:4) Sum 81, pp.
  548-9.
"Portrait of a Mexican Barber." Kayak (57) 81, p. 60.
"Ribcage Behind a Meat Counter." Kayak (57) 81, p. 62.
"Snapshot." Ploughs (6:4) 81, p. 48.
"Travelling and Sitting Still" (for Robert Bly). PoetryE (4/5) Spr-Sum
  81, p. 196.
"Whalebone." Kayak (57) 81, p. 61.
"The Wise Guys." CharR (7:1) Spr 81, p. 45.

RAY, Kalyan
"Bedtime Story." BelPoJ (31:4) Sum 81, p. 1.

RAY, Robert Beverley
"The Aesthetics of Annotation." Poetry (138:6) S 81, pp. 318-319.

RAYMOND, Kathy
"For My Favorite Bartender." Wind (10:39) 80, p. 36.

RAZ, Hilda
"Journal Entry: the Tropics." Peb (21) 81, pp. 1-2.
"Long Night." Peb (21) 81, p. 6.
"Look." Peb (21) 81, p. 3.
"She Speaks." Peb (21) 81, pp. 4-5.
"Small Shelter." Peb (21) 81, p. 7.

READ, Ralph
"Bakunin: Or the Anarchy of Words" (tr. of Horst Bienek). NewOR
  (8:3) Aut 81, pp. 236-7.

REARDON, Patrick
"Dream 6." StoneC (9: 1-2) Aut-Wint 81/82, p. 55.
"A Foreign Thing." Tele (17) 81, p. 41.
"Ill." Wind (11:41) 81, p. 40.
"Romance." Wind (11:41) 81, p. 40.
"Three." StoneC (9: 1-2) Aut-Wint 81/82, p. 54.

REBAY, Luciano
"After Palio" (tr. of Eugenio Montale). NewYRB (28:1) 5 F 81, p. 23.

REBORA, Orlando Vicente
"Continuidad." Mairena (3:7) 81, pp. 82-83.
"Simultaneidad." Mairena (3:7) 81, p. 82.
"Sueño." Mairena (3:7) 81, p. 83.

RECIPUTI, Natalie S.
"Three Ways of Not Looking at It." PoetryNW (22:2) Sum 81, pp. 15-
  16.

RECK, Michael
"Contemporary." DenQ (16:2) Sum 81, p. 59.

RECTOR, Liam
"As With One Hand." Shen (31:4) 80, p. 27.
"We Colored Your Leaving." Kayak (56) 81, p. 33.

REDA, Jacques
"I brake so suddenly" (tr. by Linda Orr). SenR (10:2/11:1) 79-80, p.
113.
"Je freine si brusquement." SenR (10:2/11:1) 79-80, p. 112.
"On the Rue des Tournelles" (tr. by Linda Orr). SenR (10:2/11:1) 79-
80, p. 115.
"Rue des Tournelles." SenR (10:2/11:1) 79-80, p. 114.

REDGROVE, Peter
"Bees and Moss." Pequod (13) 81, pp. 57-58.
"Island of Women." Pequod (13) 81, pp. 59-60.

REED, John R.
"Colleani Chapel: Bergamo." Ploughs (6:4) 81, p. 11.
"Repairs: Florence." Ploughs (6:4) 81, p. 12.

REES, Enis
"At the Crossroads." SouthernR (17:2) Spr 81, p. 394.
"At the Resort Pool." SouthernR (17:2) Spr 81, pp. 395-6.

REES, Richard
"White Bikini." HangL (39) Wint 80-81, p. 23.

REEVE, F. D.
"A Girl's Adventure." WestHR (35:2) Sum 81, p. 124.
"Nocturne." WestHR (35:2) Sum 81, p. 134.
"Winter View of New Haven." NewYorker (56:46) 5 Ja 81, p. 36.

REIBSTEIN, Regina
"Pray for Famine." CapeR (16:2) Sum 81, p. 22.

REID, Alastair
"Injustice" (tr. of Pablo Neruda). Nat (232:12) 28 Mr 81, p. 376.
Nine Poems (tr. of Pablo Neruda). AmerPoR (10:3) My-Je 81, pp. 21-
27.
"Suddenly, A Ballad" (tr. of Pablo Neruda). Nat (232:19) 16 My 81,
p. 606.

REID, Robert Sims
"An Elegy for Leila." CutB (16) Spr-Sum 81, p. 46.
"A Family Portrait." CutB (16) Spr-Sum 81, pp. 47-48.
"South of Cascade." CutB (16) Spr-Sum 81, pp. 44-45.

REIFLER, Samuel
"Love Dance." KanQ (13:1) Wint 81, p. 112.

REISS, James
"Elegy for Jay Silverheels (1920-1980)." SouthwR (66:4) Aut 81, p.
393.

REITER, Thomas
"Black Bass Will Take Them in Dry Weather." PoetryNW (22:2) Sum
81, pp. 29-30.
"Buds and Leaf Scars: V-J Day." CimR (55) Ap 81, p. 29.

"The Interceptions" (for A. K.). PoetryNW (22:4) Wint 81-82, pp. 24-
    25.
"Looking Out from Here. " KanQ (13:3/4) Sum-Aut 81, p. 144.
"Ten Miners Lake. " Northeast (3:10) Wint 81, pp. 18-19.

RENDLEMAN, Danny
    "Crazy Man. " PoNow (6:1 issue 31) 81, p. 27.
    "Lice. " PoNow (6:1 issue 31) 81, p. 27.

RENO, Janet
    "Grant Avenue. " Northeast (3:10) Wint 81, p. 15.

REPP, John
    "Baseball. " HiramPoR (29) Aut-Wint 81, p. 33.

RETALLACK, Joan
    "Biographia Literaria. " SunM (11) Spr 81, pp. 86-87.
    "Portfolio B: Earth Heaven and Hell. " LittleM (13:1/2) Spr-Sum 79,
        c1981, pp. 52-54.
    "Why Are There So Many Dead Porcupines on the Roads in Maine?"
        ThRiPo (17/18) 81, p. 54.

RETALLACK, John
    "Arizona Antiphony. " SoDakR (19:3) Aut 81, pp. 101-102.

REVARD, Carter
    "Earth and Diamonds. " WebR (6:1) 81, pp. 69-72.
    "Planet of Blue-Eyed Cats. " WebR (6:1) 81, pp. 67-68.
    "Rock Shelters" (for John Joseph Mathews). Nimrod (25:1) Aut-Wint
        81, pp. 86-88.

REVEAL, David
    "Fireflies. " PoNow (6:3 issue 33) 81, p. 46.

REVERE, Elizabeth
    "Happy Anniversary. " CapeR (17:1) Wint 81, p. 8.

REXROTH, Kennoth
    "Life In The Palace" (tr. of Lady Hua Jui, w/ Ling Chung). UnmOx
        (22) Wint 81, pp. 15-16.

REYES, Carlos
    "Walking Along The Hills Above Cloonanaha I Pause To Replace A Stone
        Atop A Wall. " AntR (39:4) Aut 81, pp. 452-453.

REYES, Edwin
    "Parte precoz para una fecha sin traidores. " Claridad/En Rojo (22:
        1500) 30 O-5 N 81, p. 12.
    "Son cimarrón por Adelfina Villaneuva. " Claridad/En Rojo (22:1461)
        30 Ja-5 F 81, pp. 2-5.

REYES DAVILA, Marcos F.
    "¿Cómo era?" Mairena (3:7) 81, p. 67.
    "La estrella del norte. " Mairena (3:7) 81, pp. 66-7.
    "El mar que te decía. " Mairena (3:7) 81, p. 67.
    "Puerto Rico entre fragmentos" (A J. L. González). Mairena (2:6) 80,
        pp. 68-9.
    "Qué te estás. " Mairena (2:6) 80, p. 68.
    "Ya sé que estás ahí, mar. " Mairena (3:7) 81, p. 65.

REYES RIVERA, Louis
"Just In Case." Calib (3:2) Aut-Wint 80, pp. 51-52.
"Recognition." Calib (3:2) Aut-Wint 80, p. 53.
"What Would You Call It." Calib (3:2) Aut-Wint 80, pp. 49-50.

REYNOLDS, Diane Jones
"Gravity." SouthernPR (21:2) Aut 81, pp. 63-64.
"Learning to Sleep." SouthernPR (21: 1) Spr 81, pp. 22-23.

REYNOLDS, Gay
"A Poet in the Artist's Studio." Meadows (2:1) 81, p. 41.

RHODENBAUGH, Suzanne
"The Gold Rain" (To Heidi; To Justine). Vis (7) 81, n. p.

RHODES, Dee Schenck
"Gift." Sam (116) 81, p. 31.
"Satellites." Sam (116) 81, p. 29.

RHYNER, Judy Ann
"Bordertown Visit." Sam (109) 81, p. 63.

RIANCHO, Providencia
"Abrí mi puerta." Mairena (2:5) Aut 80, p. 66.
"Nocturno." Mairena (2:5) Aut 80, p. 66.
"Rapsodia del recuerdo." Mairena (2:5) Aut 80, p. 66.

RIBERA CHEVREMONT, Evaristo
"La palabra deseada." Mairena (2:6) 80, pp. 33-4.

RICAPITO, Joseph V.
"Untitled Poem." Confr (22) Sum 81, p. 105.

RICE, Pamela
"Santa Elena Crossing." CutB (17) Aut-Wint 81, pp. 53-54.

RICH, Adrienne
"Coast to Coast." Cond (7) Spr 81, pp. 102-103.
"Transit." Cond (7) Spr 81, pp. 104-105.
"What is Possible." Cond (7) Spr 81, pp. 106-108.

RICHARDSON, James
"Out of the Sun." Ploughs (7:2) 81, pp. 56-59.

RICHARDSON, Verlena Orr
"In the Steam Room." PortR (27: 2) 81, p. 97.

RICHMOND, Steve
"Gagaku." WormR (81/82) 81, pp. 13-14.

RICHTER, Robert
"Roadhome." Peb (21) 81, pp. 55-61.

RICKEL, Boyer
"Pablo Neruda." MissouriR (4:3) Sum 81, p. 29.
"The Public Garden." NoAmR (266:4) D 81, p. 36.

RIDLAND, John
    "Burning An American Flag." ThRiPo (17/18) 81, p. 57.
    "Mountain Music" (Chain Saw Couplets). Atl (248:4) O 81, p. 88.

RIEKE, Susan
    "A Fall Prayer." Focus (14:89) N 80, p. 10.
    "What Are Facts?" Focus (14:89) N 80, p. 10.

RIFAT, Oktay
    "Kirlangic." StoneC (8: 3) Spr 81, p. 30.
    "Semsiye." StoneC (8: 3) Spr 81, p. 30.
    "Swallows" (tr. by Ozcan Yalim, William A. Fielder, and Dionis Coffin
        Riggs). StoneC (8: 3) Spr 81, p. 30.
    "Umbrella" (tr. by Ozcan Yalim, William A. Fielder, and Dionis Coffin
        Riggs). StoneC (8: 3) Spr 81, p. 30.

RIFQA, Fu'ād
    "A Gift" (tr. by Michael Beard and Adnan Haydar). Nimrod (24: 2)
        Spr/Sum 81, p. 36.
    "God of Time" (tr. by Michael Beard and Adnan Haydar). Nimrod
        (24: 2) Spr/Sum 81, p. 37.
    "My beloved says" (tr. by Michael Beard and Adnan Haydar). Nimrod
        (24: 2) Spr/Sum 81, p. 38.
    "Smoke" (tr. by Michael Beard and Adnan Haydar). Nimrod (24: 2)
        Spr/Sum 81, p. 35.
    "A Tale" (tr. by Michael Beard and Adnan Haydar). Nimrod (24: 2)
        Spr/Sum 81, p. 37.
    "Verdura" (tr. by Michael Beard and Adnan Haydar). Nimrod (24: 2)
        Spr/Sum 81, p. 38.

RIGGS, Dionis Coffin
    "Swallows" (tr. of Oktay Rifat, w/ Ozcan Yalim and William A. Field-
        er). StoneC (8: 3) Spr 81, p. 30.
    "This Beautiful Weather" (tr. of Orhan Veli, w/ Ozcan Yalim and Wil-
        liam A. Fielder). StoneC (8: 3) Spr 81, p. 31.
    "Those Trees" (tr. of Melih Cevdet Anday, w/ Ozcan Yalim and Wil-
        liam A. Fielder). StoneC (8: 3) Spr 81, p. 31.
    "Umbrella" (tr. of Oktay Rifat, w/ Ozcan Yalim and William A. Field-
        er). StoneC (8: 3) Spr 81, p. 30.

RILEY, Judas Mary-Ellen
    "Grace Allen." Bound (9:2) Wint 81, pp. 156-161.

RILEY, Michael D.
    "The Contemporary Artist Reports on His Search for Higher Things."
        Poem (41) Mar 81, p. 8.
    "Drinking Song." CapeR (17:1) Wint 81, p. 33.
    "Winter Words." Poem (41) Mar 81, p. 7.
    "Words/Birds." CapeR (17:1) Wint 81, p. 33.

RILKE, Rainer Maria
    "The Angels" (tr. by Bernhard Frank). WebR (6:2) 81, p. 28.
    "Buddha" (tr. by Steven Lautermilch). LitR (24:4) Sum 81, p. 517.
    "The Buddha in Glory" (tr. by Steven Lautermilch). LitR (24:4) Sum
        81, p. 518.
    "The Carousel" (tr. by David Young). Field (25) Aut 81, p. 66.
    "Dear Neighbor God" (tr. by Steven Lautermilch). LitR (24:4) Sum 81,
        p. 516.

"Erinnerung." SenR (12:1/2) 81, p. 6.
"Fall" (tr. by Norbert Krapf). PoNow (5:6 issue 30) 81, p. 40.
"The Flamingos" (tr. by Bernhard Frank). WebR (6:2) 81, p. 28.
"Fox Fire" (tr. by Robert Bly). PoetryE (4/5) Spr-Sum 81, p. 27.
"I Keep Finding You" (tr. by Steven Lautermilch). LitR (24:4) Sum 81,
     p. 517.
"Imaginary Biography" (tr. by Robert Bly). PoetryE (4/5) Spr-Sum 81,
     p. 26.
"It seems we are asleep, blind at the bottom" (tr. by Stanley Plumly).
     SenR (12:1/2) 81, p. 5.
"Just As the Winged Energy of Delight" (tr. by Robert Bly). PoetryE
     (4/5) Spr-Sum 81, p. 28.
"Memory" (tr. by Franz Wright). SenR (12:1/2) 81, p. 7.
"Mourning" (tr. by Robert Bly). PoetryE (4/5) Spr-Sum 81, p. 25.
"The Panther" (tr. by Bernhard Frank). WebR (6:2) 81, p. 29.
"Sonnets to Orpheus" (tr. by Steven Lautermilch). LitR (24:4) Sum 81,
     pp. 514-515.
Ten poems (tr. by Stephen Mitchell). ParisR (23:82) Wint 82, pp. 111-
     128.
"Vielleicht, dass ich durch schwere Berge gehe." SenR (12:1/2) 81, p.
     4.

RINALDI, Nicholas
     "Cactus Dream." ColEng (43:8) D 81, p. 792.
     "Harbor Rescue." ColEng (43:8) D 81, p. 793.
     "Policemen's Ball." Vis (7) 81, n. p.

RINCON FERRANDEZ, Vicente
     "Palabras A Media Luz." Puerto Wint 81, p. 45.

RIND, Sherry
     "The Hawk in the Back Yard." SouthernPR (21:2) Aut 81, pp. 68-69.
     "This Time." PoetryNW (22:4) Wint 81-82, pp. 25-26.

RINGROSE, Katrina V.
     "The Meal." CalQ (18/19) 81, p. 49.
     "The Neighbors." CalQ (18/19) 81, p. 48.
     "Orchestra Pit" (after a painting by Edgar Degas). SoCaR (14: 1) Aut
          81, p. 122.
     "Shadows Are The Man." SoCaR (14: 1) Aut 81, p. 122.

RIO, Emilio del
     "Alondras castellanas para Jorge Manrique." Mairena (3:7) 81, pp. 52-
          53.
     "Campana en la tarde acorde." Mairena (3:7) 81, pp. 55-56.
     "Concierto de mediodía." Mairena (3:7) 81, p. 56.
     "Juventud y muerte." Mairena (3:7) 81, p. 54.

RIOS, Alberto
     "Lost on September Trail, 1967." CutB (16) Spr-Sum 81, pp. 9-11.

RIOS, Andrés Castro see CASTRO RIOS, Andrés

RIOS, Soleida
     "También me canto." Areito (7: 27) 81, p. 23.

RIOS RUIZ, Manuel
     "Empeño y gesta del cautivo." Os (13) Aut 81, p. 20.
     "Modo de señalar." Os (13) Aut 81, p. 20.

RISTAU, Harland
"Disturbance on the Block." BelPoJ (31:3) Spr 81, p. 3.
"Evening, Coon Valley." Northeast (3:10) Wint 81, p. 28.

RITCHIE, Elisavietta
"from Country of Lakes" (tr. with Eugene Prostov of Radovan Pavlov-
ski). Vis (5) 81, n. p.
"Crossing Colette's Palm" (for Cotette Inez). Wind (11:40) 81, pp. 27-
28.
"Drawing on an Ancient Vase" (tr. of Krassin Himmirsky, w/ Krassin
Himmirsky). PoNow (5:6 issue 30) 81, p. 18.
"Fait Divers" (correction of 1980 Index entry). Vis (4) 80.
"Elegy from Vesletza (To my mother)" (tr. of Krassin Himmirsky,
with the author). Vis (5) 81, n. p.
"Fire" (tr. of Krassin Himmirsky, with the author). Vis (5) 81, n. p.
"Krali Marko (The Giant hero of old Bulgarian epic)" (tr. of Krassin
Himmirsky with the author). Vis (5) 81, n. p.
"Masks" (tr. of Krassin Himmirsky, w/ Krassin Himmirsky). PoNow
(5:6 issue 30) 81, p. 18.
"Night Skyscrapers" (tr. of Krassin Himmirsky, with the author). Vis
(5) 81, n. p.
"Tasting the Names." PoNow (6:2 issue 32) 81, p. 21.
"Thistle Gift." Wind (11:40) 81, p. 28.

RITSOS, Yánnis
"Ablutions" (tr. by Kimon Friar). PoNow (6:2 issue 32) 81, p. 40.
"After a Settlement of Debts" (tr. by Kimon Friar and Kostas Myr-
siades). PoNow (5:6 issue 30) 81, p. 24.
"Announcement" (tr. by Kimon Friar and Kostas Myrsiades). Hudson
(34:2) Sum 81, p. 171.
"At Least" (tr. by Edmund Keeley). Antaeus (40/41) Wint-Spr 81, p.
376.
"Boubo Aggelma." SenR (12:1/2) 81, p. 20.
"The Coloured Beads" (tr. by John Constantine Stathatos). Mund (12/
13) 80-81, p. 356.
"Continued Waiting" (tr. by Edmund Keeley). Antaeus (40/41) Wint-Spr
81, p. 378.
"Danger Outstripped" (tr. by Kimon Friar). Mund (12/13) 80-81, p.
356.
"The Dark Shop" (tr. by Kimon Friar and Kostas Myrsiades). PoNow
(5:6 issue 30) 81, p. 24.
"Dilettantism" (tr. by Kimon Friar and Kostas Myrsiades). Ploughs
(6:4) 81, pp. 198-199.
Eight poems (tr. by Edmund Keeley). AmerPoR (10:4) Jl-Ag 81, p. 22.
Eight poems (tr. by Martin McKinsey). AmerPoR (10:4) Jl-Ag 81, pp.
23-29.
"Elation" (tr. by Edmund Keeley). OntR (14) Spr-Sum 81, p. 49.
Eleven poems (tr. by Edmund Keeley). Chelsea (40) 81, pp. 38-45.
"Elegy" (tr. by Edmund Keeley). OntR (14) Spr-Sum 81, p. 47.
"Enlightenment" (tr. by Edmund Keeley). OntR (14) Spr-Sum 81, p. 50.
"False Discoveries" (tr. by Kimon Friar and Kostas Myrsiades).
ArizQ (37:3) Aut 81, p. 244.
"Fragmented" (tr. by Edmund Keeley). Antaeus (40/41) Wint-Spr 81,
p. 376.
"The Get-Away" (tr. by Kimon Friar and Kostas Myrsiades). PoNow
(5:6 issue 30) 81, p. 24.
"The Hill" (tr. by Kimon Friar). PoNow (6:2 issue 32) 81, p. 40.
"Improvised Achievement" (tr. by Kimon Friar and Kostas Myrsiades).

Ploughs (6:4) 81, p. 199.
"The Iron Mosaic" (tr. by Kimon Friar and Kostas Myrsiades).
    Ploughs (6:4) 81, p. 196.
"The Laugh" (tr. by Kostas Myrsiades). SenR (12:1/2) 81, p. 23.
"Level Duration" (tr. by Kimon Friar and Kostas Myrsiades). Hudson
    (34:2) Sum 81, p. 169.
"Like Travelers" (tr. by Kimon Friar and Kostas Myrsiades). Hudson
    (34:2) Sum 81, p. 170.
"Limits" (tr. by Edmund Keeley). Antaeus (40/41) Wint-Spr 81, p.
    377.
"Multidimensional" (tr. by Kostas Myrsiades). SenR (12:1/2) 81, p.
    25.
"Narrowness" (tr. by Edmund Keeley). OntR (14) Spr-Sum 81, p. 48.
"Our Land" (tr. by Edmund Keeley). Antaeus (40/41) Wint-Spr 81, p.
    375.
"Penelope's Despair" (tr. by Kostas Myrsiades). NewOR (8:1) Wint 81,
    p. 14.
"Perpetual" (tr. by Kimon Friar and Kostas Myrsiades). Hudson (34:2)
    Sum 81, p. 169.
"Polydiastato." SenR (12:1/2) 81, p. 24.
"Remembrances" (tr. by Kimon Friar and Kostas Myrsiades). Hudson
    (34:2) Sum 81, p. 172.
"Return" (tr. by Edmund Keeley). NewYRB (28:17) 5 N 81, p. 18.
"The Roots" (tr. by Kimon Friar and Kostas Myrsiades). Hudson (34:
    2) Sum 81, pp. 170-171.
"Silent Message" (tr. by Edmund Keeley). SenR (12:1/2) 81, p. 21.
"The Scarecrow" (tr. by Kimon Friar and Kostas Myrsiades). Ploughs
    (6:4) 81, p. 197.
"Startled" (tr. by Edmund Keeley). Antaeus (40/41) Wint-Spr 81, p.
    377.
"To Gelio." SenR (12:1/2) 81, p. 22.
"Traces" (tr. by Kimon Friar and Kostas Myrsiades). Hudson (34:2)
    Sum 81, p. 172.
"Untitled Events" (tr. by Edmund Keeley). Antaeus (40/41) Wint-Spr
    81, p. 377.
"Winter Approaches" (tr. by Kimon Friar). PoNow (6:2 issue 32) 81,
    p. 40.

RITTER, Roman
    "Die Neutronenbombe." Mund (11:2) 79, p. 120.
    "The Neutron Bomb" (tr. by Von Underwood). Mund (11:2) 79, p. 121.

RITTY, Joan
    "Excuses." Comm (108:8) 24 Ap 81, p. 242.

RIVERA, Guillermo Rodríguez see RODRIGUEZ RIVERA, Guillermo

RIVERA, Louis Reyes see REYES RIVERA, Louis

RIVERA, Marina
    "For Celia" (no. 1). DenQ (16:3) Aut 81, p. 25.
    "For Celia" (no. 2). DenQ (16:3) Aut 81, p. 26.
    "For Celia" (no. 3). DenQ (16:3) Aut 81, p. 27.

RIVERA APONTE, René
    "Cancerberos de la Cultura." Claridad/En Rojo (22: 1490) 21-27 Ag
        81, p. 12.
    "Décimas del Patio Democracia en tres actos." Claridad/En Rojo (22:

1507) 18-23 D 81, p. 10.
"Retratos" (Doña Leti). Claridad/En Rojo (22: 1490) 21-27 Ag 81, p.
   12.

RIVERA RODRIGUEZ, Luis A.
   "A Esther." Mairena (2:6) 80, pp. 85-6.
   "El eco de mi voz." Mairena (2:6) 80, pp. 44-5.

RIVEREND, Pablo Le see Le RIVEREND, Pablo

RIVERS, J. W.
   "Esterhazy on the Departure of a Little Brother in the Trobriand Is-
      lands." StoneC (8: 3) Spr 81, p. 18.
   "Esterhazy's Wife." StoneC (8: 3) Spr 81, p. 18.
   "Hope." SouthwR (66:3) Sum 81, p. 291.
   "A Tunnel Made with a Bucket in a Chicago January." HiramPoR (29)
      Aut-Wint 81, pp. 34-35.

RIVIELLO, Vito
   "Paganini's Devil" (tr. by Lawrence Venuti). Chelsea (40) 81, p. 53.

RIZZA, Peggy
   "Amnios." Atl (247:2) F 81, p. 71.

ROBATTO, Matilde Albert see ALBERT ROBATTO, Matilde

ROBBINS, Andrew
   "Christmas 1978." Sulfur (3) 82, pp. 107-108.
   "Ibidem." Sulfur (3) 82, pp. 109-110.
   "A Hieroglyph for Joe and Mark and Angela." Sulfur (3) 82, pp. 111-
      112.

ROBBINS, Kate L.
   "The Little Boy that Died." NowestR (19:1/2), pp. 29-31.
   "Sunrise in Camp." NowestR (19:1/2), pp. 31-2.

ROBBINS, Martin
   "Again the Improbable Ceremony." Os (13) Aut 81, p. 23.
   "The Day Improvised." StoneC (8: 3) Spr 81, p. 15.
   "From An August Field." StoneC (9: 1-2) Aut-Wint 81/82, p. 60.
   "Nearing Midnight." Os (13) Aut 81, p. 21.
   "Pictures Seen by Luck." Os (12) Spr 81, p. 9.
   "Plaza San Martin." SewanR (89:1) Wint 81, p. 30.
   "Plot." StoneC (9: 1-2) Aut-Wint 81/82, p. 62.
   "Summer's Tent." Im (7:2) 1981, p. 11.
   "This Longest Night of Winter." Os (13) Aut 81, p. 22.
   "The Uniforms I've Worn:." CapeR (17:1) Wint 81, p. 29.

ROBBINS, Richard
   "First Day Over 60, April 1980." QW (12) Spr-Sum 81, p. 51.
   "Leaping The Chasm At Stand Rock Wisconsin Dells, 1887." QW (12)
      Spr-Sum 81, p. 50.
   "Prairie: Gordon, Nebraska, August 1916." CutB (16) Spr-Sum 81,
      pp. 17-18.
   "Time After Time." Thrpny (5) Spr 81, p. 21.
   "Topographical" (for K.R.). CarolQ (34:2) Aut 81, p. 89.

ROBBINS, Tim
   "The Bower." HangL (39) Wint 80-81, p. 66.

"Country Scene." HangL (39) Wint 80-81, p. 66.
"Credulity Recovered." HangL (40) Aut 81, p. 68.
"For Ken." HangL (39) Wint 80-81, p. 68.
"The Punisher, It Is He That Is Asleep." HangL (39) Wint 80-81, p. 67.
"Redemption Blues." HangL (40) Aut 81, p. 69.

ROBERTS, Dorothy
"The Sun." Hudson (34:2) Sum 81, p. 247.
"Women and Light." Hudson (34:2) Sum 81, p. 248.

ROBERTS, Helen Wade
"A Genealogical Cousin." CapeR (16:2) Sum 81, p. 40.

ROBERTS, Len
"Either Way." NowestR (19:1/2), pp. 74-5.
"White Pigeon." CarolQ (34:2) Aut 81, p. 42.

ROBERTS, Stephen R.
"An Elegy for Lee Starr." Wind (11:40) 81, p. 29.
"From Here to There." SoCaR (14: 1) Aut 81, pp. 17-18.
"A Note I'll Give You Tomorrow" (for Amy Buchholz). SoCaR (14: 1) Aut 81, p. 19.
"Winter Feed." WindO (38) Spr-Sum 81, p. 43.

ROBERTS, Susan
"Discreet. it's a party." Tele (17) 81, pp. 56-57.
"Things to be whispered." Tele (17) 81, p. 57.

ROBERTSON, Kirk
"Exactly Eight Degrees." Meadows (2:1) 81, p. 53.
"Hindsight." PoNow (6:2 issue 32) 81, p. 37.
"Mustard Colored Man." PoNow (6:2 issue 32) 81, p. 37.

ROBERTSON, Patrika
"Balancing Act." MalR (57) Ja 81, p. 162.
"Family Portrait: Christmas 1978." MalR (57) Ja 81, p. 160.
"Fifteen." MalR (57) Ja 81, p. 159.
"Ken's Deli at Midnight: Boston, 1979." MalR (57) Ja 81, p. 161.

ROBIN, Ralph
"This Moment, Walking." NewL (47:4) Sum 81, pp. 90-91.
"Second Stories." NewL (67:4) Sum 81, p. 90.

ROBINS, Natalie
"Waiting for Rain." OP (31/32) Aut 81, pp. 130-131.

ROBINSON, James Miller
"The Dreamer." WormR (84) 81, p. 102.
"The Keeper of the Herd." Wind (11:43) 81, p. 30.

ROBINSON, Leonard Wallace
"Envy's Stinging." Wind (11:41) 81, pp. 39-40.
"Yes." CutB (17) Aut-Wint 81, p. 55.

ROBLES, Tina Alvarez see ALVAREZ ROBLES, Tina

ROBY, Gayle
"Eve out of Eden, to Adam." PraS (55:4) Wint 81-82, p. 30.

ROCHA, Adrian
"The Only Nuclear War." Sam (106) 81, p. 15.

RODGERS, Frederick
"Mount St. Helens--Mid-Winter." PortR (27: 2) 81, p. 16.

RODGERS, Gordon
"Floating Houses." PottPort (3) 81, p. 10.
"Woodcraft." PottPort (3) 81, p. 11.

RODRIGUEZ, Andrés
"Hunters Tell at Midnight." Maize (4:3/4) Spr-Sum 81, p. 75.
"Irises." Maize (4:3/4) Spr-Sum 81, p. 75.
"The Island." Maize (4:3/4) Spr-Sum 81, p. 74.

RODRIGUEZ, Luis
"El Maestro enfermo." Claridad/En Rojo (22: 1493) 11-17 S 81, p.
    12.

RODRIGUEZ, Luis A. Rivera see RIVERA RODRIGUEZ, Luis A.

RODRIGUEZ, Norman
"Canto a la mujer." Mairena (3:7) 81, pp. 32-34.
"Canto a la mujer mulata." Mairena (3:7) 81, pp. 34-5.
"El sí...." Mairena (3:7) 81, p. 36.
"Era domingo...." Mairena (3:7) 81, p. 36.

RODRIGUEZ, Rafael Hernández see HERNANDEZ RODRIGUEZ, Rafael

RODRIGUEZ, Reina María
"Ella no murió de amor." Areito (7: 27) 81, p. 22.

RODRIGUEZ FRESE, Marcos
"Ejercicios." Mairena (2:6) 80, p. 75.

RODRIGUEZ NUÑEZ, Victor
"Mujer desconocida." Areito (7: 27) 81, p. 22.

RODRIGUEZ RIVERA, Guillermo
"Un fantasma recorre América Central." Areito (7: 26) 81, p. front-
    cover.
"Nostalgia de Eva." Areito (27: 28) 81, p. 50.

ROESKE, Paulette
"Edens Expressway." WebR (6:2) 81, p. 59.
"Tending the Jade Plant." WebR (6:2) 81, p. 60.

ROGERS, Pattiann
"Being Accomplished." PoetryNW (22:3) Aut 81, pp. 4-5.
"A Daydream of Light." PoetryNW (22:3) Aut 81, pp. 3-4.
"Discovering Your Subject." Poetry (138:1) Ap 81, pp. 28-29.
"The Dream of the Marsh Wren: Reciprocal Creation." PoetryNW (22:
    3) Aut 81, pp. 5-6.
"Exposing the Future with Conviction." Poetry (138:1) Ap 81, pp. 31-
    32.
"The Faulty Realization of the Hoary Puccoon." PoetryNW (22:4) Wint
    81-82, pp. 5-6.
Fifteen poems. ArkRiv (5:1) 81, pp. 22-38.

"First Notes From One Born and Living in an Abandoned Barn."
PoetryNW (22:4) Wint 81-82, pp. 4-5.
"For Stephen Drawing Birds." NewYorker (57:3) 9 Mr 81, p. 44.
"The Gift of Reception." PoetryNW (22:3) Aut 81, pp. 6-7.
"Her Delight." PoetryNW (22:4) Wint 81-82, pp. 6-7.
"Justification of the Horned Lizard." Iowa (12:1) Wint 81, pp. 100-
101.
"The Last Blessing." Poetry (138:1) Ap 81, p. 30.
"Love Song." PoetryNW (22:4) Wint 81-82, pp. 3-4.
"Maintaining the Indistinguishable." Iowa (12:1) Wint 81, pp. 102-103.
"Mastering the Calm." PoetryNW (22:3) Aut 81, pp. 7-8.
"Parlor Game on a Snowy Winter Night." Kayak (56) 81, pp. 24-25.
"The Possible Advantages of the Expendable Multitudes." Poetry (138:1)
Ap 81, pp. 33-34.
"Raising the Eyes that High." PoetryNW (22:4) Wint 81-82, p. 8.
"Struck Seven Times." SouthernR (17:2) Spr 81, pp. 379-380.
"Teaching a Sea Turtle Suddenly Given the Power of Language, I Begin
by Saying." Iowa (12:1) Wint 81, pp. 104-105.
"Watching Dreams." SouthernR (17:2) Spr 81, pp. 378-9.

ROGERS, Timothy J.
"15 (Autobiografía)" (tr. of Etelvina Astrada). WebR (6:2) 81, p. 18.

ROHMAN, Simone
"Dichotomy." Confr (22) Sum 81, p. 149.

ROHRER, Jane
"Reading At Breakfast." AmerPoR (10:6) N-D 81, p. 34.
"Wedding." AmerPoR (10:6) N-D 81, p. 34.
"Zen Poem." AmerPoR (10:6) N-D 81, p. 34.

ROJAS, Gonzalo
"Quién Dijo Videncia?" Inti (9) Spr 79, p. 95.
"Uptown." Inti (9) Spr 79, pp. 94-95.

ROJAS CRUZADO, Nydia
"Nuestro siglo veinte." Mairena (2:6) 80, pp. 84-5.

ROJO, María Elena Sancho see SANCHO ROJO, María Elena

ROJO LEON, Armando
"Versos del Mar." Puerto Wint 81, p. 46.

ROMAÑA, Valdir Peyceré see PEYCERE ROMAÑA, Valdir

ROMER, Stephen
"An Afternoon in the Parc Monceau." Stand (22: 2) 81, p. 29.

ROMTVEDT, David
"The Heavenly Mistakes Amid So Much Golfing." PoNow (6:1 issue 31)
81, p. 41.
"A Short Novel About a Cheesecutter." PoNow (6:1 issue 31) 81, p. 41.
"Stop." PoNow (6:1 issue 31) 81, p. 41.

RONAN, Richard
"Fools" (for G.). AmerPoR (10:1) Ja-F 81, pp. 31-32.

RONCI, Ray
"Submerged" (for Thomas Lux). ThRiPo (17/18) 81, p. 69.

RONSARD, Pierre De see De RONSARD, Pierre

ROOT, William Pitt
 "Awake on an Island." CharR (7:1) Spr 81, p. 27.
 "Coot and the Sperm Bank." CutB (16) Spr-Sum 81, p. 56.
 "Dear Jeffers" (A Note From Sheridan to Carmel-By-The-Sea). CutB
   (16) Spr-Sum 81, pp. 54-55.
 "Don't Blink." NoAmR (266:2) Je 81, p. 67.
 "Fireclock." Nimrod (25:1) Aut-Wint 81, pp. 77-85.
 "How the Pygmy Forest Works" (fragment of a conversation). PoNow
   (6:1 issue 31) 81, p. 37.
 "Listening with the World's Ear." ColEng (43:6) O 81, p. 578.
 "Walking in Chaparral." PoNow (6:2 issue 32) 81, p. 21.
 "Waking to the Comet." PoNow (6:1 issue 31) 81, p. 45.
 "Wheel Turning on the Hub of the Sun." CimR (57) O 81, p. 56.

ROSADO, Gabriel
 "Florecimiento de la Poesía." Inti (9) Spr 79, p. 101.
 "Metamorfosis." Inti (9) Spr 79, p. 102.

ROSBERG, Rose
 "Walk over Water." Wind (11:41) 81, p. 38.

ROSE, Jennifer
 "Intentions" (for Helena Minton). Tendril (11) Sum 81, pp. 63-64.

ROSE, Lynne Carol
 "Three Mile Island." HiramPoR (29) Aut-Wint 81, p. 36.

ROSE, Mike
 "At Doctor Konrad's." Vis (6) 81, n. p.
 "The Bookkeeper at Springtime." Vis (6) 81, n. p.
 "Italian Wine Stop." Vis (7) 81, n. p.

ROSE, Wendy
 "Sunday Morning: Eating a Hamburger in Iowa City." Cond (7) Spr 81,
   pp. 63-64.

ROSELIEP, Raymond
 "Elizabeth Ann's Picnic." Im (7:2) 1981, p. 8.
 "Entry." PoNow (6:2 issue 32) 81, p. 5.
 "Nobel Recipient." ChrC (98:36) 11 N 81, p. 1150.
 "Parent." ChrC (98:24) 29 Jl-5 Ag, 81, p. 769.
 "Shrine." ChrC (98:2) 21 Ja 81, p. 37.
 "Sistine Chapel." ChrC (98:3) 28 Ja 81, p. 70.
 "Spring Stroll." ChrC (98:12) 8 Ap 81, p. 382.
 "Temple." ChrC (98:33) 21 O 81, p. 1047.
 "Transience." ChrC (98:23) 15-22 Jl 81, p. 731.

ROSEN, Kenneth
 "Bat." Shen (31:4) 80, p. 91.
 "Plum Season." MassR (22:4) Wint 81, pp. 623-624.
 "Rimini Diary." MassR (22:4) Wint 81, pp. 621-622.

ROSEN, Michael
 "Hidden Pictures." NewEngR (3:4) Sum 81, pp. 596-7.
 "Into the Heartland." Focus (14:89) N 80, p. 10.
 "June." CarolQ (34:2) Aut 81, p. 70.

ROSENBERG, Chuck
  "Envoy From The Dog-People." AmerPoR (10:2) Mr-Ap 81, p. 33.
  "Landfall." AmerPoR (10:2) Mr-Ap 81, p. 33.
  "Noodling Around In The Natural Order." AmerPoR (10:2) Mr-Ap 81,
    p. 33.

ROSENBERG, D. M.
  "Halwit." BallSUF (22:4) Aut 81, p. 47.
  "Manta Bay." BallSUF (22:4) Aut 81, p. 22.

ROSENBERG, David
  "Jacob and the Angel" (tr. of Yehuda Amichai). Nat (232:17) 2 My 81,
    p. 545.
  "Songs for a Woman" (tr. of Yehuda Amichai). Nat (233:1) 4 Jl 81,
    p. 24.
  "Tourist" (tr. of Yehuda Amichai). Nat (232:17) 2 My 81, p. 545.

ROSENBERG, L. M.
  "The Angels Inform the World." NewYorker (57:8) 13 Ap 81, p. 38.
  "The Christmas Cactus." NewYorker (56:51) 9 F 81, p. 36.
  "Eating the Cow." Bound (9:1) Aut 80, p. 125.
  "What the Trees Suffer." GeoR (35:2) Sum 81, p. 380.

ROSENBERG, Theodore
  "After Williams." BelPoJ (31:3) Spr 81, p. 2.
  "The Mona Lisa" (for L. D.). BelPoJ (31:3) Spr 81, p. 2.
  "To Voluptuous Plumpness." BelPoJ (31:3) Spr 81, p. 3.

ROSENBERGER, F. C.
  "Light Verse." ArizQ (37:2) Sum 81, p. 136.

ROSENBLATT, Herta
  "Valentine's Day." StoneC (8: 3) Spr 81, p. 24.

ROSENBLATT, Suzanne
  "The Men in Her Life." Confr (21) Wint 81, p. 25.
  "Trepidation." Confr (21) Wint 81, p. 24.

ROSENMAN, John B.
  "After We Met." Wind (11:40) 81, p. 9.
  "Cycle." BallSUF (22:1) Wint 81, p. 51.
  "If God Were an Imagist Poem." BallSUF (22:1) Wint 81, p. 41.
  "Patterns." BallSUF (22:4) Aut 81, p. 20.

ROSENSTONE, Caroline
  "The Boarder." MassR (22:1) Spr 81, p. 32.

ROSENTHAL, M. L.
  "Lines In Dejection." MassR (22:3) Aut 81, p. 423.
  "In Praise Of Sweet Chance." MassR (22:3) Aut 81, p. 424.

ROSENWALD, John
  "The Other." LitR (24:3) Spr 81, p. 394.

ROSENZWEIG, Gerry
  "The Lake." SmPd (18:3) Aut 81, p. 9.

ROSENZWEIG, Phyllis
  "Untitled." SunM (11) Spr 81, pp. 146-148.

ROSETTA, Govan
  "Justify Your Manhood When There's Nothing Left." WindO (39) Wint
    81/82, p. 18.

ROSS, Aden Kathryn
  "Quatidian Leda." PoetryNW (22:4) Wint 81-82, pp. 40-43.

ROSS, Bob
  "Poem for Margaret." Peb (21) 81, p. 107.
  "To Loven Eiseley." Peb (21) 81, pp. 108-109.

ROSS, Carolyn
  "In the Dark Room" (For the C.). AmerS (50:4) Aut 81, pp. 499-500.

ROSSI, Vinio
  "Little Comedy" (tr. of Giovanni Raboni, w/ Stuart Friebert). Field
    (24) Spr 81, p. 11.
  "Magdalen's Fears" (tr. of Giovanni Raboni, w/ Stuart Friebert). Field
    (24) Spr 81, p. 12.
  "This Is the Catalogue" (tr. of Giovanni Raboni, w/ Stuart Friebert).
    Field (24) Spr 81, p. 10.

ROTELLA, Alexis
  "Dusk." WindO (39) Wint 81/82. On calendar.
  "His finger." WindO (39) Wint 81/82. On calendar.
  "Listening to the silence." WindO (39) Wint 81/82. On calendar.
  "To be able." WindO (39) Wint 81/82. On calendar.

ROTELLA, Alexis Kaye
  "Visit to the Herb Farm." WindO (39) Wint 81/82, p. 4.

ROTELLA, Guy
  "Housing." SmPd (18:2) Spr 81, p. 4.
  "Remains." Tendril (10) Wint 81, p. 39.

ROTHENBERG, Jerome
  "Europe" (for Pierre Jaris). Sulfur (3) 82, pp. 97-99.
  "Hunger." Sulfur (1) 81, pp. 11-14.
  "Terror." Sulfur (2) 81, pp. 173-176.
  "War." Sulfur (3) 82, pp. 94-96.

ROTHFORK, John
  "Shiva." Vis (6) 81, n. p.

ROTHMAN, David
  "The Elephant's Chiropracter." LitR (24:3) Spr 81, p. 393.

ROTHSTEIN, Margaret
  "Administrative Hierarchies of the Public Schools." EngJ (70:5) S 81,
    p. 25.
  "Behavior Gap." EngJ (70:4) Ap 81, p. 44.

ROTONDARO, Len
  "Track Season." WindO (39) Wint 81/82, p. 9.

ROUGHTON, Becke
  "Dream in the House of Hell." SouthernPR (21: 1) Spr 81, p. 25.
  "My Grandmother's Pain." PoNow (6:3 issue 33) 81, p. 35.
  "The Man Without." PoNow (6:3 issue 33) 81, p. 35.

ROUTE, Deborah
    "Silverware." CentR (25:1) Wint 81, pp. 45-46.

ROY, Teresa
    "And I was My Child." Kayak (57) 81, p. 9.
    "Make Me Anonymous." Kayak (57) 81, p. 8.

ROYSTER, Philip M.
    "Mama." Obs (6:1/2) Spr-Sum 80, pp. 207-208.
    "Questions." Obs (6:1/2) Spr-Sum 80, p. 209.
    "Variations." Obs (6:1/2) Spr-Sum 80, p. 208.

ROZEWICZ, Tadeusz
    "Golden Mountains" (tr. by Victor Contoski). PoNow (5:6 issue 30) 81,
        p. 25.
    "In Haste" (tr. by Victor Contoski). PoNow (5:6 issue 30) 81, p. 25.
    "Purgatory" (tr. by Antoni Gronowicz). WebR (6:2) 81, p. 33.
    "The Survivor" (tr. by Pawel Mayewski). Mund (12/13) 80-81, p. 231.
    "To the Heart" (tr. by Victor Contoski). PoNow (5:6 issue 30) 81, p.
        25.

RUANO, Isabel de los Angeles
    "No son muchos." Maize (4:1/2) Aut-Wint 80-81, p. 63.
    "El cadáver." Maize (4:1/2) Aut-Wint 80-81, p. 62.

RUARK, Gibbons
    "Essay On Solitude." AmerPoR (10:1) Ja-F 81, p. 14.
    "Horse And Willow Tree In The Moonlight: Chines, Sung Dynasty" (for
        J. L.). AmerPoR (10:1) Ja-F 81, p. 14.
    "Lost Letter to James Wright, With Thanks for a Map of Fano."
        NewRep (184:7) 14 F 81, p. 28.
    "With Our Wives in Late October (for James Wright)." NewEngR (3:4)
        Sum 81, p. 540.

RUBENFELD, Florence
    "The Bridegrooms At The Center." PartR (48:2) 81, p. 256.

RUBENSTEIN, Carol
    "Lizard Island." PoNow (6:3 issue 33) 81, p. 36.

RUBENSTEIN, Elaine
    "Waltz." VirQR (57:4) Aut 81, pp. 634-636.

RUBIN, Larry
    "Ancestors (Wakulla Springs, Florida)." SouthernHR (15:3) Sum 81, p.
        228.
    "Lines to an Elderly Friend, Preparing to Remarry." SouthernHR (15:
        3) Sum 81, p. 242.
    "Locked Out, But Only Temporarily." Comm (108:22) 4 D 81, p. 698.
    "Venice Again." PraS (55:1/2) Spr-Sum 81, p. 286.

RUBIN, Stan Sanvel
    "Towel." PoNow (6:3 issue 33) 81, p. 35.

RUDD, Gail
    "The Prisoner." KanQ (13:3/4) Sum-Aut 81, p. 143.
    "Susan." KanQ (13:3/4) Sum-Aut 81, p. 143.

RUDENKO, Mykola
"At Least, You" (tr. by Askold Melnyczuk). Agni (14) 81, p. 98.
"The Flower" (tr. by Askold Melnyczuk). Agni (14) 81, p. 99.
"The King of Tasmania" (tr. by Askold Melnyczuk). Agni (14) 81, pp.
    96-97.
"Spring" (tr. by Askold Melnyczuk). Agni (14) 81, p. 100.

RUDMAN, Mark
"An Even More Sultry Dawn" (tr. of Boris Pasternak, w/ Bohdan Boy-
    chuk). AmerPoR (10:4) Jl-Ag 81, p. 38.
"Balashov" (tr. of Boris Pasternak, w/ Bohdan Boychuk). AmerPoR
    (10:4) Jl-Ag 81, p. 39.
"The Blood of Captive Women" (tr. of Mykola Bazhan, w/ Bohdan
    Boychuk). PoNow (5:6 issue 30) 81, p. 6.
"Concerning These Poems" (tr. of Boris Pasternak, w/ Bohdan Boy-
    chuk). PoNow (5:6 issue 30) 81, p. 35.
"Darling--the terror! It comes back!" (tr. of Boris Pasternak, w/
    Bohdan Boychuk). PoNow (5:6 issue 30) 81, p. 34.
"The End of the World" (tr. of Gohdan Antonych, w/ Bohdan Boychuk).
    PoNow (6:1 issue 31) 81, p. 43.
"Log (Journey to 'Four Corners')." Pequod (12) 81, pp. 86-89.
"Our Thunderstorm" (tr. of Boris Pasternak, w/ Bohdan Boychuk).
    PoNow (5:6 issue 30) 81, p. 34.
"The Picture" (tr. of Boris Pasternak, w/ Bohdan Boychuk). PoNow
    (5:6 issue 30) 81, p. 35.
"Prince Igor's Campaign" (tr. of Mykola Bazhan, w/ Bohdan Boychuk).
    PoNow (5:6 issue 30) 81, p. 6.
"Rain" (tr. of Boris Pasternak, w/ Bohdan Boychuk). AmerPoR (10:4)
    Jl-Ag 81, p. 39.
"Returning to New York from Cortez." Pequod (12) 81, p. 90.
"The Road" (tr. of Mykola Bazhan, w/ Bohdan Boychuk). PoNow (5:6
    issue 30) 81, p. 6.
"The Substitute" (tr. of Boris Pasternak, w/ Bohdan Boychuk).
    AmerPoR (10:4) Jl-Ag 81, p. 38.
"A Sultry Night" (tr. of Boris Pasternak, w/ Bohdan Boychuk). PoNow
    (5:6 issue 30) 81, pp. 34-35.

RUDNIK, Raphael
"Frank 207." OP (31/32) Aut 81, p. 143.

RUDOLF, Anthony
"The Dialogue of Anguish and Desire" (tr. of Yves Bonnefoy). Mund
    (12/13) 80-81, pp. 218-220.

RUDY, D. L.
"Meridian." Poem (42) Jul 81, pp. 18-19.
"On Meeting an Old Friend at a Cocktail Party." Wind (10:39) 80, p.
    37.

RUEFLE, Mary
"As When I Did Not Exist." VirQR (57:2) Spr 81, pp. 268-270.
"The Tomb in Ghent." Chelsea (40) 81, pp. 140-141.

RUENZEL, David
"Call from Home on My 25th Birthday." KanQ (13:3/4) Sum-Aut 81, p.
    181.

RUESCHER, Scott
"On a Globe Harging by Wire From a Classroom Ceiling." PoetryNW

(22:3) Aut 81, pp. 20-21.
"The Situation." PoetryNW (22:3) Aut 81, pp. 19-20.
"The Snow on the Ice on the Water of the Reservoir." PoetryNW (22:
   3) Aut 81, p. 21.
"X." Iowa (11:2/3) Spr-Sum 80, pp. 202-203.

RUFFUS, Stephen
   "After the Lights Go Down" (for Emmett Kelly). QW (12) Spr-Sum 81,
      p. 12.
   "My Mother Climbs Mt. Timpanogos." QW (12) Spr-Sum 81, p. 13.

RUGGLES, Eugene
   "Oath in a Railway Terminal" (for Muriel Rukeyser 1913-1980).
      PoetryNW (22:2) Sum 81, pp. 11-12.
   "Song of One." PoetryNW (22:2) Sum 81, pp. 12-13.

RUISSEAUX, Pierre Des
   "La mer répétée." Os (12) Spr 81, p. 6.

RUIZ, José O. Colón see COLON RUIZ, José O.

RUIZ de la CUESTA, Francisco
   "Silencios." Mairena (2:5) Aut 80, p. 75.
   "Sin fuego en los brazos abiertos." Mairena (2:5) Aut 80, pp. 75-6.

RUIZ ESCOBAR, Jaime
   "VII." Mairena (2:6) 80, p. 46.

RUKEYSER, Muriel
   "Fire" (tr. of Vicente Aleixandre). Mund (12/13) 80-81, p. 405.

RUMMEL, Mary Kay
   "How the cold comes" (autumn). Prima (6/7) 81, p. 85.

RUNCIMAN, Lex
   "Guernseys." CharR (7:1) Spr 81, p. 12.

RUSSELL, CarolAnn
   "Affair With a Watercolor River." PortR (27: 1) 81, p. 11.
   "The Colors." PoetryNW (22:3) Aut 81, pp. 24-25.
   "Confessions." CutB (16) Spr-Sum 81, pp. 12-13.
   "For All You Know." CutB (16) Spr-Sum 81, pp. 14-15.
   "Relations." QW (13) Aut/Wint 81/82, p. 26.

RUSSELL, Hilary
   "The Schoolteacher Thinks of Moving." BelPoJ (32:1) Aut 81, pp. 18-
      19.

RUSSELL, Norman H.
   "The Black Jay." KanQ (13:3/4) Sum-Aut 81, p. 83.
   "The Catskillers." OP (31/32) Aut 81, p. 71.
   "Going Inside." WebR (6:1) 81, p. 73.
   "Many Marches and Camps." KanQ (13:3/4) Sum-Aut 81, p. 83.
   "Waiting the Fish to Come." WebR (6:1) 81, p. 74.
   "A Work of Many Days." KanQ (13:3/4) Sum-Aut 81, p. 84.
   "Wren." Aspect (77/79) 81, p. 167.

RUSSELL, Timothy
   "The Possibility of Turning To Salt." BelPoJ (31:4) Sum 81, p. 33.

"The Possibility of Turning to Salt." PoNow (6:3 issue 33) 81, p. 47.

RUSSO, Albert
  "Journey Under a Microscope." Confr (21) Wint 81, p. 128.

RUTAN, Catherine
  "Women in the Rain." GeoR (35:1) Spr 81, pp. 124-125.

RUTSALA, Vern
  "The Dream." PoNow (6:1 issue 31) 81, p. 7.
  "East of Here." QW (12) Spr-Sum 81, pp. 114-5.
  "Haunting the All Night Stores." MinnR (17) Aut 81, p. 21.
  "Hello to the Back Row." ThRiPo (17/18) 81, p. 59.
  "Helpless Day." QW (12) Spr-Sum 81, p. 116.
  "How Things Go." MassR (22:2) Sum 81, p. 395.
  "Invitation." MassR (22:2) Sum 81, p. 396.
  "Moonlight Walk: Li Po." GeoR (35:4) Wint 81, p. 801.
  "Out There." MinnR (17) Aut 81, p. 20.

RYAN, Dennis
  "Raspberry Slump." PoNow (6:3 issue 33) 81, p. 36.

RYAN, Michael
  "First Exercise." AmerPoR (10:3) My-Je 81, p. 13.
  "In Winter." AmerPoR (10:3) My-Je 81, p. 13.
  "Memory." AmerPoR (10:3) My-Je 81, p. 13.

RZEZAK, Elisa Ruth
  "Casi todo." Mairena (3:7) 81, p. 68.
  "Combate." Mairena (3:7) 81, p. 68.
  "Matutino." Mairena (3:7) 81, p. 68.

SAARIKOSKI, Pentti
  from Invitation to the Dance: (II, III, XXV, XXVII, XXX, XXXIV,
    XLVII, L, LIV, LVIII) (tr. by Herbert Lomas). PoetryE (6) Aut
    81, pp. 35-38.
  from The Dance-Floor on the Mountain: "Today, I walk another way"
    (tr. by Anselm Hollo). PoetryE (6) Aut 81, pp. 38-40.

SABINES, Jaime
  "I Always Thought a Walk in the Dark" (tr. by Naomi Lindstrom).
    CharR (7:1) Spr 81, p. 52.

SACHS, Nelly
  "Three Poems" (tr. by Robert Hauptman). WebR (6:2) 81, p. 104.

SADOFF, Ira
  "Early April Morning: Fairfield, Maine." Ploughs (7:1) 81, p. 100.
  "Gathering Kindling." NewYorker (57:38) 9 N 81, p. 50.
  "The Kreutzer Sonata." OP (31/32) Aut 81, pp. 82-83.
  "My Old German Girl Friend's." MissouriR (4:3) Sum 81, p. 20.
  "On First Sighting a Man." VirQR (57:3) Sum 81, pp. 467-468.
  "Summer Solstice In Praise of the Bourgeoise." Ploughs (7:1) 81, p.
    101.
  "Villains." MissouriR (4:3) Sum 81, p. 21.
  "Walking Down Castro Street After Frank O'Hara." PartR (48:1) 81,
    p. 129.

SAGAN, Miriam
"Mary to Shelley." HolCrit (18:3 [i. e. 4]) O 81, p. 9.
"Notes for America." Cond (7) Spr 81, pp. 61-62.
"Some Ghazals for the Neighbors." Wind (11:40) 81, p. 22.

SA'ID, Ali Ahmad see ADONIS

SAID, Ali Ahmed see ADONIS

ST. CLAIR, Philip
"Red Jacket." HiramPoR (30) Spr-Sum 81, p. 37.

SAISER, Marjorie
"Antithesis." Peb (21) 81, p. 72.

SAITO, Mokichi
"Flies" (tr. by Graeme Wilson). DenQ (16:4) Wint 81, p. 29.

SAKELLARIOU, Becky
"Sisters." 13thM (5:1/2) 80, p. 105.

SALINA, Luis Omar
"What Is This Something." CharR (7:1) Spr 81, p. 30.

SALINGER, Herman
"Behavior In Fair Weather" (tr. of Karl Krolow). Mund (12/13) 80-81,
    p. 57.
"Forever" (tr. of Karl Krolow). Mund (12/13) 80-81, p. 58.
"The Skin Into Which One Is Put" (tr. of Karl Krolow). Mund (12/13)
    80-81, p. 60.
"Small Change" (tr. of Karl Krolow). Mund (12/13) 80-81, p. 58.
"Summer. Forms" (tr. of Karl Krolow). Mund (12/13) 80-81, p. 59.
"Too Late" (tr. of Karl Krolow). Mund (12/13) 80-81, p. 57.

SALKEY, Andrew
"Away (for Charles Hyatt)." MassR (22:1) Spr 81, p. 58.
"Breaking the Ice." Stand (22: 4) 81, p. 13.
"El Mío Mar (for Nicolás Guillén)." MassR (22:1) Spr 81, p. 59.
"La Tierra Cubana" (in memory of Lourdes Casal). Areito (27: 28) 81,
    p. frontcover.
"Two." Ploughs (6:4) 81, p. 56.
"Veranda Prayer." Ploughs (6:4) 81, p. 57.
"White Metallic Element." NewL (47:4) Sum 81, p. 52.

SALLAH, Tijan M.
"Birds." Obs (6:1/2) Spr-Sum 80, p. 210.
"On Denton Bridge." Obs (6:1/2) Spr-Sum 80, p. 210.

SALLI-DAWSON, Donna
"The Heart." QW (12) Spr-Sum 81, p. 72.

SALOMON, I. L.
"Las Animas" (tr. of Mario Luzi). Mund (12/13) 80-81, pp. 232-233.

SALSICH, Albert
"Fantasy Dance." KanQ (13:3/4) Sum-Aut 81, p. 159.
"Men Together." KanQ (13:3/4) Sum-Aut 81, p. 160.

SALTER, Mary Jo
"For an Italian Cousin." NewEngR (4:1) Aut 81, pp. 53-4.

SALZMANN, Jerome
"Napoleon." PikeR (2) Sum 81, p. 27.
"System Maker." PikeR (2) Sum 81, p. 26.

SAMUEL, Jean
"Tigers the Color of Light." Prima (6/7) 81, p. 39.

SANCHEZ, Rubén
"Amor y sus cuatro letras Como lo es la mujer con un clavo crucifi-
    cada sin cruz." Metam (3:2/4:1) 80-81, p. 75.
"La violencia." Metam (3:2/4:1) 80-81, p. 76.

SANCHEZ PELAEZ, Juan
"They ignore me" (tr. by Ann McBride and Mary McBride). Mund
    (12/13) 80-81, pp. 106-107.

SANCHO ROJO, María Elena
"Rimas." Mairena (3:7) 81, p. 100.

SANDEEN, Ernest
"Predicting the Past." Poetry (139:3) D 81, p. 156.

SANDERS, Mark
"The Empty Farm Place." Peb (21) 81, p. 23.
"19." Northeast (3:11) Sum 81, p. 29.
"10." Northeast (3:11) Sum 81, p. 28.

SANDSTROEM, Yvonne L.
"The Butterfly" (tr. of Harry Martinson). Mund (12/13) 80-81, p. 112.
"Elegy for a Dead Labrador" (tr. of Lars Gustafsson). NewYorker
    (57:27) 24 Ag 81, p. 34.
"Lines for the Count of Venosa" (tr. of Lars Gustafsson). Mund (12/
    13) 80-81, pp. 94-98.

SANDY, Stephen
"Family Album." Salm (52/53) Spr/Sum 81, pp. 63-64.
"Odes, Book I. v" (tr. of Horace). SenR (12:1/2) 81, p. 33.
"Post Partem Blue." Salm (52/53) Spr/Sum 81, p. 61.
"Survivor, Walking." Poetry (137:4) Ja 81, pp. 197-198.
"When April." Salm (52/53) Spr/Sum 81, pp. 62-63.
"Young Man With Infant." Salm (52/53) Spr/Sum 81, p. 64.

SANER, Reg
"The Blue Changes." CreamCR (7:1) 81, pp. 68-69.
"Bright Sun & Windstorm up Glacier Gorge." CreamCR (7:1) 81, p.
    67.
"The Man-In-The-Moon." Poetry (139:3) D 81, pp. 152-153.
"Nostalgia for Creede, Colorado." CreamCR (7:1) 81, pp. 65-66.
"Poem." CreamCR (7:1) 81, p. 63.
"Skiing Alone Near the Divide." PoNow (6:2 issue 32) 81, p. 16.
"To Take Yourself by Surprise." CreamCR (7:1) 81, p. 64.
"The Tongue As Red Dog." ThRiPo (17/18) 81, p. 68.
"Wearing Breakfast for Two." CreamCR (7:1) 81, p. 70.

SANFILIPPO, Amelia
"The New Dress." Sam (117) 81, p. 27.

SANFORD, Richard
  "Nerve Gas." Outbr (6/7) Aut 80-Spr 81, pp. 107-108.

SANGE, Gary
  "Gramps." LitR (24:3) Spr 81, pp. 395-396.
  "The Lifter." PoNow (6:2 issue 32) 81, p. 44.
  "The poolhall at noon is a hoard of dark." PoNow (6:1 issue 31) 81,
    p. 31.

SANGE, Sally Harris
  "The Intensive Care Nursery: From Maternity." Comm (108:22) 4 D
    81, p. 698.
  "The Intensive Care Nursery: The Waiting." Comm (108:22) 4 D 81,
    p. 698.

SANGER, Peter
  "The Man in the Woods." PottPort (3) 81, p. 21.
  "Ruffed Grouse." PottPort (3) 81, p. 4.
  "The White Lady" (Margaret Webster, Chebogue Union, Churchyard Ca.
    1820). PottPort (3) 81, p. 34.

SANTAMARIA, Carmen Isabel
  "Poema al Guadalquivir." Puerto Wint 81, p. 47.

SANTIAGO, José Manuel Torres see TORRES SANTIAGO, José Manuel

SANTIAGO, William M. Mena
  "Amor camarada." Mairena (3:7) 81, p. 70.
  "Discúlpenme si digo y si no digo." Mairena (3:7) 81, pp. 71-72.
  "Mañana." Mairena (3:7) 81, pp. 70-71.

SANTIAGO BERMUDEZ, Ariel
  "El niño del campo." Mairena (2:6) 80, pp. 46-7.

SANTOS, Sherod
  "The Art of Cruel Colors." NewYorker (57:35) 19 O 81, p. 44.
  "The Breakdown." Poetry (138:5) Ag 81, pp. 285-286.
  "Burning The Fields." QW (13) Aut/Wint 81/82, pp. 90-91.
  "The Coming of Fall." Poetry (138:5) Ag 81, p. 290.
  "The Evening Light Along the Sound." Poetry (138:5) Ag 81, pp. 287-
    288.
  "The Garden Party" (after K. M.). Antaeus (43) Aut 81, pp. 43-44.
  "Second Person Singular." QW (13) Aut/Wint 81/82, pp. 92-93.
  "Terra Incognita." Antaeus (43) Aut 81, p. 42.
  "View From the Hotel Lobby." Poetry (138:5) Ag 81, p. 288.
  "Waiting for the Storm." Poetry (138:5) Ag 81, p. 289.
  "Winter Landscape With a Girl In Brown Shoes." Nat (232:4) 31 Ja 81,
    p. 118.

SANTOS SILVA, Loreina
  "Soledad." Mairena (2:6) 80, p. 67.
  "XXX." Mairena (3:7) 81, p. 97.
  "XXXI." Mairena (3:7) 81, p. 97.

SANTOS TIRADO, Adrián
  "Retorno." Mairena (2:5) Aut 80, p. 76.
  "Vendrá entonces la lluvia." Mairena (2:6) 80, pp. 47-8.

SANZ, Yolanda Fernández see FERNANDEZ SANZ, Yolanda

SAPHIRE, Jonathan J.
"Untitled." Wind (11:43) 81, p. 31.

SAPIA, Yvonne
"Burning the Leaves in Winter." CapeR (17:1) Wint 81, p. 11.
"The River Farmers." CapeR (16:2) Sum 81, p. 11.

SAPPHO
"Déduke mèn 'a selánna." SenR (12:1/2) 81, p. 2.
"The westering moon has gone" (tr. by Robert Fitzgerald). SenR (12:
1/2) 81, p. 3.

SARGENT, Robert
"Mississippi Jukejoint: Highway 51." CimR (54) Ja 81, p. 4.

SARRERA, Danielle
"C'est d'une seule âme." SenR (10:2/11:1) 79-80, p. 126.
"I write the third gospel" (tr. by Linda Orr). SenR (10:2/11:1) 79-80,
p. 123.
"If we consider" (tr. by Linda Orr). SenR (10:2/11:1) 79-80, p. 125.
"It is from a single soul" (tr. by Linda Orr). SenR (10:2/11:1) 79-80,
p. 127.
"J'écris le troisième évangile." SenR (10:2/11:1) 79-80, p. 122.
"The Knight of the Trepan" (tr. by Lydia Davis). ParisR (23:81) Aut
81, pp. 106-109.
"Si nous considérons." SenR (10:2/11:1) 79-80, p. 124.

SARRETT, Sylvia
"In This My Thirteenth Year of Teaching." EngJ (70:4) Ap 81, p. 22.
"II. B. In 50 Words or Less, Explain Why You Want to Teach." EngJ
(70:8) D 81, p. 43.

SATEL, Sally
"On Reading a Book of Arbus Photographs." Prima (6/7) 81, p. 52.
"Waterglass." Prima (6/7) 81, p. 52.

SATHERLEY, David
"Map Under The Skin." PottPort (3) 81, p. 4.
"Quid Pro Quo." PottPort (3) 81, p. 27.

SATO, Harou
"Quatrain" (tr. by Graeme Wilson). DenQ (16:4) Wint 81, p. 36.

SAULS, Roger
"Prayer." OhioR (26), p. 56.
"Woman Smoking." OhioR (26), p. 57.

SAUNDERS, Geraldine
"Waiting in Line." US1 (14/15) Aut/Wint 81, p. 9.

SAVAGE, Tom
"All (Wo)men Created Equal To The Task." Tele (17) 81, pp. 69-71.
"Androgyny." Tele (17) 81, p. 68.

SAVITT, Lynne
"After the Rape" (for my son, Matthew). PoNow (6:1 issue 31) 81, p.
17.
"First Love Song." PoNow (6:1 issue 31) 81, p. 17.
"Prison Poem #32." 13thM (5:1/2) 80, p. 124.

SAVOIE, Terry
"Day-Book." NoAmR (266:4) D 81, p. 37.

SAVORY, Teo
"Rocks" (tr. of Eugène Guillevic). Mund (12/13) 80-81, pp. 234-236.

SAWA, Yuki
"Four Thousand Days And Nights" (tr. of Ruichi Tamura, w/ Edith Shiffert). Mund (12/13) 80-81, p. 36.

SAYEGH, Tawfiq
"No, And Why" (tr. by Sargon Boulus). Mund (12/13) 80-81, p. 302.

SCANNELL, Vernon
"Some Pictures of the 'Thirties." Stand (22: 1) 80, p. 50.

SCANTLEBURY, Mark
"The Second Coming." Wind (11:43) 81, p. 34.
"Other Levels of Significance." SouthernPR (21: 1) Spr 81, p. 68.

SCARPA, Vivien C.
"The Gamut." Wind (11:41) 81, p. 41.
"Through Windows." Wind (11:41) 81, pp. 41-42.

SCATES, Maxine
"Home." PraS (55:4) Wint 81-82, pp. 39-40.
"Island." BelPoJ (31:3) Spr 81, pp. 26-27.
"The Weavers." PraS (55:4) Wint 81-82, pp. 38-9.
"Your Children" (for Cecelia Hagen). PraS (55:4) Wint 81-82, pp. 40-41.

SCHAECHTERLE, Carol
"Michael, Just Baptized." Peb (21) 81, pp. 63-64.

SCHAEFER, Ted
"The Attic." KanQ (13:3/4) Sum-Aut 81, p. 107.
"Chicago River Poem." CapeR (17:1) Wint 81, p. 37.
"Danaë Leaves Wisconsin." Vis (7) 81, n. p.
"The Empire." KanQ (13:3/4) Sum-Aut 81, p. 108.
"The Hunting Camp's Collective Love Song." NewL (48:1) Aut 81, p. 53.
"The Liberty Asphalt Corporation." KanQ (13:3/4) Sum-Aut 81, p. 107.
"Pigweed." PoNow (6:2 issue 32) 81, p. 37.
"Realtors in Spring." PoNow (6:2 issue 32) 81, p. 37.
"The Swan Wife and the Seal Wife." Vis (7) 81, n. p.
"Welcoming the Sears Men." CapeR (17:1) Wint 81, p. 37.

SCHAEFFER, Susan Fromberg
"Below." BallSUF (22:4) Aut 81, p. 34.
"Cobalt." PraS (55:1/2) Spr-Sum 81, p. 299.
"Falling Snow." CentR (25:1) Wint 81, p. 41.
"The Garden." ThRiPo (17/18) 81, p. 62.
"Gifts." CentR (25:3) Sum 81, pp. 257-259.
"Hunting the Lily." StoneC (8: 3) Spr 81, pp. 34-35.
"I Will Sink." CentR (25:3) Sum 81, pp. 259-260.
"Mercury." PraS (55:1/2) Spr-Sum 81, pp. 297-8.
"She Asks for Help." OP (31/32) Aut 81, p. 69.
"Sleeping Last." OP (31/32) Aut 81, pp. 169-170.

"Spring." CentR (25:1) Wint 81, pp. 41-42.
"The Trees." BallSUF (22:4) Aut 81, p. 23.
"Uranium." PraS (55:1/2) Spr-Sum 81, pp. 300-302.

SCHARNHORST, Gary
  "Sonnet in Subjunctive Mood." BallSUF (21:4) Aut 80, p. 4.

SCHAUM, Melita
  "Selections From The Letters." DenQ (16:1) Spr 81, pp. 46-47.

SCHEDLER, Gilbert
  "The Difficulties of Being a Gandhian in California." ChrC (98:32) 14
    O 81, p. 1020.
  "Divine Rites." ChrC (98:4) 4-11 F 81, p. 104.
  "Family." ChrC (98:27) 9 S 81, p. 853.
  "Sermons." ChrC (98:28) 16 S 81, p. 906.

SCHEELE, Roy
  "The Earth Coming Green Again." Peb (21) 81, p. 110.
  "Last Watch." ThRiPo (17/18) 81, p. 34.
  "Near Dorchester, in Dorset, from the Train." Peb (21) 81, p. 111.

SCHEER, Linda
  "Have You Noticed?" (tr. of Marco Antonio Montes de Oca). PoNow
    (5:6 issue 30) 81, p. 31.
  "My Brothers Left Little by Little" (tr. of Marco Antonio Campos).
    PoNow (6:1 issue 31) 81, p. 42.
  "Variations Without A Theme" (tr. of Marco Antonio Montes de Oca).
    PoNow (5:6 issue 30) 81, p. 31.

SCHELL, Gary
  "Naked Trees." PoNow (6:3 issue 33) 81, p. 36.

SCHELLING, Andrew
  "A First Winter's Rain." Thrpny (4) Wint 81, p. 17.
  "The Redtail Hawks." Ploughs (7:1) 81, p. 149.
  "Words of a Go-Between." Ploughs (7:1) 81, p. 148.

SCHEMM, Ripley
  "Eugène Boudin's 'The Gleanor'--1856." CutB (16) Spr-Sum 81, p. 6.
  "Lolly Doo Dum Day with My Daughter." CutB (16) Spr-Sum 81, p. 7.
  "View from the Kitchen." CutB (16) Spr-Sum 81, p. 8.

SCHENKER, Donald
  "Excerpts." WormR (81/82) 81, pp. 4-5.

SCHENWIESE, Ernst
  "Alles Ist Nur." Mund (11:2) 79, p. 76.
  "Everything Is Only" (tr. by Herbert Kuhner). Mund (11:2) 79, p. 77.

SCHERZER, Joe
  "Bruckner boulevard." PikeR (2) Sum 81, p. 16.
  "Lines for daisy." PikeR (2) Sum 81, p. 17.
  "Quick kiss." PikeR (2) Sum 81, p. 17.
  "Upstate." PikeR (2) Sum 81, p. 16.

SCHEVILL, James
  "Death of a Teacher" (to George W. Taylor). Im (7:2) 1981, p. 6.

"The Last New England Transcendentalist" (for Hyatt Waggoner).
MichQR (20:2) Spr 81, pp. 92-93.
"The Last New England Transcendentalist Tries to Fly His Soul As a
Kite." ThRiPo (17/18) 81, pp. 64-65.
"The Quiet Man of Simplicity" (for Robert Francis). PoNow (6:2 issue
32) 81, p. 39.
"Sitting on the Porch at Dawn." Im (7:2) 1981, p. 6.
"The T-Shirt Phenomenon in Minnesota On The Fourth of July." MinnR
(17) Aut 81, pp. 43-44.

SCHIFF, Jeff
"Written Christmas Eve." CreamCR (6:1) Aut 80, p. 26.

SCHLANGER, Judith
From "Liesse." SenR (10:2/11:1) 79-80, pp. 128-130.
From "Wild Rejoicing" (tr. by Linda Orr). SenR (10:2/11:1) 79-80, pp.
129-131.

SCHLICK, Karen
"Phases of the Moon." PottPort (3) 81, p. 50.

SCHLOSS, David
"City of Angels." Iowa (11:2/3) Spr-Sum 80, p. 92.
"Globe." Iowa (11:2/3) Spr-Sum 80, pp. 90-91.

SCHLOSSER, Robert
The Humidity Readings. Sam (113) 81, Entire issue.

SCHMID, Vernon
"Pentecost." ChrC (98:20) 3-10 Je 81, p. 637.
"Sunday Morning Sanctuaries." ChrC (98:30) 30 S 81, p. 965.

SCHMIDT, Augusto Frederico
"Dead Star" (tr. by Alexis Levitin). PortR (27: 2) 81, p. 31.

SCHMITZ, Dennis
"Birds." CimR (57) O 81, p. 4.
"Dressing Game." Iowa (11:2/3) Spr-Sum 80, pp. 101-102.
"Finding the Way." Tendril (11) Sum 81, p. 65.
"Marriage." Tendril (11) Sum 81, p. 66.
"On a Dark Afternoon." Field (25) Aut 81, p. 62.
"Singing." Antaeus (40/41) Wint-Spr 81, pp. 379-380.
"Uncle Lucien." Field (25) Aut 81, pp. 60-61.

SCHNACK, Asger
"The Ambercollectors" (tr. by Asger Schnack and Alexander Taylor).
PoNow (5:6 issue 30) 81, p. 40.

SCHNACKENBERG, Gjertrud
"Advent Calendar." Atl (248:6) D 81, p. 69.

SCHNEEBERGER, Susan
"Colorado Sea-bird." SmPd (18:1) Spr 81, p. 30.

SCHNEIDER, Pat
"Mother Goose." MinnR (17) Aut 81, p. 35.
"This is a River." MinnR (17) Aut 81, p. 36.

SCHNEIDERMAN, Steven
"Archery." PoNow (6:3 issue 33) 81, p. 36.

SCHNORBUS, Frank
"Oak Leaves." ArizQ (37:3) Aut 81, p. 196.

SCHOB, E. M.
"Death." SouthernPR (21: 1) Spr 81, p. 42.

SCHOOLFIELD, George
"Advice to Happy Folk" (tr. of Lars Huldén). PoetryE (6) Aut 81, p. 27.
"Bulletin from Staff-Headquarters" (tr. of Lars Huldén). PoetryE (6) Aut 81, pp. 21-22.
"The Children Were Packed Off" (tr. of Lars Huldén). PoetryE (6) Aut 81, pp. 23-24.
"Countryside Organizations" (tr. of Lars Huldén). PoetryE (6) Aut 81, pp. 22-23.
"Like a Cautious Flier" (tr. of Lars Huldén). PoetryE (6) Aut 81, p. 25.
"Today God" (tr. of Lars Huldén). PoetryE (6) Aut 81, p. 26.
"When the Church Burned" (tr. of Lars Huldén). PoetryE (6) Aut 81, p. 24.

SCHOR, Patricia
"Eyes" (tr. of Carolina D'Antin). LetFem (7:2) Aut 81, p. 64.

SCHOR, Sandra
"Death of an Audio Engineer." Ploughs (6:4) 81, pp. 188-190.
"Gestorben In Zurich." Ploughs (6:4) 81, pp. 191-192.

SCHOTT, Carol
"The Mother." Poem (42) Jul 81, p. 64.
"The Retarded Boy in 306." Poem (42) Jul 81, p. 63.

SCHRAMM, Richard
"Blood Child." QW (12) Spr-Sum 81, p. 52.

SCHREIBER, Jan
"Saturday Morning." SouthernR (17:3) Sum 81, p. 582.

SCHREIBER, Ron
"The end of Leo." Wind (11:42) 81, p. 33.
"The gay beach, Boca Raton." Wind (11:42) 81, pp. 34-35.
"The line." Wind (11:42) 81, p. 34.
"To G--." Ascent (77/79) 81, p. 184.

SCHUCHMAN, Dorothy
"The Old Lady Retires." HolCrit (18:3) Je 81, pp. 10-11.

SCHULMAN, Grace
"Flight Commands." Poetry (138:5) Ag 81, pp. 261-262.
"Hemispheres." Nat (233:20) 12 D 81, p. 650.
"Judgement" (tr. of T. Carmi). Pequod (13) 81, p. 1.
"Losses." GeoR (35:4) Wint 81, p. 853.
"The Messenger." Antaeus (40/41) Wint-Spr 81, p. 381.
"Miracles" (tr. of T. Carmi). Pequod (13) 81, p. 3.

"The Stars and the Moon." Hudson (34:3) Aut 81, p. 370.
"This Sunset" (tr. of T. Carmi). Pequod (13) 81, p. 2.

SCHULTE, Rainer
   "Glance that the morning invades" (tr. of Claude Esteban). Mund (12/
      13) 80-81, p. 92.
   "One day I will find a word" (tr. of Roberto Juarróz, w/ Sergio Mon-
      dragón). Mund (12/13) 80-81, p. 23.
   "No one yet against the sky" (tr. of Claude Esteban). Mund (12/13)
      80-81, p. 92.
   "With each stone" (tr. of Claude Esteban). Mund (12/13) 80-81, pp.
      92-93.

SCHULTZ, Philip
   "A Person." NewOR (8:2) Sum 81, p. 177.

SCHULTZ, Robert
   "The Light on the Wall." Hudson (34:2) Sum 81, pp. 246-247.

SCHULZE, Axel
   "Die Schienenleger." SenR (12:1/2) 81, pp. 16-18.
   "The Tracklayers" (tr. by Frederic Will). SenR (12:1/2) 81, pp. 17-
      19.

SCHUYLER, James
   "August First, 1974." AmerPoR (10:3) My-Je 81, p. 16.
   "Back." ParisR (23:79) Spr 81, p. 252.
   "Blizzard." ParisR (23:79) Spr 81, p. 253.
   "Heather and Calendulas." ParisR (23:79) Spr 81, pp. 251-252.
   "Linen." ParisR (23:79) Spr 81, p. 254.
   "Pastime." ParisR (23:79) Spr 81, pp. 253-254.
   "Red Brick And Brown Stone." AmerPoR (10:3) My-Je 81, p. 17.
   "Self-Pity Is A Kind Of Lying, Too." AmerPoR (10:3) My-Je 81, p.
      17.
   "We Walk." ParisR (23:79) Spr 81, p. 251.

SCHWARTZ, Hillel
   "Edel's Tattoos." PraS (55:4) Wint 81-82, pp. 65-6.
   "Elmer's Museum, Chamber of Commerce (Open Every Day)." Tendril
      (11) Sum 81, pp. 68-69.
   "Helen's Corset Heaven." Tendril (11) Sum 81, p. 67.
   "Immigrant." Comm (108:15) 28 Ag 81, p. 467.
   "Negatives." Thrpny (6) Sum 81, p. 21.
   "Painting in an Old Office." Nimrod (25:1) Aut-Wint 81, p. 90.
   "Princess Naomi, Reader of Palms." Tendril (11) Sum 81, p. 72.
   "Sayings from The Yiddish." CalQ (18/19) 81, pp. 117-119.
   "Sideshow." Nimrod (25:1) Aut-Wint 81, p. 90.
   "Xerxes Signs." Tendril (11) Sum 81, pp. 70-71.

SCHWARTZ, Jeffrey
   "Contending with the Dark." Ascent (77/79) 81, p. 190.
   "Faces of Egypt" (for E.W.W.). Ascent (77/79) 81, p. 189.
   "Florida (A Land of Flowers)." Ascent (77/79) 81, p. 188.
   "Insomnia." HangL (40) Aut 81, p. 55.
   "The Lady in the Window of the Island Hotel." Ascent (77/79) 81, p.
      191.
   "A Word About Self-Defense." Ascent (77/79) 81, p. 188.

SCHWARTZ, Lloyd
    "Interior Monologue." Shen (31:4) 80, pp. 10-11.
    "Mental Cases." MassR (22:1) Spr 81, pp. 153-162.
    "Villanelle." Ploughs (7:2) 81, p. 138.

SCHWARTZ, S. G.
    "Fears and Imaginations." LitR (24:3) Spr 81, pp. 403-404.

SCHWERNER, Armand
    "Pantoum, With Some Material From George Oppen And Robert Dun-
        can." PartR (48:2) 81, p. 254.

SCHWERTFEGER, Ruth
    "Factory Streets by Day" (tr. of Paul Zech, w/ James Liddy). DenQ
        (16:1) Spr 81, p. 68.
    "To God" (tr. of Else Lasker-Schüler, w/ James Liddy). DenQ (16:1)
        Spr 81, p. 69.

SCOTELLARO, Robert
    "He Wants." WormR (84) 81, p. 120.
    "Ode To The 2 Thin Curls Still Left From The Old Dynasty On The
        Front Of My Head." WormR (84) 81, p. 120.
    "Scarecrow." WormR (84) 81, p. 120.
    "Stand Off On The Front Steps." WormR (84) 81, p. 121.

SCOTELLARO, Rocco
    "Charity of my Village" (tr. by Ruth Feldman and Brian Swann).
        PoNow (5:6 issue 30) 81, p. 41.
    "The City Sweetheart" (tr. by Ruth Feldman and Brian Swann). PoNow
        (5:6 issue 30) 81, p. 41.
    "The Dawn is Always New" (tr. by Ruth Feldman and Brian Swann).
        PoNow (5:6 issue 30) 81, p. 25.
    "The Grain of the Sepulchre" (tr. by Ruth Feldman and Brian Swann).
        PoNow (5:6 issue 30) 81, p. 41.
    "Journeys" (tr. by Ruth Feldman and Brian Swann). PoNow (5:6 issue
        30) 81, p. 25.
    "Now that July Rules" (tr. by Ruth Feldman and Brian Swann). PoNow
        (5:6 issue 30) 81, p. 25.
    "Rainbow" (tr. by Ruth Feldman and Brian Swann). PoNow (5:6 issue
        30) 81, p. 41.
    "The Rule" (tr. by Ruth Feldman and Brian Swann). PoNow (5:6 issue
        30) 81, p. 41.
    "Vico Tapera" (tr. by Ruth Feldman and Brian Swann). PoNow (5:6
        issue 30) 81, p. 25.

SCOTT, Dennis
    "Solution." Mund (12/13) 80-81, p. 303.

SCOTT, Herbert
    "As She Enters Her Seventieth Year She Dreams of Milk." Nimrod
        (25:1) Aut-Wint 81, pp. 49-53.
    "On the Missouri." PoNow (6:2 issue 32) 81, p. 7.
    "Oklahoma Sunset." PoNow (6:1 issue 31) 81, p. 19.
    "The Other Life" (for James Wright, in memoriam). Nimrod (25:1)
        Aut-Wint 81, p. 54.

SCRIBNER, Douglas
    "Crazy As A Loon." Sam (116) 81, p. 18.

SCULLY, James
  "Housekeeping Progress." MinnR (17) Aut 81, pp. 24-25.
  "Taking Liberties." MinnR (17) Aut 81, pp. 23-24.

SEABAUGH, Alan
  "Two Dead Children." CapeR (17:1) Wint 81, p. 30.

SEABURG, Alan
  "The Hucky." CapeR (16:2) Sum 81, p. 2.

SEARS, Janet
  "The Hitchhiker." PottPort (3) 81, p. 44.

SEARS, Peter
  "Day of Calm Sea." PoNow (6:1 issue 31) 81, p. 33.

SECREAST, Donald
  "To Robin, Who Is Taking Up Fish and a New Name." HiramPoR (30)
    Spr-Sum 81, p. 38.

SEE, Molly
  "In the Rains of Late October." WestHR (35:3) Aut 81, p. 251.
  "Walking Out to Feed the Horses." WestHR (35:3) Aut 81, p. 252.

SEIDEL, Frederick
  "Flame." ParisR (23:79) Spr 81, p. 255.
  "Our Gods." NewYRB (28:5) 2 Ap 81, p. 37.
  "Scotland." AmerPoR (10:3) My-Je 81, p. 3.

SEIDMAN, Hugh
  "The Best Thing." Pequod (13) 81, p. 9.
  "The Last Or The First." UnmOx (22) Wint 81, p. 43.
  "The Mother." ParisR (23:81) Aut 81, pp. 134-135.
  "Promised Land." Pequod (13) 81, p. 10.
  "Screen Dream." UnmOx (22) Wint 81, p. 42.
  "We Knew." UnmOx (22) Wint 81, p. 44.

SEIFERT, Edward
  "The Redeemed." ChrC (98:14) 29 Ap 81, p. 470.

SELLERS, Bettie
  "After the Very Last Frost." Poem (43) Nov 81, p. 12.
  "In a Dark Wood" (for Barth). GeoR (35:4) Wint 81, pp. 836-837.
  "Letter Written in Darkness." BelPoJ (31:3) Spr 81, p. 35.
  "Miss Essie Bell and Papa Hemingway." Poem (43) Nov 81, p. 11.
  "A Routine Surgical Procedure" (for D., dying in April). BelPoJ (31:3)
    Spr 81, p. 34.

SELTZER, Joanne
  "Dead Rats." PoNow (6:3 issue 33) 81, p. 36.

SELVAGGIO, Marc
  "On Cypress Avenue." PoNow (6:3 issue 33) 81, p. 37.
  "To Fillmore Holly, Reedman, Who Only Recorded One Session--Chi-
    cago, October, 1923--With Berny Young's Creole Jazz Band."
    PoNow (6:3 issue 33) 81, p. 37.
  "Looking for Bear." PoNow (6:3 issue 33) 81, p. 37.

SEMENOVICH, Joseph
    "Calligraphies." WebR (6:2) 81, pp. 63-64.
    "A fall Poem." SmPd (18:2) Spr 81, p. 25.

SEMONES, Charles
    "For a Suicide of 1979." Wind (11:40) 81, pp. 30-31.
    "South Georgia Fantasy" (for S. D. S.). Wind (11:40) 81, p. 29.

SENA, Jorge de
    "Last Request" (tr. by Alexis Levitin). Im (7:2) 1981, p. 10.

SERENI, Vittorio
    from Holland: "Amsterdam" (tr. by Ruth Feldman and Brian Swann).
        PoNow (5:6 issue 30) 81, p. 42.
    from Holland: "The Interpreter" (tr. by Ruth Feldman and Brian
        Swann). PoNow (5:6 issue 30) 81, p. 42.
    from Holland: "Volendam" (tr. by Ruth Feldman and Brian Swann).
        PoNow (5:6 issue 30) 81, p. 42.

SETO, Thelma
    "Diving." PortR (27: 2) 81, p. 4.
    "My Father's Friends." PortR (27: 2) 81, p. 5.
    "Ledger." PortR (27: 2) 81, p. 92.
    "Lyric for Khomeini." PortR (27: 2) 81, p. 4.
    "Sunrise at Nag's Head." PortR (27: 2) 81, p. 4.
    "The Well-Cultivated Garden." PortR (27: 2) 81, p. 5.

SEVERY, Bruce
    "Bust on Sunset Blvd." PoNow (6:3 issue 33) 81, p. 37.
    "Glenn Eagle, in the Pelican, Fort Yates, N. D. " PoNow (6:1 issue
        31) 81, p. 44.

SEVOV, Kolyo
    "At the Beach" (tr. by Greg Gatenby and Dobrina Nikolova). PortR
        (27: 1) 81, p. 14.
    "Besides Rhodes" (tr. by Greg Gatenby and Dobrina Nikolova). PortR
        (27: 1) 81, p. 14.

SEXTON, Anne
    "Admonitions To A Special Person." ParisR (23:79) Spr 81, pp. 268-269.
    "The Children." Mund (12/13) 80-81, pp. 343-344.
    "Rowing." Mund (12/13) 80-81, pp. 342-343.

SEXTON, Tom
    "Landlord." ColEng (43:8) D 81, p. 791.

SHAFER, Margaret
    "Photograph: Nina." Poetry (137:5) F 81, p. 278.

SHAKA, Nattt Moziah
    "Dominion Atlantic Railway" (for Susan). PottPort (3) 81, p. 38.
    "North Atlantic." PottPort (3) 81, p. 46.

SHANTIRIS, Kita
    "The Good Guy." Poetry (138:2) My 81, pp. 73-74.

SHAPIRO, Alan
    "Bad Debts." AmerS (50:1) Wint 80-81, p. 100.

"On the Eve of the Warsaw Uprising." ChiR (32:4) Spr 81, pp. 32-33.
"Rain" (for my Grandmother). Ploughs (7:2) 81, pp. 91-92.

SHAPIRO, David
   "To The Earth" (to Meyer Schapiro). ParisR (23:79) Spr 81, p. 270.

SHAPIRO, Harvey
   "At the Shore." Hudson (34:4) Wint 81, pp. 509-510.
   "Brooklyn Heights." Epoch (30:1) Aut 80, p. 41.
   "City." Epoch (30:1) Aut 80, p. 42.
   "Epitaph." Epoch (30:1) Aut 80, p. 44.
   "From the Greek Anthology." Epoch (30:1) Aut 80, p. 44.
   "The Parable about a Turkey." Epoch (30:1) Aut 80, p. 43.

SHARETT, Deirdre
   "My Mind Doesn't Run Toward Creation Myths" (for Louis Patler).
      Tele (17) 81, p. 115.

SHARTSE, Olga
   "Life's Beginning" (tr. of Petrus Brovka). PoNow (5:6 issue 30) 81,
      p. 11.

SHATTUCK, Roger
   "Moving Picture" (for Eileen). NewRep (184:13) 28 Mr 81, p. 24.
   "Palimpsest." Poetry (138:6) S 81, p. 320.
   "Street Scene." Poetry (138:6) S 81, p. 321.

SHAW, Robert B.
   "Blues Remembered." YaleR (71: 1) Aut 81, p. 94.
   "Early Natural History." Poetry (138:5) Ag 81, pp. 278-279.
   "Just Here and Now." YaleR (71: 1) Aut 81, pp. 95-96.

SHEA, Maggie
   "Beginnings." Poem (43) Nov 81, p. 55.
   "The Maple Trees." Poem (43) Nov 81, p. 56.
   "On the Beach." Poem (43) Nov 81, p. 57.

SHEARS, Judith
   "Letting the Poem Go." BelPoJ (31:3) Spr 81, p. 13.
   "Protective Coloration." BelPoJ (31:3) Spr 81, pp. 13-14.

SHECK, Laurie
   "Doll House." Ploughs (7:1) 81, pp. 140-141.
   "House." PoetryNW (22:1) Spr 81, pp. 22-23.
   "Käthe Kollwitz." VirQR (57:2) Spr 81, p. 274.
   "Scar." VirQR (57:2) Spr 81, pp. 272-273.
   "Simone Weil At Le Puy." MissouriR (4:2) Wint 81-82, p. 17.
   "Swallows." PraS (55:3) Aut 81, p. 73.
   "Twelve poems." ArkRiv (5:1) 81, pp. 39-52.

SHEEHAN, Marc J.
   "How The Dawn Comes." PoNow (6:3 issue 33) 81, p. 38.

SHEEHE STARK, Sharon see STARK, Sharon Sheehe

SHEFFLER, Natalie R.
   "Woman with a Blue Face, I." Wind (11:40) 81, p. 32.
   "Woman with a Blue Face, II." Wind (11:40) 81, p. 33.

SHELDON, Glenn
    "Death in Black and White." CreamCR (7:1) 81, p. 48.

SHEPARD, Neil
    "In the Dark." PikeR (2) Sum 81, p. 13.
    "Wilderness" (for Bill Hunt). PikeR (2) Sum 81, pp. 14-15.

SHEPHERD, J. Barrie
    "Easter Overture." ChrC (98:12) 8 Ap 81, p. 384.
    "Immigrant's Child." ChrC (98:38) 25 N 81, p. 1221.
    "Morning Pipe." ChrC (98:20) 3-10 Je 81, p. 638.
    "Season of Preparation." ChrC (98:41) 16 D 81, p. 1307.
    "Traveler." ChrC (98:43) 30 D 81, p. 1357.

SHEPPARD, Patricia
    "After Sappho." AntR (39:2) Spr 81, p. 207.
    "The Twin Pines." AntR (39:2) Spr 81, p. 206.

SHERBURNE, James C.
    "Hobby." Wind (11:41) 81, pp. 43-44.

SHERIDAN, David
    "Owen Roe O'Sullivan." HiramPoR (30) Spr-Sum 81, p. 39.

SHERLOCK, Karl
    "A Mourning Prayer." CreamCR (6:2) 81, pp. 125-26.
    "This Face." CreamCR (7:1) 81, pp. 98-99.

SHERMAN, Susan
    "What I Want." 13thM (5:1/2) 80, p. 75.

SHERRY, James
    "Prince Valiant." SunM (11) Spr 81, pp. 102-108.

SHETTERLY, Susan Hand
    "The Lobsterman's Death." BelPoJ (31:3) Spr 81, p. 33.

SHEVIN, Jonathan
    "Incident." ThRiPo (17/18) 81, p. 88.

SHIFFERT, Edith
    "Four Thousand Days And Nights" (tr. of Ruichi Tamura, w/ Yuki
        Sawa). Mund (12/13) 80-81, p. 36.

SHIMAZAKI, Toson
    "The Way" (tr. by Graeme Wilson). DenQ (16:4) Wint 81, p. 27.

SHIMER, Michael
    "Insomniloquy." SmPd (18:1) Wint 81, p. 20.
    "Insomniloquy." SmPd (18:2) Spr 81, p. 15.

SHINN, Sharon
    "Student Union." Poetry (137:6) Mr 81, p. 334.

SHIRAISHI, Kazuko
    "Street" (tr. by Graeme Wilson). DenQ (16:4) Wint 81, p. 50.

SHIRLEY, Aleda
    "Detail of a Portrait of a Man Reading a Volume of James." Shen
        (31:3) 80, p. 26.
    "Some of the Windows." SouthernPR (21: 1) Spr 81, p. 52.

SHIRLEY, Betty
    "If I Am Me." Meadows (2:1) 81, p. 68.

SHISLER, Barbara Esch
    "Baby." ChrC (98:34) 28 O 81, p. 1085.

SHNEY, Rinah
    "My Child" (tr. by Bernhard Frank). PoNow (5:6 issue 30) 81, p. 42.

SHOLL, Betsy
    "Humpty Dumpty." PoetryNW (22:4) Wint 81-82, pp. 14-15.
    "Love Poem." Ascent (77/79) 81, p. 193.
    "Narcissus." Ascent (77/79) 81, p. 192.

SHORE, Jane
    "Aubade." Ploughs (6:4) 81, p. 16.
    "Literature." Poetry (137:6) Mr 81, pp. 321-322.
    "Possessives." MissouriR (4:3) Sum 81, p. 18.
    "The Russian Doll." Ploughs (6:4) 81, pp. 13-15.
    "Sleeping Beauty." Poetry (137:6) Mr 81, pp. 324-325.
    "Tender Acre." Poetry (137:6) Mr 81, p. 323.
    "Young Woman on the Flying Trapeze." Poetry (137:6) Mr 81, pp.
        326-327.

SHOWS, Hal Steven
    "Traveller's Song." LittleM (13:1/2) Spr-Sum 79, c1981, p. 50.

SHU NING LIU, Stephen   see   LIU, Stephen Shu Ning

SHUCARD, Alan
    from Doberman Poems: "III. Another Lament." KanQ (13:3/4) Sum-
        Aut 81, p. 151.
    from Doberman Poems: "IV. Yet Another Love Song." KanQ (13:3/4)
        Sum-Aut 81, p. 151.

SHUMAKER, Peggy
    "A Cotton Chopper Arches." ThRiPo (17/18) 81, p. 90.
    "Night Fishing." ThRiPo (17/18) 81, p. 91.

SHUMWAY, Mary
    "Accidental." DenQ (16:2) Sum 81, pp. 66-67.
    "Fragment (found while walking seaward near Donegal Bay)" (for Mike
        McNamara 1940-1979). DenQ (16:2) Sum 81, p. 65.
    "Morgenstern." PraS (55:1/2) Spr-Sum 81, p. 287.
    "Morning After." DenQ (16:2) Sum 81, p. 68.

SHUNAN, Thomas F.
    "Cat Scan." CapeR (17:1) Wint 81, p. 28.

SHURIN, Aaron
    "The Calling." Thrpny (6) Sum 81, p. 5.

SHUTTLE, Penelope
    "Fire." Pequod (13) 81, p. 61.

SHUTTLEWORTH, Paul
  "An Invitation" (for Dwight Fullingim). Peb (21) 81, pp. 37-38.
  "Antelope." PoNow (6:1 issue 31) 81, p. 46.
  "A Day Short." OntR (15) Aut-Wint 81-82, p. 92.
  "The Failure of Open Hands." OntR (15) Aut-Wint 81-82, p. 91.

SIBLEY, Frederic
  "Sunday in the Song of the Morning." Shen (32:1) 80, pp. 83-84.

SIBLEY, Lawrence
  "The Tidal Bore." PottPort (3) 81, p. 50.

SICOLI, Dan
  "Rest Stop." CapeR (16:2) Sum 81, p. 4.

SIGNORE, Richard
  "She." HiramPoR (30) Spr-Sum 81, p. 40.

SILBERT, Layle
  "Resurrection." NewL (47:4) Sum 81, p. 97.

SILEN, Iván
  "La Fátida." Lugar (1:1) 79, p. 15.
  "La Hija de Dios." Lugar (1:1) 79, p. 15.

SILVA, Beverly
  "Easter Sunday." Vis (6) 81, n. p.

SILVA, Loreina Santos see SANTOS SILVA, Loreina

SILVA ESTRADA, Alfredo
  "Over the Limit" (tr. by Willis Barnstone). Mund (12/13) 80-81, pp.
    124-125.

SILVERBERG, Dan
  "Education." Sam (106) 81, p. 11.

SILVERMAN, Stuart Jay
  "How the Animals Buried the Hunter." PoetryNW (22:4) Wint 81-82,
    pp. 30-32.

SILVERSTEIN, Shel
  "Rosalie's Good Eats Café." Playb (28:12), pp. 251-259.

SIMCOX, Helen Earle
  "Poker Player." ChrC (98:25) 12-19 Ag 81, p. 801.

SIMIC, Charles
  "Astral Matters." Field (24) Spr 81, p. 42.
  "Crows." Atl (247:5) My 81, p. 43.
  "Dark Farmhouses." Field (24) Spr 81, p. 46.
  "Drawing the Triangle." Field (24) Spr 81, p. 45.
  "February." NewYorker (56:51) 9 F 81, p. 40.
  "History." Antaeus (40/41) Wint-Spr 81, p. 382.
  "Hurricane Season." CarolQ (34:2) Aut 81, p. 88.
  "Interlude." Field (24) Spr 81, p. 43.
  "Madonnas Touched Up With a Goatee." Ploughs (6:4) 81, p. 166.
  "Old Mountain Road." Field (24) Spr 81, p. 47.

"One Evening" (tr. of Ljubomir Simović). Mund (12/13) 80-81, p. 265.
"Pawnshop." Field (24) Spr 81, p. 44.
"Severe Figures." GeoR (35:4) Wint 81, p. 835.
"Strictly Bucolic." Ploughs (6:4) 81, p. 167.
"Voices of the Dead" (tr. of Ivan V. Lalić). Mund (12/13) 80-81, pp.
    350-351.

SIMMERMAN, Jim
    "A Brief Introduction." Iowa (11:4) Aut 80, pp. 62-63.
    "The Dead Madonnas of Santiago." Antaeus (40/41) Wint-Spr 81, pp.
        383-384.
    "In Her Sparse Season." DenQ (16:4) Wint 81, p. 111.
    "On an Unconceived Painting by Lautrec." Iowa (11:4) Aut 80, p. 64.
    "Open Season." WestHR (35:1) Spr 81, pp. 43-44.
    "Ricky Ricardo Drinks Alone." Iowa (11:4) Aut 80, pp. 65-66.

SIMMONS, Al
    "A lock of my true love's hair." Tele (17) 81, p. 78.
    "The Prophet of Doom Poem." Tele (17) 81, p. 79.
    "Sonnetto." Tele (17) 81, p. 78.

SIMMONS, Edgar
    "The Poet." CEACritic (43:3) Mr 81, p. 28.

SIMMONS, Jes
    "Biloxi Beach: 5 A.M." CEACritic (43:3) Mr 81, p. 26.
    "Notebook Hieroglyphics." CEACritic (43:3) Mr 81, p. 26.
    "October Sunday." CEACritic (43:3) Mr 81, p. 27.
    "Poison." CEACritic (43:3) Mr 81, p. 26.
    "Species." CEACritic (43:3) Mr 81, p. 27.

SIMMS, Michael
    "Aubade." SouthwR (66:2) Spr 81, p. 128.

SIMON, John Oliver
    "Seedcraft Minus 13046." PortR (27: 2) 81, p. 69.
    "Seedcraft Plus 15140." PortR (27: 2) 81, p. 69.
    "Seedcraft Plus 9977491-19381265." PortR (27: 2) 81, p. 69.
    "Since You Asked." PoNow (6:1 issue 31) 81, p. 35.

SIMON, Maura
    "Once I Thought the Dark Legs of Piers To Be the Pillars of Heaven."
        CreamCR (7:1) 81, pp. 46-47.

SIMONE, Judith
    "Ballroom Rehearsal." Prima (6/7) 81, p. 94.
    "Goodbyes." Prima (6/7) 81, p. 95.

SIMONOVIC, Simon
    "Early Works" (tr. by Stephen Stepanchev). PoNow (5:6 issue 30) 81,
        p. 42.

SIMONSON, Conrad
    "Resurrection." ChrC (98:1) 7-14 Ja 81, p. 16.

SIMONSUURI, Kirsti
    "Mother Tongues" (tr. by Aili Flint and Austin Flint). PoetryE (6) Aut
        81, p. 6.

SIMOVIC, Ljubomir
   "One Evening" (tr. by Charles Simic). Mund (12/13) 80-81, p. 265.

SIMPSON, Grace Pow
   "Looking at My Face on Somebody Else." SmPd (18:1) Wint 81, p. 25.

SIMPSON, Louis
   "American Classic." PoNow (6:2 issue 32) 81, p. 26.
   "Magritte Shaving." ParisR (23:79) Spr 81, p. 271.
   "The Mexican Woman." PoNow (6:2 issue 32) 81, p. 26.

SIMPSON, Mark
   "For X, Who is Sad." Peb (21) 81, p. 40.
   "Riding With You and Your Cello on the Bus in Lincoln, Nebraska
      March 23, 1974." Peb (21) 81, p. 39.
   "X, Oh X." Peb (21) 81, p. 41.

SIMPSON, Nancy
   "Lives in One Lifetime." GeoR (35:2) Sum 81, p. 337.

SIMS, Harry DeMott
   "Pursuing My Students with Packaged Words." EngJ (70:1) Ja 81, p.
      33.

SIMS, Lawrence
   from Poems by Leontes (I, IV). Epoch (30:1) Aut 80, pp. 37-40.

SINISGALLI, Leonardo
   "The Bell's Clanging at the End of the Line" (tr. by W. S. Di Piero).
      Pequod (12) 81, p. 27.
   "Concentric Circles" (tr. by W. S. Di Piero). PoNow (5:6 issue 30)
      81, p. 43.
   "Easter 1952" (tr. by W. S. Di Piero). Agni (14) 81, pp. 15-16.
   "Freightyard at Narni-Amelia" (tr. by W. S. Di Piero). Pequod (12)
      81, p. 26.
   "Holly Saturday in Manfredonia" (tr. by W. S. Di Piero). Agni (14)
      81, p. 14.
   "Reliquary" (tr. by W. S. Di Piero). PoNow (5:6 issue 30) 81, p. 43.
   "The Snow Owl" (tr. by W. S. Di Piero). PoNow (6:2 issue 32) 81,
      p. 41.
   "Technique" (tr. by W. S. Di Piero). PoNow (5:6 issue 30) 81, p. 43.
   "Triangulations" (tr. by W. S. Di Piero). PoNow (5:6 issue 30) 81,
      p. 43.
   "The Valley" (tr. by W. S. Di Piero). PoNow (5:6 issue 30) 81, p.
      43.

SINOPOULOS, Takis
   "Waiting Room" (tr. by Kimon Friar). Mund (12/13) 80-81, pp. 254-
      255.

SINYARD, William J.
   "Bouncer." Wind (11:40) 81, p. 26.

SIROWITZ, Hal
   "Refusing to Float." HangL (39) Wint 80-81, p. 39.
   "Remember Me." LittleM (13:1/2) Spr-Sum 79, c1981, p. 105.

SISSON, Jonathan
  "The Crows of St. Thomas." Poetry (139:3) D 81, pp. 139-141.
  "Diana's Baths." ParisR (23:81) Aut 81, pp. 138-139.

SJÖBERG, Leif
  "The Dolphin" (tr. of Thorkild Bjørnvig, w/ William Jay Smith).
    PoetryE (6) Aut 81, pp. 77-88.
  "I: The thewed horses slept" (tr. of Erik Akerlund, w/ John Currie).
    SenR (12: 1/2) 81, p. 182.
  "II: They don't carry away much" (tr. of Erik Akerlund, w/ John
    Currie). SenR (12: 1/2) 81, p. 183.
  "With Old Eyes I Look Back" (tr. of Pär Lagerkvist, w/ W. H.
    Auden). Mund (12/13) 80-81, pp. 326-328.

SKEEN, Anita
  "Going Back" (for JB). Outbr (6/7) Aut 80-Spr 81, pp. 79-80.
  "The Minstrel." Outbr (6/7) Aut 80-Spr 81, p. 80.
  "More Than Just the Moon." KanQ (13:1) Wint 81, p. 28.
  "Tracking." KanQ (13:1) Wint 81, p. 29.

SKELTON, Robin
  "The Short Cut." Poetry (137:4) Ja 81, pp. 213-214.
  "Triptych." Poetry (137:4) Ja 81, pp. 215-216.

SKINNER, Jeffrey
  "Nominal Acrostic." PraS (55:1/2) Spr-Sum 81, p. 286.
  "Song Beginning in Summer." GeoR (35:2) Sum 81, p. 407.

SKINNER, Knute
  "Pissing on Thistles." PoNow (6:1 issue 31) 81, p. 29.

SKLAREW, Myra
  "Certainty." WebR (6:2) 81, pp. 89-92.

SKLOOT, Floyd
  "The Clues." NowestR (19:3), p. 94.
  "New England Nights." SouthernPR (21: 1) Spr 81, pp. 56-57.

SKLUTE, Larry
  "Litera Troili." LitR (24:3) Spr 81, pp. 409-410.

SKY-PECK, Kathryn
  "Inspiration." Tendril (10) Wint 81, p. 40.

SLEIGH, Tom
  "A Formal Occasion." NewYorker (57:30) 14 S 81, p. 157.

SLESINGER, Warren
  "Our Bedroom In The Fields" (for Y. A.). AmerPoR (10:3) My-Je 81,
    p. 42.

SLOTE, Bernice
  "Afternoon in the Cloisters." PraS (55:1/2) Spr-Sum 81, p. 52.
  "The Game." PraS (55:1/2) Spr-Sum 81, p. 57.
  "Grandfather." PraS (55:1/2) Spr-Sum 81, p. 58.
  "Invitation: Debate of Body and Soul." PraS (55:1/2) Spr-Sum 81, p.
    55.
  "Nevada." PraS (55:1/2) Spr-Sum 81, p. 53.

"Of Certain Men." PraS (55:1/2) Spr-Sum 81, p. 57.
"Old House." PraS (55:1/2) Spr-Sum 81, p. 54.
"Student: 8 A. M." PraS (55:1/2) Spr-Sum 81, p. 56.

SMALLFIELD, Edward
    "Poem For My Grandmother." ThRiPo (17/18) 81, p. 36.

SMART, Ernest
    "Miss Mallarme's Fan" (tr. of Stephane Mallarme). Stand (22: 1) 80,
       p. 38.

SMETZER, Michael
    "Late-Night Cafe in Missouri." PoNow (6:3 issue 33) 81, p. 38.

SMITH, Annette
    "Batoque" (tr. with Clayton Eshleman of Aimé Césaire). Sulfur (1) 81,
       pp. 212-218.

SMITH, Annick
    "Old Woman to the River." CutB (16) Spr-Sum 81, pp. 112-113.

SMITH, Arthur
    "Crosscut." NowestR (19:3), p. 93.
    "Elegy on Independence Day." Nat (232:20) 23 My 81, p. 637.
    "In Praise of Violence." PoNow (6:1 issue 31) 81, p. 29.
    "In the White Fog." Nat (233:12) 17 O 81, p. 386.

SMITH, Bruce
    "Garvey, Radiant." Iowa (11:4) Aut 80, p. 86.
    "Her Back." NewEngR (4:1) Aut 81, p. 89.
    "Plumy Clay Waits for Her Lover." NewEngR (4:1) Aut 81, pp. 87-8.
    "The Wooing of Katie O'Keefe." NewEngR (4:1) Aut 81, pp. 90-1.

SMITH, Bryan
    "Daily Draughts." PottPort (3) 81, p. 5.

SMITH, Crichton
    "The Church." Stand (22: 3) 81, p. 23.
    "Coronary." Stand (22: 3) 81, p. 23.

SMITH, Dave
    "Crab." NewEngR (3:4) Sum 81, pp. 482-485.
    "Turn-of-the-Century House." NewYorker (57:13) 18 My 81, p. 42.
    "White Beach, Black Beach: Buckroe, Virginia." NewEngR (3:4) Sum
       81, pp. 479-82.
    "Wildfire." Atl (247:1) Ja 81, p. 53.

SMITH, Jared
    "In The Dark Of The Station." StoneC (8: 3) Spr 81, p. 39.

SMITH, Jordan
    "For Dulcimer & Doubled Voice." GeoR (35:4) Wint 81, pp. 870-871.
    "Constable Hall" (C. , N.Y.). Agni (14) 81, p. 41.
    "The Hawk." Agni (14) 81, p. 42.
    "Hymns: For the Orthodox" (M.T. , 1892-1941). Agni (14) 81, pp.
       34-40.
    "Niagara, 1804." Agni (15) 81, pp. 115-121.
    "A Side of Beef" (CS, 1925). Agni (14) 81, pp. 43-44.

"Six Poems--after the drawings and paintings by Edvard Munch: Two Pen and Ink for 'Despair'." (1 & 2). Chelsea (40) 81, pp. 88-89.
"Six Poems...: Inheritance." Chelsea (40) 81, p. 90.
"Six Poems...: Mephistopheles II: Split Personality." Chelsea (40) 81, p. 91.
"Six Poems...: Self Portrait With Skeleton Arm." Chelsea (40) 81, p. 90.
"Six Poems...: Uninvited Guests." Chelsea (40) 81, p. 91.

SMITH, Kay
"Prelude." PottPort (3) 81, p. 11.

SMITH, Larry
"Learning to Read." PoNow (6:2 issue 32) 81, p. 12.
"A Story of Little." WormR (81/82) 81, pp. 42-43.
"Why Suppertime is Sacred." PoNow (6:2 issue 32) 81, p. 12.

SMITH, Lawrence R.
"Resurrection After the Rain" (tr. of Alfredo Giuliani). PoNow (5:6 issue 30) 81, p. 16.

SMITH, Louise Robb
"Exploration of a Mood." WebR (6:2) 81, pp. 85-86.
"Sonnets to a Newborn Child." WebR (6:2) 81, p. 84.

SMITH, Margoret
"Surveyor's Chain." PoetryNW (22:2) Sum 81, pp. 39-41.

SMITH, Pat Hollis
"Caprice" (tr. of Alfonsina Storni). LetFem (7:2) Aut 81, pp. 66-67.
"Loves" (tr. of Dulce María Loynaz). LetFem (7:2) Aut 81, p. 65.

SMITH, R. T.
"Believing in a Circle." KanQ (13:1) Wint 81, p. 78.
"A Brady Photograph of Lee." SouthernHR (15:1) Wint 81, p. 66.
"From The High Dive In Late August." Poem (42) Jul 81, pp. 38-39.
"Ice House." PoNow (6:2 issue 32) 81, p. 47.
"Imagine" (for Jim Mathis). Poem (42) Jul 81, pp. 40-44.
"Mentor, Then." Poem (42) Jul 81, p. 45.
"Night Class Demonstration." Wind (11:43) 81, pp. 32-33.
"Threading the Last Needle." Poem (42) Jul 81, p. 46.
"A Victory." SouthernPR (21: 1) Spr 81, p. 50.

SMITH, Rick
"hills" (gayle's poem). Ascent (77/79) 81, p. 194.
"the Lake" (for arbus). Ascent (77/79) 81, p. 194.

SMITH, Robert L.
"Caminante, Son Tus Huellas" (tr. with Judith Candullo of Antonio Machado). WebR (6:2) 81, p. 27.
"It Was Yesterday My Sorrows" (tr. of Antonio Machado, w/ Judith Candulo). StoneC (9: 1-2) Aut-Wint 81/82, p. 57.
"The Last Suburban Train" (tr. of Andrei Vosnesensky, w/ Sylvia Maizell). StoneC (9: 1-2) Aut-Wint 81/82, pp. 11-12.

SMITH, Ronald
"Black Piano." Kayak (57) 81, p. 21.
"The Myth of Surrealism." Kayak (57) 81, p. 21.

SMITH, Sandra
"Reverend Malthus On The Beach" (tr. of Gabriel Zaid, w/ Sergio
    Mondragón). Mund (12/13) 80-81, p. 156.
"Thousand and One Nights" (tr. of Gabriel Zaid, w/ Sergio Mondragón).
    Mund (12/13) 80-81, p. 156.

SMITH, Stephen E.
"A Three-D Afternoon in Easton, Maryland, Circa Sept. 1956." PoNow
    (6:3 issue 33) 81, p. 40.

SMITH, Sybil
"For Your Bones, Your Hair." 13thM (5:1/2) 80, pp. 50-51.
"I Want to Know" (for my dead mother). 13thM (5:1/2) 80, p. 49.
"The Origin Of The Dog." Sam (116) 81, pp. 54-55.
"Remembering The Appleman." Sam (117) 81, pp. 28-29.
"To Provide." Epoch (30:3) Spr-Sum 81, pp. 188-189.

SMITH, Thomas
"Military Duties." HiramPoR (30) Spr-Sum 81, p. 41.

SMITH, Tom
"Déjà Vu." EnPas (12), 81, p. 29.
"Wake." EnPas (12), 81, p. 29.

SMITH, William Jay
"The Dolphin" (tr. of Thorkild Bjørnvig, w/ Leif Sjöberg). PoetryE
    (6) Aut 81, pp. 77-88.

SMITH-BOWERS, Cathy
"ADA 1912." SouthernHR (15:4) Aut 81, pp. 324-325.
"Among the Mysterious Missing." SouthernPR (21: 1) Spr 81, pp. 8-9.
"Watching for Meteors." PikeR (2) Sum 81, p. 5.

SMYKLO, Pat
"Cambodian Woman: Famine 1979." WebR (6:1) 81, p. 76.
"Mount Nyiru." WebR (6:1) 81, p. 75.

SMYRES, Craig
"A body and a box." Meadows (2:1) 81, p. 34.

SMYTH, Paul
"After the Windstorm." Poetry (137:5) F 81, p. 283.
"A Little Night Music." EnPas (12), 81, p. 36.

SNIVELY, Susan
"The Chambered Nautilus of Edward Weston" (from the Daybrooks).
    Thrpny (6) Sum 81, p. 21.
"Their Foot Shall Slide in Due Time." Ploughs (6:4) 81, pp. 158-159.

SNOTHERLY, Mary C.
"Three Horses in a Field...." SouthernPR (21:2) Aut 81, p. 60.

SNOW, Karen
"Words." BelPoJ (31:4) Sum 81, pp. 2-3.
"Bread." BelPoJ (32:2) Wint 81-82, pp. 25-28.

SNOW, Walter
"The 'Nigger' He Killed" (for New York Timesman Richard Severo).
    OP (31/32) Aut 81, p. 66.

SNYDAL, James
  "Friends See Each Other Now and Then Forever." PoNow (6:3 issue
    33) 81, p. 40.

SNYDER, Gary
  "Up Branches Of Duck River." UnmOx (22) Wint 81, p. 40.

SO, Kyong-Dok
  "The Fool on the Mountain" (tr. by Michael Stephens). Pequod (13) 81,
    p. 75.

SO, Reynaldo Pérez see PEREZ SO, Reynaldo

SO, Sakon
  "Tomb of a Fabled Creature" (tr. by Graeme Wilson). DenQ (16:4)
    Wint 81, p. 46.

SOBEK, María Herrera see HERRERA SOBEK, María

SOBIN, Anthony
  "Cabin Fever." AmerPoR (10:5) S-O 81, p. 41.
  "Eccentric Painting: 'Aftermath With Kitchen Chair'." AmerPoR (10:5)
    S-O 81, p. 41.
  "Picasso Postcard with Pigeons." PoetryNW (22:1) Spr 81, pp. 40-41.

SOBIN, Gustaf
  "Draft: For Santa Cruz." Pequod (13) 81, pp. 5-8.
  "The Poem." Pequod (13) 81, p. 4.
  "Sudden Essays on Shadow and Substance." Sulfur (1) 81, pp. 15-18.

SOCOLOW, Liz
  "Hollyhocks and the War." US1 (14/15) Aut/Wint 81, p. 9.
  "Stocking the Stream." US1 (14/15) Aut/Wint 81, p. 9.

SÖDERGRAN, Edith
  "Autumn's Final Flower" (tr. by Rika Lesser). PoetryE (6) Aut 81, pp.
    42-43.
  "The Condition" (tr. by Lennart Bruce). PoNow (5:6 issue 30) 81, p.
    43.
  "The Day Cools" (tr. by Rika Lesser). PoetryE (6) Aut 81, pp. 41-42.
  "The Foreign Lands" (tr. by Lennart Bruce). PoNow (5:6 issue 30)
    81, p. 43.
  "The Land That Is Not" (tr. by Rika Lesser). PoetryE (6) Aut 81, p.
    43.
  "Northern Spring" (tr. by Rika Lesser). PoetryE (6) Aut 81, p. 41.
  "Tantalus, Fill Your Goblet" (tr. by Lennart Bruce). PoNow (5:6 issue
    30) 81, p. 43.
  "Which Is My Homeland" (tr. by Lennart Bruce). PoNow (5:6 issue 30)
    81, p. 43.

SOKOLSKY, Helen H.
  "Last Visit." Wind (11:40) 81, p. 34.

SOLDOFSKY, Alan
  "Choosing the Name." PoetryE (6) Aut 81, p. 61.
  "Descendant." PoetryE (6) Aut 81, p. 60.

SOLHEIM, James
  "Light." Tendril (11) Sum 81, p. 73.

SOLOMAR, David
"Inventory for a Dying Year." SmPd (18:3) Aut 81, pp. 11-12.

SOLWAY, David
"The Games." Atl (248:5) N 81, p. 76.
"My Mother's Chess." Atl (247:1) Ja 81, p. 48.

SOMERVILLE, Jane
"Heavenly Bodies." SoCaR (14: 1) Aut 81, p. 124.
"Oh oh oh you pretty thing." OhioR (26), p. 120.
"Who Would Count On A Man Like That?" SoCaR (14: 1) Aut 81, p.
   125.

SONNEVI, Göran
"An untitled poem" (tr. by Jan Karlsson and Cynthia Hogue). AmerPoR
   (10:6) N-D 81, p. 32.
"Clearness." Mund (12/13) 80-81, p. 107.
"Ground" (tr. by Robin Fulton). Mund (12/13) 80-81, p. 107.

SØRHEIM, Thor
"Cracks and Springs" (tr. by Katherine Powell). Field (25) Aut 81, p.
   40.
"Pinetrees and Large Heavy Rowboats" (tr. by Katherine Powell).
   Field (25) Aut 81, p. 38.
"Rails, Poles and Barbed Wire" (tr. by Katherine Powell). Field (25)
   Aut 81, p. 39.

SORKIN, Nelson C.
"Ice Cube." Poem (43) Nov 81, p. 27.
"Paper Houses." Poem (43) Nov 81, pp. 28-30.

SORNBERGER, Judith
"Rose Diary." Peb (21) 81, pp. 112-115.

SORRENTINO, Gilbert
"The Disappearance Of Oilcloth." PartR (48:3) 81, p. 461.
"Paul Blackburn." UnmOx (22) Wint 81, p. 34.

SOTO, Gary
"Her." Poetry (138:4) Jl 81, p. 220.
"Hitchhiking with a Friend and a Book That Explains the Pacific Ocean."
   Poetry (138:4) Jl 81, p. 218.
"Making Money: Drought Year in Minkler, California." Thrpny (6)
   Sum 81, p. 16.
"Walking with Jackie, Sitting with a Dog." Poetry (138:4) Jl 81, p.
   219.

SOTOMAYOR, Aurea M.
"El dolor reconoce otros desplantes (Jorge Musto)." Mairena (2:6) 80,
   p. 48.

SOTO VEGA, Jenaro
"Si tuviereís fe...." Mairena (2:6) 80, p. 90.

SOTO VELEZ, Clemente
"A la hora del relampago." Claridad/En Rojo (22: 1463) 13-19 F 81,
   p. 24.
"Clemente Soto Vélez." Claridad/En Rojo (22: 1463) 13-19 F 81, p. 20.

"Estrellas de cinco puntas." Claridad/En Rojo (22: 1463) 13-19 F 81,
    p. 16.
from La Tierra Prometida: "56," "60," "80." Claridad/En Rojo (22:
    1463) 13-19 F 81, pp. 17-19.
from La Tierra Prometida: "Toros de transparencia u ondas."
    Claridad/En Rojo (22: 1463) 13-19 F 81, p. 17.
"Lo conocí" (1, 3, 4, 7, 11, 16, 19, 21). Claridad/En Rojo (22: 1463)
    13-19 F 81, pp. 20-23.
"O en Washington." Claridad/En Rojo (22: 1463) 13-19 F 81, p. 20.

SOUPAULT, Philippe
    "Face to Face" (tr. by Paulette Weinstock). Mund (12/13) 80-81, pp.
    250-252.

SOUTHWICK, Marcia
    "The Body." AmerPoR (10:2) Mr-Ap 81, p. 48.
    "Small Difficulties." AmerPoR (10:2) Mr-Ap 81, p. 48.
    "Solo." Ploughs (7:1) 81, p. 39.
    "The Woman Who Buried a Stone." OP (31/32) Aut 81, pp. 101-103.

SPACKS, Barry
    "Essence." Hudson (34:1) Spr 81, p. 73.
    "Glory Learnt from Roses." SewanR (89:1) Wint 81, pp. 31-32.
    "Living Simply." Poetry (139:3) D 81, pp. 150-151.
    "Neilsen." Hudson (34:1) Spr 81, p. 73.
    "A Sense of Change." Tendril (11) Sum 81, p. 74.
    "Song: After the Party." SewanR (89:1) Wint 81, p. 31.
    "The Thought of Light." SewanR (89:1) Wint 81, p. 32.
    "Tree in a Bowl." SewanR (89:1) Wint 81, p. 33.
    "What's Fine." Poetry (139:3) D 81, p. 151.

SPANCKEREN, Kathryn Van see VAN SPANCKEREN, Kathryn

SPANN, Mark
    "Runner." CapeR (16:2) Sum 81, p. 1.

SPARK, Muriel
    "Conversation Piece." NewYorker (57:40) 23 N 81, p. 54.

SPAULDING, John
    "The S.S. Coptic." AmerPoR (10:3) My-Je 81, p. 20.

SPEAR, Cindy
    "Grace." PottPort (3) 81, p. 45.

SPEAR, Roberta
    "The Last Gift." SouthernPR (21:2) Aut 81, pp. 56-60.

SPECTOR, Robert D.
    "Rabbi" (for Rev. Joseph Spector). Confr (22) Sum 81, p. 47.

SPEER, Laurel
    "Shelley's Last Boat Trip." PoNow (6:2 issue 32) 81, p. 46.
    "Winter Apples." PoNow (6:2 issue 32) 81, p. 46.

SPENCE, Michael
    "Cornbelt In Summer." QW (13) Aut/Wint 81/82, p. 98.
    "Crossing the Ice Lake." CharR (7:1) Spr 81, p. 24.

"The Fireman's Cremation." CharR (7:1) Spr 81, pp. 24-25.
"The Galactic Circus." PoNow (6:3 issue 33) 81, p. 38.
"Here." CreamCR (7:1) 81, p. 5.
"The Lost People." HiramPoR (30) Spr-Sum 81, p. 42.

SPICER, David
"Lost Astronaut." PoNow (6:3 issue 33) 81, p. 41.
"The Man Who Hit Triples." PoNow (6:2 issue 32) 81, p. 17.

SPIEGEL, Robert
"Delivering Papers." Wind (11:41) 81, pp. 45-46.

SPIELBERG, Peter
"St. Valentine's Day Massacre." OP (31/32) Aut 81, pp. 85-86.

SPILMAN, Richard
"After Hours at Pandora's." KanQ (13:3/4) Sum-Aut 81, p. 106.
"Suspension." KanQ (13:3/4) Sum-Aut 81, p. 106.
"Wet Day in San Francisco." KanQ (13:3/4) Sum-Aut 81, pp. 106-107.

SPIRES, Elizabeth
"Dark Night on Cape Cod." Antaeus (40/41) Wint-Spr 81, p. 385.
"Sun in an Empty Room" (after the Edward Hopper painting). Antaeus
    (40/41) Wint-Spr 81, p. 386.
"The Telescope." PartR (48:1) 81, p. 132.
"The Travellers." GeoR (35:1) Spr 81, pp. 26-27.

SPIVACK, Kathleen
"A Letter." 13thM (5:1/2) 80, p. 125.
"Crystal Night: Berlin 1938." Poetry (138:5) Ag 81, pp. 280-281.
"Fifteen." Agni (14) 81, p. 60.
"He Doesn't Move." Poetry (138:5) Ag 81, p. 282.
"I Think." MinnR (17) Aut 81, p. 22.
"Night Skier." Ploughs (6:4) 81, pp. 147-148.
"Photography As The Effect Of Light." AmerPoR (10:2) Mr-Ap 81, p.
    12.
"Point of View." Tendril (11) Sum 81, pp. 75-76.
"Three Generations." PoNow (6:1 issue 31) 81, p. 9.
"White Sheets." PoNow (6:2 issue 32) 81, p. 43.

SPIVACK, Susan Fantl
"The Bird and the Baby Opera." HangL (40) Aut 81, p. 13.
"Grief" (for Lois). HangL (40) Aut 81, p. 14.

SPIVAK, Dawnine
"The Weight of the Body." Ploughs (6:4) 81, p. 150.

SPRAGUE, J. Barnes
"As." CapeR (17:1) Wint 81, p. 23.
"Experience, the Sea." BelPoJ (31:3) Spr 81, p. 11.
"For One." CapeR (17:1) Wint 81, p. 23.

SQUIER, Charles L.
"The Bard Enchaîné." OP (31/32) Aut 81, pp. 89-90.

SQUIRES, Con
"Where the Fishermen Stood in Winter." BelPoJ (32:1) Aut 81, p. 17.

STADLER, Ernst
    "Troubled Hour" (tr. by Francis Golffing). PoNow (5:6 issue 30) 81,
      p. 44.

STAFFORD, Kim R.
    "Cadillac." CutB (17) Aut-Wint 81, p. 51.

STAFFORD, Kim Robert
    "History at North Star." SoCaR (14: 1) Aut 81, pp. 83-84.

STAFFORD, William
    "Ardmore." MissouriR (4:2) Wint 81-82, p. 16.
    "August." AmerPoR (10:6) N-D 81, p. 3.
    "A Correspondence In Poetry" (w/ Marvin Bell) (23, 27, 29, 31, 37,
      39, 41). AmerPoR (10:6) N-D 81, pp. 4-7.
    "For The Barn At Bread Loaf." AmerPoR (10:6) N-D 81, p. 3.
    "Enlightenment." StoneC (9: 1-2) Aut-Wint 81/82, p. 22.
    "Maybe." Field (25) Aut 81, p. 83.
    "Mutability." Field (25) Aut 81, p. 84.
    "Notice: A Bly Prescription." PoetryE (4/5) Spr-Sum 81, p. 8.
    "One of the Ways." ParisR (23:79) Spr 81, p. 272.
    "108 East Nineteenth." Atl (248:6) D 81, p. 60.
    "Priorities At Friday Ranch." AmerPoR (10:6) N-D 81, p. 3.
    "Remembering Brother Bob." Iowa (11:2/3) Spr-Sum 80, p. 113.
    "Revelation." Field (25) Aut 81, p. 86.
    "Some of the Ways." VirQR (57:1) Wint 81, pp. 76-78.
    "Starting a Reading at Stephens." OP (31/32) Aut 81, p. 117.
    "Textures." AmerPoR (10:6) N-D 81, p. 3.
    "The Chair In The Meadow." AmerPoR (10:6) N-D 81, p. 3.
    "Things I Learned Last Week." AmerS (50:3) Sum 81, p. 328.
    "Vocatus Atque Non Vocatus." Field (25) Aut 81, p. 87.
    "Walking through Texas." SouthwR (66:2) Spr 81, p. 202.
    "What You See." Iowa (11:2/3) Spr-Sum 80, p. 111.
    "The Weather Beyond the Weather." ThRiPo (17/18) 81, p. 70.
    "Where I Live." Iowa (11:2/3) Spr-Sum 80, p. 112.
    "Why I Look Far Away." Im (7:3) 81, p. 10.
    "Yellow Cars." Field (25) Aut 81, p. 85.

STAGG, Barry
    "Unlike The Muted Plague." PottPort (3) 81, p. 38.

STAINTON, Albert
    "Dinner at Ting's." Ascent (77/79) 81, p. 195.

STALLMAN, R. W.
    "Tiberius." SouthernR (17:2) Spr 81, p. 403.
    "Where Am I?" SouthernR (17:2) Spr 81, p. 404.

STALLWORTHY, Jon
    "The Old Park" (tr. of Boris Pasternak, w/ Peter France). Hudson
      (34:4) Wint 81, pp. 550-551.
    "Winter approaches" (tr. of Boris Pasternak, w/ Peter France).
      Hudson (34:4) Wint 81, p. 549.

STAMBLER, Peter
    "Father Pernin in Seclusion, 1874." BelPoJ (31:3) Spr 81, pp. 15-25.

STANDING, Sue
    "Shooting Pool." Ploughs (7:1) 81, p. 139.

STANESCU, Nichita
  "The Ghost" (tr. by Mariana Carpinisan and Mark Irwin). SenR (12:
    1/2) 81, p. 137.
  "Marina" (tr. by Mariana Carpinisan and Mark Irwin). SenR (12:1/2)
    81, p. 135.
  "Marina." SenR (12:1/2) 81, p. 134.
  "Vedenia." SenR (12:1/2) 81, p. 136.

STANFORD, Ann
  "Makers." StoneC (9: 1-2) Aut-Wint 81/82, p. 31.

STANFORD, Frank
  "Poem: When the rain hits...." OP (31/32) Aut 81, p. 56.

STANFORD, Michael
  "Insomnia" (tr. of Osip Mandelstam). SenR (12:1/2) 81, p. 27.
  "To Olga Arbenina" (tr. of Osip Mandelstam). SenR (12:1/2) 81, p.
    29.
  "The Sestina on the Lady Pietra" (tr. of Dante). SenR (12:1/2) 81, pp.
    35-7.

STANHOPE, Rosamond
  "From January to January." WebR (6:2) 81, p. 45.

STANSBERGER, Richard
  "A Piece of Tooth." Thrpny (7) Aut 81, p. 3.
  "Sylvia." HiramPoR (29) Aut-Wint 81, p. 37.

STAP, Don
  "A Letter at the End of Winter." NoAmR (266:4) D 81, p. 46.

STAR, Gregory
  "Canto with Typo." UnmOx (22) Wint 81, pp. 5-7.

STARBUCK, George
  "Amazing Gracious Living on I-93." Ploughs (6:4) 81, pp. 168-169.
  "Mykonos: Wall With Mailbox." Ploughs (6:4) 81, p. 170.
  "Sunday Brunch in the Boston Restoration." (for G. and B.). Agni (14)
    81, pp. 18-21.

STARK, Sharon
  "Nightdrowning." BelPoJ (32:2) Wint 81-82, p. 24.

STARK, Sharon Sheehe
  "View From Home." BelPoJ (32:1) Aut 81, p. 1.

STATHATOS, John Constantine
  "The Coloured Beads" (tr. of Yánnis Rítsos). Mund (12/13) 80-81, p.
    356.

STAUDACHER, Carol
  "A Farewell." Prima (6/7) 81, p. 8.

STAW, Jane
  "On April 8" (tr. of Emmanuel Hocquard). SenR (12:1/2) 81, p. 65.
  "On August 5" (tr. of Emmanuel Hocquard). SenR (12:1/2) 81, p. 69.
  "On January 1" (tr. of Emmanuel Hocquard). SenR (12:1/2) 81, p. 63.
  "On July 15" (tr. of Emmanuel Hocquard). SenR (12:1/2) 81, p. 67.

STEARNS, Martha
   "Why They Endure." Ploughs (7:1) 81, pp. 142-143.

STEELE, Paul Curry
   "Juniperus Virginiana." Wind (11:42) 81, p. 37.

STEELE, Peggy
   "I Know A Man." PoNow (6:3 issue 33) 81, p. 47.

STEELE, Timothy
   "1816." ChiR (33:1) Sum 81, p. 59.
   "Near Olympic" (West Los Angeles). Thrpny (6) Sum 81, p. 12.
   "Summer." ChiR (33:1) Sum 81, p. 58.

STEFENHAGENS, Lyn
   "The Bones." StoneC (8: 3) Spr 81, p. 22.
   "The Snake Mother." StoneC (8: 3) Spr 81, pp. 23-24.

STEIN, Agnes
   "At the White Pansy Bed" (tr. of Sarah Kirsch). PoNow (5:6 issue 30)
     81, p. 21.
   "I'm to Go Into an Airplane" (tr. of Sarah Kirsch). PoNow (5:6 issue
     30) 81, p. 21.
   "Long Journey" (tr. of Sarah Kirsch). PoNow (5:6 issue 30) 81, p. 21.
   "Music on the Water" (tr. of Sarah Kirsch). PoNow (5:6 issue 30) 81,
     p. 21.

STEIN, Charles
   from A Book of Confusions. Sulfur (1) 81, pp. 51-55.

STEIN, Dona
   "Le déjeuner sur L'herbe." Aspect (77/79) 81, p. 196.

STEIN, Hadassah
   "Beyond Contention" (For S.). BelPoJ (31:4) Sum 81, p. 38.
   "My Child's Leopard." CalQ (18/19) 81, p. 47.
   "Signals." PoetryNW (22:3) Aut 81, p. 45.
   "The Waterfall." CalQ (18/19) 81, p. 46.

STEIN, Paul
   "Goat." OhioR (26), p. 98.

STEIN, Suzana Albornoz see ALBORNOZ STEIN, Suzana

STEINBERG, Alan L.
   "The Birth of Our Daughter." PortR (27: 2) 81, p. 95.
   "My Wife in Labor." PortR (27: 2) 81, p. 95.

STEINER, Carolyn
   "The Death Mask" (tr. of Renê Char, w/ Franz Wright). SenR (12:
     1/2) 81, p. 47.
   "The Dowry of Maubergeonne" (tr. of Renê Char, w/ Franz Wright).
     SenR (12: 1/2) 81, p. 49.
   "Fastes" (tr. of Renê Char, w/ Franz Wright). SenR (12: 1/2) 81, p.
     45.
   "Line of Faith" (tr. of Renê Char, w/ Franz Wright). SenR (12: 1/2)
     81, p. 45.
   "The Tree Frog" (tr. of Renê Char, w/ Franz Wright). SenR (12: 1/2)
     81, p. 49.

STEINER, Karen
"The River Goes. " PoNow (6:3 issue 33) 81, p. 38.

STEINGASS, David
"Mythology of Rock. " PoNow (6:1 issue 31) 81, p. 13.
"Two Love Poems While Driving in Wisconsin" (1, 2). PoNow (6:1
   issue 31) 81, p. 13.

STELMASZYNSKI, Wojtek
"Opus 12, A Comedy" (tr. of Krzysztof Ostaszewski). MichQR (20:4)
   Aut 81, p. 423.
"Opus 30" (tr. of Krzysztof Ostaszewski). MichQR (20:4) Aut 81, pp.
   423-24.
"Opus 75" (tr. of Krzysztof Ostaszewski). MichQR (20:4) Aut 81, p.
   424.

STEPANCHEV, Stephen
"Disaster. " PoNow (6:1 issue 31) 81, p. 29.
"Early Works" (tr. of Simon Simovic). PoNow (5:6 issue 30) 81, p.
   42.
"Everyday Encounters" (tr. of Dejan Tadic). PoNow (5:6 issue 30) 81,
   p. 44.
"In Colorado. " PoNow (6:2 issue 32) 81, p. 19.
"Meeting" (tr. of Husein Basic). PoNow (5:6 issue 30) 81, p. 7.
"The Steeple of Misa" (tr. of Milan Uzelac). PoNow (5:6 issue 30) 81,
   p. 46.
"Talk About Poetry" (tr. of Bazidar Milidragovic). PoNow (5:6 issue
   30) 81, p. 31.

STEPHENS, Jack
"Eight. " AmerPoR (10:1) Ja-F 81, p. 28.
"Four Dredging. " AmerPoR (10:1) Ja-F 81, pp. 27-28.
"Six Cockroach. " AmerPoR (10:1) Ja-F 81, p. 28.
"Thirteen. " AmerPoR (10:1) Ja-F 81, p. 29.
"Two. " AmerPoR (10:1) Ja-F 81, p. 27.

STEPHENS, Michael
"Azaleas" (tr. of Kim Sowol). Pequod (13) 81, p. 71.
"Breaking the Branch" (tr. of Hongnang). Pequod (13) 81, p. 69.
"Budding" (tr. of Kim Sowol). Pequod (13) 81, p. 72.
"The Fool on the Mountain" (tr. of So Kyong-Dok). Pequod (13) 81, p.
   75.
"Full Moon in Pear Blossoms" (tr. of Yi Chonyon). Pequod (13) 81, p.
   76.
"If I Had Been As I Am Now" (tr. of Myong-Ok). Pequod (13) 81, p.
   74.
"Kisaeng Song" (after a translation by Peter H. Lee) (tr. of Anony-
   mous). Pequod (13) 81, p. 67.
"O Mothers O Sisters" (tr. of Kim Sowol). Pequod (13) 81, p. 73.
"A Passing Woman" (tr. of Chong-Chol). Pequod (13) 81, p. 68.
"Poem 12" (tr. of Yi Sang). Pequod (13) 81, p. 77.
"Rock-Ledge" (tr. of Yi Sang). Pequod (13) 81, p. 78.
"What Is A Girl To Do?" (tr. of Hwang-Chini). Pequod (13) 81, p. 70.

STERN, Gerald
"Arthur's Lily. " Field (24) Spr 81, p. 36.
"St. Patrick's Day, 1979. " ParisR (23:80) Sum 81, p. 127.
"Dear Mole. " ParisR (23:80) Sum 81, p. 128.

"For Night to Come." Iowa (11:4) Aut 80, pp. 93-94.
"Hanging Scroll." AmerPoR (10:2) Mr-Ap 81, p. 19.
"Here I Am Walking." ParisR (23:80) Sum 81, pp. 125-126.
"In These Shadows." MissouriR (4:2) Wint 81-82, p. 22.
"June First." ParisR (23:79) Spr 81, p. 273.
"My Hand." ParisR (23:80) Sum 81, p. 126.
"The Picasso Poem." Iowa (11:2/3) Spr-Sum 80, pp. 81-82.
"The Red Coal." ParisR (23:80) Sum 81, pp. 123-124.
"There Is Wind, There Are Matches." Field (24) Spr 81, pp. 34-35.

STERNBERG, Ricardo da Silveira Lobo
"Moonlight In Any City..." (tr. of Carlos Drummond de Andrade, w/
Duane Ackerson). Mund (12/13) 80-81, p. 271.

STERRETT, Jane
"The Examination." ConcPo (14:1) Spr 81, p. 104.

STETLER, Charles
"Administration." WormR (84) 81, p. 100.
"The First Of The Month." WormR (84) 81, p. 100.
"The Pet Hitman." WormR (84) 81, p. 99.

STETSER, Virginia M.
"Sunbread." FourQt (30:2) Wint 81, p. 12.

STEURY, Tim
"In the Barn." SouthernPR (21: 1) Spr 81, p. 33.

STEVENS, Alex
"Regard and Other Rings: A Brief Exposition." Shen (32: 4) 81, pp.
52-53.

STEVENSON, Anne
"The Garden." Pequod (13) 81, p. 63.
"Moirae." Pequod (13) 81, p. 62.

STEVENSON, Diane
"Day and Night." SouthernPR (21: 1) Spr 81, p. 12.
"Turnings." SouthernPR (21: 1) Spr 81, pp. 13-14.

STEWART, Frank
"The Geese." ThRiPo (17/18) 81, p. 74.

STEWART, H. K.
"The Child of Patient People." PoNow (6:3 issue 33) 81, p. 39.
"Still Life." SouthernPR (21:2) Aut 81, p. 38.

STEWART, Jack
"I Met a Girl with Green and Yellow Hair." PoNow (6:3 issue 33) 81,
p. 39.
"In the City." PoNow (6:3 issue 33) 81, p. 39.

STEWART, Michael
"Michael Stewart's Alphabet Book." BallSUF (22:4) Aut 81, pp. 11-16.

STEWART, Pamela
"October." Ploughs (6:4) 81, p. 53.

STEWART, Robert
"Among the Plumbing: A Sequence." Nimrod (25:1) Aut-Wint 81, pp.
91-93.

STEWART, Susan
"Every True Miracle." PoNow (6:3 issue 33) 81, p. 26.
"Terror." PoNow (6:3 issue 33) 81, p. 26.

STILLWELL, Marie
"Waiting For the Indians-." WebR (6:2) 81, p. 65.

STILLWELL, Mary Kathryn
"To Adele." PortR (27: 2) 81, p. 87.
"Song Parts of a New Year." PortR (27: 2) 81, p. 87.
"The Three Sisters." MassR (22:2) Sum 81, p. 333.

STINCHCOMBE, Bobby
"Cool of Summer." Prima (6/7) 81, p. 84.

STIX, Judith Saul
"Affair." PoNow (6:3 issue 33) 81, p. 39.

STOCK, Bud
"Passages." Poem (42) Jul 81, p. 4.

STOCKDALE, J. C.
"Seasonally Adjusted." PottPort (3) 81, p. 39.

STOKES, Terry
"Adopting a Character." Shen (31:4) 80, pp. 92-94.
"The Ballistics Expert." ChiR (33:1) Sum 81, p. 61.
"Driving Through Any Old Place." Confr (22) Sum 81, p. 27.
"I Don't Think It's So Funny." CreamCR (6:1) Aut 80, p. 32.
"If It's All the Same to You." Confr (21) Wint 81, p. 69.
"Leave me Alone." PoNow (6:1 issue 31) 81, p. 35.
"True Devotion." CreamCR (6:1) Aut 80, p. 33.
"Untitled." PartR (48:1) 81, p. 136.
"When Spring Falls Off the Roof of the Garage." ChiR (33:1) Sum 81,
p. 60.

STOKESBURY, Leon
"Chance of Showers (for Matt Horan)." NewEngR (4:2) Wint 81, pp.
194-6.
"A Few Words for Frank Stanford." NewEngR (4:2) Wint 81, pp. 191-
3.
"If I Could Open You." NewEngR (3:3) Spr 81, p. 384.
"The Party's End." NewEngR (3:3) Spr 81, p. 382.
"Unsent Message to My Brother in His Pain." NewEngR (3:3) Spr 81,
p. 383.

STOLOFF, Carolyn
"Dinner time." HangL (39) Wint 80-81, p. 41.
"From Her Ledge." HangL (39) Wint 80-81, p. 40.
"In the Blind." MichQR (20:4) Aut 81, p. 443.

STONE, Arlene
"Dinner Party." PoNow (6:2 issue 32) 81, p. 28.

"2 South. " 13thM (5:1/2) 80, p. 8.
"Weird Sister. " 13thM (5:1/2) 80, p. 9.

STONE, Jeanette
"Absolute Auction. " Wind (11:43) 81, p. 33.

STONE, Nancy
"California Autumn. " SouthernPR (21: 1) Spr 81, p. 58.

STONEY, Leland
"On A Lawn, Growing Older. " PortR (27: 2) 81, p. 79.
"Room R. " PortR (27: 2) 81, p. 15.

STORCH, Franz
"Reflection" (tr. by Herbert Kuhner). WebR (6:2) 81, p. 37.

STORK, Gerry
"Warning the Deer. " Harp (263:1575) Ag 81, p. 70.

STORNI, Alfonsina
"Caprice" (tr. by Pat Hollis Smith). LetFem (7:2) Aut 81, pp. 66-67.

STOTT, Antonia
"A Rare Fish" (tr. of Giuseppe Belli, w/ Robert Garioch). Stand (22:
    4) 81, p. 4.
"The Vou" (tr. of Giuseppe Belli, w/ Robert Garioch). Stand (22: 4)
    81, p. 5.
"The Wee Thief's Mither" (tr. of Giuseppe Belli, w/ Robert Garioch).
    Stand (22: 4) 81, p. 4.

STOUT, Robert Joe
"After Meditation on Maidu Peak. " FourQt (30:4) Sum 81, p. 31.
"First Night With The Blonde From The Jade Room. " Sam (116) 81,
    p. 63.
"Night Bus: Carrollton Street, New Orleans. " Northeast (3:10) Wint
    81, p. 28.
"Our Garden. " PortR (27: 2) 81, p. 95.
"Outside the 10th Street Mission. " PoNow (6:2 issue 32) 81, p. 42.
"Self-Portrait. " Sam (106) 81, p. 34.
"Tools, Trees. " Confr (22) Sum 81, p. 148.
"Truce. " Northeast (3:10) Wint 81, p. 27.
"Witnesses at the Extortion Trial. " HiramPoR (29) Aut-Wint 81, p.
    38.

STOUTENBURG, Adrien
"Listening To The Silence. " StoneC (9: 1-2) Aut-Wint 81/82, pp. 28-
    29.
"Potato Dream. " PoNow (6:2 issue 32) 81, p. 21.

STRACK, Angela
"Wild Jack. " SoCaR (14: 1) Aut 81, p. 16.

STRADAL, Helmut H.
"Words Between You and Me" (tr. by Herbert Kuhner). Mund (11:2) 79,
    p. 77.
"Worte Zwischen Dir Und Mir. " Mund (11:2) 79, p. 76.

STRAHAN, B. R.
    "Happily Ever After." Vis (7) 81, n. p.
    "Mexican Two Step." Vis (6) 81, n. p.

STRAHAN, Barak
    "Charlene." Vis (6) 81, n. p.
    "Last Door" (correction of 1980 Index entr). Vis (3) 80.

STRAND, Mark
    "José" (tr. of Carlos Drummond de Andrade). SenR (12:1/2) 81, pp.
        89-91.
    "My Mother on an Evening in Late Summer." AntR (39:1) Wint 81, pp.
        121-122.
    "The Onset of Love" (tr. of Carlos Drummond de Andrade). NewYorker
        (57:28) 31 Ag 81, p. 40.
    "Shooting Whales" (for J. and L. M.). AntR (39:1) Wint 81, pp. 119-
        120.
    "Story of the Dress" (tr. of Carlos Drummond de Andrade). Antaeus
        (40/41) Wint-Spr 81, pp. 276-281.

STRICKLAND, Stephanie
    "Mother: Dressed Up." Agni (14) 81, p. 58.
    "Rite: A Life." Cond (7) Spr 81, pp. 59-60.

STRINGER, A. E.
    "Woman Fishing" (after the drawing by Seurat). Antaeus (40/41) Wint-
        Spr 81, p. 387.

STRIPLING, Kathryn
    "Elegy." Hudson (34:3) Aut 81, pp. 385-386.

STROBLAS, Laurie
    "The Silver Spring Diner." PortR (27: 2) 81, p. 97.

STROTHER, Garland
    "Dorothy Day, 1897-1980." ChrC (98:27) 9 S 81, p. 865.

STRUTHERS, Betsy
    "The Season of Blood." MalR (57) Ja 81, pp. 128-129.

STRYK, Dan
    "An Event." Comm (108:11) 5 Je 81, p. 342.
    "Away from Things." HolCrit (18:2) Ap 81, p. 19.
    "Bethlehem St., Chicago." PoNow (6:3 issue 33) 81, p. 27.
    "Elegy for an Unemployed Brakeman." PoNow (6:3 issue 33) 81, p.
        27.
    "Mayflies of Ferry Landing" (for my father). HiramPoR (29) Aut-Wint
        81, p. 39.

STRYK, Lucien
    "Memorial Day." CharR (7:2) Aut 81, p. 6.
    "Nomads" (Meshed, Iran). CharR (7:2) Aut 81, pp. 6-7.
    "Why I Write." CharR (7:2) Aut 81, p. 5.
    "Winter." GeoR (35:4) Wint 81, p. 838.

STUART, Floyd C.
    "Huntington Gorge." PoNow (6:3 issue 33) 81, p. 47.

STUCKEY, William
    "For H. D. Thoreau." ArizQ (37:1) Spr 81, p. 46.

STULL, Richard
    "Early Fall." Pequod (13) 81, pp. 16-17.

STURN, John Edward
    "Taking No Risks." Wind (11:40) 81, p. 35.

SUARDIAZ, Luis
    "A Most Peculiar Girl" (tr. by Steve Kowit). PoNow (5:6 issue 30) 81,
        p. 44.
    "Chicago in the afternoon." Areito (7: 26) 81, p. backcover.
    "Questions and Answers" (tr. by Reginald Gibbons). Mund (12/13) 80-
        81, p. 104.
    "Witness for the Prosecution" (to Jorge and Noel Navarro) (tr. by
        Steve Kowit). PoNow (5:6 issue 30) 81, p. 44.

SUAREZ, Elena
    "Aniquilación (Para José Emilio)." Mairena (2:5) Aut 80, p. 78.
    "Nostalgias (A Mario)." Mairena (2:5) Aut 80, p. 78.

SUAREZ, Nicomedes
    "Listen" (tr. of Carmen Naranjo). Mund (12/13) 80-81, p. 119.

SUDERMAN, Elmer F.
    "Two Shadows." ChrC (98:13) 22 Ap 81, p. 447.

SU-JANG, Kim
    "Disdain" (tr. by Graeme Wilson). WestHR (35:2) Sum 81, p. 152.

SUK, Julie
    "Hungry as Always." PoNow (6:2 issue 32) 81, p. 35.
    "Now We Come." PoNow (6:3 issue 33) 81, p. 27.
    "Remnants." PoNow (6:3 issue 33) 81, p. 27.

SULLINS, Max
    "To Forgive Is Always There." ChrC (98:39) 2 D 81, p. 1254.

SULLIVAN, Dennis
    "September Tenth." StoneC (8: 3) Spr 81, p. 19.

SULLIVAN, Francis
    "The Life of the Soul at Fifty." LittleM (13:1/2) Spr-Sum 79, c1981,
        p. 21.

SULLIVAN, James
    "The Railroad Bridge at Argenteuil." Comm (108:15) 28 Ag 81, p.
        467.

SULLIVAN, Nancy
    "The O'Rourkes Mull Over the Seven Deadly Sins." NewL (48:1) Aut
        81, pp. 57-69.

SUMMERS, Hollis
    "Man Walking." PoNow (6:1 issue 31) 81, p. 18.

SUPERVIELLE, Jules
    "Champs Elysées" (tr. by George Bogin). AmerPoR (10:4) Jl-Ag 81,

p. 48.
"The Drop of Rain (God Speaks)" (tr. by George Bogin).   ChiR (33:1)
   Sum 81, p. 83.
"La Goutte de Pluie (Dieu Parle). " ChiR (33:1) Sum 81, p. 82.
"In Memory of Odilon-Jean Périer" (tr. by Dorothy B. Aspinwall).
   WebR (6:2) 81, p. 20.

SURIA, Violeta López see LOPEZ SURIA, Violeta

SURPRENANT, Dominic
   "Ginseng Poem. " PikeR (2) Sum 81, p. 38.

SUSSKIND, Harriet
   "A Different Number. " Prima (6/7) 81, p. 40.

SUTHERLAND, Fraser
   "The Death and Life of Doctor Bethune. " PottPort (3) 81, pp. 47-49.

SUTHERLAND, Joan
   "Remembering a Dream" (tr. of Li Qingzhao, w/ Peter Levitt).   SenR
   (12:1/2) 81, p. 117.

SUTTER, Barton
   "In the Bell Museum of Natural History. " NoAmR (266:3) S 81, p. 17.

SUTZKEVER, Abraham
   "For My Child" (tr. by Seymour Mayne).   Stand (22: 3) 81, p. 6.
   "Mother" (tr. by Seymour Mayne).   Stand (22: 3) 81, pp. 7-9.
   "Self-Portrait" (tr. by Seymour Mayne).   Stand (22: 3) 81, pp. 4-5.

SVEHLA, John
   "The Sound of November. " Wind (11:43) 81, p. 22.

SVOBODA, Robert J.
   "Housewarming Gift. " SmPd (18:1) Wint 81, p. 27.

SVOBODA, Terese
   "Dance for the Sun. " GeoR (35: 3) Aut 81, p. 552.
   "Family Court. " VirQR (57:3) Sum 81, pp. 462-463.
   "Scouting Locations for a Commercial. " VirQR (57:3) Sum 81, pp. 461-
   462.

SWANDER, Mary
   "Lost Lake. " MissouriR (4:3) Sum 81, p. 42.

SWANGER, David
   "Caught. " Tendril (10) Wint 81, p. 41.
   "Postcard from South Africa. " NewL (48:1) Aut 81, p. 47.

SWANN, Brian
   "Aubade for Autumn. " PartR (48:3) 81, p. 460.
   "Baedeker" (tr. of Bartolo Cattafi, w/ Ruth Feldman). PoNow (5:6
   issue 30) 81, p. 12.
   "Brindisi" (tr. of Vittorio Bodini, w/ Ruth Feldman).   PoNow (5:6 issue
   30) 81, p. 9.
   "But in the Hour" (tr. of Vittorio Bodini, w/ Ruth Feldman).   PoNow
   (5:6 issue 30) 81, p. 9.
   "Center. " MalR (57) Ja 81, p. 34.

"Chains" (tr. of Melih Cevdet Anday, w/ Talat S. Halman). WebR (6: 1) Spr 81, p. 18.

"Charity of my Village" (tr. of Rocco Scotellaro, w/ Ruth Feldman). PoNow (5:6 issue 30) 81, p. 41.

"The City Sweetheart" (tr. of Rocco Scotellaro, w/ Ruth Feldman). PoNow (5:6 issue 30) 81, p. 41.

"Climbing." MalR (57) Ja 81, p. 33.

"Cloth" (tr. of Bartolo Cattafi, w/ Ruth Feldman). Mund (12/13) 80-81, p. 346.

"Comet" (tr. of Rafael Alberti). PoNow (5:6 issue 30) 81, p. 2.

"Copper Age" (tr. of Melih Cevdet Anday, w/ Talat S. Halman). LitR (24:3) Spr 81, p. 405-406.

"Danger" (tr. of Rafael Alberti). PoNow (5:6 issue 30) 81, p. 2.

"The Dawn is Always New" (tr. of Rocco Scotellaro, w/ Ruth Feldman). PoNow (5:6 issue 30) 81, p. 25.

"Do Not Dump Rubbish Here" (tr. of Rafael Alberti). PoNow (5:6 issue 30) 81, p. 2.

"Earthquake Country." NoAmR (266:1) Mr 81, p. 51.

"Following Through." Kayak (56) 81, p. 18-23.

"The Grain in the Sepulchre" (tr. of Rocco Scotellaro, w/ Ruth Feldman). PoNow (5:6 issue 30) 81, p. 41.

"His Voice." SewanR (89:2) Ap-Je 81, p. 187.

from Holland: "Amsterdam" (tr. of Vittorio Sereni, w/ Ruth Feldman). PoNow (5:6 issue 30) 81, p. 42.

from Holland: "Volendam" (tr. of Vittorio Sereni, w/ Ruth Feldman). PoNow (5:6 issue 30) 81, p. 42.

from Holland: "The Interpreter" (tr. of Vittorio Sereni, w/ Ruth Feldman). PoNow (5:6 issue 30) 81, p. 42.

"Journeys" (tr. of Rocco Scotellaro, w/ Ruth Feldman). PoNow (5:6 issue 30) 81, p. 25.

"Knowledge" (tr. of Nina Cassian, w/ Michael Impey). Mund (12/13) 80-81, p. 347.

"Laboma." PoNow (6:2 issue 32) 81, p. 13.

"Laughing Stock" (tr. of Gulten Akin, w/ Talat Halman). PoNow (5:6 issue 30) 81, p. 2.

"Like A Blade" (tr. of Bartolo Cattafi, w/ Ruth Feldman). Mund (12/13) 80-81, p. 346.

"Like Boats." NewYorker (57:19) 29 Je 81, p. 36.

"Lizard" (tr. of Rafael Alberti). PoNow (5:6 issue 30) 81, p. 2.

"Moving Westward." SouthernPR (21:2) Aut 81, pp. 18-24.

"Nexus." LitR (24:3) Spr 81, p. 407.

"Now that July Rules" (tr. of Rocco Scotellaro, w/ Ruth Feldman). PoNow (5:6 issue 30) 81, p. 25.

"Oblivion is Birds" (tr. of Melih Cevdet Anday, w/ Talat S. Halman). WebR (6: 1) Spr 81, p. 15.

"Oracles of Light." DenQ (16:4) Wint 81, pp. 112-113.

"The Package" (tr. of Bartolo Cattafi, w/ Ruth Feldman). PoNow (5:6 issue 30) 81, p. 12.

"A Pair of Threes" (tr. of Rafael Alberti). PoNow (5:6 issue 30) 81, p. 2.

"Pig Moon, Turtle Moon." ChiR (33:1) Sum 81, pp. 40-41.

"Quarrel With Chaos" (tr. of Nina Cassian, w/ Michael Impey). Mund (12/13) 80-81, p. 347.

"Rainbow" (tr. of Rocco Scotellaro, w/ Ruth Feldman). PoNow (5:6 issue 30) 81, p. 41.

"A Reach Away." PoetryNW (22:3) Aut 81, pp. 35-36.

"Reflections." SewanR (89:2) Ap-Je 81, pp. 186-187.

"The Rowboat" (tr. of Melih Cevdet Anday, w/ Talat S. Halman). WebR

(6: 1) Spr 81, p. 17.
"The Rule" (tr. of Rocco Scotellaro, w/ Ruth Feldman).   PoNow (5:6 issue 30) 81, p. 41.
"The Sky."   YaleR (70: 3) Spr 81, p. 412.
"Sobre Los Animales."   MinnR (17) Aut 81, pp. 39-40.
"Song of the Game of Silence."   PoetryNW (22:3) Aut 81, pp. 36-37.
"Sound" (tr. of Melih Cevdet Anday, w/ Talat S. Halman).   WebR (6: 1) Spr 81, p. 16.
"Touch."   VirQR (57:2) Spr 81, pp. 280-281.
"Toward Bastions and Warriors" (tr. of Bartolo Cattafi, w/ Ruth Feldman).   PoNow (5:6 issue 30) 81, p. 12.
"Vico Tapera" (tr. of Rocco Scotellaro, w/ Ruth Feldman).   PoNow (5:6 issue 30) 81, p. 25.
"A Visit to the Old Country."   SouthernPR (21: 1) Spr 81, pp. 60-62.
"Visitors."   SouthwR (66:4) Aut 81, p. 359.

SWANSON, R. A.
    "Nitecap."   MalR (60) O 81, p. 139.
    "Untitled."   MalR (60) O 81, p. 139.

SWANSON, Robert
    "Hobo Camp."   HiramPoR (30) Spr-Sum 81, p. 43.
    "The Voice of the Field."   HiramPoR (30) Spr-Sum 81, p. 43.

SWARTS, Helene
    "Soon."   ChrC (98:24) 29 Jl-5 Ag, 81, p. 758.
    "In Tangier."   ChrC (98:2) 21 Ja 81, p. 44.

SWEDE, George
    "Ashes."   Northeast (3:10) Wint 81, p. 19.
    "Lives."   Northeast (3:10) Wint 81, p. 19.

SWEENEY, Theresa
    "MacSweeney's Lament."   Nat (232:10) 14 Mr 81, p. 313.
    "St. Martin of Tours."   Nat (233:16) 14 N 81, p. 510.

SWEET, Nanora
    "Squares, and the Light."   Confr (22) Sum 81, p. 44.

SWENSON, Karen
    "The Fun House Fable."   Kayak (57) 81, p. 63.

SWENSON, May
    "From A Daybook."   ParisR (23:79) Spr 81, pp. 274-276.

SWETMAN, Glenn Robert
    "How Civilization Fell."   KanQ (13:1) Wint 81, p. 148.

SWILKY, Jody
    "Some Streets" (after Vallejo).   Chelsea (40) 81, p. 98.

SWISS, Thomas
    "Autumnal."   Iowa (11:2/3) Spr-Sum 80, p. 85.
    "Rounds."   Iowa (11:2/3) Spr-Sum 80, pp. 86-87.

SWIST, Wally
    "In May."   Tele (17) 81, p. 97.

SYKES, Graham
    "Upon This Rock." <u>Wind</u> (10:39) 80, p. 38.

SYLVESTER, Bill
    "The Beet Movement: Herbs dried and collected by Bill Sylvester."
        <u>Chelsea</u> (40) 81, pp. 112-116.

SZYMBORSKA, Wislaw
    "Any Case" (tr. by Grazyna Drabik and Sharon Olds). <u>Pequod</u> (12) 81,
        p. 1.

SZYMBORSKA, Wislawa
    "The Number Pi" (tr. by Grazyna Drabik and Sharon Olds). <u>AntR</u> (39:
        1) Wint 81, p. 77.

TADA, Chimako
    "Dead Sun" (tr. by James Kirkup). <u>Mund</u> (12/13) 80-81, p. 141.

TADIC, Dejan
    "Everyday Encounters" (tr. by Stephen Stepanchev). <u>PoNow</u> (5:6 issue
        30) 81, p. 44.

TAFOLLA, Carmen
    "Caminitos." <u>Maize</u> (4:3/4) Spr-Sum 81, p. 76-7.

TAGGART, John
    "See What Love." <u>NowestR</u> (19:3), pp. 21-25.

TAGLIABUE, John
    "American Complicated with Integrity: Homage to Muriel." <u>Harp</u>
        (262:1571) Ap 81, p. 39.
    "Another vegetable occasion to thank the Chutes." <u>ChiR</u> (32:4) Spr 81,
        p. 15.
    "Back in the Tuileries." <u>Chelsea</u> (40) 81, p. 94.
    "Dancers Emerge from Silence Like Fireworks and Return to It Like
        Flowers to the Divine Ground." <u>Epoch</u> (30:3) Spr-Sum 81, p. 220.
    "For years, many, I've succumbed to them." <u>ChiR</u> (32:4) Spr 81, p.
        12.
    "From a French Travel Journal." <u>NewL</u> (48:1) Aut 81, p. 45.
    "The Immortal Name of Solomon Can Only Be Written by God." <u>Epoch</u>
        (30:3) Spr-Sum 81, p. 218.
    "Impossible--Ma Bravo." <u>Epoch</u> (30:3) Spr-Sum 81, p. 219.
    "Lettuce does not let us alone." <u>ChiR</u> (32:4) Spr 81, p. 13.
    "My and Paolo Uccello's BATTLE SCENES and 'Quella Benedetta Per-
        spettiva!'" <u>Epoch</u> (30:3) Spr-Sum 81, pp. 218-219.
    "Nympheas and momentous Celebration in evolution." <u>Chelsea</u> (40) 81,
        p. 94.
    "On the way to Alexander of Rhode Island, 9 days old." <u>NewL</u> (48:1)
        Aut 81, p. 46.
    "Poem." <u>CentR</u> (25:3) Sum 81, pp. 260-261.
    "Poems from a French Travel Journal." <u>Chelsea</u> (40) 81, pp. 92-93.
    "Related to the Present from the Mt. Vernon poets and farmers."
        <u>ChiR</u> (32:4) Spr 81, p. 14.
    "Under the Commandments and Commotion of the Sun." <u>Epoch</u> (30:3)
        Spr-Sum 81, p. 220.

TAKACS, Nancy
    "Fort Larue, With Words, And Distance." <u>Nat</u> (232:20) 23 My 81, p.
        637.

TAKAMI, Jun
    "Blackboard" (tr. by Graeme Wilson). DenQ (16:4) Wint 81, p. 44.

TAKAMURA, Kotaro
    "Artless Story" (tr. by Graeme Wilson). DenQ (16:4) Wint 81, p. 30.

TAKAMURA, Kotaroh
    "The Cathedral Beaten By Rain" (tr. by Gary Steven Corseri and
        Tsuyoshi Itoh). WebR (6:2) 81, pp. 21-24.

TAKENAKA, Iku
    "Enchantress" (tr. by Graeme Wilson). DenQ (16:4) Wint 81, pp. 43-
        44.

TALL, Deborah
    "Anima." Poetry (138:4) Jul 81, pp. 210-211.
    "Memorabilia." Poetry (138:4) Jl 81, pp. 212-213.
    "Ninth Life." MalR (58) Ap 81, pp. 92-95.

TAMMARO, Thom
    "Sarah Schaffer." BallSUF (22:4) Aut 81, p. 21.

TAMURA, Ruichi
    "A Distant Land." Mund (12/13) 80-81, pp. 34-35.
    "Four Thousand Days and Nights" (tr. by Edith Shiffert and Yuki Sawa).
        Mund (12/13), 80-81, p. 36.
    "October Poem." Mund (12/13) 80-81, p. 35.
    "The Withered Leaves" (tr. by Sam Grolmes and Yumiko Tsumura).
        Mund (12/13) 80-81, p. 34.

TAMURA, Ryuichi
    "Ghost Watcher (3)" (tr. by Graeme Wilson). DenQ (16:4) Wint 81, p.
        47.

TANIKAWA, Shuntaro
    "Growth" (tr. by Graeme Wilson). DenQ (16:4) Wint 81, p. 51.

TAO, Chien
    "Sons" (tr. by Graeme Wilson). WestHR (35:3) Aut 81, p. 240.

TAPSCOTT, Stephen
    "Because She Is Pregnant and Full of Her California." MissouriR (4:3)
        Sum 81, p. 15.
    "In the Darkness of the Body." MissouriR (4:3) Sum 81, p. 12.
    "Lobster." LitR (24:3) Spr 81, pp. 389-390.
    "Narcissus." Antaeus (40/41) Wint-Spr 81, pp. 388-389.
    "Irises." MissouriR (4:3) Sum 81, p. 14.
    "This." LitR (24:3) Spr 81, p. 390.

TARLEN, Carol
    "Work Slows Down At The Plant." Sam (109) 81, pp. 32-33.

TARN, Nathaniel
    Eight poems (tr. of Héctor Manjarrez). Sulfur (2) 81, pp. 59-64.

TARRIUS LOPEZ, Edith
    "Canto a la Tierra en el Campesino." Puerto Wint 81, p. 48.

TATE, James
  "Autochthonous." MassR (22:4) Wint 81, p. 631.
  Eight poems. AmerPoR (10:1) Ja-F 81, pp. 3-5.
  "It Wasn't Me." Poetry (138:5) Ag 81, p. 269.
  "Jelka." Kayak (56) 81, p. 6.
  "The Mink Cemetery." MassR (22:4) Wint 81, p. 632.
  "Promised Land." Kayak (56) 81, p. 7.
  "Red Bricks and Camphor Trees." Poetry (138:5) Ag 81, p. 270.
  "Soldier Without a Gun." Antaeus (40/41) Wint-Spr 81, pp. 392-393.
  "Summer Night." Antaeus (40/41) Wint-Spr 81, pp. 390-391.
  "To Fuzzy." Poetry (138:5) Ag 81, pp. 267-268.

TAYLOR, Alexander
  "The Ambercollectors" (tr. of Asger Schnack). PoNow (5:6 issue 30)
    81, p. 40.
  "It's Fall. It's Raining in the Woods" (tr. of Kirsten Thorup, w/
    Nadia Christensen). PoNow (5:6 issue 30) 81, p. 26.
  "37° C" (tr. of Kirsten Thorup, w/ Nadia Christensen). PoNow (5:6
    issue 30) 81, p. 26.
  "Trieste II" (tr. of Kirsten Thorup, w/ Nadia Christensen). PoNow
    (5:6 issue 30) 81, p. 26.

TAYLOR, Duane
  "Parley Porter Picks up a Hitchhiker and Rides through Cana County."
    BelPoJ (31:4) Sum 81, pp. 26-27.
  "Parley's Story Features a Famous Sinner to the Which He's Previously
    Alluded." BelPoJ (31:4) Sum 81, pp. 27-28.

TAYLOR, Eleanor Ross
  "Daymother with Forks." Shen (31:3) 80, p. 77.
  "In Case of Danger." Ploughs (7:2) 81, pp. 34-35.
  "A Little Obituary." VirQR (57:1) Wint 81, p. 69.
  "Nightmother Putting Up Her Hair." Shen (31:3) 80, p. 77.
  "Order and Law." VirQR (57:1) Wint 81, pp. 69-70.
  "Over a Stone." Poetry (138:1) Ap 81, p. 15.
  "The Painted Bridge." Ploughs (7:2) 81, pp. 36-37.
  "Rachel Plummer's Dream Winter 1836." Shen (31:3) 80, pp. 74-76.
  "Women's Terminal Ward." VirQR (57:1) Wint 81, pp. 71-72.

TAYLOR, Henry
  "Hawk." HolCrit (17:6 [i.e. 18:1?]) F 81, p. 19.
  "Sick in Soul and Body Both." WestHR (35:1) Spr 81, p. 12.

TAYLOR, John
  "Jukebox Tune." NewL (47:4) Sum 81, p. 88.

TAYLOR, K. P. A.
  "Prayer." SewanR (89:4) Aut 81, p. 518.
  "A Seacoast in Bohemia." SewanR (89:4) Aut 81, p. 519.
  "A Well Wishing." SewanR (89:4) Aut 81, pp. 516-517.

TAYLOR, Keith
  "Innocent Confusion." HiramPoR (30) Spr-Sum 81, p. 44.

TAYLOR, Laurie
  "Nightpiece." Im (7:3) 81, p. 4.
  "Visitation Rights, Summer, 1968." CapeR (16:2) Sum 81, p. 29.

TAYLOR, Stephaine Parrish
    "The Albino." BlackALF (15:1) Spr 81, p. 30.

TAYLOR, Tommie Nell
    "Children After It Rains." Obs (6:1/2) Spr-Sum 80, p. 146.
    "Love Like Toenails." Obs (6:1/2) Spr-Sum 80, p. 147.
    "Made Down." Obs (6:1/2) Spr-Sum 80, p. 147.
    "Moored." Obs (6:1/2) Spr-Sum 80, p. 146.

TEAGUE, Toney
    "Assault on Second Avenue." Poetry (138:4) Jl 81, p. 221.
    "Woman in White." Poetry (138:4) Jl 81, p. 222.

TEMPLETON, Fiona
    "America Language Women Abstraction Anarchy Empiricism Eating
        Emotion and Credibility." SunM (11) Spr 81, pp. 3-5.

TENNER, Andy
    "Jerusalem" (tr. of Muzaffar al-Nawwab, w/ Michael Beard). Nimrod
        (24: 2) Spr/Sum 81, pp. 135-138.

TENORIO, Harold Alvarado see ALVARADO TENORIO, Harold

TEPFER, Karen
    "The Figurehead." ThRiPo (17/18) 81, p. 40.

TERADA, Wini
    "Kalihi Home." PoNow (6:3 issue 33) 81, p. 41.
    "Waimea Bay" (for Bijei). PoNow (6:3 issue 33) 81, p. 41.

TERRANELLA, Ron
    "Joggers." PoNow (6:3 issue 33) 81, p. 41.

TERRILL, Kathryn
    "The Darker Side of Mary Worth." Poetry (137:6) Mr 81, p. 331.

TERRILL, Richard
    "The Good Places to Hide in the Human Heart." CarolQ (33:1) Wint 81,
        p. 51.
    "The Miracle." CarolQ (33:1) Wint 81, p. 50.
    "Some Days." CarolQ (34:2) Aut 81, pp. 59-60.

TERRIS, Susan
    "A Lesson in Tense." PoetryNW (22:4) Wint 81-82, p. 40.

TERRIS, Virginia
    "Arrangements." Confr (21) Wint 81, p. 124.
    "The Ugly Woman." PoetryE (6) Aut 81, p. 64.

TETI, Zona
    "Late Afternoon" (for R. Z.). BelPoJ (32:2) Wint 81-82, p. 23.

THALMAN, Mark
    "Eagle Rock." CharR (7:1) Spr 81, p. 21.
    "Rockfishing." CalQ (18/19) 81, p. 129.
    "Swallows at Walterville." CharR (7:1) Spr 81, pp. 20-21.

THENON, Susana
    "from Distances" (tr. by Renata Treitel and Charles Kemnitz). NewOR

(8:1) Wint 81, p. 37.
"Medea" (tr. by Renata Trietel and Charles Kemnitz). PoNow (5:6 issue 30) 81, p. 45.
"The woman of many names will return" (tr. by Renata Trietel and Charles Kemnitz). PoNow (5:6 issue 30) 81, p. 45.

THEOBALDY, Jürgen
"Something Like Peace" (tr. by Von Underwood). Mund (11:2) 79, p. 123.
"Wie Friede." Mund (11:2) 79, p. 122.

THERIAULT, Marie José
"VI: Arañas." Os (12) Spr 81, pp. 16-17.
"II: He hablado de ti a los pinos y a las piedras." Os (12) Spr 81, p. 18.
"I: Encendida la vela." Os (12) Spr 81, p. 15.

THOMAS, Colette
"Answer." Vis (6) 81, n. p.
"April Mushrooms." Vis (6) 81, n. p.

THOMAS, D. M.
"The Myth." AmerS (50:2) Spr 81, p. 178.

THOMAS, Dylan
"On a Wedding Anniversary." Antaeus (40/41) Wint-Spr 81, p. 547.
"On a Wedding Anniversary." Antaeus (40/41) Wint-Spr 81, p. 548.

THOMAS, Elizabeth
"Without Me." QW (12) Spr-Sum 81, pp. 14-15.

THOMAS, Gail
"Drought." HiramPoR (30) Spr-Sum 81, p. 45.
"Wintering." HiramPoR (30) Spr-Sum 81, p. 46.

THOMAS, Graham
"All About Peter." Pequod (13) 81, p. 64.

THOMAS, Harry
"Contagion." SewanR (89:2) Ap-Je 81, p. 188.

THOMAS, Jim
"Captive." KanQ (13:1) Wint 81, p. 147.
"Currents." CapeR (17:1) Wint 81, p. 47.
"Growth Factors." KanQ (13:1) Wint 81, p. 148.
"View From The Lot." CapeR (16:2) Sum 81, p. 27.

THOMAS, Linda
"Believing" (for K. D.). AmerPoR (10:4) Jl-Ag 81, p. 35.
"Shorebird." AmerPoR (10:4) Jl-Ag 81, p. 35.

THOMAS, Peter
"Legacy." Wind (10:39) 80, pp. 39-40.

THOMAS, Richard
"Pillow Cards." PartR (48:2) 81, p. 252.

THOMASON, Helen
   "Circles Closing." Obs (7:1) Spr 81, p. 12.
   "When I Play My Music Loud." Obs (7:1) Spr 81, p. 11.

THOMPSON, Gary
   "As For Living." ThRiPo (17/18) 81, p. 29.

THOMPSON, Hilary
   "The Death Watch." PottPort (3) 81, p. 45.
   "The Enemy." PottPort (3) 81, p. 5.

THOMPSON, Jeanie
   "The Songs Beyond Hearing." NewEngR (4:2) Wint 81, pp. 246-9.

THOMPSON, Joanna
   "Farewell to Dead Parents." SouthwR (66:4) Aut 81, p. 394.
   "Picnic Day." Confr (21) Wint 81, p. 122.

THOMPSON, Nancy-Jean
   "Untitled." PottPort (3) 81, p. 40.

THOMPSON, Phyllis H.
   "What We Learned." ThRiPo (17/18) 81, p. 73.

THOMSEN, Barbara
   "Evergreen." Poem (42) Jul 81, p. 11.
   "Hurdle Mills, NC." Atl (247:2) F 81, p. 70.
   "Snake." Thrpny (5) Spr 81, p. 17.
   "Thaw." Poem (42) Jul 81, p. 9.
   "Winter Pumpkins." Poem (42) Jul 81, p. 10.

THOMSON, Sharon
   "Mother." ThRiPo (17/18) 81, p. 9.

THORNBURG, Thomas R.
   "Newspaperobitspoem." BallSUF (22:1) Wint 81, pp. 79-80.

THORNE, Evelyn
   "Astronaut After the First Moon Landing for B. A." WebR (6:2) 81, p.
      69.
   "Grouchy Poem On The First Day Of Summer." WindO (38) Spr-Sum
      81, p. 11.

THORPE, Michael
   "Exit March." StoneC (9: 1-2) Aut-Wint 81/82, p. 29.

THORUP, Kirsten
   "It's Fall, It's Raining in the Woods" (tr. by Nadia Christensen and
      Alexander Taylor). PoNow (5:6 issue 30) 81, p. 26.
   "37° C" (tr. by Nadia Christensen and Alexander Taylor). PoNow
      (5:6 issue 30) 81, p. 26.
   "Trieste II" (tr. by Nadia Christensen and Alexander Taylor). PoNow
      (5:6 issue 30) 81, p. 26.

THRONE, Marilyn
   "Summer Night: The Young Men." CapeR (17:1) Wint 81, p. 1.

THUMAN, Michiela
   "Baba and the Buffalo" (with love to Adnan). Peb (21) 81, pp. 67-68.

"Ode to the Lennon-like Unicorn" (with admiration, to Matt). Peb (21)
    81, pp. 65-66.

THURN, Janice
    "We Will All Wait." ThRiPo (17/18) 81, p. 95.

THURSTON, Bonnie Bowman
    "Plant Parable." ChrC (98:36) 11 N 81, p. 1156.

TICHY, Susan
    "Artillery." AntR (39:4) Aut 81, p. 447.
    "In an Arab Town." AntR (39:4) Aut 81, pp. 449-450.
    "Irrigation." AntR (39: 4) Aut 81, p. 446.
    "Lying on My Cot." AntR (39: 4) Aut 81, p. 448.
    "A Meditation in Perthshire, Scotland." BelPoJ (32:1) Aut 81, pp. 2-
    3.
    "Painting the Fence." AntR (39: 4) Aut 81, p. 445.
    "Volunteers." AntR (39: 4) Aut 81, pp. 450-451.

TILENA, Franco
    "Lucanian Cemeteries" (tr. by Lawrence Venuti). Chelsea (40) 81, p.
    52.

TILLINGHAST, Richard
    "Nativity" (tr. of Miodrag Pavlovic). Ploughs (7:2) 81, p. 61.
    "Sewanee in Ruins, Part One." Ploughs (7:1) 81, pp. 66-71.
    "Sewanee in Ruins, Part Two." Ploughs (7:2) 81, pp. 99-104.

TIMMERMAN, John H.
    "Burr Oak Lake." Wind (11:43) 81, pp. 35-36.

TIO, Elsa
    "A Arnaldo Darío Rosado y a Carlos Soto Arriví." Caribe (2: 2/3) 80/
    81, p. 63.

TIRADO, Adrián Santos see SANTOS TIRADO, Adrián

TISDALE, Charles
    "October." AntR (39:3) Sum 81, p. 339.

TIXIER, Jean-Max
    "Deux poèmes." Os (13) Aut 81, p. 10.

TODD, Harris
    "The Day He Killed The Sheep." Wind (10:39) 80, p. 42.
    "I'm Not Caring for Details These Days." Wind (10:39) 80, p. 41.

TODD, Jane
    "Elegy." Wind (11:42) 81, pp. 36-37.
    "Spectrum Shift." Wind (11:42) 81, p. 36.

TODD, Theodora
    "The Missing Person." BelPoJ (32:2) Wint 81-82, pp. 8-14.
    "The Separation." HangL (40) Aut 81, p. 56.

TOLLEFSEN, Astrid
    "Bonjour Monsieur Gaugin" (tr. by Nadia Christensen). PoNow (5:6
    issue 30) 81, p. 45.

TOLSA, Sanna
  "Pyres" (tr. of Arto Melleri, w/ Austin Flint).   PoetryE (6) Aut 81,
    pp. 29-30.

TOME, Jesús
  "De cómo los terrores me amparan del terror."   Mairena (2:6) 80, pp.
    63-4.
  "Expósito (A la memoria de un curtidor que era mi abuelo)."   Mairena
    (2:6) 80, pp. 62-3.
  "Un lugar como destino."   Mairena (2:6) 80, p. 62.

TOMEI, Miguel A.
  "Isla de Puerto Rico."   Mairena (2:6) 80, p. 84.
  "La palabra castellana."   Mairena (2:6) 80, pp. 83-4.

TOMKIW, Lydia
  "Insomnia."   Kayak (57) 81, p. 44.
  "Lethargy."   Kayak (57) 81, p. 42.
  "Night Travellers."   Kayak (57) 81, p. 42.
  "Praxis."   Wind (11:43) 81, p. 37.
  "Praying for a Revolver."   Wind (11:43) 81, pp. 37-38.
  "Recalling the Last Encounter."   Kayak (57) 81, p. 43.

TOMLINS, Jack E.
  "Sadness in Heaven" (tr. of Carlos Drummond de Andrade).   Mund
    (12/13) 80-81, p. 270.
  "To Be" (tr. of Carlos Drummond de Andrade).   Mund (12/13) 80-81,
    pp. 270-271.

TOMLINSON, Charles
  "The Epilogue."   Hudson (34:1) Spr 81, p. 14.
  "The Flood."   Hudson (34:1) Spr 81, pp. 9-11.
  "Giovanni Diodati" (tr. of Attilio Bertolucci).   Stand (22: 3) 81, p. 21.
  "In the Estuary."   Hudson (34:1) Spr 81, p. 13.
  "Programme Note."   ParisR (23:79) Spr 81, pp. 277-278.
  "Severnside."   Hudson (34:1) Spr 81, p. 12.
  "Snow Signs."   Stand (22: 3) 81, p. 20.

TOMLINSON, Rawdon
  "Letter" (for Amie).   Wind (10:39) 80, p. 43.

TONG, Raymond
  "A Private Person."   WormR (84) 81, p. 89.
  "Solution."   WormR (84) 81, p. 90.

TORGERSEN, Eric
  "First Shot."   PoNow (6:2 issue 32) 81, p. 13.

TORNES, Beth
  "The Break" (tr. of Delmira Agustini, w/ Linda Wine).   SenR (12:1/2)
    81, p. 109.
  "My Lovers" (tr. of Delmira Agustini).   SenR (12:1/2) 81, pp. 97-101.
  "A Soul" (tr. of Delmira Agustini).   SenR (12:1/2) 81, p. 107.
  "The Sweet Reliquaries" (tr. of Delmira Agustini).   SenR (12:1/2) 81,
    p. 105.
  "While You Slept" (tr. of Delmira Agustini).   SenR (12:1/2) 81, p. 103.

TORRES, Daniel
  "Te he hallado." Mairena (3:7) 81, p. 96.

TORRES, Eladio
  "Contrapunto de la lluvia." Mairena (2:6) 80, p. 49.

TORRES, Gerardo Moreno see MORENO TORRES, Gerardo

TORRES MELENDEZ, Carlos "La Sombra"
  "Músico Revolucionario" (A Juan Mari Bras). (Pedro Baiges Chapel).
      Claridad/En Rojo (22: 1471) 10-16 Ap 81, p. 12.
  "Sobre Juan Mari Bras." Claridad/En Rojo (22: 1471) 10-16 Ap 81, p.
      12.
  "Zapatero, Revolucionario y Abogado" (Dedicada al compañero Pedro
      Baiges Chapel). Claridad/En Rojo (22: 1471) 10-16 Ap 81, p. 5.

TORRES SANTIAGO, José Manuel
  "Cuscatlán." Claridad/En Rojo (22: 1476) 15-21 My 81, p. 12.
  "Panorama." Claridad/En Rojo (22: 1476) 15-21 My 81, p. 12.
  "Poética." Claridad/En Rojo (22: 1476) 15-21 My 81, p. 12.
  "Sucesos." Claridad/En Rojo (22: 1476) 15-21 My 81, p. 12.
  "Testimonio." Claridad/En Rojo (22: 1476) 15-21 My 81, p. 12.

TORRES VEGA, Armando
  "Mentores del Garrote." Claridad/En Rojo (22: 1507) 18-23 D 81, p.
      11.
  "Rebeldía patria." Claridad/En Rojo (22: 1501) 6-12 N 81, p. 12.

TORRESON, Rodney
  "A Missionary Comes to Oakdale Country Church." BelPoJ (32:2) Wint
      81-82, p. 17.

TOSTESON, Heather
  "Membranes." SmPd (18:2) Spr 81, p. 16.

TOUMI, Ann J.
  "The Sick Gypsy Boy" (tr. of Josef Haltrich). Northeast (3:10) Wint
      81, p. 31.

TRACHTENBERG, Paul
  "Lamp Post in Storm." PoNow (6:3 issue 33) 81, p. 42.
  "Love is More Than a Four Letter Word." PoNow (6:3 issue 33) 81,
      p. 42.
  "The Raven." PoNow (6:3 issue 33) 81, p. 42.
  "Thickening." PoNow (6:3 issue 33) 81, p. 42.

TRAKL, Georg
  "Declension" (tr. by Francis Golffing). PoNow (6:1 issue 31) 81, p.
      43.
  "Evening in Lans" (tr. by Paul Morris). PoNow (5:6 issue 30) 81, p.
      45.
  "Landscape" (tr. by Paul Morris). PoNow (5:6 issue 30) 81, p. 45.
  "The Rats" (tr. by Paul Morris). PoNow (5:6 issue 30) 81, p. 45.

TRANSTRÖMER, Tomas
  "After a Long Dry Spell" (tr. by Robert Bly). Pequod (12) 81, p. 93.
  "Answers to Letters" (tr. by Robin Fulton). Pequod (13) 81, p. 107.
  "At Funchal" (tr. by Robert Bly). Pequod (12) 81, p. 91.

"The Black Mountain" (tr. by Robert Bly). Pequod (12) 81, p. 92.
"Brief Pause in the Organ Recital" (tr. by Robin Fulton). Pequod (13) 81, pp. 108-109.
"From the Winter of 1947" (tr. by Robert Bly). PoNow (5:6 issue 30) 81, p. 26.
"Övergångsstället." PoetryE (4/5) Spr-Sum 81, p. 232.
"The Scattered Congregation" (tr. by Robert Bly). Mund (12/13) 80-81, p. 90.
"Street Crossing" (tr. by Robert Bly). PoetryE (4/5) Spr-Sum 81, p. 233.
"Street Crossing" (tr. by Robert Bly). PoNow (5:6 issue 30) 81, p. 26.
"Winter's Gaze" (tr. by Robin Fulton). Pequod (13) 81, p. 110.

TRAVIS, Byall
    "Hanging Upside-Down from a Bridge Railing." MissouriR (4:3) Sum 81, p. 32.

TRAXLER, Patricia
    "The Glasscutters: II. Eleven Glass Dreams in Winter." HangL (39) Wint 80-81, pp. 42-46.

TREAN, Mick
    "Forest (His Memory of Existence)" (tr. by Larry Couch). Vis (5) 81, n. p.

TREITEL, Margot
    "At Nightfall, Algeria Awakes." MinnR (17) Aut 81, p. 5.
    "Bearing the Witness." SouthernPR (21: 1) Spr 81, p. 19.
    "The Coming and Going of Cyprian Ikeme." MinnR (17) Aut 81, p. 6.
    "Here and Now, Years Later." DenQ (16:2) Sum 81, p. 51.
    "The Host Country's Language." ColEng (43:5) S 81, p. 493.
    "Jane Street, Number 84." DenQ (16:2) Sum 81, p. 48.
    "Moving Pictures." CarolQ (34:1) Sum 81, p. 22.
    "The Names of the Demonstrators and Defectors." DenQ (16:2) Sum 81, p. 49.
    "The Old Presence Française." DenQ (16:2) Sum 81, p. 50.
    "Reconstructing Her Girlhood Home." HiramPoR (30) Spr-Sum 81, p. 47.
    "Re-entry." HolCrit (18:3 [i. e. 4]) O 81, p. 18.
    "Slogans on the Wall." MinnR (17) Aut 81, p. 7.
    "Snowstorm and Shipwreck by Turner." LitR (24:3) Spr 81, p. 348.
    "Somewhere The Snow Is Falling Heavily." StoneC (9: 1-2) Aut-Wint 81/82, p. 20.
    "What Happens in Algeria Every Day." DenQ (16:2) Sum 81, p. 47.
    "The Woodcarver's Song to a Tree." MinnR (17) Aut 81, p. 8.

TRETHEWAY, Eric
    "Garbage." SouthernPR (21:2) Aut 81, pp. 54-55.

TREVIÑO, Gloria Velásquez see VELASQUEZ TREVIÑO, Gloria

TRIETEL, Renata
    from "Distances" (tr. of Susana Thénon, w/ Charles Kemnitz). NewOR (8:1) Wint 81, p. 37.
    "Medea" (tr. of Susana Thénon, w/ Charles Kemnitz). PoNow (5:6 issue 30) 81, p. 45.
    "Three Images From the Plitvice Lakes" (tr. of Margherita Guidacci, w/ Manly Johnson). WebR (6:2) 81, pp. 25-26.
    "The woman of many names will return" (tr. of Susana Thénon, w/

Charles Kemnitz). PoNow (5:6 issue 30) 81, p. 45.

TRIMBLE, Mary
    "Nothing Today." Ascent (7:1) 81, p. 40.

TRIMPI, Wesley
    "For the Living" (to the memory of A. Y. W.). SouthernR (17:4) Aut 81,
    p. 679.

TRITEL, Barbara
    "Apotheosis in The Laundromat." CalQ (18/19) 81, p. 130.

TRIVELPIECE, Laurel
    "Waiting for Water." PraS (55:4) Wint 81-82, p. 83.

TROTTA de BASCIANO, Irma
    "Pablo en el recuerdo." LetFem (7:1) Spr 81, p. 89.

TROUPE, Quincy
    "After the Holocaust." Mund (12/13) 80-81, pp. 178-179.

TROWBRIDGE, William
    "Christmas Poem." Wind (10:39) 80, p. 44.
    "Happy Hour." HiramPoR (29) Aut-Wint 81, p. 40.
    "Retrospective: An SS Photo of a Man About to be Shot." BelPoJ (32:
    1) Aut 81, pp. 36-37.
    "A Timely Message." Wind (10:39) 80, pp. 44-45.
    "War Baby." KanQ (13:3/4) Sum-Aut 81, p. 150.

TROWELL, I. Douglas
    "Fair Sex." PottPort (3) 81, p. 33.
    "Flocks in Shock." PottPort (3) 81, p. 52.

TROYER, Gene van see Van TROYER, Gene

TRUDELL, Dennis
    "Watch Them Die." GeoR (35:3) Aut 81, p. 596.

TRUMP, John P.
    "The Flower." Tele (17) 81, p. 32.

TSCHACBASOV
    "The Bird's Last Roost." Chelsea (39) 81, p. 191.
    "Logic-Twisting Heads." Chelsea (39) 81, p. 193.
    "The Image Grew." Chelsea (39) 81, p. 190.
    "Night Belongs to Life." Chelsea (39) 81, p. 194.
    "Pavilions of the Winds." Chelsea (39) 81, p. 192.

TSCHERNISCH, Garth
    "More Praise From the Barnyard Suite No. 2." Sulfur (2) 81, pp. 177-
    179.

TSUMURA, Yumiko
    "A Distant Land" (tr. of Ruichi Tamura, w/ Sam Grolmes). Mund
    (12/13) 80-81, pp. 34-35.
    "October Poem" (tr. of Ruichi Tamura, w/ Sam Grolmes). Mund (12/
    13) 80-81, p. 35.
    "The Withered Leaves" (tr. of Ruichi Tamura, w/ Sam Grolmes).
    Mund (12/13) 80-81, p. 34.

TU, Fu
  "The Winding River" (tr. by C. H. Kwan). MalR (58) Ap 81, p. 38.

TU, Mu
  "Autumn Evening" (tr. by C. H. Kwan). MalR (58) Ap 81, p. 37.

TUCKER, Larry
  "Yes Gray." Tele (17) 81, p. 125.

TUCKER, Liza
  "By the River Oka." Pequod (12) 81, pp. 6-7.

TUCKER, Martin
  "The Inveterate Hesitater." Confr (21) Wint 81, p. 128.
  "Poetry and the New Science." Confr (22) Sum 81, p. 120.

TUDOR, Stephen
  "The House of Your Head." OP (31/32) Aut 81, p. 139.

TUENI, Nadia
  "Exile" (tr. by Elaine Gardiner). Mund (12/13) 80-81, p. 253.
  "Inventory" (tr. by Elaine Gardiner). Mund (12/13) 80-81, p. 253.

TULLOSS, Rod
  "A Series of Messages." US1 (14/15) Aut/Wint 81, p. 8.
  "At the end of Rising." US1 (14/15) Aut/Wint 81, p. 8.
  "I." US1 (14/15) Aut/Wint 81, p. 8.

TURCO, Lewis
  "Attic Poem." SewanR (89:2) Ap-Je 81, p. 189.
  "Cancer." SewanR (89:2) Ap-Je 81, p. 190.
  "Querule." NewOR (8:1) Wint 81, p. 76.
  "The Stockyard." ThRiPo (17/18) 81, p. 75.

TURGEON, Gregoire
  "A Girl Distracted a Hundred Years." PoNow (6:3 issue 33) 81, p. 42.
  "Interior Near Copake, New York, 1933." Tendril (10) Wint 81, p. 42.
  "Letter From the Shore." Tendril (10) Wint 81, p. 43.

TURNER, A.
  "Three Fears." LittleM (13:1/2) Spr-Sum 79, c1981, p. 124.

TURNER, Alison
  "Cobble Hill." Hudson (34:3) Aut 81, pp. 388-389.
  "Nightwalk." Hudson (34:3) Aut 81, p. 389.

TURNER, Keith
  "Raleigh Returning from Guyana." Pequod (13) 81, p. 65.

TWICHELL, Chase
  "Holy Night." CharR (7:1) Spr 81, p. 19.
  "Like A Caretaker." Ploughs (6:4) 81, p. 185.
  "Nostalgia For the Future." Ploughs (6:4) 81, pp. 186-187.
  "This Was a Farm." PoNow (6:3 issue 33) 81, p. 28.
  "Watercress & Ice." PoNow (6:3 issue 33) 81, p. 28.
  "When the Rapture Comes, I Will Depart Earth." CharR (7:1) Spr 81,
     p. 20.

TYNDALL, Paul
"Lines Written For A Summer's Evening" (to Margot).   PottPort (3) 81,
   p. 9.

TYSH, Chris
   "Alix."   SunM (11) Spr 81, p. 84.
   "Chanel."   SunM (11) Spr 81, p. 85.
   "Schiaparelli."   SunM (11) Spr 81, p. 83.

TYSH, George
   "Heart."   Tele (17) 81, p. 63.
   "Ida Lupino" (for Chris).   Tele (17) 81, pp. 62-63.
   "In Les Yeux Verts."   Tele (17) 81, p. 62.

TYSON, Tina C.
   "The Cold and the Grey."   Meadows (2:1) 81, p. 66.

UCAR, Gina del
   "A Puerto Rico 1981" (sombra de Gautier).   Claridad/En Rojo (22:
      1503) 20-26 N 81, p. 12.
   "Desahucio."   Claridad/En Rojo (22: 1462) 6-12 F 81, p. 12.
   "Meditación."   Claridad/En Rojo (22: 1462) 6-12 F 81, p. 12.

UCETA, Acacia
   "Paseo por el parque de San Julián."   LetFem (7:2) Aut 81, pp. 43-44.
   "Primavera."   LetFem (7:2) Aut 81, pp. 45-46.
   "Primer día de frío."   LetFem (7:2) Aut 81, pp. 41-42.
   "Soneto a Cuenca."   LetFem (7:2) Aut 81, p. 40.

UDA, Emperor
   from The Kokinshu: "Estuary at Twighlight" (tr. by Graeme Wilson).
      WestHR (35:4) Wint 81, p. 346.

ULLMAN, Leslie
   "Each Year."   OP (31/32) Aut 81, p. 118.
   "The Grocery."   AmerPoR (10:1) Ja-F 81, p. 13.
   "Loyalty."   AmerPoR (10:1) Ja-F 81, p. 13.
   "Porch Light."   AmerPoR (10:1) Ja-F 81, p. 13.
   "The Split."   ThRiPo (17/18) 81, p. 78.

ULLOA, Yolanda
   "Pequeña biografía de una lavandera."   Areito (7: 27) 81, p. 19.

UMBREIT, Paula
   "Fjordic Spring."   Wind (11:43) 81, p. 40.

UNGARETTI, Giuseppe
   "The Seasons" (tr. by Dora Pettinella).   Mund (12/13) 80-81, pp. 378-
      379.
   "Silence" (tr. by Dora M. Pettinella).   Mund (12/13) 80-81, p. 377.

UNGARO de FOX, Lucia
   "Necropolis and Perspectives" (tr. by Ben Belitt).   Mund (12/13) 80-81,
      p. 113.

UNGER, Barbara
   "Magenta Gloves."   SouthernPR (21: 1) Spr 81, p. 37.

UNGER, David
    "The Bait Truck." PoNow (6:1 issue 31) 81, p. 46.
    "Dostoevsky and Physical Beauty" (tr. of Luis Cernuda). PoNow (5:6 issue 30) 81, p. 13.
    "It's Not Possible Now" (tr. of Vicente Aleixandre, w/ Lewis Hyde). PoNow (5:6 issue 30) 81, p. 3.
    "Love's Cutting Edge" (tr. of Vicente Aleixandre, w/ Lewis Hyde). PoNow (5:6 issue 30) 81, p. 3.
    "Marta Kuhn-Weber" (tr. of Enrique Lihn). PoNow (5:6 issue 30) 81, p. 28.
    "No Man's Land" (tr. of Vicente Aleixandre, w/ Lewis Hyde). PoNow (5:6 issue 30) 81, p. 3.
    "Seagulls in the Parks" (tr. of Luis Cernuda). PoNow (5:6 issue 30) 81, p. 13.

UNGER, Suzie
    "Jackie Z." Bound (9:2) Wint 81, pp. 155-156.

UNTERECKER, John
    "The Dancers" (for Theone). UnmOx (22) Wint 81, p. 36.
    "Discarded Typewriter Ribbon: Friends: Maile Leaves." Wind (10:39) 80, p. 47.
    "Explorer." PoNow (6:2 issue 32) 81, p. 9.
    "Evensong: All of Our Sad Violins." Tendril (11) Sum 81, p. 77.
    "Interview." Kayak (57) 81, pp. 45-47.
    "Pennsylvania Summer." PoNow (6:2 issue 32) 81, p. 9.
    "River Song." Wind (10:39) 80, pp. 46-47.
    "The Room." NewEngR (3:4) Sum 81, pp. 543-5.
    "Videotape: Eight Second Pause." Kayak (56) 81, pp. 36-37.
    "Winter Night." Wind (10:39) 80, p. 46.

UPDIKE, John
    "Crab Crack." Harp (263:1574) Jl 81, p. 80.
    "Penumbrae." NewYorker (57:30) 14 S 81, p. 54.

UPTON, Lee
    "Come Out." PoNow (6:3 issue 33) 81, p. 42.
    "Emergency Cannibals." MassR (22:4) Wint 81, p. 694.
    "Love of Ornament." Confr (21) Wint 81, p. 123.
    "Rolling Dogs." MassR (22:4) Wint 81, p. 693.
    "A Single Drop." ConcPo (14:1) Spr 81, p. 51.

URDANG, Constance
    "The Dream-Addict." PoNow (6:2 issue 32) 81, p. 25.
    "History Is a Single Savage Act." CharR (7:2) Aut 81, p. 9.
    "Safe Places." PoNow (6:2 issue 32) 81, p. 25.
    "Why They Turned Back/Why They Went On." CharR (7:2) Aut 81, p. 8.

URDANG, Elliot
    "Tomorrow The Past Comes" (tr. of Ion Caraion, w/ Marguerite Dorian). Mund (12/13) 80-81, p. 305.
    "Unornamentation" (tr. of Ion Caraion, w/ Marguerite Dorian). Mund (12/13) 80-81, p. 305.

URPI, Xavier
    "Alto Voltaje." Lugar (1:1) 79, p. 19.

URQUHART, Jane
"Other." MalR (58) Ap 81, p. 117.
"Time After." MalR (58) Ap 81, p. 116.

URRUTIA, Angel
"Clavado a la Agonía." Puerto Wint 81, p. 49.

USCHUK, Pamela
"A Dream, My Child." Nimrod (25:1) Aut-Wint 81, p. 94.
"Light from Dead Stars." Nimrod (25:1) Aut-Wint 81, pp. 94-96.
"Watching Falling Stars at the Rancho De Lucks." CutB (16) Spr-Sum
    81, p. 114.

USHER, Ann Carter
"Remembering the Landscape." Northeast (3:10) Wint 81, p. 8.

UZELAC, Milan
"The Steeple of Misa" (tr. by Stephen Stepanchev). PoNow (5:6 issue
    30) 81, p. 46.

VACANTE, Jane
"Shard." FourQt (30:4) Sum 81, p. 15.

VACAS, Francisco José
"Apelación inconsumable (A un Rafael Alberti)." Mairena (3:7) 81, pp.
    6-8.
"Exploración de júbilo." Mairena (3:7) 81, pp. 10-11.
"Incorporación (A Paco Ibáñez)." Mairena (3:7) 81, pp. 8-9.
"Motivo de cristal." Mairena (3:7) 81, pp. 11-12.
"Vosotros." Mairena (3:7) 81, p. 12.

VAETH, Kim
"A Flute in the Middle of the Night." OP (31/32) Aut 81, pp. 167-
    168.

VAIL, Amy
"Cynicism." WormR (84) 81, p. 104.
"Ode On A Piece Of Salt Water Taffy." WormR (84) 81, p. 104.

VAKALO, Eleni
from Planet Education, V (tr. by Kimon Friar). Poetry (139:2) N 81,
    p. 81.

VALDES, Gina
"Back to School." Maize (4:1/2) Aut-Wint 80-81, p. 45.
"Buscando una casa nueva." Maize (4:1/2) Aut-Wint 80-81, pp. 46-7.
"Caminaba en la pradera." Maize (4:1/2) Aut-Wint 80-81, p. 47.
"Ko." Maize (4:1/2) Aut-Wint 80-81, p. 48.
"Platicamos como se acostumbra." Maize (4:1/2) Aut-Wint 80-81, p.
    48.

VALDEZ, Ramiro
"Cornered" (tr. by Leland H. Chambers). DenQ (16:3) Aut 81, p. 96.
"Stones" (tr. by Leland H. Chambers). DenQ (16:3) Aut 81, p. 95.

VALENTA, H.
"Photograph from Costa Rica." CreamCR (7:1) 81, p. 125.

VALENTA, Helen
"Champaign County." Wind (11:41) 81, p. 44.
"Cleopatra in the Bath." Ascent (6:3) 81, p. 9.

VALENTE, José Angel
"The Adolescent" (tr. by Willis Barnstone). Mund (12/13) 80-81, p. 146.
"The Bet" (tr. by Willis Barnstone). Mund (12/13) 80-81, p. 146.
"Prohibition of Incest" (tr. by Willis Barnstone). Mund (12/13) 80-81, p. 147.

VALENTINE, Jean
"Birthday Letter from South Carolina" (for Sarah, 21). ParisR (23:81) Aut 81, p. 143.

VALENZUELA de PEREZ, Ilma
"Juana de América." LetFem (7:1) Spr 81, pp. 87-8.

VALERO, Roberto
"Dreams Weaver" (A Maru). Notarte (6:2) F 81, p. 10.
"Guerreros enigmáticos." Notarte (6:2) F 81, p. 10.

VALK, E. M.
"Sheep, Looked at Another Way" (tr. of Robert Musil). Pequod (12) 81, pp. 32-33.

VALLE, Carmen
"Por que yo." Mairena (2:6) 80, pp. 49-50.

VALLONE, Anthony
"The Crow" (for Bitsey Kemp and Lorna Cohen). SouthernPR (21:2) Aut 81, pp. 42-48.

van BRUNT, H. L.
"Hatching Out." Wind (11:41) 81, p. 7.
"In the Looking Glass." Confr (22) Sum 81, p. 64.
"Perseid (August 12, 1978)." Wind (11:41) 81, p. 6.
"Speaking In Tongues." NewL (47:4) Sum 81, p. 87.

VANCE, Vera
"If Not a War." NewEngR (4:1) Aut 81, pp. 80-82.

Van der MOLEN, Robert
"Howard & His Silence." Epoch (30:2) Wint-Spr 81, pp. 132-134.
"Howard's Marriage." Epoch (30:2) Wint-Spr 81, pp. 135-137.

van DUYN, Mona
"Dreaming of Mark Strand." Ploughs (6:4) 81, pp. 39-40.
"Fall" (for James). GeoR (35:4) Wint 81, p. 789.
"Lives of the Poets." GeoR (35:4) Wint 81, pp. 788-789.
"Photographs." Poetry (138:3) Je 81, pp. 151-155.
"Saleswomen in Bakery Shops." MassR (22:2) Sum 81, pp. 358-9.
"The Stream." MichQR (20:3) Sum 81, pp. 190-193.
"The Vision Test." MassR (22:2) Sum 81, pp. 359-60.

van HOUTEN, Lois
"Almonds." StoneC (9: 1-2) Aut-Wint 81/82, p. 41.

van SPANCKEREN, Kathryn
"The Time in Baja California." Aspect (77/79) 81, p. 198.

van TROYER, Gene
"Cat" (tr. of Yamanoguchi Baku). PortR (27: 2) 81, p. 30.
"Comfort" (tr. of Yamanoguchi Baku). PortR (27: 2) 81, p. 30.
"Is it just because." PortR (27: 1) 81, p. 33.
"The Starfarers" (1-4) (w/ Robert Frazier). PortR (27: 2) 81, pp. 70-72.

van WALLEGHEN, Michael
"The Great Cornflake Mystery." Ascent (6:3) 81, p. 52.

van WINCKEL, Nance
"Bringing Stones To the Midwest." CalQ (18/19) 81, pp. 136-137.
"Husbands in Bad Weather." PoetryNW (22:1) Spr 81, pp. 12-14.
"The Trainmaster's Thunder." PoetryNW (22:1) Spr 81, pp. 14-15.

VARELA, Blanca
"The Things I Say Are True" (tr. by Donald A. Yates). Mund (12/13) 80-81, p. 334.

VARVITSIOTIS, Takis
"Reposing Under the Cold Stone" (tr. by Kimon Friar). Poetry (139:2) N 81, p. 76.

VAS, Istvan
"Anacreontics" (tr. by Jascha Kessler). Confr (21) Wint 81, p. 23.

VAS DIAS, Robert
"The Color Beginning" (for L.C.). Stand (22: 3) 81, p. 45.

VAUGHAN, Kathy
"Untitled." PottPort (3) 81, p. 11.
"Zooming In On An Angel." PottPort (3) 81, p. 26.

VAUL, Diane De see DeVAUL, Diane

VAVRA, Linda
"Baby Poem 4." Field (24) Spr 81, p. 37.

VEAZEY, Mary
"Gas Girl." Poem (43) Nov 81, p. 14.
"To a Country Boy." Poem (43) Nov 81, p. 13.

VECCHIO, Gloria del see Del VECCHIO, Gloria

VEGA, Armando Torres see TORRES VEGA, Armando

VEGA, Janine Pommy
"Jameson's Whiskey." Aspect (77/79) 81, p. 181.

VEGA, Janine Pomy
"Poem For Mad Marcus The Dark." UnmOx (22) Wint 81, p. 35.

VEGA, Jenaro Soto see SOTO VEGA, Jenaro

VEGA, José Luis
"Ataraxia." Mairena (2:6) 80, p. 55.

"Bajo los efectos de la poesía." Mairena (2:6) 80, p. 54.
"Mensaje de adhesión." Mairena (2:6) 80, p. 54.

VELASQUEZ TREVIÑO, Gloria
"Metamorfosis." Metam (3:2/4:1) 80-81, p. 84.
"Solitaria." Metam (3:2/4:1) 80-81, p. 84.

VELEZ, Clemente Soto see SOTO VELEZ, Clemente

VELI, Orhan
"This Beautiful Weather" ("Güzel Havalar") (tr. by Ozcan Yalim, William A. Fielder, and Dionis Coffin Riggs). StoneC (8: 3) Spr 81, p. 31.

VENCLOVA, Tomas
"Nel mezzo del cammin di nostra vita" (to the memory of Konstantin Bogatyrev) (tr. by David McDuff). Stand (22: 2) 81, p. 15.
"Villanelle" (tr. by David McDuff). Stand (22: 2) 81, p. 14.

VENN, George
"Five Six Minutes in March." PoetryNW (22:2) Sum 81, pp. 19-20.
"Conjuring a Basque Ghost" (for Jean Ospital). CutB (16) Spr-Sum 81, pp. 107-108.
"My Mother is This White Wind Cleaning." PoetryNW (22:2) Sum 81, pp. 21-22.
"Safeway Conversation." PoetryNW (22:2) Sum 81, pp. 20-21.
"Winter Sailor." PortR (27: 2) 81, p. 86.

VENTSIAS, Roberta
"Drowning." ThRiPo (17/18) 81, p. 63.

VENUTI, Lawrence
"Feast Day" (tr. of Ordenio Loberto). Chelsea (40) 81, p. 51.
"Lucanian Cemeteries" (tr. of Franco Tilena). Chelsea (40) 81, p. 52.
"Luisa of the Slums, Demoiselle D'Avignon" (tr. of Antonio Lotierzo). Chelsea (40) 81, p. 50.
"Nipple" (tr. of Bruno Moretti). Chelsea (40) 81, p. 51.
"Paganini's Devil" (tr. of Vito Riviello). Chelsea (40) 81, p. 53.
"Shipwreck" (tr. of Nicola Iacobacci). Chelsea (40) 81, p. 49.
"Sleep Is the Death of the Aged" (tr. of Nicola Iacobacci). Chelsea (40) 81, p. 48.

VERNON, William
"The Valley of Mud." HiramPoR (30) Spr-Sum 81, p. 48.

VERON GORMAZ, José
Eight poems. Mairena (3:7) 81, pp. 23-28.

VERVAECKE, Kris
"Dane Church Standing Empty Outside Red Cloud" (for Paul Olson). Peb (21) 81, p. 16.

VEST, Debra Kay
"Children of the Glassblower." CreamCR (6:2) 81, p. 33.
"Familiar Sails." Poem (42) Jul 81, pp. 33-35.

VETERE, Richard
"Sestina" (for Little Guy). Im (7:2) 1981, p. 5.

VIAU 368

VIAU, Théophile De see De VIAU, Théophile

VICTOR-ROOD, Juliette
"Plain" (tr. of Johannes Bobrowski). DenQ (16:1) Spr 81, p. 67.
"Tale" (tr. of Johannes Bobrowski). DenQ (16:1) Spr 81, p. 64.
"The Wanderer" (tr. of Johannes Bobrowski). DenQ (16:1) Spr 81, p. 66.
"Unsaid" (tr. of Johannes Bobrowski). DenQ (16:1) Spr 81, p. 65.

VICTORIA, Carlos
"Escorzo." Notarte (6:11) N 81, p. 19.
"Números." Notarte (6:11) N 81, p. 19.
"Nuestros héroes." Notarte (6:11) N 81, p. 19.

VIERECK, Peter
"Anniversary" (tr. of Stefan George). PoNow (5:6 issue 30) 81, p. 16.
"Drunk on Bread." MassR (22:3) Aut 81, pp. 509-517.
"Guardianship" (tr. of Stefan George). PoNow (5:6 issue 30) 81, p. 16.
"Three for Eve." WebR (6:2) 81, pp. 40-44.
"Welcome to Tarsus." PoNow (6:2 issue 32) 81, pp. 2-5.

VILHJALMSSON, Thor
"Fall I" (tr. by Frederic Will). SenR (12:1/2) 81, p. 175.
"Haust I." SenR (12:1/2) 81, p. 174.

VILLANUA, Robert
"En el taller del pintor" (tr. by Carmen Lugo and Robert Villanua). Claridad/En Rojo (22: 1470) 3-9 Ap 81, p. 11.
"Enrique" (tr. by Carmen Lugo and Robert Villanua). Claridad/En Rojo (22: 1470) 3-9 Ap 81, p. 10.
"El imperfecto que más" (tr. by Carmen Lugo and Robert Villanua). Claridad/En Rojo (22: 1470) 3-9 Ap 81, p. 11.
"Lenguaje afectado" (tr. by Carmen Lugo and Robert Villanua). Claridad/En Rojo (22: 1470) 3-9 Ap 81, p. 10.
"Pointe-a-Pitre/Burdeos" (tr. by Carmen Lugo and Robert Villanua). Claridad/En Rojo (22: 1470) 3-9 Ap 81, p. 10.
"Telegrama" (tr. by Carmen Lugo and Robert Villanua). Claridad/En Rojo (22: 1470) 3-9 Ap 81, p. 11.
"El tulipán africano" (tr. by Carmen Lugo and Robert Villanua). Claridad/En Rojo (22: 1470) 3-9 Ap 81, p. 10.

VILLANUEVA, Alma
"The Curse: A One-Act Play, and a Poem." Metam (3:2/4:1) 80-81, pp. 95-100.
"The Labor of Buscando la Forma." Metam (3:2/4:1) 80-81, pp. 33-34.
"Passion." Metam (3:2/4:1) 80-81, p. 32.

VILLARRUBIA, Jan
"Fever." Vis (7) 81, n. p.
"Grandpa." Wind (11:43) 81, p. 39.

VILLASEÑOR, Laura
"At Sea Level" (tr. of Marco Antonio Montes de Oca). Mund (12/13) 80-81, pp. 256-257.
"Light in Readiness" (tr. of Marco Antonio Montes de Oca). Mund (12/13) 80-81, p. 257.
"Prelude" (tr. of José Gorostiza). Mund (12/13) 80-81, pp. 375-377.

VILLAURRUTIA, Xavier
"Cezanne" (tr. by Anthony Edkins). Chelsea (40) 81, p. 87.

VILMORIN, Louise de
"Mazurka" (tr. by James P. Gilroy). DenQ (16:1) Spr 81, p. 79.
"Postlude: Polonaise" (tr. by James P. Gilroy). DenQ (16:1) Spr 81,
p. 80.

VINZ, Mark
"Father to Father." NoAmR (266:2) Je 81, p. 27.
"The Trouble With Cemeteries. " QW (13) Aut/Wint 81/82, p. 49.

VITALE, Ida
"Answer of the Dervish" (tr. by Lisa Bradford). Mund (12/13) 80-81,
p. 103.

VITIELLO, Justin
"Non di una maschera" (tr. of Danilo Dolci). PortR (27: 2) 81, p. 35.
"Ti affascina" (tr. of Danilo Dolci). PortR (27: 2) 81, p. 35.

VITIER, Cintio
"Each Time I Return To You" (tr. by Ena Hollis). Mund (12/13) 80-
81, pp. 21-22.
"Viaje a Nicaragua. " Areito (7: 26) 81, pp. 46-51.
"The Word" (tr. by Ena Hollis). Mund (12/13) 80-81, p. 21.

VIZCARRONDO de QUIÑONES, Clara Luz
"Desde que te fuiste...." Mairena (2:6) 80, p. 50.

VOGELSANG, Arthur
"California. " PartR (48:1) 81, p. 126.

VOGELWEIDE, Walther von der
"Künc Constantin de Gap sô Vil" (tr. by Ezra Pound). Iowa (12:1) Wint
81, p. 49.
"Solt Ich den Pfaffen Râten an den Triuwen Mîn" (tr. by Ezra Pound).
Iowa (12:1) Wint 81, p. 48.

VOIGHT, Ellen Bryant
"Alba. " MissouriR (4:2) Wint 81-82, p. 14.
"The Apology. " Nat (233:13) 24 O 81, p. 417.
"The Bat. " NewYorker (57:4) 16 Mr 81, p. 66.
"Eurydice. " Ploughs (6:4) 81, p. 142.
"January. " GeoR (35:4) Wint 81, p. 804.
"Letter from Vermont. " Antaeus (40/41) Wint-Spr 81, p. 394.
"Liebesgedicht. " MissouriR (4:2) Wint 81-82, p. 15.
"A Marriage Poem. " Ploughs (6:4) 81, pp. 143-144.
"Pastoral. " Atl (247:5) My 81, p. 52.
"Talking the Fire Out. " NewYorker (57:43) 14 D 81, p. 44.
"Turning from a Loss. " Antaeus (43) Aut 81, p. 41.

von der VOGELWEIDE, Walther see VOGELWEIDE, Walther von der

von FREYTAG-LORINGHOVEN, Elsa see FREYTAG-LORINGHOVEN, Elsa
von

von HUTTEN, Katrine see HUTTEN, Katrine von

Von UNDERWOOD
"Additional Poem" (tr. of Michael Krüger). Mund (11:2) 79, p. 33.
"The Neutron Bomb" (tr. of Roman Ritter). Mund (11:2) 79, p. 121.
"Poem About a Walk By the Reservoir and About Poems" (tr. of
Michael Krüger). Mund (11:2) 79, pp. 35-37.
"Something Like Peace" (tr. of Jürgen Theobaldy). Mund (11:2) 79, p.
123.

VORIS, Linda
"Chevy Chase Drive, L. A. " CalQ (18/19) 81, p. 121.
"Iambic Pentameter. " CalQ (18/19) 81, pp. 120-121.

VOSNESENSKY, Andrei
"The Last Suburban Train" (tr. by Robert L. Smith and Sylvia Maizell).
StoneC (9: 1-2) Aut-Wint 81/82, pp. 11-12.

VYAZEMSKY, Prince P. A.
"The Russian God" (tr. by Alan Myers). NewYRB (28:2) 19 F 81, p.
31.

WADE, Cory
"Seeing Silver. " SouthernR (17:3) Sum 81, pp. 558-9.

WADE, John Stevens
"Life-Style. " Aspect (77/79) 81, p. 199.
"The Old Drunk. " Poem (41) Mar 81, p. 51.
"Old Song. " Aspect (77/79) 81, p. 199.

WADE, Seth
"Beginning. " SmPd (18:2) Spr 81, p. 17.

WADSWORTH, Sarah
"The Annual Hot Air Balloon Fiesta" (Albuquerque, NM). WindO (38)
Spr-Sum 81, pp. 15-16.
"For Mama. " WindO (38) Spr-Sum 81, p. 14.

WAGNER, Anneliese
"Odor. " PoNow (6:3 issue 33) 81, p. 43.

WAGNER, Charles
"Sunbathing. " PoNow (6:3 issue 33) 81, p. 43.

WAGNER, Kathy
"The Baltimore Riots: 1968. " MidwQ (23:1) Aut 81, p. 59.
"Late Elegy for Elizabeth Bishop. " MidwQ (23:1) Aut 81, p. 60.
"Near Emily Dickinson's House. " MidwQ (23:1) Aut 81, pp. 61-2.
"Returning to the City by Boat. " MidwQ (23:1) Aut 81, p. 58.

WAGONER, David
"The Art of Surrender. " GeoR (35:4) Wint 81, p. 757.
"At the Timberline. " PoetryE (6) Aut 81, p. 53.
"Big Game. " Poetry (138:5) Ag 81, p. 253.
"Breath Test. " NewRep (184:11) 14 Mr 81, p. 30.
"Crossing the Divide. " Atl (248: 1) Jl 81, p. 53.
"Dipper. " NowestR (19:3), p. 18.
"Feeding. " Iowa (12:1) Wint 81, pp. 111-112.
"Found Poem: Deportment for Young Gentlemen. " Kayak (57) 81, pp.
56-57.

"Golden Retriever." NewYorker (57:25) 10 Ag 81, p. 40.
"In the Booking Room." NewRep (184:11) 14 Mr 81, p. 30.
"Kingfisher." Iowa (12:1) Wint 81, p. 113.
"The Land Behind the Wind." Antaeus (43) Aut 81, pp. 92-102.
"Lifesaving." Poetry (138:5) Ag 81, p. 254.
"The Lost Stones." WestHR (35:1) Spr 81, pp. 27-28.
"Love Song During a Penumbral Eclipse." NewEngR (4:1) Aut 81, p.
   33.
"March for a One-Man Band." Poetry (138:5) Ag 81, p. 252.
"The Old Racoon." Poetry (138:5) Ag 81, p. 253.
"Poem About Breath." Poetry (138:5) Ag 81, pp. 249-250.
"Round Dance." Chelsea (40) 81, pp. 142-143.
"Snowflakes" (In memory of James Wright). AntR (39:4) Aut 81, p.
   456.
"To a Farmer Who Hung Five Hawks on His Barbed Wire." Poetry
   (138:5) Ag 81, pp. 251-252.
"Trying to Sing in the Rain." AntR (39:1) Wint 81, p. 69.
"Walking into a Spider's Web." PoNow (6:1 issue 31) 81, p. 9.

WAISMAN, Ana
   "A Color Used to Call Him Juan (To the Memory of Juan Gris)" (tr.
      of Juan Larrea). DenQ (16:1) Spr 81, p. 59.
   "Occupied" (tr. of Juan Larrea). DenQ (16:1) Spr 81, p. 57.
   "Provisional Spring" (tr. of Juan Larrea). DenQ (16:1) Spr 81, p. 58.

WAKOSKI, Diane
   "For Clint on the Desert." Tendril (11) Sum 81, pp. 78-79.
   "Green Thumb." Iowa (11:2/3) Spr-Sum 80, pp. 94-98.
   "Little Tricks of Linear B." Ploughs (7:2) 81, pp. 72-79.
   "Nell's Birthday." ThRiPo (17/18) 81, pp. 84-85.
   "Peaches." PraS (55:1/2) Spr-Sum 81, p. 121.
   "The Rose." SouthernPR (21:2) Aut 81, pp. 65-66.
   "Sailor's Daughter" (for Edward Abbey). PraS (55:1/2) Spr-Sum 81, p.
      120.
   "Stillife: Michael, Silver Flute, and Violets (for M.R.)." Mund (12/
      13) 80-81, pp. 332-333.
   "Why I Am a Poet Not a Painter." Sulfur (1) 81, pp. 195-198.

WALCOTT, Derek
   "Early Pompeian (for Norline)." Nat (232:6) 14 F 81, pp. 182-3.
   "Europa." Antaeus (40/41) Wint-Spr 81, p. 398.
   "From This Far" (for R.G.). Antaeus (40/41) Wint-Spr 81, pp. 395-
      397.
   "Greece." Antaeus (40/41) Wint-Spr 81, pp. 399-400.
   "The Hotel Normandie Pool." NewYorker (56:46) 5 Ja 81, pp. 30-31.
   "Store Bay." NewYorker (57:32) 28 S 81, p. 48.

WALD, Diane
   "A Silent Wind Over the Islet." Ploughs (6:4) 81, pp. 37-38.
   "Olenska." Ploughs (6:4) 81, pp. 36-37.

WALDMAN, Anne
   "Trains & Clouds." PartR (48:3) 81, p. 458.

WALDROP, Keith
   "Communication." OP (31/32) Aut 81, pp. 64-65.
   "Elegy." Sulfur (2) 81, pp. 218-230.
   "The Ruins of Providence." OP (31/32) Aut 81, p. 161.
   "Song: Paper." OP (31/32) Aut 81, pp. 42-43.

WALDROP, Rosmarie
    "And How Do You See Yourself, Mrs. Waldrop?" OP (31/32) Aut 81,
        p. 53.
    "Come Dreams." OP (31/32) Aut 81, p. 162.

WALEY, Arthur
    From "The Letter" (tr. of Po Chu-I). NowestR (19:1/2), p. i.

WALKER, Brian
    "By the old log." PortR (27: 1) 81, p. 33.
    "Half a yellow elm." PortR (27: 1) 81, p. 33.
    "Poem: Words pouring forth." FourQt (30:4) Sum 81, p. 23.

WALKER, Carol Bridge
    "This Cloud Between." SouthernHR (15:4) Aut 81, p. 325.
    "Wife-song." SouthernHR (15:4) Aut 81, p. 300.

WALKER, David
    "For Robert Lowell (1917-1977)." SouthernPR (21:2) Aut 81, p. 74.
    "Slips." NowestR (19:1/2), pp. 88-90.

WALKER, Jeanne Murray
    "The Arrest: Lumberton, N.C." KanQ (13:3/4) Sum-Aut 81, p. 121.
    "The Butcher." NoAmR (266:3) S 81, p. 11.
    "The Uncle." KanQ (13:3/4) Sum-Aut 81, p. 122.

WALKER, Jim
    "Lilies." CapeR (17:1) Wint 81, p. 34.

WALKER, John David
    "A Memory." PoNow (6:1 issue 31) 81, p. 34.
    "Plano Nursing Home." PoNow (6:1 issue 31) 81, p. 34.

WALKER, Kath
    "The Bunyip." DenQ (16:4) Wint 81, p. 61.
    "Civilization." DenQ (16:4) Wint 81, p. 62.
    "Municipal Gum." DenQ (16:4) Wint 81, p. 59.
    "The Past." DenQ (16:4) Wint 81, p. 60.

WALLACE, Anthony
    "The Web." Wind (11:40) 81, p. 36.
    "Metamorphosis." Wind (11:40) 81, p. 36.

WALLACE, D. M.
    "Girl." NewL (48:1) Aut 81, p. 49.

WALLACE, Robert
    "In the First Place." ThRiPo (17/18) 81, p. 81.
    "Poetry." OP (31/32) Aut 81, p. 49.
    "A Sunny, Winter Day." PoNow (6:1 issue 31) 81, p. 11.

WALLACE, Ron
    "The Worrier." Northeast (3:11) Sum 81, p. 10.

WALLACE, Ronald
    "Bird Study." PoetryNW (22:1) Spr 81, pp. 15-17.
    "Clayton House." Im (7:2) 1981, p. 3.
    "Constipation." Im (7:2) 1981, p. 3.

"First Love." Im (7:2) 1981, p. 3.
"Geography." PoetryNW (22:1) Spr 81, pp. 17-18.
"Grandmother Grace." NewL (48:1) Aut 81, pp. 48-49.
"Windfall Bucker." NewOR (8:2) Sum 81, p. 154.

WALLER, Ray
    "Because." Obs (7:1) Spr 81, p. 33.
    "Crucifixion" (For Darlene). Obs (7:1) Spr 81, p. 33.
    "Once A Soldier." Obs (7:1) Spr 81, p. 29.
    "Third Homage To A Lizardskin Woman." Obs (7:1) Spr 81, p. 30.
    "To Mikhail Baryshnikov." Obs (7:1) Spr 81, p. 32.
    "Woman Waiting." Obs (7:1) Spr 81, p. 31.

WALLIN, Stephen
    "Your Dimple" (for Trisha). OP (31/32) Aut 81, pp. 132-133.

WALLING, Rachel
    "American Sentiment" (w/ Elinor Nauen). Tele (17) 81, p. 13.
    "Dinner With The Folks" (w/ Elinor Nauen). Tele (17) 81, p. 13.

WALLS, Doyle Wesley
    "A Graduate Teaching Assistant's Nightmare." CEAFor (12:1) O 81,
        p. 18.

WALLS, Jerry L.
    "The Rich Man's Might." ChrC (98:11) 1 Ap 81, p. 340.

WALSH, Des
    "Don't leave me she said." PottPort (3) 81, p. 51.
    "Untitled." PottPort (3) 81, p. 13.

WALSH, Donald
    "Colloquy of Sadness" (Variations on text by Kathleen Agena; tr. of
        Angel Cuadra). PartR (48:4) 81, pp. 595-6.
    "I Got" (tr. of Nicolás Guillén). AmerPoR (10:3) My-Je 81, p. 34.
    "In some far-off place" (tr. of Roberto Fernández Iglesias). Mund
        (12/13) 80-81, p. 331.
    "Police Efficiency" (Variation on text by Kathleen Agena; tr. of Angel
        Cuadra). PartR (48:4) 81, p. 596.
    "Vision of the Keys" (Variation on text by Kathleen Agena; tr. of Angel
        Cuadra). PartR (48:4) 81, p. 597.
    "Word" (tr. of Manuel del Cabral). AmerPoR (10:3) My-Je 81, p. 34.
    "You saw her growing" (tr. of Roberto Fernández Iglesias). Mund (12/
        13) 80-81, p. 331.

WALSH, Donald D.
    "The Buried One" (tr. of Manuel del Cabral). DenQ (16:1) Spr 81, p.
        63.
    "To a Newborn Child" (tr. of Manuel del Cabral). DenQ (16:1) Spr 81,
        p. 62.

WALSH, Joan
    "In Trust." Comm (108:8) 24 Ap 81, p. 242.

WALSH, Larry
    "At the End After the Suicides." PoNow (6:3 issue 33) 81, p. 43.
    "Mothra." PoNow (6:3 issue 33) 81, p. 43.
    "A Night to Remember." PoNow (6:3 issue 33) 81, p. 43.

WALSH, Marty
  "A Field Guide." HiramPoR (30) Spr-Sum 81, p. 49.
  "To You, Anne Sexton." WindO (38) Spr-Sum 81, pp. 41-42.
  "Vegetable Woman." WindO (38) Spr-Sum 81, p. 41.

WALSH, Phyllis
  "The Last Equestrienne." Northeast (3:10) Wint 81, p. 16.

WALTHALL, Hugh
  "Mixed Blessings." Shen (32:2) 81, p. 102.
  "Love Poem." Shen (32:2) 81, p. 103.

WANEK, Connie
  "A Night in July." PoNow (6:3 issue 33) 81, p. 43.

WANG, An-shih
  "Hibiscus" (tr. by C. H. Kwan). MalR (58) Ap 81, p. 37.

WANG, Orrin N. C.
  "I Am Lying to You Every Time I Speak." PoNow (6:1 issue 31) 81,
      p. 47.

WANIEK, Marilyn
  "Mama's Murders." GeoR (35:4) Wint 81, pp. 849-851.

WARD, Albert M.
  "Images of Tall Warriors." Obs (7:1) Spr 81, p. 19.
  "For Brothers and Other Men." Obs (7:1) Spr 81, pp. 22-23.
  "Love the Children." Obs (7:1) Spr 81, pp. 20-22.

WARD, Jerry
  "In memory of walter rodney." Obs (6:1/2) Spr-Sum 80, p. 185.
  "Knot 6.18.78." Obs (6:1/2) Spr-Sum 80, pp. 182-185.

WARD, Matt
  "John Ashbery Reads at the Guggenheim." Shen (31:4) 80, pp. 75-76.

WARD, Matthew
  "Striking a Match." Shen (32: 4) 81, p. 22.

WARD, Michael
  "Willie in Winter." Aspect (77/79) 81, p. 200.

WARMBROD, Nancy Compton
  "Generations." Poem (43) Nov 81, p. 22.
  "Pawnbroker." Poem (43) Nov 81, p. 21.

WARNER, Michael
  "At the Sheerar Cultural Center, Sillwater, Oklahoma." KanQ (13:3/4)
      Sum-Aut 81, p. 202.

WARNER, Val
  "Never Such Light" (Dundee). Pequod (13) 81, p. 66.

WARREN, Larkin
  "Temperature Drop" (for David and Jan). Tendril (10) Wint 81, p. 44.

WARREN, Robert Penn
  "Afterward." AmerPoR (10:1) Mr-Ap 81, p. 4.

"Aging Painter Sits Where the Great Tower Heaves Down Midnight."
 GeoR (35:4) Wint 81, pp. 768-774.
"At the Corner of the Eye." Atl (247:4) Ap 81, p. 97.
"Basic Syllogism." Atl (247:6) Je 81, p. 71.
"Convergences." SewanR (89:3) Sum 81, pp. 311-314.
"Caribou Near Arctic." NewYorker (57:41) 30 N 81, p. 46.
"Dawn." AmerPoR (10:2) Mr-Ap 81, p. 5.
"Dead Horse In Field." AmerPoR (10:2) Mr-Ap 81, p. 3.
"Death Of Time." AmerPoR (10:2) Mr-Ap 81, p. 4.
"Eternity." Ploughs (7:1) 81, p. 65.
"Fear and Trembling." GeoR (35:1) Spr 81, p. 13.
"Glimpses of Seasons." SouthernR (17:3) Sum 81, pp. 551-4.
"Going West." NewYorker (57:1) 23 F 81, p. 40.
"If." AmerPoR (10:2) Mr-Ap 81, p. 5.
"Minneapolis Story" (To John Knox Jessup). NewYRB (28:12) 16 Jl 81,
 p. 40.
"Nameless Thing." AmerPoR (10:2) Mr-Ap 81, p. 5.
"Paradox of Time." NewYorker (57:12) 11 My 81, pp. 36-7.
"The Rumor." Antaeus (40/41) Wint-Spr 81, pp. 401-402.
"Stars (A Note on Mycology)." NewYorker (57:20) 6 Jl 81, p. 38.
"Summer Rain in Mountains." Antaeus (40/41) Wint-Spr 81, pp. 403-
 404.
"Sunset Scrupulously Observed." NewYorker (57:23) 27 Jl 81, p. 36.
"Twice Born." SewanR (89:1) Wint 81, pp. 22-23.
"Vermont Thaw." AmerPoR (10:2) Mr-Ap 81, p. 3.
"What Voice at Moth-Hour." NewYorker (56:48) 19 Ja 81, p. 34.

WARREN, Rosana
 "Antietam Creek." NewEngR (4:2) Wint 81, p. 253.
 "Visitation." SouthernR (17:3) Sum 81, pp. 572-73.

WARROCK, Anna M.
 "Monet." Aspect (77/79) 81, p. 201.

WARSHAWSKI, Morrie
 "Dancer Fixing Her Shoulder Strap." Aspect (77/79) 81, p. 202.

WASHBURN, Katharine
 "Conversation in the Mountains" (tr. with Margaret Guillemin of Paul
 Celan). ParisR (23:80) Sum 81, pp. 215-220.

WATERHOUSE, Elizabeth
 "Rearranging the Seasons." Ploughs (7:2) 81, pp. 89-90.

WATERMAN, Andrew
 from Out for the Elements: "I am invited to a christening." Hudson
 (34:2) Sum 81, pp. 186-194.

WATERS, Mary Ann
 "Climbing Alone." PoetryNW (22:1) Spr 81, pp. 35-36.
 "Moving." PoNow (6:3 issue 33) 81, p. 44.
 "On the Trail." PoetryNW (22:1) Spr 81, pp. 34-35.

WATERS, Michael
 "Anniversary of the Air." GeoR (35:1) Spr 81, pp. 48-49.

WATKINS, Alison
 "Demonstration of a Need." Sulfur (3) 82, p. 30.

"Esperanto is the name...." Sulfur (3) 82, p. 26.
"In her dream...." Sulfur (3) 82, pp. 28-29.
"Mantic Core." Sulfur (3) 82, p. 27.
"The Tugboat Captain." Sulfur (3) 82, p. 31.

WATKINS, Edward
"Sunflowers." Confr (22) Sum 81, p. 50.

WATSON, Charlotte D.
"Uncle Ben (or the Man Who Can Live with Bakke)." Obs (6:1/2) Spr-
Sum 80, p. 153.

WATSON, Elaine
"New Hearing Room." BallSUF (22:4) Aut 81, p. 35.

WATTERS, Doug
"Although he's old...." PottPort (3) 81, p. 41.
"Balance." PottPort (3) 81, p. 27.

WAUGAMAN, Charles A.
"Cathedral Triptych." CapeR (17:1) Wint 81, pp. 38-39.
"Etching." CapeR (16:2) Sum 81, p. 25.
"On the Banks of Avon." CapeR (16:2) Sum 81, p. 24.
"Reverie in January Rain." Wind (10:39) 80, p. 40.
"Son Among Poppies" (for S.). CapeR (16:2) Sum 81, p. 26.
"A Song for Grunewald's "Crucifixion"." Wind (11:43) 81, pp. 40-41.

WAYMAN, Tom
"Hearing Sam Astrachan Read Excerpts from His Novel Katz-Cohen in
Room 400, State Hall." MinnR (16) Aut 81, p. 52.
"Marketing" (for Jacqui and Mike). LittleM (13:1/2) Spr-Sum 79, c1981,
pp. 5-6.
"Raincoast Archaeology." OntR (15) Aut-Wint 81-82, p. 24.
"Receding." OntR (15) Aut-Wint 81-82, pp. 25-26.
"Reply to a Citizen, Using Lots of Nasty Words After Victor García
Robles." MinnR (17) Aut 81, pp. 46-51.
"Roses." Confr (22) Sum 81, p. 43.

WAYNE, Jane O.
"Braiding Your Hair." Poetry (138:2) My 81, p. 95.
"First Freeze." Poetry (138:2) My 81, p. 94.
"Kitchen Midden." PoetryNW (22:4) Wint 81-82, pp. 9-10.
"Looking Both Ways." PoetryNW (22:4) Wint 81-82, p. 9.
"The Only Cure." KanQ (13:3/4) Sum-Aut 81, p. 84.
"With Solitude." Poetry (138:2) My 81, pp. 93-94.

WEATHERS, Winston
"Mezzo Cammin: Ten Poems." Poem (41) Mar 81, pp. 13-18.

WEAVER, M. S.
"For Milton Obote President Hopeful of Uganda." BlackALF (15:2) Sum
81, p. 73.
"Inner Harbor Visions." BlackALF (15:2) Sum 81, p. 72.

WEBBER, Dawn
"Easter 1978." CreamCR (6:1) Aut 80, p. 107.
"For Shadows." CreamCR (6:1) Aut 80, p. 105-106.
"Hung Velvet Overtaken Me." CreamCR (7:1) 81, pp. 61-62.

WEBER, R. B.
"The Judge." PoNow (6:3 issue 33) 81, p. 28.
"The Only Man I Ever Cared For." PoNow (6:3 issue 33) 81, p. 28.
"The Widow Wagner." PoNow (6:3 issue 33) 81, p. 28.

WEBER, Ron
"Always." PoNow (6:2 issue 32) 81, p. 34.
"Don't You Think." PoNow (6:2 issue 32) 81, p. 34.
"Tristeza." PoNow (6:2 issue 32) 81, p. 34.

WEBSTER, W. G.
Twelve poems. LittleR (7:1, issue 15) 81, pp. 12-15.

WECHSLER, Peter
"Citrus Fruit." HangL (39) Wint 80-81, p. 68.
"The Garbagemen." HangL (39) Wint 80-81, p. 69.

WEDGE, George F.
"Catullan Variations." KanQ (13:3/4) Sum-Aut 81, p. 54.
"A Stillness above the Radishes." KanQ (13:1) Wint 81, pp. 136-137.

WEEDEN, Craig
"And Then He Tips His Cap to the Cows." PoNow (6:1 issue 31) 81,
    p. 32.
"Another Bestseller." PoNow (6:3 issue 33) 81, p. 44.
"The Battered Suitcase." PoNow (6:1 issue 31) 81, p. 32.
"Such Friends." PoNow (6:2 issue 32) 81, p. 33.
"We'll Call You." PoNow (6:1 issue 31) 81, p. 32.

WEEDON, Syd
"Cupped hands." Sam (116) 81, p. 64.
"The fool mocks." Sam (109) 81, p. 51.
"I sit with the beast." Sam (116) 81, p. 57.
"My Norman Bethune Poem." Sam (109) 81, p. 46.
"One Touch." Sam (117) 81, p. 26.
"'Sacrifice,' Priest-King says." Sam (109) 81, p. 50.

WEEKS, Ramona
"Slide, Kelly, Slide" (a painting by Frank O. Small, 1880's, in the
    Boston Public Library). Thrpny (7) Aut 81, p. 21.

WEHLAGE, Deborah
"Late Evening." PoNow (6:2 issue 32) 81, p. 47.

WEI, Chuang
"The Beautiful Regions South of the Yangtse River" (tr. by C. H.
    Kwan). MalR (58) Ap 81, p. 37.

WEIDMAN, Phil
"Safety Check." WormR (81/82) 81, p. 3.
"Wise Button." WormR (81/82) 81, p. 3.

WEIGEL, Tom
"Metropolis." Tele (17) 81, p. 14.

WEIGL, Bruce
"Catch" (for Andrew Grossbardt in memoriam). CimR (55) Ap 81, p.
    4.

"Hotel Florence." CimR (55) Ap 81, p. 62.
"The Last Lie." PoNow (6:2 issue 32) 81, p. 22.
"The Man Who Made Me Love Him." PoNow (6:2 issue 32) 81, p. 26.
"Sparrows." PoNow (6:2 issue 32) 81, p. 26.
"Survivors." PoNow (6:2 issue 32) 81, p. 22.

WEIGL, Etta Ruth
"Conspirator." PoNow (6:3 issue 33) 81, p. 44.
"Meltwater." PoNow (6:3 issue 33) 81, p. 44.

WEIL, Eric
"A Horse at the Hirshhorn." AmerS (50:3) Sum 81, p. 354.

WEINBERGER, Eliot
"The Fountain" (tr. of San Juan de la Cruz, version for Karin Les-
    sing). Sulfur (3) 82, pp. 87-89.

WEINER, Rebecca
"Birds." Poetry (138:4) Jl 81, p. 214.
"Driving Around." Poetry (138:4) Jl 81, pp. 215-217.

WEINERMAN, Chester
"Halloween Night Pastiche." AmerPoR (10:4) Jl-Ag 81, p. 12.
"Last Supper At Ann's." AmerPoR (10:4) Jl-Ag 81, p. 12.

WEINGARTEN, Roger
"After the Death of a Poet." SenR (11:2) 81, p. 65.
"The Afterlife." Poetry (138:4) Jl 81, pp. 208-209.
"Aura, Cry, Fall, and Fit" (for Brenda, Susan, and Phillipe). Shen
    (32:2) 81, pp. 18-23.
"Epistolary." MissouriR (4:2) Wint 81-82, p. 30.
"Medium Walking the Sea of Serenity." SenR (11:2) 81, pp. 66-68.
"Shadow Shadow." Poetry (137:4) Ja 81, pp. 202-203.

WEINMAN, Paul
"At Night the Gnomes." PoNow (6:2 issue 32) 81, p. 34.
"Hands of Bone." Wind (11:40) 81, p. 37.
"Lizards Scuttle Angularly." Wind (11:40) 81, pp. 37-38.
"Never Use a Stainless Steel Spoon." PoNow (6:2 issue 32) 81, p. 34.
"Tree Frogs Were Silent." Wind (11:40) 81, p. 37.

WEINSTOCK, Paulette
"Face to Face" (tr. of Philippe Soupault). Mund (12/13) 80-81, pp.
    250-252.

WEIR, Karen
"Anorexic." SouthernHR (15:4) Aut 81, p. 346.
"Learning the Cold." Poem (43) Nov 81, p. 24.
"The Lost Things." Poem (43) Nov 81, p. 23.
"Reciprocal Memory." Wind (11:43) 81, p. 41.

WEISNER, Ken
"A Hundred Thousand Thanks" (tr. of Carlos Belli). SenR (12:1/2) 81,
    p. 111.

WEISS, David
"At the Cloisters." NewYorker (57:39) 16 N 81, p. 60.
"Closing Time." Poetry (139:3) D 81, pp. 146-147.
"In an Orchard on Thanksgiving." Poetry (139:3) D 81, p. 148.

WEISS, Sanford
    "The Glass of the Sea." Kayak (56) 81, p. 31.
    "Habits of the Mirror." Kayak (56) 81, p. 32.
    "The Map." Kayak (56) 81, p. 30.
    "Song." Kayak (56) 81, p. 30.

WEITZMAN, Sarah Brown
    "Etymology." Tendril (10) Wint 81, p. 64.
    "in the desert." Tendril (10) Wint 81, pp. 68-69.
    "in the middle of the night" (for Arthur). Tendril (10) Wint 81, pp.
        66-67.
    "not the ones you wrote." Tendril (10) Wint 81, p. 65.
    "Questions of Origin." Tendril (10) Wint 81, pp. 70-72.

WELBURN, Ron
    "The Black Sea." Obs (6:1/2) Spr-Sum 80, p. 148.
    "In Of." Obs (6:1/2) Spr-Sum 80, pp. 151-152.
    "Gerschwin." Obs (6:1/2) Spr-Sum 80, p. 150.
    "The Oracle." Obs (6:1/2) Spr-Sum 80, p. 149.
    "The Sleeper." Obs (6:1/2) Spr-Sum 80, pp. 148-149.

WELCH, Dennis M.
    "Morphine." LittleR (7:1, issue 15) 81, p. 18.

WELCH, Don
    "The Limbus." Epoch (30:2) Wint-Spr 81, p. 121.
    "The Unicorn." Epoch (30:2) Wint-Spr 81, pp. 120-121.

WELCH, Liliane
    "The Body Warm Under The Blankets." StoneC (9: 1-2) Aut-Wint 81/
        82, p. 42.

WELLMAN, John
    "Tenth Satire: Having Led a Charmed Life, He Had to Be Hanged
        Twice." SunM (11) Spr 81, pp. 109-115.

WELLS, Katherine
    "Spring." Kayak (56) 81, p. 17.

WELSH, Marjorie
    "Mobile." DenQ (16:2) Sum 81, p. 85.
    "Pastoral." DenQ (16:2) Sum 81, pp. 86-87.

WEN, Ting-yun
    "Keeping Watch in Vain By a Flowing River" (tr. by C. H. Kwan).
        MalR (58) Ap 81, p. 40.

WEÖRES, Sandor
    "Self-Portrait" (tr. by Emory George). PoNow (5:6 issue 30) 81, p.
        47.

WERNICK, Dinah E.
    "Balcony." Tele (17) 81, p. 49.

WESTERFIELD, Nancy G.
    "Accommodations." OntR (14) Spr-Sum 81, p. 65.
    "Beachcombers: Padre Island." SouthwR (66:3) Sum 81, p. 254.
    "Beans: Their Recipe." ChrC (98:14) 29 Ap 81, p. 469.

WESTON   380

"Intermission." ChrC (98:27) 9 S 81, p. 867.
"The Judgment of Paris." Confr (22) Sum 81, p. 54.
"Learning to Read the Sky." KanQ (13:1) Wint 81, p. 91.
"Porchlight." OntR (14) Spr-Sum 81, p. 66.
"Terrarium." Comm (108:15) 28 Ag 81, p. 467.

WESTON, Lee
"For H. C. Anderson's Little Mermaid." PortR (27: 2) 81, p. 82.

WETTEROTH, Bruce
"Burning Rubber." PoetryNW (22:4) Wint 81-82, pp. 22-23.

WEXELBLATT, Robert
"Charming." SouthernHR (15:4) Aut 81, pp. 334-335.
"Poem: Yesterday morning it lay still where I...." SouthernHR (15:4)
Aut 81, p. 345.

WHEELER, Susan
"Frame for a Clapboard House." ModernPS (10:2/3), pp. 117-118.
"Grandfather I: In The Attic." ModernPS (10:2/3), p. 119.
"Grandfather II: At The Wake." ModernPS (10:2/3), p. 119.
"Martha Olive/Photograph 1932." ModernPS (10:2/3), p. 118.

WHEELER, Sylvia
"Taking Down Chagall's Blue Bull." CharR (7:1) Spr 81, p. 14.
"A Woman Guards the Mona Lisa." Northeast (3:11) Sum 81, p. 27.

WHISLER, Robert F.
"Diffusions V, Machines." SmPd (18:3) Aut 81, p. 10.
"Diffusions II, War." PortR (27: 2) 81, p. 91.
"For Sails and Falling Starfish." SouthernPR (21: 1) Spr 81, p. 64.
"A Nagshead Legend." HiramPoR (29) Aut-Wint 81, p. 41.
"Too Vain." HolCrit (18:5) D 81, p. 18.

WHITE, Gail
"The Apprentice Ascetic." KanQ (13:3/4) Sum-Aut 81, p. 81.
"The Grower." KanQ (13:3/4) Sum-Aut 81, p. 81.
"Holding it Together." Northeast (3:10) Wint 81, p. 13.
"If My Son Sees Me Crying." Northeast (3:10) Wint 81, p. 12.
"Pregnant, I Always Wanted." Northeast (3:10) Wint 81, p. 12.

WHITE, James L.
"Little Deaths." Northeast (3:10) Wint 81, p. 17.

WHITE, James P.
"Bowlbound." Mund (12/13) 80-81, p. 127.

WHITE, Mary Jane
"Crossing The Courtyard." AmerPoR (10:6) N-D 81, p. 47.
"In Our Leisure." AmerPoR (10:6) N-D 81, p. 47.
"OK, OK." Iowa (11:2/3) Spr-Sum 80, p. 205.
"Walking on a Field." Iowa (11:2/3) Spr-Sum 80, pp. 206-207.

WHITE, Sarah
"God Creates Eve On a Prayer-Book Page." Chelsea (40) 81, pp. 80-81.

WHITE, Steven
"The Drowned Horse" (tr. of Pablo Antonio Cuadra). NewOR (8:3) Aut
81, p. 250.

WHITEBIRD, J.
    "Truce." StoneC (9: 1-2) Aut-Wint 81/82, p. 13.

WHITEHEAD, James
    "For President Jimmy Carter on His Homecoming." NewEngR (3:4)
        Sum 81, p. 471.

WHITING, Nathan
    "Kerenhappuch." HangL (40) Aut 81, p. 57.
    "Mister, You Give Me 10¢ for Caps?" HangL (40) Aut 81, p. 60.
    "Organized Guerilla Attack on a Volkswagen." HangL (40) Aut 81, pp.
        58-60.

WHITNEY, Nancy
    "Presence." Meadows (2:1) 81, p. 11.

WHITTAKER, S.
    "True Love (maybe)." Ploughs (7:1) 81, p. 150.

WICKELHAUS, Martha
    "Snow: A Portrait of my Father." CimR (56) Jl 81, p. 61.

WIESELTIER, Me'ir
    "Near Morning" (tr. by Bernhard Frank). PoNow (5:6 issue 30) 81, p.
        47.
    "'Our Piss,' She Said" (tr. by Bernhard Frank). PoNow (5:6 issue 30)
        81, p. 47.
    "Sadness Pursues Me" (tr. by Bernhard Frank). PoNow (5:6 issue 30)
        81, p. 47.

WIGAN, Susan
    "Six different bowls of flowers." Stand (22: 2) 81, p. 33.

WIGGIN, Neurine
    "At Sixteen." SmPd (18:2) Spr 81, p. 26.
    "Pregnant." BelPoJ (31:4) Sum 81, p. 40.

WILBORN, William
    "The Disconsolate Cowboy" (for John Burt). Poetry (137:6) Mr 81, p.
        332.
    "For Aunt Lizzie." Poetry (137:6) Mr 81, p. 333.

WILBUR, Richard
    "Mirabeau Bridge" (tr. of Guillaume Apollinaire). ParisR (23:81) Aut
        81, p. 110.
    "Some Differences." MassR (22:4) Wint 81, pp. 778-779.

WILCOX, Patricia
    "Dramatic Monologue #7: Her Things." ThRiPo (17/18) 81, p. 87.

WILD, Peter
    "Bighorn Sheep." Im (7:3) 81, p. 10.
    "Circuses." CreamCR (6:2) 81, p. 101.
    "Cheeseweed." CharR (7:2) Aut 81, p. 26.
    "Climbers." PraS (55:1/2) Spr-Sum 81, p. 35.
    "Dawn." CharR (7:2) Aut 81, pp. 25-26.
    "Dinosaur Tracks." CreamCR (6:1) Aut 80, p. 75.
    "Eating Carp." Ploughs (7:1) 81, pp. 154-155.

"Family Man." CreamCR (6:1) Aut 80, p. 74.
"Getting Ready For A Date." MichQR (20:4) Aut 81, p. 420.
"Gold." QW (12) Spr-Sum 81, p. 5.
"Haying." CutB (16) Spr-Sum 81, p. 106.
"Indians." ChiR (32:4) Spr 81, p. 16.
"Martin Luther." CreamCR (6:2) 81, p. 100.
"Miner." PoNow (6:1 issue 31) 81, p. 26.
"Mountain Lion." Im (7:3) 81, p. 10.
"Oatmeal." PoNow (6:2 issue 32) 81, p. 28.
"Paper Bags." NowestR (19:3), p. 16.
"Pioneers." AmerPoR (10:1) Ja-F 81, p. 18.
"Planting the Eucalyptus." SouthernPR (21: 1) Spr 81, pp. 29-30.
"Rapids." Aspect (77/79) 81, p. 205.
"Survivors." PoNow (6:1 issue 31) 81, p. 26.
"Trees." NoAmR (266:3) S 81, p. 50.
"Turtles." AmerPoR (10:1) Ja-F 81, p. 18.
"Washing Windows." MichQR (20:4) Aut 81, p. 419.
"Whipping the Cactus." CutB (16) Spr-Sum 81, p. 105.
"Wyoming." ThRiPo (17/18) 81, p. 89.

WILER, John
"Baskets." US1 (14/15) Aut/Wint 81, p. 14.
"Five Fifty Seven Runs Straight Through the Pine Barrens." US1 (14/
    15) Aut/Wint 81, p. 14.
"Handyman at the End of the World." US1 (14/15) Aut/Wint 81, p. 14.

WILEY, Harold
"The Ghost." BelPoJ (31:3) Spr 81, pp. 28-29.

WILJER, Robert
"Cheerio." Poetry (139:1) O 81, p. 20.

WILKINSON, Anne
"Ah! You've Come Back" (tr. of Anna Akhmatova, w/ Judith Hemsche-
    meyer). Hudson (34:4) Wint 81, pp. 553-554.
"Confession" (tr. of Anna Akhmatova, w/ Judith Hemschemeyer).
    PoNow (5:6 issue 30) 81, p. 1.
"For Us to Lose Freshness" (tr. of Anna Akhmatova, w/ Judith
    Hemschemeyer). Hudson (34:4) Wint 81, p. 553.
"I came as the poet's guest" (to Alexander Blok) (tr. of Anna Akhma-
    tova, w/ Judith Hemschemeyer). Stand (22: 2) 81, p. 4.
"Kiev" (tr. of Anna Akhmatova, w/ Judith Hemschemeyer). Hudson
    (34:4) Wint 81, pp. 552-553.
"My imagination obeys me" (tr. of Anna Akhmatova, w/ Judith
    Hemschemeyer). Stand (22: 2) 81, p. 4.
"One heart isn't chained to another" (tr. of Anna Akhmatova, w/ Judith
    Hemschemeyer). PoNow (5:6 issue 30) 81, p. 1.
"Song of Our Last Meeting" (tr. of Anna Akhmatova, w/ Judith
    Hemschemeyer). PoNow (6:1 issue 31) 81, p. 43.
"The Twenty-First" (tr. of Anna Akhmatova, w/ Judith Hemschemeyer).
    Hudson (34:4) Wint 81, p. 554.
"They didn't bring me a letter today" (tr. of Anna Akhmatova, w/ Judith
    Hemschemeyer). PoNow (5:6 issue 30) 81, p. 1.
"Under the Icon" (tr. of Anna Akhmatova, w/ Judith Hemschemeyer).
    Hudson (34:4) Wint 81, p. 552.
"Verses about Petersburg" (tr. of Anna Akhmatova, w/ Judith Hemsche-
    meyer). Stand (22: 2) 81, p. 3.
"We are drinkers and fornicators here, one and all" (tr. of Anna

Akhmatova, w/ Judith Hemschemeyer). PoNow (5:6 issue 30) 81,
    p. 1.
"When you're drunk you're so much fun!" (tr. of Anna Akhmatova, w/
    Judith Hemschemeyer). PoNow (5:6 issue 30) 81, p. 1.

WILL, Frederic
    "An Everyday Psalm" (tr. with Leszek Elektorowicz of Tadeusz Nowak).
        SenR (12:1/2) 81, p. 113.
    "Betty." NowestR (19:3), pp. 14-15.
    from the Claudopteron Suite: "Four Poems Celebrating Her." Kayak
        (56) 81, pp. 11-13.
    "The dark forces, yes that's it." Aspect (77/79) 81, p. 207.
    "Fall I" (tr. of Thor Vilhjálmsson). SenR (12:1/2) 81, p. 175.
    "He wondered and wondered ... etc." Aspect (77/79) 81, p. 207.
    "I Bedded Down." NoAmR (266:2) Je 81, p. 53.
    "Man of the House." Aspect (77/79) 81, p. 206.
    "Me and the Wrecked Ornaments." NoAmR (266:2) Je 81, p. 53.
    "Mine or yours who cares." NowestR (19:3), p. 13.
    "From Moirologhia" (tr. of Alvaro Mutis). SenR (12:1/2) 81, pp. 85-
        87.
    "My Mother" (tr. of Bernd Jentzsch). SenR (12:1/2) 81, p. 15.
    "The New Sounds in the Garden." PoNow (6:2 issue 32) 81, p. 13.
    "Peace" (tr. of Jón Oskar). SenR (12:1/2) 81, pp. 177-79.
    "The Tracklayers" (tr. of Axel Schulze). SenR (12:1/2) 81, pp. 17-19.
    "A Word" (tr. of Alvaro Mutis). SenR (12:1/2) 81, pp. 81-83.

WILLERTON, Chris
    "Nursery Home." HiramPoR (29) Aut-Wint 81, pp. 42-43.

WILLIAMS, C. K.
    "From My Window." ParisR (23:81) Aut 81, pp. 140-142.

WILLIAMS, Elizabeth
    "Any Excuse (Venus in a Puddle)" (tr. of Dmitry Bobyshev, w/ Olga
        Bobyshev). CreamCR (6:2) 81, p. 16.
    "The Claw" (tr. of Dmitry Bobyshev, w/ Olga Bobyshev). CreamCR
        (6:2) 81, pp. 14-15.

WILLIAMS, John D.
    "Death Notice I: The Singing of Death" (A Ballad) (for Frank). Calib
        (3:2) Aut-Wint 80, pp. 86-87.

WILLIAMS, Jonathan
    "In Marsden Hartley's Hand." Sulfur (1) 81, pp. 193-194.

WILLIAMS, Karen
    "Clinging to Banisters." CentR (25:2) Spr 81, pp. 162-163.
    "The Price of Innocence." CentR (25:2) Spr 81, pp. 163-164.

WILLIAMS, Loren
    "Schumann." LittleM (13:1/2) Spr-Sum 79, c1981, p. 96.

WILLIAMS, Miller
    "The Chair." NewOR (8:1) Wint 81, p. 28.
    "Deciding to Be Insane He Explains How It Is." PoetryNW (22:4) Wint
        81-82, pp. 20-21.
    "In Defense of Uncertainty and Disarray." CharR (7:2) Aut 81, p. 12.
    "Late Show." ThRiPo (17/18) 81, p. 92.

"Letters" (for WW). CharR (7:2) Aut 81, p. 13.
"Love." PoetryNW (22:4) Wint 81-82, pp. 19-20.
"Natural History." CharR (7:2) Aut 81, p. 13.
"Sir." NewEngR (3:4) Sum 81, p. 470.
"We." PoetryNW (22:4) Wint 81-82, p. 20.

WILLIAMS, Milton Vishnu
"Alter the Method of Your Coming." Stand (22: 1) 80, p. 39.

WILLIAMS, Otis C. , Jr.
"For Your Future Reference." GeoR (35:1) Spr 81, pp. 14-15.

WILLIAMS, Phil
"The Janitor." Wind (11:43) 81, p. 36.

WILLIAMS, Tyrone
Eight poems. Obs (7:1) Spr 81, pp. 7-10.

WILLIAMSON, Alan
"Airports." MassR (22:3) Aut 81, pp. 569-570.
"Art Roman." Sulfur (1) 81, pp. 219-220.
"The Last Supper" (tr. of Miodrag Pavlovic). Ploughs (7:2) 81, pp. 64-
    65.
"Late Words To C." MassR (22:3) Aut 81, pp. 570-572.
"Old Toys Come Back" (for my daughter Elizabeth). Poetry (139:1) O
    81, p. 19.
"Times at Cassis." Ploughs (7:2) 81, pp. 66-67.
"The Transfiguration" (tr. of Miodrag Pavlovic). Ploughs (7:2) 81, pp.
    62-63.

WILMER, Clive
"Among Bric-à-brac." SouthernR (17:3) Sum 81, p. 562.
"Gothic Polyphony." SouthernR (17:3) Sum 81, p. 564.
"Narcissus, Echo" (for Julia Dale). SouthernR (17:3) Sum 81, p. 563-
    4.
"Venice." SouthernR (17:3) Sum 81, p. 564.

WILNER, Eleanor
"Candied." AmerPoR (10:6) N-D 81, p. 13.
"Eleusis." AmerPoR (10:6) N-D 81, p. 14.
"Hunting Manual." AmerPoR (10:6) N-D 81, p. 15.
"Meditation On The Wēn-Fu" AmerPoR (10:6) N-D 81, p. 13.

WILSON, Don
"The Face of Peace" (tr. of Paul Eluard). PoetryE (6) Aut 81, pp.
    89-92.

WILSON, Gary
"Fog" (tr. of Alphonze Piche). HolCrit (18:5) D 81, p. 12.
"The Old House." BallSUF (22:4) Aut 81, p. 65.

WILSON, Gary D.
"An Arrangement of Pieces." CapeR (17:1) Wint 81, p. 35.

WILSON, Graeme
"Appendix" (tr. of Gottfried Benn). WestHR (35:3) Aut 81, pp. 216-17.
"Artless Story" (tr. of Takamura Kotaro). DenQ (16:4) Wint 81, p. 30.
"Battleship" (tr. of Ono Tosaburo). DenQ (16:4) Wint 81, p. 42.

"Blackboard" (tr. of Takami Jun). DenQ (16:4) Wint 81, p. 44.
"Cat" (tr. of Yamamura Bocho). DenQ (16:4) Wint 81, p. 31.
"Disdain" (tr. of Kim Su-Jang). WestHR (35:2) Sum 81, p. 152.
"Enchantress" (tr. of Takenaka Iku). DenQ (16:4) Wint 81, pp. 43-44.
"Evening" (tr. of Lu Yu). WestHR (35:1) Spr 81, p. 68.
"Flea" (tr. of Yagi Yokichi). DenQ (16:4) Wint 81, p. 40.
"Flies" (tr. of Saito Mokichi). DenQ (16:4) Wint 81, p. 29.
"Ghost Watcher (3)" (tr. of Tamura Ryuichi). DenQ (16:4) Wint 81, p. 47.
"Growth" (tr. of Tanikawa Shuntaro). DenQ (16:4) Wint 81, p. 51.
from The Kokinshu: "Estuary at Twighlight" (tr. of Emperor Uda). WestHR (35:4) Wint 81, p. 346.
from The Kokinshu: "Grebe" (tr. of Oshikochi no Mitsune). WestHR (35:4) Wint 81, p. 347.
"Lighthouses" (tr. of Yamamoto Taro). DenQ (16:4) Wint 81, p. 48.
"Love and Fever" (tr. of Miyazawa Kenji). DenQ (16:4) Wint 81, p. 39.
"Love Song" (tr. of Nakae Toshio). DenQ (16:4) Wint 81, p. 52.
"National Flag of the Sky" (tr. of Horiguchi Daigaku). DenQ (16:4) Wint 81, p. 37.
"Old Man" (tr. of Ishikawa Takuboku). DenQ (16:4) Wint 81, p. 32.
"Other Men's Wives" (tr. of Anzai Hitoshi). DenQ (16:4) Wint 81, p. 45.
"Pleasing Oneself" (tr. of the Abbot Ikkyu). WestHR (35:1) Spr 81, p. 58.
"Prisoner" (tr. of Yosano Akiko). DenQ (16:4) Wint 81, p. 28.
"Quatrain" (tr. of Sato Haruo). DenQ (16:4) Wint 81, p. 36.
"Return in Winter" (tr. of An Min-yong). WestHR (35:4) Wint 81, p. 330.
"Rhinoceros and Lion" (tr. of Maruyama Kaoru). DenQ (16:4) Wint 81, p. 38.
"Running" (tr. of Ibaragi Noriko). DenQ (16:4) Wint 81, p. 49.
"Sickbed" (tr. of Natsume Soseki). DenQ (16:4) Wint 81, p. 26.
"Sickroom" (tr. of Hagiwara Sakutaro). DenQ (16:4) Wint 81, p. 34.
"Sons" (tr. of Tao Chien). WestHR (35:3) Aut 81, p. 240.
"Stories" (tr. of Miyoshi Tatsuji). DenQ (16:4) Wint 81, p. 41.
"Street" (tr. of Shiraishi Kazuko). DenQ (16:4) Wint 81, p. 50.
"Summer Flower" (tr. of Muro Saisei). DenQ (16:4) Wint 81, p. 35.
"Tea Master" (tr. of Kitahara Hakashu). DenQ (16:4) Wint 81, p. 33.
"Tomb of a Fabled Creature" (tr. of So Sakon). DenQ (16:4) Wint 81, p. 46.
"The Way" (tr. of Shimazaki Toson). DenQ (16:4) Wint 81, p. 27.

WILSON, John R.
    "Atlanta Whispers" (Commemorating the twenty-one black children of Atlanta). BlackALF (15:2) Sum 81, p. 71.

WILSON, Miles
    "The Will to Fail." SouthernPR (21: 1) Spr 81, pp. 72-73.

WILSON, Rob
    "Ananda Air, III." Poetry (138:6) S 81, pp. 322-323.
    "Nothing." Poetry (138:6) S 81, p. 323.

WILSON, Robley, Jr.
    "Desire." Poetry (139:1) O 81, pp. 28-29.
    "Endsong." Poetry (139:1) O 81, p. 27.
    "A Literary Lesson" (For the lady's memory). Poetry (137:5) F 81,

p. 279.
"Vertebrae." Atl (248:6) D 81, p. 74.

WINE, James
"The Law of the Sea" (for my father). SunM (11) Spr 81, pp. 89-91.
"The Loom And The Weave." Tele (17) 81, pp. 28-32.

WINE, James Michael
"Adrift." Wind (10:39) 80, p. 48.
"Ankh." Wind (10:39) 80, p. 49.
"Encompass." Wind (10:39) 80, p. 48.

WINE, Linda
"The Break" (tr. of Delmira Agustini, w/ Beth Tornes). SenR (12:1/2)
81, p. 109.

WINKLER, M.
"Fall" (tr. by Bernhard Frank). PoNow (5:6 issue 30) 81, p. 47.
"Your white breasts" (tr. by Bernhard Frank). PoNow (5:6 issue 30)
81, p. 47.

WINN, Howard
"Anthology." Wind (11:41) 81, pp. 48-49.
"History." Wind (11:41) 81, p. 47.
"Living." Wind (11:41) 81, pp. 47-48.
"Other World." SouthernHR (15:2) Spr 81, p. 170.
"Sexist." SouthernHR (15:2) Spr 81, p. 165.
"Teaching Modern Poetry." KanQ (13:1) Wint 81, p. 77.

WINNER, Robert
"Dawn." PoNow (6:2 issue 32) 81, p. 46.

WINSLOW, Pete
"Hurricane Fred." OP (31/32) Aut 81, p. 35.

WINTER, Griselle Duchesne see DUCHESNE WINTER, Griselle

WINTERS, Anne
from The Watch (Vigie) (tr. of Robert Marteau). Ploughs (7:2) 81, p.
60.

WINTERS, Yvor
from: "Song from an Academic Bower." SouthernR (17:4) Aut 81, p.
108.
"To the Moon." SouthernR (17:4) Aut 81, p. 680.

WIPLINGER, Peter Paul
"End" (tr. by Herbert Kuhner). PortR (27: 2) 81, p. 35.
"Legends" (tr. by Herbert Kuhner). PortR (27: 2) 81, p. 35.

WITT, Harold
from American Lit: "Spoon River Anthology." HiramPoR (30) Spr-Sum
81, p. 50.
"Dream." NewL (47:4) Sum 81, p. 95.
"Ed Williams, Philosopher." MidwQ (23:1) Aut 81, p. 64.
"In These Home Movies." CharR (7:1) Spr 81, p. 9.

"Millayish." Im (7:2) 1981, p. 5.
"Shirley 'Sharee' Le Doux." PoNow (6:1 issue 31) 81, p. 30.
"Sneezing and Wheezing." WindO (39) Wint 81/82, p. 11.
"Soma." WindO (39) Wint 81/82, p. 11.
"Some of these Seashore Mornings." SouthwR (66:3) Sum 81, p. 266.
"Tiny Starker, Arsonist." MidwQ (23:1) Aut 81, p. 63.
"Whitmanesque." Im (7:2) 1981, p. 5.

WITTE, John
    "Artist's Proof." OntR (14) Spr-Sum 81, p. 89.
    "Atlas." OntR (14) Spr-Sum 81, pp. 86-87.
    "Clear Lake." OntR (14) Spr-Sum 81, p. 84.
    "Deer Island." OntR (14) Spr-Sum 81, p. 91.
    "Gathering Mushrooms." Antaeus (40/41) Wint-Spr 81, p. 405.
    "Grandmother." OntR (14) Spr-Sum 81, p. 88.
    "Islesboro." OntR (14) Spr-Sum 81, p. 90.
    "Victoria." NewYorker (57:26) 17 Ag 81, p. 38.
    "The Wagon." OntR (14) Spr-Sum 81, p. 85.

WITTLIN, Josef
    "Lamentación del Carnero Sacrificado." Lugar (1:1) 79, p. 18.

WITTLINGER, Ellen
    "The Dog At The End." Aspect (77/79) 81, p. 208.
    "For the Girl Drowned Off the Provincetown Breakwater, March 1975."
        Aspect (77/79) 81, p. 209.

WIXON, Vincent
    "Dark." PoNow (6:1 issue 31) 81, p. 47.
    "Cash Crop." PortR (27: 2) 81, p. 86.
    "Exercise to a Poem by William Carlos Williams." PortR (27: 2) 81,
        p. 86.

WOESSNER, Warren
    "The Bonner Players." PoNow (6:1 issue 31) 81, p. 32.
    "The Diagnosis." Northeast (3:10) Wint 81, p. 34.
    "Misty Freeze." PoNow (6:2 issue 32) 81, p. 31.

WOHMANN, Gabriele
    "A Subject for Writing" (tr. by Allen H. Chappel). NewOR (8:2) Sum
        81, p. 134.

WOJAHN, David
    "Elegy for James Wright." Poetry (138:2) My 81, pp. 79-80.
    "Matins." Poetry (138:2) My 81, pp. 84-85.
    "Miracles" (for Mary Logue). Poetry (138:2) My 81, pp. 81-83.

WOLF, Joan
    "Early Planting" (for FLW). Poem (42) Jul 81, pp. 28-29.
    "Poem After Kabir." WebR (6:2) 81, p. 67.
    "The Rape: Two Voices." Poem (42) Jul 81, p. 27.

WOLF, Leslie
    "Afterward: Homage To Movies." AmerPoR (10:2) Mr-Ap 81, p. 31.
    "Pause." AmerPoR (10:2) Mr-Ap 81, p. 31.
    "The Slip Of Many Colors." AmerPoR (10:2), Mr-Ap 81, p. 31.

WOLFE, Gene
    "After the Runaway." PortR (27: 2) 81, p. 52.
    "The Computer Iterates the Greater Trumps." PortR (27: 2) 81, p.
        52.

WOLFER, Cynthia
    "Impressions Of A Frightened World." Sam (109) 81, p. 24.

WOLFERT, Adrienne
    "Flying Grampa's Pigeons." Poem (41) Mar 81, pp. 43-45.
    "To My Lost Sister." Poem (41) Mar 81, pp. 46-47.

WOLLENBERG, Bruce
    "One Man's Life." ChrC (98:7) 4 Mr 81, p. 227.

WONG, Deborah
    "Destroying The Abbey: 1539." AmerPoR (10:1) Ja-F 81, p. 7.

WONG, Nellie
    "How to Guard Our Dead?" HangL (39) Wint 80-81, p. 54.
    "My Sister Dreams." HangL (39) Wint 80-81, p. 58.
    "Ode to Two Sisters in the Sun." HangL (39) Wint 80-81, p. 55.
    "Reminiscing About a Chinese Restaurant." 13thM (5:1/2) 80, pp. 29-
        31.
    "Window Full of Shoes." HangL (39) Wint 80-81, pp. 56-57.

WOOD, C. Roger
    "To the Painkillers." Poem (43) Nov 81, p. 25.
    "Stranded." Poem (43) Nov 81, p. 26.

WOOD, John A.
    "Elegy for a Colleague." BallSUF (22:4) Aut 81, pp. 67-68.
    "Jam." PoNow (6:3 issue 33) 81, p. 44.

WOOD, Peter
    "Suite: Five Pieces for Tambourine." US1 (14/15) Aut/Wint 81, p. 4.
    "The Title of This Poem Is Sex Manual." US1 (14/15) Aut/Wint 81, p.
        5.
    "A Woman's Possessions." US1 (14/15) Aut/Wint 81, p. 5.

WOOD, Robert E.
    "Apologia for May." ConcPo (14:1) Spr 81, p. 52.
    "Exit Wounds." ConcPo (14:1) Spr 81, p. 52.
    "Honeymoon." Confr (22) Sum 81, p. 130.
    "November." SoCaR (14: 1) Aut 81, p. 123.

WOOD, Susan
    "Fourth of July, Texas, 1956." Ploughs (7:1) 81, p. 45.
    "Pink Vista." Ploughs (7:1) 81, p. 44.

WOODRUFF, Tim
    "El Salvador: Interview With A Rebel" (hiding in Panama City when
        poem was written) (tr. of Anonymous). Sam (116) 81, p. 56.

WOODS, John
    "Crocus." PoetryNW (22:4) Wint 81-82, pp. 11-12.
    "Disorder and the Fear of Spring." Field (24) Spr 81, p. 9.
    "So Much Down, So Much a Week." PoetryNW (22:4) Wint 81-82, pp.
        12-13.

WOOLFOLK, Anne
"The Grandfather." US1 (14/15) Aut/Wint 81, p. 16.
"Macchu Picchu." US1 (14/15) Aut/Wint 81, p. 16.
"Scene from a Medieval French Calendar." US1 (14/15) Aut/Wint 81,
p. 16.
"Tarheel, in Memory of my Uncle, Benjamin." US1 (14/15) Aut/Wint
81, p. 16.
"Twister." US1 (14/15) Aut/Wint 81, p. 16.

WOOLSON, Peter
"Evolutionary Theory of Poison." Epoch (30:2) Wint-Spr 81, p. 119.

WORLEY, James
"After the Quarrel." ChrC (98:18) 20 My 81, p. 568.
"Could Eve Un-apple." ChrC (98:3) 28 Ja 81, p. 76.
"The Day My Uncle Left." ChrC (98:24) 29 Jl-5 Ag, 81, p. 765.
"Her Grace" (Of Flannery O'Connor). ChrC (98:6) 25 F 81, p. 198.

WORLEY, Jeff
"At a Zen Reading My Libido Acts Up Again (after Lucien Stryk)."
Northeast (3:11) Sum 81, p. 11.

WORMSER, Baron
"The Brothers." PoNow (6:3 issue 33) 81, p. 46.
"Bureaucrats Investigated." Poetry (138:2) My 81, pp. 65-66.
"A History of Photography." Poetry (138:2) My 81, pp. 69-70.
"A Mania." NewEngR (4:2) Wint 81, pp. 219-20.
"Numerous Questions." Poetry (138:2) My 81, p. 66.
"Of Small Towns." Poetry (138:2) My 81, pp. 63-64.
"Pets." NoAmR (266:4) D 81, p. 36.
"Servants." Poetry (138:2) My 81, pp. 67-68.
"The Spirit That Speaks." Poetry (138:2) My 81, p. 70.
"Student Population." NewEngR (4:2) Wint 81, p. 219.

WORMUTH, Diana W.
"The American Woman" (tr. of Artur Ludkvist). LitR (24:4) Sum 81,
pp. 543-44.
"Demon and the Bible" (tr. of Artur Lundkvist). LitR (24:4) Sum 81,
p. 546.
"Tigers" (tr. of Artur Lundkvist). LitR (24:4) Sum 81, p. 547.
"You Met A Beggar" (tr. of Artur Lundkvist). LitR (24:4) Sum 81, pp.
544-45.

WORTH, Douglas
"Breakthrough." Aspect (77/79) 81, p. 205.

WOSTER, Kevin
"Recovery." SoDakR (19:3) Aut 81, pp. 49-50.

WRIGHT, A. J.
"Knots." Vis (6) 81, n.p.

WRIGHT, Carolyne
"After We Received the News of the 100-Mile Wind." PoNow (6:2 issue
32) 81, p. 27.
"Celebration for the Cold Snap." Poetry (139:3) D 81, pp. 154-155.
"The Custody of the Eyes" (for Madeline DeFrees). Nimrod (25:1) Aut-
Wint 81, pp. 35-36.

"Early Fall." MalR (57) Ja 81, p. 126.
"The Extraordinary Courage of the Trees." Nimrod (25:1) Aut-Wint 81, p. 31.
"Farm Outside Oswego." Nimrod (25:1) Aut-Wint 81, pp. 34-35.
"Herons at Tahuya (Hoods Canal, Washington)." NoAmR (266:4) D 81, p. 38.
"How to Dress a Squid." SouthernPR (21:2) Aut 81, pp. 52-53.
"Leaving Northern New York State." QW (12) Spr-Sum 81, p. 68.
"The Loveliest Country of Our Lives." PoNow (6:2 issue 32) 81, p. 27.
"Mandamientos: Lover to Beloved." Wind (10:39) 80, p. 50.
"The Morning Mail: A Brief Irreverie." MalR (57) Ja 81, p. 127.
"Night Walk Around Green Lakes." Nimrod (25:1) Aut-Wint 81, p. 33.
"Seasons" (tr. of Angel Leiva). DenQ (16:1) Spr 81, p. 61.
"Transit." Wind (10:39) 80, p. 51.
"Walk in Mid-Winter." Wind (10:39) 80, p. 53.
"Walk in Mid-Winter: a Clearing South of Town." Nimrod (25:1) Aut-Wint 81, p. 32.
"What You Teach." Wind (10:39) 80, pp. 52-53.
"Zone" (tr. of Angel Leiva). DenQ (16:1) Spr 81, p. 60.

WRIGHT, Charles
"Ars Poetica." Antaeus (40/41) Wint-Spr 81, p. 406.
"Bar Giamaica, 1959-60." NewYorker (56:47) 12 Ja 81, p. 36.
"Gate City Breakdown." PoNow (6:1 issue 31) 81, p. 44.
"Laguna Blues." ParisR (23:79) Spr 81, p. 279.
"Landscape with Seated Figure and Olive Trees." Shen (31:4) 80, p. 14.
"Lost Bodies." Field (24) Spr 81, pp. 48-52.
"Lost Souls." Field (24) Spr 81, pp. 53-56.
"New Year's Eve, 1979." Iowa (11:2/3) Spr-Sum 80, p. 216.
"The Southern Cross." ParisR (23:80) Sum 81, p. 165-179.

WRIGHT, Franz
"The Death Mask" (tr. of René Char, w/ Carolyn Steiner). SenR (12: 1/2) 81, p. 47.
"The Dowry of Maubergeonne" (tr. of René Char, w/ Carolyn Steiner). SenR (12: 1/2) 81, p. 49.
"Fastes" (tr. of René Char, w/ Carolyn Steiner). SenR (12: 1/2) 81, p. 45.
"Line of Faith" (tr. of René Char, w/ Carolyn Steiner). SenR (12: 1/2) 81, p. 45.
"Memory" (tr. of Rainer Maria Rilke). SenR (12: 1/2) 81, p. 7.
"The Tree Frog" (tr. of René Char, w/ Carolyn Steiner). SenR (12: 1/2) 81, p. 49.

WRIGHT, James
"Against Surrealism." Poetry (139:2) N 81, p. 72.
"At Peace With The Ocean Off Misquamicut." ParisR (23:81) Aut 81, p. 100.
"Come, Look Quietly." NewYorker (57:42) 7 D 81, p. 52.
"Entering The Kingdom Of The Moray Eel." ParisR (23:81) Aut 81, pp. 99-100.
"A Fishing Song." ParisR (23:81) Aut 81, p. 101.
"The Fox At Eype." ParisR (23:81) Aut 81, p. 101.
"Honey." GeoR (35:4) Wint 81, p. 761.
"In View of the Protestant Cemetery in Rome." Nat (233:16) 14 N 81, p. 516.

"May Morning." Poetry (139:2) N 81, p. 73.
"Old Bud." GeoR (35:4) Wint 81, p. 760.
"Petition to the Terns." ThRiPo (17/18) 81, p. 94.
"The Sumac in Ohio." OhioR (26), p. 3.
"To the Adriatic Wind, Becalmed." NewYorker (57:42) 7 D 81, p. 52.
"A True Voice" (for Robert Bly). GeoR (35:4) Wint 81, p. 761.
"With the Gift of a Fresh New Notebook I Found in Florence."
    NewYorker (57:42) 7 D 81, p. 53.
"Yes, But." NewYorker (57:42) 7 D 81, pp. 52-3.

WRIGHT, Martha
    "If I Wanted to Explain My Days" (tr. of Eledino Paraguez). PortR
    (27: 2) 81, p. 94.

WRIGLEY, Robert
    "The Collector of Old Lumber." PortR (27:2) 81, p. 22.
    "Heart Attack." QW (13) Aut/Wint 81/82, pp. 24-25.
    "Killing Them." NowestR (19:1/2), p. 83.
    "Message." QW (13) Aut/Wint 81/82, p. 23.

WUEST, Barbara
    "Faith un-Healing." Wind (11:40) 81, pp. 39-40.
    "The Order of Freezing Rain." Wind (11:40) 81, p. 39.

WURSTER, Michael
    "The Cruelty of the Desert." FourQt (30:2) Wint 81, p. 33.

WYMAN, Peter
    "Grandpa's Funerals." PottPort (3) 81, p. 15.

WYNAND, Derk
    "Hidden Behind Flowers" (tr. of Peter Paul Fersch). Mund (12/13) 80-
    81, p. 123.
    "Winterscape" (tr. of Peter Paul Fersch). Mund (12/13) 80-81, p.
    123.

WYRICK, Green D.
    "Elegy for Dottie." CapeR (17:1) Wint 81, pp. 12-13.

WYTTENBERG, Victoria
    "Where is the music?" PortR (27: 2) 81, p. 97.

YAGI, Yokichi
    "Flea" (tr. by Graeme Wilson). DenQ (16:4) Wint 81, p. 40.

YALIM, Ozcan
    "This Beautiful Weather" (tr. of Orhan Veli, w/ William A. Fielder,
    and Dionis Coffin Riggs). StoneC (8: 3) Spr 81, p. 31.
    "Swallows" (tr. of Oktay Rifat, w/ William A. Fielder and Dionis Cof-
    fin Riggs). StoneC (8: 3) Spr 81, p. 30.
    "Those Trees" (tr. of Melih Cevdet Anday, w/ William A. Fielder, and
    Dionis Coffin Riggs). StoneC (8: 3) Spr 81, p. 31.
    "Umbrella" (tr. of Oktay Rifat, w/ William A. Fielder and Dionis Cof-
    fin Riggs). StoneC (8: 3) Spr 81, p. 30.

YAMAMATO, Judith
    "A Small Tent." PartR (48:3) 81, p. 462.

YAMAMOTO, Taro
"Lighthouses" (tr. by Graeme Wilson). DenQ (16:4) Wint 81, p. 48.

YAMAMURA, Bocho
"Cat" (tr. by Graeme Wilson). DenQ (16:4) Wint 81, p. 31.

YAMANOGUCHI, Baku
"Cat" (tr. by Gene Van Troyer). PortR (27: 2) 81, p. 30.
"Comfort" (tr. by Gene Van Troyer). PortR (27: 2) 81, p. 30.

YARROW, Bill
"If Dogs Should Come." Confr (22) Sum 81, p. 50.

YATES, David C.
"The Odd Man in the Bleachers." PoNow (6:2 issue 32) 81, p. 18.
"The Way It Was with Luckies." PoNow (6:2 issue 32) 81, p. 44.

YATES, Donald A.
"Adolescence" (tr. of Vicente Aleixandre). Mund (12/13) 80-81, p.
405.
"The Things I Say Are True" (tr. of Blanca Varela). Mund (12/13)
80-81, p. 334.

YATES, James
"Confusions at the Entrance to the Birdhouse." NoAmR (266:4) D 81,
p. 39.
"The Inherent Sadness of Baseball." PoNow (6:3 issue 33) 81, p. 45.
"Mousing." BelPoJ (31:3) Spr 81, pp. 8-9.

YATES, Peter
"Watts Towers." OP (31/32) Aut 81, p. 73.
"Whoever Cannot Believe the Good." OP (31/32) Aut 81, p. 113.

Y CASTRO, Antonio Castro see CASTRO Y CASTRO, Antonio

YEAGLEY, Joan
"Persimmons." PoNow (6:1 issue 31) 81, p. 18.

YERGEAU, Robert
"Dépassement de l'ombre." Os (13) Aut 81, pp. 8-9.

YI, Chonyon
"Full Moon in Pear Blossoms" (tr. by Michael Stephens). Pequod (13)
81, p. 76.

YI, Sang
"Poem 12" (tr. by Michael Stephens). Pequod (13) 81, p. 77.
"Rock-Ledge" (tr. by Michael Stephens). Pequod (13) 81, p. 78.

YOSANO, Akiko
"Prisoner" (tr. by Graeme Wilson). DenQ (16:4) Wint 81, p. 28.

YOUMANS, Marlene
"A Lady, Near Charleston, 1870." CarolQ (33:1) Wint 81, pp. 85-86.

YOUNG, David
"The Carousel" (tr. of Rainer Maria Rilke). Field (25) Aut 81, p. 66.
"The Self: A Sonnet Sequence." MissouriR (4:2) Wint 81-82, p. 34.

YOUNG, Gary
"The Bed." OntR (15) Aut-Wint 81-82, pp. 85-86.
"The Elegies." OntR (15) Aut-Wint 81-82, p. 87.
"Loch Lomond" (for my Father). Poetry (137:6) Mr 81, p. 337.
"Monday." Poetry (137:6) Mr 81, p. 335.
"Tornado Watch, Bloomington, Indiana." Poetry (137:6) Mr 81, p.
   336.

YOUNG, Karl
"Maya Vocabulary." SunM (11) Spr 81, pp. 79-82.

YOUNG, Robert De see DeYOUNG, Robert

YOUNG, Virginia Brady
"On Picking Up the Phone While Writing a Poem." KanQ (13:3/4) Sum-
   Aut 81, p. 82.

YOUNGBLOOD, Sarah
"On Receiving a Poem of Emily Dickinson's, Sent by a Friend, After
   a Gift of Books." Ploughs (6:4) 81, p. 149.

YU, Lu
"Evening" (tr. by Graeme Wilson). WestHR (35:1) Spr 81, p. 68.

YURKIEVICH, Saúl
"Adivina Adivinador." Lugar (1:1) 79, p. 21.
"Anticuerpo." Inti (9) Spr 79, pp. 91-93.
"Bramadero." Lugar (1:1) 79, pp. 20-21.

YUSIF, Sa'di
"A Stone" (tr. by Sargon Boulus). Mund (12/13) 80-81, p. 31.

ZABLE, Jeffrey
"The Dark Year." Wind (11:43) 81, p. 42.
"8 A.M." Wind (11:43) 81, p. 42.

ZAID, Gabriel
"Reverend Malthus on the Beach." Mund (12/13) 80-81, p. 156.
"Thousand and One Nights" (tr. by Sergio Mondragón and Sandra Smith).
   Mund (12/13) 80-81, p. 156.

ZAMORA, Bladimir
"Como quien da buenos días" (a Celia). Areito (7: 27) 81, p. 22.

ZAMORA, Sheila
"Clearing." SenR (10:2/11:1) 79-80, pp. 44-46.
"Of Return, The Palo Verde and Dusk." SenR (10:2/11:1) 79-80, pp.
   49-52.
"Only the Wind" (after a painting). SenR (10:2/11:1) 79-80, p. 48.
"Prologue: From a Small Plane." SenR (10:2/11:1) 79-80, p. 41.
"The View from the Blue Hills" (for Connie). SenR (10:2/11:1) 79-80,
   pp. 42-43.
"Window." SenR (10:2/11:1) 79-80, p. 47.

ZAMVIL, Stella
"Veteran's Day." Sam (106) 81, p. 45.

ZANDER, William
"Allergic to Cats." Wind (11:42) 81, pp. 38-39.
"Man." HiramPoR (30) Spr-Sum 81, p. 51.

ZANETTI, Carol
"Thanks." Meadows (2:1) 81, p. 25.

ZARZYSKI, Paul
"Retiring Ol' Gray." CutB (16) Spr-Sum 81, p. 109.

ZAVRIAN, Suzanne Ostro
"Alphabet One." OP (31/32) Aut 81, p. 44.
"For Peter." StoneC (9: 1/2) Aut-Wint 81/82, p. 53.
"2/23." StoneC (9: 1/2) Aut-Wint 81/82, p. 52.

ZAWAKIWSKY, Christine
"Before It Gets Cold." StoneC (9: 1-2) Aut-Wint 81/82, pp. 72-73.
"Clay." Ascent (77/79) 81, p. 210.
"Cyanide." OP (31/32) Aut 81, pp. 87-88.
"Pearls." StoneC (9: 1-2) Aut-Wint 81/82, p. 73.
"Targets." OP (31/32) Aut 81, p. 114.

ZEBRUN, Gary
"Bethlehem, Pa., 1930." MassR (22:1) Spr 81, p. 184.

ZECH, Paul
"Factory Streets by Day" (tr. by James Liddy and Ruth Schwertfeger).
DenQ (16:1) Spr 81, p. 68.

ZEIDNER, Lisa
"Light." LittleM (13:1/2) Spr-Sum 79, c1981, pp. 106-107.

ZEIGER, David
"If I forget Thee." LitR (24:3) Spr 81, p. 378.

ZEIGER, L. L.
"Designer Condoms." PoNow (6:3 issue 33) 81, p. 45.
"Gratitude." PoNow (6:3 issue 33) 81, p. 45.
"Simplification (Note to a Poet)." PoNow (6:3 issue 33) 81, p. 45.

ZEIS, Gabriel
"After This, Then He Sleeps." ChrC (98:5) 18 F 81, p. 164.

ZELLIKOFF, Louis
"Haymaking" (tr. of Simon Chikovani). PoNow (5:6 issue 30) 81, p.
13.

ZELVIN, Elizabeth
"Family Party." 13thM (5:1/2) 80, p. 34.

ZENKER, Helmut
"Note" (tr. by Herbert Kuhner). Mund (11:2) 79, p. 79.
"Notiz." Mund (11:2) 79, p. 78.

ZENON CRUZ, Isabel
"El amor: camino incansable" (Diálogo entre el desnudo y el desvestido)
(Para Angela María Dávila). Claridad/En Rojo (22: 1488) 7-13 Ag
81, p. 12.

ZEPEDA, Rafael
"John Doesn't Like Washing Dishes." WormR (84) 81, p. 103.
"John's Garden." WormR (84) 81, p. 104.
"A Logical Procession Of Terms." WormR (84) 81, p. 103.

ZICHLINSKY, Rajzel
"The Camel" (tr. by Mark Kanter). PortR (27: 1) 81, p. 25.
"On Sunny Days" (tr. by Joseph Leftwitch). PortR (27: 1) 81, p. 25.

ZICKE, Getachew
"The Locked Mind." BlackALF (15:2) Sum 81, p. 71.
"A Proposal to Beneatha." BlackALF (15:2) Sum 81, p. 71.

ZIDE, Arlene
"Memorial Day." Prima (6/7) 81, p. 82.
"Signifying." Prima (6/7) 81, p. 60.
"Waiting by the Seaside for Messages from Home." Prima (6/7) 81,
    p. 81.

ZIMMER, Paul
"Christian Fearing the Sky." PoNow (6:1 issue 31) 81, p. 26.
"The King's Religion." PoetryNW (22:4) Wint 81-82, p. 16.
"Wanda and Zimmer in the Tenderloin." PoNow (6:1 issue 31) 81, p.
    26.
"Wanda kissed me very wet." PoNow (6:1 issue 31) 81, p. 26.

ZIMUNYA, Musa B.
"Ifulaimachina (Flying-machine)." Stand (22: 2) 81, p. 30.

ZINNES, Harriet
"The Key" (tr. of Jacques Prevert). PoNow (6:1 issue 31) 81, p. 42.
"Good Young Weather" (tr. of Jacques Prevert). PoNow (6:1 issue 31)
    81, p. 42.
"Mates(Pantoum)." CentR (25:1) Wint 81, p. 43.
"Spring: My Son Rides His Bicycle." PoNow (6:1 issue 31) 81, p. 41.

ZISQUIST, Linda
"Living in History." ThRiPo (17/18) 81, p. 46.
"Ritual Bath." Nimrod (25:1) Aut-Wint 81, p. 58.

ZOHARA
"La Borinqueña." Claridad/En Rojo (22: 1468) 20-26 Mr 81, p. 12.

ZOLYNAS, Al
"Air Poem." PoNow (6:2 issue 32) 81, p. 13.

ZORZUT, Emilse
"De tu partida, Rapsodia en Gris." Mairena (3:7) 81, pp. 45-6.
"Hilvano las nubes...." Mairena (3:7) 81, p. 44.
"No partiré más." Mairena (3:7) 81, p. 44.
"Plenitud." Mairena (3:7) 81, p. 43.
"Rima." Mairena (3:7) 81, p. 46.
"Si besas mi boca." Mairena (3:7) 81, p. 45.

ZU-BOLTON II, Ahmos
"Beachhead Preachment." OP (31/32) Aut 81, p. 148.

ZUCKER, Jack
"House with Five Pillars." PoetryNW (22:3) Aut 81, pp. 16-19.

ZWEIG, Paul
"Aunt Lil." AmerPoR (10:3) My-Je 81, p. 9.
"The Danger." ParisR (23:80) Sum 81, pp. 131-132.
"Eternity's Woods." AmerPoR (10:3) My-Je 81, p. 8.
"Father." AmerPoR (10:3) My-Je 81, p. 8.
"Life Story." AmerPoR (10:3) My-Je 81, p. 9-10.
"Snow." ParisR (23:80) Sum 81, p. 132.

ZWETTLER, Michael
from On the Magic Carpet: "Canto 3: The Slave" (tr. of Fawzī Ma'-
lūf). Nimrod (24: 2) Spr/Sum 81, pp. 59-60.

ZYDEK, Frederick
"Figure Skater." PoNow (6:2 issue 32) 81, p. 16.

ZYDEK, Fredrick
"Bright Wing Cannot Reach The Wind." Wind (11:41) 81, pp. 50-51.
"Getting What You Need" (for Sarah Jo). Poem (42) Jul 81, p. 12.
"Lady on the Hill" (for Leslie). Wind (11:41) p. 50.
"No Weather Tomorrow." CapeR (16:2) Sum 81, p. 8.
"Places for a Storm." Confr (22) Sum 81, p. 82.
"Summa" (for T. A.). CapeR (17:1) Wint 81, p. 25.
"A Sunday Sort of Thief" (for Lee John). CapeR (17:1) Wint 81, p. 26.